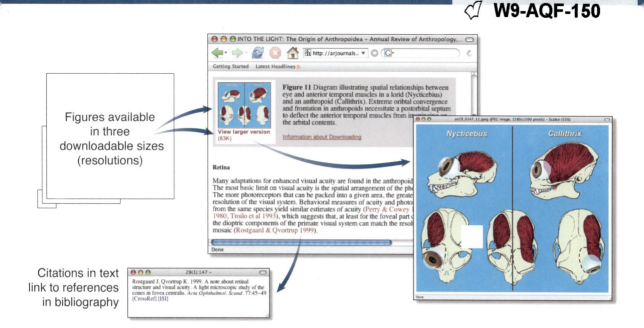

Figures available in three downloadable sizes (resolutions)

Citations in text link to references in bibliography

References in Annual Reviews article bibliography link out to sources of cited articles online

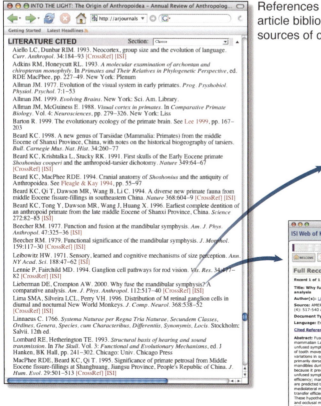

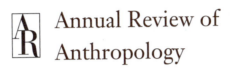

Annual Review of
Anthropology

Annual Review of Anthropology

Volume 38, 2009

Donald Brenneis, *Co-Editor*
University of California, Santa Cruz

Peter T. Ellison, *Co-Editor*
Harvard University

www.annualreviews.org • science@annualreviews.org • 650-493-4400

Annual Reviews
4139 El Camino Way • P.O. Box 10139 • Palo Alto, California 94303-0139

AR

Annual Reviews

Palo Alto, California, USA

International Standard Serial Number: 0084-6570
International Standard Book Number: 978-0-8243-1938-0
Library of Congress Catalog Card Number: 72-821360

TYPESET BY APTARA
PRINTED AND BOUND BY MALLOY INCORPORATED, ANN ARBOR, MICHIGAN

Holism and Anthropology

Along with the two-hundredth anniversaries of the births of Abraham Lincoln and Charles Darwin, the year 2009 saw the fiftieth anniversary of C.P. Snow's "Two Cultures" address as the Rede Lecture at Cambridge University. Although not as momentous an upheaval as those associated with the names of Lincoln and Darwin, Snow's address publicly marked—and subsequently helped shape—a tectonic chasm that was opening in the academic world. An irreversible drift seemed to be isolating practitioners of humanities and sciences on different intellectual continents as the universe of knowledge that gave the university its name began to break up. Fifty years later it is hard to dispute that we live in an expanding universe of knowledge and information with increasing specialization driven not by the desire to focus on less and less but by the challenge to cope with more and more.

The expanding universe of knowledge increases the distance between disciplines of inquiry as the techniques and theories that are developed at the advancing edges of fields become ever more remote from their common roots. Two different reactions that have arisen in response to this new intellectual topography are interdisciplinarity and multidisciplinarity. The first is an effort to address the areas of overlap as well as the interstices between fields. The second is an effort to marshal experts from different fields to address a common problem.

The field of anthropology has long aspired to a third position: holism. More than just a cobbling together of disparate perspectives, anthropology has historically attempted to cultivate a comprehensive approach to the human condition. This quixotic mission has always set it apart. When Abraham Lincoln established the National Academy of Sciences of the United States of America in the midst of the Civil War, anthropology was represented among the ten original sections of the organization. Yet it was a difficult discipline to categorize even then. The section name was Ethnology, but it was grouped with Geology, Zoology, Botany, and Anatomy and Physiology in the "Class of Natural History."

Today, many anthropology departments feel themselves sitting uncomfortably astride the great fault lines of the modern university, part humanities, part social science, part life science. Some (like the home department of one of us) have succumbed to the tensions of this situation and divided into separate departments. Others have let go of their foothold in one or more or the traditional subfields of anthropology and have consolidated themselves on less ambiguous terrain.

The *Annual Review of Anthropology* remains committed to the spirit of holistic inquiry, engagement, and debate that has long animated our discipline. We seek not only to represent within its pages reviews of contemporary research in the various subfields of anthropology, but in every volume to group articles in themes that bridge those divisions, where scholars and students interested in cultivating a holistic approach can find food for thought, material for teaching, and inspiration for research. The two themes in this issue, "Current Research on Gender" and "Anthropology and Human Health," are excellent examples of that practice. The Overview chapter by Patty Jo Watson also presents the remarkably holistic perspective of one of the leading figures in contemporary anthropology.

No one has exemplified the holistic spirit better than Bill Durham during his 15 years as Editor. The fact that the editorial torch has now passed to two of us, each in different subfields of anthropology, should not, however, be seen as a worrying token of the erosion of holistic perspective in the *ARA*. Both of us remain committed to that perspective ourselves and expect to be better able to realize it together. We are grateful for the enthusiastic engagement of a wonderful editorial board, who together constitute a "dream department" of colleagues. We particularly thank Cynthia Beall and Carla Sinopoli as they rotate off the board, having contributed enormously to the success of the *ARA* during their tenures. Cognizant of the challenges, we are excited to help steer the *ARA* in the years ahead.

Don Brenneis and Peter Ellison
Co-Editors

**Annual Review of
Anthropology**

Volume 38, 2009

Contents

Indexes

Errata

An online log of corrections to *Annual Review of Anthropology* articles may be found at
http://anthro.annualreviews.org/errata.shtml

Related Articles

Annual Reviews is a nonprofit scientific publisher established to promote the advancement of the sciences. Beginning in 1932 with the *Annual Review of Biochemistry*, the Company has pursued as its principal function the publication of high-quality, reasonably priced *Annual Review* volumes. The volumes are organized by Editors and Editorial Committees who invite qualified authors to contribute critical articles reviewing significant developments within each major discipline. The Editor-in-Chief invites those interested in serving as future Editorial Committee members to communicate directly with him. Annual Reviews is administered by a Board of Directors, whose members serve without compensation.

Patty Jo Watson

Archaeology and Anthropology: A Personal Overview of the Past Half-Century

Patty Jo Watson

Missoula, Montana 59803; email: pjwatson@artsci.wustl.edu

Annu. Rev. Anthropol. 2009. 38:1–15

The *Annual Review of Anthropology* is online at anthro.annualreviews.org

This article's doi:
10.1146/annurev-anthro-091908-164458

Key Words

origins of agriculture, Eastern Agricultural Complex, ethnoarchaeology, New Archaeology, processual archaeology, postprocessual archaeology

Abstract

Having begun graduate work in anthropology and prehistoric archaeology at a time (early 1950s) and place (University of Chicago) where the two were closely linked, I subsequently participated in work devoted to early agricultural economies in Western Asia and Eastern North America; to the relations among archaeology, history, and science; and to the place of anthropological archaeology in the contemporary world. In this article I discuss my personal experiences within each of these areas of endeavor.

INTRODUCTION

AAA: American Anthropological Association

NSF: National Science Foundation

When I entered the University of Chicago's pre-MA program in the fall of 1952, I encountered a small community of faculty and students pursuing a bewildering array of research trajectories: Totonac phonetics and phonemics, agricultural origins in ancient Mesopotamia, functional anatomy of nonhuman primates, contemporary Mayan kinship systems and village life, domestic economies among the Sauk and Fox Indian tribes. This was very exciting but also confusing for someone fresh from the cornfields of northern Iowa who just wanted to learn how to be an archaeologist. It helped a great deal, however, that these scholars were all self-declared anthropologists, members of a single discipline dedicated to the study of humankind throughout time and space. Before the end of fall quarter, I thought of myself as an anthropologist committed to investigating the cultural histories of prehistoric human groups: an anthropologist first and an archaeologist second. I joined the American Anthropological Association (AAA) in the spring of my first year as an anthropology grad student and have been on its rolls ever since. Thoroughly imprinted in the unity of the discipline, I completed a PhD in 1959 and began my career in the 1960s as an anthropological archaeologist specializing in Near Eastern prehistory, especially the origins and early development of agropastoral economies.

ORIGINS OF AGRICULTURE IN SOUTHWEST ASIA, THEN AND NOW

Then (1950s)

The center of my grad school orbit was Robert J. Braidwood's office on the third floor of the Oriental Institute (known to habitués as the Orinst, its cable address, or the OI).

I enrolled in all Braidwood's seminars—held in his OI office—but also took courses in social anthropology (from Eggan and Redfield, plus a class on Aboriginal Australia offered by Lloyd Warner, which featured the Murngin controversy, and one by Simon Ottenberg on African

ethnology), physical anthropology (Washburn), and linguistics (McQuown).

Braidwood was well known as the excavator of Jarmo in the foothills of northern Iraq, then the oldest known food-producing community in the world. The 1950–1951 Jarmo field season (Braidwood 1953; Braidwood & Braidwood 1950, 1953) had been a big success, and plans were well underway for the 1954–1955 season by the time I became a Braidwood advisee. Braidwood's views on how, where, and when the first West Asian plants and animals were domesticated (the Hilly Flanks theory) centered on regional floral, faunal, and climatic data. These data indicated to him that the earliest evidence for farming and herding should be found in geographic locales where wild ancestral populations were native, i.e., in the rain-watered uplands above the Fertile Crescent, stretching from the Levantine coast across northern Mesopotamia to the Tigris and Euphrates.

For the 1954–1955 Jarmo season, Braidwood wanted to take with him to Iraq experts who could identify and interpret physical remains of Jarmo animals and plants, representing as they did the oldest known domestic goats, sheep, pigs, wheat, and barley. He included a zoologist (Charles Reed), an archaeobotanist (Hans Helbaek), and a radiocarbon expert (Fred Matson) in his National Science Foundation (NSF) proposal, in addition to the geologist (Herbert Wright) who had begun work at Jarmo in 1950–1951. This proposal was the first ever received by NSF for archaeological fieldwork in the Near East. It was funded. The natural scientists and other staff members were signed on, and I was included as the most junior member.

Just prior to and during the 1954–1955 Iraq-Jarmo season, Kathleen Kenyon's excavations in basal levels at the big mound of Tell es-Sultan (ancient Jericho) in Jordan produced results that directly challenged Braidwood's Hilly Flanks theory. The long stratigraphic sequence her team documented revealed evidence of a prehistoric settlement at the oasis of Jericho, far from the Hilly Flanks—a settlement not only bigger and fancier than Jarmo, but also several millennia older (Braidwood 1957; Davis 2008, pp. 11, 118–120, 128–150; Kenyon 1957).

During ensuing decades, many other archaeologists took up the interdisciplinary agricultural/pastoral origins focus pioneered by the Braidwoods at Jarmo. Although Braidwood is still widely recognized as the first Near Easternist to take natural scientist colleagues to the field, he himself always insisted that Raphael Pumpelly (1908) initiated interdisciplinary archaeological fieldwork in Asia.

The state of knowledge now is, of course, far more complex than it was 50 years ago. Besides many more sites and much more data, methods and techniques now provide new categories of information, such as ancient sheep/goat herd structures, DNA analyses of wild-to-domestic animal and plant lineages, and much more precise radiocarbon dating than was possible in the mid-twentieth century.

Now (Early 2000s)

Subsequent to the Jarmo-Jericho debate, Braidwood's interdisciplinary team carried out one season of fieldwork in the Iranian Zagros (the return to Jarmo planned for 1958–1959 having been cancelled owing to the nationalist revolution in Iraq) but then moved to Ergani, Diyarbakır Vilayet, in southeastern Turkey. The Joint Istanbul-Chicago Prehistoric Project, directed by Halet Çambel and Bob Braidwood, continued for the next 30 years, its major focus being Çayönü, a site significantly larger than Jarmo, more complex architecturally, and at least a millennium older (Çambel & Braidwood 1980).

Another big, fancy, prehistoric Turkish site—Çatalhöyük—had been preliminarily excavated during the 1970s by James Mellaart (1967). A second generation of work at Çatalhöyük was begun in 1993 by Ian Hodder (2007). Çatalhöyük is somewhat younger than basal Çayönü, representing what Braidwood called "established village-farming," although the site is quite different from the early established village-farming communities known when he coined that phrase. In fact, the whole

latter-day agropastoral origins archaeological enterprise is so large and active that topical, regional, and general syntheses appear frequently (e.g., Cappers & Bottema 2002, Colledge & Conolly 2007, Denham et al. 2007, Naderi et al. 2008, Simmons 2007, Zeder 2008).

The general picture is that most of the animal and plant species identified as key players by Braidwood's Jarmo colleagues are now known to have been domesticated during the early Holocene at various times and places within the Hilly Flanks and the southern Levant: sheep and goats by ~11,000 years ago, pigs by ~10,500 years ago, cattle by ~10,000 years ago; wheat, barley, peas, and lentils by ~10,500 years ago. Accelerator mass spectrometer (AMS) radiocarbon techniques provide precise dating of the floral and faunal remains themselves, whereas new analytical procedures enable archaeobotanists and archaeozoologists to detect subtle patterns in bone and plant remains indicating "predomestication" managing many centuries prior to the emergence of morphological traits clearly attesting to domesticated status (Hillman & Davies 1992, Hillman 2000, Weiss et al. 2006, Zeder 2008). The entire Near Eastern complex of domestic plants and animals was present by 9500 years ago in the earliest established village-farming communities. Furthermore, many of those communities were very large and sustained complex ritual activities.

AGRICULTURAL ORIGINS IN THE EASTERN WOODLANDS OF NORTH AMERICA

While Braidwood's teams, as well as those of his colleagues, students, and successors, were pursuing the origins of agropastoral economies in western Asia, evidence for a very different food-producing system was emerging in the Eastern Woodlands of North America (Fritz 1990, 2007; Gremillion 2002; Smith 2002, 2006; Watson 1997; Yarnell 1969, 1974, 1994).

Having, in the summer of 1955, married into a speleological group (the Cave Research Foundation) carrying out research within and adjacent to Mammoth Cave National Park, Kentucky, I was drawn toward dark-zone cave archaeology in the early 1960s (Benington et al. 1962; Watson 1969, 1974, 1999b; Watson & Yarnell 1966). The cave—Salts Cave, Mammoth Cave National Park—where I began research contained many miles of dry passages well known to prehistoric inhabitants of the region. There is a significant amount of historic traffic and disturbance in the upper levels of Salts Cave, but there are several lower-level passages undisturbed since the end of the aboriginal caving period here 2000 years ago. Everything left in such passages is preserved in situ, including ample evidence of prehistoric diet, primarily in the form of human fecal deposits. Desiccated human paleofeces—readily dated by AMS radiocarbon techniques—are marvelous data repositories containing information about the environment (inferred from floral and faunal contents, including pollen) as well as subsistence, sex, and DNA data for the defecators and DNA data for the fragments of plant and animal tissue in each specimen (Poinar et al. 2001; Sobolik et al. 1996; Watson & Yarnell 1986; Yarnell 1969, 1974).

Introduction of wet-screening and flotation techniques to Eastern Woodlands archaeology in the 1970s and 1980s enabled retrieval of charred plant fragments and various categories of microfaunal remains (e.g., fish scales, tiny rodent bones and teeth) missed by standard dry-screening (Chapman & Watson 1993). Evidence accumulated rapidly for a previously unsuspected form of indigenous agriculture east of the Mississippi that began about 4000 years ago and was well developed by the time prehistoric cavers roamed the passages of Salts and Mammoth Caves (Smith & Yarnell 2009).

For most of the twentieth century, scholars of early agriculture in North America focused heavily on Mexico (especially the origins of maize) and the U.S. Southwest. Reference was frequently made to the Three Sisters—maize, squash, and beans—grown by many American Indian groups at the time of European contact. These crops were all believed to have been domesticated originally in pre-Hispanic Mexico, diffused north as a package to the U.S. Southwest, and eventually across the Plains to the Eastern Woodlands. The retrieval revolution in Americanist archaeology and development of the requisite specialties, as had been the case in the Near East during and after the Braidwoodian era, replaced older understandings with much more detailed knowledge. The Eastern Agricultural Complex was one result and is now known to be among the very few, independently created agricultural systems in the entire human past. The exact number of autochthonous developments of food-producing economies varies somewhat from expert to expert but is fewer than ten. The usual lineup includes Western Asia, Eastern Asia, Oceania (New Guinea), Eastern North America, Mexico, tropical South America, and sub-Saharan Africa.

Emergence of agricultural economies in the Americas—North, Central, and South—is currently a hot topic characterized by considerable difference of opinion on many details (Browman et al. 2009), but it has been clear for some time that the earlier notion of a single Mexican package (the Three Sisters) diffused north and south is wrong. Each region north of Mexico, for example, has its own plant-use story. Some locales include an early-agriculture narrative, whereas others are characterized by only occasional or seasonal use of one or more domesticated (or cultivated or propagated) species to supplement wild fruits, nuts, and other forest, prairie, or desert foods.

Maize did come into the U.S. Southwest from Mexico and was present by 4000 years ago. Squash appears by 3500 years ago, but Mexican beans did not appear until 2000 years ago. The premaize Eastern Agricultural Complex, present by 3000 years ago in parts of the Midwest and Midsouth, included sunflower (genus *Helianthus*), sumpweed or marshelder (*Iva*, a relative of sunflower that also produces oily seeds), *Chenopodium* (goosefoot, lambsquarter), maygrass (*Phalaris*), a thick-walled squash (*Cucurbita pepo ovifera*, pepo gourd), and bottle gourd (*Lagenaria*). Knotweed (*Polygonum*) and tobacco (*Nicotiana*) show up later, as does maize [*Zea*, which appeared in the U.S. Midwest ~2000 years ago, but at only one site that early (Riley et al. 1994)]. Maize became widespread ~1500–1200 years ago and later, with considerable regional variation and many places where it was not grown at all prior to European contact. Finally, ~800 years ago, Mexican beans are present at a few sites.

While this agricultural origins excitement was going on at ground level in Eastern North America during the 1970s, 1980s, and 1990s, stirring events were taking place in the rarified atmosphere surrounding major methodological and theoretical issues relevant to all of Americanist anthropological archaeology.

A much-discussed topic during the 1970s and 1980s, ethnographic fieldwork in the interests of archaeological interpretation, is one that Braidwood periodically brought up in his 1950s seminars at the Oriental Institute.

FROM ARCHAEOLOGICAL ETHNOGRAPHY TO ETHNOARCHAEOLOGY: BACK TO JARMO

Staff members for the first Jarmo field season of 1950–1951 included a recent Chicago graduate student in Anthropology, Frederik Barth [MA 1949]. Braidwood asked Barth to remain for several weeks after the Jarmo dig closed, so he could document archaeologically relevant architectural and economic details in nearby Kurdish villages. Barth (1953) produced a fine social anthropological monograph, but it contained no data on construction and maintenance of puddled-adobe houses, details of wheat and barley farming, specifics about sheep and goat herds, etc. (see Barth 2007, p. 2, for his account of this early stage in his anthropological career). Hence, when I became one of his advisees, Braidwood was still lacking farming, herding, and architectural details from contemporary Iraqi Kurdistan. After the 1954–1955 Iraq-Jarmo season, he suggested that my dissertation project could be the archaeological ethnographic one yet to be undertaken in the Jarmo locale.

I never did any archaeological ethnography in living villages around Jarmo, however, because the 1958–1959 Iraq season was cancelled subsequent to the 1958 revolution. Braidwood did succeed in fielding his interdisciplinary team in western Iran during a nine-month period in 1959–1960, so it was in Iranian villages that I recorded information meant to aid better interpretations for ancient villages such as Jarmo (Watson 1979).

The empirical aspects of archaeologically oriented ethnography seemed quite straightforward to me at the time I was doing it. In the minds of 1970s archaeological theorists, however, the relations between archaeology and ethnography were highly problematic (even without considering the negative opinions of some ethnologists about ethnographic skills of those archaeologists invading their scholarly turf). The standard reference on epistemological aspects of ethnographic analogy is "The Reaction Against Analogy" by philosopher of science Alison Wylie (1985; see also Wylie 1982, David & Kramer 2001). My own modest efforts to sort through the most troubling problems from the perspective of a practicing archaeologist are detailed in a 1999 essay, "Ethnographic Analogy and Ethnoarchaeology" (also Watson et al. 1971, pp. 49–51, and Watson 2008, pp. 30–31), the essential point being that ethnographic analogies—whether simple or complex—are trial formulations (hypotheses, models) subject to testing like all such propositions.

Ethnoarchaeology was just one of the theoretical issues central to Americanist anthropological archaeology during the later 1960s through the 1970s and 1980s, a period when New Archaeology—also known as processual archaeology—became dominant. Archaeological practitioners within the United States during the mid-1970s were also struggling with the transformation of their discipline in response to passage by Congress of the Archeological and Historic Preservation Act, giving rise to Cultural Resource Management (CRM). This Act formally added archaeological (prehistoric and historic) sites and materials (cultural heritage properties) to environmental protection

CRM: Cultural Resource Management

legislation, mandating (and recommending a certain amount of federal funding for) archaeological survey with subsequent mitigation (documentation, excavation) of resources scheduled to be disturbed or destroyed by federally funded projects (e.g., roads, dams).

The most pressing problems in the immediate aftermath of the Preservation Act were pragmatic, the first being clear description of requisite expertise for archaeologists certified to carry out work in advance of federally funded projects. Regulations sufficiently general to be applicable throughout the entire country and across the entire prehistoric and historic span covered by the archaeological record in the United States were also necessary. Moreover, Americanist archaeology, a small group of avocational or academic scholars, now had to include a rapidly growing subset of practitioners employed by public agencies (e.g., the National Park Service) or private construction firms, or those who were in business for themselves as contract archaeologists.

Because more than 95% of all archaeological fieldwork in the United States is now CRM archaeology, major impacts have been made on teaching, training, and public outreach (King 2008). Nevertheless, these effects are often rather distant from theoretical debates carried on by the small minority of non-CRM (ivory-tower) archaeologists, to whom I now return.

PROCESSUAL, POSTPROCESSUAL, AND POST-POSTPROCESSUAL ARCHAEOLOGY

New Archaeology/Processual Archaeology (1960s–1970s)

I use the terms New Archaeology and processual archaeology interchangeably, although some scholars make a distinction (Johnson 2008). In any case, Lewis Binford was the leader of this movement that shifted Americanist archaeology from highly particularistic, historicist foci toward generalizing, explicitly social scientific, anthropological ones.

> Archaeology must accept a greater responsibility in the furtherance of the aims of anthropology. Until the tremendous quantities of data which the archaeologist controls are used in the solution of problems dealing with cultural evolution or systemic change, we are not only failing to contribute to the furtherance of the aims of anthropology but retarding the accomplishment of these aims. We as archaeologists have available a wide range of variability and a large sample of cultural systems. Ethnographers are restricted to the small and formally limited extant cultural systems. .... As archaeologists, with the entire span of culture history as our "laboratory," we cannot afford to keep our theoretical heads buried in the sand. We must shoulder our full share of responsibility within anthropology.... (Binford 1962, p. 224)

Binford's call to revise and broaden anthropological archaeology was not the first (Bennett 1943, Kluckhohn 1940, Steward & Setzler 1938, Taylor 1948), but it was certainly the most successful. Although Binford was on the Anthropology faculty at Chicago when he published his 1962 paper, I had left some years prior to his arrival and—not being a New World archaeologist at that time—did not know much about his radical ideas until 1968. During the fall of that year, my husband Richard (Red) Watson and I and our five-year-old daughter Anna, resided in Ergani, Turkey, together with other staff members of Halet Çambel and Robert Braidwood's Turkish Prehistoric Project (Watson 1999c). Red was geological field assistant cooperating with the Turkish Geological Survey to find and document obsidian sources and to sample each one. I was field supervisor for the excavation of a Halafian site (Girikihaciyan, GK for short; Watson & LeBlanc 1990) several millennia younger and a few miles away from Çayönü, the primary focus of the Project.

Two University of Chicago graduate students were also members of the Project staff: Geoffrey Clark and Charles Redman. Geoff and Chuck were steeped in 1960s Binfordian New Archaeology and eager to apply it at Girikihaciyan and/or Çayönü. I was an easier mark than Bob or Halet, let alone the codirectors in combination, so they set about giving me an intense tutorial. Their efforts were aided significantly by the fact that Turkish Antiquities law prohibits one expedition from excavating two sites simultaneously. Hence, the 1968 GK sondage had to await completion of work at Çayönü. There was no rule against nondigging, surface work, however, so we got permission from Halet and Bob to carry out systematic surface collection at GK. The results were very rewarding, and I became an enthusiastic convert to New Archaeology. Halet and Bob were also favorably impressed to the extent that they allowed us to surface-collect Çayönü, too (Redman & Watson 1970).

By the next Turkish season in the fall of 1970, Steven LeBlanc had entered the predoctoral graduate program in Anthropology at Washington University and was in search of a dissertation project. He joined the GK field staff in place of Chuck, who was Çayönü dig supervisor in 1970. Between those two seasons, the three of us had collaborated on a book manuscript. This was LeBlanc's idea. He thought that a substantive but brief exposition of New Archaeology for a general archaeological audience, students and professionals, was badly needed. Chuck secured the interest of an editor at Columbia University Press, and the book came out soon after the 1970 Turkish season (Watson et al. 1971). It was sufficiently controversial to be a big seller, becoming what one critic (pejoratively) called a *locus classicus* of 1970s New Archaeology.

Just about the time it seemed the battle was over and processualist New Archaeology had won, English archaeologist Ian Hodder published an essay describing a distinctly contrasting approach (Hodder 1982). He followed that account of his radical views with numerous others, as well as many talks at meetings in Europe

and the United States. In 1985, he published a synthesis of European perspectives entitled "Postprocessual Archaeology" (Hodder 1985).

Postprocessual Archaeology

Although Binford himself asserted that entire past cultural systems could be and should be inferred from the archaeological record (Binford 1962), in practice Binfordian processualist archaeology of the 1960s and 1970s was focused on paleoenvironment, paleoecology, and subsistence economies of ancient societies. Relations between ancient communities and their physical environments were highlighted; explicitly scientific research designs were stressed and insisted on by peer review panels of the NSF and other funding agencies. The major goal of Americanist anthropological archaeology was to formulate and test generalizations about human sociocultural behavior (Watson et al. 1971), but the generalizations sought were nearly always in the realm of what Robert Hall (1977) succinctly characterized as "econothink." Hall and a few other anthropological archaeologists (e.g., Kehoe & Kehoe 1974) advocated more broadly based interpretive frameworks than those of the New Archaeologists, but they were a very small minority.

A much bigger theoretical/methodological fuss was stirred up by Binford himself and by Michael Schiffer during the 1970s and early 1980s (Binford 1976, 1980, 1981; Schiffer 1972, 1987). The crux of this debate was the nature of the archaeological record. Archaeologists were ignoring the complexities inherent to prehistoric human/environmental relations. They also gave insufficient attention to cultural and noncultural agents, events, and processes that rearrange, remove, or obliterate original cultural deposits and their original sedimentary contexts. Binford's and Schiffer's publications impelled an intense focus on site formation and deformation (e.g., Goldberg et al. 1993; Goldberg & Sherwood 2006; Stein 1983, 2005a,b; Stein & Farrand 1985).

All this site formation debate and work, however, was very much within the prevailing processualist mode. What concerned Ian Hodder and other British and European archaeologists of the 1980s and later was an altogether different set of theoretical matters, as indicated by Hodder's coining of the term postprocessual archaeology. The phrase covers a multitude of perspectives, some (various Marxian emphases, for instance) fairly congruent with processualist archaeology, others antagonistic (e.g., extreme structuralist-symbolic or critical-theory approaches).

My own initial close encounters with postprocessual archaeology—in 1982 and 1989—made significant impacts on my subsequent thoughts and actions.

LeBlanc, Redman, and I had carried out two explicitly New Archaeology–oriented field seasons in New Mexico during the summers of 1972 and 1973 (Watson et al. 1980), after which the two of them became career Southwesternists while I shifted to cave and shell mound archaeology in the Eastern Woodlands of North America (Watson 1999b).

As already noted, cave archaeology in and around Mammoth Cave National Park fortuitously enabled me to continue research on an agricultural origins story very different from that being pursued by Braidwood, his codirectors, and collaborators in Iraq, Iran, and Turkey. By 1974, I was thoroughly immersed in fieldwork at Salts Cave, Mammoth Cave, and other underground locales, as well as Bill Marquardt's and my investigations of shell mounds along Green River downstream from Mammoth Cave National Park (Marquardt & Watson 2005; Watson 1969, 1974). My job as a new faculty member in the Anthropology Department (recently split off from Sociology) at Washington University in St. Louis was also very demanding. After the main New Archaeology period of the 1960s and ensuing debates about ethnoarcheology and site formation, I slid away from abstract theoretical issues and scholarly disputes to pressing matters of departmental and campus politics vital to our small Anthropology unit on the one hand and exhilarating field and lab research in my new persona as an Americanist archaeologist on the other.

So I was a little slow to focus on what was happening in European archaeological theory during the 1980s, and even on developments within 1970s–1980s sociocultural anthropology. I received a valuable introduction to some crucial postprocessualist issues, however, during a 1982 visit to Birzeit University in the West Bank/Israeli Occupied Territories. The trip was arranged by Albert E. Glock, an archaeologist who had recently accepted a position at Birzeit. The central administration there wanted to establish a curriculum in regional archaeology, which they hired Glock to create. Having found several promising West Bank students, he was planning to help them secure graduate degrees from archaeological programs in Europe and the United States so they could return to staff the Birzeit department. Glock invited me to come to Jerusalem, stay with him and his wife Lois, meet the students, and discuss current developments in archaeology with them, especially ethnoarchaeology.

I spent several days with Glock and his students, being toured around archaeological sites on the West Bank, talking with them about work they had already done and work planned for the future. Glock was very explicit about his goal. He was preparing this select group of bright, well-educated indigenous young scholars to carry out their own archaeological research in their own country and to guide future generations of Birzeit students in learning about their own cultural history.

My stay in the West Bank made a profound impression. There are few places in the world where every aspect of archaeological research is so politicized and where practitioners must remain so continuously aware of the political intricacies integral to everything they say and do.

Further lessons were forthcoming in other categories addressed by postprocessualists when I participated in a 1989 conference at Southern Illinois University, Carbondale. The conference organizer was Robert Preucel, then Scholar in Residence at the Center for Archaeological Investigations. This appointment meant he could work on his own research all year, except that he was responsible for organizing and chairing a conference on the theme he proposed when applying for this position. Preucel's theme was Processual versus Post-Processual Archaeology. Proponents on both sides of the Atlantic and of the theoretical/methodological divide were invited, and Preucel asked me to provide general commentary at the close of the conference.

The group assembled for the get-acquainted reception at A Touch of Nature, the woodland retreat that lodged the conference. While talking with a Norwegian archaeologist, Bjørnar Olsen, I received my first clue concerning significant differences between European perspectives and my own. Olsen remarked that he saw no need for consensus or accommodation among proponents of different views on archaeological theory. Why should archaeologists not continually dispute their positions as philosophers do?

As the conference ran its course, I became increasingly anxious about my putative contribution. The presentations (by advocates much more skilled at debating than I) were diverse, sometimes contradictory, and drew on literature of which I was fairly or completely ignorant. The names of the favorite social theorists—even those I'd heard of and knew a little about—were menacing: Adorno, Bourdieu, Giddens, Foucault, Heidigger, Horkheimer, Ladurie, Marcuse, Merleau-Ponty, Ricoeur. I stayed up most of the night before my presentation to compose it.

In spite of my qualms, it turned out all right (interested readers can judge for themselves by consulting Preucel 1991). I used Olsen's comment to make a point about the funding of archaeological research: How can we expect NSF or the National Endowment for the Humanities (NEH) to provide money to a scholarly group who cannot agree about the empirical nature (if any) of the archaeological record, and what the most important goals (if any) should be for archaeology in general? Moreover, given the nature of field archaeology in the United States a decade and a half into the CRM era, how could the large group of CRM archaeologists maintain their professional activities (successfully bidding on contracts in response to Requests-for-Proposals, carrying out Phase I and/or II, and/or III work, preparing the final report under budget and before deadline) while also keeping up with fast-moving scholarly debates that draw primarily on the vast literature of European social theory?

My experiences at the Touch of Nature conference and on the West Bank were valuable in many ways, central among them being a much clearer understanding of the basic critiques than I would have gained from simply studying postprocessualist publications.

So what do, or did, the 1980s postprocessualists want? Some of their accusations and demands for change were justified. For example, processualist archaeologists neglected ideational issues and individual agency in past societies they were studying and virtually completely ignored the sociopolitical context of contemporary archaeology. Hence, processualists were vulnerable to many charges leveled against them by postprocessualists voicing archaeologically relevant portions of the postmodernist program that had surfaced a decade or so earlier in sociocultural anthropology. Perhaps most importantly, postprocessualists denied that direct, unproblematic, unbiased access to "the real past" was possible.

Preucel's edited volume was, of course, not the only product of the processual-postprocessual conflict. Argumentation included direct confrontations in person (Stone 1989) and in print between Binford and Hodder (Binford 1987, Binford & Stone 1988, Hodder 1988). Many books and journal articles addressing the general debate and issues raised by it appeared and continue to do so (e.g., Gero & Conkey 1991, Hall 1997, Hodder & Hutson 2003, Nelson 2007, World Archaeol. Congr. 2005, Wylie 2002).

There is also by now something along the lines of postpostprocessualist archaeology represented by archaeological theorists who have taken up themes from, for example, poststructuralism, embodiment, and neosemiotics (Bapty & Yates 1990, Hamilakis et al. 2002, Preucel 2006).

Meanwhile, CRM continues to be a major focus within the U.S. archaeological community. In 1990, strong impetus in a direction congruent with the postprocessual emphasis on indigenous and descendant populations was provided by passage of the Native American Graves Protection and Repatriation Act (NAGPRA). NAGPRA requires all U.S. institutions to inventory Native American human remains, grave goods, and other relevant materials in their possession and to send copies of these inventories to all 600+ federally recognized Indian tribes. Those tribes can then, via their legally appointed representatives (e.g., Tribal Historic Preservation Officers), request repatriation of such remains and items they establish as part of their cultural patrimony.

There are many examples of negotiations among American Indian tribes, museums, and other curational facilities and between tribal groups and archaeological research teams. Hundreds of human skeletal remains excavated between 1915 and 1925 during A.V. Kidder's Pecos Project (New Mexico) have been repatriated by Harvard University's Peabody Museum and reburied. A single skull labeled "Pawnee," obtained from a nineteenth-century battlefield and eventually donated to the anatomy department of a St. Louis hospital, was formally conveyed to a designated Pawnee representative. In some cases, agreements are drawn up whereby human remains and/or grave goods, ancient or historic, continue to be curated, by the institutions holding them, in a manner deemed appropriate by descendant groups.

Some years ago I was contacted by speleologists working in the Southern Rocky Mountains who had come upon human bone in the dark zone of a cave they were investigating. The skeletal remains turned out to be several thousand years old. Because the cave is on Forest Service land, the Forest Service archaeologist informed the appropriate Native American group so that their cultural heritage representative could join us to assist and oversee the proposed research. We determined that the ancient man had died in the cave, which meant that it was a burial site, hence a sacred site, so the Forest Service closed it to the public. The skeletal remains were examined and thoroughly documented then formally conveyed to a Forest Service repatriation specialist, who presented them to the cultural heritage representative.

As a scientist, I found this a wrenching experience because the most fundamental axiom of science is public accessibility to the primary evidence. We had done our best to document the ancient physical remains, but nothing is a satisfactory substitute for the bones themselves. Nevertheless, science and scientists function in the real world of the present and are subject to regulations and laws of the nations and administrative boundaries wherein they work. Long before CRM and NAGPRA, archaeology in the United States, as everywhere else, was constrained by many factors: shortage of time and money, inimical weather, hostile flora and/or fauna, sickness and accidents, uncooperative landowners or provincial officials, friction among the staff, and many other major and minor logistical problems, including destruction of some or all the primary evidence [e.g., by fire, floods, looting, warfare (Löw 2003, Emberling & Hanson 2008)].

As already noted, repatriation and reburial or other sequestration are not always the final result of a NAGPRA situation, but even if they are, those results can be ameliorated by benefits to both sides from working closely with each other. In fact, a very salubrious effect of postprocessual critiques together with legislation requiring attention to the rights of indigenous groups is that archaeologists everywhere are now much more aware of their responsibilities to local communities. It has become routine to confer and consult with the local people where one is planning to work. A good example is reported by the Center for Desert Archaeology (Duff et al. 2008; see also Colwell-Chanthaphonh & Ferguson 2007; Killion 2008; Little & Shackel 2007; SAA 2008a,b).

WHAT NEXT?

Anthropological archaeology in the Americas is an enterprise vastly different from what it was 30 years ago, let alone 50 years ago when I was completing graduate work. Both the AAA and the SAA are much larger than at any earlier time in their histories: ~11,000 members for the AAA and 7650 for the SAA. When the *Guide to Departments of Anthropology* was first published in 1962, only 44 PhD-granting departments containing 522 anthropologists were listed. In that same year, the SAA had 1706 members, including avocational as well as academic and museum personnel.

The AAA was reorganized in the 1980s, taking on its current configuration of multiple units called associations, councils, divisions, sections, or societies. According to the 2008–2009 AAA *Guide*, there are 37 of these (one of the founding units being the Archeology Division), plus six interest groups. The 13-member Executive Board includes representatives for five major subfields plus Student and Minority seats. The AAA governance group, like that of the SAA, has been for many years thoroughly engaged in contemporary national concerns including public outreach.

The SAA was also reorganized during the 1980s, having previously carried out its business affairs via the AAA headquarters office. Under the guidance of the first SAA Executive Director, Jerome Miller (hired in 1983), the mid to late 1980s were exciting years (Fowler et al. 1997). Under Miller's guidance, membership increased, *American Antiquity* was printed and distributed by an independent publishing company, and the SAA established its own Washington, DC, office and hired its own lobbyist on The Hill (after learning that a nonprofit organization can legally devote up to 20% of its income to direct lobbying of Congressional personnel).

Size increase for the restructured SAA was accompanied by increases in diversity, both in ethnicity and in gender. There is still work to be done (Zeder 1997), but SAA membership includes American Indian, African American, and Latin American archaeologists as well as many more women than it had previously. The percentage of members based in public or private sectors (i.e., federal, state, county, or municipal

agencies vis-à-vis free-lance CRM businesses, or large contracting firms that carry out an array of environmental consulting work) is roughly equal to that of academic and museum archaeologists, and CRM training is the norm for student archaeologists. There is also considerable concern with applied archaeology directed to retrieving past technology and knowledge for use in the present (e.g., Erickson 1998) and with other archaeological contributions to solving contemporary problems (Sabloff 2008).

The highly parochial character of early- to mid-twentieth-century ivory-tower archaeology is much diminished. Strong scholarly traditions with striking contrasts from one country to another, or interregionally within a single country, have given way to an international archaeological community (sustained by global email systems) wherein major and minor data-based questions as well as theoretical, methodological, and political ones are discussed and debated. The World Archaeological Congress is the largest of these networks, but there are also many smaller e-lists (e.g., cave archaeology) that are—thanks to the Internet—equally global in coverage. Globally accessible Web sites maintained by individual projects or individual archaeologists are legion. The Internet has (so long as the electronic infrastructure can be maintained) solved the problems of archaeological data manipulation, storage, retrieval, and public access that loomed so large through the 1970s and early 1980s. It has also greatly facilitated international interdisciplinary research.

Themes now common to Americanist archaeology and world archaeology include those central to Old Archaeology (time-space systematics, cultural histories specific to places and peoples), New Archaeology (archaeology as science, evolutionary archaeology; paleoenvironment, paleoecology, paleoeconomy of past societies and cultures), postprocessual archaeology (paleo-cognition, critical theory, multivalent interpretations of the past, archaeology as history, individual action in the past, domination and resistance), and

SAA: Society for American Archaeology

post-postprocessual archaeology (phenomenological perspectives, embodiment and the human body as a universal referent).

And that is just with reference to archaeological theory and to the sociology and ethnography of archaeological scholars. Archaeological technology has become much more complex, much more expensive, and much more international in scope. Radiocarbon dating, integral to the practice of archaeology since the 1950s, as well as trace element analysis, ancient DNA analysis, and the whole panoply of archaeochemistry and archaeophysics are routinely employed in addition to the subdisciplines now standard to archaeological practice everywhere (archaeobotany, archaeometry, archaeozoology, ethnoarchaeology, and geoarchaeology). It's a brave new archaeological world.

But that brave new world is a fragile one because—like every other scholarly pursuit—archaeology, prehistoric or historic, anthropological or classical, is one very small component of a global human population that is currently highly politicized and severely threatened by planet-wide problems ranging from fiscal crises to pollution of the oceans and the atmosphere, desertification, epidemic diseases, and inadequate subsistence systems affecting millions of people.

Archaeology and anthropology alone cannot save the real world. Nor does it matter, I suppose, whether we explicitly profess allegiance to what used to be a unified field called "anthropology." But it is supremely important that anthropologists of all varieties continue to participate in the work that has always engaged anthropological scholars and practitioners, work that no other discipline can undertake: Providing more and better understandings about the whole of humankind—viewed biologically, culturally, socially—from origins millions of years ago to the present day. If a global human community is to be created and sustained on this endangered planet, then the real world needs those understandings desperately.

DISCLOSURE STATEMENT

The author is not aware of any affiliations, memberships, funding, or financial holdings that might be perceived as affecting the objectivity of this review.

ACKNOWLEDGMENTS

I am grateful to Cyndi J. Mosch for permission to publish the image appearing here as the frontispiece.

LITERATURE CITED

Bapty I, Yates T, eds. 1990. *Archaeology after Structuralism: Introductory Readings in Post-Structuralism and Archaeology*. Cambridge, UK: Cambridge Univ. Press

Barth F. 1953. *Principles of Social Organization in Southern Kurdistan*. Oslo: Univ. Etnog. Mus.

Barth F. 2007. Overview: sixty years in anthropology. *Annu. Rev. Anthropol.* 36:1–16

Benington F, Melton C, Watson PJ. 1962. Carbon dating prehistoric soot from Salts Cave, Kentucky. *Am. Antiq.* 18:238–41

Bennett JW. 1943. Recent developments in the functional interpretation of archaeological data. *Am. Antiq.* 9:208–19

Binford LR. 1962. Archaeology as anthropology. *Am. Antiq.* 28:217–25

Binford LR. 1976. Forty-seven trips: a case study in the character of some formation processes of the archaeological record. In *Contributions to Anthropology: The Interior Peoples of Northern Alaska*, ed. E Hall Jr, pp. 299–381. Archaeol. Survey Can. Paper 49. Ottawa: Natl. Mus.

Binford LR. 1980. Willow smoke and dogs' tails: hunter-gatherer settlement systems and archaeological site formation. *Am. Antiq.* 45:4–20

Binford LR. 1981. *Bones: Ancient Men and Modern Myths*. New York: Academic

Binford LR. 1987. Data, relativism and archaeological science. *Man* 22:391–404

Binford LR, Stone N. 1988. Correspondence: archaeology and theory. *Man* 23:374–76

Braidwood LS. 1953. *Digging Beyond the Tigris*. New York: Schuman

Braidwood RJ. 1957. Jericho and its setting in Near Eastern prehistory. *Antiquity* 31:73–81

Braidwood RJ, Braidwood LS. 1950. Jarmo: a village of early farmers in Iraq. *Antiquity* 24:189–95

Braidwood RJ, Braidwood LS. 1953. The earliest village communities of Southwestern Asia. *J. World Hist.* 1:278–310

Browman DL, Fritz GJ, Watson PJ. 2009. Origins of food-producing economies in the Americas. In *The Human Past*, ed. C Scarre, pp. 306–49. New York: Thames & Hudson. 2nd ed.

Çambel H, Braidwood RJ. 1980. *Prehistoric Research in Southeastern Anatolia I*. Publ. 2589. Istanbul: Univ. Istanbul, Fac. Lett. Press

Cappers RTJ, Bottema S, eds. 2002. *The Dawn of Farming in the Near East*. Stud. Near East. Prod. Subsist. Environ. No. 6. Berlin: Ex Oriente

Colledge S, Conolly J, eds. 2007. *The Origin and Spread of Domestic Plants in Southwest Asia and Europe*. Walnut Creek, CA: Left Coast

Chapman J, Watson PJ. 1993. The Archaic Period and the flotation revolution. In *Foraging and Farming in the Eastern Woodlands of North America*, ed. M Scarry, pp. 27–38. Gainesville: Univ. Press Fla.

Colwell-Chanthaphonh C, Ferguson TJ, eds. 2007. *Collaboration in Archaeological Practice: Engaging Descendant Communities*. Lanham, MD: Altamira

David N, Kramer C, eds. 2001. *Ethnoarchaeology in Action*. Cambridge, UK: Cambridge Univ. Press

Davis MC. 2008. *Dame Kathleen Kenyon: Digging Up the Holy Land*. Walnut Creek, CA: Left Coast

Denham TP, Kriarte J, Vrydaghs L, eds. 2007. *Rethinking Agriculture: Archaeological and Ethnoarchaeological Perspectives*. Walnut Creek, CA: Left Coast

Duff AI, Ferguson TJ, Bruning S, Whiteley P. 2008. Collaborative research in a living landscape: Pueblo land, culture, and history in west-central New Mexico. *Archaeol. Southwest* 22:1–2

Emberling G, Hanson K, eds. 2008. *Catastrophe! The Looting and Destruction of Iraq's Past*. Chicago: Orient. Inst.

Erickson CL. 1998. Applied archaeology and rural development: archaeology's potential contribution to the future. In *Crossing Currents: Continuity and Change in Latin America*, ed. M Whiteford, S Whiteford, pp. 34–45. Upper Saddle River, NJ: Prentice Hall

Fowler D, Dincauze D, Leone M, Sabloff J. 1997. Jerome Miller, 1922–1996. *SAA Bull.* 15:22–23

Fritz GJ. 1990. Multiple pathways to farming in precontact Eastern North America. *J. World Prehist.* 4:387–435

Fritz GJ. 2007. Keepers of Louisiana's levees: early mound builders and forest managers. See Denham et al. 2007, pp. 189–209

Gero J, Conkey M, eds. 1991. *Engendering Archaeology: Women and Prehistory*. Oxford: Basil Blackwell

Goldberg P, Nash D, Petraglia M, eds. 1993. *Formation Processes in Archaeological Context*. Monogr. World Archaeol. 17. Madison, WI: Prehistory Press

Goldberg P, Sherwood S. 2006. Deciphering human prehistory through the geoarchaeological study of cave sediments. *Evolutionary Anth.* 15:20–36

Gremillion KJ. 2002. The development and dispersal of agricultural systems in the Woodland Period Southeast. In *The Woodland Southeast*, ed. DG Anderson, RJ Mainfort Jr, pp. 483–501. Tuscaloosa: Univ. Ala. Press

Hall RL. 1977. An anthropocentric perspective for Eastern U.S. prehistory. *Am. Antiq.* 42:499–518

Hall RL. 1997. *An Archaeology of the Soul: North American Indian Belief and Ritual*. Urbana: Univ. Ill. Press

Hamilakis Y, Pluciennik M, Tarlow S, eds. 2002. *Thinking through the Body: Archaeologies of Corporality*. New York: Plenum

Hillman GC. 2000. Overview: the plant-based components of subsistence in Abu Hureyra 1 and 2. In *Village on the Euphrates: From Foraging to Farming at Abu Hureyra*, ed. AMT Moore, GC Hillman, AJ Legge, pp. 416–22. Oxford: Oxford Univ. Press

Hillman GC, Davies MS. 1992. Domestication rate in wild wheats and barley under cultivation: preliminary results and archaeological implications of field measurements of selection coefficient. In *Préhistoire de L'Agriculture: Nouvelles Approches Expérimentale et Ethnografique*, ed. P Anderson, pp. 113–58. Cent. Rech. Archéol. Monogr. 6. Paris: CNRS

Hodder I. 1982. Theoretical archaeology: a reactionary view. In *Symbolic and Structural Archaeology*, ed. I Hodder, pp. 1–16. Cambridge, UK: Cambridge Univ. Press

Hodder I. 1985. Postprocessual archaeology. *Adv. Archaeol. Method Theory* 8:1–26

Hodder I. 1988. Correspondence: archaeology and theory. *Man* 23:373–74

Hodder I. 2007. Çatalhöyük in the context of the Middle Eastern Neolithic. *Annu. Rev. Anthropol.* 36:105–20

Hodder I, Hutson S. 2003. *Reading the Past: Current Approaches to Interpretation in Archaeology*. Cambridge, UK: Cambridge Univ. Press. 3rd ed.

Johnson A. 2008. Processual archaeology. In *Encyclopedia of Archaeology*, ed. D Pearsall, pp. 1894–96. Oxford: Elsevier

Kehoe AB, Kehoe TF. 1974. Cognitive models for archaeological interpretation. *Am. Antiq.* 38:150–54

Kenyon K. 1957. Reply to Professor Braidwood. *Antiquity* 31:82–84

Killion TW, ed. 2008. *Opening Archaeology: Repatriation's Impact on Contemporary Research and Practice*. Santa Fe, NM: Sch. Am. Res.

King TF. 2008. *Cultural Resource Laws and Practice*. Lanham, MD: Altamira

Kluckhohn C. 1940. The conceptual structure in Middle American studies. In *The Maya and their Neighbors*, ed. CL Hay, RL Linton, SC Lothrop, HL Shapiro, GC Vaillant, pp. 41–51. New York: Appleton-Century

Little BJ, Shackel PA. 2007. *Archaeology as a Tool of Civic Engagement*. Lanham, MD: Altamira

Löw U. 2003. Die plünderungen der kulterellen einrichtungen im Irak under besonderer berüksichtigung des Nationalmuseums in Baghdad. *Mitteilungen der deutschen Orient-Gesellschaft* 135:13–56

Marquardt WH, Watson PJ, eds. 2005. *Archaeology of the Middle Green River Region, Kentucky*. Fla. Mus. Nat. Hist., Inst. Archaeol. Paleoenviron. Stud. Monog. 5. Gainesville: Univ. Press Fla.

Mellaart J. 1967. *Çatal Hüyük: A Neolithic Town in Anatolia*. London: Thames and Hudson

Naderi S, Rezaei H-R, Pompanon F, Blum MGB, Negrini R, et al. 2008. The goat domestication process inferred from large-scale mitochondrial DNA analysis of wild domestic individuals. *Proc. Natl. Acad. Sci. USA* 105:17659–64

Nelson SM, ed. 2007. *Identity and Subsistence: Gender Strategies for Archaeology*. Lanham, MD: Altamira

Poinar HN, Kuch M, Sobolik KD, Barnes I, Stankiewicz AB, et al. 2001. A molecular analysis of dietary diversity for three Archaic Native Americans. *Proc. Natl. Acad. Sci. USA* 98:4317–22

Preucel R, ed. 1991. *Processual and Post-Processual Archaeologies: Multiple Ways of Approaching the Past*. Cent. Arch. Investig. Occas. Pap. 10. Carbondale: South. Ill. Univ. Press

Preucel R. 2006. *Archaeological Semiotics*. Oxford: Blackwell Sci. Ltd.

Pumpelly R, ed. 1908. *Explorations in Turkestan. Expedition of 1904. Prehistoric Civilizations of Anau: Origins, Growth, and Influence of Environment*. Vols. 1, 2. Washington DC: Carnegie Inst. Wash.

Redman CL, Watson PJ. 1970. Systematic, intensive surface collection. *Am. Antiq.* 35:279–91

Riley TJ, Walz GR, Bareis CJ, Fortier AC, Parker KE. 1994. Accelerator mass spectrometry (AMS) dates confirm early Zea mays in the Mississippi River valley. *Am. Antiq.* 59:490–98

Sabloff J. 2008. *Archaeology Matters: Action Archaeology in the Modern World*. Walnut Creek, CA: Left Coast

Schiffer MB. 1972. Archaeological context and systematic context. *Am. Antiq.* 37:372–75

Schiffer MB. 1987. *Formation Processes of the Archaeological Record*. Albuquerque: Univ. N. M. Press

Simmons AH. 2007. *The Neolithic Revolution in the Near East: Transforming the Human Landscape*. Tucson: Univ. Ariz. Press

Smith BD. 2002. *Rivers of Change*. Washington, DC: Smithson. Inst. Press

Smith BD. 2006. Eastern North America as an independent center of plant domestication. *Proc. Natl. Acad. Sci. USA* 103:12223–28

Smith BD, Yarnell RA. 2009. Initial formation of an indigenous crop complex in eastern North America. *PNAS Early Ed.* **http://www.pnas.org/cgi/doi/10.1073/pnas.0901846106**

Sobolik KD, Gremillion KJ, Whitten PL, Watson PJ. 1996. Sex determination of prehistoric human paleofeces. *Am. J. Phys. Anthropol.* 101:283–90

Soc. Am. Archaeol. (SAA) 2008a. Special issue: international cooperative research. In *The Archaeological Record*, Vol. 8, no. 2, ed. A Duff, pp. 7–24. Washington, DC: Soc. for Am. Archaeol.

Soc. Am. Archaeol. (SAA) 2008b. Special section: international cooperative research. In *The Archaeological Record*, Vol. 8, no. 3, ed. A Duff, pp. 6–27. Washington, DC: Soc. for Am. Archaeol.

Stein JK. 1983. Earthworm activity: a source of potential disturbances of archaeological sediments. *Am. Antiq.* 48:277–89

Stein JK. 2005a. Environment of the Green River sites. See Marquardt & Watson 2005, pp. 19–39

Stein JK. 2005b. Formation processes of the Carlston Annis shell midden. See Marquardt & Watson 2005, pp. 121–57

Stein JK, Farrand WR, eds. 1985. *Archaeological Sediments in Context.* Orono, ME: Cent. Study Early Man, Inst. Quat. Stud., Univ. Maine

Steward JH, Setzler FH. 1938. Function and configuration in archaeology. *Am. Antiq.* 4:4–10

Stone NM. 1989. Symposium: *Advice and dissent: an exchange of views about archaeological issues confronting the 1990s.* Transcript of comments by and dialogue among L Binford, M Conkey, R Dunnell, I Hodder, M Leone, C Renfrew, M Schiffer, PJ Watson. Annu. Meet. Soc. Am. Archaeol., 57th, Atlanta, GA

Taylor WW. 1948. *A Study of Archeology.* Mem. 69. Menasha, WI: Am. Anthropol. Assoc.

Watson PJ, ed. 1969. *The Prehistory of Salts Cave, Kentucky.* Rep. Investig. 16. Springfield: Ill. State Mus.

Watson PJ, ed. 1974. *Archeology of the Mammoth Cave Area.* New York: Academic

Watson PJ. 1979. *Archaeological Ethnography in Western Iran.* Viking Fund Publ. 57, Wenner-Gren Found. Tucson: Univ. Ariz. Press

Watson PJ. 1997. The shaping of modern paleoethnobotany. In *People, Plants, and Landscapes: Case Studies in Paleoethnobotany*, ed. KJ Gremillion, pp. 13–22. Tuscaloosa: Univ. Ala. Press

Watson PJ. 1999a. Ethnographic analogy and ethnoarchaeology. In *Archaeology, History, and Culture in Palestine and the Near East: Eassays in Memory of Albert E. Glock*, ed. T Kapitan. American Schools of Oriental Research, ASOR Books, vol. 3, pp. 47–65

Watson PJ. 1999b. From the Hilly Flanks of the Fertile Crescent to the Eastern Woodlands of North America. In *Grit-Tempered: Early Women Archaeologists in the Southeastern US*, ed. NM White, LP Sullivan, RA Marrinan, pp. 286–97. Gainesville, FL: Univ. Fla. Press

Watson PJ. 1999c. The Prehistoric Project, 1968 and 1970: a familial memoir. In *Light on Top of the Black Hill: Studies presented to Halet Çambel*, ed. G Arsebük, M Mellink, W Schirmer, pp. 759–61. Istanbul: Ege Yayınları

Watson PJ. 2008. Processualism and after. In *Handbook of Archaeological Theories*, ed. RA Bentley, HDG Maschner, C Chippindale, pp. 29–38. Lanham, MD: Altamira

Watson PJ, LeBlanc SA. 1990. *Girikihaciyan: A Halafian Site in Southeastern Turkey.* Los Angeles: Inst. Archaeol., Univ. Calif. Los Angeles

Watson PJ, LeBlanc SA, Redman CL. 1971. *Explanation in Archeology.* New York: Columbia Univ. Press

Watson PJ, LeBlanc SA, Redman CL. 1980. Aspects of Zuni prehistory. *J. Field Archaeol.* 7:201–18

Watson PJ, Yarnell RA. 1966. Archaeological and paleoethnobotanical investigations in Salts Cave, Mammoth Cave National Park, Kentucky. *Am. Antiq.* 31:842–49

Watson PJ, Yarnell RA. 1986. Lost John's last meal. *Mo. Archaeol.* 47:241–55

Weiss E, Kislev ME, Hartmann A. 2006. Autonomous cultivation before domestication. *Science* 312:1608–10

World Archaeol. Congr. 2005. *Archaeologies: Journal of the World Archaeological Congress*, Vol. 1, Number 1. New York: Springer

Wylie MA. 1982. An analogy by any other name is just as analogical: a commentary on the Gould-Watson dialogue. *J. Anthropol. Archaeol.* 1:382–401

Wylie MA. 1985. The reaction against analogy. *Adv. Archaeol. Method Theory* 8:63–111

Wylie A. 2002. *Thinking From Things: Essays in the Philosophy of Archaeology.* Berkeley: Univ. Calif. Press

Yarnell RA. 1969. Contents of human paleofeces. See Watson 1969, pp. 41–54

Yarnell RA. 1974. Plant foods and cultivation of the Salts Cavers. See Watson 1974, pp. 113–22

Yarnell RA. 1994. Investigations relevant to the native development of plant husbandry in Eastern North America: a brief and reasonably true account. In *Agricultural Origins and Development in the Midcontinent*, ed. W Green, pp. 7–24. Rept. 19. Iowa City: Off. State Archaeol., Univ. Iowa

Zeder MA. 1997. *The American Archaeologist: A Profile.* Walnut Creek, CA: Altamira

Zeder MA. 2008. Domestication and early agriculture in the Mediterranean basin: origins, diffusion, and impact. *Proc. Natl. Acad. Sci. USA* 105:11597–604

New Paths in the Linguistic Anthropology of Oceania

Matt Tomlinson[1] and Miki Makihara[2]

[1] Discipline of Anthropology, Monash University, Clayton, Victoria 3800, Australia;
email: matt.tomlinson@arts.monash.edu.au

[2] Department of Anthropology, Queens College and the Graduate Center, City University
of New York, Flushing, New York 11372; email: miki.makihara@qc.cuny.edu

Annu. Rev. Anthropol. 2009. 38:17–31

First published online as a Review in Advance on
June 12, 2009

The *Annual Review of Anthropology* is online at
anthro.annualreviews.org

This article's doi:
10.1146/annurev-anthro-091908-164438

0084-6570/09/1021-0017$20.00

Key Words

agency, entextualization, language ideologies, *mana*, personhood

Abstract

The linguistic anthropology of Oceania has seen vigorous and productive analysis of language ideologies, ritual performance, personhood, and agency. This article points to three related paths of inquiry that are especially promising. First, language ideologies are analyzed for the ways they shape expectations and interpretations of effective action and social identity. Second, processes of entextualization are examined with reference to Bible translation because Christianity is a dominant social force in contemporary Oceania. Third, prominent recent work on personhood and agency is reviewed, and scholars are urged to reconsider the classic Oceanic term *mana* in relation to changing understandings of power, including those wrought by religious transformations. These paths of inquiry are intertwined and cross-cutting and can lead to productive new understandings of ideologies and practices of stability and transformation.

INTRODUCTION

Personhood:
grammatical
configuration of social
selves

Agency:
responsibility for
action

Entextualization: the
process in which
segments of discourse
gain apparent fixity
that facilitates their
public circulation

As scholars increasingly focus on culture's "public, mobile, traveling" qualities (Ortner 2006, p. 18), anthropologists ask how certain categories and identities come to seem stable and durable for our interlocutors. Rightly wary of essentialisms, anthropologists nonetheless recognize that discourse of fixity and permanence is a prominent feature of many cultural contexts and is a means of shaping unfolding practice. The study of language use has been at the forefront of efforts to understand relationships between ideologies and practices of stability and transformation, and in the past 20 years the linguistic anthropology of Oceania has played a vital role in developing relevant theoretical approaches with careful attention to ethnographic detail. (See sidebar, Oceanic Boundaries.)

Three areas of investigation in which the linguistic anthropology of Oceania has been especially illuminating are (*a*) language ideologies, (*b*) ritual performance, and (*c*) personhood and agency. In each of these areas, interplays between stability and transformation are manifest in discourse about tradition, authority, and efficacy. This article reviews recent work in these areas and points to three interconnected paths of inquiry.

We begin by examining language ideologies, shared notions about the nature of language, including reflexive representations of language characteristics, use, and effects. Language ideologies, which often treat stability and transformation as both subjects and criteria of evaluation, have become a major area of research because of the ways they "envision and enact links of language to group and personal identity, to aesthetics, to morality, and to epistemology ... [and] often underpin fundamental social institutions" (Woolard & Schieffelin 1994, pp. 55–56). Anthropology has vigorously taken up research on language ideologies throughout Oceania and across a range of local settings and, in doing so, has illuminated culture's "public, mobile, traveling" qualities in new ways. Next we turn to entextualization, focusing on the intersection of ritual performance and translation practices, paying special attention to studies of Bible translation. We take this approach because Christianity is a dominant social force in modern Oceania and is increasingly the subject of intensive ethnographic analysis. Finally, in the third section we address topics of personhood and agency. Anthropologists have used detailed grammatical and pragmatic analyses of subjects such as "segmentary persons," the "heroic I," and ergativity to illuminate the ways that personhood and agency are constituted and contested in Oceanic linguistic-cultural contexts. We argue that work on personhood and agency in Oceania can be enriched through fresh critical attention to *mana*, a term whose cognates are found in languages throughout the region.

OCEANIC BOUNDARIES

"Oceania" conventionally denotes the Pacific islands, extending from New Guinea and the Northern Mariana Islands in the west and northwest to Rapa Nui (Easter Island) in the east, and from New Zealand in the south to Hawai'i in the north. In 1832, d'Urville classified the islands in three groups: Melanesia, Micronesia, and Polynesia (Besnier 2004, p. 97). These labels have come under scholarly criticism; archaeologists have proposed a new distinction between "near Oceania" and "remote Oceania" on the basis of migration and settlement histories (Green 1991, Kirch 1997). Despite such criticism, the terms have become accepted within the region and applied to such entities as states (the Federated States of Micronesia), economic zones (the Melanesian Spearhead Group), and religious organizations (the Anglican Diocese of Polynesia).

The two major language groups in Oceania are Austronesian and Papuan, with the former extending to southeast Asia and Madagascar. Papuan languages, which unlike Austronesian ones do not share a common ancestor (Foley 1986, 2000), are found largely in New Guinea. Oceanic, a subgroup of Austronesian, includes ~450 languages (Pawley & Ross 1995, p. 39). All Polynesian languages are Oceanic; all Micronesian languages are Oceanic except for two, Chamorro and Palauan (Lynch et al. 2002, p. 4).

LANGUAGE IDEOLOGIES

Language ideologies—shared notions about the nature of language—inform worldviews, shape verbal behaviors, and contour social interactions. As such, they help construct social realities, personhood, identity, agency, aesthetic sensibilities, and sentiments (Kroskrity 2000, Schieffelin et al. 1998, Woolard & Schieffelin 1994). They do so not only through the use of language in which propositional meaning is created, but also, and perhaps more significantly, through the semiotic working of language, where social actors use or interpret "contextualization cues" (Gumperz 1982, 1992), in particular those with indexical and iconic properties linking linguistic elements to social and affective meanings.[1]

Fine-grained analysis of the relationship between linguistic structure and practice and language ideologies has provided a tool for understanding social and cultural formations' reproduction and transformation. Through close examination of verbal acts and their sociocultural contexts, linguistic anthropologists have demonstrated how verbal behaviors can constitute innovative, experimental, reproductive, and transformative acts, thereby illuminating the dynamic, processual relationships among what Williams (1977) called "emergent," "residual," and "dominant" cultural formations. Verbal behaviors themselves are shaped by the linguistic dispositions and ideologies of their speakers, which are continually reconfirmed or revised as they shape verbal interaction.

One of the reasons why Oceania has offered rich case studies of the links between language and social life is the central place of talk and oratory in the construction of social life in many Pacific societies, where talk figures prominently in the regulation of social relations, in the formation of group and personal identities, and in negotiations of power and interpersonal and group conflict (e.g., Arno 1993; Besnier 2004; Brenneis & Myers 1984; Makihara & Schieffelin 2007a,b; Watson-Gegeo 1986; Watson-Gegeo & White 1990). Several scholars working in Melanesia have undertaken pioneering work on the dense and complex interconnections among forms of linguistic and material exchange [Merlan & Rumsey 1991; Robbins 2001b, 2007; Schieffelin 1990; see also Keane's (1997) influential work on Indonesia]. In addition, Oceanic societies exhibit enormous diversity in language varieties, practices, and ideologies, even across small speech communities. Small speech communities also often experience sociolinguistic change at an accelerated rate, with transformation depending on innovations and strategic language choices on the part of fewer individuals.

Recent anthropological work on language ideologies and sociocultural reproduction and transformation has benefited in particular from Ochs's and Schieffelin's innovative writings on language socialization (Ochs & Schieffelin 1984; Schieffelin & Ochs 1986a, 1986b). Socialization is a lifelong process of interaction and participation. Through careful linguistic and ethnographic examination of verbal interactions involving caretakers and children, Ochs and Schieffelin have demonstrated how participants structure communication to construct culturally specific worldviews in Samoa and Papua New Guinea (Ochs 1988, Schieffelin 1990). Ochs (1992) presents a theory of indexicality grounded in comparisons of the links between gender identities and language in a comparative study of Samoan and middle-class Anglo-American mothers. Through their verbal strategies of accommodation (such as the use or nonuse of a baby talk register) and evaluation (such as praise), Samoan and American mothers position themselves differently vis-à-vis children. Ochs demonstrates how use of linguistic resources indirectly indexes gender identity through stances, acts, and activities. Schieffelin's (1990)

Language ideologies: shared notions about the nature of language

---

[1]Included in contextualization cues are auditory and visual dimensions of prosody and paralanguage, which are nondiscrete, suprasegmental, and largely iconic. Such meaning construction is often performed in multisensory communication contexts where kinesic and musical modalities are intertwined with language (Feld & Fox 1994, Feld & Brenneis 2004, Feld et al. 2004).

study brings attention to the ways in which the communication of emotion in socialization is central to the construction of notions of self. Her work among the Kaluli resonates with Kulick's (1992b) among Gapun villagers, also in Papua New Guinea, highlighting the ways in which these societies host quite divergent views of children and their verbal expressions of emotions, and how this difference has led to distinct cultural expectations and preferences regarding actions and notions of self.

Sites of language socialization are sites of sociocultural reproduction and transformation. For example, Schieffelin's examination of Bosavi church sermons in terms of participant structure, language use, and cultural content demonstrates how missionizing practices involve language socialization and effect linguistic and cultural change (Kulick & Schieffelin 2004; see also Schieffelin 2007). In his study of language shift in Gapun, Kulick (1992a,b) describes two aspects of the self: *save* ("knowledge"), associated positively with Christianity, modernity, education, civilization, and men; and *hed* ("head"), associated negatively with paganism, the past, ancestors, backwardness, lack of education, and women. These two expressions of the self have come to be associated with the national language, Tok Pisin, and the local vernacular, Taiap, respectively. Kulick argues that the change in conceptions of personhood and language as enacted in children's language socialization practices has motivated the loss of Taiap and shift to Tok Pisin.[2]

Other works have focused on language ideology to investigate questions of agency, performance, and participation. They have shown how different kinds of actors in diverse situations can objectify and manipulate language to constitute new social realities and how such activities are culturally organized and historically contingent. For example, in her studies of language, status, and gender in Pohnpei, Micronesia, Keating details how power and status are achieved in, and constructed by, collaborative semiotic practices involving honorific language usage, food, and the body. Local cultural notions of language and body, as well as gender and honor, inform the semiotic choices Pohnpeian speakers make in claiming entitlement to prestige and in negotiating their places in the status hierarchy (Keating 1997, 1998a,b, 1999, 2000, 2005; Keating & Duranti 2006). Similarly, in his work on gossip and politics in Tuvalu, Besnier (2009) analyzes interconnections among language performance and local notions of hierarchy, egalitarianism, and gender. In examining the construction of power, agency, emotion, and morality in language use, he uncovers telling complexities beneath the local discourse of consensus and homogeneity and points to the partialness and unevenness of cultural knowledge and practices across individuals and situations. In comparison, Philips (2000, 2004) analyzes Tongan magistrate's court interactions to show how multiple language ideologies manifest themselves in nationalist discourses that contribute to the making of the Tongan nation-state, combining modern and traditional images of the constitutional monarchy.[3]

Taken together, these studies show that language structure does not necessarily shape social reality as an earlier variety of Whorfian linguistic relativism would describe it, but rather that what people do with language has the potential to change social reality, as well as to change language structure, which is differentially opened to objectification and

---

[2] See also Riley (2007), who describes language socialization practices in Marquesas, French Polynesia. French language ideology has contributed to language shift toward French by objectifying and alienating the local language, 'Enana; Riley finds, however, that family interactions, which continue to use the indigenous teasing genre and codeswitching speech styles, have contributed to increasing communicative competence in 'Enana among children.

[3] Other notable sources on these topics include Meyerhoff (1999) on the use of "sorry" in Bislama in Vanuatu, demonstrating that gender differences in linguistic strategies are linked to the different sources of social power to which men and women have access; Brison (1992) on the political importance of gossip and rumor in Kwanga villages in Papua New Guinea; and Philips's (2007) historical analysis of how missionaries and Tongan elites shaped nation-state formation through scholarly representations of honorific language.

manipulation (see e.g., Brenneis 1984, 1987; Duranti 1994; Robbins 2007; Schieffelin 2007). Moreover, such studies challenge anthropologists to think critically of their own presuppositions about social reality and ethnographic enterprises. For example, Robbins & Rumsey (2008, p. 408) have recently noted that one assertion often heard in Oceanic discourse—that one cannot know other people's thoughts and feelings—can be used productively "to force a rethinking of some fairly settled approaches to topics such as the nature of theories of mind, the role of intention in linguistic communication and social interaction more generally, and the importance of empathy in human encounters and in anthropological method."

The culturally organized and historically contingent nature of verbal activity is especially marked in cases of cross-cultural contact (Makihara & Schieffelin 2007a,b). The introduction of a new language involves much more than the acquisition of new vocabulary and grammar by community members. Stasch (2007) describes how the Korowai of West Papua have understood and incorporated a new lingua franca, Bahasa Indonesia, in their ethnolinguistic landscape and analyzes the development of a local ideology of linguistic difference characterized by the coexistence of estrangement and attraction. The Korowai consider Bahasa to be a "demon language," something foreign and dangerous but also alluring, existing in a parallel world: "Indonesian's strangeness, summarized in the 'demon language' label, is an important part of why Korowai are learning the language and why they are using it in the ways they do" (2007, p. 110). In situations of language contact, language hierarchies often develop in accord with the political and economic balance between groups. The formation and transformation of such hierarchies are a result of the verbal practices of actors who base their actions on their own situated, but changing, understandings of language, identity, and power. For example, Makihara (2004) describes the rise of new Spanish–Rapa Nui syncretic speech styles on Easter Island, where symbolic values attached to these new varieties as well as to the native Rapa Nui language are leading to the breakdown of the previously established "colonial diglossia"—a sociolinguistic hierarchy and associated diglossic separation of the functions of colonial and local languages.[4] In this context, where the balance of political power has steadily shifted toward the local Rapa Nui, community members have begun to develop a purist Rapa Nui language ideology. Seemingly opposed language ideologies—syncretic and purist—may be drawn upon within the same context or even by the same individuals (Makihara 2007).

ENTEXTUALIZATION, TRANSLATION, AND CHRISTIANITY

The term entextualization denotes the ways in which segments of discourse gain apparent fixity that facilitates their public circulation (see e.g., Bauman & Briggs 1990, Briggs & Bauman 1992, Duranti & Goodwin 1992, Kuipers 1990, Silverstein & Urban 1996). Drawing on models of culture as textual inscription and performance, per Ricouer and Geertz, Silverstein & Urban (1996, p. 1) observe that entextualization and contextualization "are the central and ongoing practices within cultural orders," processes in which people objectify social learning and facilitate its public circulation. Translation can be seen as a kind of entextualization, a variety distinguished by the crossing of linguistic codes in an attempt to replicate something from an original inscription such as semantic meaning or performative force.

The past two centuries have seen massive and ongoing efforts at rendering the Bible in diverse local tongues in Oceania, and these translation projects have had deep social consequences. Tahitian was the first Oceanic language in which a book of the Bible was printed (Luke, in 1818), as well as the first New

---

[4]See also Jourdan (2007, 2008) on changing language hierarchy in the Solomon Islands where Pijin, with its association with cosmopolitanism and individualism, has become the (de facto) national language and the new language of urban youth identity.

Testament (1829) and complete Bible (1838; see Murray 1888, Rickards 1996). By 1918, 15 languages of the Oceanic subgroup had full Bible translations (Rickards 1996, p. 463); a half century later, this number had increased to 21, with 54 languages receiving at least one book of the Bible in translation (United Bible Soc. 1974). In the mid-1950s, members of the Summer Institute of Linguistics (SIL), an organization dedicated to the task of Bible translation, were dismayed to learn how many distinct languages existed in the islands of the Pacific—well over 1000, and New Guinea itself has a large share—because they intended to translate Scripture into every single tongue (Handman 2007). At present, SIL aims to begin a translation in every remaining language of the world by 2025 (Handman 2007).

Processes of Bible translation are notable not just for their global scope but also their local impact, including changes within indigenous grammar, vocabulary, and ideology (Schieffelin 2000, 2007). For example, Besnier (1995) describes how Samoan missionaries reshaped local linguistic practices as they worked in Tuvalu from the mid-1860s under the aegis of the London Missionary Society. The missionaries introduced literacy so new congregants could read the Bible, but the Bibles they brought were Samoan translations; as a result, a diglossic situation arose in which Samoan came to represent education, church, and government authority. Although Tuvaluan has replaced Samoan in many contexts over the past century, and islanders have energetically turned literacy to purposes other than Bible reading, a distinct Samoan imprint on the dialect of Nukulaelae atoll is evident in grammar, vocabulary, and phonology (Besnier 1995, pp. 54–55). In Fiji, by comparison, British missionaries of the Wesleyan Methodist Missionary Society worked with their Tongan and Fijian counterparts to produce Fijian-language Bibles almost as soon as they arrived. In 1843, the missionaries selected the dialect of Bau Island as the standard for their translations, partly because of Bau's political status. Through the middle of the nineteenth century they kept translating, revising,

and publishing Scripture in Bauan, and the wide circulation of their Bibles fostered the development of a national language now referred to as Standard Fijian. Bauan, Standard Fijian, and the language of the Bible all diverge in significant ways; our point is simply that the establishment of modern Standard Fijian began with missionaries' Bible translation efforts (Cammack 1962, Clammer 1976, Geraghty 1989, Schütz 1972).

Connections between Christianity's universalist trajectories and its local appropriations are revealed through close attention to the use of particular Bible passages. For example, Robbins (2004, p. 163) notes that for the Urapmin of highland Papua New Guinea, who are obsessed with the end of the world and how to prepare for it, Revelation is the Bible book that "they pore over more than any other"; Romans is the second most popular because "statements in Romans that pertain to the divine legitimacy of the state have become key texts in Urapmin attempts to think about their current situation" within the nation (Robbins 2004, p. 170). Also in Papua New Guinea, Schieffelin notes how the gospel of Mark was the first translation project for Protestant missionaries to the Bosavi "because its narrative was seen as relatively simple for nonliterate indigenous people to understand" (2007, p. 148). It was taken up enthusiastically, becoming "the most popular and often repeated of the Gospels," with the first 12 verses of the second chapter especially favored because they gave Bosavi a persuasive new understanding of illness and Jesus's role in healing (Schieffelin 2007, pp. 145, 148–49).

Yet both Robbins and Schieffelin demonstrate how Bible translation is never a simple or straightforward process, but instead a problematic and open-ended encounter. Translators confront grammatical incommensurability, culturally presupposed meanings that require extensive elaboration, the pervasive significance of contexts of performance, and the force of different language ideologies. Schieffelin describes how Bosavi pastors have difficulty reading Tok Pisin Bible verses aloud and translating them into Bosavi as they go along—even though this is a prominent ritual action during church services—partly because their reading skills are inexpert, but also because their Tok Pisin Bibles contain metalinguistic and metapragmatic elements that are difficult to reconcile with Bosavi cultural principles (see also Schieffelin 2008). Robbins notes Urapmin interest in, but difficulties with, the verse John 1:1, "In the beginning was the Word, and the Word was with God, and the Word was God." The verse troubles Urapmin because of its opaqueness bordering on incoherence, but it also appeals to them because it reflects their understanding of speech's centrality to Christian ritual. They often say that "God is nothing but talk," a phrase that Robbins notes sounds insulting to Urapmin speakers (as well as English speakers) but one that indicates "problems many Urapmin people have with the Christian promotion of speech to the center of religious life" (Robbins 2001a, p. 905; see also Robbins 2004, 2007). Robbins and Schieffelin show that although missionaries commonly aim for clarity in their Bible translations, incoherence is sometimes valued and treated as a source of interpretive motivation for local audiences (see also Engelke & Tomlinson 2006).[5]

Sermons are key sites for tracing articulations among texts, performances, and broad patterns of ideology and practice. Analyzing congregationalist preaching in Tuvalu, Besnier (1995, pp. 116–68) shows that the effectiveness of sermons—and Christian ritual generally—depends on a sense of orderliness conveyed by an emphasis on literacy. Preachers base their sermons on handwritten texts, which vary from short notes to full scripts read aloud verbatim. Preachers may lend their scripts to kin,

circulating the written productions as they do customary forms of knowledge. Gender ideologies are reinforced in sermon script production and circulation because women never write their own. In addition, sermons highlight models of individual personhood, as preachers use pronouns and patterns of parallelism in distinctive ways that "centralize the separate individuality of the preacher and of each audience member" (1995, p. 147). Finally, sermons both reflect and shape local passion for understanding "truth," which is ideologically linked to a sense of completeness (see also Duranti 1993, Miyazaki 2004). This concern with truth leads to heavy quotation of the Bible in sermons, and Besnier notes that "quoted and quoting voices merge" (1995, p. 150), crowning preachers with an aura of divine authority, at least in contexts of performance.

These examples show the force of entextualization in social life. Missionaries created newly circulating texts as they translated Scripture into diverse local tongues, and their products were taken up selectively and deployed creatively by local audiences who shaped new practices—and new texts, and new ideologies—in response. These engagements often focused people's attention on processes and interplays of stability and transformation. Christianity arrived as a new cultural product, but it thrived in some places because it was recast as something primordial, whereas in other places it took hold precisely because of its novelty. This complicated relationship between stability and transformation is shown vividly in Watson-Gegeo & Gegeo's (1991) analysis of differences in communication styles between Anglican and evangelical Kwara'ae speakers in the Solomon Islands. Anglicans, who present themselves as more respectful of pre-Christian tradition, give a high degree of prestige to formal "high rhetorical" Kwara'ae speaking styles, whereas evangelicals, oriented to nonindigenous forms associated with the West, consider Kwara'ae language to be uniformly less prestigious than English and Solomon Islands Pijin. For markedly religious terms such as "baptize," "pastor," "heaven," and "sin," Anglicans use

---

[5]Positive evaluations of incoherent language are not limited to contexts of Christianity or conversion. Lindstrom (1990, p. 121) notes that "[v]aluable Melanesian knowledge . . . typically includes a lot of nonsense words," which, he argues, "permits people to seem to be revealing their knowledge while maintaining its secrecy, privacy, and thus its continuing exchange value." Crowley (2001), drawing on Lindstrom's observations and his own data from Erromango, Vanuatu, implies that a group holding such appreciation of "opaque nonsense" might readily accept grammatically awkward translations of new sacred texts precisely because of this appreciation.

(or have developed) Kwara'ae equivalents, whereas evangelicals tend to borrow English terms. Grammatically, evangelicals speak everyday Kwara'ae in a simplified, repetitive form molded by the simplified, repetitive Bible translation they use, and phonologically, they imitate certain non-Kwara'ae pronunciations. Because of these differences, evangelicals' "Kwara'ae sounds[s] like 'babytalk' (children's speech) to Anglicans. In turn, the Anglican penchant for using high-rhetoric Kwara'ae forms associated with traditional practices make[s] [Anglican] Kwara'ae sound *wikit* 'wicked, sinful'... and old-fashioned to Evangelicals" (1991, p. 541).[6]

The practical importance of Christianity in contemporary Oceania cannot be overstated. The missiologist Charles Forman characterized Oceania in the 1970s as "in all probability, the most solidly Christian part of the world" (Forman 1982, p. 227), and in the decades since he wrote this, the influence of churches has arguably increased, as missionary efforts continue (with newer evangelical groups challenging established denominations) and Christian leaders assert their presence in national political processes in places such as Fiji. Anthropologists have come to pay increasing attention to Christianity as a dominant social force in Oceania (Barker 1990). In doing so, many have found language to be a fruitful field of investigation, especially for apprehending people's ideologies and practices of stability and transformation.

PERSONHOOD, AGENCY, *MANA*

Innovative writings on personhood have been a hallmark of Melanesian anthropology (e.g., Leenhardt 1979); Strathern put forth the influential argument that Melanesian personhood is not predicated on a parts-whole relationship between individuals and a reified society, but instead follows a logic in which dividual persons condense social relationships with different relationships "elicited" in different contexts (e.g., Strathern 1988, 1992, pp. 90–116; compare Scott 2007). Such scholarship, which developed partly in response to dissatisfaction with Africanist descent theory's application to highlands Papua New Guinea, raises complicated questions about interrelationships among representation, action, and identity.

Linguistic anthropologists have contributed to this field of inquiry by investigating the precise ways in which social identities are generated and shaped through language use, and the ways in which identities are linked to attributions of agency (Ahearn 2001). For example, Merlan & Rumsey (1991) argue that persons who are discursively configured as agents in formal oratory in the western Nebilyer Valley of highlands Papua New Guinea are often neither solitary individuals nor stable social groups but "segmentary persons." Such "persons" are social units frequently designated by first- and second-person singular pronouns and associated verb markings. A group is often referred to by speakers in formal oratory as "I" or "you"; indeed, such pronominal reference is more common than overt designation by "tribal" name. The fact that pronominal referents can be shifting and ambiguous offers orators strategic potential because they are able to treat groups as presupposed and also render their claims "less available to overt contestation than the use of segmentary identity and personal names" (Merlan & Rumsey 1991, p. 139).

The designation of groups by singular pronouns is also seen in Polynesian use of the "heroic I," an "I" whose author and principal (per Goffman 1981) are considered to be ancestors and polity rather than the person uttering the words. Analysis of the heroic I is most strongly developed in the work of Sahlins, who treats it as an integral part of his theoretical project of reconciling structure and agency, culture and history: "By the heroic I—and various complements such as perpetual

---

[6]Watson-Gegeo & Gegeo (1991) show how these emblematic differences in speaking styles are correlated with differences in habitus: Anglicans aim for quiet, serious, respectful comportment and speaking styles, whereas evangelicals carry and express themselves exuberantly. On the construction of emblematic differences between mainline and evangelical denominations elsewhere in Oceania, see also Besnier (n.d.), Brison (2007), Jebens (2005), Miyazaki (2004), and Philips (2007).

kinship—the main relationships of society are at once projected historically and embodied currently in the persons of authority" (Sahlins 1985, p. 47; see also Sahlins 1981, 1991). This Polynesian expansion of "I" to encompass social wholes might seem to be at odds with Melanesian partible personhood per Strathern (see Mosko 1992), thus perhaps redrawing boundaries between Melanesia and Polynesia that were set in earlier discussions about distinctions between big-men and chiefs (e.g., Sahlins 1963). Rumsey (2000) argues, however, that these different models of personhood can be reconciled through close attention to the linguistic practices in which persons are made discursively present, especially the use of pronouns. Building partly on the work of Urban (1989), Rumsey argues that dividual, partible personhood follows a logic of anaphora, whereas heroic, encompassing personhood follows a logic of direct indexicality, both of which are possible with the first-person singular pronoun. Because both relationships exist within any language, both possibilities exist in any social system. That is, "these two contrary tendencies, the simultaneous amplification of the everyday self and partial eclipse of it," are copresent (Rumsey 2000, p. 109). The value of such an insight is that although different cultural configurations of personhood and agency are evident, no system is treated as closed or immutable: Melanesian personhood can be encompassing (as in the example of segmentary persons described above) as well as partible, and Polynesian personhood can be partible as well as encompassing.

Such scholarship encourages close attention to linguistic practices' political effects, a subject on which anthropologists working in Oceania have produced several invaluable studies (e.g., Brenneis & Myers 1984, Duranti 1994, Watson-Gegeo & White 1990). A previous review article on the linguistic anthropology of Oceania noted that "[t]he interconnection between speech-making and politics has been a continuing interest in the Pacific, where oratorical skills are critical to many forms of leadership" (Watson-Gegeo 1986, p. 153). A well-known ethnographic illustration is Duranti's (1994) monograph on Samoan political oratory in the context of the *fono*, a formal village council where speakers discuss contentious issues. A key difference in speaking strategies concerns use of the ergative particle (*e*), which marks subjects of transitive clauses. That is, *e* explicitly identifies agents, as opposed to other roles such as actors and instruments (Duranti 1994, pp. 122–23). Noting that use of the ergative particle is somewhat rare in everyday speech, and that speakers do not need to use it to represent a subject as an agent, Duranti argues that analysis of its use is an insightful way to link grammar and politics: To mark agency explicitly in the *fono* is often to praise or to blame because one is either giving credit for effective action or offering criticism for it.

In making this argument, Duranti notes that "the use of transitive clauses with explicit agents often seems to contribute to the actualization of Polynesian *mana*, meant as an unstable and mobile potency that needs to be activated in concrete acts, speech acts included" (Duranti 1994, p. 129). He does not extend this observation, however, and ironically does not ask how the term *mana* itself is configured grammatically and pragmatically. Here, we want to argue that rethinking the classic topic of *mana* is a key task for anthropologists. *Mana* is an old favorite that urgently needs fresh scholarly attention, especially close linguistic analysis of its use and transformations.

The term *mana* (and its cognates) is found in many Oceanic languages across the divisions of Melanesia, Polynesia, and Micronesia, although in Melanesia its extent is not as well established (Blust 2007, Blevins 2008). The earliest well-known English definition of *mana* came from Codrington, whose letter on the subject to Max Müller was included in the latter's Hibbert Lectures in 1878 (Blust 2007, p. 406; Smith 2004, pp. 125–26). In his classic statement from 1891, Codrington wrote that "[t]he Melanesian mind is entirely possessed by the belief in

Mana: an Oceanic term often denoting efficacy, but which has a wide range of meanings cross-culturally and in different contexts

a supernatural power or influence, called almost universally *mana*. This is what works to effect everything which is beyond the ordinary power of men, outside the common processes of nature" (1957, pp. 118–19). Theorists including Frazer, Durkheim, Marett, Hubert, and Mauss saw a golden opportunity for evolutionary classification, and "many early accounts of *mana* do seem caught up in the attempt to propose religion as the ordering principle of homo-oceaniens as a genus of homo-primitive" (Mawyer 2006, p. 420). A generation of anthropologists observed closely but also speculated freely; Hocart, for example, wrote a sober article comparing Fijian *mana* and truth (1914) but followed it with a short piece recklessly characterizing *mana* as "one of the more archaic forms of a belief that has spread to the uttermost bounds of the earth" (1922, p. 141; see also Hocart 1927). In response to such claims, Firth observed wryly that *mana* was in danger of becoming "a technical term describing a specialized abstraction of the theoretical anthropologist" and called for more rigorous attention to contextualizing speakers' use of the term (1940, pp. 487–88; see also Evans-Pritchard 1965; Keesing 1984, 1985; Shore 1989; compare Lévi-Strauss 1987).

As a term found widely in Oceania, *mana* offers rich possibilities for comparative studies—but one might justifiably wonder, in light of the extensive attention it has already received, why it is worth general reconsideration at this point. We argue that the main reason is that conceptions of power are changing in significant ways in Oceania owing to evangelism, global capitalism, national independence, and other forces (variously generated, coopted, adapted, channeled, and resisted) that are glossed as "modernity," although this term is not one we want to debate here. Ironically, as anthropological attention to power and resistance waxed in theoretical sophistication during the past decades, precise attention to *mana* waned; however, we argue, focusing on *mana* can reveal a great deal about how global forces are engaged with and how those engagements reshape their own terms.

For example, as we argue in the preceding section, Christianity has been an especially transformative cultural force in Oceania. It should be no surprise, then, that Christian institutions, speakers, and genres have newly configured *mana* in distinct and consequential ways. White (1991, p. 194) shows that Anglican missionaries in Santa Isabel, Solomon Islands, appropriated the indigenous concept of *mana* so effectively that "[b]y the 1930s, extraordinary mana was attributed only to persons identified with church knowledge and ritual."[7] Tomlinson (2006, 2007) argues that Methodist missionaries helped change indigenous Fijian uses and understandings of the term and concept *mana* through their biblical translation practices, shifting use of *mana* as a verb denoting achievement toward *mana* as a noun in the classical Polynesian sense (see also Blust 2007, p. 409).

The more widely the term circulates, the more it becomes available for appropriation, and in some ways *mana* is becoming commodified—used in the names of commercial ventures, staged entertainment, magazines, and other products. At the same time, the term has become a marker of specifically indigenous efficacy; for example, the Hawaiian anthropologist Tengan (2008, p. 211) writes of the success of a Maori political party in New Zealand as "a direct outcome of the collective Maori mana" generated by a huge protest march. Within indigenous political contexts, *mana* may also be associated with gendered activities and identities (Keating 1998b, p. 126; Linnekin 1990; Tengan 2008). In short, whether understood as the "unstable and mobile potency" described by Duranti or as a stable and eternal force in Christian cosmologies (emanating from Jehovah) or indigenous politics, the term *mana* is a keystone in ideologies of stability and transformation and rewards close analysis of its usage.

---

[7] The local term *nolaghi* is apparently not cognate with *mana*, but White (1991, p. 38) notes that "[s]peakers of Cheke Holo refer to spiritual potency as *nolaghi*, and readily equate the term with the word *mana* used by their Bughotu neighbors."

CONCLUSION

The path is a common diagrammatic icon in Oceanic discourse (Parmentier 1987), and here we have invoked it to signal some promising directions in which the linguistic anthropology of Oceania can travel. Language ideologies, Christianity, entextualization, personhood, and agency are not uniquely Oceanic topics, but work done on these subjects by anthropologists in the region has proven both substantial and provocative. These paths of investigation are intertwined and cross-cutting, and many of the topics raised here can be investigated most fruitfully by tracing interconnections. For example, as we have suggested for the term *mana*, its key contribution to anthropological theory should be the way it links these topics in distinct and consequential configurations.

All these subjects are urgent ones for anthropologists and demand attention because they are enmeshed in wider debates about ideologies and practices of stability and transformation. Vital new conceptualizations of culture, discourse, ritual, and power need ethnographic investigations attuned to the concrete details of situated practices, and this is precisely what the linguistic anthropology of Oceania has been developing and promises to offer in newly vivid, productive ways.

DISCLOSURE STATEMENT

The authors are not aware of any affiliations, memberships, funding, or financial holdings that might be perceived as affecting the objectivity of this review.

ACKNOWLEDGMENTS

For advice that improved this article, we especially thank Amelia Bonea, Andrew Pawley, Karen Peacock, Joel Robbins, Bambi Schieffelin, and Albert J. Schütz.

LITERATURE CITED

Ahearn L. 2001. Language and agency. *Annu. Rev. Anthropol.* 30:109–37

Arno A. 1993. *The World of Talk on a Fijian Island: An Ethnography of Law and Communicative Causation.* Norwood, NJ: Ablex

Barker J, ed. 1990. *Christianity in Oceania: Ethnographic Perspectives.* Lanham, MD: Univ. Press Am.

Bauman R, Briggs CL. 1990. Poetics and performance as critical perspectives on language and social life. *Annu. Rev. Anthropol.* 19:59–88

Besnier N. 1995. *Literacy, Emotion, and Authority: Reading and Writing on a Polynesian Atoll.* Cambridge, UK: Cambridge Univ. Press

Besnier N. 2004. Diversity, hierarchy, and modernity in Pacific Islands communities. See Duranti 2004, pp. 95–120

Besnier N. 2009. *Gossip and the Everyday Production of Politics.* Honolulu: Univ. Hawai'i Press. In press

Blevins J. 2008. Some comparative notes on Proto-Oceanic *mana: inside and outside the Austronesian family. *Ocean. Ling.* 47(2):253–74

Blust R. 2007. Proto-Oceanic *mana revisited. *Ocean. Ling.* 46(2):404–23

Brenneis D. 1984. Grog and gossip in Bhatgaon: style and substance in Fiji Indian conversation. *Am. Ethnol.* 11(3):487–506

Brenneis D. 1987. Performing passions: aesthetics and politics in an occasionally egalitarian community. *Am. Ethnologist* 14(2):236–50

Brenneis DL, Myers FR, eds. 1984. *Dangerous Words: Language and Politics in the Pacific.* New York: N.Y. Univ. Press

Briggs CL, Bauman R. 1992. Genre, intertextuality, and social power. *J. Linguist. Anthropol.* 2(2):131–72

Brison KJ. 1992. *Just Talk: Gossip, Meetings, and Power in a Papua New Guinea Village*. Berkeley: Univ. Calif. Press

Brison KJ. 2007. *Our Wealth Is Loving Each Other: Self and Society in Fiji*. Lanham, MD: Lexington Books

Cammack FM. 1962. *Bauan grammar*. PhD thesis, Cornell Univ.

Clammer JR. 1976. *Literacy and Social Change: A Case Study of Fiji*. Leiden: Brill

Codrington RH. 1957 [1891]. *The Melanesians: Studies in Their Anthropology and Folk-Lore*. New Haven: HRAF Press

Crowley T. 2001. The indigenous linguistic response to missionary authority in the Pacific. *Aust. J. Linguist.* 21(2):239–60

Duranti A. 1993. Truth and intentionality: an ethnographic critique. *Cult. Anthropol.* 8(2):214–45

Duranti A. 1994. *From Grammar to Politics: Linguistic Anthropology in a Western Samoan Village*. Berkeley: Univ. Calif. Press

Duranti A, Goodwin C, eds. 1992. *Rethinking Context: Language as an Interactive Phenomenon*. Cambridge, UK: Cambridge Univ. Press

Duranti A, ed. 2004. *A Companion to Linguistic Anthropology*. Malden, MA: Blackwell

Engelke M, Tomlinson M, eds. 2006. *The Limits of Meaning: Case Studies in the Anthropology of Christianity*. New York: Berghahn

Evans-Pritchard EE. 1965. *Theories of Primitive Religion*. Oxford: Clarendon

Feld S, Brenneis D. 2004. Doing anthropology in sound. *Am. Ethnol.* 31(4):461–74

Feld S, Fox AA. 1994. Music and language. *Annu. Rev. Anthropol.* 23:25–53

Feld S, Fox A, Porcello T, Samuels D. 2004. Vocal anthropology: from the music of language to the language of song. See Duranti 2004, pp. 321–45

Firth R. 1940. The analysis of *mana*: an empirical approach. *J. Polyn. Soc.* 49(4):483–510

Foley WA. 1986. *The Papuan Languages of New Guinea*. Cambridge, UK: Cambridge Univ. Press

Foley WA. 2000. The languages of New Guinea. *Annu. Rev. Anthropol.* 29:357–404

Forman CW. 1982. *The Island Churches of the South Pacific: Emergence in the Twentieth Century*. Maryknoll, NY: Orbis

Geraghty P. 1989. Language reform: history and future of Fijian. In *Language Reform: History and Future*, Vol. IV, ed. I Fodor, C Hagège, pp. 377–95. Hamburg: Helmut Buske Verlag

Goffman E. 1981. *Forms of Talk*. Philadelphia: Univ. Penn. Press

Green RC. 1991. Near and remote Oceania—disestablishing "Melanesia" in culture history. In *Man and a Half: Essays in Pacific Anthropology and Ethnobiology in Honour of Ralph Bulmer*, ed. A Pawley, pp. 491–502. Auckland: Polyn. Soc.

Gumperz JJ. 1982. *Discourse Strategies*. Cambridge, UK: Cambridge Univ. Press

Gumperz JJ. 1992. Contextualization and understanding. See Duranti & Goodwin 1992, pp. 229–52

Handman C. 2007. Speaking to the soul: on native language and authenticity in Papua New Guinea Bible translation. See Makihara & Schieffelin 2007, pp. 166–88

Hocart AM. 1914. Mana. *Man* 14:97–101

Hocart AM. 1922. Mana again. *Man* 22:139–41

Hocart AM. 1927. *Kingship*. London: Oxford Univ. Press

Jebens H. 2005. *Pathways to Heaven: Contesting Mainline and Fundamentalist Christianity in Papua New Guinea*. New York: Berghahn

Jourdan C. 2007. Linguistic paths to urban self in postcolonial Solomon Islands. See Makihara & Schieffelin 2007, pp. 30–48

Jourdan C. 2008. Language repertoires and the middle class in urban Solomon Islands. See Meyerhoff & Nagy 2008, pp. 43–67

Keane W. 1997. *Signs of Recognition: Powers and Hazards of Representation in an Indonesian Society*. Berkeley: Univ. Calif. Press

Keating E. 1997. Honorific possession: power and language in Pohnpei, Micronesia. *Lang. Soc.* 26(2):247–68

Keating E. 1998a. Honor and stratification in Pohnpei, Micronesia. *Am. Ethnol.* 25(3):399–411

Keating E. 1998b. *Power Sharing: Language, Rank, Gender, and Social Space in Pohnpei, Micronesia*. New York: Oxford Univ. Press

Keating E. 1999. Contesting representations of gender stratification in Pohnpei, Micronesia. *Ethnos* 64(3):350–71

Keating E. 2000. Moments of hierarchy: constructing social stratification by means of language, food, space, and the body in Pohnpei, Micronesia. *Am. Anthropol.* 102(2):303–20

Keating E. 2005. The sociolinguistics of status in Pohnpei. *Int. J. Soc. Lang.* 172(1):7–30

Keating E, Duranti A. 2006. Honorific resources for the construction of hierarchy in Samoan and Pohnpeian. *J. Polynesian Soc.* 115(2):145–72

Keesing RM. 1984. Rethinking *mana*. *J. Anthropol. Res.* 40(1):137–56

Keesing RM. 1985. Conventional metaphors and anthropological metaphysics: the problematic of cultural translation. *J. Anthropol. Res.* 41(2):201–17

Kirch PV. 1997. *The Lapita Peoples: Ancestors of the Oceanic World*. Malden, MA: Blackwell

Kroskrity PV, ed. 2000. *Regimes of Language: Ideologies, Polities, and Identities*. Santa Fe: Sch. Am. Res. Press

Kuipers J. 1990. *Power in Performance: The Creation of Textual Authority in Weyewa Ritual Speech*. Philadelphia: Univ. Penn. Press

Kulick D. 1992a. Anger, gender, language shift and the politics of revelation in a Papua New Guinean village. *Pragmatics* 2(3):281–96

Kulick D. 1992b. *Language Shift and Cultural Reproduction: Socialization, Self, and Syncretism in a Papua New Guinean Village*. New York: Cambridge Univ. Press

Kulick D, Schieffelin B. 2004. Language socialization. See Duranti 2004, pp. 349–68

Leenhardt M. 1979. *Do Kamo: Person and Myth in the Melanesian World*, transl. BM Gulati. Chicago: Univ. Chicago Press

Lévi-Strauss C. 1987. *Introduction to the Work of Marcel Mauss*, transl. F Baker. London: Routledge & Kegan Paul

Lindstrom L. 1990. *Knowledge and Power in a South Pacific Society*. Washington, DC: Smithson. Inst. Press

Linnekin J. 1990. *Sacred Queens and Women of Consequence: Rank, Gender, and Colonialism in the Hawaiian Islands*. Ann Arbor: Univ. Mich. Press

Lynch J, Ross M, Crowley T. 2002. *The Oceanic Languages*. Richmond, UK: Curzon

Makihara M. 2004. Linguistic syncretism and language ideologies: transforming sociolinguistic hierarchy on Rapa Nui (Easter Island). *Am. Anthropol.* 106(3):529–40

Makihara M. 2007. Linguistic purism in Rapa Nui political discourse. See Makihara & Schieffelin 2007, pp. 49–69

Makihara M, Schieffelin B, eds. 2007a. *Consequences of Contact: Language Ideologies and Sociocultural Transformations in Pacific Societies*. New York: Oxford Univ. Press

Makihara M, Schieffelin B. 2007b. Cultural processes and linguistic mediations: Pacific explorations. See Makihara & Schieffelin 2007, pp. 3–29

Mawyer AD. 2006. *"TV talk" and processes of media receptivity in the production of identities in the Gambier Islands, French Polynesia*. PhD thesis. Univ. Chicago

Merlan F, Rumsey A. 1991. *Ku Waru: Language and Segmentary Politics in the Western Nebilyer Valley, Papua New Guinea*. Cambridge, UK: Cambridge Univ. Press

Meyerhoff M. 1999. Sorry in the Pacific: defining communities, defining practices. *Lang. Soc.* 28(2):247–68

Meyerhoff M, Nagy N, eds. 2008. *Social Lives in Language—Sociolinguistics and Multilingual Speech Communities: Celebrating the Work of Gillian Sankoff*. Amsterdam: John Benjamins

Miyazaki H. 2004. *The Method of Hope: Anthropology, Philosophy, and Fijian Knowledge*. Stanford, CA: Stanford Univ. Press

Mosko MS. 1992. Motherless sons: 'Divine kings' and 'partible persons' in Melanesia and Polynesia. *Man* 27(4):697–717

Murray AW. 1888. *The Bible in the Pacific*. London: James Nisbet

Ochs E. 1988. *Culture and Language Development: Language Acquisition and Language Socialization in a Samoan Village*. New York: Cambridge Univ. Press

Ochs E. 1992. Indexing gender. See Duranti & Goodwin 1992, pp. 335–58

Ochs E, Schieffelin BB. 1984. Language acquisition and socialization: three developmental stories and their implications. In *Culture Theory: Essays on Mind, Self, and Emotion*, ed. RA Shweder, RA LeVine, pp. 276–320. Cambridge, UK: Cambridge Univ. Press

Ortner SB. 2006. *Anthropology and Social Theory: Culture, Power, and the Acting Subject*. Durham, NC: Duke Univ. Press

Parmentier R. 1987. *The Sacred Remains: Myth, History, and Polity in Belau*. Chicago: Univ. Chicago Press

Pawley A, Ross M. 1995. The prehistory of Oceanic languages: a current view. In *The Austronesians: Historical and Comparative Perspectives*, ed. P Bellwood, JJ Fox, D Tryon, pp. 39–74. Canberra: Dep. Anthropol., Res. Sch. Pac. Asian Stud., Aust. Natl. Univ.

Philips SU. 2000. Constructing a Tongan nation state through language ideology in the courtroom. See Kroskrity 2000, pp. 229–57

Philips SU. 2004. The organization of ideological diversity in discourse: Modern and neotraditional visions of the Tongan state. *Am. Ethnologist* 31:231–50

Philips SU. 2007. Changing scholarly representations of the Tongan honorific lexicon. See Makihara & Schieffelin 2007, pp. 189–215

Rickards R. 1996. *In Their Own Tongues: The Bible in the Pacific*. Suva, Fiji: Bible Soc. South Pac.

Riley K. 2007. To tangle or not to tangle: shifting language ideologies and the socialization of *charabia* in the Marquesas, French Polynesia. See Makihara & Schieffelin 2007, pp. 70–95

Robbins J. 2001a. God is nothing but talk: modernity, language, and prayer in a Papua New Guinea society. *Am. Anthropol.* 103(4):901–12

Robbins J. 2001b. Ritual communication and linguistic ideology. *Curr. Anthropol.* 42(5):591–99

Robbins J. 2004. *Becoming Sinners: Christianity and Moral Torment in a Papua New Guinea Society*. Berkeley: Univ. Calif. Press

Robbins J. 2007. You can't talk behind the Holy Spirit's back: Christianity and changing language ideologies in a Papua New Guinea society. See Makihara & Schieffelin 2007, pp. 125–39

Robbins J, Rumsey A. 2008. Introduction: cultural and linguistic anthropology and the opacity of other minds. *Anthropol. Q.* 81(2):407–20

Rumsey A. 2000. Agency, personhood and the 'I' of discourse in the Pacific and beyond. *J. R. Anthropol. Inst.* 6(1):101–15

Sahlins M. 1963. Poor man, rich man, big man, chief: political types in Melanesia and Polynesia. *Comp. Stud. Soc. Hist.* 5(3):285–303

Sahlins M. 1981. *Historical Metaphors and Mythical Realities: Structure in the Early History of the Sandwich Islands Kingdom*. Ann Arbor: Univ. Mich. Press

Sahlins M. 1985. *Islands of History*. Chicago: Univ. Chicago Press

Sahlins M. 1991. The return of the event, again; with reflections on the beginnings of the great Fijian war of 1843 to 1855 between the Kingdoms of Bau and Rewa. In *Clio in Oceania: Toward a Historical Anthropology*, ed. A Biersack, pp. 37–99. Washington, DC: Smithsonian Inst. Press

Schieffelin BB. 1990. *The Give and Take of Everyday Life: Language Socialization of Kaluli Children*. New York: Cambridge Univ. Press

Schieffelin BB. 2000. Introducing Kaluli literacy: a chronology of influences. See Kroskrity 2000, pp. 293–327

Schieffelin BB. 2007. Found in translating: reflexive language across time and texts in Bosavi, Papua New Guinea. See Makihara & Schieffelin 2007, pp. 140–65

Schieffelin BB. 2008. Tok bokis, tok piksa: translating parables in Papua New Guinea. See Meyerhoff & Nagy 2008, pp. 111–34

Schieffelin BB, Ochs E. 1986a. Language socialization. *Annu. Rev. Anthropol.* 15:163–91

Schieffelin BB, Ochs E, eds. 1986b. *Language Socialization across Cultures*. New York: Cambridge Univ. Press

Schieffelin BB, Woolard KA, Kroskrity PV, ed. 1998. *Language Ideologies: Practice and Theory*. New York: Oxford Univ. Press

Schütz AJ. 1972. *The Languages of Fiji*. Oxford: Clarendon

Scott MW. 2007. *The Severed Snake: Matrilineages, Making Place, and a Melanesian Christianity in Southeast Solomon Islands*. Durham, NC: Carolina Acad.

Shore B. 1989. *Mana* and *tapu*. In *Developments in Polynesian Ethnology*, ed. A Howard, R Borofsky, pp. 137–73. Honolulu: Univ. Hawaii Press

Silverstein M, Urban G. 1996. The natural history of discourse. In *Natural Histories of Discourse*, ed. M Silverstein, G Urban, pp. 1–17. Chicago: Univ. Chicago Press

Smith JZ. 2004. Manna, mana everywhere and / ˘ / ˘ /. In *Relating Religion: Essays in the Study of Religion*, pp. 117–44. Chicago: Univ. Chicago Press

Stasch R. 2007. Demon language: the otherness of Indonesian in a Papuan community. See Makihara & Schieffelin 2007, pp. 96–124

Strathern M. 1988. *The Gender of the Gift: Problems with Women and Problems with Society in Melanesia*. Berkeley: Univ. Calif. Press

Strathern M. 1992. *Reproducing the Future: Essays on Anthropology, Kinship and the New Reproductive Technologies*. New York: Routledge

Tengan TPK. 2008. *Native Men Remade: Gender and Nation in Contemporary Hawai'i*. Durham: Duke Univ. Press

Tomlinson M. 2006. Retheorizing mana: Bible translation and discourse of loss in Fiji. *Oceania* 76(2):173–85

Tomlinson M. 2007. Mana in Christian Fiji: the interconversion of intelligibility and palpability. *J. Am. Acad. Religion* 75(3):524–53

United Bible Soc. 1974. *Scriptures of the World*. Stuttgart: United Bible Soc.

Urban G. 1989. The "I" of discourse. In *Semiotics, Self, and Society*, ed. B Lee, G Urban, pp. 27–51. Berlin: Mouton de Gruyter

Watson-Gegeo KA. 1986. The study of language use in Oceania. *Annu. Rev. Anthropol.* 15:149–62

Watson-Gegeo KA, Gegeo DW. 1991. The impact of church affiliation on language use in Kwara'ae (Solomon Islands). *Lang. Soc.* 20(4):533–55

Watson-Gegeo KA, White GM, eds. 1990. *Disentangling: Conflict Discourse in Pacific Societies*. Stanford, CA: Stanford Univ. Press

White GM. 1991. *Identity Through History: Living Stories in a Solomon Islands Society*. Cambridge, UK: Cambridge Univ. Press

Williams R. 1977. *Marxism and Literature*. Oxford: Oxford Univ. Press

Woolard KA, Schieffelin BB. 1994. Language ideology. *Annu. Rev. Anthropol.* 23:55–82

Social Reproduction in Classrooms and Schools

James Collins

Department of Anthropology, University at Albany, State University of New York, Albany, New York 12222; email: Collins@albany.edu

Annu. Rev. Anthropol. 2009. 38:33–48

First published online as a Review in Advance on June 12, 2009

The *Annual Review of Anthropology* is online at anthro.annualreviews.org

This article's doi:
10.1146/annurev.anthro.37.081407.085242

0084-6570/09/1021-0033$20.00

Key Words

language, social class, social inequality, education, ethnographies, multilevel analysis

Abstract

Social reproduction theory argues that schools are not institutions of equal opportunity but mechanisms for perpetuating social inequalities. This review discusses the emergence and development of social reproduction analyses of education and examines three main perspectives on reproduction: economic, cultural, and linguistic. Reproduction analyses emerged in the 1960s and were largely abandoned by the 1990s; some of the conceptual and political reasons for this turning away are addressed. New approaches stress concepts such as agency, identity, person, and voice over the structural constraints of political economy or code, but results have been mixed. Despite theoretical and methodological advances—including new approaches to multilevel analysis and alertness to temporal processes—the difficult problem remains to understand how social inequality results from the interplay of classrooms, schools, and the wider society.

INTRODUCTION

Concern with the processes whereby societies and cultures perpetuate themselves has an ancient pedigree, traceable back to Aristotle's (1959) analysis of the domestic economy in political orders. Researchers have suggested that scholastic institutions were important sites of cultural reproduction in classical Greece (Lloyd 1990), imperial Rome (Guillory 1993), medieval Europe (Bloch 1961), and modern France (Durkheim 1977). Overt concern with social reproduction is, however, a product of post–World War II social dynamics, especially the political and intellectual ferment of the 1960s. It is a product of concern with inequality. As a framework of inquiry, it draws from diverse disciplines but is typically rooted in dialogue with Marxist traditions of social analysis.

Early studies of social reproduction in education emerged in the 1960s and 1970s in the United States, Britain, and France. Foundational works include Bowles & Gintis's (1976) *Schooling in Capitalist America* (United States), Willis's (1977) *Learning to Labor* (Britain), and Bourdieu & Passeron's (1977) *Reproduction in Education, Culture, and Society* (France). Although these works differed in regard to theorization, scope of analysis, and methodology, each attempted to trace links between economic structures, schooling experience, and modes of consciousness and cultural activity. Their analyses responded to debates concerning central contradictions of these postwar societies. In each country, public education was officially understood and presented as a meritocratic institution in which talent and effort alone predicted outcomes, but by the post–World War II period considerable evidence indicated otherwise (e.g., Coleman 1966, Jencks 1972).

The basic reproductionist argument was that schools were not exceptional institutions promoting equality of opportunity; instead they reinforced the inequalities of social structure and cultural order found in a given country. How they were understood to do so depended on the theoretical perspective of analysts, the sites they prioritized for study, and a varying emphasis on top-down structural determination versus bottom-up agency by individuals or small groups. Early research on educational reproduction provided structuralist accounts, identifying systematic features of language, culture, and political economy, which were reflected in the conduct and organization of classrooms and curricula and assigned a causal role in perpetuating linguistic, cultural, and economic inequalities (Bernstein 1975, Bourdieu & Passeron 1977, Bowles & Gintis 1976). The economic perspective on reproduction (Bowles & Gintis 1976) attracted criticism for its treatment of culture as secondary to economics and politics. "Cultural reproduction" analyses, when they emerged, often attempted to integrate class analyses with analysis of race or gender formation and to investigate the social practices of small groups. An early, influential and highly controversial argument about class and education focused on the role of language (Bernstein 1960, 1964). It was quickly taken up for criticism and exploration by sociolinguistic and anthropological researchers in the United States but with an emphasis on ethnicity and culture and a focus on situated communication, especially in classrooms (Cazden et al. 1972).

Although the reproductive thesis is simple to state in academic terms, it has been and continues to be quite unpalatable to many of those who work in schools or educational systems more generally (Rothstein 2004). This is probably because it presents a direct challenge to meritocratic assumptions and seems to dash egalitarian aspirations. Early arguments and analyses of reproduction were also of their era, the 1960s and early 1970s, when economic and social stability seemed more secure than it has in recent decades. They were also formulated with a structuralist intellectual confidence that has not survived the intervening decades of reflexive, postmodern uncertainty (Bauman 1997). By the early 1990s, there was a turning away from arguments about social reproduction and education, whether focused on economic, cultural, or linguistic dimensions. This is puzzling in some respects because the problem of inequality remains a central feature of the contemporary world, within nations and on a global scale (Henwood 2003; Stiglitz 2002), and the centrality of straightforward economic factors in school performance appears little changed over more than 40 years (Coleman 1966, U.S. Dep. Educ. 2001).

This review surveys studies developing economic, cultural, and linguistic perspectives on social reproduction in classrooms and schools. After examining work using each lens, it then discusses why the reproduction framework was largely abandoned, exploring the conceptual and political dilemmas that seem to have motivated the turn to new approaches and assessing the achievements and limitations of subsequent efforts. Last, it takes up the question of "What now?" arguing that the issue of social reproduction in education and society remains highly relevant but that its study requires new conceptual tools as well as a reworking of old findings and insights. Two central theses inform the overall argument. The first is that to understand social reproduction we have to consider multiple levels of social and institutional structure as well as microanalytic communicative processes and cultural practices. The second is that social class matters profoundly but that analysts struggle to understand its protean nature, including its intricate interplay with other principles of inequality, such as race and gender.

ECONOMIC REPRODUCTION

Althusser's (1971) essay on "Ideological State Apparatuses" was an early and influential argument about education and social reproduction. It conceptualized the school as an agency of class domination, achieving its effects through ideological practices that inculcated knowledge and dispositions in class-differentiated social subjects, preparing them for their dominant or dominated places in the economy and society. The foundational work on economic reproduction, however, was *Schooling in Capitalist America* (Bowles & Gintis 1976). In this account, classroom experience, and school knowledge more generally, emphasized

discrete bits of knowledge and discipline for those bound for blue-collar occupations, alongside more synthetic, analytic knowledge and self-directedness for those destined for middle-class professions. It provided a straightforward argument in which school curricula and classroom procedure reflected the organization of class-differentiated adult dispositions, skills, and work experiences and transmitted similar dispositions and skills to subsequent generations. The argument quickly attracted criticism, in part because it maintained considerable distance conceptually and empirically from actual schools and classrooms (Giroux 1983). However, the basic thesis that schooling as a system rations kinds of knowledge to class- and ethnically-stratified student populations has been empirically confirmed by a number of studies (Anyon 1981, 1997; Carnoy & Levin 1985; Oakes 1985). Published in translation at about the same time, *Reproduction in Education, Culture and Society* (Bourdieu & Passeron 1977) dealt with France. It provided a more nuanced analysis, both in its framework, which related forms of symbolic value (economic, cultural, and social "forms of capital") to economic and political arenas, and in its attention to forms of pedagogic discourse, which hypothesized systemic miscommunication in classrooms (1977, Chapter 2). It also attracted many critics of its "determinism" (Giroux 1983, Levinson & Holland 1996) because it argued that class-based differences in material resources were ultimate causes in the reproduction of cultural and educational inequality.

According to critics, a primary deficiency in all the early formulations was their neglect of the problem of agency and change (Giroux 1983, MacLeod 1987). Instructive criticism in this regard is provided by Apple (1982). As does *Schooling in Capitalist America*, this work takes as its starting point that certain shared principles govern the organization of schooling and work. It argues that in essence schooling is organized to provide individuated, technical knowledge to select strata of consumer-workers (largely white, middle class, and compliant). The abstract and schematic treatment of social dynamics and the education process is enriched, however, by Apple's argument that "cultures and ideologies" are "filled with contradiction" and "produced . . . in contestation and struggle." (pp. 24, 26). In support of this argument, Apple turns to sociological case studies and educational ethnographies. The first of these address adults in work situations and show, for example, male factory workers and female salespeople as they slow down, disrupt, and otherwise exert informal control over work processes. Such studies document how class-situated practices of resistance subvert the formal procedures and control mechanisms of the workplace bureaucracy (see also Scott 1998, pp. 310–11).

The ethnographic studies Apple discusses focus on class conflicts in society and in relation to school. One of these, Willis's *Learning to Labor* (1977), is a classic because of its detailed observation of peer group behavior and its provocative theorization of cultural agency and reproduction. The study examines how working-class English lads penetrate the school's meritocratic ideology. Through peer group solidarities analogous to their fathers' shop-floor tactics for controlling the flow of factory work, they disrupt classroom procedure with humor and aggression, ubiquitously calling into question the classroom social contract whereby compliance is exchanged for knowledge and grades. They celebrate masculine solidarity and power through partying, fighting, and "having a laff"; they also oppress girls, deride ethnoracial minorities, and fail in school. Another study is McRobbie's (1978) "Working Class Girls and the Culture of Femininity." It is an ethnographic analysis of both class and sexuality, theorized as structures of domination that are lived as partially autonomous cultural formations, zones of practice and meaning wherein working-class girls assert femininity and sexuality against the prudish compliance expected of good girls in school. Like their working-class mothers, these girls form bonds of self and solidarity through gender expression, but they also disengage from schooling and its prospects of social mobility and enact self-limiting rituals of sexual subordination.

In these two studies, rather than reproductive processes that involve congruence across multiple levels of organizations and actors (e.g., by parents, teachers, and education bureaucracies), we instead find oppositional practices that nonetheless reproduce social relations. We have sophisticated accounts of how the winner loses. Adolescent class- and gender-based solidarities draw from parental legacies of class and gender struggles, and the students building these solidarities develop considerable insight into the selective, class-biased nature of school curriculum and normative classroom conduct. They disrupt the logic of schooling, but their group- and practice-based insights are limited "penetrations" (Willis 1977, chapters 5 and 6) because their class expressions also reinforce ethnoracial antagonism, gender oppression, and educational failure.

Carnoy & Levin (1985) share Apple's emphasis on education as a site of class conflict and social contradiction, and they emphasize the role of the state. They argue that schooling serves primarily as an instrument of class domination but that it is also a site of struggles for equality. As does Apple, they also turn to ethnographies to understand reproductive processes, focusing on comparative ethnographic studies of schools serving upper- and lower-middle-class communities in California. Analyzing teacher beliefs and classroom practices regarding work-relevant knowledge and dispositions; parental views of schooling, their children, and their occupational futures; and state education criteria for adequate and nonadequate performance on core subjects, they find a lockstep pattern of teacher and parental beliefs, classroom practices, and state performance criteria that "reinforce the differential class structure in preparing the young for future occupational roles" (p. 141).

Lareau's *Home Advantage* (1989) provides a further perspective on class conditions and school experiences, focusing especially on families. It comparatively analyzes how working and middle class adults with elementary-age children view education and interact with school, thus influencing their children's school experiences. Lareau finds that what might be called work process shapes families' tacit theories of the home/school relation. Does parents' office work come home with them? If so, expect (middle-class) parents and children to perceive and enact many home/school connections. Does parental work end at the factory gate or retail shop door? If so, expect (working-class) parents and children to perceive and enact a clear separation of home and school, viewing school as the place for schooling and home as a needed respite. The study reports a salient home advantage: Middle-class parents, especially mothers, are avid and effective school minders. When well-resourced, school-confident women set the standard for normal parenting, their blue-collar counterparts inevitably lag behind. School personnel often view working-class parents as insufficiently involved in their children's education (Freeman 2004, Luttrell 1997, Thompson 1995).

CULTURAL REPRODUCTION

Lareau uses the concept of cultural capital to analyze cultural knowledge as class advantage in educational areas. This concept, from Bourdieu (Bourdieu 1984, Bourdieu & Passeron 1977), has been applied in numerous studies of social advantage and classroom processes (e.g., Collins 1999a, Heller 1994, Nespor 1987). Key extended works on cultural reproduction focused on the relative autonomy of cultural forms and practices vis-à-vis political economy, investigating the interplay of class with other significant social relations, especially those of gender and race. They often analyze how social relations are produced and reproduced in encounters between adolescents and their peers in a variety of school settings, including classrooms.

Foley's (1990) *Learning Capitalist Culture* proposes to show "how schools are sites for popular cultural practices that stage or reproduce social inequality" (p. xv). It reports on a south Texas town and high school in the ferment of 1970s civil rights reforms. Investigating the dynamics of class in relation to other axes of inequality, it analyzes the staging and reproducing of class and racial hierarchies at multiple sites: football games, the dating scene, beer parties, and classrooms. Foley argues that class relations take priority over ethnic affiliations but that class is expressive rather than structural in the usual sense. More particularly, he argues that middle-class Anglo and Latino cohorts, of athletes and other popular cliques, share greater commonalities in their presentation of self (Goffman 1959, 1967), whether in classrooms or elsewhere, than they share with ostensible working-class counterparts, whether Anglo "shitkickers" or Chicano "vatos." In this account, capitalist culture is fundamentally "communicative action" (Habermas 1987), and class culture is a "situational speech performance" (pp. 178–81, 192–94) enacted and learned in many places, including the classroom; it crosscuts and informs the staging and reproduction of ethnic identities. Essentially, middle-class expressive culture is highly instrumental: Middle-class kids, whether Anglo or Chicano, play the classroom "game," appearing interested while discreetly mocking teacher authority and school knowledge. Working-class expressive culture is less strategic for various reasons: Working-class kids do not play the classroom game as well; they are either passive and exclude themselves from classroom interaction or openly defiant and likely to provoke confrontations with teachers.

What adds additional substance to Foley's ethnography of social reproduction is its companion analysis *From Peones to Politicos* (Foley 1988), a historical treatment of the changing political economy of the town and region in which the more detailed school/community study is situated. This study analyzes the broad movement of adult Chicanos from field laborers to civil rights advocates, as the region's economy transforms over an 80-year period from feudalized ranching to modern capitalist agriculture. It shows the space made for an expanded Latino middle class, investigates the role of public institutions such as schools in class-stratified ethnic social mobility, and provides the broader compass for the social scenes, institutional processes, and face-to-face conduct explored in *Learning Capitalist Culture*.

Despite its strengths, Foley's analysis of capitalist culture gave short shrift to questions of gender (Collins 1992). Other studies have addressed this lack; a pair by Weis is particularly valuable. *Working Class Without Work* (Weis 1990) takes up issues of gender, race, and aspiration in the context of identity, social movements, feminism, and class restructuring. It examines how white high-school students in "Freeway," a working-class suburb of Buffalo, New York, in the throes of late 1980s deindustrialization and job loss, phrase their aspirations, behave in classrooms, and relate to each other on the basis of their gender and race. The study calls for attention to the production of class identities, rather than the reproduction of class conditions. It argues that social movements of feminism and New Right populism inform female and male responses to the loss of traditional working-class livelihoods, deeply influencing the meaning of school and providing alternative, conflicting paths of identity formation. In particular, girls are analyzed as proto-feminists, aspiring to education and socially mobile work independent of the patriarchal domination endured by their mothers and grandmothers; they do not have the resentment of institutional authority that boys have. Boys, for their part, seem more attuned to a social conservative agenda; they aspire to a restoration of their fathers' world of good wages and good jobs with the women at home, and they avoid and resist schoolwork and teacher authority. *Working Class Without Work* portrays class formation in a time of uncertain transition (the late 1980s), arguing that class legacies of underachievement in schooling can be reshaped by social movements that speak to gender and racial as well as class identities.

Class Reunion (Weis 2004) is a follow-up investigation conducted with many of the women and men originally studied as students at Freeway High. The heart of *Class Reunion* is

an analysis of class in relation to both gender and race dynamics in an era of global economic reconstruction. Talking with earlier research participants about their adult lives, Weis finds predictable outcomes as well as instructive surprises. Few of the men have successfully pursued tertiary education; with the ongoing loss of industrial work, most make livings in lower-wage service-sector jobs. Many of the women have completed college and hold white-collar jobs, challenging assumptions that family background simply predicts educational attainment. Weis finds—unexpectedly—that many men have given up their aspirations to the patriarchal authority and privilege embedded in an earlier white, working-class masculinity. They have opted of necessity for domestic partnerships in which economic resources are shared along with domestic work, including child care. But this kinder, gentler domestic realm shows a harsher face to the outside world: These men and women forge new domestic alliances as whites, protecting "their communities" from African Americans and "Arabs" (Weis 2004).

Those "Arabs," whom Weis's research participants see as racial others, are predominantly of Yemeni origin. Yemeni immigrants are also the subjects of Sarroub's (2005) *All American Yemeni Girls*, a study of high-school girls who are members of a working-class immigrant community in Dearborn, Michigan. The contrasts of site and study are instructive. Sarroub finds very different gender dynamics in this working-class community. In the 1990s, there appears to have been plenty of factory work in Dearborn, supporting a multigenerational Yemeni community that is devoutly Islamic and starkly patriarchal. In Sarroub's analysis, school-focused, society-wide cultural reproduction of the sort proposed by Bourdieu & Passeron (1977) is rejected. Schools are not the site of social reproduction; instead classrooms are "an oasis" where talk flows relatively freely between girl and boy, Yemeni and native-born American, and where educational achievement is sought and aspirations flower. Home and community are where diasporic Yemeni identities are reinforced through transnational marital strategies; a locally construed Muslim faith entails a very close monitoring of female dress, speech, and conduct; and achievement in school is appreciated but firmly subordinated to marriage and family. Documenting "the religious and cultural traditions that are in fact reproduced and reconstructed within the Yemeni family, and by the girls," Sarroub convincingly shows that "cultural tools and traditions may have little bearing on learning and achievement [in school] but may serve the purpose of easing cultural or religious tensions as home and school worlds collide" (p. 12). Some outcomes of that collision—desperation as high-school graduation approaches, flight from family, and ostracism from community for girls who do choose education and jobs over submission to patriarchal authority—are sober reminders that identity can be anguished as well as reassuring and that the meanings of class, gender, and race vary widely.

This variation and its challenges for social analysis are central issues in Bettie's (2003) *Women Without Class*. Studying Latina and Anglo adolescents, Bettie documents that working-class style and demeanor were both sexualized and racialized. School personnel judged working-class Anglos and Latinas as overly sexualized; both girls and school personnel saw upwardly mobile Latina girls as "acting white" (pp. 83–86). Theoretically focused on the interplay of class, gender, and race, Bettie argues that class should be understood as both performance and performative. It is performance because there is an indirect fit between background and style: Some working-class and middle-class "performers" depart from family origins. It is performative because family and community origins constrain the class expressions with which people are comfortable: Class expressivity is "an effect of social structure" (pp. 49–56). Examining working-class Latinas' expressivity, she explores how class is deflected into sexuality, negatively judged by school personnel, feeding into curriculum tracking processes that lead these "class performers" to working-class futures (chapter 3).

LINGUISTIC REPRODUCTION

Language pervades formal education as the primary means of teaching and learning (Cazden 2001). As shown by the fields of sociolinguistics and linguistic anthropology, as well as some of the work on cultural reproduction just reviewed, language is also a primary means of expressing social identities, affiliating with cultural traditions, and building relations with others (Gee 2001, Harris & Rampton 2003, Schieffelin & Ochs 1986). A third major approach to social reproduction has focused on language and communication conduct in and out of schools, and with such studies we see the emergence of research into public debates about schools and society, often with unintended consequences.

Bernstein provided the major early theoretical and empirical work arguing for the role of class and language in social reproduction (Bernstein 1960, 1964, 1975). Briefly, he argued that the experience of work process reinforces kinds of family role relations, themselves realized as discursive identities that are carried by "elaborated" and "restricted" codes (1964). The codes are seen as the "genes of social class," the semiotic-communicative sources of identities that are congruent with or disjunctive from the expressive styles required in school (Bernstein 1986, p. 472). Because of its schematic formulation of relations between classes and codes and its uptake in American debates about "cultures of poverty" and "linguistic deficit," Bernstein's account attracted much criticism (see Atkinson 1985, Collins 1988, Edwards 1976 for reviews).

Bernstein's early work on language and class had been picked up in the 1960s by American researchers who argued that poor people, especially poor African Americans concentrated in cities, performed inadequately in school because they were linguistically or culturally deprived (Bereiter & Englemann 1966, Deutsch 1967). This began the first iteration of controversies over linguistic deprivation explanations for educational failure. Anthropologists and other critics of the deficit model argued that minorities did poorly in school not because of their language per se but because they were treated differently in schools (Leacock 1969, 1971; Rist 1970).

Functions of Language in the Classroom (Cazden et al. 1972) is an influential response to the deficit arguments in which linguistic anthropologists, socially minded psychologists, sociologists, and educators investigate the relationships between group-based communicative styles and classroom interactional dynamics that might lead to poor educational outcomes. Among the contributors, Bernstein (1972) criticizes facile notions of compensatory education, and Hymes (1972) argues for the need to investigate community-specific "communicative competencies" underlying language use that might be perceived as deficient in classroom settings. Some contributions analyze ethnically grounded preferences for collaborative approaches to socializing and learning, including Hawaiian-American traditions of "talk story" (Boggs 1972) and Native American preferences for peer-based "participation structures" (Philips 1972); others explore stigmatizing assumptions about Standard English versus other languages (Spanish) or varieties (Black English), which result in differential treatment in classrooms (Gumperz & Hernandez-Chavez 1972, Mitchell-Kernan 1972). The volume established a standard for arguments about communicative differences, which departed from middle-class white and school-based practice but had an underlying logic or rationale. Many findings led to additional research and analysis, either confirming and elaborating the original phenomena (Au 1980, Erickson & Mohatt 1992, Philips 1983) or applying concepts to new domains, such as literacy learning (Michaels 1981) and mathematics instruction (O'Connor & Michaels 1996).

The major contribution in this tradition, however, is Heath's (1983) *Ways With Words*. It melds Bernstein's concerns with work, socialization, language, and schooling and the linguistic anthropological concerns with community-based differences in communicative style that appeared to influence classroom processes and learning outcomes. The book painstakingly analyzes three different communities in the Carolina Piedmont: a mixed-race middle-class cohort of "Townspeople"; a black working-class neighborhood of "Trackton"; and a white working-class neighborhood of "Roadville." It documents striking differences in language and literacy socialization among the three groups, relates these differences to expectations about language held by classroom teachers and embedded in school curriculum, and compellingly argues that ethnographic inquiry by research participants (children and teachers) can lessen the mismatch between home and school. Despite its strengths, the book is circumspect about the perpetuation of race and class inequalities clearly implied by its findings, perhaps in part owing to methodological modesty, but also in part because it ignores power relations, in particular, the larger state-level political forces that roll back the classroom reforms, which are only mentioned in a final Postscript (Collins & Blot 2003, chapters 3 and 5; de Castell & Walker 1991).

Drawing on the now-established school/home mismatch framework, a series of studies in the 1980s and early 1990s closely examined teacher-student and student-student interaction to demonstrate disadvantages faced by working-class African American students in standard classroom literacy lessons (Collins 1986; Gee 1996; Michaels 1981, 1986) and the advantages of classroom innovation (Foster 1987, Lee 1993). Others drew similar conclusions from analyses of community-based "funds of knowledge" possessed by working-class Latino students but largely ignored by public schools (Gonzalez et al. 2005, Moll et al. 1992). Few studies in this period explicitly thematized the reproductive aspects of class- or race-inflected classroom encounters with literacy (Bigler 1996; Collins 1988, 1989).

In early 1997, however, a second iteration of the linguistic deprivation debate occurred after the Oakland Unified School District proposed to treat Ebonics (African American Vernacular English) as a classroom language resource. In making sense of the firestorm of protest this proposal unleashed, analysts drew on the *Functions of Language* tradition of trying to understand community-based ways of speaking as resources for learning (Delpit & Perry 1998). They also pointed to the larger cultural-political processes that systematically devalued African American Vernacular (i.e., working-class) ways with words (Baugh 2000). Some explicitly treated it as an ideological conflict that revealed the reproductive nature of standard school language hierarchies and procedures in the United States (Collins 1999b) and internationally (Long 2003).

In recent years, the ways in which linguistic differences correlate with class differences have been getting renewed attention because of debates about school reform and the failure of the Bush administration's *No Child Left Behind* mandates and programs (No Child Left Behind Act 2001). This is an ambitious national intervention in public education that was supposed to change long-standing patterns of educational inequality but has not done so (Rothstein 2007, Tough 2006). In the search for explanations and alternatives, research making linguistic difference or deficit arguments is being considered in policy discussions and schools reforms. This development has largely escaped published discussion in anthropology (but see Bomer et al. 2008).

Two studies are relevant for our discussion because of the substance of their claims and the way they have been picked up in policy debates. Both studies provide accounts of class-based differences in language and interactional dispositions and argue why they matter for schooling. Hart & Risley's (1995) *Meaningful Differences* is a study of child socialization, based on a substantive, longitudinal sampling of language use in family settings. It makes strong claims about social class and language use, and it has had influential uptake in discussions of compensatory literacy programs for poor children. The book is explicitly cast as a dialogue with Bernstein's claims about class and code, and the analysis concentrates on the amount of vocabulary, specific sentence types, and specific interactional features of talk directed to children in "professional," "working-class" and "welfare"

homes during their infant, preschool, and early primary years. Hart & Risley argue that the cumulative vocabulary differences they found have direct effects on early literacy. Although no commentators seem to have noticed, the specific literacy measures they study do not support their claim, nor do their findings show a regular class distribution. Compounding the problem of the flawed analysis of class and language, Hart & Risley subsequently simplified their results and promoted them in policy discussions as a "catastrophic" linguistic disadvantage for the poor (Hart & Risley 2003), and this version of findings has been used to justify strict pedagogical regimes aimed at the inner-city poor (Brook-Gunn et al. 2003, Tough 2006).

Lareau's (2003) *Unequal Childhoods* is a more measured work investigating child-rearing practices among poor, working-class, and affluent, professional white and black families living in Philadelphia and its suburbs. It supports and elaborates Bernstein's and Heath's arguments about class and language socialization, showing a disjuncture between poor and working-class language practices and those expected in public arenas such as school or the (white-collar) workplace. It also explores how the differences in child-rearing are rooted in class-based cultural models that unite ideas about parents, children, and learning. Middle-class families believe in "concerted cultivation," whereas their working-class counterparts view child development as akin to "natural growth" (Lareau 2003, chapter 1; see Heath 1983, chapters 3 and 7 for evidence of similar beliefs). The professional patterns go together with school achievement, the working-class patterns do not, and these class differences supersede otherwise notable white/black differences. Lareau is frank about the "power of class" (Chapter 12) in shaping child language socialization, schooling experiences, and life chances, and although her findings are not part of a deficit argument, they have been picked up in the same commentary as those of Hart & Risley.

There is reason to take *Meaningful Differences* (Hart & Risley 1995) seriously. Stripped of its alarmist rhetoric and read closely, the study reports findings commensurable with those of Lareau (2003) and Heath (1983) and the body of work in England supporting Bernstein's early arguments (Cook-Gumperz 1973, Hawkins 1977). The recurrent deprivation debates, which have not ended, are an indication of the difficulties of understanding the dynamic interactions among racial formations, class conditions, and language. The fact that the most recent iteration of the debate has attracted little attention from sociolinguists or linguistic anthropologists calls to mind Hymes's (1972) observation regarding Bernstein in the 1970s:

> Bernstein is in the complex, difficult position of defending a kind of communication he calls a "restricted code" and of insisting on its limitations. His position will please few. Those who defend children by placing all blame on the schools, and those who explain the failures of schools by the language of the children, will both be offended. (p. xlvi)

THE TURN FROM REPRODUCTION AND THE CURRENT SCENE

The "difficult position" to which Hymes refers has largely been abdicated. Although there are exceptions, by the late 1980s efforts to understand social reproduction in classrooms and schools had largely been abandoned. This was not because social inequality had lessened in the latter part of the twentieth century; indeed, as numerous analysts have demonstrated, it has increased in the United States and internationally since the early 1970s (Henwood 2003, Kuttner 2007), but concern with reproduction as a conceptual focus was set aside in favor of other approaches. Instead analysts have given priorities that emphasize individual or group initiative—"agency," "identity," "person," and "voice"—over the structural constraints of political economy or linguistic code. Economic reproduction models, the first formulated, were also the first criticized, most pointedly for neglecting the role of ethnoracial formations and gender relations in capitalist

political economies and class relations (Bettie 2003, Foley 1990, Weis 1990).

The difficulties of formulating multifaceted accounts of race, class, and gender in relation to schooling have been formidable, however, and the new directions are informative for both their achievements and their limitations. Weis (1990) argued for a shift away from analyzing class reproduction to analyzing identity formation, and her subsequent study (2004) supports the earlier argument that schools are not simply about reproducing class relations to education. However, it does not show that social movements posited in 1990 as sources of identity formation do in fact serve such a role; the discussion of ideology and consciousness is the weakest part of the latter work. The collection in Levinson et al. (1996) represents an anthropological option, arguing against cultural reproduction models as too deterministic and for the priority of the "cultural production of person" in schools, with a wider diversity of kinds of person than is allowed by the broad social categories of class, race, and gender. It is not clear, however, whether their project of studying the schooled production of persons has continued. Bettie (2003) explicitly analyzes class in relation to gender and race, and her conceptualizing class as "performance" and "performativity" moves forward the study of class-as-expression (see also Rampton 2006). However, although she argues against reproductionist accounts, she reports outcomes of class-expressive behavior very similar to Willis's and McRobbie's findings—that is, while dismissing reproduction models, she presents straightforward reproductive outcomes (Bettie 2003, chapter 3).

On the language front, there has been a dramatic turning away from models of structure and code (Rampton et al. 2008), and this has left a troubling situation. On the one hand, there are currently very sophisticated accounts of practice, semiosis, and indeterminacy in the relation between language and social order; on the other hand, the new approaches would appear to have little to say about the substantive projects, just discussed, that report strong links between class background and language use. This aversion to social reproduction analysis can be seen in a recent *Annual Review* essay. Wortham (2008) presents a cogent account of the "Linguistic Anthropology of Education." What is notable in his treatment of this field is the emphasis on the contextual indeterminacy of language use, on the constructed, contested nature of language ideologies, and in general on the creative, flexible aspect of social life in educational settings. This is not so much wrong as it is one sided. He presents a "compositionist" view of social orders (Kontopoulos 1993), acutely aware of language use by persons and creativity in small group processes, but inattentive to the nature of institutions and vague about hierarchy or power. Thus studies addressing ethnic inequalities are lauded for avoiding "simple reproductionist accounts" (Erickson & Schultz 1982) and for not arguing "simply that minority languages are devalued" (Rampton 1995) (Wortham, 2008, p. 42). Research that deals with language ideologies that organize nation-state hierarchies of language, class, and ethnorace (Blommaert 1999, Heller 1999), is euphemistically described as showing that "language policies...differentially position diverse populations" (Wortham 2008, p. 44). Discussing an analysis of narrative and identity among Latino dropouts in an alternative school in Southern California (Rymes 2001), Wortham stresses the speakers' narrative creativity but omits any mention of the author's sobering discovery that despite rich hybrid narratives, alternative schools can be quickly shut down by higher administrative powers (Rymes 2001, chapter 9). In brief, this linguistic anthropology of education is attuned to the performative dimensions of language use, but not to structural constraint or social conflict.

CONCLUSION

A federally commissioned study in the 1960s sought to determine the influence of schools in educational attainment and occupational outcomes. It found that differences among schools mattered much less than assumed and that family socioeconomic status was the strongest influence on a child's educational achievement and life chances (Coleman 1966). More than four decades later, that generalization still holds (Jencks & Phillips 1998, Kingston 2000, U.S. Dep. Educ. 2001); furthermore, this pattern is found in most nations (Lemke 2002). This is a sobering feature of our world, and efforts to understand such enduring social and educational inequality have occupied a wide range of scholars. The Marxian paradigm of social reproduction provided one angle on the question but arguably proved both too narrow (excluding gender and race) and too rigid (failing to account for agency or identity). But efforts to go beyond this framework—studying class identity as a result of social movements, drawing on performance theory, or stressing the contextual creativity of language in educational settings—have not provided comprehensive accounts that enable us better to understand the gross distribution of class-linked statuses and resources. Although this is a stalemate, there are lessons to be learned. Here are two worth thinking about.

First, it is necessary to conceptualize and study multiple social levels to understand mechanisms that might produce such large-scale structural inequality. The need to move beyond a micro-macro dichotomy of individual and society has been long-established (Bourdieu 1977, Ortner 1993); there are now sophisticated, theoretically and empirically robust accounts of "heterarchical structures" (Kontopoulos 1993) that presume neither bottom-up construction of the social world by aggregate individual action nor top-down determination by large-scale entities but allow instead for emergence over time and complex feedback among structures and processes. Such approaches are needed to understand the internal ecologies of educational systems or the external relations between schools and other social institutions, such as families. Regarding the internal ecologies, heterarchical models can help formulate the place of classrooms and schools in larger educational systems, as a structured but not predetermined process, shedding light on studies of schools as sites of innovation and resistance that can quickly be reversed by higher bureaucratic levels, as both Heath (1983) and Rymes (2001) discover. Such models can also provide insight into organizational and interactive processes that produce class-differentiated curricula, which have such inegalitarian outcomes (Anyon 1981, 1997; Carnoy & Levin 1985, Leacock 1969, Oakes 1985). Regarding the external relationships between schools and other social institutions, such as families, heterarchical models are needed to analyze the interplay between schools and social-class-based dispositions to intervene in schools (Lareau 1989, 2003); between such class-based dispositions and the disabling stigma of working-class parents, especially mothers (Freeman 2004, Luttrell 1997, Thompson 1995); or between the class-specific, family-inculcated gender expressivity and school tracking decisions (Bettie 2003, Luttrell 1996).

Second, understanding reproductive processes requires alertness to patterns that become evident only over longer periods of time. Some patterns follow the school year. For example, classroom processes such as formal lessons show a structured interplay among immediate face-to-face exchanges, event-level topical coherences, and such things as patterns of differential response to vernacular speech or second languages that unfold over the course of a year (Bartlett 2007, Collins 1996); the acquisition of problematic identities in schools (as, say, "troublemaker" or "learning disabled") is a process that occurs in face-to-face exchanges as they occur over time and across multiple institutional domains (as Wortham 2008 insightfully discusses; see also Rogers 2003, Wortham 2006). Other patterns reveal themselves in what might be called the time of the life course. Weis's (2004) discovery of the significance of gender both for working-class educational attainment and the reworking of family organization depended on a longitudinal research strategy that followed high-school students into their adult lives. It would be valuable to have such a perspective on the life trajectories of Sarroub's (2005) research participants, allowing us to see whether their plight is transitional or enduring. This question brings us to the issue of the temporality of more abstract political and economic processes as they bear on more tangible cultural dynamics. Heightened diasporization—as described by Sarroub—seems to be a characteristic of the contemporary globalization, now some three to four decades into its course (Friedman 2003). Foley's (1990) study of reproductive class cultures derives its insight into interplay of class and ethnicity in school settings and other social arenas in part because of the companion study (Foley 1988) analyzing the community's transitions over an 80-year period.

Attention to multilevel processes and alertness to differing time frames would show that reproductive processes need not be simple to be systematic, nor to be consequential over the long term. Despite theoretical and methodological advances of work in the postreproduction period, there is much to be done to understand how social inequality results from the interplay of classrooms, schools, and the wider society.

DISCLOSURE STATEMENT

The author is not aware of any affiliations, memberships, funding, or financial holdings that might be perceived as affecting the objectivity of this review.

ACKNOWLEDGMENTS

I am grateful to many people who contributed to this review: Greg Urban, who responded to an early prospectus, raising useful questions about scope; Laura Hallgren Flynn, who provided a number of stimulating references and insights into the changing nature of "linguistic reproduction" in classroom contexts and wider educational arenas; Fiona Thompson, who listened to many ideas-in-progress and carefully read a presubmission draft; and Rosa Collins, who provided valuable (paid) clerical assistance compiling the large bibliography.

LITERATURE CITED

Althusser L. 1971. Ideology and ideological state apparatuses. In *Lenin and Philosophy*, pp. 127–86. New York: NLB

Anyon J. 1981. Social class and school knowledge. *Curric. Inq.* 11:3–42

Anyon J. 1997. *Ghetto Schooling: A Political Economy of Urban Educational Reform.* New York: Teachers Coll. Press

Apple M. 1982. *Education and Power.* Boston: Routledge & Kegan Paul

Aristotle. 1959. *Aristotle's Politics.* Oxford: Clarendon

Atkinson P. 1985. *Language, Structure, and Reproduction: An Introduction to the Sociology of Basil Bernstein.* London: Methuen

Au K. 1980. Participation structures in a reading lesson with Hawaiian children: analysis of a culturally appropriate instruction event. *Anthropol. Educ. Q.* 11:91–115

Bartlett L. 2007. Bilingual literacies, social identification, and educational trajectories. *Linguist. Educ.* 18:215–31

Baugh J. 2000. *Beyond Ebonics: Linguistic Pride and Racial Prejudice.* New York: Oxford Univ. Press

Bauman Z. 1997. *Postmodernity and Its Discontents.* New York: Routledge

Bereiter C, Englemann S. 1966. *Teaching Disadvantaged Children in the Pre-School.* Englewood Cliffs, NJ: Prentice Hall

Bernstein B. 1960. Language and social class. *Br. J. Sociol.* 11:271–76

Bernstein B. 1964. Elaborated and restricted codes: their social origins and some consequences. *Am. Anthropol.* 66(No. 6, Part 2):55–69

Bernstein B. 1972. A critique of the concept of compensatory education. See Cazden et al. 1972, pp. 135–51

Bernstein B. 1975. *Class, Codes, and Control.* London: Routledge & Kegan Paul

Bernstein B. 1986. A sociolinguistic approach to socialization; with some reference to educability. In *Directions in Sociolinguistics: The Ethnography of Communication*, ed. J Gumperz, D Hymes, pp. 465–97. New York: Blackwell

Bettie J. 2003. *Women Without Class: Girls, Race, and Identity.* Berkeley: Univ. Calif. Press

Bigler E. 1996. Telling stories: on ethnicity, exclusion, and education in upstate New York. *Anthropol. Educ. Q.* 27:186–203

Bloch M. 1961. *Medieval Society.* Chicago: Univ. Chicago Press

Blommaert J. 1999. *State Ideology and Language in Tanzania.* Koln: Rudiger Koppe Verlag

Boggs S. 1972. The meaning of questions and narratives to Hawaiian children. See Cazden et al. 1972, pp. 299–327

Bomer R, Dworin J, May L, Semington P. 2008. Miseducating teachers about the poor: a critical analysis of Ruby Payne's claims about poverty. *Teach. Coll. Rec.* ID Number: 14591. **http://www.tcrecord.org**

Bourdieu P. 1977. *Outline of a Theory of Practice.* Cambridge, UK: Cambridge Univ. Press

Bourdieu P. 1984. *Distinction: A Social Critique of the Judgement of Taste.* Cambridge, MA: Harvard Univ. Press

Bourdieu P, Passeron J-C. 1977. *Reproduction in Education, Society, and Culture.* Beverly Hills: Sage

Bowles S, Gintis H. 1976. *Schooling in Capitalist America.* New York: Basic Books

Brooks-Gunn J, Klebanov P, Smith J, Duncan G, Lee K. 2003. The black-white test score gap in young children: contributions of test and family characteristics. *Appl. Dev. Sci.* 7:239–52

Carnoy M, Levin H. 1985. *Schooling and Work in the Democratic State.* Stanford, CA: Stanford Univ. Press

Cazden C. 2001. *Classroom Discourse: The Language of Teaching and Learning.* Cambridge, MA: Harvard Univ. Press

Cazden C, Hymes D, John V, eds. 1972. *Functions of Language in the Classroom.* New York: Teachers Coll. Press

Coleman J. 1966. *Equality of Educational Opportunity.* Washington, DC: US Gov. Print. Off.

Collins J. 1986. Differential treatment in reading groups. See Cook-Gumperz 1986, pp. 117–37

Collins J. 1988. Language and class in minority education. *Anthropol. Educ. Q.* 19:299–326

Collins J. 1989. Hegemonic practice: literacy and standard language in public education. *J. Educ.* 171:9–35

Collins J. 1992. Review of *Learning Capitalist Culture* (Douglas E. Foley). *Latin Am. Anthropol. Rev.* 4:83–84

Collins J. 1996. Socialization to text: structure and contradiction in schooled literacy. In *Natural Histories of Discourse*, ed. M Silverstein, G Urban, pp. 203–28. Chicago: Univ. Chicago Press

Collins J. 1999a. The culture wars and shifts in linguistic capital: for combining political economy and cultural analysis. *Int. J. Qual. Res. Educ.* 12:269–86

Collins J. 1999b. The Ebonics controversy in context: literacies, subjectivities, and language ideologies in the United States. In *Language Ideological Debates*, ed. J Blommaert, pp. 201–34. New York: Mouton de Gruyter

Collins J, Blot R. 2003. *Literacy and Literacies: Texts, Power, and Identity*. Cambridge, UK: Cambridge Univ. Press

Cook-Gumperz J. 1973. *Social Control and Socialization*. London: Routledge & Kegan Paul

Cook-Gumperz J, ed. 1986. *The Social Construction of Literacy*. New York: Cambridge Univ. Press

de Castell S, Walker T. 1991. Identity, metamorphosis and ethnographic research: What kind of story is 'Ways with Words'? *Anthropol. Educ. Q.* 22:3–20

Delpit L, Perry T, eds. 1998. *The Real Ebonics Debate: Power, Language, and the Education of African-American Children*. New York: Beacon

Deutsch M, ed. 1967. *The Disadvantaged Child*. New York: Basic Books

Durkheim E. 1977. *The Evolution of Educational Thought: Lectures on the Formation and Development of Secondary Education in France*. London: Routledge & Kegan Paul

Edwards A. 1976. *Language, Education, and Class*. London: Heinemann

Erickson F, Mohatt G. 1992. Participation structures in two communities. In *Doing the Ethnography of Schooling*, ed. G Spindler. New York: Holt, Rinehart and Winston

Erickson F, Schultz J. 1982. *The Counselor as Gatekeeper: Social Interaction in Interviews*. New York: Academic

Foley D. 1988. *From Peones to Politicos: Class and Ethnicity in a South Texas Town, 1900–1987*. Austin: Univ. Tex. Press

Foley D. 1990. *Learning Capitalist Culture: Deep in the Heart of Tejas*. Philadelphia: Univ. Penn. Press

Foster M. 1987. "It's cookin' now": a performance analysis of the speech events of a black teacher in an urban community college. *Lang. Soc.* 18:1–29

Freeman M. 2004. Toward a rearticulation of a discourse on class within the practice of parental involvement. *Qual. Inq.* 10:566–80

Friedman J. 2003. Globalizing languages: ideologies and realities of the contemporary global system. *Am. Anthropol.* 105:744—52

Gee J. 1996. *Social Linguistics and Literacies*. London: Taylor & Maxwell

Gee J. 2001. Identity as an analytic lens for research in education. *Rev. Res. Educ.* 25:99–125

Giroux H. 1983. Theories of reproduction and resistance in the new sociology of education. *Harv. Educ. Rev.* 53:257–93

Goffman E. 1959. *The Presentation of Self in Everyday Life*. Garden City, NY: Anchor Doubleday

Goffman E. 1967. *Interaction Rituals: Essays on Face-to-Face Interaction*. New York: Anchor

Gonzalez N, Moll L, Amanti C, eds. 2005. *Funds of Knowledge: Theorizing Practice in Households, Communities, and Classrooms*. Mahwah, NJ: Erlbaum

Guillory J. 1993. *Cultural Capital: The Problem of Literary Canon Formation*. Chicago: Univ. Chicago Press

Gumperz J, Hernandez-Chavez E. 1972. Bilingualism, bidialectalism, and classroom interaction. See Cazden et al. 1972, pp. 85–108

Habermas J. 1987. *Lifeworld and System: A Critique of Functionalist Reason. The Theory of Communicative Action*. Boston, MA: Beacon Press

Harris R, Rampton B, eds. 2003. *The Language, Ethnicity and Race Reader*. New York: Routledge

Hart B, Risley T. 1995. *Meaningful Differences*. Baltimore, MD: Brookes

Hart B, Risley T. 2003. The early catastrophe: the 30 million word gap by age 3. *Am. Educ.* 17:110–18

Hawkins P. 1977. *Social Class, the Nominal Group and Verbal Strategies*. London: Routledge & Kegan Paul

Heath S. 1983. *Ways with Words: Language, Life, and Work in Communities and Classrooms*. New York: Cambridge Univ. Press

Heller M. 1994. *Crosswords: Language, Education and Ethnicity in French Ontario*. New York: Mouton de Gruyter

Heller M. 1999. *Linguistic Minorities and Modernity*. Paramus, NJ: Prentice Hall

Henwood D. 2003. *After the New Economy*. New York: New Press

Hymes D. 1972. Introduction. See Cazden et al. 1972, pp. xi–lvii

Jencks C. 1972. *Inequality: A Reassessment of the Effect of Family and Schooling in America*. New York: Basic Books

Jencks C, Phillips M, eds. 1998. *The Black-White Test Score Gap*. Washington, DC: Brookings Inst. Press

Kingston P. 2000. *The Classless Society*. Stanford, CA: Stanford Univ. Press

Kontopoulos K. 1993. *The Logics of Social Structure*. New York: Cambridge Univ. Press

Kuttner R. 2007. *The Squandering of America*. New York: Alfred A. Knopf

Lareau A. 1989. *Home Advantage: Social Class and Parental Intervention Elementary Education*. New York: Falmer

Lareau A. 2003. *Unequal Childhoods: Class, Race and Family Life*. Berkeley: Univ. Calif. Press

Leacock EB. 1969. *Teaching and Learning in City Schools: A Comparative Study*. New York: Basic Books

Leacock EB, ed. 1971. *The Culture of Poverty: A Critique*. New York: Simon & Schuster

Lee C. 1993. *Signifying as a Scaffold for Literary Interpretation: The Pedagogical Implications of an African American Discourse Genre*. Urbana, IL: NCTE

Lemke M. 2002. *Outcomes of Learning. Results From the 2000 Program for International Student Assessment of 15-Year-olds in Reading, Mathematics, and Science Literacy*. NCES 2002–115. Washington, DC: US Dep. Educ., Off. Educ. Res. Improv.

Levinson B, Holland D. 1996. The cultural production of the educated person: an introduction. See Levinson et al. 1996, pp. 1–54

Levinson B, Holland D, Foley D, eds. 1996. *The Cultural Production of the Educated Person: Critical Ethnographies of Schooling and Local Practice*. Albany: State Univ. NY

Lloyd GER. 1990. *Demystifying Mentalities*. Cambridge: Cambridge Univ. Press

Long M. 2003. Ebonics, language and power. In *Language and Social Identity*, ed. R Blot, pp. 147–70. Westport, CT: Praeger

Luttrell W. 1996. Taking care of literacy: one feminist's critique. *Educ. Policy* 3:342–65

Luttrell W. 1997. *Schoolsmart and Motherwise: Working-Class Women's Identity and Schooling*. New York: Routledge

MacLeod J. 1987. *Ain't No Makin' It: Aspirations and Attainment in a Low-Income Neighborhood*. Boulder, CO: Westview

McRobbie A. 1978. Working class girls and the culture of feminity. In *Women Take Issue: Aspects of Women's Subordination*, ed. Women's Study Group. London: Hutchinson

Michaels S. 1981. "Sharing time": children's narrative styles and differential access to literacy. *Lang. Soc.* 10:423–41

Michaels S. 1986. Narrative presentations: an oral preparation for literacy with first graders. See Cook-Gumperz 1986, pp. 94–116

Mitchell-Kernan C. 1972. On the status of Black English for native speakers: an assessment of attitudes and values. See Cazden et al. 1972, pp. 195–210

Moll L, Amanti C, Neff D, Gonzalez N. 1992. Funds of knowledge for teaching: using a qualitative approach to connect homes and classrooms. *Theory Into Pract.* 31:133–41

Nespor J. 1987. The construction of school knowledge: a case study. *J. Educ.* 169:34–54

No Child Left Behind Act of 2001. 2002. Public Law No. 107–110

Oakes J. 1985. *Keeping Track: How Schools Structure Inequality*. New Haven, CT: Yale Univ. Press

O'Connor MC, Michaels S. 1996. Shifting participation structures: orchestrating thinking practices in group discussion. In *Discourse, Learning, and Schooling*, ed. D Hicks, pp. 63–103. New York: Cambridge Univ. Press

Ortner S. 1993. Theory in anthropology since the sixties. In *Culture/Power/History: A Reader in Contemporary Social Theory*, ed. N Dirks, G Eley, S Ortner, pp. 372–411. Princeton, NJ: Princeton Univ. Press

Philips S. 1972. Participant structures and communicative competence: Warm Springs children in community and classroom. See Cazden et al. 1972, pp. 370–94

Philips S. 1983. *The Invisible Culture: Communication in Classroom and Community on the Warm Springs Indian Reservation*. Highland Park, IL: Waveland

Rampton B. 1995. *Crossing: Language and Ethnicity among Adolescents*. London: Longman

Rampton B. 2006. *Language in Late Modernity: Interaction in an Urban School*. New York: Cambridge Univ. Press

Rampton B, Harris R, Collins J, Blommaert J. 2008. Language, class and education. In *Kluwer Encyclopedia of Language and Education*, ed. N Hornberger, S May, pp. 71–81. New York: Springer

Rist R. 1970. Student social class and teacher expectations: the self-fulfilling prophecy in ghetto education. *Harv. Educ. Rev.* 40:411–51

Rogers R. 2003. *A Critical Discourse Analysis of Family Literacy Practices: Power In and Out of Print*. Mahwah, NJ: Erlbaum

Rothstein R. 2004. *Class and Schools: Using Social, Economic, and Educational Reform to Close the Black-White Achievement Gap*. New York: Teachers Coll. Press

Rothstein R. 2007. *What schools can (and cannot) do*. (Plenary lecture, *Every Child Counts*, NYSUT Symp. Albany, NY, Oct. 27)

Rymes B. 2001. *Conversational Borderlands: Language and Identity in an Alternative Urban High School*. New York: Teachers Coll. Press

Sarroub L. 2005. *All American Yemeni Girls: Being Muslim in a Public School*. Philadelphia: Univ. Penn. Press

Schieffelin B, Ochs E, eds. 1986. *Language Socialization Across Cultures*. Cambridge, UK: Cambridge Univ. Press

Scott J. 1998. *Seeing Like a State: How Certain Schemes to Improve the Human Condition Have Failed*. New Haven, CT: Yale Univ. Press

Stiglitz J. 2002. *Globalization and Its Discontents*. New York: Norton

Thompson F. 1995. *An exploration of the use of cultural capital in home-school interactions around homework*. PhD thesis, Temple Univ. 323pp.

Tough P. 2006. What it takes to make a student. *New York Times*, Nov. 26:27

U.S. Dep. Educ. 2001. *The Condition of Education*. Washington, DC: NCES

Weis L. 1990. *Working Class without Work: High School Students in a De-Industrialized Economy*. New York: Routledge

Weis L. 2004. *Class Reunion: The Remaking of the American White Working Class*. New York: Routledge

Willis P. 1977. *Learning to Labor: How Working Class Kids Get Working Class Jobs*. New York: Teachers Coll. Press

Wortham S. 2006. *Learning Identity: The Mediation of Social Identity through Academic Learning*. New York: Cambridge Univ. Press

Wortham S. 2008. Linguistic anthropology of education. *Annu. Rev. Anthropol.* 37:37–51

The Commodification of Intimacy: Marriage, Sex, and Reproductive Labor

Nicole Constable

Department of Anthropology, University of Pittsburgh, Pittsburgh, Pennsylvania 15260;
email: constabl@pitt.edu

Annu. Rev. Anthropol. 2009. 38:49–64

First published online as a Review in Advance on
June 12, 2009

The *Annual Review of Anthropology* is online at
anthro.annualreviews.org

This article's doi:
10.1146/annurev.anthro.37.081407.085133

Key Words

domestic work, sex work, cross-border marriage, gendered migration,
transnationalism

Abstract

Over the past three decades, scholars have paid greater attention to the
intensification and complex interconnectivity of local and global processes. Anthropological studies of cross-border marriages, migrant domestic workers, and sex workers have burgeoned, demonstrating growing scholarly interest in how social relations have become evermore
geographically dispersed, impersonal, mediated by and implicated in
broader political-economic or capitalist processes. At the same time,
intimate and personal relations—especially those linked to households
and domestic units, the primary units associated with reproductive
labor—have become more explicitly commodified, linked to commodities and to commodified global processes (i.e., bought or sold; packaged
and advertised; fetishized, commercialized, or objectified; consumed;
assigned values and prices) and linked in many cases to transnational
mobility and migration, presenting new ethnographic challenges and
opportunities. This review highlights contemporary anthropological
and ethnographic studies of the transnational commodification of intimacy and intimate relations, related debates, themes, and ethnographic
challenges.

INTRODUCTION

> The proliferation of consumption practices and domains in late capitalism, including the commodification even of fetuses and the means of reproduction, creates doubts as to what—if anything—exists outside of commodity exchange.
>
> –Russ 2005, p. 142

> In employment market terms, European demand is strong for migrant women in three areas: cleaning, cooking and housekeeping inside private houses; caring for sick, disabled, elderly and young people inside private houses; and providing sex in a wide variety of locales.
>
> –Augustín 2007a, p. 53

> To label a payment as a gift (tip, bribe, charity, expression of esteem) rather than an entitlement (pension, allowance, rightful share of gains) or compensation (wages, salary, bonus, commission) is to make claims about the relationship between payer and payee.
>
> –Zelizer 2000, p. 826

Over the past three decades, anthropologists have paid attention to the intensification and complex interconnectivity of local and global processes (Appadurai 1996, Basch et al. 1994, Gupta & Ferguson 1992). They have criticized and analyzed the myriad ways in which social relations have become evermore geographically dispersed, impersonal, mediated by and implicated in broader political-economic or capitalist processes. Scholars have examined the ways in which aspects of intimate and personal relations—especially those that are linked to households and domestic units, the primary units associated with reproductive labor—are increasingly and evermore explicitly commodified, seemingly linked to commodities and to commodified global processes, or under assault by "market biographies" or lives that are shaped by market demands that characterize modernity (Beck & Beck-Gernscheim 1995, Shumway 2003, Zelizer 2005).

In Marxist terms, commodification refers to the process of assigning market value to goods or services that previously existed outside of the market (Marx 1978). This review focuses on how anthropologists have recently contributed to analyses of the real or imagined commodification of intimate relations, particularly those involving marriage, sex, and reproductive labor. By commodification, I refer to the ways in which intimacy or intimate relations can be treated, understood, or thought of as if they have entered the market: are bought or sold; packaged and advertised; fetishized, commercialized, or objectified; consumed or assigned values and prices; and linked in many cases to transnational mobility and migration, echoing a global capitalist flow of goods.

The term intimate relations refers here to social relationships that are—or give the impression of being—physically and/or emotionally close, personal, sexually intimate, private, caring, or loving. Such relationships are not necessarily associated with or limited to the domestic sphere, but discourses about intimacy are often intertwined with ideas about gender and domesticity, gifts as opposed to markets. In many cases, intimate relations are related to reproductive labor or care work in the broadest sense including, most notably, child care, nursing, and hospice care (Hochschild 1983, Russ 2005) and also to entertainment such as stripping, erotic dancing, hostessing, and other types of sex work. This review draws selectively and not exhaustively from a vast and rapidly growing literature on transnational intimacies, including intimate labor and intimate relations, although much of the literature is not self-identified as such or unified around this theme. Topically, primary examples are taken from three broad types of intimate relations: cross-border marriages, migrant domestic workers and care workers, and migrant sex workers, as they relate directly or indirectly to commodification. These three broad categories represent of course only a small range of possible intimate relations that are related to reproductive labor, but these are three areas in which a significant literature has developed in recent years. This review focuses on the ways in which ethnographic scholarship contextualizes, problematizes, and theorizes the commodification and consumption of intimate reproductive labor, especially within an increasingly global or transnational context since the 1980s and concludes with a discussion of possible future directions.[1]

GENDERED MIGRATION

Gender is a central topic and primary subject of criticism in the literature on transnational marriage migration, sex work, and care work. Since the 1970s, studies of migration were criticized for focusing almost exclusively on male migrants (without attention to gender) or for treating female migrants as though they were simply appendages of migrant men (Brettell & deBerjeois 1992; Hondagneu-Sotelo 1994; Morokvasic 1983, 1984; Piper 2006). Since then, many influential studies have focused on the feminization of migrant labor (Ehrenreich & Hochschild 2003, Parreñas 2001, Sassen 2000). More recently, the scholarly focus on migrant women (instead of gender) as well as the heteronormative focus of most migrant studies have also been subject to criticism, pointing in new directions for future research (Babb 2006, Donato et al. 2006, Mahler & Pessar 2006, Manalansan 2006).

In her influential essay entitled "Love and Gold," Hochschild argues that the care and love provided by third world women is a resource that is not unlike "the nineteenth-century extraction of gold, ivory, and rubber from the Third World" (2003a, p. 26; 2003b). In the contemporary version of imperialist extraction, she argues, love and care are "the new gold" because emotional labor is extracted from poorer regions of the world to benefit richer ones at a low cost (2003a). The edited volume *Global Woman* focuses primarily on such feminized labor and is aptly subtitled "Nannies, Maids, and Sex Workers in the New Economy" (Ehrenreich &

Hochschild 2003). The articles in *Global Woman* illustrate how globalization has resulted in increased opportunities for intimacy across and despite vast geographic distances.

Numerous studies and analyses of global relationships and processes point to wide variations in gendered patterns of mobility that involve men as well as women. Men from poorer regions of the so-called Global South migrate for work—as in the case of construction workers and seamen from the Philippines and Indonesia—to the oil-rich countries of the Middle East. Immigrant male doctors provide intimate care, and men are also involved in sexual and reproductive labor. But such men, with few notable exceptions (e.g., Espiritu 2002; Margold 1995; Padilla 2007a,b), are rarely approached as a gendered topic of study. The issue of intimacy is far more often applied to the physical and emotional labor of women (Augustín 2007a,b; Donato et al. 2006; Ehrenreich & Hochschild 2003).

Scholars have attempted to shift the analytical focus away from "women" per se toward gendered analyses more broadly. Building on cultural geographer Massey's notion of "power geometry" (Massey 1994), in which some people are in charge of mobility (their own and that of others), Pessar & Mahler (2001) call for attention to "gendered geographies of power" in which one's social location relative to power influences opportunities for geographic mobility. Massey, Pessar & Mahler, and others query the variety of factors that determine who moves and who controls or influences the movements of others. Following Appadurai's notion of global ethnoscapes (1996), scholars have examined a variety of "marriage-scapes" (e.g., Abelmann & Kim 2005; Chao 2005; Constable 2005a,b; Freeman 2005; Oxfeld 2005; Schein 2005; Suzuki 2005; Thai 2005) and "sex-scapes" (Brennan 2004, 2007).

Ethnographic research thus describes varied patterns of gendered marital mobility and gendered sex and care work in a global context, illustrating new gendered geographies of power in which certain women have opportunities for mobility that are unavailable to men,

---

[1] Drawing from Hochschild's work on emotional labor (1983), Frank uses the term "commodification of intimacy" to refer to the "authentic experience" that is created for regular male customers at a U.S. strip club (2002).

and certain classes of men and women have the ability to determine their own mobility and that of others. Despite the burgeoning number of studies of caregivers, domestic workers, and cross-border marriages, studies of migrant sex workers, particularly of male sex workers, male care givers, and same sex-intimacy, have been slower to appear (Augustín 2007a; Cheng 2005, 2007, 2010; Constable 2000; Manalansan 2003; Padilla 2007a,b; Sim 2007, 2009).

Gendered geographies of mobility point to different class ends of the migratory spectrum. On one end are elite "astronaut families" (in which the family members are divided across regions; for example, the male breadwinner may go work in one country and the wife accompanies the children to another country to facilitate their education) and immigrant professionals (Ong 1999; Piper & Roces 2003; Shen 2005, 2008; Shih 1999; Yeoh et al. 2005), many of whom have the privilege to choose to remain at home or whose "home" becomes multiple and flexible. On the other end of the spectrum are growing numbers of documented and undocumented women and men from poorer countries who provide benefits for the more privileged residents of wealthier regions (Ong 2006) as maids (Anderson 2000, Adams & Dickey 2000, Lan 2006, Parreñas 2001, Sim & Wee 2009), sex workers (Augustín 2007a,b; Cheng 2007, 2010; Parreñas 2008), wives (Constable 2003, 2005a; Oxfeld 2005; Roces 2003; Thai 2005, 2008), or adoptees (Cohen 2007, Dorow 2006, Volkman 2005), all of whom contribute to what Parreñas has called a "chain of love."

Studies of contemporary global migratory processes point to the importance of socioeconomic class transformations and related conflicts for workers and employers or clients. The "middle-class" educated identity of Filipina maids, for example, may be threatening to Taiwan or Hong Kong employers when the home is also an intimate workplace (Constable 2007b, Lan 2006) or can increase their perceived value relative to other nationalities of workers (de Regt 2008, Lan 2006). Conflicts exist between the class and educational identity of migrant Vietnamese or Chinese wives and

their U.S. working-class husbands, and in the gendered desires of men who seek "traditional wives" abroad and women who seek "modern husbands" (Constable 2003, 2005b; Thai 2005, 2008). In a fascinating study of Brazilian erotic dancers in New York City, Maia (2007) illustrates the class/gender complexities of the situation as educated middle-class Brazilian women opt to work as dancers in nightclubs (as opposed to working as maids) where they provide intimate labor for working-class—or less-educated middle-class—U.S. men. In such cases, class identity is an important mediating factor in constructing and resisting commodified migrant subjectivities.

Ethnographies of migrant workers have examined a single ethnic group/nationality of workers in one location, for example, Filipina domestic workers in Hong Kong (Constable 1997) or Mexican and Central American maids in Los Angeles (Hondagneu-Sotelo 2001). More recent studies have adopted more ambitious multisited research methodologies including multiple destinations, sending and receiving countries, and migrant workers as well as family members who are left behind (Cheng 2007, 2010; Frantz 2008; Gamburd 2000; Parreñas 2001, 2005a,b; Sim & Wee 2009). As Liebelt (2008) argues, migrant maids and caregivers often do not simply move back and forth from home to a single migrant destination and back again, but rather on and on from one destination to another that is higher on the global hierarchy of employment possibilities, thus requiring mobile research methodologies.

Clearly not all geographic mobility involves travel or migration of women or men from poorer countries to wealthier ones for work. A rich area of research examines movements of residents of richer countries, as in the case of tourists (Brennan 2004; Padilla 2007a,b; Wilson 2004) and astronaut families described above (Ong 1999, 2006; Piper & Roces 2003; Yeoh et al. 2005). Men and women tourists from wealthy countries of Asia-Pacific, Western Europe, North America, and elsewhere travel to regions of Southeast Asia, the Caribbean, Latin America, Eastern Europe, the former

Soviet Union, and elsewhere for sex and in search of spouses. Whereas women also partake in sex tourism, and local men provide sexual intimacy to men and women, men from wealthy regions of the globe are widely depicted as the main beneficiaries and the consumers of such global intimacies (Brennan 2004; Cheng 2010; Frohlick 2007; Kelsky 2001; Padilla 2007a,b). Such studies increasingly consider new mobility patterns of elites and nonelites, the "costs and benefits" both to those who move and those who remain at home (Gamburd 2000, Parreñas 2005a), and, as discussed below, the role of new technologies in patterns, and the notions of love and authenticity that such relationships entail.

NEW TECHNOLOGIES OF CONSUMPTION

Arranged marriages and marriages based on correspondence are not new, nor is the employment of migrant maids or sex workers. New technologies offer unique methodological and theoretical challenges to ethnographers of transnational intimacies while also transforming the landscape of intimacy. The Internet plays a striking role in the proliferation of businesses that promote international marital introduction services (or offer mail-order brides). It shapes new procedures for recruiting, interviewing, and employing foreign maids across great geographic distances, and it proffers new opportunities to advertise and locate sexual services. Internet technology plays a central role in the commodification of intimacy and in shaping new movements and geographic and electronic landscapes of intimacy for individuals who are otherwise geographically dispersed (Brennan 2004; Constable 2003, 2007a). New technologies offer migrant workers new means to create and maintain a sense of intimacy with family members far away, as in the case of "long distance mothering" (Parreñas 2005a,b; Yeoh et al. 2005), to facilitate intimate communications between sex workers and boyfriends/clients (Brennan 2004, Cohen 1986), and to provide opportunities for

prospective spouses to develop online intimacy before they meet face to face (Constable 2007a).

Since the early 1990s when so-called mail order bride catalogs began to be published and accessible online, the number of introduction agencies geared toward English speakers has rapidly proliferated (Constable 2005b). Recent studies of cross-border marriages, courtships, dating, and sexual partnerships of various sorts have pointed to new patterns of commodification and to rapid growth of profit-oriented and electronically mediated forms of matchmaking or marital introduction that facilitate wider global patterns of cross-border relationships (Johnson 2007, Johnson-Hanks 2007). Some marriage brokers promote international marriage partners as though they were commodities or offer services to facilitate the process of meeting and selecting partners from a wider globally defined "marriage market" (Constable 2003, 2005a; Freeman 2005, 2006; Piper & Roces 2003; Simons 2001; Thai 2008; Wang & Chang 2002).

Processes of online and electronic communication have influenced the purchase of sexual services because individual sex workers increasingly advertise online and communicate with prospective clients via the internet and without the need for middlemen or intermediaries (Agustin 2007a,b; Bernstein 2007a). As Bernstein's sensitive and fine-grained analysis shows, electronic communication leads to new opportunities and possibilities for intimate encounters and individual businesses and have literally redefined the spaces of sexual labor. As opposed to depending on older assumptions about red light districts and street walkers, patrons and clients can now advertise and locate one another invisibly and privately through the Internet.

The Internet has also had a major impact on the marketing and consumption of migrant domestic workers (Constable 2007b, Julag-Ay 1997, Lan 2006, Tyner 2009). Internet technology is one tool of domestic worker employment agencies (replacing videotapes and CDs with live Internet interviews). As is the case with online escort and dating services and marriage introduction services, the success of the business is based on creating and anticipating the desires of consumers or clients. The more "high quality" products or services they offer, the better the chance of selling the agency's services. A number of scholars have examined the role of domestic worker recruitment and employment agencies in marketing and selling products, distinguishing among different nationalities of workers, objectifying workers by offering specials, sales, markdowns, free replacements, and guarantees—in short, using the language of commodity markets to refer to workers—but less has been done in terms of analyzing its importance in creating new markets and transforming the spaces of labor. Unlike Bernstein's study of the spaces of sex work and the historical impact of technological change on both the meaning and consumption of sexual services, parallel analyses have yet to be produced in relation to domestic labor and the terrain of marriage.

An intellectual bridge is also needed to connect the technology of marriage, domestic work, and sex work to transformations and redefinitions of the meaning of family, drawing from the many insights of studies of technologically assisted parenting and the reproduction of children. Adoption and new reproductive technologies have provided a rich arena for anthropologists to revisit older theories of kinship and definitions of family (Edwards et al. 1993; Franklin & McKinnon 2000, 2002; Franklin & Ragoné 1998; Schneider 1968). Commodified processes of reproductive labor have led to important studies of diverse family forms that challenge prevailing patterns of heteronormativity (Lewin 1993, Weston 1991). New critiques of biologically deterministic theories of kinship have offered insights about commodified global and transnational processes (Bowie 2005, Cohen 2007, Dorow 2006, Howell 2003, McKinnon 2005, Orobitg & Salazar 2005, Padilla et al. 2007, Volkman 2005). Anthropologists have examined the sociocultural and political-economic implications of new procreative or reproductive services and mechanisms such as surrogate parenthood, egg or sperm donation, and local and international adoption that aim at facilitating the creation of families (Bharadwaj 2003; Franklin 1995; Ginsburg & Rapp 1995; Inhorn & Birenbaum-Carmeli 2008; Modell 1994; Nahman 2006; Ragoné 1994, 1996; Sharp 2001; Strathern 1985, 1992a,b). Work remains to be done to link the insights relating to the reproductive technologies with technologically mediated and transnational intimacies.

LOVE, PERFORMANCE, AND AUTHENTICITY

The commodification of social relations in the era of industrial capitalism stands in supposed contrast to Marx's nostalgic ideal of the "social character" of familial labor in precapitalist peasant families (Marx 1978, p. 326). Yet despite common idealization of precapitalist social relations, social relationships that are represented and defined by gifts, bride wealth, dowry, and payments are not unambiguous, free of conflict, or unmarked by inequality or instrumentalism (Bloch & Parry 1989, Comaroff 1979, Mauss 1967). Commodification is likewise rarely simply given, unambiguous, or complete, as illustrated by Zelizer's analysis of monetary exchanges, intimate social relations, and legal disputes in the West (2000, 2005). The social science perspective that places moral boundaries between market and domestic spheres has been labeled the "hostile worlds view" (Zelizer 2000). The conflation of intimate social relations with monetary value is criticized by those who imagine a more altruistic or authentic precapitalist past or who view the domestic sphere as a proper shelter from the harsh and impersonal world of market capitalism. Yet the question remains of how the commodification of intimate relations is understood and experienced by those involved in such relationships and processes. A key concern is—as the title of Brennan's (2004) study of sex workers in the Dominican Republic aptly puts it—*What's Love Got to do With It?*

The historical meaning and construction of love, its performance and authenticity, are rich and promising areas of inquiry, as the following diverse examples illustrate. Whereas Brennan (2004, 2007) approaches Dominican women's relationships with foreign men, some of which result in marriage, as "performances" in which sex workers feign love to mask the economic exchange and the benefits they receive, other scholars define them in terms of "bounded authenticity" (Bernstein 2007a,b) or in terms of historical constructions of romantic intimacy (Giddens 1992, Hirsch 2007, Padilla et al. 2007).

Numerous studies examine cultural constructions of love and romance in a variety of geographic settings (Jankowiak 1995), considering how they are commodified in terms of material expectations, gift exchanges, and mass-mediated images of modern romance (Ahearn 2001, Hirsch 2004, Hirsch & Wardlow 2006, Illouz 1997, Jankowiak 1995, Padilla et al. 2007, Rebhun 1999). Commodification may be hidden, disguised, mystified, denied, or reinterpreted as a gift or experienced as liberating and modern (Russ 2005). In the context of Europe and the United States, Bernstein argues that "traditional 'procreative'" and "modern 'companionate'" models of sexuality are increasingly being supplanted by a "recreational sexual ethic" that differs from marital or ongoing relationships and is defined by "physical sensation and from emotionally bounded erotic exchanges" (2007b, p. 6). She argues that the "girlfriend experience" increasingly offered by sex workers and often located via the Internet is an example of "bounded authenticity" in which not only eroticism but also an "authentic relationship" (albeit within a bounded frame) is for sale in the marketplace (Bernstein 2007b, p.7). Allison's research among Japanese salary men who frequent hostess clubs and engage prostitutes focuses on how hostesses serve to make men "feel like men" and that men gain satisfaction from "care" they receive and the lack of ongoing responsibility that accompanies payment for sexual and intimate attention in hostess clubs and on sex tours abroad, in contrast with their domestic lives and relationships with their wives (Allison 1994).

These examples suggest that commodification of intimacy is not an analytical end in itself, but instead offers a valuable starting point for analyses of gendered social relations, cultural meanings, social inequalities, and capitalist transformations (Appadurai 1986). In a provocative volume on modernity, companionate marriage, and romantic courtship, Hirsch & Wardlow illustrate the promise of such comparative ethnographic analyses (Hirsch & Wardlow 2006). In her study of the Huli of Papua New Guinea, Wardlow notes that Seventh-Day Adventist missionaries criticized the Huli (as other Christian missionaries did of other groups) for the exchange of bride wealth, which they argued "commoditizes women and weakens the proper bonds of marriage" (Wardlow 2006, p. 66). Yet the decline of bride wealth among the Huli and in other societies has not meant that within "the context of capitalism, the home becomes ideologically demarcated as the safe haven of emotional intimacy, a place where one recovers from the alienation of the marketplace" (Wardlow 2006, p. 74). Instead, the meanings and importance of commodities are transformed in relation to particular local understandings of modernity as related to subjectivity and intimate relationships (Ahearn 2001, Chao 2005, Rebhun 1999).

Faier's work on professions of love among Filipina entertainers who marry Japanese men is groundbreaking. Instead of questioning the authenticity of women's professions of love for their husbands, or treating them as feigned performances, Faier asks how such declarations are "made meaningful through global processes" (2007, p. 148). Faier argues that Filipinas' professions of love serve to counteract the stigma of their work and to define their transnational subjectivities. Love is also associated with the care (including gifts and monetary remittances for their families) and understanding offered to women by their husbands. Following Rebhun's view of Christian love in opposition to financial gain, Faier stresses women's constructions of new gendered and sexualized subjectivities in relation to modernity, Christianity, and Philippine notions of *utang ng loob* (a debt of gratitude) that encompass the meaning of love (Faier 2007, p. 156) in relation to the notion of shame, which results from a failure to respect and repay one to whom it is owed. As discussed below, Faier's analytical approach to love also has important implications for the debate about migrant women as agents or victims of trafficking.

As scholarship on transnational intimacies illustrates, relationships assumed to be based primarily on paid work for money are often understood to involve complex forms of intimacy, love, or emotion, and those assumed to be based on love are linked in new and evolving ways to commercial practices and material desires.

BEYOND TRAFFICKED VICTIMS

A central theme in critical popular media and certain activist and feminist depictions of women who migrate from poorer countries to wealthier ones as maids, brides, or sex workers is that they are powerless "victims of trafficking."[2] So-called mail-order brides are depicted as though they are literally bought and sold and connected to human trafficking, although little actual evidence exists to support this position (Constable 2005c, Vance 2005).

Building on Foucault's idea that power is everywhere, much anthropological attention has been paid in recent decades to revealing instances of resistance and agency among the relatively powerless (Martin 1987, Ortner 2006, Parker 2005). In opposition to popular media images of helpless victims, ethnographic research has provided numerous examples of

migrant women's activism, their subtle or explicit protests, and their resistance and agency within the context of structural factors that limit the opportunities and often disempower foreign brides, migrant domestic workers, and sex workers (Brennan 2004; Constable 1997, 2009; Kempadoo 2005; Kempadoo & Doezema 1998; Parker 2005; Parreñas 2008).

Unlike popular media depictions of trafficked women as commodities devoid of agency, anthropologists point to subtle and complex forms of power and agency within the household, in public spaces, and in the wider global context. Studies of care workers reposition older arguments about emotional labor as a gift or commodity in terms of, for example, the "commodity candidacy" of care, the relationality of partners in exchange, or the phenomenology of gift and commodity in relation to the self (Appadurai 1986, Ehrenreich & Hochschild 2003, Kopytoff 1986, Russ 2005, Valeri 1994).

Scholarship on gendered migration points to striking contrasts between the gendered migration of (mostly girl) babies who are adopted from China and elsewhere by European and North American middle-class, mostly white and heterosexual, parents and the migration of foreign brides and workers who face a markedly different migration process. Whereas forming a family through adoption is viewed as the right and privilege of middle-class families, and transnational adoptees are assumed to grow up to be privileged citizens, other types of immigrants face vastly different circumstances. Whereas adoptees, like migrant brides and workers, are sometimes characterized as trafficked or as part of a commodified process, adoptees are more likely to be depicted as the fortunate beneficiaries of such a process (Anagnost 2000, Cohen 2007, Constable 2003, Dorow 2006, Volkman 2005). In her study of U.S. adoptions of Chinese children, Dorow considers how discourse and processes of commodification are counterbalanced and opposed to parental understandings of children as gifts who will also receive the gift of good life and opportunity (Dorow 2006).

---

[2]In an earlier publication, I argued against "unwarranted blurring" of different categories of migrant women, specifically brides, sex workers, and domestic workers, due to the self-ascribed subjectivities that divide them and the tendency in popular literature to gloss them all as "victims" or "trafficked women" (Constable 2006). However, studies of these three broad and overlapping categories of migrants can provide key insights for scholarly understandings and assumptions about the consumption and commodification of relationships that are often assumed to be naturally or ideally based on emotional ties, love, or caring but that increasingly involve impersonal relations, complex commercial and increasingly bureaucratic mediating processes, material benefits, and wages.

Anthropologists, sociologists, and feminist scholars have examined migratory patterns that build on or contrast with older forms of arranged marriage and matchmaking, have reconsidered older patterns of gift exchange and marriage payments, and have criticized Levi-Straussian structural assumptions about the "traffic in women" (Bloch & Parry 1989, Comaroff 1979, MacCormack & Strathern 1980, Rubin 1975). More recent scholarly research on sex work, sex tourism, prostitution, and comfort women points to the fluidity between paid sexual labor and marital relations and to interconnections between paid forms of intimacy and those that are assumed to be "free" (Bernstein 2007a,b; Brennan 2004; Cabezas 2004; Cheng 2007; Cohen 1982, 1986; Liechty 2005; Padilla 2007a,b; Piper & Roces 2003; Zelizer 2000).

The agent-victim binary has proven to be a dead end of sorts. Whereas certain feminist scholars and activists argue that all sex workers are victims, other scholars and feminists can respond with endless examples of agency and choice. Instead, scholars such as Augustín (2007a,b), Bernstein (2007a,b), Vance (2005), and others take on a critical analysis of the notion of trafficking, considering its historical specificity and the parallels between late-twentieth-century anxiety about trafficking and nineteenth-century hysteria about white slavery. Several scholars have drawn attention to both sex workers and their middle-class "social helpers" or nongovernmental workers and volunteers who often aim to help or rescue sex workers in misguided ways (Augustín 2007a, Bloch 2003, Cheng 2005). Anthropologists have also addressed methodological challenges associated with research on trafficking and have criticized rhetorical conflations of trafficking with prostitution (Brennan 2005, 2008; Vance 2005).

Faier's work (2007) discussed above offers a valuable alternative to the victim-agent binary. She focuses on the transnational gendered and sexual subjectivities of migrant women and successfully steers an analytical course away from the question of "true love versus material motivations," thus offering an important advance over the dead-end question of depicting women migrants as either passive victims who lack the ability to make choices or active agents who have full control of their circumstances. Faier's analysis illustrates unequal global power relations within the context of women's self-definitions. Loving their husbands resonates with their sense of self as moral and modern women and wives. The lure of the Japanese entertainment industry for poor and unemployed Filipinas, the opportunities that such employment offers for intimate socialization with Japanese men, and the shortage of Japanese brides in rural regions of Japan illustrate ways in which capitalist processes promote new opportunities for intimacy and marriage that are influenced by, but not entirely defined by, the entertainment or sex work industry.

CONCLUSIONS AND FUTURE DIRECTIONS

Recent studies of the changing local and global patterns, processes, and relations of intimacy build on and borrow from older critiques of overly binary models of public and private, intimate and impersonal, material and emotional, love and money, local and global, nature and culture (Franklin 2003; Franklin & McKinnon 2000, 2002; Levine 2003; McKinnon & Silverman 2005; Zelizer 2000). Some such studies refine older Marxist notions of commodification and reproductive labor or point to the ongoing importance of Maussian insights about gift exchange and the intimacy of social relationships. Collectively they draw on symbolic and interpretive analyses, critical global and feminist perspectives, and new anthropological insights that are linked to wider multisited and transnational ethnographic research that looks beyond local-global dichotomies, yet draws insight from older assumptions about kinship and social relations within increasingly global, mobile, and technologically mediated contexts.

Current anthropological studies demonstrate that in some contexts commodification of social relations are welcomed and interpreted as modern progress, as in the cases of child care and elderly care, which were once the responsibility of family members but can now be delegated to paid service providers. Yet even in such cases, commodification, or "the purchase of intimacy" (Zelizer 2000, 2005), is not the end point of the analysis nor is it devoid of countervailing personalized processes, assumptions, and anxieties. Instead, commodification and the accompanying notions of impersonal pragmatic market relations are often denied, mystified, mediated, transformed, or disguised. As the scope of commodification expands more deeply into various realms of intimacy, it involves a range of countervailing discourses and actions involving reciprocity and gift giving, claims to altruism, assertions of love, and claims to bounded authenticity.

This review has outlined some of the key contributions of the literature on cross-border marriages, domestic work, and sex work that addresses the commodification of intimacy. Methodologically, there is a marked shift toward multisited research away from narrow "area studies" approaches, toward border-crossing topics that require mobility as well as online and "deterritorialized" research (Gupta & Ferguson 1992). Promising new research has shifted from single nationalities and single locations, moving beyond binary constructions of sending and receiving locations to multiple hierarchies of sites and subjectivities.

Another key issue has been and continues to be gender and sexuality. Studies of transnational intimacies echo the shift in anthropology and migration studies more broadly, from the earliest topics of men as unexamined gendered subjects, to women, to gender more broadly. Still lacking are studies of men as intimate gendered subjects, as providers of care work and intimacy, and not just as consumers of sexual services. A fruitful direction for future research is also to question and move beyond the frames and assumptions of heteronormativity that are inherent in much of the research on transnational intimacies. As Babb (2006) proposes, "queering" love and globalization requires

reexamining assumptions about domesticity, marriage, and gender that are deeply held by research subjects and researchers. Berlant's call for cataloging "intimacy's norms, forms and crimes," asking "how public institutions use issues of intimate life to normalize particular forms of knowledge and practice and to create compliant subjects" (1998, p. 188) is well worth considering.

The value of future research therefore lies not in bemoaning the downfall of the sanctity of the domestic sphere or the demise of authentic relations outside the realm of capital, but instead, in continuing to attend to the multiple, complex, transnational, and also transgressive and transformative ways in which emotional ties and relationships are understood, formulated, or prohibited within and beyond local and global spaces. Studies such as those of Bernstein (2007a,b) and Faier (2007) point to the importance of fine-grained historically and culturally specific studies of intimacy in relation to new technologies and opportunities for mobility. Such studies continue to ask how authenticity is understood and experienced, offering opportunities as well as constraints. Globalization does not simply result in greater commodification of intimate sexual, marital, and reproductive relationships; it also offers opportunities for defining new sorts of relationships and for redefining spaces, meanings, and expressions of intimacy that can transform and transgress conventional gendered spaces and norms.

Future research would benefit by further examining the pairing of commodification and intimacy, casting them as the main topic rather than separating out topical foci on marriage, household work, sex work, nursing, adoption, etc. We must ask not only what differentiates erotic dance and hospice care, but also what such multiple and varied examples can tell us about the meaning of intimacy for all involved. The focus on transnational mobility of both elites and nonelites within neoliberal globalization and the ongoing tension between more complex microlevel patterns of power and agency and broader macro patterns of global inequality are also key. Research on the structural factors and the experiences and meanings of migrant work and marriage have made important inroads, allowing us to avoid the pitfalls of overly binary notions of victim and agent, public and private, or the trap of defining all women migrants or sex workers as trafficked victims. Yet there are risks and benefits associated with the notion of commodification. This notion both offers a way to illuminate power relations inherent in a variety of intimate relations but also can overdetermine the political-economic frame, thus masking the multiplicity of power and the potentially liberating and transformative aspects of intimate subjectivities.

DISCLOSURE STATEMENT

The author is not aware of any affiliations, memberships, funding, or financial holdings that might be perceived as affecting the objectivity of this review.

LITERATURE CITED

Abelmann N, Kim H. 2005. A failed attempt at transnational marriage: maternal citizenship in globalizing South Korea. See Constable 2005a, pp. 101–23

Adams KM, Dickey S, eds. 2000. *Home and Hegemony: Domestic Service and Identity Politics in South and Southeast Asia*. Ann Arbor: Univ. Mich. Press

Ahearn L. 2001. *Invitations to Love: Literacy, Love Letters, and Social Change in Nepal*. Ann Arbor: Univ. Mich. Press

Allison A. 1994. *Nightwork: Sexuality, Pleasure, and Corporate Masculinity in a Tokyo Hostess Club*. Chicago, IL: Univ. Chicago Press

Anagnost A. 2000. Scenes of misrecognition: maternal courtship in the age of transnational adoption. *Positions* 8:389–421

Anderson B. 2000. *Doing the Dirty Work: The Global Politics of Domestic Labor*. New York: Zed

Appadurai A. 1986. Introduction: commodities and the politics of value. In *The Social Life of Things: Commodities in Cultural Perspective*, ed. A Appadurai, pp. 3–63. Cambridge, UK: Cambridge Univ. Press

Appadurai A. 1996. *Modernity at Large: Cultural Dimensions of Globalization*. Minneapolis: Univ. Minn. Press

Augustín LM. 2007a. *Sex at the Margins: Migration, Labor Markets and the Rescue Industry*. London: Zed

Augustín LM, ed. 2007b. Special issue on the cultural study of commercial sex. *Sexualities* 10(4):473–88

Babb FE. 2006. Queering love and globalization. *GLQ: A Jr. Lesbian Gay Stud.* 13:111–24

Basch L, Schiller NG, Blanc CS. 1994. *Nations Unbound: Transnational Projects, Postcolonial Predicaments, and Deterritorialized Nation-States*. Langhorne, PA: Gordon & Breach

Beck U, Beck-Gernsheim E. 1995. *The Normal Chaos of Love*. Cambridge, MA: Blackwell

Berlant L. 1998. Intimacy: a special issue. *Crit. Inq.* 4:181–88

Bernstein E. 2007a. Temporarily yours: the sale and purchase of bounded authenticity. See Padilla et al. 2007, pp. 186–202

Bernstein E. 2007b. *Temporarily Yours: Intimacy, Authenticity, and the Commerce of Sex*. Chicago, IL: Univ. Chicago Press

Bharadwaj A. 2003. Why adoption is not an option in India: the visibility of infertility, the secrecy of donor insemination, and other cultural complexities. *Soc. Sci. Med.* 56:1867–80

Bloch A. 2003. Victims of trafficiking or entrepreneurial women? *J. Can. Woman Stud.* 22:152–58

Bloch M, Parry J. 1989. *Money and the Morality of Exchange*. New York: Cambridge Univ. Press

Bowie F. 2005. *Cross-Cultural Approaches to Adoption*. New York: Routledge

Brennan D. 2004. *What's Love Got to Do with It? Transnational Desires and Sex Tourism in the Dominican Republic*. Durham, NC: Duke Univ. Press

Brennan D. 2005. Methodological challenges in research with trafficked persons: tales from the field. *Int. Migr.* 43(1/2):35–54

Brennan D. 2007. Love work in a tourist town: Dominican sex workers and resort workers perform at love. See Padilla et al. 2007, pp. 203–25

Brennan D. 2008. Competing claims of victimhood? Foreign and domestic victims of trafficking in the United States. *Sex. Res. Soc. Policy: J. NSRC* 5(4):45–61

Brettell CB, deBerjeois PA. 1992. Anthropology and the study of immigrant women. In *Seeking Common Ground*, ed. D Gabaccia, pp. 41–63. Westport, CT: Greenwood

Cabezas AL. 2004. Between love and money: sex, tourism, and citizenship in Cuba and the Dominican Republic. *Signs* 29:987–1015

Chao E. 2005. Cautionary tales: marriage strategies, state discourse, and women's agency in a Naxi village in southwestern China. See Constable 2005a, pp. 34–52

Cheng S. 2005. The 'success' of anti-trafficking policy: women's human rights and women's sexuality in South Korea. Presented at *Ethnography and Policy: What Do We Know About Trafficking?* CS Vance, organizer. Santa Fe, NM: Sch. Adv. Res.

Cheng S. 2007. Romancing the club: love dynamics between Filipina entertainers and GIs in US military camp towns in South Korea. See Padilla et al. 2007, pp. 226–51

Cheng S. 2010. *Dreams of Flight: Sex, Love, and Labor of Migrant Entertainers*. Ithaca, NY: Cornell Univ. Press

Cohen E. 1982. Thai girls and farang men—the edge of ambiguity. *Ann. Tour. Res.* 9:403–28

Cohen E. 1986. Lovelorn farangs: the correspondence between foreign men and Thai girls. *Anthropol. Q.* 59:115–28

Cohen F. 2007. *Tracing the red thread: an ethnography of Chinese–U.S. transnational adoptions*. PhD thesis. Univ. Pittsburgh, 214 pp.

Comaroff JL. 1979. *The Meaning of Marriage Payments*. New York: Academic

Constable N. 1997. *Maid to Order in Hong Kong: Stories of Filipina Workers*. Ithaca, NY: Cornell Univ. Press

Constable N. 2000. Dolls, t-birds, and ideal workers: the negotiation of Filipino identity in Hong Kong. See Adams & Dickey 2000, pp. 221–48

Constable N. 2003. *Romance on a Global Stage: Pen Pals, Virtual Ethnography, and "Mail Order" Marriages*. Berkeley: Univ. Calif. Press

Constable N, ed. 2005a. *Cross-Border Marriages: Gender and Mobility in Transnational Asia*. Philadelphia: Univ. Penn. Press

Constable N. 2005b. A tale of two marriages: international matchmaking and gendered mobility. See Constable 2005a, pp. 166–86

Constable N. 2005c. The International Marriage Broker Regulation Act: What does it have to do with trafficking? Presented at *Ethnography and Policy: What Do We Know About Trafficking?* CS Vance, organizer. Santa Fe, NM: Sch. Adv. Res.

Constable N. 2006. Brides, maids, and prostitutes: reflections on the study of 'trafficked' women. *PORTAL: J. Multidiscip. Int. Stud.* 3(2). Special Issue: *Women in Asia*, ed. D Ghosh. **http://epress.lib.uts.edu.au/ojs/index.php/portal**

Constable N. 2007a. Love at first sight? Visual images and virtual encounters with bodies. See Padilla et al. 2007, pp. 252–69

Constable N. 2007b. *Maid to Order in Hong Kong: Stories of Migrant Workers*. Ithaca, NY: Cornell Univ. Press

Constable N. 2009. Migrant workers and the many states of protest in Hong Kong. *Crit. Asian Stud.* 41:143–64

de Regt M. 2008. High in the hierarchy, rich in diversity: Asian domestic workers, their networks and employers' preferences in Yemen. *Crit. Asian Stud.* 40:587–608

Donato KM, Gabaccia D, Holdaway J, Manalansan M, Pessar PR. 2006. A glass half full? Gender in migration studies. *Int. Migr. Rev.* 40:3–26

Dorow SK. 2006. *Transnational Adoption: A Cultural Economy of Race, Gender, and Kinship*. New York: NY Univ. Press

Edwards J, Franklin S, Hirsch E, Price F, Strathern M. 1993. *Technologies of Procreation: Kinship in the Age of Assisted Conception*. Manchester, UK: Manchester Univ. Press

Ehrenreich B, Hochschild AR, eds. 2003. *Global Woman: Nannies, Maids and Sex Workers in the New Economy*. New York: Holt/Metropolitan Books

Espiritu Y. 2002. Filipino navy stewards and Filipino health care professionals: immigration, work and family relations. *Asia Pac. Migr. J.* 11:47–66

Faier L. 2007. Filipina migrants in rural Japan and their professions of love. *Am. Ethnol.* 34:148–62

Frank K. 2002. *G-Strings and Sympathy: Strip Club Regulars and Male Desire*. Durham, NC: Duke Univ. Press

Franklin S. 1995. Postmodern procreation: a cultural account of assisted reproduction. In *Conceiving the New World Order: The Global Politics of Reproduction*, ed. FD Ginsburg, R Rapp, pp. 323–45. Berkeley: Univ. Calif. Press

Franklin S. 2003. Rethinking nature-culture: anthropology and the new genetics. *Anthropol. Theory* 3:65–85

Franklin S, McKinnon S. 2000. New directions in kinship study: a core concept revisited. *Curr. Anthropol.* 41:275–79

Franklin S, McKinnon S. 2002. *Relative Values: Reconfiguring Kinship Studies*. Durham, NC: Duke Univ. Press

Franklin S, Ragoné H. 1998. *Reproducing Reproduction: Kinship, Power, and Technological Innovation*. Philadelphia: Univ. Penn. Press

Frantz E. 2008. Of maids and madams: Sri Lankan domestic workers and their employers in Jordan. *Crit. Asian Stud.* 40:609–38

Freeman C. 2005. Marrying up and marrying down: the paradoxes of marital mobility for Chosonjok brides in South Korea. See Constable 2005, pp. 80–100

Freeman C. 2006. *Forging kinship across borders: paradoxes of gender, kinship, and nation between China and South Korea*. PhD thesis. Univ. Va. 288 pp.

Frohlick S. 2007. Fluid exchanges: the negotiation of intimacy between tourist women and local men in a transnational town in Caribbean Costa Rica. *City Soc.* 19(1):139–68

Gamburd M. 2000. *The Kitchen Spoon's Handle: Transnationalism and Sri Lanka's Migrant Housemaids*. Ithaca, NY: Cornell Univ. Press

Giddens A. 1992. *The Transformation of Intimacy: Sexuality, Love, and Eroticism in Modern Societies*. Cambridge, UK: Polity

Ginsburg FD, Rapp R. 1995. *Conceiving the New World Order: The Global Politics of Reproduction*. Berkeley: Univ. Calif. Press

Gupta A, Ferguson J. 1992. Space, identity and the politics of difference. *Cult. Anthropol.* 7(1):6–23

Hirsch JS. 2004. *A Courtship after Marriage: Sexuality and Love in Mexican Transnational Families*. Berkeley: Univ. Calif. Press

Hirsch JS. 2007. 'Love makes a family': globalization, companionate marriage, and the modernization of gender inequality. See Padilla et al. 2007, pp. 93–106

Hirsch JS, Wardlow H, eds. 2006. *Modern Loves: The Anthropology of Romantic Courtship and Companionate Marriage*. Ann Arbor: Univ. Mich. Press

Hochschild AR. 1983. *The Managed Heart: Commercialization of Human Feeling*. Berkeley: Univ. Calif. Press

Hochschild AR. 2003a. Love and gold. See Ehrenreich & Hochschild 2003, pp. 15–30

Hochschild AR. 2003b. *The Commercialization of Intimate Life: Notes from Home and Work*. Berkeley: Univ. Calif. Press

Hondagneu-Sotelo P. 1994. *Gendered Transitions: Mexican Experiences of Immigration*. Berkeley: Univ. Calif. Press

Hondagneu-Sotelo P. 2001. *Domestica: Immigrant Workers Cleaning and Caring in the Shadows of Affluence*. Berkeley: Univ. Calif. Press

Howell S. 2003. Kinning: the creation of life trajectories in transnational adoptive families. *J. R. Anthropol. Inst.* 9:465–84

Illouz E. 1997. *Consuming the Romantic Utopia: Love and the Cultural Contradictions of Capitalism*. Berkeley: Univ. Calif. Press

Inhorn MC, Birenbaum-Carmeli D. 2008. Assisted reproductive technologies and culture change. *Annu. Rev. Anthropol.* 37:177–96

Jankowiak W, ed. 1995. *Romantic Passion: A Universal Experience?* New York: Columbia Univ. Press

Johnson E. 2007. *Dreaming of a Mail Order Husband: Russian-American Internet Romance*. Durham, NC: Duke Univ. Press

Johnson-Hanks J. 2007. Women on the market: marriage, consumption, and the Internet in urban Cameroon. *Am. Ethnol.* 34:642–58

Julag-Ay C. 1997. *Correspondence marriages between Filipinas and United States men*. PhD thesis. Univ. Calif., Irvine. 206 pp.

Kelsky K. 2001. *Women on the Verge: Japanese Women, Western Dreams*. Durham, NC: Duke Univ. Press

Kempadoo K, ed. 2005. *Trafficking and Prostitution Reconsidered: New Perspectives on Migration, Sex Work, and Human Rights*. Boulder, CO: Paradigm

Kempadoo K, Doezema J, eds. 1998. *Global Sex Workers: Rights, Resistance, and Redefinition*. New York: Routledge

Kopytoff I. 1986. The cultural biography of things: commoditization as process. See Appadurai 1986, pp. 64–91

Lan PC. 2006. *Global Cinderellas: Migrant Domestic and Newly Rich Employers in Taiwan*. Durham, NC: Duke Univ. Press

Levine HB. 2003. Gestational surrogacy: nature and culture in kinship. *Ethnology* 42:173–85

Lewin E. 1993. *Lesbian Mothers: Accounts of Gender in American Culture*. Ithaca, NY: Cornell Univ. Press

Liebelt C. 2008. On sentimental orientalists, Christian Zionists, and working class cosmopolitans: Filipino domestic workers' journeys to Israel and beyond. *Crit. Asian Stud.* 40:567–85

Liechty M. 2005. Carnal economies: the commodification of food and sex in Kathmandu. *Cult. Anthropol.* 20:1–38

MacCormack C, Strathern M, eds. 1980. *Nature, Culture and Gender*. Cambridge, UK: Cambridge Univ. Press

Mahler SJ, Pessar PR. 2006. Gender matters: ethnographers bring gender from the periphery toward the center of migration studies. *Int. Migr. Rev.* 40(1):27–63

Maia SM. 2007. *Brazilian erotic dancers in New York: desire and national identity*. PhD thesis. The Graduate Cent., City Univ. NY, 303 pp.

Manalansan MF. 2003. *Global Divas: Filipino Gay Men in Diaspora*. Durham, NC: Duke Univ. Press

Manalansan MF. 2006. Queer intersections: sexuality and gender in migration studies. *Int. Migr. Rev.* 40(1):224–49

Margold J. 1995. Narratives of masculinity and transnational migration: Filipino migrant workers in the Middle East. In *Bewitching Women and Pious Men: Gender and Body Politics in Southeast Asia*, ed. A Ong, MJ Peletz, pp. 274–98. Berkeley: Univ. Calif. Press

Martin E. 1987. *The Woman in the Body: A Cultural Analysis of Reproduction*. Boston: Beacon

Marx K. 1978 (1867). The fetishism of commodities and the secret thereof. In *The Marx-Engels Reader*, ed. R Tucker, pp. 319–29. New York: Norton. 2nd ed. See also *Capital* 1:71–83

Massey D. 1994. *Space, Place and Gender*. Minneapolis: Univ. Minn. Press

Mauss M. 1967. *The Gift: Forms and Functions of Exchange in Archaic Societies*. New York: Norton

McKinnon S. 2005. On kinship and marriage: a critique of the genetic and gender calculus of evolutionary psychology. In *Complexities: Beyond Nature and Culture*, ed. S McKinnon, S Silverman, pp. 106–31. Chicago, IL: Univ. Chicago Press

McKinnon S, Silverman S, eds. 2005. *Complexities: Beyond Nature and Culture*. Chicago, IL: Univ. Chicago Press

Modell J. 1994. *Kinship With Strangers: Adoption and the Interpretation of Kinship in American Culture*. Berkeley: Univ. Calif. Press

Morokvasic M. 1983. Women in migration: beyond the reductionist outlook. In *One Way Ticket: Migration and Female Labor*, ed. A Phizacklea, pp. 13–31. London: Routledge

Morokvasic M. 1984. Birds of passage are also women. *Int. Migr. Rev.* 18(4):886–907

Nahman M. 2006. Materializing Israeliness: difference and mixture in transnational ova donation. *Sci. Cult.* 15(3):199–213

Ong A. 1999. *Flexible Citizenship: The Cultural Logics of Transnationality*. Durham, NC: Duke Univ. Press

Ong A. 2006. *Neoliberalism as Exception: Mutations in Citizenship and Sovereignty*. Durham, NC: Duke Univ. Press

Orobitg G, Salazar C. 2005. The gift of motherhood: egg donation in a Barcelona infertility clinic. *Ethnos* 70:31–51

Ortner SB. 2006. *Anthropology and Social Theory: Culture, Power, and the Acting Subject*. Durham, NC: Duke Univ. Press

Oxfeld E. 2005. Cross-border hypergamy? Marriage exchanges in a transnational Hakka community. See Constable 2005a, pp. 17–33

Padilla M. 2007a. *Caribbean Pleasure Industry: Tourism, Sexuality, and AIDS in the Dominican Republic*. Chicago: Univ. Chicago Press

Padilla M. 2007b. Tourism and tigueraje: the structures of love and silence among Dominican male sex workers. See Padilla et al. 2007, pp. 38–69

Padilla M, Hirsch JS, Munoz-Laboy M, Sember RE, Parker RG, eds. 2007. *Love and Globalization: Transformations of Intimacy in the Contemporary World*. Nashville, TN: Vanderbilt Univ. Press

Parker L, ed. 2005. *The Agency of Women in Asia*. Singapore: Marshall Cavendish

Parreñas RS. 2001. *Servants of Globalization: Women, Migration and Domestic Work*. Stanford, CA: Stanford Univ. Press

Parreñas RS. 2005a. *Children of Global Migration: Transnational Families and Gendered Woes*. Stanford, CA: Stanford Univ. Press

Parreñas RS. 2005b. Long distance intimacy: class, gender and intergenerational relations between mothers and children in Filipino transnational families. *Glob. Netw.* 5(4):317–36

Parreñas RS. 2008. *The Force of Domesticity: Filipina Migrants and Domesticity*. New York: NY Univ. Press

Pessar PR, Mahler SJ. 2001. *Gender and transnational migration*. Transnatl. Communities Program Work. Pap. Ser. WPTC-01-20. **http://www.transcomm.ox.ac.uk/working_papers.htm**

Piper N. 2006. Gendering the politics of migration. *Int. Migr. Rev.* 40:133–64

Piper N, Roces M, eds. 2003. *Wife or Worker? Asian Women and Migration*. New York: Rowman & Littlefield

Ragoné H. 1994. *Surrogate Motherhood: Conception in the Heart*. Boulder, CO: Westview

Ragoné H. 1996. Chasing the blood tie: surrogate mothers, adoptive mothers and fathers. *Am. Ethnol.* 23:352–65

Rebhun LA. 1999. *The Heart Is an Unknown Country: Love and the Changing Economy of Northeast Brazil*. Stanford, CA: Stanford Univ. Press

Roces M. 2003. Sisterhood is local: Filipino women in Mount Isa. See Piper & Roces 2003, pp. 73–100

Rubin G. 1975. The traffic in women: notes on the "political economy" of sex. In *Toward an Anthropology of Women*, ed. R Reiter, pp. 157–210. New York: Mon. Rev.

Russ AJ. 2005. Love's labor paid for: gift and commodity at the threshold of death. *Cult. Anthropol.* 20:128–55

Sassen S. 2000. Countergeographies of globalization: the feminization of survival. *J. Int. Aff.* 53(2):503–24

Schein L. 2005. Marrying out of place: Hmong/Miao women across and beyond China. See Constable 2005a, pp. 53–79

Schneider DM. 1968. *American Kinship: A Cultural Account*. Englewood Cliffs, NJ: Prentice Hall

Sharp LA. 2001. Commodified kin: death, mourning, and competing claims on the bodies of organ donors in the United States. *Am. Anthropol.* 103:112–33

Shen HH. 2005. "The first Taiwanese wives" and the "Chinese mistresses": the international division of labor in familial and intimate relations across the Taiwan Strait. *Glob. Netw.* 5(4):419–37

Shen SS. 2008. The purchase of transnational intimacy: women's bodies, transnational masculine privileges in Chinese economic zones. *Asian Stud. Rev.* 32:57–75

Shih SM. 1999. Gender and the geopolitics of desire: the seduction of Mainland women in Taiwan and Hong Kong media. In *Spaces of Their Own*, ed. MM Yang, pp. 278–307. Minneapolis: Univ. Minn. Press

Shumway DR. 2003. *Modern Love: Romance, Intimacy and the Marriage Crisis*. New York: New York Univ. Press

Sim ASC. 2007. *Women in transition: Indonesian domestic workers*. PhD thesis. Univ. Hong Kong, 352 pp.

Sim ASC. 2009. Transitional sexuality among women migrant workers: Indonesians in Hong Kong. In *As Normal as Possible: Negotiating Sexuality in Hong Kong and China*, ed. C Yau. Hong Kong: Univ. Hong Kong Press. In press

Sim ASC, Wee V. 2009. Undocumented Indonesian workers: the human outcome of colluding interests. *Crit. Asian Stud.* 41:165–88

Simons LA. 2001. *Marriage, migration, and markets: international matchmaking and international feminism*. PhD thesis. Univ. Denver, 344 pp.

Strathern M. 1985. Kinship and economy: constitutive orders of a provisional kind. *Am. Ethnol.* 12:191–209

Strathern M. 1992a. The meaning of assisted kinship. In *Changing Human Reproduction: Social Science Perspectives*, ed. M Stacey, pp. 148–69. London: Sage

Strathern M. 1992b. *Reproducing the Future: Essays on Anthropology, Kinship and the New Reproductive Technologies*. New York: Routledge

Suzuki N. 2005. Tripartite desires: Filipina-Japanese marriages and fantasies of transnational traversal. See Constable 2005a, pp. 124–44

Thai HC. 2005. Clashing dreams in the Vietnamese diaspora: highly educated overseas brides and low-wage U.S. husbands. See Constable 2005a, pp. 145–65

Thai HC. 2008. *For Better or Worse: Vietnamese International Marriages in the New Global Economy*. New Brunswick, NJ: Rutgers Univ. Press

Tyner JA. 2009. *The Philippines: Mobilities, Identities, Globalization*. New York: Routledge

Valeri V. 1994. Buying women but not selling them: gift and commodity exchange in Huaulu alliance. *Man* 29:1–26

Vance CS, ed. 2005. Ethnography and policy: What do we know about trafficking? Presented at *Ethnography and Policy: What Do We Know About Trafficking?* CS Vance, organizer. Santa Fe, NM: Sch. Adv. Res.

Volkman TA, ed. 2005. *Cultures of Transnational Adoption*. Durham, NC: Duke Univ. Press

Wang HZ, Chang SM. 2002. The commodification of international marriages: cross-border marriage business between Taiwan and Viet Nam. *Int. Migr.* 40:93–116

Wardlow H. 2006. All's fair when love is war: romantic passion and companionate marriage among the Huli of Papua New Guinea. See Hirsch & Wardlow 2006, pp. 51–77

Weston K. 1991. *Families We Choose: Lesbians, Gays, Kinship*. New York: Columbia Univ. Press

Wilson A. 2004. *The Intimate Economies of Bangkok: Tomboys, Tycoons, and Avon Ladies in the Global City*. Berkeley: Univ. Calif. Press

Yeoh BSA, Huang S, Lam T. 2005. Transnationalizing the "Asian" family: imaginaries, intimacies, and strategic intents. *Glob. Netw.* 5:307–15

Zelizer VA. 2000. The purchase of intimacy. *Law Soc. Inq.* 25:817–48

Zelizer VA. 2005. *The Purchase of Intimacy*. Princeton, NJ: Princeton Univ. Press

Identity and Difference: Complicating Gender in Archaeology

Pamela L. Geller

Department of Anthropology, University of Miami, Coral Gables, Florida 33124;
email: pgeller@mail.as.miami.edu

Annu. Rev. Anthropol. 2009. 38:65–81

First published online as a Review in Advance on
June 17, 2009

The *Annual Review of Anthropology* is online at
anthro.annualreviews.org

This article's doi:
10.1146/annurev-anthro-091908-164414

0084-6570/09/1021-0065$20.00

Key Words

feminism, bioarchaeology, race, sexuality, postmodernism

Abstract

From its inception, the archaeology of gender was entwined with feminism. Engagement has engendered reconstructions of complex, diverse peoples and practices that are more equitable, relevant, and sound. Yet, for many archaeologists, the connection with feminist perspectives has frayed in recent years. Their studies of gender articulate dated ideas about women and epistemological frames that highlight duality and universality. Examinations of labor divisions typify shortcomings. To advance gender's study and archaeology, practitioners need to consider several concerns about identity and difference emerging from third-wave feminism. Gender is envisioned as intersection. Bioarchaeology, especially, will benefit from feminist approaches that reflect critically and regard gender in nonnormative and multiscalar terms. To this end, resistance to feminism must fade. Opposition stems from its imagined relationship with postmodernism, but conflation misconstrues feminism's sociopolitical commitment to emancipatory change. For their part, archaeologists can utilize feminist perspectives to diversify the field, explore difference, and tackle archaeological issues with sociopolitical resonance.

BEGINNINGS

Her reputation of reading a great deal hung about her like the cloudy envelope of a goddess in an epic; it was supposed to engender difficult questions. . .

–Henry James, *The Portrait of a Lady*

To conceive this review, I first revisited a scholarly touchstone: Conkey & Spector's "Archaeology and the Study of Gender" (1984). Unsurprisingly, I found its key points still cogent after 25 years. To expose presentism, androcentrism, and ethnocentrism, Conkey & Spector advocated for critical theory building. The authors endeavored to detect material traces of gender roles and relations, identities and ideology. They did not suggest that inquiry be limited to women. Rather, the past that Conkey & Spector envisioned was diversely peopled, dynamic, and complex. Such efforts, they concluded, would ultimately transform archaeology's practice and scholarship. But, a study of gender could not be extricated from feminist perspectives. Thus, this catalytic piece represents fruition of its authors' deep-rooted personal and professional engagements with feminism (Wylie 2002, p. 189).

Tracking her intellectual history, Conkey (2007b) identifies formative familial inspirations, undergraduate activism, and professional actualization as playing important parts in the publication's conception. Spector shared similar experiences (2007). In fact, the feminist movement, which battles against institutionalized sexism on professional and personal fronts, resonated globally for many early archaeologists of gender. One European happening was the Norwegian Archaeological Association's 1979 workshop, "Were They All Men?" Publication of proceedings followed in time (Bertelsen et al. 1987), and the event triggered subsequent conferences, conscious raising, and collaborations (Engelstad 2007).

In North America, archaeologists heeded Conkey & Spector's call for critical evaluation and expansion of research interests. Conferences and sessions at professional meetings in turn generated edited volumes (e.g., Claassen 1992, Gero & Conkey 1991) that have bloomed into a sizeable corpus. Yet, when Conkey & Gero reviewed this literature in 1997, they discovered that many archaeologists disregarded feminist perspectives, making for woefully undertheorized and oversimplified studies of gender. So, what do archaeologists' study of gender and their grasp of feminism look like in the twenty-first century?

Assessment of work conducted from 2000 to the present reveals that archaeologists' study of gender has innovated and transformed the discipline. At best, this review is representative because it cannot be comprehensive. At worst, I generalize to underscore conceptual trends. Other reviews—Meskell (2002) on social identity, Joyce (2005) on the body, Voss (2008b) on sexuality—also demonstrate how feminist approaches to gender's archaeological study have branched skyward. These authors do not see gender as the central root but as intertwined with age, sexuality, ethnicity, class, etc. As such, we might unearth identity and lived experience within shifting social and spatial settings. Bifurcation demonstrates the productivity of applying feminist theory to diverse concerns.

Yet, many archaeologists who undertake gender work reflect cursorily on feminists' contributions, if they do so at all. By investigating gender independent of feminism, these practitioners have not truly addressed early calls or later assessments (Hays-Gilpin 2000, Nelson 2006, Wylie & Conkey 2007). Assorted academic feminists have long theorized about gender, and archaeologists' neglect of this corpus is puzzling. Such a lacuna is akin to examining class relations with nary a reference to Marx or evolution with minimal mention of Darwin. Perhaps, Simone de Beauvoir does not come as trippingly from the lips. Inattention to feminist scholarship that has ebbed and flowed over several waves—an imperfect metaphor but useful heuristic device—makes for a deficient study of the lives of past peoples, as well as an archaeological practice that increasingly has less relevance in our modern world.

SINS OF OUR MOTHERS

Shortcomings with second-wave feminism are numerous, though two are especially glaring. Gynocentric foci and questions are as reductive and imbalanced as androcentric ones (Harding 1987), and evaluation of binary oppositions before application avoids projection of a "Western folk model" onto cultures distanced from our own in space and/or time (Collier & Yanagisako 1987). Indeed, Ortner's (1974) influential query, "Is female to male as nature is to culture?" which posited universal, structuralist dualities, was later critiqued by feminist anthropologists (Moore 1988) and revised by Ortner (1996) herself. Sins of early second-wave feminist foremothers, however, are realized today when archaeologists study gender as Woman, a monolithic and essentialized category, and fail to interrogate reliance on dichotomy as a universal epistemological frame. Persistent disinclination to address difference in the past illustrates how archaeologists may revel in dirt but loath mess. Comparison of the 1989 and 2004 Chacmool Conferences presents an intriguing case.

An early endeavor, the 1989 Chacmool Conference "The Archaeology of Gender," is significant for its tackling of androcentrism. Published proceedings assembled writings about gender bias in scientific endeavors, topics long misrepresented or neglected, and equity issues (Walde & Willows 1991). In hindsight, participants' "discovery" of women qualifies their contributions as gynocentric and dualistic. But, engendering archaeologists' study of gender was a conference goal, and so these ideas are not particularly troublesome if situated historically. Of greater cause for concern was that feminist thought did not inform many contributors' queries (Hanen & Kelley 1992, Wylie 1992). Because feminism has long destabilized deep-rooted sexism, its repudiation—whether unconscious or intentional—appears counterintuitive. Not situating disciplinary gender bias within a larger context of feminist practice, politics, and perspectives rendered past people as undifferentiated "faceless blobs" (Tringham 1991).

Given its title, "Que(e)rying Archaeology," the 2004 conference promised to expand beyond gynocentric matters and dichotomous frames. Following from 15 years of intellectual and sociopolitical growth, archaeologists' engagement with third-wave feminism and queer scholarship seemed a foregone conclusion. But, if review of the program is any indication (proceedings have yet to be published), many archaeologists' studies of gender demonstrate stymied conceptual development and minimal critical assessment. "Gender," as Conkey intuited, "is still often just another variable that has been added to an unreflexive, positivist approach" (2003, p. 876). And, like the 1989 conference, "feminist" or "feminism" appears in only 4% of contributors' abstracts (6 of 141 total abstracts). Dated feminist ideas—reductive duality, conflation of gender and sex, stereotypical representations—were especially at issue in considerations of labor organization. Twenty-two presentations (15.6% of all presentations) indicated that the timeworn topic remains focal in the archaeology of gender. Predominantly, participants explored ancient "sexual" divisions of labor, which led to reconstructions of normal social roles and relations (i.e., gender).

Certainly, not all participants committed such transgressions (or, more appropriately, failed to transgress). One presentation published elsewhere was Cobb's (2005) thought-provoking que(e)rying of hunting-gatherer studies. She demonstrates how subtle heteronormativity has informed researchers' mainstream investigations of Mesolithic Europe. Presentist reconstructions and heterosexist interpretations, Cobb reproaches, produce an inadequate study of the past and naturalize modern social interactions and activities (see also Dowson 2006). Additionally, Stockett (2005) questions if gender hierarchy and complementarity are the only models for understanding ideology, relations, and practices in pre-Columbia Mesoamerica, since "both are rooted in Western understandings of the sexual division of labor" (pp. 566–567; see also Gero & Scattolin 2002). Attention to social differences, gender fluidity, and performative contexts is also necessary for illumining the complexity of past peoples' practices of identity in daily life and extraordinary events. Mulling over lows and highs, the conference gives me pause for thought about developments (or setbacks) in the broader archaeological literature.

Despite several decades of feminist appraisal, initiated in response to man-the-hunter models (e.g., Dahlberg 1981, Slocum 1975), characterization of sexual divisions of labor as natural persists in mainstream scholarship (e.g., Elston & Zeanah 2002, Hildebrandt & McGuire 2002, Surovell 2000). Many studies are devoid of feminism, or when investigators acknowledge critiques of androcentrism, they remain unaware of theorizing beyond the early second wave that troubles duality, universality, and reductivism. Waguespack (2005) proclaims, "Whether construed as the de facto result of different physical capabilities or the product of reproductive goals, the division of labor exists as an empirical fact in all hunter-gatherer societies" (p. 668). That her Clovis case study is an archaeological one roots this fact deep in time. As physiological differences provide the basis for labor divisions, she implies that sex is gender. Her brief mention of the Agta from the Philippines, a culture in which women hunted, presents the group as a statistical anomaly rather than a potential complication to universal division. Yet, she offers no additional thoughts on why they might "deviate from the pattern" (p. 670). In addition to plant procurement and processing that required negligible technical knowledge or skill, as opposed to men's specialized hunting, women labored as house maintainers and "drudges-on-hides" (Gifford-Gonzalez 1993)—not necessarily the radical new answer to an old question despite its billing as such in *American Anthropologist*.

Many bioarchaeologists' studies of sexual division of labor are similarly deficient. Yet, presentist, ethnocentric, and heteronormative ideas are more worrying because investigators analyze skeletal materials to make inferences about social organization. As such, they may advocate, albeit inadvertently so, for biological determinism. When concurrently studying pelvic differences and skeletal markers of habitual activities, bioarchaeologists often deduce that males were highly mobile and/or active regardless of the culture, period, or pursuit—hunting, trading, farming, herding, fishing (e.g., Eshed et al. 2004; Maggiano et al. 2008). In these same studies, little is stated about Woman's activities, insinuating that her primary responsibilities involved childbearing, childcaring, lactation, and family maintenance. One finds only nominal explanation when sex differences are insignificant or females exhibit "male-like" characteristics (e.g., Marchi et al. 2006, Sládek et al. 2007). Rather, the tendency is to represent men and women as homogenous and distinct.

The deeper in time their studies take them, the more stridently do some investigators avow that contemporary practices have ancient precursors. Paleolithic archaeologists Kuhn & Stiner (2006) argued that a sexual division of economic labor in the early Upper Paleolithic signals our species' humanity. The narrow range of subsistence activities that monolithic Neanderthals enacted presaged their demise. In Neolithic studies, skeletal analysts utilize biological data to reify these preconceived notions. Of social organization at Abu Hureyra, Molleson (2007) contends that that people likely lived at the origins of "the sort of family structure with which we are familiar today" (p. 190). From this presumption the conceptual leap to a "natural" and rigid sexual division of labor is a short one, especially because "a division of roles between the sexes is ubiquitous in the animal kingdom" (p. 192). Labor divisions wedded to domesticity then facilitated craft specialization's emergence. One female's teeth may have born the marks of basket weaving. Yet, Molleson does not explain how females would have had time to specialize, given the extensive and exhaustive domestic responsibilities they performed to sustain nuclear families. Potential complications to this picture—insignificant morphological differences between the sexes she identifies at Catalhöyük—go unpondered (compare Peterson 2002).

Conversely, many archaeologists inspired by recent feminist theorizing move beyond grand, exclusionary narratives when studying labor (e.g., Owen 2005, Pyburn 2004, Robin & Brumfiel 2008). Too often androcentrism or inadvertent omission in ethnographic and colonial period sources, they caution, obscures certain activities, relations, or persons. Brumbach & Jarvenpa (2006) have urged scholars to evaluate these materials critically to discern "complex and variegated subsistence tasks *actually performed* by women and men regardless of, and sometimes in contradiction to, the normative constructions of gender fostered by their own cultures" (p. 306, emphasis in original). Additionally, to treat labor activities in homogeneous terms or as the domain of a specific gender oversimplifies actual practices. Envisioning the heterogeneity of labor entails thinking about age, ability, class, ethnicity, or religion, and these variables may cross-cut gender or structure individuals' identities and activities to a greater extent (e.g., Brumfiel 2006, Rotman 2006, Wright 2008).

For example, Robin's (2006) analysis of Chan Nòohol, Belize, a Late Classic community, dispels the myth of "Man-the-Farmer" prevalent in Maya studies. From artifacts, ecofacts, soil chemistry, and architecture, she opens a window into daily activities, local landscapes, and broader socioeconomic interactions. Contrary to historic and ethnographic sources, farming was not strictly men's work. Rather than strict compartmentalization according to gender or public/private spaces, farming involved collaborative family work. Robin takes a multiscalar approach, revealing how individuals exercised agency to maneuver within and against structures. Similarly, Jarvenpa & Brumbach (2006) have slain "Man-the-Hunter." Their cross-cultural ethnoarchaeological studies unearthed varied people and processes involved in hunting—stalking, killing, processing, storing, distributing. In doing so, they uncovered community members' interdependence and individual strategizing in the face of specific circumstances. Were Waguespack to mine their study of the Chipewyan, Khanty, Iñupiaq, and Sámi for information, she would have to rethink her "facts"

about hunter-gatherers' sexual divisions of labor. The Agta would no longer seem quite so deviant.

"We must eradicate the sexual division of labor on which our society is based," declared radical feminist Bonnie Kreps in 1972 (p. 75). That social organization is constructed not inevitable, however, is immaterial to (bio)archaeologists who conceive of ancient sexual divisions of labor as universal, timeless, and rigid. Applying presentist and ethnocentric lenses presumes too much and proves too little. To presume is not without disturbing ramifications, namely naturalization of the modern status quo. Such studies, then, justify professional inequities, stereotypical and narrow depictions of women's and men's work, and legislation legitimizing heteronormativity. Disinclination to conceive of difference as continuum not duality borders on a willful history of forgetting or chauvinistic dismissal of feminist literature from the mid-1980s onward.

THIRD-WAVE FEMINISM AND ARCHAEOLOGY

Bailey (1997) remarks, "Assigning to a particular social movement the name 'wave'…can be done only in retrospect, because, like a swimmer in the water, we are *in* the social medium" (p. 18, emphasis in original). Clarification of third-wave feminism is therefore challenging, unless 10+ years after Bailey's statement we have drifted onward. Unlike second-wave feminism, the third wave emerged in a political climate indifferent to revolutionary and massive social movement and change (Kinser 2004, p. 131). Today, we see the Equal Rights Amendment not ratified and 2008 legislation outlawing same-sex marriages (e.g., California's Proposition 8, Florida's Amendment 2). Although queer activism extends feminist agendas, both seem to be making little sociopolitical headway. Hence, many second-wave concerns remain relevant (i.e., reproductive strategies) or unresolved. We are far from postfeminist.

Within the academy, the third wave did generate significant shifts in thinking about women, gender, and sexuality. Scholarly inquiry is then one type of praxis, as academics work to change minds, which may eventually lead to amending social policies. Third-wave feminists have reacted to second-wave identity politics that often essentialized women's experiences (Bailey 1997). Significant precursors notwithstanding (e.g., Sojourner Truth, Emma Goldman), one can see formal inclusion of and internal critiques by critical race theorists (Davis 1981, Moraga & Anzaldúa 1981), gay and lesbian scholars (Rich 1980, Rubin 1984), and postcolonial academics (Mohanty 1984, Spivak 1985). Gender remains a core structuring principle but it is not always the central principle to constitute an individual's identity in a given social or historical context. Consideration of age, sexuality, ethnicity, race, class, etc.—not added but relational to gender—captures the complexity, contradiction, and plurality of lived experiences. Scholars also attend to the exclusionary social processes of how groups become different, the process of differentiation (Scott 1996). To do so avoids second-wave tendencies to naturalize differences and the postmodern pitfall of seeing differences everywhere but losing sight of shared experiences (Raddeker 2007, p. 139).

Despite some recent statements (Hamilton et al. 2007b, Whitehouse 2007), archaeology fortified by contemporary feminism does not eschew women. Rather, archaeologists have taken third-wave feminist ideas in hand to examine past women's identities as contextual and to complicate stereotypical notions of "women's work" (e.g., Ardren 2002, Wilkie 2003, Voss 2008a). Wedding age to gender has also highlighted the dynamism of identity—the processes and performances of socializations from cradle to grave (e.g., Geller 2004, Joyce 2000a, Lorentz 2008, Meskell 2000). Yet, researchers of childhood, a growing concern in the archaeology of gender (Baxter 2008), should tread lightly when seeking to find evasive little ones—i.e., children are the new women. To make something visible does not remedy "the basic problem that underwrites all processes of designation, that is, the lack of engagement with what

resides outside names and categories, things that remain 'unsaid' or 'invisible'" (Lazzari 2003, p. 195). Emphasizing in/visibility ultimately eclipses how an individual acquires personhood in a given cultural and social context.

Feminist-inspired studies of gender's intersection with ethnicity, class, and race have also materialized difference and differentiation (e.g., Clark 2003, Delle et al. 2000). Conkey (2005), for example, outlines the potentials of an intersectional approach melding feminist and Indigenous concerns. Franklin (2001) recognizes that engagement with black feminist–inspired theory avoids homogenization of enslaved and freed Africans' experiences by exposing "the simultaneous analysis of different vectors of oppression, including gender" (p. 112). Feminist-informed examinations of the African diaspora have indeed advanced archaeological inquiry (e.g., Battle 2004, Galle & Young 2004). Wilkie's (2003) consideration of mothering and midwifery in the nineteenth and early-twentieth centuries is a persuasive example. Chronicling the experiences of Lucrecia Perryman, a freed African American woman, mother, and midwife from Mobile, Alabama, Wilkie presents a politics and materiality of everyday life. By concentrating on the convergence of gender, race, and class, she elucidates black women's oppression and negotiation of structural violence and inequities. Ultimately, theoretical intersection imparts history to the historically marginalized and dismantles the structural hierarchies of white supremacy. This decolonization is as much a political act as it is an intellectual one.

Additionally, feminist critiques of dichotomous, universalizing epistemology facilitate study of masculinity's cultural construction and the diversity of men's roles and relationships with others (Connell 1995, Gutmann 1997). That is, there are other ways to be a man than as a patriarchal, white, Western heterosexual. Archaeologists' seminal studies of men and masculinity (e.g., Knapp 1998, Yates 1993), however, have yet to proliferate in the new millennium, exceptions notwithstanding (e.g., Alberti 2001, Ardren & Hixson 2006, Dean 2001,

Joyce 2000b). Perhaps the possible hazards are off-putting: reiteration of dichotomous, static thinking about gender; the possibility of masculinity's irrelevance in an ancient context; unintended conveyance of modern ideas about violence, power, and sexuality. For example, masculinity and men are central in aforementioned studies of labor divisions, but interpretative shortcomings are obvious. The past is not diversely peopled and differentiation is not adequately addressed. Alberti (2006) stresses that archaeologists see material culture as constituting not reflecting identity. They can then identify the embodiment of masculinity in specific sociohistorical settings, as well as ascertain multiple and transgressive masculinities. The latter depart from idealized, hegemonic representations that may be presentist and/or exclusionary. Hence, the study of masculinity provides a bridge between feminist and queer studies.

Although some scholars regard queer studies as an intellectual departure, Jagose (1996) asserts that such scholarship "developed out of—and continues to be understandable in terms of—feminist knowledges" (p. 119). Her avowal echoes in the writings of those who question normative social structures, destabilize heterosexism, and allay homophobia (e.g., Butler 1990, 1993; de Lauretis 1991; Sedgwick 1990). Queer archaeologists similarly champion these efforts. They are aware that transplanting heteronormative notions into the past naturalizes contemporary Western social arrangements (Dowson 2000). To destabilize necessitates formulation of "queer" as a verb (Sullivan 2003, p. 50). Cobb's (2005) aforementioned consideration of heteronormative hunter-gatherer studies provides one example, as does my own scrutiny of skeletal analysts' determination of biological sex and subsequent social inferences (Geller 2005, 2008, 2009).

Queering also sheds light on "nonnormative" sexual relations not reducible to heterosexual procreation (Boellstorff 2007, Rubin 2002). For their part, archaeologists consider space, materiality, and imagery as evidence of same-sex intimacies (Casella 2000, Reeder 2000), religious celibacy (Gilchrist

2000), nonprocreative activities (Gero 2004), violent victimizations (Scott 2001), and commodified interactions (Seifert et al. 2000, Yamin 2005). Yet, it is crucial to exercise care with terminology (compare Bevan 2001, Schmidt 2002). For example, same-sex relations have a long (pre)history, but "homosexuality" is a nineteenth-century invention, which signals a paradigm shift in scientific understandings of sexuality and categorizations of psychological deviance and anatomical difference (Somerville 1997, pp. 37–38). To historicize acknowledges that persons who embodied transgressive identities or bent gender in archaeological contexts cannot be reduced to homosexuals [see Hollimon's (2006) literature review].

Hollimon's (1997, 2000, 2001) study of Native American two-spirits serves as an excellent case in point. Drawing on osteological, historic, and artifactual data, she determined that two-spirits, or 'aqi, served as mortuary specialists in Chumash communities. For such persons, nonbinary gender categorizations applied, and nonprocreative sexual interactions were defining. Celibates, postmenopausal women, and third-gender males were all eligible. Inasmuch as Hollimon regards the body in terms of lived experience, she also offers a counterpoint to traditional investigations of labor divisions that assume much about sex, gender, and sexuality. To study embodied identity, then, one need not begin with queries about sexual difference predicated on reproductive ability. To this end, scholarship about the body fomented by postmodern, practice, and feminist theorists has been instructive (Bourdieu 1977; Butler 1990, 1993; Foucault 1978). Archaeologists expand these efforts by materializing embodiment and performance (Joyce 2005). Ultimately, consideration of individuals' repetitive bodily performances or habitual practices, as transgression or reiteration of dominant ideology, facilitates interpretations about internalization and (re)formation of gender identities.

Many who study physical bodies are wary of applying abstract theorizing, however. In bioarchaeology, interchangeability of "sex" and "gender" is prevalent. Some concede conceptual differences between the two but embrace second-wave understandings and lay investigative emphasis on sex (e.g., Armelagos 1998, Walker & Cook 1998). Or, some researchers assume that sexuality is biologically inaccessible, not realizing that concern for reproductive potential conveys heteronormative ideas about compulsory procreation and heterosexuality. Nonetheless, bioarchaeological inquiry informed by recent feminist-inspired theorizing will innovate studies about labor, health, warfare, violence, ritual, etc. (e.g., Hanks 2008, Lambert 2001, Novak 2006, Sofaer 2006). Perry's (2004) study of a fourteenth-century Ancestral Pueblo, for instance, tested "whether symbolic gender divisions observed in multiple dimensions of social life indeed correspond to embodied (skeletal) realities in the practice of habitual labor" (p. 23). Skeletal signatures of key habitual activities indicated a sexual division of labor, verifying ethnographic accounts. Bone chemistry and mortuary studies also suggested that women were nutritionally disadvantaged and socially exploited. Although Perry's study characterizes difference as dichotomy, she provides evidence for rather than presumes gendered labor divisions during a specific historical juncture. Comparing this period to preceding ones illuminates the processes of differentiation at work (Perry & Joyce 2001). However, Perry & Joyce (2001) also recognize that following formalization of *lhamanas*' ritual roles during this period, these transgendered persons may have used gender performances to transgress social regulations. Hence, bioarchaeological identification of these individuals will address how hegemonic structures are reproduced and subverted.

Bioarchaeology would be well suited to meet the challenges of "evidential constraints" (Wylie 1992) were it to complement the range of empirical resources utilized in studies with feminist perspectives. This approach also sees gender as multiscalar, from the long term and large scale to the local, everyday, and personal (Conkey 2003, Tringham 1994). The benefit is not one-way. Physiological processes are neither dismissed nor represented as destiny. Rather, bringing materiality and expansive temporal scale to the fore effectively grounds lived experiences via contextualized examination of bodies, spaces, and artifacts (Joyce 2008). These studies are a middle ground between biological determinism and postmodern nihilism, the latter being an accusation often leveled at third-wave feminism and queer studies.

ARCHAEOLOGY "UNDER ATTACK"

Studies of ancient bodies underscore that much intellectual labor is required to make often ethereal feminist ideas viable when analyzing the variability and materiality of gender. The difficulty of this effort is perhaps one reason why many archaeologists' gender studies are unfeminist. I am intrigued by sustained resistance, and put forward additional explanations besides aversion for the highly conceptual.

As Conkey (2007a) discusses, archaeologists frequently slight theory building. Rather, fieldwork renders one a "real" practitioner of the discipline. More specifically, some scholars are ambivalent about theories that reveal contradictions, open new spaces, or challenge assumptions (p. 296). Perhaps opponents see the change effected as portending the field's demise. I am reminded of one scholar's recent comments that anthropological archaeology has been "under attack from postmodernism, postcolonialism, and feminism" (Flannery 2006, p. 1). Suffice it to say, prevailing positivist ideas, which simply reiterate common sense, are significantly less threatening.

Lather (2007, p. 113) suggests that conflation of -isms is a reaction born of androcentrism. Although this may be true, some women who undertake "gender archaeology" also shun contemporary feminist perspectives (e.g., Sørenson 2000, Whitehouse 2007). For instance, in their introductory words to the edited volume *Archaeology and Women*, Hamilton and coauthors (2007b) believe that archaeologists who subscribe to the third wave co-opt "feminist scholarship in the service of the postmodernist agenda...an attack on objectivity and enlightenment" (p. 15). Third-wave scholarship, for them, emerged from Foucault's analysis of sexuality and interrogation of sex's fixity. Yet, the role of other gay and lesbian scholars goes unremarked upon, as does critical race theorists and postcolonial intellects' shifting of the paradigm. The abbreviated, historical overview by Hamilton et al. therefore has the potential to generate misunderstanding of feminism's intellectual developments and convergences.

To clarify, although feminism and postmodernism both destabilize Western thought's epistemological foundations and grand narratives (Hekman 1990), their agendas are far from identical. Postmodernism's deconstruction of objectivity and truth may be read as "an inversion that serves the interests of those who have always benefited from gender, race, and class privilege" (Wylie 2002, p. 190). Feminism's commitment to decentering androcentric bias—whether from the vantage of socialist, radical, Black, lesbian, postcolonial, or postmodern feminisms—offers a challenge and different direction. Even feminists who engage with postmodern perspectives recognize the difficulty of reconciling the latter's relativism with the former's political agenda (e.g., Hekman 1990, Nicholson 1990). At issue is theory's relationship to practice, a point MacKinnon (1991) articulates. Without denying the diversity of women's lived experiences, she asserts, "The postmodern version of the relation between theory and practice is discourse unto death.... It proceeds as if you can deconstruct power relations by shifting their markers around in your head" (p. 13). Granted, MacKinnon chastises a version of postmodernism that may be passé in the twenty-first century. Yet, her point about the centrality of praxis in feminism remains salient. To put feminist theory into practice emancipates all from social intolerance, professional discrimination, and oppressive political policies.

Feminism's introduction into the academy was driven by scholars' personal and political leanings. In turn, academic feminists' scientific critiques and expanded research interests had an impact outside of the academy walls. Yet, feminist archaeologists' overt acknowledgment of sociopolitical causes and effects continues to induce angst (Wylie 2007). Perhaps adversaries imagine guerrillas in their midst and look to defend themselves against further attacks. Or, do some archaeologists of gender believe we are postfeminist and see politicization as gratuitous? Hamilton and coauthors (2007b) have commented that "marked androcentric bias ... has characterized the discipline *until recently*" (p. 18; emphasis added). Because their volume also contains a chapter about the underrepresentation of women in British contract archaeology [by Hamilton (2007) herself], it is not clear to me how the discipline is less androcentric of late. So, is archaeology no longer androcentric, or is androcentrism in archaeology no longer so marked? For those who wish to see gender gain mainstream acceptance in archaeological inquiry but concomitantly spurn feminist perspectives (e.g., Sørenson 2000), the latter seems to be the case. Yet, to study gender exposes significant shortcomings in mainstream archaeology, not the least of which are the subtle institutional practices and ideological beliefs that have marginalized the topic. A shift in the mainstream is imperative.

ARCHAEOLOGY OF GENDER AND SOCIOPOLITICAL AGENDAS

Feminist archaeologists see a sociopolitical commitment to emancipation as transforming the discipline's present-day practices and reconstructions of the past. Both aims hinge on diversification of the field. Early on, critical feminist perspectives effectively revealed professional gender disparity (e.g., Nelson et al. 1994). Remedying such inequity has been another matter. Recent findings indicate that engendering gender parity is an exercise in imagination not realization. An American Association of University Professors report found that women faculty earn less than men do and are less likely to hold full-time positions, especially tenure-track ones (West & Curtis 2006, p. 6). An "extremely optimistic" hypothetical projection that parity will be achieved in 57 years, provided hiring and retention of men and women stay equal (p. 8), will assuredly try even the most patient.

Closer to home, the Committee on the Status of Women in Anthropology's *Academic Climate Report* drew similar conclusions (Wasson et al. 2008). Compilers were confounded: "Since we tend to think of anthropology as a discipline populated by fairly progressive people, we were surprised at the extent of the gender inequities that we uncovered" (p. 2). Leaky pipelines, maternal walls, and old boys' networks remain obstacles. The report also assessed anthropology's climate in terms of plurality—the impact that practitioners' race, ethnicity, sexual orientation, age, and national identity have on representation and experience. It is telling that aside from race, quantitative analysis was unfeasible given insufficient numbers for "statistically valid conclusions" (p. 22). An inability to quantify difference perhaps speaks to the lack of it.

It is unsurprising then that the subfield of archaeology does not diverge from broader trends. Persistence of gender disparity provides evidence of sustained resistance to incorporate feminist-inspired critiques. Women archaeologists account for almost half of the Society for American Archaeology's membership. Yet, as Conkey (2007a, p. 295) pronounces, they "are still grossly under-represented among the faculty of our major PhD institutions." *The 2005 Salary Survey* offers support. According to the survey, with few exceptions, a gendered disparity in salary exists regardless of the primary employer (i.e., university, CRM firm, federal or state government, private nonprofit, museum). On average, women make substantially less than men do, $46,786 to $53,210 respectively (p. 2). Additionally, the number of men exceeds women in all positions aside from ones that are temporary or stress "housekeeping" (per Gero 1985). As of 2001, females account for ~40% of PhDs awarded in archaeology (Patterson et al. 2004), but the pipeline leaks as

one ascends the hierarchical structure. Age and experience cannot wholly account for such gaps. The masculinist frame of intellectual socialization and practical training contributes to some of this inequality (Conkey 2007a, Moser 2007). Continued accumulation of dis/advantage resulting from entrenched gender schema (Valian 1998) is certainly a factor, as well.

I have yet to unearth surveys about professional disparity with regard to archaeologists' race, ethnicity, or sexual orientation. From informal documentation, there are 17 living Native Americans who have completed PhDs in archaeology or on issues that bridge sociocultural anthropology and archaeology, and ~5 students are currently undertaking doctoral research (K. Thompson, personal communication, 2009). And, Franklin (1997) has lamented, "There are only a handful of African Americans in the US with PhDs who specialize in anthropological archaeology (four, by my count)" (p. 799). Although this number may have increased, even if quadrupled it would be insignificant in light of the fact that the SAA boasts over 7000 members. Promotion of a more equitable, diverse field is crucial. And, to this end, Norder & Rizvi (2008) make several recommendations to the SAA pertaining to accountability, mentoring, liaising, and lobbying.

Of course the critical may question why we need a more diverse field. As Wylie (2002) explains professional gender equity can ameliorate "androcentric or sexist bias in the content of archaeological accounts" (p. 188). She finds Gero's (1993) assessment of Paleoindian researchers (who are mostly male) and their primary research interests (which are mostly stereotypical male activities like big game hunting) to be an illustrative example. Beyond gender, several feminist-inspired archaeologists have drawn from their own marginalized positions, personal experiences, and embodied differences to pose questions that diverge from traditional inquiries about race, ethnicity, or sexuality (e.g., Battle-Baptiste 2007, Dowson 2006). If we allow that knowledge is situated, per Haraway (1988), then diversification of the field will permit exploration of different ways to be human, an outcome that benefits the discipline as a whole.

By subverting received wisdom about difference, feminist archaeology can contribute to pressing sociopolitical concerns. Several issues bandied about in popular and political forums are problematically painted as universal and natural. Much discussed in today's political climate is the sanctity of marriage as only and ever between a man and a woman. Archaeologists' aforementioned studies of same-sex intimacies, therefore, have the potential to dispel the myth of the naturalness of the marital contract and subsequently mitigate homophobia. Additionally, exploration of reproductive strategizing—without essentializing or naturalizing—can unearth information about culturally specific birthing practices, folk knowledge, and natural contraceptives and abortifacients (e.g., Geller & Stockett 2006a, Wilkie 2003). Such studies may provide alternatives to modern political rhetoric and biomedical practices that disempower or do women harm.

CONCLUDING THOUGHTS AND BIGGER PICTURES

An archaeology of gender undergirded by feminist perspectives peoples the past and diversifies the present. It also requires practitioners to reflect on self and scientific production. To this end, such a study begs a bigger question that all archaeologists need ponder: Why do we investigate the past? What follows is my answer to this query.

Like many academic archaeologists, I teach an introductory course to the subfield. Feminist-inspired thought grounds the course's content, critical lens, and pedagogy (see also Arnold 2005, Hendon 2006). This approach is less obvious to undergraduates who often have little exposure to archaeology and even less to feminism. At other junctures in the semester, however, the use of a feminist perspective is explicit. Namely, I assign students Spector's (1993) *What This Awl Means*, a book that eloquently illustrates the aims, issues, and practice of feminist archaeology per Wylie's criteria (2007, pp. 211–13). Spector begins from a place of everyday, personal experience; asks questions that challenge oppressive sex/gender systems and racist attitudes; reflects critically on her social context and knowledge production; and democratizes and decolonizes archaeological practice by collaborating with the descendant Dakota community. After 16 years, *What This Awl Means* remains cogent and relevant.

In conjunction with this book, I use a mainstream textbook by Renfrew & Bahn, *Archaeology: Theories, Methods, and Practices*. In recent qualitative teaching evaluations, few students commented on this text, aside from remarks about its density. Regarding our foray into feminist archaeology, however, one student wrote, "The whole feminism thing rubbed me the wrong way. I had signed up for an archaeology class not a gender studies class." Did my anonymous reviewer's disquietude signal a failure on my part to instruct and inspire? Perhaps. But, such anxiety may also signal a raised conscious, a boundary transgressed, which—in the spirit of hooks' engaged pedagogy—heralds "the necessary conditions where learning can most deeply and intimately begin" (1994, p. 13).

An archaeology inspired by feminism can empower those whom we educate in a way that is germane, interesting, accessible, and transformative. Accordingly, archaeology will remain relevant in the twenty-first century within and beyond the academy. As it stands now, however, the field has become insular if our interactions with varied publics are any indicator. Clearly, nonarchaeologists have an interest in the past. There is constant usurpation and consumption—by students, museum patrons, tourists, antiquities collectors, religious fundamentalists, and popular media. Archaeologists, however, are frequently not responsible for dissemination of information. And, all too often the research questions we pose, the reconstructions we create, are of little interest to anyone other than specialists. Though not the only ones to find this inability to communicate with nonarchaeologists vexing, feminist archaeologists have produced creative ways to interact with publics, digital media and hypertext narratives being two recent developments (Joyce & Tringham 2007).

Yet, as my student's comments remind me, to implement a feminist-inspired archaeology, in the study of gender specifically and the discipline more broadly, does not always mean that others will gain comfort by the demands of such engagement. And, we need to be okay with their unease at our destabilizing and reconstructing. Such is the only way to effect change.

DISCLOSURE STATEMENT

The author is not aware of any affiliations, memberships, funding, or financial holdings that might be perceived as affecting the objectivity of this review.

ACKNOWLEDGMENTS

Writing this review has been a humbling experience given the enormity of the corpus. Clearly, much scholarship was omitted not because of its quality but because of constraints beyond this author's control. I acknowledge the unnamed, as well as Miranda Stockett, Wendy Ashmore, Joan Gero, Jane Buikstra, and Bob Preucel who—depending on the day—have served in the capacities of teacher, colleague, mentor, sounding board, and/or friend. I also thank Kerry Thompson and Desiree Martinez for generously sharing information about Native Americans' representation in archaeology.

LITERATURE CITED

Alberti B. 2001. Faience goddesses and ivory bull-leapers: the aesthetics of sexual difference at Late Bronze Age Knossos. *World Archaeol.* 33(2):189–205

Alberti B. 2006. Archaeology, men, and masculinities. See Nelson 2006, pp. 401–34

Ardren T, ed. 2002. *Ancient Maya Women*. Walnut Creek, CA: AltaMira

Ardren T, Hixson D. 2006. The unusual sculptures of Telantunich, Yucatan: phalli and the concept of masculinity in ancient Maya thought. *Camb. Archaeol. J.* 16:1–20

Armelagos GJ. 1998. Introduction: sex, gender, and health status in prehistoric and contemporary populations. In *Sex and Gender in Paleopathological Perspective*, ed. AL Grauer, P Stuart-Macadam, pp. 1–10. Cambridge, UK: Cambridge Univ. Press

Arnold B. 2005. Teaching with intent: the archaeology of gender. *Archaeologies* 1(2):83–93

Bailey C. 1997. Making waves and drawing lines: the politics of defining the vicissitudes of feminism. *Hypatia* 12(3):17–28

Battle WL. 2004. *A yard to sweep: race, gender and the enslaved landscape*. PhD thesis. Univ. Tex., Austin. 181 pp.

Battle-Baptiste WL. 2007. The other from within: a commentary. In *Past Meets Present: Archaeologists Partnering with Museums Curators, Teachers, and Community Groups*, ed. JH Jameson, S Baugher, pp. 101–6. New York: Springer

Baxter JE. 2008. The archaeology of childhood. *Annu. Rev. Anthropol.* 37:159–75

Bertelsen R, Lillehammer A, Naess J-R, eds. 1987. *Were They All Men? An Examination of Sex Roles in Prehistoric Society*. Acts from a workshop held at Ulstein Kloster, Rogaland, Nov. 2–4, 1979. Stavanger, Nor.: Arkeol. Mus. Stavanger

Bevan L, ed. 2001. *Indecent Exposure: Sexuality, Society and the Archaeological Record*. Glasgow: Cruithne

Boellstorff T. 2007. Queer studies in the house of anthropology. *Annu. Rev. Anthropol.* 36:17–35

Bolger D, ed. 2008. *Gender through Time in the Ancient Near East*. Walnut Creek, CA: AltaMira

Bourdieu P. 1977. *Outline of a Theory of Practice*. Cambridge, UK: Cambridge Univ. Press

Brumbach HJ, Jarvenpa R. 2006. Gender dynamics in hunter-gatherer society: archaeological methods and perspectives. See Nelson 2006, pp. 503–35

Brumfiel EM. 2006. Cloth, gender, continuity, and change: fabricating unity in anthropology. *Am. Anthropol.* 108(4):862–77

Butler J. 1990. *Gender Trouble: Feminism and the Subversion of Identity*. New York: Routledge

Butler J. 1993. *Bodies that Matter: On the Discursive Limits of Sex*. New York: Routledge

Casella EC. 2000. 'Doing trade': a sexual economy of nineteenth-century Australian female convict prisons. See Dowson 2000, pp. 209–21

Claassen C, ed. 1992. *Exploring Gender through Archaeology: Selected Papers from the 1991 Boone Conference*. Madison, WI: Prehistory Press

Clark BJ. 2003. *On the edge of purgatory: an archaeology of ethnicity and gender in Hispanic Colorado*. PhD thesis. Univ. Calif., Berkeley. 307 pp.

Cobbs H. 2005. Straight down the line? A queer consideration of hunter-gatherer studies in north-west Europe. *World Archaeol.* 73:630–36

Collier JF, Yanagisako SJ. 1987. Toward a unified analysis of gender and kinship. In *Gender and Kinship: Essays toward a Unified Analysis*, ed. J Collier, SJ Yanagisako, pp. 14–52. Stanford, CA: Stanford Univ. Press

Conkey MW. 2003. Has feminism changed archaeology? *Signs* 28(3):867–80

Conkey MW. 2005. Dwelling at the margins, action at the intersection? Feminist and indigenous archaeologies. *Archaeologies* 1(1):9–80

Conkey MW. 2007a. Questioning theory: Is there a gender of theory in archaeology? *J. Archaeol. Method Theory* 14(3):285–310

Conkey MW. 2007b. *Personal histories retrospect*. Seminar at the Univ. Cambridge, organized by PJ Smith, 22 Oct. **http://www.arch.cam.ac.uk/podcast/personal-histories-retrospect-2007.mp3**

Conkey MW, Gero JM. 1997. Programme to practice: gender and feminism in archaeology. *Annu. Rev. Anthropol.* 26:411–37

Conkey MW, Spector JD. 1984. Archaeology and the study of gender. In *Advances in Archaeological Method and Theory*, Vol. 7, ed. MB Schiffer, pp. 1–39. New York: Academic

Connell RW. 1995. *Masculinities*. Berkeley: Univ. Calif. Press

Dahlberg F, ed. 1981. *Woman the Gatherer*. New Haven: Yale Univ. Press

Davis AY. 1981. *Women, Race, and Class*. New York: Random House

Dean C. 2001. Andean androgyny and the making of men. In *Gender in Pre-Hispanic America*, ed. CF Klein, pp. 143–82. Washington, DC: Dumbarton Oaks

De Lauretis T. 1991. Queer theory: lesbian and gay sexualities. *Differences* 3(2):iii–xviii

Delle JA, Mrozowski SA, Paynter R, ed. 2000. *Lines that Divide: Historical Archaeologies of Race, Class and Gender*. Knoxville: Univ. Tenn. Press

Dowson T, ed. 2000. Special issue, *Queer Archaeologies. World Archaeol.* 32(2)

Dowson T. 2006. Archaeologists, feminists, and queers: sexual politics in the construction of the past. See Geller & Stockett 2006b, pp. 89–102

Elston RG, Zeanah DW. 2002. Thinking outside the box: a new perspective on diet breadth and sexual division of labor in the Prearchaic Great Basin. *World Archaeol.* 34(1):103–30

Engelstad E. 2007. Much more than gender. *J. Archaeol. Method Theory* 14(3):217–34

Eshed V, Gopher A, Galili E, Hershkovitz I. 2004. Musculoskeletal stress markers in Natufian hunter-gatherers and Neolithic farmers in the Levant: the upper limb. *Am. J. Phys. Anthropol.* 123(4):303–15

Flannery KV. 2006. On the resilience of anthropological archaeology. *Annu. Rev. Anthropol.* 35:1–13

Foucault M. 1978. *The History of Sexuality*, Vol. 1. New York: Vintage

Franklin M. 1997. Why are there so few black American archeologists. *Antiquity* 71(274):799–801

Franklin M. 2001. A black feminist-inspired archaeology? *J. Soc. Archaeol.* 1:108–25

Galle JE, Young AL, eds. 2004. *Engendering African American Archaeology: A Southern Perspective*. Knoxville: Univ. Tenn. Press

Geller PL. 2004. *Transforming bodies, transforming identities: a consideration of pre-Columbian Maya corporeal beliefs and practices*. PhD thesis. Philadelphia: Univ. Penn. 606 pp.

Geller PL. 2005. Skeletal analysis and theoretical complications. *World Archaeol.* 37(4):597–609

Geller PL. 2008. Conceiving sex: fomenting a feminist bioarchaeology. *J. Soc. Archaeol.* 8(1):113–38

Geller PL. 2009. Biology, bodyscapes, and heteronormativity. *Am. Anthropol.* 111(4):In press

Geller PL, Stockett MK. 2006a. *Beyond the academy: feminist anthropology, archaeology, and political debates about abortion.* Presented at Annu. Meet. Am. Anthropol. Assoc., 105th, San Jose

Geller PL, Stockett MK, eds. 2006b. *Feminist Anthropology: Past, Present, and Future.* Philadelphia: Univ. Penn. Press

Gero JM. 1985. Sociopolitics of archaeology and the woman-at-home ideology. *Am. Antiquity* 50:342–50

Gero JM. 1993. The social world of prehistoric facts: gender and power in Paleoindian research. In *Women in Archaeology: A Feminist Critique,* Res. Sch. Pac. Stud., Occas. Pap. Prehistory, No. 23, ed. H du Cros, L Smith, pp. 31–40. Canberra: Aust. Natl. Univ.

Gero JM. 2004. Sex pots of ancient Peru: post-gender reflections. In *Combining the Past and the Present: Archaeological Perspectives on Society,* ed. T Oestigaard, N Anfinset, T Saetersdal, pp. 3–22. Oxford: BAR Int. Ser. 1210 pp.

Gero JM, Conkey MW, eds. 1991. *Engendering Archaeology: Women and Prehistory.* Cambridge, MA: Blackwell

Gero JM, Scattolin MC. 2002. Beyond complementarity and hierarchy: new definitions for archaeological gender relations. In *Pursuit of Gender: Worldwide Archaeological Approaches,* ed. SM Nelson, M Rosen-Ayalon, pp. 155–72. Walnut Creek, CA: AltaMira

Gifford-Gonzalez D. 1993. You can hide, but you can't run: representation of women's work in illustrations of palaeolithic life. *Vis. Anthropol. Rev.* 9:3–21

Gilchrist R. 2000. Unsexing the body: the interior sexuality of medieval religious women. See Schmidt & Voss 2000, pp. 89–103

Gutmann MC. 1997. Trafficking in men: the anthropology of masculinity. *Annu. Rev. Anthropol.* 26:385–409

Hamilton S. 2007. Women in practice: women in British contract field archaeology. See Hamilton et al. 2007a, pp. 121–46

Hamilton S, Whitehouse R, Wright KI, eds. 2007a. *Archaeology and Women: Ancient and Modern.* Walnut Creek, CA: AltaMira

Hamilton S, Whitehouse R, Wright KI. 2007b. Introduction. See Hamilton et al. 2007a, pp. 13–24

Hanen MP, Kelley J. 1992. Gender and archaeological knowledge. In *Metaarchaeology: Reflections by Archaeologists and Philosophers,* ed. L Embree, pp. 195–227. Boston: Kluwer

Hanks B. 2008. Reconsidering warfare, status, and gender in the Eurasian Steppe Iron Age. In *Are All Warriors Male? Gender Roles on the Ancient Eurasian Steppe,* ed. KM Linduff, KS Rubinson, pp. 15–34. Walnut Creek, CA: AltaMira

Haraway D. 1988. Situated knowledges: the science question in feminism as a site of discourse in the privilege of partial perspective. *Fem. Stud.* 14:575–600

Harding S. 1987. Introduction: Is there a feminist method? In *Feminism and Methodology,* ed. S Harding, pp. 1–14. Bloomington: Indiana Univ. Press

Hays-Gilpin K. 2000. Feminist scholarship in archaeology. *Ann. Am. Acad. Polit. Soc. Sci.* 571:89–106

Hekman S. 1990. *Gender and Knowledge: Elements of a Postmodern Feminism.* Cambridge, UK: Polity

Hendon J. 2006. Feminist perspectives and the teaching of archaeology: implications from the inadvertent ethnography of the classroom. See Geller & Stockett 2006b, pp. 129–42

Hildebrandt W, McGuire K. 2002. The ascendance of hunting during the California Middle Archaic: an evolutionary perspective. *Am. Antiquity* 67(2):231–56

Hollimon S. 1997. The third gender in native California: two-spirit undertakers among the Chumash and their neighbors. In *Women in Prehistory,* ed. C Claassen, RA Joyce, pp. 173–88. Philadelphia: Univ. Penn. Press

Hollimon S. 2000. Archaeology of the 'aqi': gender and sexuality in prehistoric Chumash society. See Schmidt & Voss 2000, pp. 179–96

Hollimon S. 2001. The gendered peopling of America: addressing the antiquity of systems of multiple genders. In *The Archaeology of Shamanism,* ed. N Price, pp. 123–34. London: Routledge

Hollimon S. 2006. The archaeology of nonbinary genders in Native North American societies. See Nelson 2006, pp. 435–50

hooks b. 1994. *Teaching to Transgress: Education as the Practice of Freedom.* New York: Routledge

Jagose A. 1996. *Queer Theory: An Introduction.* New York: New York Univ. Press

Jarvenpa R, Brumbach HJ. 2006. Revisiting the sexual division of labor: thoughts on ethnoarchaeology and gender. In *Integrating the Diversity of Twenty-First-Century Anthropology: The Life and Intellectual Legacies of Susan Kent*, Archeol. Pap. Am. Anthropol. Assoc., No. 16, ed. W Ashmore, M Dobres, S Nelson, A Rosen, pp. 97–107. Arlington, VA: Am. Anthropol. Assoc.

Joyce RA. 2000a. Girling the girl and boying the boy: the production of adulthood in ancient Mesoamerica. *World Archaeol.* 31(1):473–83

Joyce RA. 2000b. A PreColumbian gaze: male sexuality among the ancient Maya. See Schmidt & Voss 2000, pp. 263–83

Joyce RA. 2005. Archaeology of the body. *Annu. Rev. Anthropol.* 34:139–58

Joyce RA. 2008. *Ancient Bodies, Ancient Lives*. New York: Thames & Hudson

Joyce RA, Tringham RE. 2007. Feminist adventures in hypertext. See Wylie & Conkey 2007, pp. 328–58

Kinser AE. 2004. Negotiating spaces for/through third-wave feminism. *NWSA J.* 16(3):124–53

Knapp AB. 1998. Boys will be boys: masculinist approaches to a gendered archaeology. In *Reader in Gender Archaeology*, ed. K Hays-Gilpin, DS Whitley, pp. 365–73. London: Routledge

Kreps B. 1972. Radical feminism 1. In *Women Unite!: An Anthology of the Canadian Women's Movement*, pp. 71–75. Toronto: Can. Women's Educ. Press

Kuhn SL, Stiner MC. 2006. What's a mother to do? The division of labor among Neandertals and modern humans in Eurasia. *Curr. Anthropol.* 47(6):953–80

Lambert PM. 2001. Auditory exostoses: a clue to gender in prehistoric and historic farming communities of North Carolina and Virginia. In *Archaeological Studies of Gender in the Southeastern United States*, ed. JM Eastman, CB Rodning, pp. 152–72. Gainseville: Univ. Press Fla.

Lather P. 2007. *Getting Lost: Feminist Efforts toward a Double(d) Science*. Albany: SUNY Press

Lazzari M. 2003. Archaeological visions: gender, landscape and optic knowledge. *World Archaeol.* 3(2):194–222

Lewin E, Leap WL, eds. 2002. *Out in Theory: the Emergence of Lesbian and Gay Anthropology*. Chicago: Univ. Ill. Press

Lorentz K. 2008. From life course to *longue durée*: headshaping as gendered capital? See Bolger 2008, pp. 281–311

MacKinnon CA. 1991. From practice to theory, or, what is a white woman anyway? *Yale J. L. Feminism* 4(2):13–22

Maggiano IS, Schultz M, Kierdorf H, Sierra Sosa T, Maggiano CM, Tiesler Blos V. 2008. Cross-sectional analysis of long bones, occupational activities and long-distance trade of the Classic Maya from Xcambó–archaeological and osteological evidence. *Am. J. Phys. Anthropol.* 136(4):170–77

Marchi DO, Sparacello VS, Holt BM, Formicola V. 2006. Biomechanical approach to the reconstruction of activity patterns in Neolithic western Liguria, Italy. *Am. J. Phys. Anthropol.* 131:447–55

Meskell LM. 2000. Cycles of life and death: narrative homology and archaeological realities. *World Archaeol.* 31(3):423–41

Meskell LM. 2002. The intersections of identity and politics in archaeology. *Annu. Rev. Anthropol.* 31:279–301

Mohanty CT. 1984. Under Western eyes: feminist scholarship and colonial discourses. *boundary 2* 12(3):333–58

Molleson T. 2007. Bones of work at the origins of labor. See Hamilton et al. 2007a, pp. 185–98

Moore H. 1988. *Feminism and Anthropology*. Cambridge, UK: Polity

Moraga C, Anzaldúa G, eds. 1981. *This Bridge Called my Back: Writings by Radical Women of Color*. Watertown, MA: Persephone

Moser S. 2007. On disciplinary culture: archaeology as fieldwork and its gendered associations. See Wylie & Conkey 2007, pp. 235–63

Nelson MC, Nelson SM, Wylie A, eds. 1994. *Equity Issues for Women in Archaeology*. Washington, DC: Archaeol. Pap. Am. Anthropol. Assoc.

Nelson SM, ed. 2006. *Handbook of Gender in Archaeology*. Walnut Creek, CA: AltaMira

Nicholson L, ed. 1990. *Feminism/Postmodernism*. New York: Routledge

Norder J, Rizvi UZ. 2008. Reassessing the present for an archaeology of the future: equity, diversity, and change. *SAA Archaeol. Rec.* 8(4):12–14

Novak S. 2006. Beneath the façade: a skeletal model of domestic violence. In *The Social Archaeology of Funerary Remains*, ed. C Knüsel, R Gowland, pp. 238–52. Oxford: Oxbow Books

Ortner S. 1974. Is female to male as nature is to culture? In *Woman, Culture, and Society*, ed. MZ Rosaldo, L Lamphere, pp. 67–88. Stanford, CA: Stanford Univ. Press

Ortner S. 1996. *Making Gender: The Politics and Erotics of Culture*. Boston: Beacon

Owen LR. 2005. *Distorting the Past: Gender and the Division of Labor in the European Upper Paleolithic*. Tübingen: Kerns Verlag

Patterson TC, Geller PL, Boites SZ. 2004. *The growth and changing composition of anthropology: 1966–2002*. **http://www.aaanet.org/ar/Changing_Composition.pdf**

Perry EM. 2004. *Bioarchaeology of labor and gender in the prehispanic American Southwest*. PhD thesis. Univ. Ariz., Tucson. 442 pp.

Perry EM, Joyce RA. 2001. Providing a past for *Bodies that Matter*: Judith Butler's impact on the archaeology of gender. *Int. J. Sex. Gend. Stud.* 6(1/2):63–76

Peterson J. 2002. *Sexual Revolutions: Gender and Labor at the Dawn of Agriculture*. Walnut Creek, CA: AltaMira

Pyburn KA. 2004. Introduction: rethinking complex societies. In *Ungendering Civilization*, ed. KA Pyburn, pp. 1–46. New York: Routledge

Raddeker HB. 2007. *Sceptical History: Feminist and Postmodern Approaches in Practice*. New York: Routledge

Reeder G. 2000. Same-sex desire, conjugal constructs, and the tomb of Niankhkhnum and Khnumhotep. See Dowson 2000, pp. 193–208

Rich A. 1980. Compulsory heterosexuality and lesbian existence. *Signs* 5(4):631–60

Robin C. 2006. Gender, farming, and long-term change: Maya historical and archaeological perspectives. *Curr. Anthropol.* 47(3):409–33

Robin C, Brumfiel EM, eds. 2008. *Gender, Households, and Society: Unraveling the Threads of the Past and the Present*, Archeol. Pap. Am. Anthropol. Assoc., No. 18. Malden, MA: Blackwell

Rotman DL. 2006. Separate spheres? Beyond the dichotomies of domesticity. *Curr. Anthropol.* 47(4):666–74

Rubin G. 1984. Thinking sex: notes for a radical theory of the politics of sexuality. In *Pleasure and Danger: Exploring Female Sexuality*, ed. C Vance, pp. 287–319. Boston: Routledge & Kegan Paul

Rubin G. 2002. Studying sexual subcultures: excavating the ethnography of gay communities in urban North America. See Lewin & Leap 2002, pp. 17–68

Schmidt RA. 2002. The Iceman cometh: queering the archaeological past. See Lewin & Leap 2002, pp. 155–85

Schmidt RA, Voss BL, eds. 2000. *Archaeologies of Sexuality*. New York: Routledge

Scott E. 2001. The use and misuse of rape in prehistory. See Bevan 2001, pp. 1–18

Scott JW. 1996. After history? *Common Knowl.* 5(3):9–26

Sedgwick EK. 1990. *Epistemology of the Closet*. Berkeley: Univ. Calif. Press

Seifert DJ, O'Brien EB, Balicki J. 2000. Mary Ann Hall's first-class house: the archaeology of a capital brothel. See Schmidt & Voss 2000, pp. 117–28

Sladék V, Berner M, Sosna D, Sailer R. 2007 . Human manipulative behavior in the central European Late Eneolithic and Early Bronze Age: humeral bilateral asymmetry. *Am. J. Phys. Anthropol.* 133:669–81

Slocum S. 1975. Woman the gatherer: male bias in anthropology. In *Toward an Anthropology of Women*, ed. RR Reiter, pp. 36–50. New York: Monthly Rev. Press

Sofaer JR. 2006. *The Body as Material Culture*. Cambridge, UK: Cambridge Univ. Press

Somerville S. 1997. Scientific racism and the invention of the homosexual body. In *The Gender/Sexuality Reader: Culture, History, Political Economy*, ed. RN Lancaster, M di Leonardo, pp. 37–52. New York: Routledge

Sørensen MLS. 2000. *Gender Archaeology*. Cambridge, UK: Polity

Spector JD. 1993. *What this Awl Means: Feminist Archaeology at a Wahpeton Dakota Village*. St. Paul: Minn. Hist. Soc. Press

Spector JD. 2007. Feminist archaeology: what this all means (after all these years). In *Feminist Waves, Feminist Generations*, ed. H Aikau, K Erickson, J Pierce, pp. 46–66. Minneapolis: Univ. Minn. Press

Spivak GC. 1985. Three women's texts and a critique of imperialism. *Crit. Inq.* 12(1):243–61

Stockett MK. 2005. On the importance of difference: re-envisioning sex and gender in ancient Mesoamerica. *World Archaeol.* 37(4):566–78

Sullivan N. 2003. *A Critical Introduction to Queer Theory*. New York: NY Univ. Press

Surovell TA. 2000. Early Paleoindian women, children, mobility, and fertility. *Am. Antiquity* 65(3):493–508

Tringham RE. 1991. Household with faces: the challenge of gender in prehistoric architectural remains. See Gero & Conkey 1991, pp. 93–131

Tringham RE. 1994. Engendered places in prehistory. *Gender Place Cult.* 1(2):169–203

Valian V. 1998. *Why So Slow? The Advancement of Women*. Cambridge, MA: MIT Press

Voss BL. 2008a. Gender, race, and labor in the archaeology of the Spanish Colonial Americas. *Curr. Anthropol.* 49(5):861–93

Voss BL. 2008b. Sexuality studies in archaeology. *Annu. Rev. Anthropol.* 37:317–36

Waguespack NM. 2005. The organization of male and female labor in foraging societies: implications for early Paleoindian archaeology. *Am. Anthropol.* 107(4):666–76

Walde D, Willows ND, eds. 1991. *The Archaeology of Gender: Proc. 22nd Annu. Chacmool Conf.* Calgary: Univ. Calgary Archaeol. Assoc.

Walker PL, Cook DC. 1998. Brief communication: gender and sex: vive la difference. *Am. J. Phys. Anthropol.* 106:255–59

Wasson C, Brondo K, LeMaster B, Turner T, Cudhea M, et al. 2008. *We've Come a Long Way, Maybe: Academic Climate Report of the Committee on the Status of Women in Anthropology*. Washington, DC: Am. Anthropol. Assoc.

West MS, Curtis JW. 2006. *AAUP Faculty Gender Equity Indicators 2006*. Washington, DC: Am. Assoc. Univ. Profr.

Whitehouse RD. 2007. Gender archaeology and archaeology of women: Do we need both? See Hamilton et al. 2007a, pp. 27–40

Wilkie LA. 2003. *The Archaeology of Mothering: An African-American Midwife's Tale*. New York: Routledge

Wright RP. 2008. Gendered relations and the Ur III dynasty: kinship, property, and labor. See Bolger 2008, pp. 247–79

Wylie A. 1992. The interplay of evidential constraints and political interests. *Am. Antiquity* 57:15–35

Wylie A. 2002. The constitution of archaeological evidence: gender politics and science. In *Thinking from Things: Essays in the Philosophy of Archaeology*, pp. 185–99. Berkeley: Univ. Calif. Press

Wylie A. 2007. Doing archaeology as a feminist: introduction. See Wylie & Conkey 2007, pp. 209–16

Wylie A, Conkey MW, eds. 2007. Special issue, *Doing Archaeology as a Feminist*. *J. Archaeol. Method Theory* 14(3)

Yamin R. 2005. Wealthy, free, and female: prostitution in nineteenth-century New York. *Hist. Archaeol.* 25(4):132–55

Yates T. 1993. Frameworks for an archaeology of the body. In *Interpretive Archaeology*, ed. C Tilley, pp. 31–72. Oxford: Berg

The Early Development of Gender Differences

Matthew H. McIntyre[1] and Carolyn Pope Edwards[2]

[1] Department of Anthropology, University of Central Florida, Orlando, Florida 32816; email: mmcintyr@mail.ucf.edu

[2] Departments of Psychology and Child, Youth, and Family Studies, University of Nebraska, Lincoln, Nebraska 68588; email: cedwards@unlnotes.unl.edu

Annu. Rev. Anthropol. 2009. 38:83–97

First published online as a Review in Advance on June 17, 2009

The *Annual Review of Anthropology* is online at anthro.annualreviews.org

This article's doi:
10.1146/annurev-anthro-091908-164338

Key Words

reproductive ecology, evolutionary psychology, patriarchy, dominance, temperament

Abstract

This article reviews findings from anthropology, psychology, and other disciplines about the role of biological factors in the development of sex differences in human behavior, including biological theories, the developmental course of sex differences, and the interaction of biological and cultural gendering processes at different ages. Current evidence suggests that major biological influences on individual differences in human gender, to the extent that they exist, operate primarily in early development, during and especially prior to puberty. Biological effects are likely to be mediated by relatively simple processes, like temperament, which are then elaborated through social interactions (as with mother and peers) into more complex gendered features of adult personality. Biological anthropologists and psychologists interested in gender should direct more attention to understanding how social processes influence the development and function of the reproductive endocrine system.

INTRODUCTION

The purpose of this review is to summarize the current evidence about the role of biological factors in the development of human gender over the life course. Rather than accept the distinction between biological sex and cultural gender, we employ the term gender very broadly to include both sex differences themselves and the cultural and biological processes that shape them. At the risk of over-reaching, we address between-sex differences, related within-sex variation, and broader features of human social systems such as patriarchy. Our review begins with biological theory about gender and its application to the evolution of human sex differentiation, followed by a discussion of the developmental course of human sex differences and the various biological and social gendering processes. As such, we also consider research from many disciplines, including tentative consideration of sociocultural studies conducted from a humanistic perspective. One important topic that we unfortunately leave out is sexuality.

BIOLOGICAL THEORIES ABOUT HUMAN GENDER

Biological theory about gender (even if that term is not always used) refers to the existence, in sexually reproducing species, of two distinct reproductive strategies called parental investment and mating effort, which have been elaborated from Darwin's description of sexual selection. Parental investment encompasses activities that are costly to parents but directly contribute to the growth or survival of offspring (Trivers 1972). For some species, this investment consists almost entirely of the initial cytoplasm contained in the gametes, with no further support provided by parents, but mammals have a number of additional parental functions including lactation. Parental investment is, in principle, common to both sexual and asexual reproduction. However, finding a mate is only relevant to sexual reproduction. In some species, finding a mate may involve travel over long distances, displays of health or beauty,

physical conflict with others who are seeking mates, or coercion of the potential mates themselves (Bateman 1948, Clutton-Brock & Parker 1992, Dewsbury 1982). For reasons that are not fully understood (Kokko et al. 2006, Wade & Shuster 2002), parental investment activities of many kinds are often, but not always, enacted by one physical form, which is also often the form with larger gametes, called female, and mating activities by another physical form, often with smaller, more motile gametes, called male.

In most mammals, virtually all parental investment is done by females and all mating effort by males, resulting in more notable sex differences than in other taxa (Clutton-Brock 1989, Orians 1969). The few exceptions are in species in which roles may be partially mixed and the sexes have less notable differences, and which more often have mating systems characterized as monogamous (Jarman 1983, Plavcan 2001). The primate order includes a relatively large number of monogamous species, often characterized by some level of male parental investment (Fuentes 1998). The characterization of patterns of human parental investment and mating effort has been the subject of debate among evolutionary anthropologists (Hawkes et al. 1991, 2001; Hill & Kaplan 1993; Kaplan et al. 2000), partly because of the substantial variation among even hunter-gatherer societies in foraging and marriage systems (Wobst 1978).

Geary (2002, 2006) has suggested that evolved human psychological sex differences include (*a*) adaptations for child care in women and interpersonal dominance striving in men, both of which should be largely primitive evolutionarily in that similar sex differences are present even in nonprimate mammals, (*b*) adaptations for coalitional aggression in men, which might be homologous with chimpanzees (Wrangham 1999), and (*c*) adaptations supporting the sexual division of labor, with particular focus on hunting. The latter two domains can be considered relatively more derived as they would have evolved later.

Feminine psychological adaptations for parental care have been linked to the psychometric construct of empathy, and reduced empathy in men has been linked, in turn, to lower thresholds for aggression (Baron-Cohen 2002, Campbell 2006). Although dominance striving has been studied using a variety of techniques, it has not yet been closely linked with, or developed as, a particular psychometric construct (Burgoon et al. 1998). Weak associations with narcissism, sensation seeking, instrumental motivations, and externalizing behavior are likely, and there may be a developmental link between low empathy and dominance striving, making femininity-masculinity at least partly unidimensional (Campbell 2006, McIntyre & Hooven 2009). Theorists have proposed that the primitive sex differences in parental care and interpersonal dominance striving should be reduced in humans owing to relatively low levels of polygyny and high levels of male parental investment (Geary 2002). Despite such a reduction, it would be surprising not to find associations of basic psychological dimensions of parental investment or male-male competition with biological factors, such as sex hormones, given the established role of these factors in nonhuman sex differences. Where interesting and surprising results might be found is in the interaction of these primitive biological factors with social forces. How do the evolved processes related to biological gender operate in different cultural and economic conditions?

Human sex differences in coalitional aggression and the division of labor are of particular interest to anthropologists because of their relatively recent evolution and probable role in the origins of patriarchy (Smuts 1995). It is difficult to predict how such biological systems might operate given the relative uniqueness, among all animals, of coalitional aggression and hunting as sex dimorphic features. The psychological construct that has been most commonly proposed as reflecting adaptations for coalitional aggression is called social dominance orientation, defined as "the extent to which one desires that one's in-group dominate and be superior to out-groups" (Pratto et al. 1994, p. 742), which shows substantial sex differences. Although many physical sex differences may be related to hunting ability, the psychological dimensions investigators have proposed to support sex differences in hunting and gathering in the literature are mostly cognitive, e.g., spatial rotation and object memory, rather than related to emotions or personality, in keeping with an emphasis on cognitive changes in human evolution (Kaplan et al. 2000).

The role of the reproductive endocrine system in human sex differences has been assessed using several techniques. For concurrent effects in children and adults, concentrations of sex hormones can be measured in the blood or saliva. For prenatal effects, several indirect techniques have been used, including comparison of children with congenital adrenal hyperplasia with controls, concentrations of sex hormones in amniotic fluid, and the relative lengths of the index and ring fingers, abbreviated as 2D:4D (Cohen-Bendahan et al. 2005, McIntyre 2006).

SOME EVIDENCE FROM ADULT MEN AND WOMEN

Some evidence indicates at least a small role of the reproductive endocrine system (especially androgens, like testosterone) in the ongoing maintenance of adult sex differences in empathy and dominance striving. For example, Deady et al. (2006) found a negative association of basal testosterone concentrations with maternal ambitions in women, and Hermans et al. (2006b) found evidence that an exogenous dose of testosterone reduces empathy as assessed by unconscious facial mimicry. However, levels of testosterone in women vary over the course of the menstrual cycle and even over the course of several days (Sellers et al. 2007). A number of studies have found associations between basal or exogenous levels of testosterone and behaviors or attitudes associated with dominance striving in men and women (Dabbs 1997, Wirth & Schultheiss 2007) and women alone (Cashdan 1995, Grant & France 2001, Hermans et al. 2006a).

However, as noted by O'Carroll (O'Carroll 1998), the interpretation of these results is complicated by the interesting, and better established, observation that men's testosterone levels also fall in response to failures in dominance contests of various kinds (Archer 2006, Dabbs & Dabbs 2000, Elias 1981, Mazur & Booth 1998), especially for men who strive more for dominance (Schultheiss et al. 2005). Archer (2006) proposed that this response is part of a primitive, evolved system by which men's willingness to enter dominance contests is informed by their previous record of success. Recent evidence suggests that willingness to enter new contests is influenced by basal testosterone level (Mehta et al. 2008) and/or testosterone response to winning or losing (Carré & McCormick 2008), and the effect is probably mediated by subtle physiological, rather than psychological, shifts (van Honk et al. 2004). Of course, hormones also have many other nonpsychological functions, including the regulation of muscle mass, which could be evolutionarily meaningful (Bribiescas 2001).

In keeping with the view that male parental investment increased during human evolution, a number of studies have identified possible suppressive effects of romantic relationships, marriage, or fatherhood on testosterone levels in men from several societies and, surprisingly, lesbians (Gray 2003; Gray et al. 2002, 2004, 2006, 2007; Mazur & Michalek 1998; McIntyre et al. 2006; van Anders & Watson 2006, 2007). Many of these studies have revealed interesting interactions suggesting that social and psychological factors might play subtle roles in regulating the suppression of testosterone and mating effort.

In the case of coalitional aggression, little evidence indicates that hormones play a major role in sex differences. Burnham (2007) found that men with higher testosterone reject low offers in an economic experiment called the ultimatum game. This could be interpreted simply as a reaction to a perceived threat to personal status or dominance. However, he also noted a nonsignificant trend for men with higher testosterone to make larger offers in the game. Together these trends might suggest a role for testosterone in the establishment of reciprocal relationships through moralistic aggression. However, as we noted, social dominance orientation is the most established measure of group-level affiliation and a recent study found no association of social dominance orientation with either testosterone or 2D:4D (Johnson et al. 2006, McIntyre et al. 2007).

There are a number of established sex differences in the performance of Western adults on a number of cognitive tests, including mental rotation of shapes on which men perform better and verbal and object memory on which women perform better (Kimura 1999). However, Ecuyer-Dab & Robert (2004) have noted that there are two competing evolutionary interpretations of these differences. They may be part of the primitive systems supporting sex differences in ranging and mate seeking (Gaulin & FitzGerald 1986, Jones et al. 2003), or they may be derived specifically to support hunting by men and gathering by women (Silverman & Eals 1992). A sex difference in throwing and targeting ability might be more recently derived in response to male hunting (Westergaard et al. 2000), but the developmental trajectory of these abilities is obviously complex and includes factors such as size and strength, which are often ignored (Jones & Marlowe 2002). Some of the effects of androgens on mental rotation tasks may not be related to cognitive ability (Hooven et al. 2004), and these associations vary across cultures (Yang et al. 2007).

Given the limitations of evidence coming from adult sex differences, it is useful to consider the role of biological factors in the earlier development of sex differences in infancy and childhood. Researchers with both biological and sociocultural perspectives have turned to studies of children to reduce the complex problem of personal life histories, which result from the continuous transaction of physical, familial, and sociocultural processes with the developing individual. However, we would take this a step further and argue that a better understanding of biosocial interactions over the life course also provides valuable insights into how biological systems affect sex differences, allowing for the formulation of hypotheses about how sex differences might develop in a variety of sociocultural systems, including ones that no longer exist (and ones that might someday exist).

THE DEVELOPMENTAL COURSE OF GENDER

Edwards (1993) noted several differences between the activities of boys and girls observed in many human societies:

1. From age three, girls spend more time working, whereas boys spend more time in play.
2. When playing in groups, children self-segregate by sex, in addition to age.
3. Boys begin to spend more time than girls away from home and their mothers.
4. Girls engage in more infant contact and care.
5. Boys engage in more rough-and-tumble play than girls do.
6. Boys engage in more practice play with weapons and vehicles than girls do.
7. Girls engage in more grooming (real and play) than boys do.

Some cases, such as patterns of rough-and-tumble play in boys, the tendency for play groups to segregate by sex, and the high frequency of infant care by girls, demonstrate apparent similarities to patterns observed in other primates (Fagan 1993, Fairbanks 1993).

Sex-different patterns of behavior begin to emerge clearly in young children, during a period when biological sex differentiation is minimal, long before puberty and the development of important secondary sex differences. Patterns of sex segregation, in which children play in same-sex groups, which accompany differences in the types of games played, emerge by five years old and often earlier in many societies (Munroe & Romney 2006; Whiting & Edwards 1973, 1988). The psychologist Eleanor Maccoby (1998, 2002) has argued that this pattern of sex segregation plays a key role in the development of adult gender. Unfortunately the causes of sex segregation

remain poorly understood because most of the proposals have found limited support (Maccoby et al. 1984).

Adults play only a small role in directly encouraging sex segregation in Western societies (Aydt & Corsaro 2003, Maccoby 1998, Thorne 1993), and their role appears to be even more limited in many other societies in which children are under less supervision (Edwards 1993, 2000; Whiting & Edwards 1973, 1988). Even when adults try to encourage cross-sex play groups, children resist and quickly return to same-sex partners when adult supervision is reduced (Serbin et al. 1977). These findings are generally supported by twin studies of the heritability of individual variation in gender-related behaviors. Heritability studies allocate variation among three categories (genetic, shared environmental, and nonshared or other environmental variation) based on differential similarities between identical twins, fraternal twins, and other siblings. The role of socialization by parents should mostly appear as shared environmental. Studies of variation in adult and adolescent gender role (as with most other personality dimensions) find moderate genetic effects (25%–50%) and large nonshared environmental effects (30%–75%) with little room for substantial effects of family-based socialization (Cleveland et al. 2001, Loehlin et al. 2005). Although recent studies in young children have found larger shared environmental effects, especially in boys (Iervolino et al. 2005, Knafo et al. 2005), this difference might be explained by their use of parent reports about their children's gendered behavior. Rather than finding variation in gender-related behavior attributable to parental influence, they may have found variation in parental attitudes toward their children's gender (a type of rater bias). This is especially likely because effects were stronger in boys, and American parents are more concerned, and have stronger views, about their sons' than their daughters' gender-appropriate behavior (Fagot 1977, Langlois & Downs 1980).

Older children clearly use cognitive ideas about gender (some of which may come from cultural norms) in their play; much of the current thinking about sex segregation focuses on the importance of gender-related sociolinguistic categories to children (Bandura & Bussey 2004, Kyratzis 2004, Martin & Ruble 2004) and argues that children choose playmates on the basis of their categorical understanding of their own gender and that of other children (Powlishta et al. 1993, Serbin et al. 2001). These arguments follow Kohlberg's (1966) ideas about the importance of cognitive knowledge about gender, such as knowledge of its constancy. For example, Martin & Ruble (2004) regard children as young as four years old as "gender detectives" who are actively trying to discover exaggerated stereotypes about men and women by listening to and observing adults and often make amusing errors. Children are motivated first by the knowledge that they are boys or girls and that this will not change (gender constancy) and second by a desire for in-group dominance. This knowledge would imply a fascinating and very radical evolutionary change in which sex differences in adult behaviors, like empathetic parenting by women and dominance striving by men, which appear similar to sex differences observed in many other species, nevertheless develop in a completely novel way via cultural and cognitive processes with limited input from the reproductive endocrine system.

However, there has been some disagreement about whether cognitive knowledge about gender is necessary, especially in younger children. Differences among children in their cognitive understanding of gender are unrelated to the sex of their play partners (Munroe & Romney 2006, Serbin et al. 1994). Munroe & Romney (2006) further argue that the term sex aggregation should be used instead of segregation because larger groups of boys, which may or may not include a few girls, break out to engage in rough-and-tumble play. Children who do not join these groups (mostly girls) tend to play alone, in dyads, or in smaller groups. This occurrence implies a primary role for differences between boys and girls in the types of games played rather than in the preferred sex of the play partners. Nevertheless, the

limited evidence that exists (all from Western children) about the relationship between play-type preferences and sex-of-partner preferences has been mixed (Alexander & Hines 1994, Hoffmann & Powlishta 2001, Moller & Serbin 1996).

To the extent that segregation or "borderwork," as described by Barrie Thorne, is actively undertaken, scholars have debated its importance and source. Thorne has documented the importance of borderwork in American preschools, and girls seem to play a more important role than boys do. That is, spaces are more likely to be declared off-limits to boys than off-limits to girls (Aydt & Corsaro 2003, Thorne 1993). This observation also makes sense from Munroe & Romney's aggregation perspective if sex segregation is being driven partly by refusal on the part of some girls to participate in large-group, rough-and-tumble play.

THE ROLE OF BIOLOGICAL SEX DIFFERENCES

Secondary sex differentiation in mammals, which has usually been conceived as including behavior, is guided primarily by sex hormones produced in the fetal gonads, especially androgens, and sex differentiation in humans (Hughes 2001) and other primates (Wallen 2005) is thought to entail similar processes. As such, human researchers employing a biological approach to studying behavioral gender in children have focused primarily on prenatal androgens (Cohen-Bendahan et al. 2005, McIntyre & Hooven 2009). The evidence that childhood sex differences are directly shaped by effects of sex hormones on the brain remains somewhat weak, despite substantial research, but, to be fair, also in the face of substantial methodological limitations (McIntyre & Hooven 2009). In particular, it is difficult, for technical and ethical reasons, to directly measure prenatal hormones of fetuses in carefully designed studies. However, the possibility that sex segregation is driven partly by sex differences in play preferences provides an opportunity for biological sex differences to influence gender development in subtler ways. The construct of temperament (Kagan 2003, Rothbart 1989) might be one avenue for biological influences.

Infant boys and girls show small but consistent differences in dimensions of temperament. In particular, girls show higher fear when confronted with a novel stimulus, expressed as shorter latency to or threshold of crying (Else-Quest et al. 2006, Martin et al. 1997). Boys show a higher motor activity level (Campbell & Eaton 1999, Else-Quest et al. 2006). Some evidence indicates that individual (and perhaps sex) differences in reactive fear (DiPietro et al. 2008) and especially motor activity (Almli et al. 2001, Eaton & Saudino 1992, Groome et al. 1999) begin to develop in utero. Infant boys also show greater attention to mechanical crib mobiles than girls do (Connellan et al. 2000), but girls show greater attention to faces by 12 months old (Lutchmaya & Baron-Cohen 2002). These attentional biases have been linked with toy preferences and characterized as a primitive masculine attentional bias to movement and feminine attentional bias to people (Alexander 2003).

Infant temperament has been further linked with measures of personality later in life that are salient to the dominance/empathy paradigm. Infants with greater fear reactivity develop both greater empathy and social anxiety as toddlers (Spinrad & Stifter 2006). Although infant temperament has not been studied in relation to later dominance orientation per se in humans, male rhesus monkey infants with higher activity levels rise higher in dominance hierarchies later in life (Weinstein & Capitanio 2008), and human infants displaying lower fear reactivity (Burgess et al. 2003) and physical activity levels (Canals et al. 2006) display more externalizing behavior as children.

Increasing evidence shows that variation in infant and childhood temperament is influenced by genetic and hormonal factors. Greater attention to faces has been associated with lower prenatal testosterone concentrations measured in amniotic fluid (Lutchmaya et al. 2002). Girls with congenital adrenal hyperplasia show a preference for male-typed toys such as trucks (Meyer-Bahlburg et al. 2004, Pasterski et al. 2005).

These temperamental differences or differences in their effects on later gender development might also result, at least in part, from differential parental treatment of infant boys and girls. However, evidence to date about differential treatment of infant boys and girls has come largely from Western societies and yielded mixed results. The body of findings does not present a strong case for the effect of infant sex or gender label per se on parental treatment, particularly in younger infants (Biringen et al. 1999, Jacklin et al. 1984, Lytton & Romney 1991, Robinson et al. 1993, Stern & Karraker 1989). In American infants, individual variations in infant temperament are also almost entirely explicable by genetic variation (Goldsmith et al. 1999), and the presence of analogous sex differences in nonhuman primates (Alexander & Hines 2002, Hassett et al. 2008, Herman et al. 2003) probably argues against a major role of socialization. Many findings of caregiving variations in treatment of girl and boy infants do not remove variance contributed by what the infants themselves elicit on the basis of their activity levels, capacity for mutual gaze, emotional expressiveness, or other temperamental differences. When child characteristics are included, gender differences in maternal behavior are reduced. For instance, Moss (1967) found that mothers of three-week-old infants were observed to hold, look at, arouse, and stimulate physically sons more than daughters; however, sons were more irritable and when infant irritability was covaried in the analyses differences in holding and looking dropped out. Some researchers (e.g., Donovan et al. 2007) have attempted to remove child-temperament effects by developing experiments in which adults respond to a stranger infant (or photographs), but these studies have the weakness of measuring parental behavior in a nonnatural situation in which they are struggling to read the (often ambiguous) signals of an unknown child and, hence, are in a situation in which they would be expected to be most guided by expectations and stereotypes rather than by meaningful child cues. In sum, although it is widely assumed that adult perceptual sets and gender stereotypes influence caregiver behavior toward male versus female infants, independent of the child's characteristics, such differences have not been clearly demonstrated. The issue is complicated even further by the fact that infant girls and boys might react differently to the same caregiver behaviors in light of their own individual differences, such as differences in temperament. For example, boys tend to react more strongly than girls do to differential maternal sensitivity (Biringen et al. 1999, Warren & Simmens 2005, Weinberg et al. 2006), particularly if the infant is difficult (Warren & Simmens 2005) or in challenging social contexts (Weinberg et al. 2006). This pattern of transactions between mother and infant could lead to complex amplification of initially small differences in either infant or caregiver behavioral variation, which might also be influenced by the social context, for example, by the extent to which fathers and siblings are involved in care of the child. Bornstein et al. (2008) found that mothers from metropolitan regions were more emotionally available than were those from rural regions, and sons, but not daughters, from metropolitan regions were more responsive than were those from rural regions. These findings suggest that key developmental systems are highly sensitive to sociocultural and/or economic factors, which as Beatrice Whiting (1976) suggested are complex "packaged variables" that need to be broken down and analyzed in terms of components that really matter. Developmental studies about how biological sex differences in children operate in varied social contexts will continue to be informative, particularly as societies are radically transformed by globalization.

REFOCUSING BIOLOGICAL STUDIES OF HUMAN GENDER

We suggest that biological studies of gender can be benefited by paying more attention to (a) infancy and childhood and (b) broader social processes. Ours is certainly not the first call for complex descriptions of biocultural interactions (Edwards 1993; McIntyre & Hooven 2009; Worthman 1993, 1995). Biocultural interactions happen repeatedly over the course of life to subjects that are themselves the products of previous interactions. Therefore, we should not be tempted to think that even the bodies of infants are, so to speak, all biology and no culture. Paying attention to broader social processes is a more difficult proposition and will force evolutionary anthropologists and psychologists to gently set aside the reconstructed Paleolithic society in favor of the actual societies in which they work.

For example, some research has shifted greater focus to the individual interests and agency of the child, and adult, actors involved in the day-to-day enactment of gender (Aydt & Corsaro 2003, Knobloch et al. 2005, Kyratzis 2004). Recent analyses particularly from humanistic (Montgomery 2005), but also from biological (Crittenden & Marlowe 2008, Hrdy 2005), frameworks have argued for greater attention to the economic value of girls' labor and the roles of parental power and coercion in the establishment of gendered patterns of play and work. This approach might allow us to think about the effects of infant temperament in different ways. The temperaments of young girls, which are characterized by greater empathy, social anxiety, and social attention, might be considered more suitable for doing work around the house and caring for siblings, or they might be more cooperative with mothers owing to their greater physiological maturity and/or same-sex identification (Whiting & Edwards 1988). Boys, however, might gain agency by virtue of their high levels of physical activity and perceived irresponsibility, freeing them from some household responsibilities.

Similarly interesting questions arise with regard to social institutions outside of the home. Whereas evolutionary anthropologists and psychologists have been looking for associations between testosterone and dominance striving, McIntyre & Hooven (2009) argue that the reality in Western societies is far more complex and fascinating. Boys with high testosterone are dominant over their peers in adolescence (Tremblay et al. 1998), but as they leave the world of peers and family and come into contact with other social institutions the trajectories of their lives are more often characterized by delinquency (Rowe et al. 2004), criminal activities (Archer 2006, Archer et al. 1998), lack of education (Dabbs & Dabbs 2000), and low social prestige (Dabbs 1992, Johnson et al. 2007). Even if this tendency results from a mismatch between ancestral and current conditions, it is a mismatch worthy of careful study, if for no other reason than it is likely to affect the results of any research that we conduct. It is not possible to escape these questions by studying simpler societies.

Our suggestions are similar to those of Goodman & Leatherman's (1998) *Biocultural Synthesis*, which encourages more study of the effects of political and economic systems on human biology but applied to reproductive biology and sex differences, in addition to nutrition and growth. We also echo some of Bourdieu's observations about patriarchy. "The biological appearances and the very real effects which have been produced, in people's bodies and in their brains, by a long collective labor of socialization of the biological and of biologization of the social combine to overturn the relationship between causes and effects..." (Bourdieu 1990, p. 12). We further argue that biological work relying on insights from humanistic social science research, far from being an alternative to evolutionary explanations (Bribiescas 2001, Ellison 2003), can also make the social sciences more useful contributors to biological and evolutionary thinking about gender in other species. Recent work in a number of species, including those whose biological gender can reverse during life, has highlighted the central roles of social stratification, power differences, and coercive or violent tactics in explaining patterns of sex or gender role change (Anthes & Michiels 2007, Black & Grober 2003, Grober & Rodgers 2008, Rodgers et al. 2007). As these processes are particularly elaborated and varied in humans, the human sciences might offer rich and surprising theoretical insights, even for ichthyologists.

SUMMARY POINTS

1. For the most part, biological influences on psychological sex differences probably occur early in life via simple mechanisms such as temperament.

2. Small sex differences in temperament interact with social factors in complex ways that might result in further psychological differentiation but not always in ways that are clearly predicted by existing evolutionary theories.

FUTURE ISSUES

1. How do sex differences in physical maturity and social competence influence how children interact with one another or are treated by adults, and what are the biological or social causes of these sex differences?

2. More evidence is needed about the social processes and individual differences that result in sex segregation in children. In particular, the relative importance of gender cognitions and activity or play-style preferences remains unclear.

3. Longer-term longitudinal studies would help us to understand the role of early processes (including sex segregation) on the further consolidation of psychological sex differences during puberty and adulthood.

DISCLOSURE STATEMENT

The authors are not aware of any affiliations, memberships, funding, or financial holdings that might be perceived as affecting the objectivity of this review.

LITERATURE CITED

Alexander GM. 2003. An evolutionary perspective of sex-typed toy preferences: pink, blue, and the brain. *Arch. Sex. Behav.* 32:7–14

Alexander GM, Hines M. 1994. Gender labels and play styles—their relative contribution to children's selection of playmates. *Child Dev.* 65:869–79

Alexander GM, Hines M. 2002. Sex differences in response to children's toys in nonhuman primates (*Cercopithecus aethiops sabaeus*). *Evol. Hum. Behav.* 23:467–79

Almli CR, Ball RH, Wheeler ME. 2001. Human fetal and neonatal movement patterns: gender differences and fetal-to-neonatal continuity. *Dev. Psychobiol.* 38:252–73

Anthes N, Michiels NK. 2007. Precopulatory stabbing, hypodermic injections and unilateral copulations in a hermaphroditic sea slug. *Biol. Lett.* 3:121–24

Archer J. 2006. Testosterone and human aggression: an evaluation of the challenge hypothesis. *Neurosci. Biobehav. Rev.* 30:319–45

Archer J, Birring SS, Wu FCW. 1998. The association between testosterone and aggression among young men: empirical findings and a meta-analysis. *Aggressive Behav.* 24:411–20

Aydt H, Corsaro WA. 2003. Differences in children's construction of gender across culture—an interpretive approach. *Am. Behav. Sci.* 46:1306–25

Bandura A, Bussey K. 2004. On broadening the cognitive, motivational, and sociostructural scope of theorizing about gender development and functioning: comment on Martin, Ruble, and Szkrvbalo (2002). *Psychol. Bull.* 130:691–701

Baron-Cohen S. 2002. The extreme male brain theory of autism. *Trends Cognit. Sci.* 6:248–54

Bateman AJ. 1948. Intrasexual selection on *Drosophila*. *Heredity* 2:349–68

Biringen Z, Emde RN, Brown D, Lowe L, Myers S, Nelson D. 1999. Emotional availability and emotion communication in naturalistic mother-infant interactions: evidence for gender relations. *J. Soc. Person. Relat.* 14:463–78

Black MP, Grober MS. 2003. Group sex, sex change, and parasitic males: sexual strategies among the fishes and their neurobiological correlates. *Annu. Rev. Sex. Res.* 14:160–84

Bornstein MH, Putnick DL, Heslington M, Gini M, Suwalsky JTD, et al. 2008. Mother-child emotional availability in ecological perspective: three countries, two regions, two genders. *Dev. Psychol.* 44:666–80

Bourdieu P. 1990. La domination masculine. *Actes Rech. Sci. Soc.* 84:3–31

Bribiescas RG. 2001. Reproductive ecology and life history of the human male. *Am. J. Phys. Anthropol.* 33(Suppl.):148–76

Burgess KB, Marshall PJ, Rubin KH, Fox NA. 2003. Infant attachment and temperament as predictors of subsequent externalizing problems and cardiac physiology. *J. Child. Psychol. Psychiatry* 44:819–31

Burgoon JK, Johnson ML, Koch PT. 1998. The nature and measurement of interpersonal dominance. *Commun. Monogr.* 65:308–35

Burnham TC. 2007. High-testosterone men reject low ultimatum game offers. *Proc. R. Soc. London Ser. B Biol. Sci.* 274:2327–30

Campbell A. 2006. Sex differences in direct aggression: What are the psychological mediators? *Aggr. Violent Behav.* 11:237–64

Campbell DW, Eaton WO. 1999. Sex differences in the activity level of infants. *Infant Child Dev.* 8:1–17

Canals J, Esparo G, Fernandez-Ballart JD. 2006. Neonatal behavior characteristics and psychological problems at 6 years. *Acta Paediatr.* 95:1412–17

Carré JM, McCormick CM. 2008. Aggressive behavior and change in salivary testosterone concentrations predict willingness to engage in a competitive task. *Horm. Behav.* 54:403–9

Cashdan E. 1995. Hormones, sex, and status in women. *Horm. Behav.* 29:354–66

Cleveland HH, Udry JR, Chantala K. 2001. Environmental and genetic influences on sex-typed behaviors and attitudes of male and female adolescents. *Person. Soc. Psychol. Bull.* 27:1587–98

Clutton-Brock TH. 1989. Mammalian mating systems. *Proc. R. Soc. London Ser. B Biol. Sci.* 236:339–72

Clutton-Brock TH, Parker GA. 1992. Potential reproductive rates and the operation of sexual selection. *Q. Rev. Biol.* 67:437–56

Cohen-Bendahan CCC, van de Beek C, Berenbaum SA. 2005. Prenatal sex hormone effects on child and adult sex-typed behavior: methods and findings. *Neurosci. Biobehav. Rev.* 29:353–84

Connellan J, Baron-Cohen S, Wheelwright S, Batki A, Ahluwalia J. 2000. Sex differences in human neonatal social perception. *Infant Behav. Dev.* 23:113–18

Crittenden AN, Marlowe FW. 2008. Allomaternal care among the Hadza of Tanzania. *Hum. Nat.-Interdiscip. Biosoc. Perspect.* 19:249–62

Dabbs JM. 1992. Testosterone and occupational achievement. *Soc. Forces* 70:813–24

Dabbs JM. 1997. Testosterone, smiling, and facial appearance. *J. Nonverbal Behav.* 21:45–55

Dabbs JM, Dabbs MG. 2000. *Heroes, Rogues, and Lovers: Testosterone and Behavior*. New York: McGraw-Hill

Deady DK, Law-Smith MJ, Sharp MA, Al-Dujaili EAS. 2006. Maternal personality and reproductive ambition in women is associated with salivary testosterone levels. *Biol. Psychol.* 71:29–32

Dewsbury DA. 1982. Dominance rank, copulatory behavior, and differential reproduction. *Q. Rev. Biol.* 57:135–59

DiPietro JA, Ghera MM, Costigan KA. 2008. Prenatal origins of temperamental reactivity in early infancy. *Early Hum. Dev.* 84:569–75

Donovan W, Taylor N, Leavitt L. 2007. Maternal sensory sensitivity and response bias in detecting change in infant facial expressions: maternal self-efficacy and infant gender labeling. *Infant Behav. Dev.* 30:436–52

Eaton WO, Saudino KJ. 1992. Prenatal activity level as a temperament dimension—individual differences and developmental functions in fetal movement. *Infant Behav. Dev.* 15:57–70

Ecuyer-Dab I, Robert M. 2004. Have sex differences in spatial ability evolved from male competition for mating and female concern for survival? *Cognition* 91:221–57

Edwards CP. 1993. Behavioral sex differences in children of diverse cultures: the case of nurturance to infants. See Pereira & Fairbanks 1993, pp. 327–38

Edwards CP. 2000. Children's play in cross-cultural perspective: a new look at the six cultures study. *Cross Cult. Res.* 34:318–38

Elias M. 1981. Serum cortisol, testosterone, and testosterone-binding globulin responses to competitive fighting in human males. *Aggress. Behav.* 7:215–24

Ellison PT. 2003. Energetics and reproductive effort. *Am. J. Hum. Biol.* 15:342–51

Else-Quest NM, Hyde JS, Goldsmith HH, Van Hulle CA. 2006. Gender differences in temperament: a meta-analysis. *Psychol. Bull.* 132:33–72

Fagan R. 1993. Primate juveniles and primate play. See Pereira & Fairbanks 1993, pp. 182–96

Fagot BI. 1977. Consequences of moderate cross-gender behavior in preschool children. *Child Dev.* 48:902–7

Fairbanks LA. 1993. Juvenile vervet monkeys: establishing relationships and practicing skills for the future. See Pereira & Fairbanks 1993, pp. 212–27

Fuentes A. 1998. Re-evaluating primate monogamy. *Am. Anthropol.* 100:890–907

Gaulin SJC, FitzGerald RW. 1986. Sex differences in spatial ability: an evolutionary hypothesis and test. *Am. Nat.* 127:74–88

Geary DC. 2002. Sexual selection and human life history. *Adv. Child Dev. Behav.* 30:41–101

Geary DC. 2006. Sex differences in social behavior and cognition: utility of sexual selection for hypothesis generation. *Horm. Behav.* 49:273–75

Goldsmith HH, Lemery KS, Buss KA, Campos JJ. 1999. Genetic analyses of focal aspects of infant temperament. *Dev. Psychol.* 35:972–85

Goodman A, Leatherman T. 1998. *Building a New Biocultural Synthesis: Political-Economic Perspectives on Human Biology*. Ann Arbor: Univ. Mich. Press

Grant VJ, France JT. 2001. Dominance and testosterone in women. *Biol. Psychiatry* 58:41–47

Gray PB. 2003. Marriage, parenting, and testosterone variation among Kenyan Swahili men. *Am. J. Phys. Anthropol.* 122:279–86

Gray PB, Chapman JF, Burnham TC, McIntyre MH, Lipson SF, Ellison PT. 2004. Human male pair bonding and testosterone. *Hum. Nat. Interdiscip. Biosoc. Perspect.* 15:119–31

Gray PB, Ellison PT, Campbell BC. 2007. Testosterone and marriage among Ariaal men of Northern Kenya. *Curr. Anthropol.* 48:750–55

Gray PB, Kahlenberg SM, Barrett ES, Lipson SF, Ellison PT. 2002. Marriage and fatherhood are associated with lower testosterone in males. *Evol. Hum. Behav.* 23:193–201

Gray PB, Yang CFJ, Pope HG. 2006. Fathers have lower salivary testosterone levels than unmarried men and married nonfathers in Beijing, China. *Proc. R. Soc. London Ser. B Biol. Sci.* 273:333–39

Grober MS, Rodgers EW. 2008. The evolution of hermaphroditism. *J. Theor. Biol.* 251:190–92

Groome LJ, Swiber MJ, Holland SB, Bentz LS, Atterbury JL, Trimm RF. 1999. Spontaneous motor activity in the perinatal infant before and after birth: stability in individual differences. *Dev. Psychobiol.* 35:15–24

Hassett JM, Siebert ER, Wallen K. 2008. Sex differences in rhesus monkey toy preferences parallel those of children. *Horm. Behav.* 54:359–64

Hawkes K, O'Connell JF, Jones NGB. 1991. Hunting income patterns among the Hadza—big game, common goods, foraging goals and the evolution of the human diet. *Philos. Trans. R. Soc. London Ser. B Biol. Sci.* 334:243–51

Hawkes K, O'Connell JF, Jones NGB. 2001. Hunting and nuclear families—some lessons from the Hadza about men's work. *Curr. Anthropol.* 42:681–709

Herman RA, Measday MA, Wallen K. 2003. Sex differences in interest in infants in juvenile rhesus monkeys: relationship to prenatal androgen. *Horm. Behav.* 43:573–83

Hermans EJ, Putman P, Baas JM, Koppeschaar HP, van Honk J. 2006a. A single administration of testosterone reduces fear-potentiated startle in humans. *Biol. Psychiatry* 59:872–74

Hermans EJ, Putman P, van Honk J. 2006b. Testosterone administration reduces empathetic behavior: a facial mimicry study. *Psychoneuroendocrinology* 31:859–66

Hill K, Kaplan H. 1993. On why male foragers hunt and share food. *Curr. Anthropol.* 34:701–10

Hoffmann ML, Powlishta KK. 2001. Gender segregation in childhood: a test of the interaction style theory. *J. Genet. Psychol.* 162:298–313

Hooven CK, Chabris CF, Ellison PT, Kosslyn SM. 2004. The relationship of male testosterone to components of mental rotation. *Neuropsychologia* 42:782–90

Hrdy SB. 2005. Comes the child before the man: how cooperative breeding and prolonged postweaning dependence shaped human potentials. In *Hunter-Gatherer Childhoods*, ed. BS Hewlett, ME Lamb, pp. 65–91. Piscataway, NJ: Aldine Transaction

Hughes IA. 2001. Minireview: sex differentiation. *Endocrinology* 142:3281–87

Iervolino AC, Hines M, Golombok SE, Rust J, Plomin R. 2005. Genetic and environmental influences on sex-typed behavior during the preschool years. *Child Dev.* 76:826–40

Jacklin CN, Dipietro JA, Maccoby EE. 1984. Sex-typing behavior and sex-typing pressure in child parent interaction. *Arch. Sex. Behav.* 13:413–25

Jarman P. 1983. Mating system and sexual dimorphism in large, terrestrial, mammalian herbivores. *Biol. Rev. Camb. Philos. Soc.* 58:485–520

Johnson DDP, McDermott R, Barrett ES, Cowden J, Wrangham R, et al. 2006. Overconfidence in wargames: experimental evidence on expectations, aggression, gender and testosterone. *R. Soc. London Ser. B Biol. Sci.* 273:2513–20

Johnson RT, Burk JA, Kirkpatrick LA. 2007. Dominance and prestige as differential predictors of aggression and testosterone levels in men. *Evol. Hum. Behav.* 28:345–51

Jones CM, Braithwaite VA, Healy SD. 2003. The evolution of sex differences in spatial ability. *Behav. Neurosci.* 117:403–11

Jones NB, Marlowe FW. 2002. Selection for delayed maturity—Does it take 20 years to learn to hunt and gather? *Hum. Nat.-Interdiscip. Biosoc. Perspect.* 13:199–238

Kagan J. 2003. Biology, context, and developmental inquiry. *Annu. Rev. Psychol.* 54:1–23

Kaplan H, Hill K, Lancaster J, Hurtado AM. 2000. A theory of human life history evolution: diet, intelligence, and longevity. *Evol. Anthropol.* 9:156–85

Kimura D. 1999. *Sex and Cognition*. Cambridge, MA: MIT Press

Knafo A, Iervolino AC, Plomin R. 2005. Masculine girls and feminine boys: genetic and environmental contributions to atypical gender development in early childhood. *J. Person. Soc. Psychol.* 88:400–12

Knobloch S, Callison C, Chen L, Fritzsche A, Zillmann D. 2005. Children's sex-stereotyped self-socialization through selective exposure to entertainment: cross-cultural experiments in Germany, China, and the United States. *J. Commun.* 55:122–38

Kohlberg L. 1966. A cognitive-developmental analysis of children's sex role concepts and attitudes. In *The Development of Sex Differences*, ed. EE Maccoby, pp. 82–173. Stanford, CA: Stanford Univ. Press

Kokko H, Jennions MD, Brooks R. 2006. Unifying and testing models of sexual selection. *Annu. Rev. Ecol. Evol. Syst.* 37:43–66

Kyratzis A. 2004. Talk and interaction among children and the coconstruction of peer groups and peer culture. *Annu. Rev. Anthropol.* 33:625–49

Langlois JH, Downs AC. 1980. Mothers, fathers, and peers as socialization agents of sex-typed play behaviors in young children. *Child Dev.* 51:1237–47

Loehlin JC, Jonsson EG, Gustavsson JP, Stallings MC, Gillespie NA, et al. 2005. Psychological masculinity-femininity via the gender diagnosticity approach: heritability and consistency across ages and populations. *J. Person.* 73:1295–319

Lutchmaya S, Baron-Cohen S. 2002. Human sex differences in social and nonsocial looking preferences, at 12 months of age. *Infant Behav. Dev.* 25:319–25

Lutchmaya S, Baron-Cohen S, Raggatt P. 2002. Fetal testosterone and eye contact in 12-month-old human infants. *Infant Behav. Dev.* 25:327–35

Lytton H, Romney DM. 1991. Parents' differential socialization of boys and girls: a meta-analysis. *Psychol. Bull.* 109:267–96

Maccoby EE. 1998. *The Two Sexes: Growing Up Apart, Coming Together*. Cambridge, MA: Harvard Univ. Press

Maccoby EE. 2002. Gender and group process: a developmental perspective. *Curr. Dir. Psychol. Sci.* 11:54–58

Maccoby EE, Snow ME, Jacklin CN. 1984. Childrens dispositions and mother child interaction at 12 and 18 months—a short-term longitudinal-study. *Dev. Psychol.* 20:459–72

Martin CL, Ruble D. 2004. Children's search for gender cues—cognitive perspectives on gender development. *Curr. Dir. Psychol. Sci.* 13:67–70

Martin RP, Wisenbaker J, Baker J, Huttunen MO. 1997. Gender differences in temperament at six months and five years. *Infant Behav. Dev.* 20:339–47

Mazur A, Booth A. 1998. Testosterone and dominance in men. *Behav. Brain Sci.* 21:353–97

Mazur A, Michalek J. 1998. Marriage, divorce, and male testosterone. *Soc. Forces* 77:315–30

McIntyre MH. 2006. The use of digit ratios as markers for perinatal androgen action. *Reprod. Biol. Endocrinol.* 2:10

McIntyre MH, Barrett ES, McDermott R, Johnson DDP, Cowden J, Rosen SP. 2007. Finger length ratio (2D:4D) and sex differences in aggression during a simulated war game. *Person. Ind. Diff.* 42:755–64

McIntyre MH, Gangestad SW, Gray PB, Chapman JF, Burnham TC, et al. 2006. Romantic involvement often reduces men's testosterone levels—but not always: the moderating role of extrapair sexual interest. *J. Person. Soc. Psychol.* 91:642–51

McIntyre MH, Hooven CK. 2009. Human sex differences in social relationships: organizational and activational effects of androgens. In *Endocrinology of Social Relationships*, ed. PB Gray, PT Ellison, pp. 225–45. Cambridge, MA: Harvard Univ. Press

Mehta PH, Jones AC, Josephs RA. 2008. The social endocrinology of dominance: basal testosterone predicts cortisol changes and behavior following victory and defeat. *J. Person. Soc. Psychol.* 94:1078–93

Meyer-Bahlburg HFL, Dolezal C, Baker SW, Carlson AD, Obeid JS, New MI. 2004. Prenatal androgenization affects gender-related behavior but not gender identity in 5–12-year-old girls with congenital adrenal hyperplasia. *Arch. Sex. Behav.* 33:97–104

Moller LC, Serbin LA. 1996. Antecedents of toddler gender segregation: cognitive consonance, gender-typed toy preferences and behavioral compatibility. *Sex Roles* 35:445–60

Montgomery H. 2005. Gendered childhoods: a cross disciplinary overview. *Gend. Educ.* 17:471–82

Moss HA. 1967. Sex, age, and state as determinants of mother-infant interaction. *Merrill Palmer Q. J. Dev. Psychol.* 13:19–36

Munroe RL, Romney AK. 2006. Gender and age differences in same-sex aggregation and social behavior—a four-culture study. *J. Cross Cult. Psychol.* 37:3–19

O'Carroll RE. 1998. Placebo-controlled manipulations of testosterone levels and dominance. *Behav. Brain Sci.* 21:382–83

Orians GH. 1969. On evolution of mating systems in birds and mammals. *Am. Nat.* 103:589–603

Pasterski VL, Geffner ME, Brain C, Hindmarsh P, Brook C, Hines M. 2005. Prenatal hormones and postnatal socialization by parents as determinants of male-typical toy play in girls with congenital adrenal hyperplasia. *Child Dev.* 76:264–78

Pereira ME, Fairbanks LA, eds. 1993. *Juvenile Primates: Life History, Development, and Behavior.* New York/Oxford: Oxford Univ. Press

Plavcan JM. 2001. Sexual dimorphism in primate evolution. *Yearb. Phys. Anthropol.* 44:25–53

Powlishta KK, Serbin LA, Moller LC. 1993. The stability of individual differences in gender typing—implications for understanding gender segregation. *Sex Roles* 29:723–37

Pratto F, Sidanius J, Stallworth LM, Malle BF. 1994. Social-dominance orientation—a personality variable predicting social and political attitudes. *J. Person. Soc. Psychol.* 67:741–63

Robinson J, Little C, Biringen Z. 1993. Emotional communication in mother-toddler relationships—evidence for early gender differentiation. *Merrill Palmer Q. J. Dev. Psychol.* 39:496–517

Rodgers EW, Earley RL, Grober MS. 2007. Social status determines sexual phenotype in the bi-directional sex changing bluebanded goby *Lythrypnus dalli*. *J. Fish Biol.* 70:1660–68

Rothbart MK. 1989. Temperament in childhood: a framework. In *Temperament in Childhood*, ed. JE Kohnstamn, JE Bates, MK Rothbart, pp. 59–73. New York: Wiley

Rowe R, Maughan B, Worthman CM, Costello EJ, Angold A. 2004. Testosterone, antisocial behavior, and social dominance in boys: pubertal development and biosocial interaction. *Biol. Psychiatry* 55:546–52

Schultheiss OC, Wirth MM, Torges CM, Pang JS, Villacorta MA, Welsh KM. 2005. Effects of implicit power motivation on men's and women's implicit learning and testosterone changes after social victory or defeat. *J. Person. Soc. Psychol.* 88:174–88

Sellers JG, Mehl MR, Josephs RA. 2007. Hormones and personality: testosterone as a marker of individual differences. *J. Res. Pers.* 41:126–38

Serbin LA, Moller LC, Gulko J, Powlishta KK, Colburne KA. 1994. The emergence of gender segregation in toddler playgroups. *New Dir. Child Dev.* 65:7–17

Serbin LA, Poulin-Dubois D, Colburne KA, Sen MG, Eichstedt JA. 2001. Gender stereotyping in infancy: visual preferences for and knowledge of gender-stereotyped toys in the second year. *Int. J. Behav. Dev.* 25:7–15

Serbin LA, Tonick IJ, Sternglanz SH. 1977. Shaping interaction in same and cross-sex play. *Child Dev.* 48:924–29

Silverman I, Eals M. 1992. Sex differences in spatial abilites: evolutionary theory and data. In *The Adapted Mind: Evolutionary Psychology and the Generation of Culture*, ed. JH Barkow, L Cosmides, J Tooby, pp. 533–49. Oxford, UK: Oxford Univ. Press

Smuts B. 1995. The evolutionary origins of patriarchy. *Hum. Nat.-Interdiscip. Biosoc. Perspect.* 6:1–32

Spinrad TL, Stifter CA. 2006. Toddlers' empathy-related responding to distress: predictions from negative emotionality and maternal behavior in infancy. *Infancy* 10:97–121

Stern M, Karraker KH. 1989. Sex stereotyping of infants: a review of gender labeling studies. *Sex Roles* 20:501–22

Thorne B. 1993. *Gender Play: Girls and Boys in School.* New Brunswick, NJ: Rutgers Univ. Press

Tremblay RE, Schaal B, Boulerice B, Arseneault L, Soussignan RG, et al. 1998. Testosterone, physical aggression, dominance, and physical development in early adolescence. *Int. J. Behav. Dev.* 22:753–77

Trivers R. 1972. Parental investment and sexual selection. In *Sexual Selection and the Descent of Man, 1871–1971*, ed. B Campbell, pp. 136–79. Chicago: Aldine

van Anders SM, Watson NV. 2006. Relationship status and testosterone in North American heterosexual and nonheterosexual men and women: cross-sectional and longitudinal data. *Psychoneuroendocrinology* 31:715–23

van Anders SM, Watson NV. 2007. Testosterone levels in women and men who are single, in long-distance relationships, or same-city relationships. *Horm. Behav.* 51:286–91

van Honk J, Schutter D, Hermans EJ, Putman P. 2004. Testosterone, cortisol, dominance, and submission: biologically prepared motivation, no psychological mechanisms involved. *Behav. Brain Sci.* 27:160–62

Wade MJ, Shuster SM. 2002. The evolution of parental care in the context of sexual selection: a critical reassessment of parental investment theory. *Am. Nat.* 160:285–92

Wallen K. 2005. Hormonal influences on sexually differentiated behavior in nonhuman primates. *Frontiers Neuroendocrinol.* 26:7–26

Warren SL, Simmens SJ. 2005. Predicting toddler anxiety/depressive symptoms: effects of caregiver sensitivity on temperamentally vulnerable children. *Infant Mental Health J.* 26:40–55

Weinberg MK, Olson KL, Beeghly M, Tronick EZ. 2006. Making up is hard to do, especially for mothers with high levels of depressive symptoms and their infant sons. *J. Child. Psychol. Psychiatry* 47:670–83

Weinstein TAR, Capitanio JP. 2008. Individual differences in infant temperament predict social relationships of yearling rhesus monkeys, Macaca *mulatta. Anim. Behav.* 76:455–65

Westergaard GC, Liv C, Haynie MK, Suomi SJ. 2000. A comparative study of aimed throwing by monkeys and humans. *Neuropsychologia* 38:1511–17

Whiting BB. 1976. The problem of the packaged variable. In *The Developing Individual in a Changing World, Vol. 1: Historical and Cultural Issues,* ed. KF Riegel, JA Meacham, pp. 303–9. The Hague: Mouton

Whiting BB, Edwards CP. 1973. A cross cultural analysis of sex differences in the behavior of children aged 3 to 11. *J. Soc. Psychol.* 91:171–88

Whiting BB, Edwards CP. 1988. *Children of Different Worlds: The Formation of Social Behavior.* Cambridge, MA: Harvard Univ. Press

Wirth MM, Schultheiss OC. 2007. Basal testosterone moderates responses to anger faces in humans. *Physiol. Behav.* 90:496–505

Wobst HM. 1978. Archaeo-ethnology of hunter-gatherers or tyranny of the ethnographic record in archeology. *Am. Antiq.* 43:303–9

Worthman CM. 1993. Biocultural interactions in human devolopment. See Pereira & Fairbanks 1993, pp. 339–58

Worthman CM. 1995. Hormones, sex, and gender. *Annu. Rev. Anthropol.* 24:593–617

Wrangham RW. 1999. Evolution of coalitionary killing. *Yeab. Phys. Anthropol.* 42:1–30

Yang CFJ, Hooven CK, Boynes M, Gray PB, Pope HG. 2007. Testosterone levels and mental rotation performance in Chinese men. *Horm. Behav.* 51:373–78

The Ethnography of South Asian Foragers

Jana Fortier

Department of Anthropology #0532, University of California San Diego, La Jolla, California 92093-0532; email: jfortier@ucsd.edu

Annu. Rev. Anthropol. 2009. 38:99–114

First published online as a Review in Advance on June 23, 2009

The *Annual Review of Anthropology* is online at anthro.annualreviews.org

This article's doi: 10.1146/annurev-anthro-091908-164345

Key Words

contemporary hunter-gatherers, egalitarian societies, subsistence foraging, human ecology, cultural resilience, indigenous peoples

Abstract

Forty contemporary South Asian societies continue to carry out hunting and gathering as their primary subsistence strategy, but who are these societies? In which ways are they similar or dissimilar? Are they like contemporary foragers in other world areas? This article reviews ethnographic research concerning contemporary South Asian foragers with a focus on subsistence, cosmologies, and social organization. Major conclusions are that evolutionary/devolutionary theories about foragers during the documented ethnographic period lack reliable data and that theories of trade between farmers and foragers ignore the paramount importance of subsistence foraging practices. Currently, theories based on interpretations of foragers' own cultural categories and standpoints constitute the most reliable ethnographic studies, and notable contributions are highlighted. Contemporary foragers themselves advocate that their best chances for cultural survival depend on state governments that maintain environmentally diverse, healthy forests, provide contemporary foraging communities access to their traditional natural resources, and implement projects that foster cultural survival rather than assimilation.

INTRODUCTION

The ethnography of South Asian (SA) foragers has played an important part in the theory and historical imagination of contemporary anthropology, although specific contributions have not always been apparent. Who exactly constitutes a forager in the South Asian geographic region remains a product of particular intellectual histories and colonial projects shaping cultural identity. Foraging societies historically have been defined by subsistence practices, in the manner of Sandhwar (1978, p. 157), who distinguished foraging Korwas, whose "economy depends on food collection," from agricultural Korwas, whose "economy depends on food production." The distinction between contemporary foragers and agriculturalists nevertheless involves more than the exploitation of wild versus domesticated resources. For this review, the foraging lifestyle is modeled as a particular set of economic and social structures, which are buttressed by a variable yet characteristic cosmological worldview (Ingold 1999; Lee 1999, p. 4). It is the trio of work, sociality, and cosmology that forms the fundamental criteria distinguishing foraging from other forms of social and economic life.

Current census data list 84.3 million of India's 1 billion people as "scheduled tribes" (Census of India 2001). Including Nepal and Sri Lanka, ~1.5–2 million of South Asia's scheduled tribes rely upon hunting, gathering, and fishing and may be defined as contemporary or recent foragers (Gautam & Thapa-Magar 1994, Singh 1994). Reviewing ethnographies and census data, an estimated 150,000 people from these societies continue to derive their subsistence from foraging. To put these figures in perspective, the population of native peoples in the United States and Canada is estimated at three million, of which 150,000 people historically have been considered recent hunter-gatherers (Hitchcock & Biesele 2000, pp. 4–5); about 15,000 of them are part-time contemporary foragers who continue to garner much of their subsistence from hunting, gathering, and fishing. Thus, South Asia is home to several times more full- and part-time contemporary foragers than are other world areas. Excluding cultures described in the ethnographic literature in which foraging is a minor activity and not valorized, there are 40 contemporary societies whose work, sociality, and cosmological worldviews meet the definition of foraging societies. Their names are given below according to language family using the most common exonyms applied in scholarly literatures.

CONTEMPORARY SOUTH ASIAN FORAGING PEOPLES

The foraging societies of the SA region speak one of six language families with Dravidian languages being the most numerous and the isolate language, Kusunda, being the most distinctive in grammatical form and vocabulary (Emeneau 1989, Van Driem 2001, Watters 2006). In terms of population, Hill Kharias and Yanadis have the largest contemporary foraging populations with about 20,000 members of each ethnic group continuing subsistence foraging (Das 1931, Dash 1998, Reddy & Reddy 1987, Rao 2002, Thurston & Rangachari 1909, Vidyarthi & Upadhyay 1980). Several ethnic groups are highly endangered with less than 350 members who continue subsistence foraging. These include the Aranadan, Jarawa, Jeru, Kusunda, Onge, Shompen, Vedda, and Yerukula. Additionally, a number of ethnic groups that discontinued subsistence foraging in the 20th century are omitted from **Table 1**, below. The Nayadi, for example, are described as hunters who were being assimilated into the Hindu caste system as professional beggars at the time of ethnographic documentation (Aiyappan 1937).

Labeling foragers by ethnic names implies a cohesive ethnic identity, but in reality, there rarely is a correspondence between a named ethnicity and a mode of subsistence; three situations can arise. First, a one-to-one correspondence does exist in some situations. When virtually all people of a named ethnic group practice foraging, and few or none do not, naming is unproblematic. All Onges of the Little Andaman Islands, for example, practice foraging (Basu 1990, Pandya 1991). The

SA: South Asian

Forager: Used interchangeably with "hunter-gatherer" in this essay, one who carries out food collecting; one who hunts, gathers, and fishes for resources

South Asian geographic region: A geographical area bounded by the Indus River watershed; Brahmaputra River watershed; Andaman Sea; Sri Lanka; and Maldivian Islands

Contemporary foragers: People who carry out food collection activities presently or within the last generation

Recent foragers: communities of foragers documented in ethnographic studies who now have few or no families that rely upon food collecting

Table 1 List of contemporary South Asian foraging peoples

Language Family	Contemporary South Asian Foraging Peoples
Andamanese	Jeru, Jarawa (Eng), Onge, Puchikwar, Sentinelese
Austroasiatic	Birhor, Hill Bondo (Remo), Hill Juang, Hill Kharia, Hill Korwa, Shompen
Dravidian	Allar, Aranadan, Betta Kurumba, Chenchu, Chingathan, Cholanayakan, Jenu Kurumba, Kadu Kurumba, Kadar, Kanikkar, Malapandaram, Malamalasar (Mahamalasar), Malavedan, Mavilan, Mudugar, Nattu Malayar, Nayaka, Paliyan, Paniyar, Sholigar, Ulladar, Urali, Yanadi, Yerukula (Kurru)
Indo-European (IE)	Vedda
Isolate	Kusunda
Tibeto-Burman	Banraji, Raji, Raute, Chepang, Puroik (Sulung)

second situation arises when a named ethnic group has various subsistence pursuits and a minority of them practice subsistence foraging. For example, few Veddas pursue foraging for their livelihood, whereas others are recent foragers and the majority practice food cultivation and fishing (Brow 1978, 1990; Dharmadasa & Samarasinghe 1990; Schalk 2004; Seligman & Seligman 1911). Third, in other situations, dominant polities give several different foraging groups one ethnonym, such as "forest people" or "hill people." Examples include *Banraja* ("forest kings"), *Kurumba* ("shepherd, nomad, mountaineer, jungle people"), *Allar* ("forest people"), and *Kattunaiken* or *Kattu Nayaka* ("wild/forest leaders"). This ethnonymic merging occurs when nonforagers lump together a number of seemingly similar ethnic groups living in remote areas. For example, of the 180,000 people known as Kurumba, many of those considered foraging communities are differentiated using modifiers such as the Upland Kurumba, Elephant specialist Kurumba, Neem tree–collecting Kurumba, Honey-collecting Kurumba, and Firebrand wielding Kurumba. Most of these groups today complement part-time foraging with food cultivation. A few of these groups continue subsistence foraging such as the Jenu Kurumba, also known as Kattu Nayaka, who number ~35,000 people, with subgroups using the self-designation *Nayaka* (Bird-David 1994, 1999b, Demmer 1997, Zvelebil 1981, 1988). Thus, lumping foragers of different locations, dialects, and cultural practices obscures, yet reflects, the process and politics of ethnic naming.

From foraging peoples' perspectives, identifying social difference is based on criteria such as territory, sartorial choice, language variation, or clan group. Our list of foraging societies does not assume a one-to-one correlation between ethnic names and foraging groups and may not represent foragers' own ethnic divisions. Furthermore, contemporary forager identities are not diachronically accurate. Over time, foraging groups may splinter and create new identities through ethnogenesis (Fortier 2009, p. 27; Schalk 2004), or they may be assimilated into surrounding dominant polities (Reddy & Reddy 1987, Zvelebil 1981).

"MOST PRIMITIVE TRIBES" IN THE BRITISH AND INDIAN COLONIAL IMAGINATION

While describing the people of Ceylon (Sri Lanka) in the seventeenth century, Director van Goens of the Dutch East India Company noted, "The Veddas are the original inhabitants of old...those people neither sow nor cultivate, but live off of hunting, honey, and a type of earth-acorn [wild yam] which grows abundantly in those forests" (Valentijn 2002, pp. 208–9). Thus began a series of descriptions by colonial scholars and administrators to catalog the foraging peoples of South Asia who were given epithets such as "aboriginal tribes," "broken tribes," or "primitive tribes" (Aiyappan 1948, Ananthakrishna Iyer 1909, Atkinson 1884, Dalton 1872, Forsyth 1889, Hamilton 1819, Knox 1681, Krishna Iyer 1941, Man 1885, Parker 1909, Radcliffe-Brown 1933, Thurston

Subsistence foraging: Food collecting for a significant or major proportion of one's subsistence

Part-time foraging: food collecting for a minor proportion of one's diet and valorizing the foraging lifestyle

& Rangachari 1909). The anthropologists who followed the colonial scholars were fascinated not only by exotic forest-dwelling peoples, but with the idea of their primordialism. Evolutionists and diffusionists supposed that SA foragers represented an original state of humanity (Das 1931, Ehrenfels 1952, Fürer-Haimendorf 1943, Roy 1925, Seligman & Seligman 1911). Yet other scholars viewed them as devolved former members of agrarian society; Veddas were assumed to be Sinhalese colonists who gave up agriculture to pursue forest foraging (Parker 1909). The case for devolution to forest-based castes rested on circumstances that some tribal peoples told folk stories of once being high castes (S. Sinha 1962), whereas medieval Indic literatures described ferocious forest-dwelling peoples who paid tribute to the early states (Thapar 2001). Generally, premodern ethnographers combined descriptions of everyday practices of foraging-based communities with large doses of preconceptions, yet their works can be reread as texts containing new insights into historical interactions.

Devolutionary models have remained difficult to validate but have gained popularity in the ensuing years. Part of the popularity stems from political interests. Coveting the resources of forest-dwelling peoples, states denied foragers their rights to raw resources (Gadgil and Guha 1993, Sivaramakrishnan 1995, Skaria 1999). Some scholars even tried to fit existing data into devolutionary theories serving nation-state interests by describing foragers as "criminal tribes" (Tolen 1991) who steal forest resources from dominant state ownership. From a colonial viewpoint, it was better to treat foragers as people who needed to be reintroduced into modern society rather than people who deserved respect and territories as distinctly different forest-dwelling societies. If some anthropologists furthered state policies as the handmaidens of colonialism, others were the manservants of development. After Indian independence, numerous projects sprang up to solve the "problem of tribal isolation" (Mahendrakumar 2005), a euphenism referring to ethnic groups that had not

assimilated into the Indian state and had not succumbed to ethnocide. Some anthropologists such as Majumdar (1929) argued for the preservation of technologically simple societies. Yet many anthropologists advocated the introduction of schools, clinics, and farming technologies to the "backward tribal communities" (Tiwari 1997:1) which are now officially categorized by the Government of India as "Primitive Tribal Groups" (Bose 1963, Bhattacharjee 1980, Misra 1977, Mohanty 2002, Sharma 2006, Sinha 1968). As Shashi (1994, p. 64) noted when writing about the Yanadi, the fallout from such policies resulted in ethnocide, and "the government's denial of Yanadis to their foraging areas caused the death-knell of Yanadi traditional subsistence" (compare Raghaviah 1962). Likewise, other foragers succumbed to the loss of their resources; they became landless tenants, suffered declining birthrates, and were assimilated into complex societies (Gurung 1989, Keyes 2002, Patnaik 2006, Reinhard 1976a, Verma 1977, Vidyarthi & Upadhyay 1980, Watters 2006). Broadly speaking, SA foraging studies concerning long-term histories and evolutionary change over time are not scientifically illegitimate pursuits; rather, they are founded on colonial interests in the absorption of small-scale societies together with the capture of their forest resources. Ethnographic studies grounded in primordialist or devolutionary positions are manifestations of the colonial imagination in primitive peoples and, as such, represent untenable folk theories.

THE NATURE OF FORAGING CULTURES

SA foraging-based societies display a range of kinship systems, ideologies, and subsistence strategies, but all are marked by a set of ideologies, work, and sociality, which differ in recognizable ways from those of food cultivators. SA foragers share certain features with other foragers worldwide, such as diffusion of authority, mobile settlement patterns, sharing of resources and tools, immediate consumption of foods, limited control over others, a valuing of individual autonomy, and a valuing of food collection rather than food cultivation. Like egalitarian foragers elsewhere, SA foragers reject the notion of being part of a society; they are free from a social framework structured by political control over individuals (Ingold 1986, 1999). Instead, they live in families, bands, and clans in which decisions are achieved consensually within social systems that are marked by diffused power. Some researchers depict such micropolitical relations as anarchies, citing notable lack of authority over labor and decision-making of other group members (Barnard & Woodburn 1988, Gardner 1991, Morris 1982). Other researchers, working with formative states and complex foraging societies, depict political decisions as forms of heterarchy, in which social power is distributed along a continuum of individuals, temporary leaders, and regionally situated bands; the elements are unranked relative to one another (Crumley 1987, p. 158). SA foraging societies generally do display political decision-making that can be defined as either heterarchical or anarchic because individual decisions cannot be enforced by elders, religious edicts, or written legal systems. Instead, people learn to be good orators, using the rhetorical power of persuasion to influence other individuals. As such, various bands and individuals form their own decisions about when to move camp and what foods to forage (Fortier 2009, p. 27). SA foraging families share not only an emphasis on individual and group autonomy, but also a distinctive form of sociality, which stresses relatedness to others rather than objectifications of others. As Bird-David (1999a) noted, SA foragers ask not "What is it?" but "Who is it?" when dealing with other sentient beings (animals, wind, weather, spirits) in their environment. Another of the key features of foragers worldwide, and in the subcontinent, involves the sharing of food, materials, and skills within foraging communities. The moral economy of sharing has been explored among communities of Onge (Pandya 1991, 1993), Raute (Fortier 2000, 2001), Nayaka (Bird-David 1990), and Paliyan (Gardner 1993). Although there are

contours of difference, all the region's foraging communities demonstrate extensive sharing of materials and resources.

One means of exploring the range of SA foraging sociality involves study of the relationship of subsistence strategies to settlement practices. South Indian foragers often adopt broad-spectrum foraging patterns. Nayaka and Paliyan, for example, opportunistically hunt a broad range of mostly smaller species and incorporate flexible settlement patterns, which enable them to adopt nomadism or sedentism under different conditions (Bird-David 1992, Gardner 1985). Northern foraging groups living in steeper montane environments, such as Rautes, Puroik, and Birhor, favor more focused foraging of medium-sized prey (langur, macaque, porcupine). Such hunting necessitates nomadic, flexible settlements near ever-changing hunting patches (Fortier 2003, Kumar 2004, Roy 1925, Stoner 1952, Williams 1968). Yet others such as Hill Kharia, Raji, and Chepang favor a mixture of broad-spectrum foraging of bats, porcupines, and deer combined with semisedentary settlements (Das 1931; Fortier 2009, p. 36; Gurung 1989; Reinhard 1976b; Roy & Roy 1937). A key feature of all SA foraging societies is that they tend to carry their technology "in the mind" (Ridington 1988, p. 107); techniques and knowledge are critical to understanding forager sociality. Spear hunting, for example, involves the hunter's knowledge of animals, their location, their habits, and also hunting techniques. For example, Chenchus use a long-tip male arrow for hunting smaller game (hare, monitor lizard, jungle cat, barking deer, giant squirrel, mongoose, jungle fowl, pea fowl) but use a triangular, barbed female point for hunting larger game (nilgai, wild boar, porcupine, mouse deer, langur). Chenchu hunters also use *kattamaram* (catamarans) to hunt sambar deer wading in rivers (Fürer-Haimendorf 1943, Shashi 1994).

Other studies explore how political contingencies shape foraging strategies. For example, there have been few prohibitions against Tibetic peoples hunting langur and macaque. Whereas Rautes in Nepal rely on monkey hunting, the Banrajis in India ceased hunting monkey a century ago because of Hindu prohibitions (Atkinson 1884, p. 367). Banrajis now hunt porcupine as their favorite prey species, one more acceptable to Hindus and forestry officials (Fortier 2009, p. 173; Negi et al. 1982). In Indian forests, officials have taxed forest resources, making traditional hunting difficult. Yet Indian foragers continue to hunt the dozen primate species of the subcontinent, often surreptitiously to avoid condemnation of their activities (Adhikary 1984b, Bhanu 1989, Morris 1982). Broadly, SA foragers adapt their prey choices and techniques to protect themselves from laws and competition from agrarian settlements. Kadars discontinued archery to avoid threats from forestry officials (Ehrenfels 1952, pp. 27, 56), Paliyans and Nayakas discontinued using hunting dogs (Gardner 2000, p. 243; Naveh 2007, p. 198), and Rautes claimed that they throw deer out of their hunting nets because this prey is reserved for farmers (Fortier 2009, p. 80).

Researchers have highlighted several commonalities and differences in the hunting and gathering repertoires of SA foragers. For example, Shompen, Banraji, Raute, Onge, Jarawa, and Chepang all use wooden-tipped spears while hunting (Caughley 2000, Fortier 2009, Pandya 2000, Patnaik 2006), yet particular spear uses are distinctive. Banrajis, for example, whittle mountain ebony (*Bauhenia variegata*) into spears shortly before dispatching prey, but they may also flip one to wield as a club, mount on the shoulder as a carrying pole, establish it in a hut as a shelter pole, reconfigure it into a digging stick, or utilize it as a walking stick. The wooden-tipped spear becomes an efficient multipurpose tool and Banrajis use few other weapons. Note, however, that Banrajis give different names for these items: spear (*lo'he*), digging stick (*dzaa'to*), and mainstay pole (*khaa bung*). Thus these spears become eminently distinct cultural items rather than undifferentiated multipurpose tools. Other foragers, such as Kusundas, have also relied on spears but incorporate them into larger hunting repertoires

to complement the use of bow/arrows, poison, axes, nets, and traps (Nebesky-Wojkowitz 1959; Reinhard 1968, 1976a; Watters 2006). Investigators have found a few uncommon technologies, as well. Chepangs and Jenu Kurumba (and recent foragers, the Chidimar) attach birdlime, a gummy resin, onto bamboo poles, which they telescope into trees to stick birds, causing them to fall to the forest floor (Caughley 2000, Gautam & Thapa-Magar 1994, Kayal 2009). Although SA blow-guns are infrequently used among SA foragers (Hutton 1924), Hill Kharias employ unique bamboo blowguns fitted with darts that have an array of two or more sharp tips (Peterson 2006, p. 279). Bow-and-arrow hunting is still a common activity among Hill Bondos (Anderson & Harrison 2008, Elwin 1950).

Hunting techniques also influence settlement sizes (Kelly 1995; Roscoe 1990, 2002); larger groups of Chepang, Raute, Raji, and Soligar use communal hunting techniques. Various people carry nets, act as beaters, and dispatch multiple animals caught in nets. Among Chepangs, spread nets are flung over large fig trees where sleeping bats are then entangled and dispatched (Caughley 1976, Gurung 1995). Among Birhors and Rautes, spread nets are tied to trees, and hunters persuade monkeys to run into the nets (Fortier 2009, Roy 1925, Singh 1997). To have enough hunters, nomadic Rautes maintain a fluctuating group of 8–30 hunters within a total settlement population of 85–150 people (Fortier 2000, Reinhard 1974). Living in smaller settlements, foragers such as Chenchu, Hill Kharia, and Shompen use spears, traps, and bow and arrow to capture single prey. Hill Pandaram have been theorized as having smaller, more autonomous groups because of commercial trade (Morris 1982). Paliyans hunt individually or in small groups using spears, billhooks, and deadfall traps (Gardner 1991, 1993). Hill Korwa and Puroik have both communal and individualistic hunting techniques (Majumdar 1929, Stoner 1952). Although investigators have researched hunting and settlement patterns in other world areas, additional research is needed in South Asia to understand the relationship of settlement patterns and hunting techniques.

With the devastation of the subcontinent's faunal resources, many South Indian foragers are better known for their foraging and knowledge of plant resources, especially those living in monsoon climates with variations ranging from warm, temperate mediterranean climates to temperate or cool subtropical climates (Peel et al. 2007). They rely on key wild resources such as yams (*Dioscorea* spp.), palms (*Borassus* spp.), and taro (*Colocasia* spp.) in addition to 100+ locally available plants. In addition to edibles, SA foragers use many similar construction materials, including *Bauhenia*, *Boehmeria*, *Dendrocalamus*, *Urtica*, and *Giardinia* for thatch, rope, woven baskets, nets, and traps. Harvesting honey and beeswax has been a key feature of many SA foraging societies. The region is home to native stinging (*Apis* spp.) and stingless bees (*Melipona* spp.), giving SA foragers an added dimension to their subsistence compared with other foragers worldwide (Crane 1999, p. 11). Veddas have kept nests of stingless bees in their rock shelters (Seligman & Seligman 1911), Malapandarams collect honey from five bee species (Morris 1982, pp. 84–87), Paliyans and Rajis climb cliffs to reach combs of aggressive *Apis dorsata* bees (Gardner 1993, pp. 126–27; Valli 1998), and Birhors collect honey from the milder *Apis* species living in tree trunks (Dash 1998, p. 216). Other studies have analyzed honey-collecting rituals, fictive relationships between hunters and bees, and emotive ties of collectors and bees (Demmer 1997, 2004; Ehrenfels 1952; Fürer-Haimendorf 1943; Gardner 1993; Rai 1985). Although there appears to be a trend toward increased commercial trade of honey and other forest products, many SA foragers incorporate honey into their subsistence diets.

FORAGER SOCIALITY

Foragers' sociality must be appreciated not only through their subsistence strategies, but also through their social and kinship organizations. Most SA foraging societies feature bilateral descent reckoning, bilateral cross-cousin marriage preferences, bilocal residence patterns, and Dravidian or Hawaiian kinship nomenclature. When clans exist, they are mostly patriclans, in which children name their father's family as the consanguinal kin. Many of the foraging societies valorize marriage with either parent's cross-sex sibling's child, enabling a social balance between consanguines and affines. Such double-helix marriage preferences extend upward in generation, enabling ego to marry a variety of kin and meshing the boundaries of consanguinal and affinal kin (Fürer-Haimendorf 1943, Morab 1977, Rao 2002).

Concerning band organization, most societies are composed of clan-based groups. Clan-based kin systems indicate flexible changes in clan identities over generations; some foraging groups even adopt the clan names of neighboring food cultivators. For example, Caughley (2000, p. 332) records Chepang-speaking groups as maintaining their traditional Red-Earth and Black-Earth clans, whereas Rai (1985) records other Chepang groups recently adopting Hindu lineage names. As part of their impression management strategies with outsiders, Rautes have recently adopted Indic clan names (Raskoti, Kalyal); whereas Banrajis also have Indic clan names (Pateto, Patchpaya, Galdiyar, Barpelo) (Fortier 2009). Broadly, SA foragers' clan identities may be of apparently long duration in some cases or, in contrast, have been recently adopted in other cases. In cases of societies with clan systems, these identities have been based on totemism (i.e., Chenchu, Puroik), territorial affiliations (Raute, Korwa), or features such as hunting specialities (Hill Korwa, Mannan, Kurumba, Yanadi). In cases of societies without clan systems (e.g., Paliyan, Kusunda, Mahamalasar, and Malapandaram), social relations are based on classificatory kinship, causing consanguineal versus affinal affiliation largely to order social relations. More complex descent groups also occur, such as moiety systems (e.g., Hill Bondo) and phratries

(Kanikkar and Kadar). Matrilineal societies reportedly include the Kanikkar, Ulladar, Mahamalasar, Malavedan, and Urali (Krishna Iyer 1941).

In the subcontinent, all the foraging societies use Dravidian forms of kinship, indicating that marriage is preferred with a cross-cousin but that parallel cousin marriage is considered incestuous. The only exception involves societies of Andaman Islanders who reportedly use Hawaiian kinship systems, which merge all cousins and siblings, making cousin-marriage untenable (Basu 1990, pp. 54–65; Radcliffe-Brown 1933, pp. 53–70). Although most of the societies under discussion valorize bilateral cross-cousin marriage, the Malavedam, Kanikkar, Kharia, Kusunda, Ulladan, and Yerukula reportedly prefer matrilateral cross-cousin marriage only. This practice may be native to these groups or otherwise indicate adoption of the marriage preferences of the surrounding dominant agrarian societies.

The foragers of the subcontinent are egalitarian, yet forms of shifting authority are invested within the kinship system. Broadly, foraging groups recognize married elder men and women as having more authority: Kinship forms denote primogeniture, persuasive elders act as temporary leaders (Sanskrit: *nayaka*), and opinions of rhetorically gifted elders hold more political weight. Among patrilineal Kusundas, for example, political power varies by the relationship of ego to others in their kinship network. Ego's paternal uncle carries more authority than do other relatives, and ego addresses him by one of six names according to his marital status and relative age (Watters 2006). In dealing with outsiders, many foraging societies have designated particular male elders to speak on their behalf. For example, among Chenchus, a "big man" (*peddamanchi*) speaks with outsiders concerning administrative issues with government officials (Turin 1999, p. 254).

Just as kinship systems regulate forager sociality, so do foragers' religious and cosmological beliefs. Foragers manifest their beliefs using portable materials and techniques, with strong emotive ties to ancestral spiritual essences rather than to memorialized individual ancestors (Adhikary 1984b; Bird-David 1999a; Gardner 1991; Morris 1982; Pandya 1993). Foragers such as the Birhor, Chepang, Raute, and Vedda believe that community members become benign human spirits (Adhikary 1984b, Caughley 2000, Fortier 2009, Meegaskumbura 1990, Seligman & Seligman 1911). Onges propitiate benign and malevolent ancestral spirits (Pandya 1993, 2000); Jenu Kurumbas argue with lonely, potentially angry beings in need of reconciliation with the living (Demmer 2001).

When conducting healing ceremonies or communicating with deceased relatives, SA foraging communities conduct shamanic rituals (Bird-David 1996, Gardner 1991, Morris 1981, Reinhard 1976b). Foragers' handling of illness and injury has been examined in terms of etiological beliefs, diagnostic practices, ritual symbolism, and dialogic discourse (Bird-David 2004; Demmer 2001, 2004, 2006; Gardner 1995). Shamanic ceremonies involve cacophonous music, possession and altered states of consciousness, confrontations with deities or spirits, and night-long events (Rahman 1959, Riboli 2000, Watters 1975), and philosophically complex belief systems have been recorded among Onges (Pandya 1993). Disease etiologies of SA foragers can be related to supernatural conflicts or attributed to natural causes and treated with herbal remedies. Studies of ethnopharmacology and ethnomedical systems suggest that foragers' naturalistic medical knowledge particularly concerns both indigenous theories of disease causation (Gardner 1995) and practical knowledge concerning fractures, bruises, stomach aches, sore muscles, and bites, among others that are common to nomadic foraging lifestyles (Manandhar 1998).

Foragers' rituals and cosmologies include not only human relatives, but nonhuman relatives and other-than-human persons. Ethnographers have recorded SA foragers as recognizing rock ancestors, grandparent deities, yam beings, bee mothers and comb lords, monkey brothers, and bear kings as relatives. For example, Chenchu youths compliment a girl by comparing her to a monkey (Thurston & Rangachari 1909, pp. II, 35), and Rautes call monkeys their "little brothers" (Fortier 2000). Broadly, SA foragers create a distinctive egalitarian, relational bond with other sentient beings whom they honor as integral to their social relations. This view asserts that animism is understood as a subjective relationship with other sentient beings and has been reformulated as a relational ontology (Bird-David 1999a, Bird-David & Naveh 2008). SA foragers also honor supernatural relatives and beings. For example, the solar deity among SA foragers in central and northern areas is known by the root cognate *Gwah* among Kusunda, Raute, and neighboring foraging horticulturalists; another name uses the root form *Dar*. A detached, distant persona, the solar deity is figured as a creator-parent figure. The Birhor described themselves as the "children of the Sun (*Darha*)" (Adhikary 1984b, Roy 1925), Banrajis say the Sun (*Diho*) created yams and water before creating themselves so that they would have something to eat, and Rautes say "*Damu* created us" (Fortier 2009, p. 147). A male deity, known as *Ber*, regulates hunting among Korwa, Kharia, Juang, Birhor, and Raute, and a female deity known as *Kayu* acts similarly for Banraji and Kusunda. Chenchus propitiate *Gare(la)*, giving flowers and asking this female deity of the forests to keep them safe during hunts, to avoid predators, to find food, etc. Veddas propitiate a male hunting deity, *Kande*, with elaborate dances, and Paliyans ask male and female deities for aid during hunts. A class of impersonal supernatural forces, representing mostly thunder, earthquakes, and other weather storms, is prevalent among some of the foraging communities. The Banraji of Kumaun, for example, fear *Bayna Ha'wa*, a "great [wind] force" that causes people to die immediately (Fortier 2009, p. 156), whereas Andaman Islanders determine camp moves according to supernatural wind forces (Pandya 1993). SA foragers acknowledge many borrowed Hindu deities, yet these play a minor role; occasionally foragers conduct rituals for Hindu villagers (Gardner 1988), attend major yearly Hindu celebrations, or incorporate local Hindu deities into healing rituals.

The ritual life of SA foragers involves expressive and material culture; SA foragers learn about rituals through observing, imitating, experimenting, and mimicking their adepts (Bird-David 2005, Gardner 2000, Naveh 2007, Pandya 2005). They also incorporate expressive cultures of play and painting (Gardner 2000, Pandya 2009), wood carving (Ehrenfels 1952, Fortier 2009), and verbal and performance arts (Demmer 2006, Elwin 1950, Fortier 2002). Expressive cultures vary, but emphasize using portable materials, verbal arts, simple/repetitious design elements, empty/open design spaces, symmetry, few boundaries, and practical arts combining form and function.

TRADE, POLITICS, AND INTERCULTURAL RELATIONS

All contemporary foragers worldwide are tied to external economies and political institutions, becoming encapsulated within neighboring dominant systems (Lee 2006, Woodburn 1982). SA foragers, too, have interacted with larger polities, and a number of writings address cross-cultural politics and social relations (i.e., Morris 1982; Obeyesekere 2009; Tharakan 2003, 2007). Unlike Native Americans, or Australian Aborigenes, SA foraging societies have experienced no great transformation during which spreading farm-based societies suddenly impinged on foragers, at least in the ethnographic record. Instead, foragers of the Old World, including Africa, have managed contact and trade relations with complex agrarian societies for millenia and continued to maintain their distinctive foraging mode of production (Allchin 1958, Denbow 1984, Lukacs 1990, Morrison & Junker 2002, Robbins et al. 2000, Stiles 1993). Contemporary SA foraging societies represent those who, despite having lost many of their natural resources to deforestation and spreading farming populations, have been unwilling to cross over to food cultivation and its distinct cultural differences.

Contemporary SA foragers reflect a continuum of adaptive responses to encapsulation, encroachment, and increasingly intensive trade. Their strategies involve activities such as protecting their beliefs and practices, accepting government land allotments and development grants, and collecting forest products for trade. For example, of the 66,000 Korwa of northern India, ~3164 depend on a food collection–based economy (Majumdar 1929, Sandhwar 1978, Singh 1994). With shrinking forest resources, these remaining foragers continue broad-spectrum hunting, using bow and arrow, axes, traps, and a few old guns to hunt pig, blackbuck, deer, feral cow, sambar, rabbits, and birds. But while hunting, they have intensified their bamboo collections, chopping reeds to weave baskets that are sold in nearby villages. Whereas bamboo used to be valued for subsistence, it has increasingly become valued for exchange, causing increased social interaction between foragers and farmers. Malapandarams too now gather forest produce in exchange for rice, cloth, and iron (Morris 1982); Birhors weave and sell *Bauhenia* rope (Roy 1925); and many SA foragers trade honey to nonforagers.

Most researchers who refer to SA foragers as "professional primitives" (Bose 1956, Fox 1969, Seligman & Seligman 1911) have failed to appreciate the degree to which foraging economies have depended on forest resources for their own subsistence. While SA foragers engage in trade with others, it hinders understanding of forager economics and sociality to label them "professional primitives," as people who subsist by selling forest products in markets. Indeed, such interpretations prevented foragers from claiming cultural rights over traditional hunting and gathering territories, causing undue hardship when they were denied access to forests by state governments. In the last generation, however, foraging studies researchers appreciate better the relationship of foragers to their environments and their resources, focusing less on trade itself and more on the role of trade within foraging economies (Bird-David 1990, 1992; Fortier 2001; Gardner 1985; Tharakan 2003). Although there exist primary ethnographies on forager resource uses, contemporary researchers need to spend much more time documenting the ethnobiology of foragers' subsistence practices and beliefs (compare Dash 1998, Singh 1997).

SA foragers have conducted not only trade with others, but a variety of economic exchanges, including patron-clientage, wage labor, bonded labor, and payment of in-kind taxes of forest produce. In their dealings with agrarian societies, foragers have used a variety of intercultural exchange strategies. Gardner (1985, 2000) describes "bicultural oscillation" and "bicultural versatility" as the flexible movement to and from underclass worker to forest forager in cultural frontier settings. This notion has enabled some scholars to account for transitions in forager lifestyles and identities (e.g., Stiles 2001). Fortier (2002) sees impression management as an interactional strategy allowing foragers to engage safely in trade with outsiders. The Seligmans (1911) described Veddas performing dances for outsiders rather than delivering forest produce. Various researchers have described silent trade techniques that foragers employ. For example, Banrajis wordlessly leave wooden bowls in villagers' courtyards, expecting them to fill the bowls with grain and keep the bowls (Atkinson 1884). Kusundas leave deer in villager courtyards hoping for an exchange for villager goods (Nebesky-Wojkowitz 1959). Puroiks provide forest produce to their agrarian neighbors on occasion (Fürer-Haimendorf 1955, p. 157; Stoner 1952). One area of notable difference among SA foragers involves their perceptions of outsiders and their reactions to outsiders during trade and communication. Whereas some societies, such as Paliyans, are notably peaceful (Gardner 2004), even being characterized as "original peaceful societies" in popular literatures, others such as Sentinelese, Ongees and Jarawa are known in the literature for violent reactions to encroachment and outsiders' trade initiatives (Pandit 1990, Pandya 2000, Radcliffe-Brown 1933).

Thus, SA foragers have engaged in intercultural trade and communication through a variety of strategies. Reviewing the literature, it is notable that foragers who traded in nonrenewable resources, particularly bushmeat, often fell into patronage or peonage and/or assimilated into farming communities. Foragers who traded in quickly renewable resources (jute, rope, carved wood, bamboo, honey) apparently have experienced more cultural resilience. Such economic relations may have been based on barter in the past, but with agrarian encroachment, some foragers engage in other types of economic exchange such as wage labor and marketing. It may not matter whether SA foragers developed economies of exchange with others for them to be considered foragers; such relations affected but did not alter the fundamental realities of SA foraging as founded on hunting and gathering, kinship-based social organizations, and spirit-based religions.

EMERGING TRENDS AND CONCLUSIONS

Foraging groups throughout the subcontinent continue to share a constellation of features distinguishing them from neighboring agrarian populations. In addition to avoidance of food cultivation, contemporary SA foraging societies use simple tools, share tools and resources, rely on short-term food storage systems, consume food resources directly, avoid manipulation of uncultivated resources, live in biologically rich and diverse environments, avoid sociopolitical control over others, use kinship-based social systems, worship relatively complex groups of spirits and deities, and use animate relational ontologies to organize their cultural worlds. Compared with agrarian populations, SA hunter-gatherers are more mobile and flexible in their land use, influence others through persuasion rather than physical force, place sanctions on accumulation of property, and employ political practices to ensure that elders' authority is limited. All the contemporary foraging societies of southern Asia in this review are egalitarian rather than nonegalitarian foragers (Kelly 1995, p. 31; Woodburn 1982).

As Hymes (1973) advocated years ago, the best theory making is done among a field of theories rather than among dominant paradigms that are constantly challenged, torn down, and reconstituted. The study of SA foragers ultimately benefits from the creative theory making of many rather than the top-down theory making of a few. However, considering there are 40 distinct foraging populations in South Asia, the production of notable anthropological dissertations and monographs in the past decade has been relatively minimal (Demmer 2006, Fortier 2009, Gardner 2000, Kumar 2004, Naveh 2007, Norström 2003, Pandya 2009, Rao 2002, Riboli 2000, Samal 2000, Venkateswar 2004, Watters 2006). Offsetting this trend, however, studies of SA foraging societies are broadening and being undertaken in development studies, sociology, cultural geography, linguistics, and botany, among other disciplines (i.e., Singh 1997, Manandhar 1998).

In the near future, one should expect to see anthropological research concerning politics, identity, ethnobiology, cultural ecology, sociolinguistics, cognitive studies, native epistemologies, and human rights. For example, foraging communities soon may be able to demonstrate rights to their aboriginal territories and resources. SA area scholars will conceivably facilitate contemporary foraging peoples' efforts to gain their land and civil rights. Most groups emphasize that they need access to rich forest resources to continue their foraging lifestyles, yet many have been evicted from their traditional habitats (Gardner 2004, Reddy & Reddy 1987, Stegeborn 1999). Giving oral testimony to their hardships, researchers increasingly facilitate their endeavors to obtain rights to traditional resources (Norström 2003, Singh 1997, Venkateswar 2004). Overall, although SA foraging communities have had many different historical experiences, they all continue to depend on foraged foods and anchor their identities as people living in biologically rich and diverse environments.

DISCLOSURE STATEMENT

The author is not aware of any affiliations, memberships, funding, or financial holdings that might be perceived as affecting the objectivity of this review.

ACKNOWLEDGMENTS

Research relevant to the preparation of this article is gratefully acknowledged from the Fulbright Foundation in 2004–2005 and the Wenner-Gren Foundation for Anthropological Research in 1997 and 2001. Special thanks go to Peter Gardner for helpful comments on the manuscript.

LITERATURE CITED

Adhikary AK. 1984a. Hunters and gatherers in India: a preliminary appraisal of their structure and transformation. *J. Indian Anthropol. Soc.* 19:8–16

Adhikary AK. 1984b. *Society and world view of the Birhor: a nomadic, hunting, and gathering community of Orissa.* Calcutta: Anthropological Survey of India

Aiyappan A. 1937. Social and physical anthropology of the Nayadis of Malabar. *Bulletin of the Madras Government Museum, New Series,* II(4):1–23. Madras: Government Press

Aiyappan A. 1948. *Report on the Socio-Economic Conditions of the Aboriginal Tribes of the Province of Madras.* Madras: Gov. Press

Allchin B. 1958. The late stone age of Ceylon. *J. R. Anthropol. Soc. of Great Britain and Ireland* 88:179–201

Ananthakrishna Iyer LK. 1909. *The Cochin Tribes and Castes.* Madras: Higginbotham

Anderson G, Harrison KD. 2008. Remo (Bondo). In *The Munda Languages,* ed. G Anderson, pp. 557–632. London: Routledge

Atkinson ET. 1884. *The Himalayan District of the North-Western Provinces of India,* Vol. 2. Allahabad: North-Western Prov. Oudh Gov. Press

Barnard A, Woodburn J. 1988. Property, power, and ideology in hunting and gathering societies: an introduction. In *Hunters and Gatherers: Property, Power, and Ideology,* ed. T Ingold, D Riches, J Woodburn, pp. 4–32. New York: Berg

Basu BK. 1990. *The Onge: Negrito Hunter-Gatherers of Little Andaman.* Calcutta: Seagull Books

Bhanu BA. 1989. *The Cholanaikan of Kerala.* Calcutta: Anthropol. Survey India

Bhattacharjee B. 1980. *Cultural Oscillation: A Study on Patua [Juang] Culture.* Calcutta: Naya Prokash. Erratum. 1980. Calcutta: Naya Prakash

Bird-David N. 1990. The giving environment: another perspective on the economic system of gatherer-hunters. *Curr. Anthropol.* 31:183–96

Bird-David N. 1992. Beyond "the hunting and gathering mode of subsistence": culture-sensitive observations on the Nayaka and other modern hunter-gatherers. *Man* 27:19–44

Bird-David N. 1994. The Nilgiri tribal systems: a view from below. *Modern Asian Studies* 28:339–55

Bird-David N. 1996. Puja or sharing with the gods? On ritualized possession among Nayaka of South India. *Eastern Anthrop.* 49:259–76

Bird-David N. 1999a. "Animism" revisited: personhood, environment, and relational epistemology. *Curr. Anthropol.* 40(Suppl.):S67–91

Bird-David N. 1999b. Nayaka. See Lee & Daly 1999, pp. 57–60

Bird-David N. 2004. Illness images and joined beings. A critical/Nayaka perspective on incorporeality. *Social Anthropol.* 12:325–39

Bird-David N. 2005. Studying children in "hunter-gatherer" societies: reflections from a Nayaka perspective. In *Hunter-gatherer childhoods: evolutionary, developmental & cultural perspectives,* ed. BS Hewlett, ME Lamb, pp. 92–104. New Brunswick: Aldine Transaction

Bird-David N, Naveh D. 2008. Relational epistemology, immediacy, and conservation: Or, what do the Nayaka try to conserve? *J. Stud. Relig. Nat. Cult.* 2:55–73

Bose NK. 1956. Some observations on nomadic castes of India. *Man India* 36:1–6

Bose NK. 1963. *Fifty Years of Science in India: Anthropology and Archaeology*. Calcutta: Indian Sci. Congr. Assoc.

Brow J. 1978. *Vedda Villages of Anuradhapura: The Historical Anthropology of a Community in Sri Lanka*. Seattle: Univ. Wash. Press

Brow J. 1990. The incorporation of a marginal community within the Sinhalese nation [Anuradhapura Veddas]. *Anthropol. Q.* 63:7–17

Caughley R. 1976. Chepang whistled talk. In *Speech Surrogates: Drum and Whistle Systems*, ed. T Sebeok, D Umiker, pp. 966–92. New York: Mouton

Caughley RC. 2000. *Dictionary of Chepang: A Tibeto-Burman Language of Nepal*. Canberra: Aust. Natl. Univ.

Census of India. 2001. *Total population, population of scheduled castes and scheduled tribes and their proportions to the total population*. **http://www.censusindia.net**

Crane E. 1999. *The World History of Beekeeping and Honey Hunting*. London: Routledge

Crumley CL. 1987. A dialectical critique of hierarchy. In *Power Relations and State Formation*, ed. TC Patterson, CW Gailey, pp. 155–68. Washington, DC: Am. Anthropol. Assoc. Occas. Publ.

Dalton ET. 1872. *Descriptive Ethnology of Bengal*. Calcutta: Off. Supt. Gov. Print.

Das T. 1931. *The Wild Kharias of Dhalbhum*. Calcutta: Univ. Calcutta

Dash J. 1998. *Human Ecology of Foragers: A Study of the Kharia (Savara), Ujia (Savara), and Birhor in Similipal Hills*. New Delhi: Commonwealth

Demmer U. 1997. Voices in the forest. The field of gathering among the Jenu Kurumba. In *Blue Mountains Revisited: Cultural Studies on the Nilgiri Hills*, ed. P Hockings, pp. 164–91. Delhi: Oxford Univ. Press

Demmer U. 2001. Always an argument: persuasive tools in the death rituals of the Jenu Kurumba. *Anthropos* 96:475–90

Demmer U. 2004. Visible knowledge: a test case from South India. *Vis. Anthropol.* 17:107–16

Demmer U. 2006. *Rhetorik, Poetik, Performanz: Das Ritual und Seine Dynamic bei den Jenu Kurumba (Südindien)*. Berlin: Münster

Denbow J. 1984. Prehistoric herders and foragers of the Kalahari: the evidence for 1500 years of interaction. In *Past and Present in Hunter Gatherer Studies*, ed. Carmel Schrire, pp. 175–93. Orlando: Academic Press

Dharmadasa KNO, SWR de A Samarsinghe, eds. 1990. *The Vanishing Aborigines: Sri Lanka's Veddas in Transition*. New Delhi: Vikas

Ehrenfels UR. 1952. *Kadar of Cochin*. Madras: Univ. Madras

Elwin V. 1950. *Bondo Highlander*. Bombay: Oxford Univ. Press

Emeneau MB. 1989. The Languages of the Nilgiris. *Blue Moutains: The ethnography and biogeography of a south Indian region*. Delhi: Oxford Univ. Press

Forsyth J. 1889. *The Highlands of Central India: Notes on Their Forests and Wild Tribes, Natural History and Sports*. London: Chapman and Hall

Fortier J. 2000. Monkey's thigh is the shaman's meat: ideologies of sharing among the Raute of western Nepal. *Senri Ethnol. Ser.* 53:113–47

Fortier J. 2001. Sharing, hoarding, and theft: exchange and resistance in forager-farmer relations. *Ethnology* 40:193–211

Fortier J. 2002. The arts of deception: verbal performances by the Raute of Nepal. *J. R. Anthropol. Inst.* 8(2):233–57

Fortier J. 2003. Reflections on Raute identity. *Stud. Nep. Hist. Soc.* 8:317–48

Fortier J. 2009. *Kings of the Forest: The Cultural Resilience of Himalayan Hunter Gatherers*. Honolulu: Univ. Hawai'i Press

Fox R. 1969. Professional primitives: hunters and gatherers of nuclear South Asia. *Man India* 49:139–60

Fürer-Haimendorf Cv. 1943. *The Chenchus: Jungle Folk of the Deccan*. London: Macmillan

Fürer-Haimendorf Cv. 1955. *Himalayan Barbary*. London: J Murray

Gadgil M, Guha R. 1993. *This Fissured Land: An Ecological History of India*. Berkeley: Univ. Calif. Press

Gardner PM. 1985. Bicultural oscillation as a long-term adaptation to cultural frontiers: cases and questions. *Hum. Ecol.* 13:411–32

Gardner PM. 1988. Pressures for Tamil propriety in Paliyan social organization. In *Hunters and Gatherers 1: History, Evolution, and Social Change*, ed. T Ingold, D Riches, J Woodburn, pp. 91–106. Oxford: Berg

Gardner PM. 1991. Foragers' pursuit of individual autonomy. *Curr. Anthropol.* 32:543–72

Gardner PM. 1993. Dimensions of subsistence foraging in South India. *Ethnology* 32:109–44

Gardner P. 1995. Illness and response among South Indian foragers. *Medical Anthropol.* 16:119–35

Gardner PM. 2000. *Bicultural Versatility as a Frontier Adaptation among Paliyan Foragers of South India*. Lewiston, NY: Edwin Mellen

Gardner PM. 2004. Respect for all: the Paliyans of South India. In *Keeping the Peace: Conflict Resolution and Peaceful Societies around the World*, ed. G Kemp, DP Fry, pp. 53–71. New York: Routledge

Gautam R, Thapa-Magar AK. 1994. *Tribal Ethnography of Nepal*. Delhi: Book Faith India

Gurung GM. 1989. *The Chepangs: A Study in Continuity and Change*. Lalitpur: SB Shah

Gurung GM. 1995. *Report from a Chepang Village*. Kathmandu: S Gurung

Hamilton FB. 1819. *An Account of the Kingdom of Nepal and of the Territories Annexed to this Dominion by the House of Gurkha*. Edinburgh: Archibald Constable

Hitchcock RK, Biesele B. 2000. Introduction. In *Hunters and Gatherers in the Modern World*, ed. PP Schweitzer, RK Hitchcock, M Biesele, pp. 1–28. New York: Berghahan

Hutton JH. 1924. The occurence of the blow-gun in Assam. *Man* 24:104–6

Hymes D. 1973. Speech and language: on the origins and foundations of inequality among speakers. *Daedalus* 102(3):59–86

Ingold T. 1986. *The Appropriation of Nature: Essays on Human Ecology and Social Relations*. Manchester, UK: Manchester Univ. Press

Ingold T. 1999. On the social relations of the hunter-gatherer band. See Lee & Daly 1999, pp. 399–410

Kayal R. 2009. *Somanna on Indigenous Knowledge of Jenu Kurubar, Part 2*. 5 min., 36 sec. Windows Media Video. **http://www.youtube.com/watch?v=DizTiIjnmTM**

Kelly R. 1995. *The Foraging Spectrum*. Washington, DC: Smithson. Inst. Press

Keyes C. 2002. Peoples of Asia—science and politics in the classification of ethnic groups in Thailand, China, and Vietnam. *J. of Asian Studies* 61(4):1163–1203

Knox R. 1681. *An Historical Relation of the Island Ceylon, in the East-Indies*. London: Richard Chiswell

Krishna Iyer LA. 1941. *The Travancore Tribes and Castes*. Vol. 3. Trivandrum: Gov. Press

Kumar S. 2004. *The Birhors of Chotanagpur region: A Study in Tribal Geography*. New Delhi: Rajesh

Lee RB, Daly R, eds. 1999. *The Cambridge Encyclopedia of Hunters and Gatherers*. Cambridge, UK: Cambridge Univ. Press

Lee RB. 2006. Twenty-first century indigenism. *Anthropol. Theory* 6:455–79

Lukacs J. 1990. On hunter-gatherers and their neighbors in prehistoric India: contact and pathology. *Curr. Anthropol.* 31:183–6

Majumdar DN. 1929. The Korwas of the United Provinces. *Man India* 1:237–50

Man EH. 1885. *On the Aboriginal Inhabitants of the Andaman Islands*. London: R. Anthropol. Inst.

Manandhar NP. 1998. Native phytotherapy among the Raute tribes of Dadeldhura district, Nepal. *J. Ethnopharmacol.* 60:199–206

Meegaskumbura PB. 1990. Religious beliefs of the Veddas in relation to their world-view. See Dharmadasa & Samarasinghe 1990, pp. 99–140

Misra PK. 1977. The Jenu Kurubas. In *The Primitive Tribes: The First Steps*, ed. S Sinha, BD Sharma, pp. 103–31. New Delhi: Gov. India

Mohanty SC. 2002. *Development of Primitive Tribal Groups in India*. Delhi: Gyan Books

Morab SG. 1977. *The Soliga of Biligiri, Rangana Hills*. Calcutta: Anthropol. Survey India

Morris B. 1981. Hill gods and ecstatic cults: notes on the religion of a hunting and gathering people. *Man in India* 61:203–36

Morris B. 1982. *Forest Traders*. London: Althone

Morrison KD, Junker L. 2002. *Forager-Traders in South and Southeast Asia: Long-Term Histories*. Cambridge, UK: Cambridge Univ. Press

Naveh D. 2007. *Continuity and change in Nayaka epistemology and subsistence economy: a hunter-gatherer case from South India*. PhD thesis. Univ. Haifa, Israel

Nebesky-Wojkowitz R. 1959. Kusunda and Chepang: notes on two little-known tribes of Nepal. *Bull. Int. Com. Urgent Anthropol. Ethnol. Res.* 2:77–84

Negi RS, Raha MK, Das JC. 1982. The Raji and their economy. In *Economies of the Tribes and their Transformation*, ed. KS Singh, pp. 153–58. New Delhi: Concept

Norström C. 2003. '*They call for us*': *Strategies for securing autonomy among the Paliyans, hunter-gatherers of the Palni Hills, South India*. Stockholm: Stockholm Univ.

Obeyesekere G. 2009. Colonial histories and Vaada primitivism: an unorthodox reading of Kandy Period texts. **http://vedda.org/obeyesekere1.htm**

Pandit TN. 1990. *The Sentinelese*. Kolkata: Seagull Books

Pandya V. 1991. Tribal cosmology: displacing and replacing processes in Andamanese places. In *Tribal Thought and Culture: Essays in Honor of Surajit Chandra Sinha*, ed. B Saraswati, pp. 81–103. New Delhi: Concept

Pandya V. 1993. *Above the Forest: A Study of Andamanese Ethnoanemology, Cosmology, and the Power of Ritual*. Delhi: Oxford Univ. Press

Pandya V. 2000. Making of the other: vignettes of violence in Andamanese culture. *Crit. Anthropol.* 20:359–91

Pandya V. 2005. Deforesting among Andamanese children: political economy and history of schooling. In *Hunter-Gatherer Childhoods: Evolutionary, Developmental and Cultural Perspectives*, ed. BS Hewlett, ME Lamb, pp. 385–406. New Brunswick, NJ/London: Aldine Trans.

Pandya V. 2009. *In the Forest: Visual and Material Worlds of Andamanese History (1858–2006)*. New York: Univ. Press Am.

Parker H. 1909. *Ancient Ceylon: An Account of the Aborigines and a Part of the Early Civilisation*. London: Luzac

Patnaik R. 2006. The last foragers: ecology of Forest Shompen. In *Anthropology of Primitive Tribes*, ed. PD Sharma, pp. 116–29. New Delhi: Ser. Publ.

Peel MC, Finlayson BL, McMahon TA. 2007. Updated world map of the Köppen-Geiger climate classification. *Hydrol. Earth Syst. Sci. Discuss.* 4:439–73

Peterson J. 2006. *Kharia-English Lexicon*. Osnabrück: Univ. Osnabrück

Radcliffe-Brown AR. 1933 (1922). *The Andaman Islanders*. Cambridge, UK: Cambridge Univ. Press

Raghaviah V. 1962. *The Yanadis*. New Delhi: Bharatiya Adimjati Sevak Sangh

Rahman R. 1959. Shamanistic and related phenomena in northern and middle India. *Anthropos* LIV:681–760

Rai N. 1985. *People of the Stones: The Chepangs of Central Nepal*. Kathmandu: Cent. Nepal. Asian Stud.

Rao NS. 2002. *Ethnography of a Nomadic Tribe: A Study of Yanadi*. New Delhi: Concept

Reddy PS, Reddy AM. 1987. The displaced Yanadis of Sriharikota Island: a study of changing interactions between environment and culture. *Mankind Q.* 27:435–45

Reinhard J. 1968. The Kusunda: ethnographic notes on a hunting tribe of Nepal. *Bull. Int. Com. Urgent Anthropol. Ethnol. Res.* 10:95–110

Reinhard J. 1974. The Raute: notes on a nomadic hunting and gathering tribe of Nepal. *Kailash* 2:233–71

Reinhard J. 1976a. The Bana Rajas—a vanishing Himalayan tribe. *Contrib. Nepal. Stud.* 4:1–22

Reinhard J. 1976b. Shamanism among the Raji of Southwest Nepal. In *Spirit Possession in the Nepal Himalayas*, ed. J Hitchcock, R Jones, pp. 263–92. Warminster: Aris and Phillips

Riboli D. 2000. *Tunsuriban, Shamanism in the Chepang of Southern and Central Nepal*. Kathmandu: Mandala Book Point

Ridington R. 1988. Knowledge, power, and the individual in subarctic hunting societies. *Am. Anthropol.* 90:98–110

Roscoe P. 1990. The bow and spreadnet: ecological origins of hunting technology. *Am. Anthropol.* 92:691–701

Roscoe P. 2002. The hunters and gatherers of New Guinea. *Curr. Anthropol.* 43:153–62

Roy SC. 1925. *The Birhors, A Little-Known Jungle Tribe of Chota Nagpur*. Ranchi: Man in India Off.

Roy SC, Roy RC. 1937. *The Kharias*. Ranchi: Man in India Off.

Samal P. 2000. *Van Rawats: A Tribe in Peril*. Nainatal: Gyanodaya Prakashan

Sandhwar AN. 1978. *The Korwa of Palamau: A Study of Their Society and Economy*. Wien, Föhrenau: Elisabeth Stiglmayr

Schalk P. 2004. *Vädi into Vanniyalatto: Transformation of Images of the Lankan Vaddo*. Uppsala: Uppsala Univ.

Seligman CG, Seligman B. 1911. *The Veddas*. Cambridge, UK: Cambridge Univ. Press

Sharma PD (editor). 2006. *The Anthropology of Primitive Tribes in India*. New Delhi: Serials Publications.

Shashi SS. 1994. *Encyclopedia of Indian tribes*. New Delhi: Anmol

Singh KS. 1994. *The Scheduled Tribes*. Delhi: Oxford Univ. Press

Singh NB. 1997. *The Endangered Raute Tribe: Ethnobiology and Biodiversity*. Kathmandu: GLORECA

Sinha DP. 1968. *Culture Change in an Intertribal Market*. New York: Asia Publ. House

Sinha S. 1962. State formation and Rajput myth in tribal Central India. *Man India* XLII:35–80

Sivaramakrishnan K. 1995. Colonialism and forestry in India: imagining the past in present politics. *Comp. Stud. Soc. Hist.* 37:3–40

Skaria A. 1999. *Hybrid Histories: Forests, Frontiers and Wildness in Western India*. Delhi: Oxford Univ. Press

Stegeborn W. 1999. The Wanniyala-aetto (Veddahs) of Sri Lanka. See Lee & Daly 1999, pp. 269–73

Stiles D. 2001. Hunter-gatherer studies: the importance of context. *African study monographs supplment* 26:41–65

Stiles D. 1993. Hunter-gatherer trade in wild forest products in the early centuries A.D. with the Port of Broach, India. *Asian Perspect.* 32:153–67

Stoner CR. 1952. The Sulung tribe of the Assam Himalayas. *Anthropos* 47:947–62

Thapar R. 2001. Perceiving the forest: early India. *Stud. Hist.* 2:1–16

Tharakan CG. 2003. The mixed economy of the South Indian Kurumbas. *Ethnology* 42:323–34

Tharakan CG. 2007. The Mudugua and Kurumba of Kerala, south India and the social organization of hunting and gathering. *J. Ecol. Anthropol.* 11:5–24

Thurston E, Rangachari K. 1909. *Castes and Tribes of Southern India*. Madras: Gov. Press

Tolen RJ. 1991. Colonizing and transforming the criminal tribesman: the Salvation Army in British India. *Am. Ethnol.* 18(1):106–25

Turin M. 1999. Chenchu. *The Cambridge Encyclopedia of Hunter-Gatherers*, ed. RB Lee, R Daly, pp. 252–56. Cambridge: Cambridge Univ. Press

Valentijn F. 2002 (1724). *Oud en nieuw Oost-Indiën*. Franeker: Van Wijnen

Valli E. 1998. *Hunting for Honey: Adventures with the Rajis of Nepal*. London: Thames & Hudson

Van Driem G. 2001. *Languages of the Himalayas*. Leiden: Brill

Venkateswar S. 2004. *Development and ethnocide: colonial practices in the Andaman Islands*. Somerset, N.J.: Transaction Publishers

Verma KK. 1977. *Culture, Ecology, and Population: An Anthropo-Demographic Study*. New Delhi: Natl. Pub. House

Vidyarthi LP, Upadhyay VS. 1980. *The Kharia, Then and Now: A Comparative Study of Hill, Dhelki, and Dudh Kharia of the Central-Eastern Region of India*. New Delhi: Concept

Watters DE. 1975. Siberian shamanistic traditions among the Kham-Magars of Nepal. *Contrib. Nepalese Stud.* 2:123–68

Watters DE. 2006. Notes on Kusunda grammar: a language isolate of Nepal. *Himal. Ling. Arch.* 3:1–182

Williams B. 1968. The Birhor of India and some comments on band organization. In *Man the Hunter*, ed. RB Lee, I DeVore, pp. 126–31. Chicago: Aldine

Woodburn J. 1982. Egalitarian societies. *Man* 17:431–51

Zvelebil K. 1981. Problems of identification and classification of some Nilagiri tribes. *Anthropos* 76:467–528

Zvelebil K. 1988. Jenu Kurumba: brief report on a "tribal" language of the Nilgiri area. *J. Am. Orient. Soc.* 2:297–301

RELATED RESOURCES

Nepalnews.com. 2009. Rautes seek guarantee of their right to live in forest. 3 min., 17 sec. **http://www.youtube.com/watch?v=h7YdRfDGNZ4**

Puttagunta SM. 2008. *Chenchus: Children of the forest*. Srujana Movies. 22 min., 11 sec. **http://www.youtube.com/watch?v=-6IZzWSMJTU**

Zahieruddin Z. 2009. Sri Lanka (ceylon)—Vedda ceremonial song. 2 min. 29 sec. **http://www.youtube.com/watch?v=9XDwIubm4UI**

The Biology of Paternal Care in Human and Nonhuman Primates

Eduardo Fernandez-Duque,[1,2] Claudia R. Valeggia,[1,2] and Sally P. Mendoza[3]

[1]Department of Anthropology, University of Pennsylvania, Philadelphia, Pennsylvania 19104; email: eduardof@sas.upenn.edu, valeggia@sas.upenn.edu

[2]Centro de Ecología Aplicada del Litoral-Conicet, Corrientes 3400, Argentina

[3]California National Primate Research Center, University of California, Davis, California 95616; email: spmendoza@ucdavis.edu

Annu. Rev. Anthropol. 2009. 38:115–30

First published online as a Review in Advance on June 23, 2009

The *Annual Review of Anthropology* is online at anthro.annualreviews.org

This article's doi: 10.1146/annurev-anthro-091908-164334

0084-6570/09/1021-0115$20.00

Key Words

fatherhood, alloparenting, monogamy, attachment, development

Abstract

Among primates, intense paternal care is manifested in only a few distantly related species, including humans. Thus, neither purely phylogenetic nor socioecological hypotheses can explain its presence or the variability in the expression of paternal behaviors. Traditional theoretical models for the evolution of paternal care can now be reexamined, focusing on male-female interactions as a possible key to understanding parental strategies. At a proximate level, the existing evidence implies a common physiological substrate for both paternal behavior and pair-bonds. Vasopressin, and perhaps prolactin and testosterone, apparently underlies the endocrinological bases of paternal care, and neuroanatomical reward pathways may be involved in the formation of attachment bonds. Understanding of the genetic structure of primate populations and the neurogenetics of social behavior is also emerging. A multidisciplinary approach that also considers epigenetic and transgenerational effects promises to open new avenues to explain the flexible nature of paternal care in primates.

INTRODUCTION

Paternal care:
behaviors performed
by putative/social
fathers, which appear
to have positive effects
on infant development,
growth, well-being,
and/or survival

Paternal investment:
behaviors performed
by putative/social
fathers, which increase
the probability of the
infant's survival

Few aspects of primate behavior are so intriguing, yet so poorly understood, as the expression of intense paternal care. Although rare, paternal care in a few primate species and some human societies includes providing protection from predators and other conspecifics, sharing food, playing, grooming, carrying infants, teaching hunting skills, and singing lullabies. All avian and mammalian males face the uncertainty of paternity because of internal fertilization. Participation of mammalian fathers in the most essential parental activities is further constrained by pregnancy and lactation. Yet, in spite of these limitations, some primate males display intense paternal care (Gubernick & Klopfer 1981, Kleiman 1985, Kleiman & Malcolm 1981, Smuts & Gubernick 1992, Whitten 1987, Wright 1990).

Field and laboratory data on primate paternal care have accumulated to the point where a synthesis of its expression is possible. Paternal care among primates, illustrated in its extreme form by our research on a few nonhuman primate species and some human societies, is varied (Di Fiore et al. 2007; Fernandez-Duque et al. 2008, 2009; Mendoza & Mason 1986a,b; Rotundo et al. 2005; Valeggia 2009; Wolovich et al. 2008). Using information from disciplines as disparate as evolutionary biology and neuroscience, we provide an initial attempt to understand this variation, ecological and social determinants, and common proximate mechanisms.

A TAXONOMY OF PATERNAL CARE

Paternal Care and Paternal Investment

Paternal/parental care, biparental care, paternal/parental investment, and alloparental care are terms regularly mentioned in the primate literature. Given the different ways in which they are used, it is important to state that our work has focused on paternal care, not paternal investment. Paternal care and paternal investment are frequently used interchangeably, and wrongly so (Sheldon 2002). Thus, we do not attempt to relate the two terms or to use paternal care as proxy for paternal investment.

Paternal care is a suite of behaviors performed by a mature male (the putative/social father of the immature young), which would not be performed in the absence of the young. These behaviors are directed to the infant and have a positive effect on infant development, growth, well-being, or survival. They may include carrying, grooming, playing, sharing food, feeding, cleaning, retrieving, huddling, babysitting, defending, and teaching. Some of these behaviors may continue beyond the stage of development when they are necessary for infant survival. This is so because infant primates, unlike other mammals, experience a long period of dependency during which they require significant assistance.

Infants play an active role in directing their own development and have considerable skill in eliciting care behaviors. Generally the mother is the primary target of the infant's solicitation of care, but in many primate species other group members are also responsive to infants. Alloparental care, care provided by nonmothers, has received significant attention recently (Hrdy 2005, 2008; Ross & MacLarnon 2000; Tardif 1997), but here we are concerned with the relatively rare situation where alloparental care is provided by the putative father.

Paternal care, as defined above, is widespread among birds and fish and is occasionally present in amphibians, insects, and worms (Beltran & Boissier 2008, Clutton-Brock 1991, Trumbo 2006, Zeh & Smith 1985). On the other hand, paternal care is relatively rare in mammals. Among the mammalian orders, it is more frequent in carnivores, rodents, and primates (Kleiman & Malcolm 1981, Woodroffe & Vincent 1994).

Paternal Care in Nonhuman Primates

In most primates, males may be tolerant of infants, or they may occasionally interact affiliatively with them without any clear direct or indirect paternal care provided (Whitten 1987, Wright 1990). The most conclusive evidence for the benefits that infants may accrue from these infrequent interactions with males comes from studies of wild savannah baboons (*Papio cynocephalus*). Adult males selectively support their offspring in agonistic disputes with a direct effect on the offspring fitness (Buchan et al. 2003, Charpentier et al. 2008). It is still not fully understood whether fathers can somehow recognize offspring likely to be their own or if it is a generalized response to all infants. Still, the putative father interacts affiliatively with infants only in very particular and restrictive circumstances.

It is only among a handful of primate genera that the relationship between males and infants takes on a qualitatively different form. Among siamangs, tamarins, marmosets, titi monkeys, owl monkeys, and some human societies, paternal care is direct, conspicuous, and sustained across time and circumstance. These taxa are only distantly related, suggesting that paternal care may result from evolutionary trajectories developing under different social and ecological conditions (**Figure 1**, see color insert; Di Fiore & Fernandez-Duque 2007).

Paternal care among siamangs is intriguing. All hylobatids (i.e., gibbons, lesser apes) show the traditional correlates of paternal care—social monogamy, territoriality, and reduced sexual dimorphism—but it is only the siamangs (*Symphalangus syndactylus*) that show paternal care. Female siamangs take exclusive care of the infants during the first year of life, but adult males and older juveniles carry infants beginning in the second year (Chivers 1974, Lappan 2008).

Generalized sharing of infant transport is also exhibited by the callitrichids of South America (**Figure 1**). Alloparental care (also called cooperative breeding) is the norm, and the mother, father, siblings, and other group members share in the care of the twins (or triplets) that are born twice a year (Bales et al. 2000, Tardif et al. 2002, Tardif & Garber 1994, Zahed et al. 2007, Ziegler 2000). The infants appear to be highly attractive to group members who often compete for the opportunity to carry dependent infants.

Nowhere is paternal care more extensive and more obligate than among titi monkeys (*Callicebus*) and owl monkeys (*Aotus*, **Figures 2** and **3**, see color insert). Both genera live in small groups consisting of an adult pair and 2–4 young (Fernandez-Duque 2007, Norconk 2007). Females give birth to a single infant each year and the male is the primary carrier for the infant, each assuming their roles soon after birth. Dependent infants may be carried as much as 90% of the time by their putative fathers and transfer to the mother for brief periods usually surrounding active nursing bouts (Dixson & Fleming 1981, Fernandez-Duque et al. 2009, Fragaszy et al. 1982, Mendoza & Mason 1986b, Wright 1984). Siblings very infrequently participate in transport of the infant (Fernandez-Duque et al. 2008). In titi monkeys, infants develop a preference for their fathers over their mothers (Mendoza & Mason 1986b), demonstrated via a strong pituitary-adrenal stress response when separated from their fathers but not from their mothers (Hoffman et al. 1995).

Paternal Care in Human Societies

Human societies vary in the expression of paternal care, from complete absence or aloofness to great intimacy and direct care. A range of variation manifested even within foraging societies. At one end, Aché fathers of the Paraguayian forests seldom hold or interact with infants and young children (Hill & Hurtado 1996). At the other end, male Aka Pygmies are heavily involved in paternal care, spending up to 22% of their time holding young infants (Hewlett 1991).

Societies in both developed and developing countries, with varying levels of industrialization fall within this broad spectrum of expression of paternal care. Intercultural variability in fathering seems to be associated with the local ecology and social environment. Household composition, availability of mating opportunities and resources, the extent of extrinsic mortality, and pathogen stress have all been identified as potential correlates of paternal care in humans (Hewlett 1991, 1992; Marlowe 1999; Quinlan 2007).

In addition to the great variability in paternal care among human groups, there is usually significant variation among men within societies known for their high levels of paternal care. In those societies, some men do not participate in child care, whereas others cannot do more (Hewlett 1991). Even though human mothers clearly need a considerable amount of help rearing their offspring, paternal care among humans is highly variable and far from a universal trait. This disconnect leads anthropologist Sarah Hrdy to talk about "the paradox of facultative fathering" in the human species (Hrdy 2005, 2008).

EVOLUTION OF PATERNAL CARE

The 1970s and 1980s brought a series of predominantly qualitative theoretical models that attempted to explain the evolution of parental investment or parental care (Dawkins & Carlisle 1976, Hamilton 1984, Kurland & Gualin 1984, Lancaster & Lancaster 1983, Maynard Smith 1977, Trivers 1972). The models emphasized primarily parental investment with a focus on cost-benefit analyses. Nonetheless, two hypotheses remain particularly relevant in attempting to explain the evolution of paternal care.

The first hypothesis is that paternal care evolved in response to the necessity of obligate biparental care to rear offspring successfully (Achenbach & Snowdon 2002; Fite et al. 2005; Hill & Hurtado 1996; Key & Aiello 2000; Miller et al. 2006; Smucny et al. 2004; Tardif 1997; Tardif et al. 2005; Van Schaik & Kappeler 1997; Wright 1984, 1990; Ziegler et al. 2006). This hypothesis seems particularly relevant for explaining the evolution of alloparental care in the callitrichids. The mother, whose body mass is often exceeded by the combined body mass of her infants is incapable of raising the offspring on her own and even a male-female pair have difficulty raising

twins successfully. Her situation is further compounded by a postpartum estrous that results in females being simultaneously and continuously pregnant and lactating. Most callitrichids have elaborate behavioral and physiological mechanisms that prevent nondominant group members from participating in reproduction and thereby facilitate paternity certainty. The care provided by the male (or other conspecifics) contributes to reducing the metabolic costs to the female of raising the offspring as illustrated by the fact that callitrichid males lose weight when they are providing most infant transport. The obligate biparental care hypothesis has less appeal for other species exhibiting intense paternal care, such as titi and owl monkeys.

The second hypothesis considers the affiliative interactions between males and infants as a mating strategy by males that helps them develop a relationship with a female and secure a position in the larger social network. The hypothesis has been useful to examine male-infant interactions in taxa where there is no conspicuous and direct care (Smuts & Gubernick 1992), and more recently in humans (Marlowe 2000). The relationship between paternal care and the development of emotional attachments (or pair-bonds) in humans has played a central role in evolutionary models of human behavior (Geary & Flinn 2001, Hawkes 2004; see sidebar, Attachment Bonds). Investigators have historically argued that pair-bonds evolved given the female need for paternal infant care and provisioning. For example, men in Xhosa (South Africa) invested the most (in terms of money and time) in their coresiding putatively biological children and the least in the stepoffspring of a former partner (Anderson et al. 1999, 2007). However, biological children living with a former partner and stepchildren of current partners receive similar levels of investment. Among the Hazda of Tanzania, biological children receive more care (both direct and indirect) than do stepchildren (Marlowe 1999). Thus men provide care to their partner's offspring as a component of their mating strategy, but they tend to provide more to their own offspring. This tendency suggests that paternity confidence plays an important role in shaping men's relationships with women and with their putative genetic children (Anderson 2006). These studies illustrate problems inherent in quantifying and differentiating parental investment and parental care. This is true particularly when men may be providing investment or care for children that will have benefits only in the very long term (e.g., college tuition, teaching hunting skills).

These early models were extremely influential and shaped the research on paternal care and parental investment during the next decades. Their impressive contributions notwithstanding, it cannot be overemphasized that they were developed and evaluated on very limited data. Bateman's and Trivers' contributions have recently been reexamined with some fascinating new insights (Parker & Schwagmeyer 2005, Queller 1997, Wade & Shuster 2002). Wade & Shuster (2002, p. 291) proposed that "differences in initial parental investment between the sexes are likely to arise from rather than lead to sexual selection favoring increased mate numbers in males and emphasis on parental care by females." This effectively reverses the direction of causality between sexual selection and parental investment and would lead, if accepted, to a major reconsideration of sex differences in parental care (Kokko & Jennions 2003). Other authors continue to remind us of the need to abandon the now untenable traditional view of coy females and ardent males championed by Bateman and Trivers and followed dogmatically ever since (Snyder & Gowaty 2007, Tang-Martinez & Ryder 2005). We have enough evidence in a wide range of taxa, primates included, to show that the relative contributions of males and females in the shaping of social systems and in the provision of care are better understood as the outcome of a conflict between the sexes. A conflict during which females regularly exercise choice and control and during which female promiscuity is far from an exception (Gowaty 1996, 2004; Hrdy 2000).

ATTACHMENT BONDS

In many species, infants are highly motivated to form an emotional bond with their mothers (Bowlby 1969) and, in the absence of the mother, will direct filial attachment to the closest individual (Mason & Kenney 1974). Ainsworth (1969) elaborated the elements of attachment bonds to include the following: (*a*) individual recognition, (*b*) specific preference, and (*c*) separation distress (Mendoza et al. 1980). Infant monkeys will return to their attachment figure when distressed, suggesting that stress-buffering or secure base is also a component of attachment (Suomi 1999). Using these criteria it is possible to determine whether affiliative relationships qualify as attachment or something more akin to friendship (Mendoza et al. 1991). In titi monkeys, infants form a unidirectional attachment bond with their fathers, which persists into adulthood; mothers are less effective attachment figures in the absence of the father (Hoffman et al. 1995, Mendoza & Mason 1986b). Mothers and fathers do form attachment bonds with each other, but not with their offspring. Other nonattachment relationships among family members are amicable (including close following, play, food sharing, and passive contact). Thus it is not possible to distinguish attachment bonds on the basis of proximity or contact alone, as has been often incorrectly assumed.

ENDOCRINE, GENETIC, AND NEURAL SUBSTRATES OF PATERNAL CARE

Hormonal Substrates of Paternal Behavior

The hormonal correlates of paternal care in mammals have not been as extensively studied as those of maternal care (Bridges 2008). In females, mechanisms regulating maternal behavior may be derived from processes involved in birth or, for mammals, in the regulation of lactation. Sudden changes in progesterone, estrogen, oxytocin, and prolactin, all involved in birth or lactation, are also implicated in maternal behavior. Therefore, although it is reasonable to suppose there is overlap between mechanisms supporting maternal and paternal behavior, it is unlikely that they are the same ones related to birth and lactation, which obviously do not have male parallels. When examining the hormonal basis of paternal care, we are compelled to signal the correlational nature of most of the evidence and the bidirectionality of hormone-behavior interactions (Almond et al. 2008, Schradin & Anzenberger 2002).

Prolactin, a peptide secreted by the anterior pituitary gland, has long been associated with maternal care in birds and mammals (Ziegler 2000). Prolactin also appears to be involved in paternal care in a variety of species (Schradin & Anzenberger 1999, Wynne-Edwards & Timonin 2007, Ziegler 2000). Among some of the neotropical primates that display intense paternal behavior, adult reproductive males show changes in prolactin levels associated with fatherhood (Schradin et al. 2003). The way prolactin changes are associated with paternal care widely varies, and this variation could reflect the different ways in which males experience and express infant care. In humans, the role of prolactin in paternal care is not straightforward. Parental experience affects men's prolactin responses, but recent contact with infants and individual differences in responses to infant cues may be responsible for the hormonal changes rather than the reverse (Delahunty et al. 2007, Fleming et al. 2002, Gray et al. 2007). No evidence as yet indicates that elevations in prolactin actually contribute to the expression of paternal behavior. Because prolactin is stress responsive and is regulated by each of the monoamine systems involved in emotion regulation, the prolactin changes attendant to interactions with the infant may be epiphenomenal.

Investigators have conclusively associated two other peptide hormones, oxytocin and vasopressin, with parental care. Oxytocin is implicated in maternal behavior and in female reproduction through its role in parturition, milk let down during lactation, sexual behavior, and sperm transport (Pedersen et al. 2006, Pedersen & Prange 1985). Although oxytocin may underlie the expression of paternal behaviors (Parker & Lee 2001), contradicting evidence indicates otherwise (Bales et al. 2004a). Vasopressin has been implicated in other sociosexual behaviors

including courtship, male-male competition, and pair-bonding (Lim et al. 2004a, Moore 1992). Both sexes respond to both peptides, but oxytocin seems to be more relevant in females and vasopressin in males (Bales et al. 2004b, Carter 2007, Carter et al. 2008b). The sexually dimorphic physiological and behavioral effects of oxytocin and vasopressin appear to be conserved in humans as well (Feldman et al. 2007, Gray et al. 2007, Sanchez et al. 2009).

Testosterone is a steroid hormone strongly associated to reproduction and infant care. One seminal idea in behavioral endocrinology is that testosterone is antagonistic to infant care, and males may have to make trade-offs between mating effort and parental care (Ketterson & Nolan 1999, Wingfield et al. 1990). For example, marmoset males who carried infants the most had the lowest urinary testosterone levels (Nunes et al. 2001) and the most significant declines in gonadal steroids (Nunes et al. 2000). Male titi monkeys do not show changes in gonadal steroids with the birth of infants, but changes in adrenal steroids suggest that the animals become more stress responsive with the advent of new infants (Reeder 2001). Among humans, several cross-cultural studies indicate that married men with young children tend to have lower testosterone levels than single, unpaired men and married men with no children (Berg & Wynne-Edwards 2001; Gray et al. 2006, 2007; Muller et al. 2008; Storey & Walsh 2000). Although the evidence is not wholly in line with the idea that testosterone is inimical to paternal behavior, the evidence is strong that steroid hormones are involved in expression of paternal behavior.

Genetic Substrates of Paternal Behavior

Genetic studies are making significant contributions in at least two aspects relevant to understanding paternal care. First, they provide data on the biological relatedness between care providers and infants. The presentation of these data will be a most crucial contribution because theoretical formulations have generally assumed that care providers will adjust their investment on the basis of paternity certainty, which may not always be true (Queller 1997, Sheldon 2002). Second, they are helping us understand the neurogenetic basis of social behavior.

Paternal care and paternity. Molecular genetic studies, combined with long-term behavioral and demographic data, are required to determine biological relatedness and reproductive success. Most primate studies of genetic structure have focused on polygynous species (Altmann et al. 1996, Di Fiore & Fleischer 2005, Gagneux et al. 1999, Keane et al. 1997). Genetic evidence has been used to suggest that some males in polygynous species intervene in agonistic disputes or defend infants from infanticidal males in a manner that directly favors the development and/or survival of their offspring (Borries et al. 1999, Buchan et al. 2003, Charpentier et al. 2008). That said, even if it is shown that males are somehow intervening in favor of their offspring, the nature of their interventions are qualitatively different from those observed in taxa in which there is direct and conspicuous care. Thus, the genetic substrates of the neurobiological mechanisms underlying a tendency to interfere in agonistic disputes would be expected to be different from the ones underlying behaviors such as infant retrieval, transport, and active food sharing.

Unfortunately, only a handful of studies have examined genetic paternity among taxa with direct paternal care. In at least one marmoset species (*Callithrix kuhlii*), genetic chimerism, mixing of two or more genomic lineages within an individual, changes the predicted pattern of 50% sharing of genetic information in siblings (Ross et al. 2007). The caregivers could apparently detect differences due to chimerism inasmuch as males carried chimeric infants more often than nonchimeric ones. Among mustached tamarins and common marmosets, most infants were sired by one male, but nonfathers participated in carrying infants (Huck et al. 2005, Nievergelt et al. 2000). Among fat-tailed dwarf lemurs, there is a high rate of extrapair paternity and social fathers provide care to extra-pair young (Fietz & Dausmann 2003, Fietz et al. 2000).

No published studies have yet described the genetic structure of populations of titis and owl monkeys in which paternal care is most intense. Still, on the basis of their dispersal patterns, serial monogamy, and mtDNA population structure (Babb et al. 2008, Bossuyt 2002, Fernandez-Duque 2009, Rodman & Bossuyt 2007), it seems likely that the potential genetic benefits of providing paternal care will need to be considered at a community level as has been suggested for gibbons (Reichard 2003). Relatively short dispersal distances and a fast rate of adult replacement may result in males providing care to young who are not their offspring but who are still closely related kin.

Genetics, pair-bonding, and paternal care. Recent attempts to examine the genetics of pair-bonding and paternal care in primates are exciting, but correlational and preliminary. Thus far, they have focused on the potential role of the distribution and quantity of neural receptors for vasopressin (Donaldson & Young 2008, Walum et al. 2008). In voles, polymorphisms in the promoter region of vasopressin receptor 1a gene (*avpr1a*) apparently contribute to behavioral differences between monogamous and polygynous males by altering gene expression and ultimately the distribution and density of vasopressin receptors in brain tissue (Hammock & Young 2005). Primate mating and social behaviors may also be influenced by variation in the number of repeat sequences in the promoter region of the *avpr1a* gene (Rosso et al. 2008, Walum et al. 2008), but evidence on a large number of rodent species strongly indicates that it is extremely unlikely that similar mechanisms are regulating such complex behaviors in humans and nonhumans alike (Fink et al. 2007).

Neural Substrates of Paternal Behavior

At this point, we know very little about the neural substrates of primate paternal behavior. Because paternal behavior co-occurs with

Genetic chimerism: a mixing within an individual of two or more populations of genetically distinct cells that originated in different zygotes

Extra-pair paternity: a male sires an infant with an individual other than the pair-mate

pair-bonding, we can use studies of pair-bonding to supplement what is known, and in doing so, we must draw heavily from studies of monogamous prairie voles (Nair & Young 2006). Two components of the neural circuitry underlie pair-bonding and paternal behavior in voles: a cognitive component required for individual recognition and an emotional component that provides the reward for engaging with particular other individuals (Lim et al. 2004b; Liu et al. 2001; Young et al. 2001, 2005). These circuits did not evolve specifically to support paternal behavior; rather they are an elaboration of existing social recognition and reward circuits that function in a variety of behaviors.

Titi monkeys seem to have neurobiological mechanisms of pair-bonding that parallel the pathways identified in voles. Male titi monkeys that were in long-term pair-bonds (conflating pair-bonding and paternal experiences) showed differences in glucose uptake when compared with males living alone (Bales et al. 2007). The lone males in that study were subsequently paired and PET scans repeated. Then, males in new pairs (without paternal experience) showed some changes in neural activity in the direction of males in long-term relationships but overall were not as different from lone males as they were from males in long-term bonds.

The neurobiological mechanisms facilitating pair-bonding and paternal care may be elaborations of mechanisms that foster sociality more generally. Familiar conspecifics attenuate behavioral and physiological stress in rodents and primates (Gust et al. 1994, Kiyokawa et al. 2004, Mendoza & Mason 1986a, Ruis et al. 1999, Terranova et al. 1999). The pathway by which the social environment influences stress responsiveness has been partially identified and is believed to include activation of oxytocin and vasopressin pathways and ultimately the dopamine and opiate reward pathways in the brain (Carter et al. 1999). Monogamous voles, as compared with nonmonogamous voles, have a greater density of oxytocin receptors in neural structures involved in the reward pathway. Male voles also have a much higher level of vasopressin receptors in structures necessary for

both reward and social cognition (Lim & Young 2006). The evidence in primates is still limited, but fatherhood apparently increases the abundance of vasopressin receptors in the brains of male marmosets (Kozorovitskiy et al. 2006). In humans, a recent review of studies using functional neuroimaging indicates that responses to infant stimuli include the same circuitry identified in rodent and nonhuman primate studies and thus are highly conserved through evolution (Swain et al. 2007).

DEVELOPMENTAL PROGRAMMING AND TRANSGENERATIONAL INFLUENCES

The studies reviewed above give strong support to hypotheses that involve certain neural and endocrine pathways in the expression of paternal care. However, evidence is accumulating that shows epigenetic effects on parental behavior and an increasingly important role of early experience in shaping its development (Carter et al. 2008a, Champagne & Meaney 2007, Michel & Tyler 2007). Laboratory experiments with prairie voles have shown that relatively subtle changes in early experience (e.g., handling of pups, licking, sniffing) have long-term consequences for later social behavior of the offspring. A single handling event in the postnatal period was associated with increased future paternal care in male offspring (Carter et al. 2008a). In turn, these differences in early experiences were correlated with changes in oxytocin and vasopressin patterns in adulthood. Variation in early experiences, then, could be translated into endocrine signals that would influence certain behavioral patterns later in life. For example, epigenetic influences on early oxytocin modulation may be implicated in social aspects of personality and may be the underlying base for some psychiatric disorders such as autism, anxiety, and depression (Carter 2007, Swain et al. 2007). Along the same lines, it is not unreasonable to expect that a stable environment during early development may modulate the establishment of neuroendocrine pathways

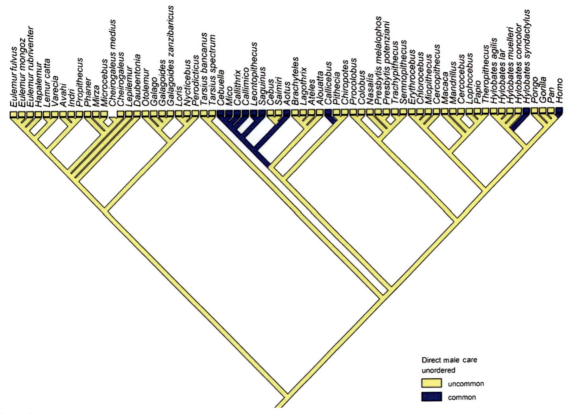

Figure 1

Primate phylogeny showing the taxa where paternal care is direct and conspicuous (*dark branches*).

Figure 2

A titi monkey infant (*Callicebus moloch*) sits in physical contact with his father.

Figure 3

An owl monkey infant (*Aotus azarai*) rides dorsally on the back of his father.

that would promote certain types of parental behaviors, on the basis of that early experience, which would be differentially expressed in the adult.

Evidence of developmental programming of social behavior via epigenetic effects introduces the possibility of transgenerational influences in the development and expression of paternal care. Hypotheses of developmental programming of parental behavior, stemming mostly from studies with biparental rodents (Michel & Tyler 2007), are receiving considerable attention. Systematic research in primates, however, is still scarce. Preliminary data from titi monkeys indicate that males with lesions to a very small part of the prefrontal cortex were more tolerant of other group members and hence spent even more time in contact with mates and offspring than is typical. The offspring of lesioned males, in turn, were more likely to engage affiliatively with their siblings (S.P. Mendoza, W.A. Mason, J. Padberg, and K. Bales, unpublished data). Significantly, these males showed more extreme differences in brain regions associated with social recognition and reward when compared with lone or newly paired males than did the nonlesioned males in long-term bonds (Bales et al. 2007). In humans, several hypotheses propose a relationship between childhood experiences and an adult focus on mating or parenting effort (Belsky et al. 1991, Chisholm 1993, Geary 2000, Quinlan 2007). According to these views, local unstable environments (e.g., high mortality risks, low resource availability) during childhood would be associated with a higher focus by men on mating rather than on parenting. This focus on mating would lead to less-responsive paternal behaviors. Although the existing evidence is scant, there may be developmental influences modulating the degree of paternal involvement.

CONCLUSIONS

Among primates, paternal care is present in a wide range of body sizes, from the small callitrichids (0.5–0.7 kg) to siamangs (5–7 kg) and humans (50–70 kg). Paternal care is present with and without simultaneous sibling care. Sometimes, within the same genus, paternal care is present in extremely varied ecological settings. For example, the owl monkey species ranging evergreen tropical forests exhibit patterns of paternal care that are similar to the ones showed by owl monkeys in relatively dry subtropical forests. In some taxa, paternal care is omnipresent, whereas in others its frequency and intensity are more variable. It seems reasonable to conclude that paternal care has evolved independently at least a few times in the radiation of the primate order.

Long-term behavioral and demographic data strongly indicate that direct, conspicuous and frequent paternal care tends to occur simultaneously with the development of a pair-bond between the mother and the putative father providing care. An association between pair-bonds and paternal care is further supported by our understanding of the proximate mechanisms underlying these aspects of the social behavior of primates. There seems to be a common biological substrate with similar neuroanatomical and neuroendocrine processes regulating the manifestation of pair-bonds, monogamy, and paternal care. Following the lead of the rodent research, it is increasingly likely that neurobiological processes underlying paternal behavior are related to mechanisms that promote social behavior generally. Still, much more work is needed to identify the precise mechanisms that are altered to facilitate expression of paternal care. The most promising research is on vasopressin and its receptor quantity and distribution, which is closest to being linked to enhanced sociality. It is unlikely that vasopressin will fully explain the intriguing role that emotional bonds seem to play in the expression of the monogamous social system in titi monkeys, but it may act on them to facilitate expression of paternal care. We tend to think in human terms that something akin to love motivates fathers to provide care for their infants. This is not the case in titi monkeys in which the fathers are tolerant, nonrejecting, and nonaggressive to their infants but show no evidence of an emotional bond with them.

Perhaps, all that is needed to bring about the expression of paternal behavior is a relatively small change in mechanisms regulating social tolerance, rather than an elaborate mechanism specifically designed for that end. For example, vasopressin may be playing a prominent role in regulating paternal care because it reduces fear and hence enhances tolerance.

The ability to form social bonds, being those pair or parental bonds, may be influenced early during development in response to individual infant rearing styles or to extrinsic environmental variables (e.g., war, famine, pathogenic load). This proposal implies the existence of a high degree of phenotypic plasticity, which is a salient feature of primate adaptation in general and human adaptation in particular (Quinlan 2007). The incorporation of, possibly adaptive, developmental programming into models of paternal care may help explain the intra- and interpopulation variation in the expression of paternal behaviors. Studies of paternal care provide an ideal model to understand the epigenesis of complex behavioral traits in model systems that are characterized in the field and the laboratory.

FUTURE ISSUES

1. From a life-history approach, the energetic costs of providing paternal care should be reflected in the life history of the species. How does paternal care affect the developmental trajectory of offspring?

2. Given the broad taxonomic distribution of paternal care, different evolutionary trajectories may have resulted in the same outcome. Titi and owl monkeys may be excellent models for studying homoplasy in paternal care.

3. Developmental programming and transgenerational effects are particularly exciting areas of future research on parental behavior. Biocultural models of developmental histories may explain the variation in the expression of paternal behavior in human societies. If so, what does this tell us about the evolution of the human family?

4. Given the flexibility in primate behavioral patterns, more data are needed on variation within and among populations. To identify successfully subtle differences among individuals in a population or among populations, data collection procedures need to be better validated across field sites, species, and researchers.

5. Genetic studies of paternity need to examine the costs and benefits of care at a community level to incorporate possible kin selection effects.

DISCLOSURE STATEMENT

The authors are not aware of any affiliations, memberships, funding, or financial holdings that might be perceived as affecting the objectivity of this review.

ACKNOWLEDGMENTS

We thank Peter Gray, Sarah Blaffer-Hrdy, and Suzette Tardif for critical comments on the manuscript and Peter T. Ellison for encouraging us to write it. The work of Fernandez-Duque and Valeggia was supported by the L.S.B. Leakey Foundation, the Wenner-Gren Foundation, the National Geographic Society, the National Scientific and Technological Council of Argentina (Cecoal-CONICET), and the University of Pennsylvania Research Funds. Fernandez-Duque's work was also supported through NSF (BCS-0621020). Valeggia received additional support from the Population Studies Center and the Population Aging Research Center (University of Pennsylvania). Mendoza's work received funding from the National Center for Research Resources (RR000169).

LITERATURE CITED

Achenbach GG, Snowdon CT. 2002. Costs of caregiving: weight loss in captive adult male cotton-top tamarins (*Saguinus oedipus*) following the birth of infants. *Int. J. Primatol.* 23:179–89

Ainsworth MDS. 1969. Object relations, dependency, and attachment: a theoretical review of the infant-mother relationship. *Child Dev.* 40:969–1025

Almond RE, Ziegler TE, Snowdon CT. 2008. Changes in prolactin and glucocorticoid levels in cotton-top tamarin fathers during their mate's pregnancy: the effect of infants and paternal experience. *Am. J. Primatol.* 70:560–65

Altmann J, Alberts SC, Haines SA, Dubach J, Muruthi P, et al. 1996. Behavior predicts genetic structure in a wild primate group. *Proc. Natl. Acad. Sci. USA* 93:5797–801

Anderson KG. 2006. How well does paternity confidence match actual paternity? Evidence from worldwide nonpaternity rates. *Curr. Anthropol.* 48:511–18

Anderson KG, Kaplan H, Lam D, Lancaster JB. 1999. Paternal care by genetic fathers and stepfathers II: reports by Xhosa High School students. *Evol. Hum. Behav.* 20:433–51

Anderson KG, Kaplan H, Lancaster JB. 2007. Confidence of paternity, divorce, and investment in children by Albuquerque men. *Evol. Hum. Behav.* 28:1–10

Babb P, Fernandez-Duque E, Gagneux P, Schurr TG. 2009. Phylogeography and population structure of mtDNA diversity in Azara's owl monkeys (*Aotus azarai azarai*) of the Argentinean Chaco. *Mol. Phylogenet. Evol.* Submitted

Bales KL, Dietz JM, Baker AJ, Miller KE, Tardif SD. 2000. Effects of allocare-givers on fitness of infants and parents in callitrichid primates. *Folia Primatol.* 71:27–38

Bales KL, Kim AJ, Lewis-Resse AD, Carter CS. 2004a. Both oxytocin and vasopressin may influence allo-parental behavior in male prairie voles. *Horm. Behav.* 45:354–61

Bales KL, Pfeifer LA, Carter CS. 2004b. Sex differences and developmental effects of manipulations of oxytocin on alloparenting and anxiety in prairie voles. *Dev. Psychobiol.* 44:123–31

Bales KL, Plotsky PM, Young LJ, Lim MM, Grotte N, et al. 2007. Neonatal oxytocin manipulations have long-lasting, sexually dimorphic effects on vasopressin receptors. *Neurosci.* 144:38–45

Bearder S, Campbell CJ, Fuentes A, MacKinnon KC, Panger M, eds. 2007. *Primates in Perspective.* Oxford, UK: Oxford Univ. Press

Belsky J, Steinberg L, Draper P. 1991. Childhood experience, interpersonal development, and reproductive strategy: an evolutionary theory of socialization. *Child Dev.* 62:647–70

Beltran S, Boissier J. 2008. Schistosome monogamy: who, how and why? *Trends Parasitol.* 24:386–91

Berg SJ, Wynne-Edwards KE. 2001. Changes in testosterone, cortisol, and estradiol levels in men becoming fathers. *Mayo Clin. Proc.* 76:582–92

Borries C, Launhardt K, Epplen C, Epplen JT, Winkler P. 1999. Males as infant protectors in Hanuman langurs (*Presbytis entellus*) living in multimale groups—defence pattern, paternity and sexual behaviour. *Behav. Ecol. Sociobiol.* 46:350–56

Bossuyt F. 2002. Natal dispersal of titi monkeys (*Callicebus moloch*) at Cocha Cashu, Manu National Park, Peru. *Am. J. Phys. Anthropol.* S34:47

Bowlby J. 1969. *Attachment and Loss. Volume I. Attachment.* New York: Basic Books

Bridges R. 2008. *Neurobiology of the Parental Brain.* Burlington, MA: Academic. 584 pp.

Buchan JC, Alberts SC, Silk JB, Altmann J. 2003. True paternal care in a multi-male primate society. *Nature* 425:179–81

Carter CS. 2007. Sex differences in oxytocin and vasopressin: implications for autism spectrum disorders? *Behav. Brain Res.* 176:170–86

Carter CS, Boone EM, Bales KL. 2008a. Early experience and the developmental programming of oxytocin and vasopressin. See Bridges 2008, pp. 417–34

Carter CS, Grippo AJ, Pournajafi-Nazarloo H, Ruscio MG, Porges SW. 2008b. Oxytocin, vasopressin and sociality. *Prog. Brain Res.* 170:331–36

Carter SC, Lederhendler II, Kirkpatrick B, eds. 1999. *The Integrative Neurobiology of Affiliation.* Cambridge, MA: MIT Press. 418 pp.

Champagne FA, Meaney MJ. 2007. Transgenerational effects of social environment on variations in maternal care and behavioral response to novelty. *Behav. Neurosci.* 121:1353–63

Charpentier MJE, Van Horn RC, Altmann J, Alberts SC. 2008. Paternal effects of offspring fitness in a multimale primate society. *Proc. R. Soc. London B Biol. Sci.* 105:1988–92

Chisholm JS. 1993. Death, hope, and sex: life-history theory and the development of reproductive strategies. *Curr. Anthropol.* 34:1–24

Chivers DJ. 1974. *The Siamang in Malaya. A Field Study of a Primate in Tropical Rain Forest.* Basel, Switz.: S. Karger AG. 335 pp.

Clutton-Brock TH. 1991. *The Evolution of Parental Care.* Princeton, NJ: Princeton Univ. Press

Dawkins R, Carlisle TR. 1976. Parental investment, mate desertion and a fallacy. *Nature* 262:131–33

Delahunty KM, McKay DW, Noseworthy DE, Storey AE. 2007. Prolactin responses to infant cues in men and women: effects of parental experience and recent infant contact. *Horm. Behav.* 51:213–20

Di Fiore A, Fernandez-Duque E. 2007. A comparison of paternal care in three socially-monogamous neotropical primates. *Am. J. Phys. Anthropol.* 132:99

Di Fiore A, Fernandez-Duque E, Hurst D. 2007. Adult male replacement in socially monogamous equatorial saki monkeys (*Pithecia aequatorialis*). *Folia Primatol.* 78:88–98

Di Fiore A, Fleischer RC. 2005. Social behavior, reproductive strategies, and population genetic structure of *Lagothrix poeppigii. Int. J. Primatol.* 26:1137–73

Dixson AF, Fleming D. 1981. Parental behaviour and infant development in owl monkeys (*Aotus trivirgatus griseimembra*). *J. Zool.* 194:25–39

Donaldson ZR, Young LJ. 2008. Oxytocin, vasopressin, and the neurogenetics of sociality. *Science* **322:900–4**

Feldman R, Weller A, Zagoory-Sharon O, Levine A. 2007. Evidence for a neuroendocrinological foundation of human affiliation: plasma oxytocin levels across pregnancy and the postpartum period predict mother-infant bonding. *Psychol. Sci.* 18:965–70

Fernandez-Duque E. 2007. The Aotinae: social monogamy in the only nocturnal haplorhines. See Campbell et al. 2007, pp. 139–54

Fernandez-Duque E. 2009. Natal dispersal in monogamous owl monkeys (*Aotus azarai*) of the Argentinean Chaco. *Behaviour* 146:583–606

Fernandez-Duque E, Di Fiore A, de Luna AG. 2009. Pair-mate relationships and parenting in equatorial saki monkeys (*Pithecia aequatorialis*) and red titi monkeys (*Callicebus discolor*) of Ecuador. In *Evolutionary Biology and Conservation of Titis, Sakis and Uacaris*, ed. LM Veiga, AA Barnett. Cambridge, UK: Cambridge Univ. Press. In press

Fernandez-Duque E, Juárez C, Di Fiore A. 2008. Adult male replacement and subsequent infant care by male and siblings in socially monogamous owl monkeys (*Aotus azarai*). *Primates* 49:81–84

Fietz J, Dausmann KH. 2003. Costs and potential benefits of parental care in the nocturnal fat-tailed dwarf lemur (*Cheirogaleus medius*). *Folia Primatol.* 74:246–58

Fietz J, Zischler H, Schwiegk C, Tomiuk J, Dausmann KH, Ganzhorn JU. 2000. High rates of extra-pair young in the pair-living fat-tailed dwarf lemur, *Cheirogaleus medius. Behav. Ecol. Sociobiol.* 49:8–17

Fink S, Excoffier L, Heckel G. 2007. Mammalian monogamy is not controlled by a single gene. *Proc. Natl. Acad. Sci. USA* 103:10956–60

Fite JE, Patera KJ, French JA, Rukstalis M, Hopkins EC, Ross CN. 2005. Opportunistic mothers: female marmosets (*Callithrix kuhlii*) reduce their investment in offspring when they have to, and when they can. *J. Hum. Evol.* 49:122–42

Fleming AS, Corter C, Stallings J, Steiner M. 2002. Testosterone and prolactin are associated with emotional responses to infant cries in new fathers. *Horm. Behav.* 42:399–413

Fragaszy DM, Schwarz S, Shimosaka D. 1982. Longitudinal observations of care and development of infant titi monkeys (*Callicebus moloch*). *Am. J. Primatol.* 2:191–200

A taxonomic-wide review of the neurobiology of social behavior and implications for our societies.

Gagneux P, Boesch C, Woodruff DS. 1999. Female reproductive strategies, paternity and community structure in wild West African chimpanzees. *Anim. Behav.* 57:19–32

Geary DC. 2000. Evolution and proximate expression of human paternal investment. *Psychol. Bull.* 126:55–77

Geary DC, Flinn MV. 2001. Evolution of human parental behavior and the human family. *Parent. Sci. Pract.* 1:5–61

Gowaty PA. 1996. Battles of the sexes and origins of monogamy. In *Partnerships in Birds: The Study of Monogamy*, ed. JM Black, pp. 21–52. Oxford: Oxford Univ. Press

Gowaty PA. 2004. Sex roles, contests for the control of reproduction and sexual selection. In *Sexual Selection in Primates*, ed. PM Kappeler, C Van Schaik, pp. 37–56. Cambridge, UK: Cambridge Univ. Press

Gray PB, Parkin JC, Samms-Vaughan ME. 2007. Hormonal correlates of human paternal interactions: a hospital-based investigation in urban Jamaica. *Horm. Behav.* 52:499–507

Gray PB, Yang C-FJ, Pope HGJ. 2006. Fathers have lower salivary testosterone levels than unmarried men and married non-fathers in Beijing, China. *Proc. R. Soc. London B* 273:333–39

Gubernick DG, Klopfer PH, eds. 1981. *Parental Care in Mammals*. New York: Plenum Press. 459 pp.

Gust DA, Gordon TP, Brodie AR, McClure HM. 1994. Effect of a preferred companion in modulating stress in adult female rhesus monkeys. *Physiol. Behav.* 55:681–84

Hamilton WJ III. 1984. Significance of paternal investment by primates to the evolution of adult male-female associations. See Taub 1984, pp. 309–35

Hammock EAD, Young LJ. 2005. Microsatellite instability generates diversity in brain and sociobehavioral traits. *Science* 308:1630–34

Hawkes K. 2004. Mating, parenting, and the evolution of human pair bonds. In *Kinship and Behavior in Primates*, ed. B Chapais, C Berman, pp. 443–73. Oxford: Oxford Univ. Press

Hewlett BS. 1991. *Intimate Fathers: The Nature and Context of Aka Pygmy Paternal Infant Care*. Ann Arbor: Univ. Mich. Press

Hewlett BS, ed. 1992. *Father-Child Relations*. New York: Aldine DeGruyter

Hill KR, Hurtado AM. 1996. *Ache Life History: The Ecology and Demography of a Foraging People*. New York: Aldine de Gruyter

Hoffman KA, Mendoza SP, Hennessy MB, Mason WA. 1995. Responses of infant titi monkeys, *Callicebus moloch*, to removal of one or both parents: evidence for paternal attachment. *Dev. Psychobiol.* 28:399–407

Hrdy S. 2000. The optimal number of fathers. Evolution, demography, and history in the shaping of female mate preferences. *Ann. N. Y. Acad. Sci.* 907:75–96

Hrdy SB. 2005. Evolutionary context of human development: the cooperative breeding model. In *Attachment and Bonding. A New Synthesis*, ed. SC Carter, L Ahnert, KE Grossmann, SB Hrdy, ME Lamb, et al., pp. 9–32. Cambridge, MA: MIT Press

Hrdy SB. 2008. Cooperative breeding and the paradox of facultative fathering. See Bridges 2008, pp. 407–16

Huck M, Lottker P, Bohle UR, Heymann EW. 2005. Paternity and kinship patterns in polyandrous moustached tamarins (*Saguinus mystax*). *Am. J. Phys. Anthropol.* 127:449–64

Keane B, Dittus WPJ, Melnick DJ. 1997. Paternity assessment in wild groups of toque macaques *Macaca sinica* at Polonnaruwa, Sri Lanka using molecular markers. *Mol. Ecol.* 6:267–82

Ketterson ED, Nolan VJ. 1999. Adaptation, exaptation, and constraint: a hormonal perspective. *Am. Nat.* 54:S4–25

Key C, Aiello LC. 2000. A prisoner's dilemma model of the evolution of paternal care. *Folia Primatol.* 71:77–92

Kiyokawa Y, Kikusui T, Takeuchi Y, Mori Y. 2004. Partner's stress status influences social buffering effects in rats. *Behav. Neurosci.* 118:798–804

Kleiman DG. 1985. Paternal care in New World primates. *Am. Zool.* 25:857–59

Kleiman DG, Malcolm JR. 1981. The evolution of male parental investment in mammals. In *Parental Care in Mammals*, ed. DG Gubernick, PH Klopfer, pp. 347–87. New York: Plenum Press

Kokko H, Jennions M. 2003. It takes two to tango. *Trends Ecol. Evol.* 18:103–4

Kozorovitskiy Y, Hughes M, Lee K, Gould E. 2006. Fatherhood affects dendritic spines and vasopressin V1a receptors in the primate prefrontal cortex. *Nat. Neurosci.* 9:1094–95

A study of fatherhood in foraging societies with an insightful discussion on the sources of variation in human paternal care among foraging societies.

The first and only evidence of attachment between mammal infant and father.

An extension of the cooperative breeding hypothesis with special reference to paternal care.

Kurland JA, Gualin SJC. 1984. The evolution of male parental investment: effects of genetic relatedness and feeding ecology on the allocation of reproductive effort. In *Primate Paternalism*, ed. DM Taub, pp. 259–306. New York: Van Nostrand Reinhold

Lancaster JB, Lancaster CS. 1983. Parental investment: the hominid adaptation. In *How Humans Adapt: A Biocultural Odyssey*, ed. DJ Ortner, pp. 33–69. Washington, DC: Smithson. Inst. Press

Lappan S. 2008. Male care of infants in a siamang (*Symphalangus syndactylus*) population including socially monogamous and polyandrous groups. *Behav. Ecol. Sociobiol.* 62:1307–17

Lim M, Young LJ. 2006. Neuropeptidergic regulation of affiliative behavior and social bonding in animals. *Horm. Behav.* 50:506–17

Lim MM, Hammock EA, Young LJ. 2004a. The role of vasopressin in the genetic and neural regulation of monogamy. *J. Neuroendocrinol.* 16:325–32

Lim MM, Wang Z, Olazabal DE, Ren X, Terwilliger EF, Young LJ. 2004b. Enhanced partner preference in a promiscuous species by manipulating the expression of a single gene. *Nature* 429:754–57

Liu Y, Curtis J, Wang ZX. 2001. Vasopressin in the lateral septum regulates pair bond formation of male prairie voles. *Behav. Neurosci.* 115:910–19

Marlowe F. 1999. Male care and mating effort among Hadza foragers. *Behav. Ecol. Sociobiol.* 46:57–64

Marlowe F. 2000. Paternal investment and the human mating system. *Behav. Processes* 51:45–61

Mason WA, Kenney MD. 1974. Redirection of filial attachments in rhesus monkeys: dogs as mother surrogates. *Science* 183:1209–11

Maynard Smith J. 1977. Parental investment: a prospective analysis. *Anim. Behav.* 25:1–9

Mendoza SP, Coe C, Smotherman W, Kaplan J, Levine S. 1980. Functional consequences of attachment: a comparison of two species. In *Maternal Influences and Early Behavior*, ed. R Bell, W Smotherman, pp. 235–52. New York: Spectrum

Mendoza SP, Lyons DM, Saltzman W. 1991. Sociophysiology of squirrel monkeys. *Am. J. Primatol.* 23:37–54

Mendoza SP, Mason WA. 1986a. Contrasting responses to intruders and to involuntary separation by monogamous and polygynous New World monkeys. *Physiol. Behav.* 38:795–801

Mendoza SP, Mason WA. 1986b. Parental division of labour and differentiation of attachments in a monogamous primate (*Callicebus moloch*). *Anim. Behav.* 34:1336–47

Michel GF, Tyler AN. 2007. Can knowledge of developmental processes illuminate the evolution of parental care? *Dev. Psychobiol.* 49:33–44

Miller KE, Bales KL, Ramos JH, Dietz JM. 2006. Energy intake, energy expenditure, and reproductive costs of female wild golden lion tamarins (*Leontopithecus rosalia*). *Am. J. Primatol.* 68:1037–53

Moore FL. 1992. Evolutionary precedents for behavioral actions of oxytocin and vasopressin. *Ann. N. Y. Acad. Sci.* 652:156–65

Muller MN, Marlowe FW, Bugumba R, Ellison PT. 2008. Testosterone and paternal care in East African foragers and pastoralists. *Proc. Biol. Sci.* 276(1655):347–54

Nair H, Young LJ. 2006. Vasopressin and pair-bond formation: genes to brain to behavior. *Physiology* 21:146–52

Nievergelt CM, Digby LJ, Ramakrishnan U, Woodruff DS. 2000. Genetic analysis of group composition and breeding system in a wild common marmoset (*Callithrix jacchus*) population. *Int. J. Primatol.* 21:1–20

Norconk MA. 2007. Sakis, uakaris and titi monkeys: behavioral diversity in a radiation of seed predators. See Campbell et al. 2007, pp. 123–38

Nunes S, Fite JE, French JA. 2000. Variation in steroid hormones associated with infant care behaviour and experience in male marmosets (*Callithrix kuhlii*). *Anim. Behav.* 60:857–65

Nunes S, Fite JE, Patera KJ, French JA. 2001. Interactions among paternal behavior, steroid hormones, and parental experience in male marmosets (*Callithrix kuhlii*). *Horm. Behav.* 39:70–82

Parker GA, Schwagmeyer PL. 2005. Male "mixed" reproductive strategies in biparental species: Trivers was probably right, but why? *Am. Nat.* 165:96–105

Parker KJ, Lee TM. 2001. Central vasopressin administration regulates the onset of facultative paternal behavior in *Microtus pennsylvanicus* (meadow voles). *Horm. Behav.* 39:285–94

Pedersen CA, Prange AJ Jr. 1985. Oxytocin and mothering behavior in the rat. *Pharmacol. Ther.* 28:287–302

Pedersen CA, Vadlamudi SV, Boccia ML, Amico JA. 2006. Maternal behavior deficits in nulliparous oxytocin knockout mice. *Genes Brain Behav.* 5:274–81

An elaboration of the interface between developmental biology and paternal care.

Queller DC. 1997. Why do females care more than males? *Proc. R. Soc. London B Biol. Sci.* Series B. 264:1555–57

Quinlan RJ. 2007. Human parental effort and environmental risk. *Proc. R. Soc. London B Biol. Sci.* 274:121–25

Reeder DM. 2001. *The biology of parenting in the monogamous titi monkey* (Callicebus moloch). PhD thesis. Univ. Calif., Davis

Reichard U. 2003. Social monogamy in gibbons: the male perspective. In *Monogamy. Mating Strategies and Partnerships in Birds, Humans and Other Mammals*, ed. UH Reichard, C Boesch, pp. 190–213. Cambridge, UK: Univ. Cambridge Press

Rodman PS, Bossuyt FJ. 2007. Fathers and stepfathers: familial relations of old and new males within groups of *Callicebus brunneus* in southeastern Perú. *Am. J. Phys. Anthropol.* 132(S44):201

Ross C, MacLarnon A. 2000. The evolution of non-maternal care in anthropoid primates: a test of the hypotheses. *Folia Primatol.* 71:93–113

Ross CN, French JA, Orte G. 2007. Germ-line chimerism and paternal care in marmosets (*Callithrix kuhlii*). *Proc. Natl. Acad. Sci. USA* 104:6278–82

Rosso L, Keller L, Kaessmann H, Hammond R. 2008. Mating system and avpr1a promoter variation in primates. *Biol. Lett.* 4(4):375–8

Rotundo M, Fernandez-Duque E, Dixson AF. 2005. Infant development and parental care in free-ranging *Aotus azarai azarai* in Argentina. *Int. J. Primatol.* 26:1459–73

Ruis MA, te Brake JH, Buwalda B, De Boer SF, Meerlo P, et al. 1999. Housing familiar male wildtype rats together reduces the long-term adverse behavioural and physiological effects of social defeat. *Psychoneuroendocrinology* 24:285–300

Sanchez R, Parkin JC, Chen JY, Gray PB. 2009. Oxytocin, vasopression, and human social behavior. In *Endocrinology of Social Relationships*, ed. PB Gray, PT Ellison, pp. 319–39. Cambridge, MA: Harvard Univ. Press

Schradin C, Anzenberger G. 1999. Prolactin, the hormone of paternity. *News Physiol. Sci.* 14:223–31

Schradin C, Anzenberger G. 2002. Why do new world monkey fathers have enhanced prolactin levels? *Evol. Anthropol.* 11:122–25

Schradin C, Reeder DM, Mendoza SP, Anzenberger G. 2003. Prolactin and paternal care: comparison of three species of monogamous new world monkeys (*Callicebus cupreus, Callithrix jacchus*, and *Callimico goeldii*). *J. Comp. Psychol.* 117:166–75

Sheldon BC. 2002. Relating paternity to paternal care. *Philos. Trans. R. Soc. London B Biol. Sci.* 357:341–50

Smucny DA, Abbott DH, Mansfield KG, Schultz-Darken NJ, Yamamoto ME, et al. 2004. Reproductive output, maternal age, and survivorship in captive common marmoset females (*Callithrix jacchus*). *Am. J. Primatol.* 64:107–21

Smuts BB, Gubernick DJ. 1992. Male-infant relationships in nonhuman primates: paternal investment or mating effort? In *Father-Child Relations. Cultural and Biosocial Contexts*, ed. BS Hewlett, pp. 1–30. New York: Aldine de Gruyter

Snyder BF, Gowaty PA. 2007. A reappraisal of Bateman's classic study of intrasexual selection. *Evolution* 61:2457–68

Storey AE, Walsh CJ. 2000. Hormonal correlates of paternal responsiveness in new and expectant fathers. *Evol. Human Behav.* 21:79–95

Suomi S. 1999. Attachment in rhesus monkeys. In *Handbook of Attachment: Theory, Research, and Clinical Applications*, ed. J Cassidy, PR Shaver, pp. 181–97. New York: Guilford

Swain JE, Lorberbaum JP, Kose S, Strathearn L. 2007. Brain basis of early parent-infant interactions: psychology, physiology, and in vivo functional neuroimaging studies. *J. Child Psychol. Psychiatry* 48:262–87

> A review of the neural basis of parental care from a psychobiological perspective.

Tang-Martinez Z, Ryder TB. 2005. The problem with paradigms: Bateman's worldview as a case study. *Integr. Comp. Biol.* 45:821–30

Tardif SD. 1997. The bioenergetics of parental behavior and the evolution of alloparental care in marmosets and tamarins. In *Cooperative Breeding in Mammals*, ed. NG Solomon, JA French, pp. 11–33. Cambridge, UK: Cambridge Univ. Press

Tardif SD, Garber PA. 1994. Social and reproductive patterns in neotropical primates: relation to ecology, body size, and infant care. *Am. J. Primatol.* 34:111–14

Tardif SD, Santos CV, Baker AJ, Van Elsacker L, Ruiz-Miranda CR, et al. 2002. Infant care in lion tamarins. In *Lion Tamarins. Biology and Conservation*, ed. DG Kleiman, AB Rylands, pp. 213–32. Washington, DC: Smithson. Univ. Press

Tardif SD, Ziegler TE, Power M, Layne DG. 2005. Endocrine changes in full-term pregnancies and pregnancy loss due to energy restriction in the common marmoset (*Callithrix jacchus*). *J. Clin. Endocrinol. Metab.* 90:335–39

Taub DM, ed. 1984. *Primate Paternalism*. New York: Van Nostrand Reinhold

Terranova ML, Cirulli F, Laviola G. 1999. Behavioral and hormonal effects of partner familiarity in periado-lescent rat pairs upon novelty exposure. *Psychoneuroendocrinology* 24:639–56

Trivers RL. 1972. Parental investment and sexual selection. In *Sexual Selection and The Descent of Man, 1871–1971*, ed. BG Campbell, pp. 136–79. Chicago: Aldine

Trumbo ST. 2006. Infanticide, sexual selection and task specialization in a biparental burying beetle. *Anim. Behav.* 72:1159–67

Valeggia CR. 2009. Flexible caretakers: responses of Toba families in transition. In *Substitute Parents: Biological and Social Perspectives on Alloparenting in Human Societies*, ed. G Bentley, R Mace. Oxford: Berghahn. In press

Van Schaik CP, Kappeler PM. 1997. Infanticide risk and the evolution of male-female association in primates. *Proc. R. Soc. London B Biol. Sci.* 264:1687–95

Wade MJ, Shuster SM. 2002. The evolution of parental care in the context of sexual selection: a critical reassessment of parental investment theory. *Am. Nat.* 160:289–92

Walum H, Westberg L, Henningsson S, Neiderhiser JM, Reiss D, et al. 2008. Genetic variation in the vasopressin receptor 1a gene (AVPR1A) associates with pair-bonding behavior in humans. *Proc. Natl. Acad. Sci. USA* 105:14153–56

Whitten PL. 1987. Infants and adult males. In *Primate Societies*, ed. BB Smuts, DL Cheney, RM Seyfarth, RW Wrangham, T Struhsaker, pp. 343–57. Chicago: Univ. Chicago Press

Wingfield JC, Hegner RE, Dufty AM, Ball GF. 1990. The Challenge Hypothesis: theoretical implications for patterns of testosterone secretion, mating systems, and breeding strategies. *Am. Nat.* 136:829–46

Wolovich CK, Perea-Rodriguez JP, Fernandez-Duque E. 2008. Food transfers to young and mates in wild owl monkeys (*Aotus azarai*). *Am. J. Primatol.* 70:211–21

Woodroffe R, Vincent A. 1994. Mother's little helpers: patterns of male care in mammals. *Trends Ecol. Evol.* 9:294–97

Wright PC. 1984. Biparental care in *Aotus trivirgatus* and *Callicebus moloch*. In *Female Primates: Studies by Women Primatologists*, ed. M Small, pp. 59–75. New York: Alan R. Liss

Wright PC. 1990. Patterns of paternal care in primates. *Int. J. Primatol.* 11:89–102

Wynne-Edwards KE, Timonin ME. 2007. Paternal care in rodents: weakening support for hormonal regulation of the transition to behavioral fatherhood in rodent animal models of biparental care. *Horm. Behav.* 52:114–21

Young L, Lim M, Gingrich B, Insel T. 2001. Cellular mechanisms of social attachment. *Horm. Behav.* 40:133–38

Young LJ, Murphy Young AZ, Hammock EAD. 2005. Anatomy and neurochemistry of the pairbond. *J. Comp. Neurol.* 493:51–57

Zahed SR, Prudom SL, Snowdon CT, Ziegler TE. 2007. Male parenting and response to infant stimuli in the common marmoset (*Callithrix jacchus*). *Am. J. Primatol.* 69:1–15

Zeh DW, Smith RL. 1985. Paternal investment by terrestrial arthropods. *Am. Zool.* 25:785–805

Ziegler TE. 2000. Hormones associated with non-maternal infant care: a review of mammalian and avian studies. *Folia Primatol.* 71:6–21

Ziegler TE, Prudom SL, Schultz-Darken NJ, Kurian AV, Snowdon CT. 2006. Pregnancy weight gain: marmoset and tamarin dads show it too. *Biol. Lett.* 2:181–83

Probably the most provocative recent evaluation of the relationship between sexual selection and parental investment theories.

Developmental Origins of Adult Function and Health: Evolutionary Hypotheses

Christopher W. Kuzawa and Elizabeth A. Quinn

Department of Anthropology, Northwestern University, Evanston, Illinois 60208;
email: kuzawa@northwestern.edu

Annu. Rev. Anthropol. 2009. 38:131–47

First published online as a Review in Advance on June 19, 2009

The *Annual Review of Anthropology* is online at anthro.annualreviews.org

This article's doi:
10.1146/annurev-anthro-091908-164350

Key Words

developmental plasticity, adaptation, fetal growth, DOHaD, reproduction, life history

Abstract

Many biological systems have critical periods that overlap with the age of maternal provisioning via placenta or lactation. As such, they serve as conduits for phenotypic information transfer between generations and link maternal experience with offspring biology and disease outcomes. This review critically evaluates proposals for an adaptive function of these responses in humans. Although most models assume an adult function for the metabolic responses to nutritional stress, these specific traits have more likely been tailored for effects during fetal life and infancy. Other biological functions are under stronger evolutionary selection later in life and thus are better candidates for predictive plasticity. Given the long human life cycle and environmental changes that are unpredictable on decadal timescales, plastic responses that evolved to confer benefits in adolescence or adulthood likely rely on cues that integrate matrilineal experiences prior to gestation. We conclude with strategies for testing the timescale and adaptive significance of developmental responses to early environments.

INTRODUCTION

Developmental plasticity: the ability of a gene to generate a range of possible phenotypes (body and behavior) contingent on environmental experience

Programming: an environmentally induced, durable biological change in the structure or function of a tissue, organ, or biological system

DOHaD: developmental origins of health and disease

CVD: cardiovascular disease

Induction: synonymous with programming

Anthropology has traditionally studied developmental plasticity as a contributor to human variation (Boas 1912) and as a mode of adaptation to environmental change (Lasker 1969, Frisancho 1993). There has recently been a resurgence of interest in developmental plasticity as research has demonstrated that nutritional, hormonal, and other aspects of the prenatal and infant environments have effects on physiology and metabolism that persist into adult life (Barker 1994). Such examples of biological programming can involve modified growth of organs and tissues and are increasingly being linked to durable epigenetic changes that modify patterns of gene expression (Waterland & Michels 2007).

The multidisciplinary enterprise that studies the developmental origins of health and disease (DOHaD) is illuminating long-standing questions of interest to anthropologists, including the origins of the high rates of diabetes among specific Native American groups (Benyshek et al. 2001), the rise of chronic diseases in the context of rapid cultural and nutritional transition (Adair & Prentice 2004), and the biology of race as manifested in the disproportionate burden of cardiovascular disease (CVD) among U.S. blacks compared with U.S. whites (Kuzawa & Sweet 2009). In addition to these health-related applications, research is increasingly addressing the role of these intergenerational processes in organismal adaptation (Wells 2003, Bateson et al. 2004, Kuzawa & Pike 2005). Most proposals assume that resources transferred from mother to offspring serve as cues of local ecology, which offspring use to adjust biological settings and developmental trajectory in anticipation of future environments. Because most developmental responses occur during fetal life and infancy, they are responses to maternal phenotype and thus can be viewed as a form of nongenomic information transfer between generations. These evolutionary models propose a process of transgenerational epigenetic adaptation that links the environmental experiences of mothers with the phenotypic variation, adaptation, and disease risk in their offspring.

This review is organized in two sections. First, we selectively review evidence that early environmental stimuli, such as nutrition, growth, and stress, have persistent effects on biological systems. A comprehensive review of the empirical work is beyond our intent, and the reader is directed to the many excellent resources devoted to this topic (McMillen & Robinson 2005, Gluckman & Hanson 2006, Goldberg 2008). These summaries serve as background for the second section of the article, which reviews the functions and evolutionary origins that have been proposed to explain these findings. We first focus narrowly on the most heavily cited ideas relating to metabolic risk factors for CVD. We then suggest orienting future work in this rapidly expanding field around the goal of developing testable hypotheses aimed at clarifying the source and timescale of ecological information conveyed to offspring via maternal cues and characterizing the mechanisms that underlie offspring phenotypic change.

EVIDENCE FOR THE INFLUENCE OF EARLY ENVIRONMENTS ON ADULT BIOLOGY AND HEALTH

Early human cohort studies revealed relationships between deprivation during childhood and subsequent adult mortality rates (Kermack et al. 1934, Forsdahl 1977). These findings are now known to trace to the effects of prenatal and infant nutrition and stress on developmental plasticity (Barker 1994), a process described as developmental programming (Lucas 1991) or induction (Bateson 2001). The same suite of disease risk factors that relate to fetal growth or prenatal nutrition in humans are induced by dietary manipulation of animal models (Langley-Evans 1999, McMillen & Robinson 2005). The alterations induced involve changes in the growth, structure, and function of tissues, organs, or systems and are increasingly being linked to epigenetic changes that influence cellular gene expression (Waterland & Michels 2007).

In humans, these relationships are often studied using proxies of the prenatal environment, such as birth weight. Birth weight relates inversely to adult CVD risk, including blood pressure (Barker 2006), cholesterol (Kuzawa & Adair 2003), insulin resistance, and Type 2 diabetes, and a tendency to deposit fat in the central, metabolically active fat depot (Harder et al. 2007, Whincup et al. 2008). Maternal diet and nutritional status during pregnancy also predict risk for these conditions in offspring (Adair 2001, Brennan et al. 2006). Rapid postnatal growth, especially when expressed as catch-up growth following fetal growth restriction, may exacerbate the physiological changes that lead to CVD and adult metabolic disease (Lucas et al. 1999, Metcalfe & Monaghan 2001, Cameron 2007). The relevant research initially focused on populations in Britain, Europe, and the United States (Barker et al. 1989). However, these processes are increasingly recognized as contributing to chronic disease emergence in populations experiencing rapid economic and nutritional transition (Benyshek et al. 2001, Adair & Prentice 2004).

As an extension of the original focus on fetal nutrition, the role of breastfeeding in biological programming is now a focus of DOHaD research (Schack-Nielsen et al. 2004; Owen et al. 2006, 2008). Many of the adult metabolic states documented in lower-birth-weight individuals, including central obesity (Grummer-Strawn & Mei 2004, Harder et al. 2007), Type 2 diabetes (Owen et al. 2006), high cholesterol (Owen et al. 2008), and elevated blood pressure (Lawlor et al. 2005, Martin et al. 2005), are less common in individuals who were breastfed as infants. Formula feeding promotes increased weight gain, which could contribute to these adult health differences (Adair 2008). In addition, human and animal work has helped elucidate the role of specific nutrients as influences on future metabolic functioning. Dietary manipulation of newborn rat pups suggests that high carbohydrate exposure at this age decreases insulin and leptin sensitivity in adulthood (Srinivasan et al. 2006) and may increase risk of CVD, diabetes,

obesity, and hyperlipidemia (Mitrani et al. 2007).

Although most work continues to focus on disease outcomes, studies are investigating the developmental origins of a wide range of traits with functional and life-history consequences (Kuzawa & Pike 2005). For instance, there is evidence for long-term effects of birth outcomes on gonadal hormone production in females and males (Jasienska et al. 2006, Nunez-de la Mora & Bentley 2008) and on future reproductive effort as reflected in offspring birth weight (Morton 2006). Different components of immune function relate to early environments (McDade 2005), as do somatic and life-history traits such as lean mass and body composition (Baker et al. 2009), stress physiology (Belsky 2008), maturational timing (Adair 2001, Chisholm & Coall 2008), and life span (Doblhammer & Vaupel 2001). Thus a wide and expanding suite of functional traits are now known to be modified by early environments, in addition to the metabolic and other adult diseases that are most extensively discussed in the literature.

THE ROLE OF CRITICAL PERIODS IN THE TRANSGENERATIONAL TRANSFER OF PHENOTYPIC INFORMATION

Some of the plastic phenotypic variation induced in response to early environments reflects incomplete buffering of development and thus requires no adaptive explanation (Lummaa 2003, Jones 2005, Chisholm & Coall 2008). For example, during periods of rapid growth, growth-restricting deficits can have large impacts on the final size, structure, and function of tissues or organs (Widdowson & McCance 1975), such as the nephron-deficient kidneys that are believed to predispose lower-birth-weight individuals to developing hypertension and renal failure (Lampl et al. 2002, Luyckx & Brenner 2005).

Lingering effects of early environments can also trace to critical periods during which

Critical period: a limited time in early development when environmental stimuli can durably influence a trait or biological outcome

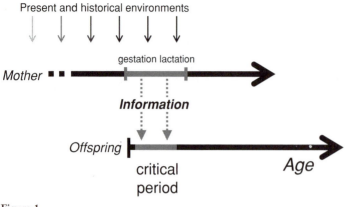

Present and historical environments

Mother

gestation lactation

Information

Offspring

critical
period

Age

Figure 1

The timing of a critical period determines the capacity for transfer of
phenotypic information between generations. Maternal phenotype comes to
embody a record of a mother's cumulative environmental experiences, and this
information is transferred via nutrients, hormones, and other cues.

developing systems permanently modify their
settings in response to environmental experience (Bornstein 1989). Many systems, such
as hormonal axes, have critical periods when
settings are dependent on and respond to social and biological cues (Worthman 1999). For
a developing biological system, a critical period effect can reflect changes in cell number, selection-driven changes in cell type (e.g.,
in neurons and lymphocytes), and epigenetic
changes in cellular gene expression that are heritable by daughter cells (Waterland & Garza
1999). That many critical periods overlap with
the timing of direct maternal provisioning via
the placenta and lactation means that these
periods are windows of opportunity for the
transfer of phenotypic information from one
generation to the next (**Figure 1**). Maternal
phenotype is expressed via nutrients, growth
factors, metabolites, hormones, and immune
factors that reflect the mother's cumulative experience of the local environment (Emanuel
1986, Drake & Walker 2004, Wells 2007b).

Investigators have provided numerous examples of developmental systems that modify
functional settings in response to cues reflecting the mother's social and physical environment. Breast milk contains the body fat–derived
hormone leptin, which is present in milk in proportion to maternal levels (Houseknecht et al.

HPT: hypothalamic-
pituitary-testicular
axis

T: testosterone

LH: luteinizing
hormone

1997) and is absorbed into the neonatal circulation (Miralles et al. 2006). In rats, perinatal administration of leptin has been shown
to reverse the metabolic phenotype established
during a stressful gestation (Vickers et al. 2005),
as does an oral dose prior to weaning (Palou &
Pico 2009). Because the leptin content of milk
may be related to maternal leptin levels (and
thus, her body fat), it could convey information about her energy stores and thus her recent
energy balance.

The hypothalamic-pituitary-testicular (HPT)
axis that regulates testosterone (T) production experiences a critical period that spans
two phases of dependency, the first during
early gestation and the second during the
months following birth. Both overlap with,
and are sensitive to, maternal resource transfer
(Worthman 1999). During the postnatal
period, pituitary secretion of luteinizing
hormone (LH) surges, leading to a temporary
rise in T to near adult levels. By roughly 6
months of age, this activity is complete and the
testes remain largely dormant until puberty.
Although the function of this postnatal surge
in HPT activity remains obscure, it likely provides opportunities for signals or experiences
to influence system settings. Because stress
may influence HPT activity, social factors
may be important. For instance, Worthman
(1987) speculates that the Kikuyu time ritual
circumcision (and resulting stress) to coincide
with this critical period, thus modifying HPT
settings. In addition, the timing of this critical
period during the first weeks after birth—likely
coinciding with exclusive breastfeeding during
much of human evolutionary history—suggests
a capacity for cues transferred via breast milk
to influence system settings. In rats, nutrient
restriction during lactation has led to lower
adult T in male offspring (Zambrano et al.
2005). This area is ripe for innovative research
(e.g. Thompson & Lampl 2007).

The timing of the critical period for somatic
growth also suggests an important role for cues
transferred via placenta and breast milk. Unlike
growth in childhood and adolescence, growth
during fetal life and infancy is insulin dependent

and thus driven by the composition and quantity of nutrients transferred across the placenta or in breast milk (Gluckman & Pinal 2003). This period of sensitivity accounts for the predominant impact of fetal, infant, and early childhood nutritional stress on adult stature in populations faced with chronic poverty and high pathogen burden (Martorell et al. 1995). The overlap of this period with direct maternal provisioning helps ensure that growth is buffered and, in contexts free from poverty and widespread childhood infections, could allow growth trajectory to be calibrated to a woman's provisioning capacity, itself reflecting the phenotypic embodiment of her cumulative nutritional experience (Wells 2003, Kuzawa 2005).

The diversity of maternal cues that have long-term effects on multiple systems in offspring suggests that many critical periods may be timed to allow signal transfer between generations. Indeed, many biological systems have a need to learn through experience, and their sensitivity to maternal phenotype hints at an ability to benefit from the mother's embodied experiential history. When a maternal cue is correlated with local conditions, this in theory allows a form of adaptive plasticity to evolve in which biological settings are established in anticipation of future environments (Mousseau & Fox 1998). Indeed, this has been the assumption of most evolutionary models of fetal plasticity in the DOHaD literature (e.g., Bateson et al. 2004), and we turn to these next.

THE THRIFTY PHENOTYPE AND FORECAST MODELS OF METABOLIC ADAPTATION

Because most DOHaD work has addressed outcomes related to CVD, the majority of speculations about the evolutionary origins of fetal and infant plasticity have focused on the cardiovascular risk factors induced by nutritional stress. Here we provide an overview of the most popular and widely cited of these ideas, and we suggest some ways in which evolutionary theory can be used to evaluate them (see also Wells 2007a).

As discussed above, individuals born small who gain excess weight as older children or adults are at elevated risk for developing metabolic risk factors for CVD. On the basis of these findings, Hales & Barker (1992) argued that the fetal response to prenatal undernutrition induces a "thrifty phenotype" characterized by insulin resistance, a shift in circulation to protect the brain ("brain sparing"), and a nutrient-conserving reduction in organ growth. They argued that these adjustments enhance immediate fetal survival but subsequently increase the risk of developing diabetes and CVD in the event that the individual later experiences nutritional excess and weight gain. This model, offered as a competing hypothesis to Neel's (1962) thrifty genotype model, proposed that high rates of diabetes among some populations might trace to stressful intrauterine environments rather than to susceptibility alleles.

As an extension of the thrifty phenotype model, Bateson (2001) suggested that fetal adjustments to prenatal nutrition are not merely designed to improve immediate survival, but also are initiated in anticipation of nutritional conditions during childhood (see also Worthman 1999, Kuzawa 2001):

> The condition of the mother in late pregnancy may be taken to provide a forecast about the state of the environment in which the child will grow. This then determines the pattern of growth and the metabolic pathways of the child. If the mother's forecast was wrong, the consequences for the child can be dire. The hypothesis is that the undernourished mother gives birth to a child who is small in size and is adapted to a thrifty environment. Conversely a well-nourished mother gives birth to a large baby who is adapted to an affluent environment. (Bateson 2001, p. 933)

According to this model, the metabolic responses of a nutritionally stressed fetus are at least in part geared toward improving survival during the postnatal period, but they also elevate risk for adult metabolic diseases in the event of excess postnatal nutrition and weight gain.

As an amendment to this proposal, Gluckman & Hanson (2004) hypothesized that, using prenatal cues, the fetus "adjusts its physiology to be appropriate for its predicted mature environmental range" (p. 1735). They suggested that a prenatally stressed individual will have a metabolism geared to cope with a nutritionally poor adult environment and would thus be poorly suited to a nutritionally rich adult environment. The resultant mismatch between expected and experienced adult environmental conditions elevates risk for diseases such as CVD. In this popular version of the forecast model, fetal metabolic responses to undernutrition are presumed to have evolved to confer benefits primarily during adulthood.

EVOLUTIONARY PRINCIPLES APPLIED TO THE THRIFTY PHENOTYPE AND FORECAST MODELS

Each of the models described above offers an explanation for a range of biological and medical observations, and as such these models have intuitive appeal. However, because they assign evolutionary origins to plasticity in metabolism, they should be evaluated on the basis of their consistency with the expectations and assumptions of evolutionary theory. We suggest the following three observations as a constructive starting point.

Selection Against Late-Life Metabolic Disease Is Minimal

First, by proposing that diabetes and CVD reflect a mismatch between expected and actual adult environments, the adult-focused version of the forecast model implies that natural selection has shaped plasticity in metabolism to avoid these late-life conditions. However, for natural selection to shape a trait into an adaptation, the trait must be variable, have a heritable component, and modify genetic fitness via effects on survival or reproduction (Lewontin 1974). Diabetes and CVD are usually asymptomatic

until postreproductive life and were likely rare prior to historically recent nutritional and economic transitions (Popkin 2004). Thus, there has been minimal selection for a capacity to adjust developmental biology to avoid such diseases because they likely had negligible impacts on genetic fitness (Williams 1966, Jones 2005, Kuzawa 2005, Worthman & Kuzara 2005, Rickard & Lummaa 2007, Wells 2007b, Chisholm & Coall 2008).

Parturition and Weaning Are Developmental Bottlenecks and Focal Points of Selection on Metabolism

Second, in contrast to the invisibility of late-life metabolic diseases to natural selection, many of the metabolic changes induced by nutritional stress could influence survival earlier in the life cycle. As Hales & Barker (1992) emphasized, the human fetus has a large, glucose-hungry brain, which must be protected during periods of shortage. The early postnatal period is similarly stressful from a metabolic perspective (Kuzawa 1998). The brain requires an uninterrupted flow of energy corresponding to roughly half of resting metabolism during much of human infancy and childhood (Holliday 1986). The challenge of meeting these needs is compounded by the nutritional and infectious disease stress of weaning, when infants may be cut off from provisioning and forced to rely on endogenous energy stores. Perhaps reflecting these selection pressures, the highly encephalized human is born with more body fat than any mammal for which data are available, and it devotes most growth expenditure to fat deposition in the months prior to weaning (Kuzawa 1998). The metabolic adjustments associated with the thrifty phenotype could improve survival during this difficult period. For instance, insulin resistance reduces peripheral glucose uptake, thus sparing glucose for the noninsulin-dependent uptake of the brain, whereas preferential deposition of visceral fat, which is innervated by sympathetic nerve fibers, allows rapid mobilization of stored fats during stress (Kuzawa 2009).

The original forecast model proposed that the thrifty phenotype was induced to match expectations to childhood nutrition rather than conditions in adulthood (Bateson 2001). From a similar but distinct perspective, Wells (2003, 2007b) has argued that thrifty adaptations are induced to match the level of likely provisioning after weaning, as reflected in the mother's life course and pregnancy nutritional exposures. These arguments assume that the primary benefit of fetal metabolic adaptations, and by implication the selection pressure that has favored their evolution, occurs after the mortality bottleneck of weaning. Yet childhood is the age of lowest mortality in the human life cycle and is characterized by very low nutritional mortality and thus minimal selection on metabolism (Kuzawa 1998). Therefore, we believe it more likely that these responses evolved to confer benefits prenatally or during infancy.

A glucose-sparing, insulin-resistant state is potentially beneficial to a nutritionally stressed fetus or neonate faced with the challenge of buffering the insulin-independent glucose uptake of a large brain (Hales & Barker 1992). These adjustments would also elevate risk for developing diabetes and CVD, especially in the event of metabolic disruption due to excess weight gain. Thus adult disease need not trace to a mismatch between anticipated and experienced adult environments; it is more likely a pleiotropic side effect of an adjustment in metabolic priorities adopted to improve fetal or infant survival (Kuzawa 2005, Rickard & Lummaa 2007).

Signal Fidelity (Predictive Ability) Decays with Time

Third, reliable predictions of environmental conditions in the distant future are not necessarily available to a human fetus or neonate. Many species do have access to early-life cues that are predictive of future conditions, and individuals of these species use this information to modify their life histories (see Bateson et al. 2004, Gluckman & Hanson 2004). However, many of these species share with humans few similarities

in life history or ecology and thus provide limited insight into how maternal-offspring signaling might operate in our species (Kuzawa 2008).

Take the example of the vole, which is often cited as a mammalian precedent for predictive plasticity. Fetuses of some vole species living in highly seasonal environments monitor maternal melatonin (reflecting day length) and chemical by-products of grass ingestion as a way to calibrate maturational timing to the summer birth season (Berger & Negus 1992, Horton 2005). This process has been described as forward-looking prediction because it adjusts life-history scheduling to match a future, changed environmental state (Kuzawa 2008). The vole is capable of forward-looking prediction because it is short lived, and the ecological variation it faces is cyclical and tightly correlated with maternal endocrine and metabolic cues that cross the placenta. The seasonal cycle that determines the optimal strategy for the individual vole involves biological entrainment to a stable (and thus highly predictable) planetary orbital process, and as such, the fidelity of the prediction does not fade once it is established. Most of the species cited as examples of predictive developmental plasticity are analogous to the vole or have life spans short enough that cues experienced early in the life cycle are good indicators of conditions later in life.

Human populations face ecological variability that operates on multiple timescales, from millennial to decadal to seasonal (Potts 1998), and which is at least partly stochastic (unpredictable) rather than cyclical or regular (for more see Kuzawa 2005, 2008). The predictive ability, or fidelity, of early-life cues will thus decay with time through the human life cycle. It may be that cue fidelity need not be high for some prediction to be useful (Gluckman et al. 2005). Even so, because humans are not forward-looking predictors like the vole, early life cues will be more tightly coupled with conditions in early life than in a distant, adult future. As discussed below, Kuzawa (2005) has hypothesized that maternal phenotype could provide integrated information that records a mother's lifelong cumulative experiences and

Stochastic: change with a random component, a trend that cannot be predicted

might have long-term predictive value, even in stochastic environments. However, even with such a (hypothetical) stabilizing influence, signal fidelity will still decay with time, and evolution will have had more opportunities to harness early life cues to set short-term strategy.

In summary, strong selection related to metabolic stress during the mortality bottlenecks of gestation and weaning, combined with the time-dependent decay in signal fidelity, implies that metabolic plasticity and the traits associated with the thrifty phenotype have the greatest opportunity to influence Darwinian fitness early in life. To the extent that they are adaptive, metabolic responses to early nutritional stress should by default be assumed to have immediate or short-term benefits rather than benefits primarily in adulthood (Kuzawa 2005; 2008; Rickard & Lummaa 2007; Wells 2007b; Chisholm & Coall 2008). Hales & Barker (1992) originally emphasized that fetal responses to nutritional stress benefit immediate survival. In our view, this remains the most plausible scenario of selection on the key plastic metabolic traits related to CVD risk (the thrifty phenotype), perhaps with an extension of similar benefits to infancy and weaning.

Whereas the above discussion applies to metabolic traits, which are the most widely studied plastic phenotypes in the DOHaD literature, other biological systems experience strong selection pressure during different parts of the life cycle. For example, adult size, maturational timing, reproduction, and neuroendocrine systems that manage social interactions are under stronger selection during adolescence or adulthood than in early life. Phenotypes such as these are better candidates for having evolved an ability to calibrate function in anticipation of adolescent or adult needs.

ON THE TIMESCALES OF MATERNAL PHENOTYPIC MEMORY

For a system to evolve such a capacity to set long-term strategy in a predictive fashion, the fetus or infant must have, as a minimal requirement, a reliable predictor of future conditions (DeWitt et al. 1998). The human generation time is several decades in length, and ecological change on this timescale is stochastic, implying that future changes are unpredictable. Some maternal cues appear to convey ecological information that has been integrated or averaged over some time period preceding gestation and, therefore, represents a better guess of average conditions likely to be experienced by offspring in the long term (Kuzawa 2005, 2008). For instance, offspring birth weight varies across women, tends to be heavier in better-nourished populations, and yet is refractory to supplementation (Morton 2006). Similarly, certain breast milk components, such as fat content and energy density, vary across women and populations in different ecological settings but are generally only poorly responsive to supplementation (Prentice 1991, Villalpando & del Prado 1999).

Some evidence indicates that this slow responsiveness of transgenerational nutritional cues reflects a lingering effect of a woman's nutritional history on nutrient transfer to offspring (Wells 2003, Kuzawa 2005). For instance, human and nonhuman primate evidence shows that a female's gestational nutritional experiences as a fetus—and thus the grandmother's nutritional history—influence her own intrauterine nutritional investment in offspring (Ounsted et al. 1986, Price et al. 1999). The resulting integration of long-term matrilineal experience, reflecting offspring responses to maternal signals of past environments, has been labeled "transgenerational phenotypic inertia" and may allow for cues that average information over decades or generations (Kuzawa 2005). Belsky (2008) has recently proposed an extension of this idea to the hypothalamic-pituitary-adrenal axis, which regulates production of the stress hormone cortisol (see also Chisholm & Coall 2008).

Building from the inertia concept, we hypothesize that offspring phenotypes that are calibrated for future function (e.g., reproduction) will be more strongly predicted by long-term maternal or matrilineal experience than by acute maternal experiences during pregnancy (**Figure 2**). The longer the window of matrilineal averaging, the less responsive the resulting cue will be to transient environmental change, and the more useful the cue will be further into the future (**Figure 3**). As a corollary, cues that are acutely responsive to transient maternal experience during pregnancy are poor candidates for calibrating phenotype to anticipated future ecology. Candidate signals for a mother's longer-term environmental experience include nutrient, metabolic, or endocrine resources that (*a*) are transferred from mother to offspring in utero or via lactation; (*b*) induce phenotypic changes (e.g., in metabolic or endocrine settings) in offspring; (*c*) vary across women or populations living in different ecologies, suggesting environmental sensitivity; and despite this, (*d*) are minimally responsive to current, transient maternal experience (e.g., supplementation or acute stress during pregnancy or lactation). Together, these qualities define a system that is sensitive to chronic rather than acute environmental change and that therefore potentially transfers a more stable environmental signal to offspring.

Although there is evidence that maternal cues can be calibrated over long time scales, other examples suggest that offspring phenotype is potentially responsive to short-term ecological variability experienced by the mother during gestation. For instance, maternal illness during pregnancy has been found to predict offspring birth outcome (Heinke & Kuzawa 2008) and adult health and function (Almond 2006), suggesting that resource transfer to the fetus and some long-term biological settings may be responsive to transient maternal experiences during gestation. Similarly, in the Gambia, individuals born in the wet season have reduced adult life expectancy (Moore et al. 1997), and season of birth has been shown to predict life span in other populations (e.g., Doblhammer & Vaupel 2001).

Unlike the short-lived vole, it is difficult to imagine how a human would benefit by adopting different adult biological strategies contingent on season of birth. Thus, such findings

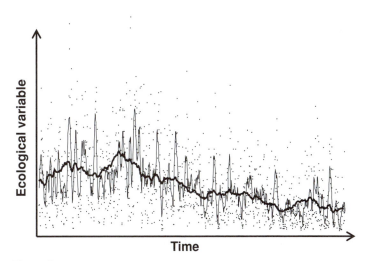

Time

Figure 2

The value of averaging as a way to identify a trend in a noisy signal, in this case representing availability of a hypothetical ecological resource. The two lines are running averages calculated across 10 time units (*thin line*) and 100 time units (*dark line*). As the window of averaging increases, an underlying long-term trend is uncovered. Transgenerational influences of maternal and grandmaternal nutritional history on fetal nutrition may help achieve a similar feat.

suggest several possible interpretations (see also Ellison & Jasienska 2007). These responses may indeed be adaptive because, as outlined earlier, there are bottlenecks of nutritional mortality in early life. To the extent that short-term cues induce adjustments in metabolic or other biological settings that allow for survival of these early challenges, their long-term effects could be tolerated as side effects. A second possibility is that acute ecological stress during gestation may permanently modify offspring biology as a result of incomplete buffering. For instance, many of the above examples involved infections rather than simple nutritional stress, and perhaps immune activation reprioritizes maternal resource allocation in a fashion that negatively impacts fetal growth.

Because both developmental impairment and short-term signaling would manifest as a response to transient conditions during gestation or lactation, they are difficult to differentiate on the basis of the inducing cue. Fortunately, certain criteria are useful for helping differentiate impairment from adaptive function. We consider this problem next.

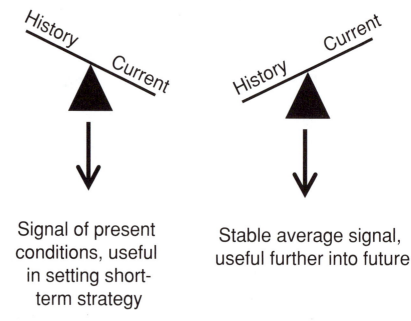

Signal of present conditions, useful in setting short-term strategy

Stable average signal, useful further into future

Figure 3

The balance of current versus historical influences on a maternal cue provides insights into its likely stability as a basis for predicting conditions into the future. Cues that respond to ecology but are refractory to transient experience during pregnancy or lactation convey information about average recent conditions and thus may be of use as a basis for calibrating long-term strategy. Cues that are sensitive to immediate experience during gestation or lactation will have poor long-term predictive ability and are therefore poor candidates for long-term signals.

EVALUATING THE REGULATORY BASIS OF OFFSPRING PHENOTYPIC CHANGE

Any proposal for an adaptive function for an induced phenotype, regardless of the presumed age of benefit, should strive to rule out the simpler interpretation of growth impairment (Gluckman et al. 2005, Worthman & Kuzara 2005, Bogin et al. 2007, Schell & Magnus 2007). Many of the outcomes predicted by early environmental conditions include physiologic, metabolic, or endocrine systems that are regulated by central (e.g., CNS) and peripheral components (e.g., an endocrine organ) linked through negative feedback. Endocrine systems regulate growth but also life history and resource allocation more generally and are thus a key coordinator of plasticity (Bribiescas & Ellison 2008). Studies investigating developmental programming of such systems should,

where feasible, document not only the downstream phenotypic effect but also the regulatory changes that underlie it because this will help clarify whether the change reflects developmental impairment or a regulatory adjustment in system settings (see Worthman 1999, Ellison & Jasienska 2007).

For illustration, once again consider the HPT axis that regulates production of T and downstream somatic and behavioral expenditures related to male life history. Low adult T in relation to low birth weight could reflect a change in central set points or a reduced sensitivity of the testes to LH (for more see Worthman 1999). Low T despite elevated LH would suggest impairment in testicular responsiveness to LH, whereas parallel reductions in both T and LH would suggest that the decline in T production is centrally mediated (**Figure 4**). The latter finding would not prove

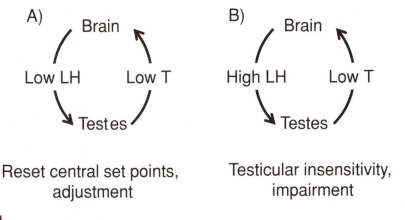

A) Brain

Low LH   Low T

Testes

Reset central set points, adjustment

B) Brain

High LH   Low T

Testes

Testicular insensitivity, impairment

Figure 4

Two possible causes for a hypothetical reduction in testosterone (T) levels found in relation to a measure of early-life nutritional stress. T is produced by the testes in response to luteinizing hormone (LH) of pituitary origin. If T and LH are both low (*a*), then the reduction in T is centrally mediated by the brain. In this instance, the central set points that set the target production of the system (the equivalent of the temperature to which a thermostat is set) have been adjusted, and the reduction in T is not a simple result of growth impairment or developmental damage to the testes due to, e.g., nutritional stress. If, however, low T is found despite high LH (*b*), then the testes are underproducing T despite high levels of LH, indicating reduced testicular sensitivity to LH. Of the two scenarios, the latter is more likely due to impaired growth or development of the peripheral organ.

that the adjustment is adaptive, but it would suggest that it is not simply a stress-induced developmental impairment of the peripheral tissue or organ.

Endocrine systems mediate trade-offs between competing functions in a context- or use-dependent fashion (Finch & Rose 1995). When evaluating effects on such systems, evidence for a change in trade-off priorities is also evidence for regulatory adjustment rather than impairment (see Ellison & Jasienska 2007). As one example, Jasienska et al. (2006) found that Polish women born as thin or fat babies were both capable of producing high estradiol as adults, but the women born thin suppressed steroid production at lower levels of physical activity. Evidence that an adult influence on a system is moderated by an early life cue suggests a change in regulatory threshold, making global impairment to the peripheral organ a less likely explanation.

The above observations suggest that adaptive plasticity will induce adjustments in central set points of affected systems. Function will not be globally impaired but will be regulated with different priorities or thresholds, which can be evaluated statistically by testing for significant interactions between early life cues and concurrent factors (e.g., diet, activity, stress) that are known to modulate system behavior.

CONCLUSION

Forensic scientists have long appreciated that the phenotype embodies a record of past experience. The ability of researchers with limited snapshots of biology, such as a single blood sample, to identify the effects of early-life experiences on adult health attests to this historical record. The direct biological connection between the mother and offspring during gestation and lactation similarly provides opportunities for offspring developmental biology to harness and use this information. For instance, an individual's chronic stress may become physically embodied in the set points and activities of the stress hormone axis, which modifies production of the hormone cortisol; cortisol may then cross the placenta to influence the development of this same hormonal axis in offspring (Worthman & Kuzara 2005). As discussed above, leptin indexes recent energy balance as reflected in body fat stores and may then transfer energetic information to offspring via breast milk. In a world without widespread obesity and metabolic dysregulation, insulin, which can cross the placenta, might reflect the nutritional sufficiency of the mother. And indeed, evidence indicates that the quantity of nutrients transferred in utero may itself reflect a woman's prior experience of nutrition, tracing back to her early formative years.

An adult phenotype is thus a storehouse of useful information about the social and physical environment. Because it interfaces directly with maternal physiology, the fetus, and later the neonate, has real-time access to this information. One recognized impediment to the evolution of adaptive plasticity is the cost of evolving and maintaining the appropriate systems of detection and response (DeWitt et al. 1998). With respect to information transferred between generations, the offspring already has the appropriate receptors and metabolic pathways in place to recognize many of these cues, which should lower these sensory costs (Kuzawa et al. 2008). A key question then is whether maternal cues are sufficiently reliable as predictors of future conditions to have allowed natural selection to shape appropriate adaptive responses to them (DeWitt et al. 1998).

To date, most work proposing such a function for fetal and infant plasticity has been inspired by findings related to the adult disease impacts of responses to early nutritional stress. As we and others have discussed, approaches grounded in adult disease–based definitions of organismal match are relevant to understanding impacts on longevity rather than on genetic success and, thus, are less than ideal as lenses into the evolutionary forces that would have shaped these responses. Opportunities for selection on the thrifty phenotype, and the potential for past cues to accurately predict current demands on these traits, are potentially high in fetal life, infancy, and early childhood and comparably low in adulthood. This fact does not make these findings uninteresting; they are

critical to understanding the health impacts of early environments, and perhaps future work will investigate any functional role of these responses during the early-life nutritional bottlenecks that likely exert strong selective pressure on them. As we have argued, systems that are under stronger selection during adolescence or adulthood, compared with early life, are better candidates for the evolution of long-term adaptive anticipatory plasticity. We are excited by the possibility and implications of predictive adaptation, and for all the reasons outlined here, we feel that it remains a viable and testable hypothesis for many systems.

All models of predictive adaptation require that the fetus or infant has access to a reliable cue. We have argued that, for a human faced with unpredictable trends in ecological change, the historical time depth of a transgenerational signal will determine how stable the prediction is and, thus, how far into the future it will retain its fidelity. Evaluating the time depth and information content of cues requires information on maternal experience prior to pregnancy, ideally collected at different ages of her prereproductive life. Creative use of historical records (e.g., Clarkin 2008) or other retrospective measures, such as leg length (Lawlor et al. 2003), fingerprint patterns (Kahn et al. 2008), and epigenetic markings in different cell lines (Waterland and Michels 2007), show promise as proxies for reconstructing maternal experiential history. We anticipate other innovative strategies to help bring the study of maternal history to developmental programming research. Such a historical approach, coupled with a focus on documenting the regulatory bases of phenotypic inductions, will clarify the possible adaptive significance of findings and help to rule out simpler interpretations such as developmental impairment (Ellison & Jasienska 2007).

The study of fetal and infant developmental plasticity is making important contributions to two central questions in anthropology: why we get sick and how we adapt. We are excited to see what discoveries future research will yield, and we hope that the ideas raised in this short review will help inspire some of this work.

SUMMARY POINTS

1. The study of developmental plasticity has a long history in anthropology and has been reinvigorated by the literature documenting effects of early environments that persist into adulthood and even to the next generation.

2. Many biological systems have critical periods during which environmental exposures can permanently change their functions. Many of these periods overlap with direct maternal provisioning via placenta or lactation and respond to maternal nutrients and hormones that reflect a woman's experience in the local environment.

3. Most evolutionary interpretations of this literature assume that the fetus sets its postnatal strategy in response to these cues.

4. Although the most widely cited evolutionary ideas propose an adult function for metabolic programming, a function for thrifty metabolic responses in fetal life or infancy is more likely.

5. Other systems are under stronger selection later in life, and these are better candidates for having evolved a capacity to adjust function in anticipation of future needs.

6. Because humans inhabit environments that change in ways that are not predictable, long-term predictive adaptation must rely on historical averaging. There is mixed evidence to support this proposition.

FUTURE ISSUES

1. A focus on reconstructing the historical information encoded in maternal cues will be key to understanding any long-term adaptive function of changes induced in offspring.

2. Studies of the regulatory basis of offspring phenotypic change can help clarify whether the response reflects a change in regulatory set points or simple developmental impairment.

3. Moving forward, the field will benefit by prioritizing hypothesis testing.

DISCLOSURE STATEMENT

The authors are not aware of any affiliations, memberships, funding, or financial holdings that might be perceived as affecting the objectivity of this review.

ACKNOWLEDGMENTS

Yarrow Axford's thoughtful comments greatly improved this manuscript.

LITERATURE CITED

Adair LS. 2001. Size at birth predicts age at menarche. *Pediatrics* 107:E59

Adair LS. 2008. Child and adolescent obesity: epidemiology and developmental perspectives. *Physiol. Behav.* 94:8–16

Adair LS, Prentice AM. 2004. A critical evaluation of the fetal origins hypothesis and its implications for developing countries. *J. Nutr.* 134:191–93

Almond D. 2006. Is the 1918 Influenza pandemic over? Long-term effects of in utero influenza exposure in the post-1940 US population. *J. Pol. Econ.* 114:672–712

Baker J, Hurtado AM, Pearson OM, Hill KR, Jones T, Frey MA. 2009. Developmental plasticity in fat patterning of Ache children in response to variation in interbirth intervals: a preliminary test of the roles of external environment and maternal reproductive strategies. *Am. J. Hum. Biol.* 21:77–83

Barker D. 1994. *Mothers, Babies, and Disease in Later Life.* London: BMJ

Barker DJ. 2006. Birth weight and hypertension. *Hypertension* 48(3):357–58

Barker DJ, Osmond C, Golding J, Kuh D, Wadsworth ME. 1989. Growth in utero, blood pressure in childhood and adult life, and mortality from cardiovascular disease. *BMJ* 298:564–67

Bateson P. 2001. Fetal experience and good adult design. *Int. J. Epidemiol.* 30:928–34

Bateson P, Barker D, Clutton-Brock T, Deb D, D'Udine B, et al. 2004. Developmental plasticity and human health. *Nature* 430:419–21

Belsky J. 2008. War, trauma and children's development: observations from a modern evolutionary perspective. *Int. J. Behav. Dev.* 32:260–71

Benyshek DC, Martin JF, Johnston CS. 2001. A reconsideration of the origins of the type 2 diabetes epidemic among Native Americans and the implications for intervention policy. *Med. Anthropol.* 20:25–64

Berger P, Negus N. 1992. Offspring growth and development responses to maternal transfer of 6-MBOA information in *Microtus montanus. Can. J. Zool.* 70:518–22

Boas F. 1912. Changes in bodily form of descendants of immigrants. *Am. Anthropol.* 14:530–62

Bogin B, Varela-Silva MI, Rios L. 2007. Life history trade-offs in human growth: adaptation or pathology? *Am. J. Hum. Biol.* 19:631–42

Bornstein MH. 1989. Sensitive periods in development: structural characteristics and causal interpretations. *Psychol. Bull.* 105:179–97

Brennan KA, Olson DM, Symonds ME. 2006. Maternal nutrient restriction alters renal development and blood pressure regulation of the offspring. *Proc. Nutr. Soc.* 65:116–24

Bribiescas RB, Ellison PT. 2008. How hormones mediate trade-offs in human health and disease. See Stearns & Koella 2008, pp. 77–94

Cameron N. 2007. Growth patterns in adverse environments. *Am. J. Hum. Biol.* 19:615–21

Chisholm JS, Coall DA. 2008. Not by bread alone. The role of psychosocial stress in age at first reproduction and health inequalities. In *Evolution and Health*, ed. W Trevathan, EO Smith, JJ McKenna, pp. 134–48. Oxford, UK: Oxford Univ. Press

Clarkin PF. 2008. Adiposity and height of adult Hmong refugees: relationship with war-related early malnutrition and migration. *Am. J. Hum. Biol.* 20:174–84

DeWitt TJ, Sih A, Wilson DS. 1998. Costs and limits of phenotypic plasticity. *Trends Ecol. Evol.* 13:77–81

Doblhammer G, Vaupel JW. 2001. Lifespan depends on month of birth. *Proc. Natl. Acad. Sci. USA* 98:2934–39

Drake AJ, Walker BR. 2004. The intergenerational effects of fetal programming: nongenomic mechanisms for the inheritance of low birth weight and cardiovascular risk. *J. Endocrinol.* 180:1–16

Ellison PT, Jasienska G. 2007. Constraint, pathology, and adaptation: How can we tell them apart? *Am. J. Hum. Biol.* 19:622–30

Emanuel I. 1986. Maternal health during childhood and later reproductive performance. *Ann. N.Y. Acad. Sci.* 477:27–39

Finch CE, Rose MR. 1995. Hormones and the physiological architecture of life history evolution. *Q. Rev. Biol.* 70:1–52

Forsdahl A. 1977. Are poor living conditions in childhood and adolescence an important risk factor for arteriosclerotic heart disease? *Br. J. Prevent Soc. Med.* 31:91–95

Frisancho AR. 1993. *Human Adaptation and Accommodation.* Ann Arbor: Univ. Mich. Press

Gluckman PD, Hanson MA. 2004. Living with the past: evolution, development, and patterns of disease. *Science* 305:1733–36

Gluckman PD, Hanson MA. 2006. *Developmental Origins of Health and Disease.* New York: Cambridge Univ. Press

Gluckman PD, Hanson MA, Spencer HG. 2005. Predictive adaptive responses and human evolution. *Trends Ecol. Evol.* 20:527–33

Gluckman PD, Pinal CS. 2003. Regulation of fetal growth by the somatotrophic axis. *J. Nutr.* 133:1741S–46

Goldberg G. 2008. *Breastfeeding: Early Influences on Later Health*. New York: Springer

Grummer-Strawn LM, Mei Z, Cent. Dis. Control Prev. Ped. Nutr. Surveill. Syst. 2004. Does breastfeeding protect against pediatric overweight? Analysis of longitudinal data from the Centers for Disease Control and Prevention Pediatric Nutrition Surveillance System. *Pediatrics* 113:e81–86

Hales CN, Barker DJ. 1992. Type 2 (noninsulin-dependent) diabetes mellitus: the thrifty phenotype hypothesis. *Diabetologia* 35:595–601

Harder T, Rodekamp E, Schellong K, Dudenhausen JW, Plagemann A. 2007. Birth weight and subsequent risk of type 2 diabetes: a meta-analysis. *Am. J. Epidemiol.* 165:849–57

Heinke D, Kuzawa CW. 2008. Self-reported illness and birth weight in the Philippines: implications for hypotheses of adaptive fetal plasticity. *Am. J. Hum. Biol.* 20:538–44

Holliday M. 1986. Body composition and energy needs during growth. In *Human Growth: A Comprehensive Treatise*, ed. F Falkner, JM Tanner, pp. 117–39. New York: Plenum. 2nd ed.

Horton TH. 2005. Fetal origins of developmental plasticity: animal models of induced life history variation. *Am. J. Hum. Biol.* 17:34–43

Houseknecht KL, McGuire MK, Portocarrero CP, McGuire MA, Beerman K. 1997. Leptin is present in human milk and is related to maternal plasma leptin concentration and adiposity. *Biochem. Biophys. Res. Commun.* 240:742–47

Jasienska G, Thune I, Ellison PT. 2006. Fatness at birth predicts adult susceptibility to ovarian suppression: an empirical test of the Predictive Adaptive Response hypothesis. *Proc. Natl. Acad. Sci. USA* 103:12759–62

Jones JH. 2005. Fetal programming: adaptive life-history tactics or making the best of a bad start? *Am. J. Hum. Biol.* 17:22–33

Kahn HS, Graff M, Stein AD, Zybert PA, McKeague IW, Lumey LH. 2008. A fingerprint characteristic associated with the early prenatal environment. *Am. J. Hum. Biol.* 20:59–65

Kermack W, McKendrick A, McKinlay P. 1934. Death rates in Great Britain and Sweden: some general regularities and their significance. *Lancet* 226:698–703

Kuzawa C. 2001. *Maternal nutrition, fetal growth, and cardiovascular risk in Filipino adolescents.* PhD diss. Emory Univ., Atlanta. 453 pp.

Kuzawa CW. 1998. Adipose tissue in human infancy and childhood: an evolutionary perspective. *Am. J. Phys. Anthropol.* 27:177–209

Kuzawa CW. 2005. Fetal origins of developmental plasticity: Are fetal cues reliable predictors of future nutritional environments? *Am. J. Hum. Biol.* 17:5–21

Kuzawa CW. 2008. The developmental origins of adult health: intergenerational inertia in adaptation and disease. See Trevathan et al. 2008, pp. 325–49

Kuzawa CW. 2009. Beyond feast-famine: brain evolution, human life history and the metabolic syndrome. In *Evolutionary Anthropology*, ed. M Muehlenbein. Cambridge, UK: Cambridge Univ. Press. In press

Kuzawa CW, Adair LS. 2003. Lipid profiles in adolescent Filipinos: relation to birth weight and maternal energy status during pregnancy. *Am. J. Clin. Nutr.* 77:960–66

Kuzawa CW, Gluckman PD, Hanson MA, Beedle A. 2008. Evolution, developmental plasticity, and metabolic disease. See Stearns & Koella 2008, pp. 253–64

Kuzawa CW, Pike IL. 2005. Introduction. Fetal origins of developmental plasticity. *Am. J. Hum. Biol.* 17:1–4

Kuzawa CW, Sweet E. 2009. Epigenetics and the embodiment of race: developmental origins of US racial disparities in cardiovascular health. *Am. J. Hum. Biol.* 21:2–15

Lampl M, Kuzawa CW, Jeanty P. 2002. Infants thinner at birth exhibit smaller kidneys for their size in late gestation in a sample of fetuses with appropriate growth. *Am. J. Hum. Biol.* 14:398–406

Langley-Evans SC. 1999. Fetal origins of adult disease. *Br. J. Nutr.* 81:5–6

Lasker GW. 1969. Human biological adaptability. The ecological approach in physical anthropology. *Science* 166(3912):1480–86

Lawlor DA, Davey Smith G, Ebrahim S. 2003. Association between leg length and offspring birthweight: partial explanation for the trans-generational association between birthweight and cardiovascular disease: findings from the British Women's Heart and Health Study. *Paediatr. Perinat. Epidemiol.* 17:148–55

Lawlor DA, Riddoch CJ, Page AS, Andersen LB, Wedderkopp N, et al. 2005. Infant feeding and components of the metabolic syndrome: findings from the European Youth Heart Study. *Arch. Dis. Child.* 90:582–88

Lewontin RC. 1974. *The Genetic Basis of Evolutionary Change*. Cambridge, UK: Cambridge Univ. Press

Lucas A. 1991. Programming by early nutrition in man. *Ciba Found. Symp.* 156:38–50; discussion 50–55

Lucas A, Fewtrell MS, Cole TJ. 1999. Fetal origins of adult disease—the hypothesis revisited. *BMJ* 319:245–49

Lummaa V. 2003. Early developmental conditions and reproductive success in humans: downstream effects of prenatal famine, birthweight, and timing of birth. *Am. J. Hum. Biol.* 15:370–79

Luyckx VA, Brenner BM. 2005. Low birth weight, nephron number, and kidney disease. *Kidney Int. Suppl.* 97:S68–77

Martin RM, Gunnell D, Smith GD. 2005. Breastfeeding in infancy and blood pressure in later life: systematic review and meta-analysis. *Am. J. Epidemiol.* 161:15–26

Martorell R, Schroeder DG, Rivera JA, Kaplowitz HJ. 1995. Patterns of linear growth in rural Guatemalan adolescents and children. *J. Nutr.* 125:1060S–67

McDade TW. 2005. Life history, maintenance, and the early origins of immune function. *Am. J. Hum. Biol.* 17:81–94

McMillen IC, Robinson JS. 2005. Developmental origins of the metabolic syndrome: prediction, plasticity, and programming. *Physiol. Rev.* 85:571–633

Metcalfe NB, Monaghan P. 2001. Compensation for a bad start: grow now, pay later? *Trends Ecol. Evol.* 16:254–60

Miralles O, Sánchez J, Palou A, Picó C. 2006. A physiological role of breast milk leptin in body weight control in developing infants. *Obesity* 14:1371–77

Mitrani P, Srinivasan M, Dodds C, Patel MS. 2007. Role of the autonomic nervous system in the development of hyperinsulinemia by high-carbohydrate formula feeding to neonatal rats. *Am. J. Physiol. Endocrinol. Metab.* 292:E1069–78

Moore SE, Cole TJ, Poskitt EM, Sonko BJ, Whitehead RG, et al. 1997. Season of birth predicts mortality in rural Gambia. *Nature* 388:434

Morton S. 2006. Maternal nutrition and fetal growth and development. See Gluckman & Hanson 2006, pp. 98–129

Mousseau T, Fox C. 1998. *Maternal Effects as Adaptations*. New York: Oxford Univ. Press

Neel J. 1962. Diabetes mellitus: a "thrifty" genotype rendered detrimental by "progress"? *Am. J. Hum. Gen.* 14:353–62

Núñez-De La Mora A, Bentley GR. 2008. Early life effects on reproductive function. See Trevathan et al. 2008, pp. 149–68

Ounsted M, Scott A, Ounsted C. 1986. Transmission through the female line of a mechanism constraining human fetal growth. *Ann. Hum. Biol.* 13:143–51

Owen CG, Martin RM, Whincup PH, Smith GD, Cook DG. 2006. Does breastfeeding influence risk of type 2 diabetes in later life? A quantitative analysis of published evidence. *Am. J. Clin. Nutr.* 84:1043–54

Owen CG, Whincup PH, Kaye SJ, Martin RM, Davey Smith G, et al. 2008. Does initial breastfeeding lead to lower blood cholesterol in adult life? A quantitative review of the evidence. *Am. J. Clin. Nutr.* 88:305–14

Palou A, Picó C. 2009. Leptin intake during lactation prevents obesity and affects food intake and food preferences in later life. *Appetite* 52:249–52

Popkin BM. 2004. The nutrition transition: an overview of world patterns of change. *Nutr. Rev.* 62:S140–43

Potts R. 1998. Environmental hypotheses of hominin evolution. *Am. J. Phys. Anthropol. Suppl.* 27:93–136

Prentice AM. 1991. Can maternal dietary supplements help in preventing infant malnutrition? *Acta Paediatr. Scand. Suppl.* 374:67–77

Price KC, Hyde JS, Coe CL. 1999. Matrilineal transmission of birth weight in the rhesus monkey (*Macaca mulatta*) across several generations. *Obstet. Gynecol.* 94:128–34

Rickard IJ, Lummaa V. 2007. The predictive adaptive response and metabolic syndrome: challenges for the hypothesis. *Trends Endocrinol. Metab.* 18:94–99

Schack-Nielsen L, Michaelsen KF, Mortensen EL, Sørensen TI, Reinisch JM. 2004. Is duration of breast-feeding influencing the risk of obesity in adult males? *Adv. Exp. Med. Biol.* 554:383–85

Schell LM, Magnus PD. 2007. Is there an elephant in the room? Addressing rival approaches to the interpretation of growth perturbation and small size. *Am. J. Hum. Biol.* 19:606–14

Srinivasan M, Aalinkeel R, Song F, Mitrani P, Pandya JD, et al. 2006. Maternal hyperinsulinemia predisposes rat fetuses for hyperinsulinemia, and adult-onset obesity and maternal mild food restriction reverses this phenotype. *Am. J. Physiol. Endocrinol. Metab.* 290:E129–34

Stearns SC, Koella JC, eds. 2008. *Evolution in Health and Disease*. Cambridge, UK: Cambridge Univ. Press. 2nd ed.

Thompson A, Lampl M. 2007. HPG activation in infancy: relationship to sex and size (Abstract). *Am. J. Hum. Biol.* 19:283

Trevathan W, Smith EO, McKenna JJ, eds. 2008. *Evolution and Health*. Oxford, UK: Oxford Univ. Press

Vickers MH, Gluckman PD, Coveny AH, Hofman PL, Cutfield WS, et al. 2005. Neonatal leptin treatment reverses developmental programming. *Endocrinology* 146:4211–16

Villalpando S, del Prado M. 1999. Interrelation among dietary energy and fat intakes, maternal body fatness, and milk total lipid in humans. *J. Mammary Gland Biol. Neoplasia* 4:285–95

Waterland RA, Garza C. 1999. Potential mechanisms of metabolic imprinting that lead to chronic disease. *Am. J. Clin. Nutr.* 69:179–97

Waterland RA, Michels KB. 2007. Epigenetic epidemiology of the developmental origins hypothesis. *Annu. Rev. Nutr.* 27:363–88

Wells JC. 2003. The thrifty phenotype hypothesis: thrifty offspring or thrifty mother? *J. Theor. Biol.* 221:143–61

Wells JC. 2007a. Environmental quality, developmental plasticity and the thrifty phenotype: a review of evolutionary models. *Evol. Bioinformatics* 3:109–20

Wells JC. 2007b. The thrifty phenotype as an adaptive maternal effect. *Biol. Rev. Camb. Philos. Soc.* 82:143–72

Whincup PH, Kaye SJ, Owen CG, Huxley R, Cook DG, et al. 2008. Birth weight and risk of type 2 diabetes: a systematic review. *JAMA* 300:2886–97

Widdowson EM, McCance RA. 1975. A review: new thoughts on growth. *Pediatr. Res.* 9:154–56

Williams GC. 1966. *Adaptation and Natural Selection*. Princeton, NJ: Princeton Univ. Press

Worthman CM. 1987. Interactions of physical maturation and cultural practice in ontogeny: Kikuyu adolescents. *Cult. Anthropol.* 2:29–38

Worthman CM. 1999. Epidemiology of human development. In *Hormones, Health and Behavior: A Socio-Ecological and Lifespan Perspective*, ed. C Panter-Brick, CM Worthman, pp. 47–104. Cambridge, UK: Cambridge Univ. Press

Worthman CM, Kuzara J. 2005. Life history and the early origins of health differentials. *Am. J. Hum. Biol.* 17:95–112

Zambrano E, Rodríguez-González GL, Guzmán C, García-Becerra R, Boeck L, et al. 2005. A maternal low protein diet during pregnancy and lactation in the rat impairs male reproductive development. *J. Physiol.* 563:275–84

Adoption of the Unrelated Child: Some Challenges to the Anthropological Study of Kinship

Signe Howell

Department of Social Anthropology, University of Oslo, 0317 Oslo, Norway;
email: signe.howell@sai.uio.no

Annu. Rev. Anthropol. 2009. 38:149–66

First published online as a Review in Advance on
June 23, 2009

The *Annual Review of Anthropology* is online at
anthro.annualreviews.org

This article's doi:
10.1146/annurev.anthro.37.081407.085115

0084-6570/09/1021-0149$20.00

Key Words

transnational adoption, fictive kinship, laws and conventions,
parenthood, biocentrism, roots and origins

Abstract

Adoption of children born by others is practiced in some form or another
in all known societies. Although ethnographic monographs from all
over the world have made numerous brief references to local adoption
and/or fostering practices, very little sustained interpretative interest
has, until recently, been directed at this social phenomenon. With the
sudden and rapid increase in transnational adoption—people in Western
Europe and North America adopt children from countries in the south
and the former Soviet empire—a new-found anthropological interest in
adoption has been observed. This review places adoption firmly within
the tradition of theoretical kinship and explores the values attached to
a perceived relationship between biological and social relatedness in a
number of different social settings in which adoption is being practiced.

INTRODUCTION

The degree to which raising nonbiological children as one's own is regarded as abnormal or problematic varies among societies and within groups of any one society and may change over time. The adoption of children born by others is practiced in some form or another in all known societies, and it is a practice that raises theoretical and analytical questions about the meaning and role of kinship. In this review I take adoption to mean the practice whereby children, for a variety of reasons, are raised by adults other than their biological parents, are treated as members of the family among whom they live, and are accepted as such by others. The adults in these cases are acknowledged to assume what one in each case would recognize as the parental responsibility of overseeing the children's care, nurturing, training, and education and of fixing them on a path of subjectivation (Faubion 2001). As a social practice, adoption goes to the heart of what we take to be kinship. And yet, with some notable exceptions (see below), it has until recently received surprisingly little sustained theoretical attention. By contrast, there is a large body of literature of psychological studies on adoption, much of which would have benefited from a perusal of the ethnographic literature.

In this review, I frame my discussion within the parameters of the relationship between biology and sociality (or the older nature/nurture debate) and raise, yet again, the question, "What is kinship all about?" Schneider's (1968 [1980]) study of American kinship, as a cultural system, led him to argue that "[k]inship is the blood relationship, the fact of shared biogenetic substances" (p. 107). This definition is equally applicable to imaginings in Western Europe, where the metaphoric statement "of my flesh and blood" exists in most languages and carries emotional and moral connotations. Arguably, we are today witnessing a renewed stress on biogenetic connectedness in the understanding of kinship (Edwards & Salazar 2009, Franklin & McKinnon 2001, Franklin & Ragone 1998, Howell 2006b, Wade 2007). In contemporary

Scandinavian law and practice, for example, to remove a child from his or her biological mother permanently—however unsuitable she is deemed to be—is regarded as the absolute final resort and its effects to be of lasting psychological damage to mother and child alike. Whether to maintain the anonymity of sperm and egg donors and of biological parents of adoptees is hotly debated in North America and Western Europe. A consensus is emerging that stresses the right to know who one's "real" parents are in such cases, and this is reflected in the laws of several countries. In the United States, the previous secrecy that surrounded adoption is being replaced by an ideologically endorsed open adoption by which a woman participates in raising her biological children who have been adopted by others (Modell 2002).

Schneider argued (1968 [1980], 1984) that in Euro-American society at large the understanding of kinship that it is predicated on biological connectedness has colored anthropologists' approaches and has made them ask wrong, irrelevant, and leading questions in alien societies. Such biocentrism has further given rise to categories such as fictive kinship (see below). Since the nineteenth century, family life, fatherhood, motherhood, and childhood in Europe and North America have been subjected to a normative discourse that emphasizes the supremacy of the nuclear family and the psychological vulnerability of the child (Gillis 1996, Melosh 2002, Rose 1999). According to Murdoch (1949), the nuclear family was "a distinct and strongly functional group in every known society" (p. 2). In a somewhat similar vein, Keesing (1975) expressed a commonly held view that kinship is "the network of relationships created by genealogical connections, and by social ties *modelled* on the 'natural' relations of genealogical parenthood" (p. 13, emphasis added). According to these views, kinship practices that disregard a distinction between nature and nurture have resulted in the commonly encountered category of fictive kinship (see below). Adoption challenges such basic assumptions. Adoption allows us truly to focus on the quality of "relationness," to elicit meanings of "kinned" relations and on processes of "kinning" (Howell 2003a, see below). Although a relationship between a woman and her biologically born child is recognized everywhere, little if anything can be assumed by the analyst about the meaning and value attributed to that relationship. By introducing terms that distinguish pater from genitor and mater from genetrix, Barnes (1973) attempted to resist the conceptual fusion of biological and social relations. His schema further gave women a conceptual space equal to that of men.

After a brief overview of the theoretical and analytic place occupied by adoption in kinship studies, I consider how a number of different societies construct kinship relationships that are not based on descent or affinity and the analytical conundrums to which this has given rise. The last section examines how the recent and rapid growth in transnational adoption from countries in the South and the former Soviet bloc to involuntarily childless couples in Western Europe and North America (more than 40,000 were adopted in 2003) has led several anthropologists to take a serious interest in this practice. In addition to questioning the meaning of kinship, transnational adoption raises further questions of anthropological interest. As it involves the movement of children from the poor South to the wealthy North, the practice also raises issues of postcolonialism, nationhood, international relations, race, and ethnicity.

ADOPTION IN KINSHIP STUDIES

Early ethnographic monographs from all over the world contain numerous descriptive references to adoption practices, but little theoretical interest was shown in the practice until the 1970s, at which point it largely disappeared from mainstream anthropological concerns along with the loss of interest in kinship more generally. Keesing (1981), for example, in his much used textbook, makes only one reference to adoption and fostering. This reference occurs in a section on domestic groups,

and the practice is not discussed in terms of challenging the understanding of kinship (p. 271). However, in an article from 1969, Jack Goody drew our attention to the potentially fruitful field of adoption and provided a very useful overview of adoption practices from ancient Greece, Rome, India, and China with a brief discussion of contemporary practices of adoption and fostering in Africa. He made the point that, in the comparative study of kinship, adoption has rarely been touched on and that in the numerous important studies on African kinship and lineage systems, "it is remarkable that adoption is rarely, if ever mentioned in these accounts of African societies" (Goody 1969, p. 55). Goody is concerned with mapping the variety in, and uneven distribution of, adoption in Eurasian and African societies and in characterizing the functions of adoption.

According to Goody (1969), the function of adoption may be divided into three main types: "To provide homes for orphans, bastards, foundlings and the children of impaired families. To provide childless couples with social progeny. To provide an individual or couple with an heir to their property" (p. 58). Although applicable to the cases discussed by Goody, and also, broadly speaking, to the situation in Western Europe and North America until the twentieth century, his is a narrow definition that does not allow for the variety in motivation encountered in other parts of the world. Goody seemed unaware of the lively interest taken in adoption practices among a group of American anthropologists with fieldwork experience from Oceania, where adoption and fostering are widely practiced. They discussed adoption in different terms—they not only contextualized the practice in terms of broader local cultural values, but also tried to find ways to theorize about the practice—and two edited volumes resulted (Brady 1976, Carroll 1970). In an article about Truk kinship, Marshall (1977) makes the point that kinship consists in part of shared biogenetic substance, but also of shared land and similar resources, and he ends by stating, "[t]hat such nurturant relationships overlay natural kinship relationships much of the time is beside the point: in Trukese kinship nurture is more than nature" (p. 657). More recently, and in line with the interest in the comparative study of notions of personhood, several anthropologists have argued that local notions of adoption and fostering are embedded in and shaped by broader understandings concerning principles of sociality and personhood (Halbmeyer 2004, Howell 2007a, Weismantel 1995). Moreover, adoption in Europe and North America during the past 50 years has primarily become a matter of emotional satisfaction on the part of involuntarily childless couples or individuals, a desire to become a "normal" family (Howell 2003a, 2006a,b; Modell 1994, 2002). This is particularly so in the case of transnational adoption, a practice that has increased dramatically in the past 20 years and which shows no signs of abating (Selman 2000, 2004).

Kinship studies have taught us to study relations, not individuals. The argument of this article is that adoption both challenges and confirms explicit and implicit notions about relatedness and sociality. As a marked social practice, adoption is meaningless without some form of a biological model for kinship as reference. But it is a two-way semantic process. Adoption provides meaning to the biological, and at the same time, the "made" relationship limits the meaning of the "natural" relationship (compare Schneider 1972).

Whenever anthropologists turn their gaze toward adoption, the results are fascinating. As mentioned above, the prevalent practice of adoption in Oceanic societies led a number of anthropologists who worked there during the 1950s and 1960s to question how it affected the anthropological understanding of kinship. Somewhat later, the work by Esther Goody (1982) and Bledsoe & Abinake (1989) from Africa demonstrated a keen awareness of the analytical challenges involved. More recently, Modell's (1994, 2002) studies from the United States and Carsten's (2000) from Scotland bring the topic back home, as do the studies of transnational adoption. Although they explore and emphasize different aspects of the practice and represent a wide variety of theoretical

stances, all these studies are thought provoking, fully validating this author's claim that adoption goes to the heart of kinship studies, a claim that is further confirmed by the articles that have appeared in some recent edited volumes (Bowie 2004, Marre & Briggs 2009, Fines 1998, Volkman 2005b) and in a special issue of *Law & Society Review* (Sterett 2002).

Conception, Birth, and Relatedness

Kinship used to occupy a central position in anthropological theory to the extent that Fox (1967) argued that "what the nude is to the painter, so kinship is to the anthropologist" (p. 10). But it lost this central position during the 1970s and 1980s. In his critique of kinship studies, Needham (1971) concluded that the dearth of theoretical advances is not due to a lack of data, but to the poverty of the conceptual frameworks of analysis (p. 2). Toward the end of the twentieth century, however, we notice a reemergence of an anthropological interest in kinship, which has provided the conceptual framework sought by Needham. Following the recent focus within anthropology on new biomedical research, including new reproductive technology, body part transplants, cloning, and same-sex couples (e.g., Edwards et al. 1999, Franklin & McKinnon 2001, Franklin & Ragoné 1998, Strathern 1992, Weston 1991), it was no longer possible to maintain a clear divide between nature and culture, a divide that had been a mainstay of traditional kinship studies but which the studies on adoption (especially those from Oceania, see below) had failed to dislodge. Strathern (1992) delivered a final death blow to nature by arguing that it is possible to replace reproduction with replication. By all accounts, one might expect that adoption would be investigated as relevant for the new discourse on procreation, but it was not until the sudden and rapidly growing demand for transnational adoption in Western Europe and North America that it caught the attention of some anthropologists who saw its potential for contributing to the theoretical debates within issues of procreation and relatedness (Gailey 1999, 2000; Howell 2003a, 2006b, 2007a; Yngvesson 2002, 2004). Today, adoption, both local (Carsten 2000; Modell 1994, 2002) and transnational (Collard 2002, Dorow 2006, Fonseca 2003, 2004; Howell 2001, 2006a,b; Howell & Marre 2006; Marre 2007; Marre & Briggs 2009; Quellette 2003; Telfer 1999, 2004; Volkman 2005a; Yngvesson 2002, 2004, 2005), is becoming a hot topic for investigation and is catching the attention of a growing number of PhD students in European and North American universities.

One possible reason for the general lack of interest in adoption beyond the three foci identified by Goody may be that, as a social category, children—much as used to be the case regarding women—have not until recently caught the theoretical attention of anthropologists. However, in contrast to the previous male-dominated field of kinship studies, most writers on assisted reproduction and adoption today are women. This may perhaps be attributed to the influence of the early feminist anthropologists (Ardener 1974, Collier & Yanagisako 1987, Ortner & Whitehead 1981, Rosaldo & Lamphere 1974, Yanagisako & Delaney 1995) who made gender and reproduction respectable. Moreover, these new practices of procreation that take place closer to home (geographically and personally) have given kinship a human face.

Some Early Interest in Adoption

Franklin & Ragoné (1998) argue that "an important genealogy of modern anthropology can readily be traced through its relationship to a core set of ideas related to reproduction, or 'the facts of life'" (p. 2). Indeed, the early founders of the discipline (Maine 1917 [1861], Morgan 1871) took a comparative study of ideas and practices of procreation—descent and marriage—as their starting point for analyzing social organization. In light of the above discussion on the analytical importance granted biological relatedness in kinship studies, and the subsequent collapse of the analytical distinction between nature and culture that derived from research in biomedicine, adoption is finding its

place in the new kinship. It is precisely because adoption challenges the very referential principle of flesh and blood in Euro-American thinking that its significance cries out for analysis.

Like marriage and divorce, birth and the raising of children, including adoption of the unrelated child, are practices that go to the heart of notions about personhood, rights, and responsibilities. These practices are everywhere subjected to rules—rules that are highly informative about broader social, cultural, and moral concerns and values in a particular sociocultural setting. In his study of American kinship, Schneider (1968 [1980]) argues that "the cultural universe of relatives in American kinship is constructed of the elements of two major cultural orders, the *order of nature* and the *order of law*" (p. 27, emphasis in original). Schneider includes adoption in the latter. If one is willing to be open-minded about the meaning of both nature and law, then the same may be said about most human societies. We know that in many places and at different times, adoption of children born by others has received the attention of the authorities and that measures to regulate the practice were perceived to be necessary. For example, the Babylonian code of Hammurabi, the oldest comprehensive set of written laws in existence, gives a prominent position to "adoption and wet-nursing" (Goody 1969, p. 55). Similarly, the laws of ancient China, India, Greece, and Rome gave adoption some attention. Adoption was linked to perpetuating agnates over time and preventing property and wealth from being alienated from the kin group. Indeed, the question of inheritance for the adopted child was a consideration that prompted the first U.S. and European adoption laws (Howell 2006a,b; Modell 1994).

Adoption was studied mostly from the point of view of the needs of the adults: to provide childless couples with social progeny and heirs to their property, to facilitate relations between groups, to provide men with more children in order to increase their number of networks, and to assist with the workload in the household, farm, workshop. The concept of "jural parenthood"—functually derived from "the social necessity to order human relations according to a code of rules in which social relationships are categorized and differently assigned rights and duties" (Goodenough 1970, p. 391)—became applied to empirical studies of adoption in the non-Western world.

In parts of West Africa, at one time, as many as half the children born were raised by individuals other than their biological parents. Childlessness does not account for this fact because the practice of polygamy usually ensures children a place in an extended household. Esther Goody, whose influential work on "social parenthood" and fostering in Africa (e.g., 1982), argued that it was rational for a society to share tasks between biological and social parents. Her main argument is that the burden of parenthood—which she divides into five roles (bearing and begetting, status entitlement, nurturance, training, and sponsorship)—can be shared between biological and social parents if the various parental roles are assumed by different people. Bledsoe & Isingo-Abanike (1989) similarly pursue a functionalist line of argument. According to them, the practices of adoption and fostering minimize the risk of famine and help to provide care for the sick and elderly. A common argument is that the system of adoption provides an enduring link between the families concerned. In a review of various non-Western practices of adoption (in which she also discusses the influence of Western adoption laws in the Third World), O'Collins (1984) makes the point that among the Kikuyu of Kenya, rights on both parental sides are not completely transferred, and the adopted child will continue to have contact with his or her biological kin. In Botswana, "Tswana customary adoption might involve a direct request for a child, and rights of inheritance depend on whether the adoption is recognized by the elders in the community" (p. 291). Indeed, adoption as a permanent rupture from the biological parents is rare, and fostering, or a form of mutual exchange of children, is not uncommon. The thrust of E. Goody's argument fits into the British structural-functionalist school. Her aim was to justify the practice as functional

and hence reasonable. These studies do not touch upon the indigenous ontological, moral, and semantic premises for the practice of adoption. The early studies from Oceania (Brady 1976, Carroll 1970, Marshall 1977, Silverman 1971) followed a different path, more in line with Schneider's approach of kinship as a cultural system, which "facilitates looking at kinship as a medium for social behavior with which people work creatively to accomplish their purposes" (Goodenough 1970, p. 14). However, it is fair to say that much recent work on adoption as a social and cultural practice has failed to consider the theoretical insights generated by this work.

Several recent studies of adoption in the South (Alber 2003, 2004; Anderson 2004; Demian 2004; Leinwater 2007, 2008; Meigs 1986; Schachter 2007; Weismantel 1995) are critical of the British "functionalist school" and ground their interpretations in local ontology and morality, which, they argue, are fundamentally different as regards the meaning of family, children, and childhood from that in contemporary Europe and North America. According to Alber (2003), one reason why the Baattombu in Northern Benin give away their infants by adoption is that it is considered better for the child not to be raised by its biological mother. Until ~60 years ago, more than 90% of all children were given up for fosterage. Biological parenthood is largely denied and "[t]here is an attitude of shame for an individual to claim ownership over his or her biological children" (p. 496). Schachter (2007) uses her research on Hawaii's customary law regarding the transfer of children to question some premises of the international conventions on international adoption.

Fictive Kinship

By and large, anthropologists have treated kinship as a complex system of culturally defined social relationships based on birth and marriage. Social practices that emphasized radically different criteria for relatedness emerged as problematic. The descent versus alliance debate provoked anthropologists to heated debates in the 1960s, as did questions about virgin birth. Later, same-sex partnership/marriage, new reproductive technology, and adoption and fostering brought a new focus on the issues. All too easily, nonbiological kinship relationships were characterized as fictive, pseudo, ritual, or artificial kinship, without asking "fictive to whom?" Thus Goody (1969) describes adoption as "quasi kinship" (p. 56) and Fox (1967) in his much used textbook *Kinship and Marriage* states, "genetic kinship is the model for fictive kinship relations" (p. 32). In his recent introductory textbook to social anthropology, Barnard (2006, p. 102) makes no reference to adoption but includes a section called fictive kinship—a concept he does not debate—in which he confines his discussion to godparenthood and compradazgo. One finds the concepts of fictive or pseudo kinship scattered throughout the anthropological literature. The many attempts to debunk it (see below) have not always met with success; for example, at the American Anthropological Association Meeting in 1998, a session entitled "Fictive Kinship" attracted a huge audience.

Anthropologists with fieldwork experience from Oceania early on questioned a general tendency to describe kinship that was neither consanguine nor affinal as fictive or artificial, implying that the relationships are somehow not real. Marshall (1977) introduced the expression "created kinship," by which he "hopes to avoid the implications that they are not an integral part of 'the nature of kinship'" (p. 644). He lists adoption as one major such relationship, together with clientship and certain kinds of friendships as acted out in Greater Trukese Society. Similarly, on the basis of his work among the Banabans in the Gilbert and Ellis Islands, Silverman suggests that another way to think about kin relationships apart from blood connection is that of being connected through land (Silverman 1971, p. 210).

Meigs (1986) maintains that the Hua of New Guinea Highlands are not interested in distinguishing between real and not-real kin, nor do they pay any attention to genealogy. Moreover,

according to Hua thinking, children are built, originally from menstrual blood and semen and later from nurture. She states that two people not related by birth can create kinship by feeding each other, or through unilateral feeding, particularly of a woman's milk, of food, and of water (p. 201). In Hua thinking, food of all kinds, including semen that builds the fetus, includes *nu*, a vital essence invested into food by the person who produces it. "Thus, when you eat a food you are . . . eating some of the *nu* vital essence of another person. Eating by this logic, relates people, making them kin because it mixes their *nu*" (p. 201). This incorporation of kin is not fictive, or some kind of pretence, she argues, but must be regarded as a different understanding of kinship (pp. 200–1).

Weismantel (1995) criticizes the persistent dichotomy between nature and culture in kinship studies and argues that the Zumbagua in the highlands of Ecuador make no such distinction in their understandings of parent-child relationships. Rather, although "[t]he physical act of intercourse, pregnancy, and birth can establish a strong bond between two adults . . . other adults, by taking a child into their family and nurturing its physical needs through the same substances as those eaten by the rest of the social group, can make of that child a son or daughter who is physically as well as jurally their own" (p. 695). Through eating the same food together and over an extended period of time, the child may become a full member of a nonbiological family—i.e., a process of kinning.

It is precisely because adoption challenges the very referential principle of flesh and blood that its significance needs to be explored. This is not to say that a notion of fictive kinship may not be relevant in particular social settings, but that it must be treated as an empirical, not a general or analytic, category.

Adoption as Social Practice

The prime motivation of contemporary Euro-American couples to adopt a child is to remedy their childlessness and create a family. Couples stress the emotional aspect of the action

(Dorow 2006; Howell 2007b; Howell & Marre 2006; Marre 2007; Volkman 2005a,b). Adoption in many other parts of the world is a well-established social practice fueled by a range of motivations, many of which are social, political, or economic as much as emotional. The reason for adoption varies enormously from society to society, even within a region, something that is explored in the edited volumes from the Pacific (Brady 1976, Carroll 1970). Among the people of the Namoluk Atol, for example, "a conspiracy of silence surrounds the adoption and it is considered to be very bad taste to tell a child that he is adopted" (Marshall 1976, p. 35). On Tonga, however, where nearly all adult people have some experience of the practice, "[t]he adoptee's continuing relationship with his natural parents may range from infrequent to almost daily contact" (Morton 1976, p. 78). However, Morton also states that the more frequent the interaction is, the higher the likelihood is for conflict to arise between the two sets of parents. On New Hebrides, young children are informed about the adoptive relationship and told the identity of their biological parents, but they are never forced to live with either (Tonkinson 1976, p. 233); and on the Manihi Atoll to the east of Tahiti, both sets of parents have an obligation to the child, but the adopted child's first obligation is to the adoptive parents (Brooks 1976, p. 53). Recent studies from Melanesia (see, e.g., work by Anderson, Demian) confirm that adoption here continues to be very common. Demian (2004) differs somewhat from the rest and criticizes the early studies, arguing that the practice is best analyzed in terms of children as commodities.

Finally, that adoption practices are no more static in traditional societies than in European ones is exemplified through reports published from the Gunantuna of the Gazelle Peninsula in Papua New Guinea. Meir, who worked among them from 1899 to 1914, described adoption as being conducted in secrecy and enacted through a payment of traditional money. Salisbury, conducting his fieldwork in the same place more than 50 years later, showed that adoption then was a very public

event, engaged in by "big men" to enhance their standing through replenishing their number of dependents (O'Collins 1984).

These studies from societies where adoption represents no challenge to indigenous ontology and epistemology clearly defy any attempt at universalizing a biogenetic understanding of procreation and kinship. They provide a useful corrective to strands in Euro-American thinking, in which the dominant discourse is one that privileges biogenetic connectedness over and above social and emotional relationships.

Laws and Conventions

Laws that regulate adoption reveal implicit and explicit values about the family and parenthood. Although anthropologists have questioned the notion of fictive kinship, their doubts are not shared by Euro-American lawmakers. Adoption laws in, inter alia, most U.S. states, Scandinavia, and the United Kingdom, all insist on the right of an adopted child to know its biological origin upon reaching legal maturity, indicating that they take biological relatedness to be the real form of parent-child relationship and that, ultimately, adoption gives rise to a fictive parent-child relationship.

Modell (1994) demonstrates how a historical perspective on changes in American adoption legislation reflects and shapes contemporary American thinking about the family. Unlike the situation in Western Europe, where virtually no local children are available for adoption (an exception is Great Britain), more than 150,000 domestic adoptions take place in the United States every year. Although many of these are step-child adoptions, it still leaves a substantial number of stranger adoptions. Domestic adoption in the United States today is almost exclusively open adoption, meaning that, not only have all records previously closed to inspection been made available to adoptees and their biological parents alike, but—more radically—biological and adoptive parents are encouraged to share in the upbringing of the child. Modell (1999, 2002) shows that it was a new focus on the reality of biogenetic relations that led to this practice, and how the law makers in the various U.S. states took account of the demands of birth parents and adoptees alike. Although open adoption emphasizes the significance of biological connectedness, it removes genealogy from the core of the American kinship system, allowing the concepts of mother and father to become plural. Elsewhere, the argument that it is a human right to know one's biological origins is gaining ground. In Norway, for example, an increased focus on biogenetics was manifested in the 2003 Biotechnology Law when the anonymity clause linked to sperm donation was removed. The argument was precisely that everyone has a right to know who their "real" parents are. So far, however, open adoption of shared parenting, a practice derived from a profound biocentric understanding of kinship, is not an issue in Norway, as regards either domestic or transnational adoption (Howell 2006a,b) and so far, no European country has introduced the practice.

As the modern welfare state takes upon itself increasingly more responsibility for the welfare of its citizens—a phenomenon that Foucault (1991) has called governmentality—the involvement of the state in people's private lives is becoming more marked. The adoption of a child from another country is a practice that gives an opportunity for the state to assert its authority; this is especially so in Scandinavia and some other European countries. The 1993 Hague Convention on Inter-Country Adoption specifies that the transaction of adoption should be carried out only between contracting states and according to a set of specified procedures. The United States, having not ratified the convention, presents a more varied picture in the role played by the authorities. Many adoptions are carried out privately, a practice that can be tainted by corruption and one that hardly occurs in Scandinavia today (Howell 2006a).

Some research undertaken on adoption is concerned with laws, both national and international (Howell 2006a,b; Modell 1994, 2002; Sterett 2002). Again, a cultural approach is pursued by most. In a comparative study of Norwegian and U.S. adoption laws, Howell (2006b) argues that the general sociopolitical climates of the two nations represent two extremes with regard to how the involvement of the state in private, family matters varies (long-established welfare state versus a more individual-centered, marked-oriented system) and that this, as a consequence, is reflected in their adoption legislation.

In her introduction to the special issue of *Law & Society Review*, which is devoted to non-biological parenting with particular attention to laws, Sterret (2002) suggests that "a legal framework of rights colors the entire discussion [of adoption]" (p. 210). To this, one might add a framework that predicates personal identity upon biological identity. This rights-based approach in part springs out of the 1986 United Nations Convention on the Rights of the Child (UNCRC). The UNCRC contains paragraphs on adoption that have become guidelines for many countries and the gist of which are replicated—and expanded—in the Hague Convention. Both conventions take for granted that biological parents provide the right and proper conditions for a child to grow up in. They hold that a child has a right to grow up in a family home and to know its identity, and that adoption—especially transnational adoption—should be a last resort. Critics of the UNCRC have argued that these conventions base their principles on an unreflected application of contemporary Euro-American ideas about childhood and family and that the dictum of the "best interest of the child" expresses Western values (Ennew 2002; Gailey 1999; Howell 2006a,b; Panter-Brick 2000; Stephens 1995; Yngvesson 2002). Moreover, Howell (2003b, 2006b) argues that owing to an imbalance in power between donor and receiving countries, the international conventions that stipulate how transnational adoption is to be carried out favor values and priorities of the receiving countries.

More recently, a discourse of rights has emerged among adults in Western Europe and North America who wish to adopt, but who are legally not acknowledged as eligible. Many argue that it is a human right to have children and that anyone who desires to adopt a child should be allowed to do so. Homosexuals, in particular, campaign for the right to adopt, and some countries are making adoption by homosexuals legal (Cadoret 2002, Howell & Marre 2006). However, no donor country will knowingly allow a child to be adopted by homosexuals, male or female.

COMMON ISSUES IN THE STUDY OF TRANSNATIONAL ADOPTION

During the twentieth century, the value accorded to having children, and the reasons for wanting them, changed dramatically. According to Scheper-Hughes, "[t]he instrumental value of children has been largely replaced by their expressive value. Children have become relatively worthless (economically) to their parents, but priceless in terms of their psychological worth" (1998, p. 12). It is precisely this emotional worth of children that makes them so necessary for the personal fulfillment of couples in present-day Europe and North America and that becomes a major reason for the increased demand for adoption by those who find themselves unable to have biological children (Howell 2003a, 2007b; Howell & Marre 2006; Volkman 2005a). In Western Europe today, people who wish to have children but are unable to do so biologically must turn to countries in Africa, Asia, Latin America, and Eastern Europe to satisfy their desires. In the United States, there are still large numbers of local children available for adoption, but for a variety of reasons, many parents wish to go outside the national boundaries to obtain a child. Although differences in values and legal requirements vary between European nations, they nevertheless have more in common with each other than they do with the United States. Because the United States has not signed the UNCRC or the Hague Convention, there is a greater degree of freedom from state supervision, which, in turn, allows for the large variety in actual regulations and infrastructure (Howell 2006b, Modell 1994). Moreover, American anthropologists (like the American general public) are generally more preoccupied with

questions of mixed race in adoptive families (Dorow 2006, Gailey 2000, Yngvesson 2004) than are the Europeans (Howell & Melhuus 2007, Marre 2007). This notwithstanding, all researchers focus on such themes as the relationship between biogenetic and social kinship and adoptees' sense of identity and their relationships with their countries of origin, and they highlight the challenges that all involved parties must face, both on the personal and familial levels and in society at large. Their writings demonstrate a difference in focus rather than in general theoretical approach. In that sense, they may be said to complement each other. The rest of this article will consider the main topics that have been investigated in the study of transnational adoption.

The Construction of the Adoptive Family

In light of a dominant Euro-American biocentrism in the understanding of kinship, most anthropologists have examined how the relationship between biological birth and social birth is handled by the adoptive parents. Adoptive parents seek to naturalize the relationship, insisting on there being no difference between their families and others except in so far as their child happens to be born by unknown others who look different from themselves. Regardless of country, prospective adoptive parents experience the process as unnecessarily restrictive and lengthy. The process of transnational adoption is often characterized as analogous to pregnancy and birth, and terms taken from biological procreation are commonly encountered. It is, however, a "pregnancy" that usually takes much longer, and the time of the "birth" is far from certain. Despite a number of important differences in procedure between the various European and North American countries, a general pattern among adoptive parents may be discerned as being characterized by a high level of emotionality, frequently accompanied by "magical thinking" and notions of fate (Howell 2007b, Howell & Marre 2006, Volkman 2005a, Yngvesson 2005).

Adoptive parents of transnationally adopted children work hard at "kinning" (Howell 2003a) their children, i.e., making them integrated members of their own family and kinship networks and—in Scandinavia at any rate—fully assimilated as family members and citizens, resulting in what Howell (2001) has described as "self-conscious kinship." Howell & Marre (2006) both argue that Spaniards and Norwegians distinguish between immigrants and adoptees, a distinction that many adoptees also express, and Howell (2003a) has argued that adoptive parents are helped in this by engaging in a process of transubstantiating the essential identity of their children. By dressing their children in Norwegian clothing from the very start, by feeding them local food, playing local games, and teaching local nursery rhymes and stories, they are, in effect, encouraging the development of Norwegian personal characteristics at the expense of those of their birth.

At the same time, "adoption upholds the biological basis for parenthood [and] inscribes the natural relationship" (Modell 1994, p. 238). Howell (2003a) agrees that adoptive families do indeed recreate the ideals embedded in notions of biological relatedness, and that in their relationships with their children, Norwegian adoptive parents alternate between foregrounding and backgrounding biology according to context. Moreover, they create a cognitive boundary between the contexts, which prevents the paradoxes from being apparent. At the same time, the shadow of biology hovers in the background. During the pregnancy and birthing stages of the adoption process, the social and emotional nature of the relationship overshadows the fact of alien biology, whereas during adolescence, when questions of identity and conditions of origin may become pressing, biology is brought out as relevant; nevertheless, in most cases, biology is still rendered inferior to sociality.

Critiques of the Practice

Transnational adoption engages the emotions and has led several (mainly) American anthropologists to adopt a somewhat critical stance vis-à-vis the practice. Yngvesson (2002) places transnational adoption within a global market economy and argues that what is presented as a "gift child" is "a product of commodity thinking" (p. 237). This is not to say that children given up for adoption between two countries are sold, but that they are nevertheless "given to other states in exchange for a donation of money, a transaction that creates an orderly (and hierarchical) relation of states to one another through the movement of valued resources (children) in adoption" (p. 237). Elsewhere, critiquing the Hague Convention's insistence on plenary (permanent) adoption, and the ideal of "a family environment," Yngvesson (2004) argues that this may not be in the best interest of the child, that it "contributes to the commodification of children's bodies and their marketing abroad as national resources" (p. 212). Dorow (2006) similarly discusses the transnationally adopted child as a gift or commodity, and Leifsen (2004) shows how market forces in Ecuador have resulted in objectification of the child through a process of commodification and desocialization (p. 183). While rejecting the commodity metaphor, Howell (2006a) also argues that an imbalance occurs in the relationship between the rich nations of the North that desire children for their childless citizens and the poor nations in the South that provide them. They supply the desired children, but they must also adhere to procedural rules formulated by the receiving state.

In a sharp criticism of interracial and transnational adoption among the white middle class in America, Gailey (1999) argues that the adopted parents she has studied show a remarkable disregard for correct procedure and a lack of interest in their child's early life experiences and that they "harbored notions of love that were performance-based, subject to evaluation and possible rejection. They only want the 'blue-ribbon babies' as part of their general pursuit of the perfect life" (p. 73). "[N]otions of love . . . were performance-based, subject to evaluation and possible rejection"

(p. 73), an observation she links to a more general trait observable in the contemporary United States, whereby performance criteria are applied not only to children—whether adopted or biological—but also to spouses and friends (p. 73; 2000, p. 308).

Yngvesson (2004) recommends that a different model altogether be applied in transnational adoption, adapted from the open adoption policy that is increasingly being practiced in the United States. She suggests that children adopted overseas be placed not in plenary adoption, but in a situation in which some degree of openness with biological relatives is maintained, allowing the adoptees to reconcile the two sides to their identity. This practice also allows the biological mothers to keep in touch with their children. Transnational family adoption whereby a child is sent via adoption to relatives in a Western country may be described as an example of this. However, it must be borne in mind that frequently the biological origin of the adoptee is not known and that some donor countries, e.g., India, refuse to release the information even if they have it.

In a study of Australian adoptive parents' preferred methods of procreation, Telfer (1999) constructed "a hierarchy of biogeneticism." The order of preference ranges from unassisted, or minimally assisted, procreation, to assisted conception with parents' own biogenetic substances, to assisted procreation with sperm donation or egg donation, to adoption, and, finally, fostering. Furthermore, he observed a hierarchy of preferences regarding types of adoptee: the first choice is generally a very young local baby with no special needs, followed by the same criterion in an overseas baby. Interestingly, prospective parents preferred a toddler child from overseas over a local toddler. At the bottom of the list was the adoption of older children from abroad. Telfer describes adoption in Australia as a "feminised field." In the adoption discourse, women are the chief subjects: The relinquishing mother and the adoptive mothers are both portrayed as suffering, albeit for different reasons. The vast majority of adoption workers—paid and voluntary—are women, and support groups are formed mainly of women. They generally assume that women know much more about adoption, are more competent at adoption-related tasks, and are naturally more interested in such matters (Telfer 2004, p. 248). No comparative studies exist, but Telfer's findings, as regards both preferences and adoption as a feminized field, would probably be reflected elsewhere. It is not irrelevant in this context to note (again) that the majority of anthropologists working on adoption are women.

The Identity of the Transnationally Adopted Person

Most children adopted from countries in the South look different from their parents. They look like immigrants, and questions of race—and racism—therefore cannot be avoided. However, as mentioned, issues of race are more in evidence in the United States than in Europe. Howell & Melhuus (2007), Howell & Marre (2006), and Marre (2007) have argued that race is not regarded as relevant in transnational adoption in Norway and Spain. Prospective adoptive parents in the Scandinavian countries may not specify racial preferences in their applications. Surveys show, however, that adoptive parents are anxious about racism as their children grow up and leave home. In Western Europe, where immigration from the South has become a major sociopolitical issue, adoptive families are at great pains to distance themselves from immigrants. By and large, the kinning activities of the parents ensure this. Unlike other immigrants, transnationally adopted persons are accepted by the population as Norwegian, Swedish, Spanish, etc. The often heard claim that transnationally adopted persons are "like coco-nuts—brown on the outside, white on the inside"—raises few eyebrows in Europe but is ideologically problematic in the United States.

Whereas Scandinavian and Spanish adoptive parents tend to have a rather superficial relationship with their child's country of origin—manifesting a "touristy approach" to cultural phenomena (Howell 2002)—American parents of transnationally adopted children, especially those from China, display a different attitude (Volkman 2005a, Dorow 2006). It is not uncommon for them to send their children to Chinese nursery schools and to encourage a serious interest in that country. According to Dorow this may be because Americans have a positive image of Chinese Americans and a highly negative one of African Americans, which limits demand for children from Africa. Unlike American adoptees, Scandinavian adoptees tend not to describe themselves with reference to their country of origins, e.g., as Norwegian-Koreans, or Norwegian-Ethiopians. Neither do they describe themselves as immigrants and tend to distance themselves from other non-European immigrants. This practice may partly be explained by the fact that non-European immigrant communities in these countries are of recent origin and that the countries from which most immigrants come usually do not coincide with the countries from which Scandinavians adopt. In the United States, on the other hand, there are large diaspora communities whose members originate from many of the same countries from which Americans adopt. As a result, it is common to hear adult transnationally adopted Americans describe themselves as Korean American or Columbian American, for example, and many of the adoptees seek contact with the diaspora community.

"Roots" and the Relationship with the Country of Origin

Perhaps the most controversial topics so far in research on transnational adoption are those that relate to the adoptees' own understanding of their identity, their attitudes to their countries of origin, and the related issue of roots. Whereas Howell (2002, 2007a) argues that the majority of adoptees in Norway experience little more than superficial interest in their roots—despite an overwhelming interest in this subject among the population at large—others (Collard 1991, Yngvesson 2005) maintain that transnational adoptees in the United States and Canada, for example, show genuine interest in such questions.

In a study of young adult Norwegian adoptees, Brottveit (1999, p. 46) develops a model of ethnic attitudes: the Norwegians, who stress the Norwegian aspects of their identity as overwhelmingly significant; the double-ethnics, who also attribute a degree of significance to their countries of birth; and the cosmopolitans, who refuse to attribute any personal significance to either country of adoption or country of birth.

An increase in the return or motherland tours by adoptive families, undertaken when the children have become teenagers or young adults, is noted by most. Arguably, this practice parallels the increasing biologization of the meaning of kinship, which adoptive parents as much as adoptees are facing today. To the adoptees, roots trips may "reveal the precariousness of 'I am'" (Yngvesson 2005, p. 28). Yngvesson's study of roots visits undertaken by Swedish families with children adopted from Chile shows that such trips can be powerful experiences for parents and their adopted children alike. To others, such visits may be little more than a pleasant holiday (Howell 2003a, 2007a).

Attitudes in Donor Countries

Transnational adoption raises questions about relations between nation states—those that send children to be adopted in other countries and those countries that receive them. Transnational adoption may be analyzed as part of globalization more generally: the movement of children from the poor South to the rich North and the movement of values from the North to the South (Howell 2003b, 2006a). As studies on the legal provisions about adoption in different countries appear, we are made aware of the profound differences in cultural values between not only the various receiving countries but also the donor countries. We also note how donor countries react differently to the practice of sending abroad. Dorow (2006) has looked at Chinese reactions, Fonseca (2003) has considered those of Brazilians, Leifsen (2004) has studied the situation in Ecuador, Howell (2006a) has examined reactions in China, India, Ethiopia, and Romania, Cartwright (2006) has studied the situation in Romania, and Yngvesson (2005) has observed attitudes in India (see also Marre & Briggs 2009). Their work shows that authorities in each country view the practice very differently: as an imposition that smacks of neo-colonialism, as shameful, as a way to handle the population explosion and/or the number of abandoned and unwanted children, or as a way to make easy money for (corrupt) politicians, lawyers, and bureaucrats. Some authorities are more positive, regarding it as a good opportunity for abandoned children to obtain a secure future. Ordinary citizens in donor countries also differ in their interpretations of the practice: as human trafficking, as a wonderful opportunity for the child, as a temporary arrangement that may be annulled once the birth parent decides to do so, as shameful, or as a source for body parts. Several countries—e.g., India (Howell 2006b, Kennedy 2007, Yngvesson 2005), China (Johnson 2005), Romania, India, China (Howell 2006a, Volkman 2005a, Yngvesson 2002)—are starting to encourage domestic adoption as a reaction against transnational adoption and/or as a result of Western encouragement.

TO CONCLUDE

The practice of adults becoming parents of a child to whom they have not given birth is found, and has been found, in some form in most societies. However, culturally and socially little if anything necessarily follows from this fact. Cultural understandings of relatedness vary between social environments and change over time. In summing up his article on adoption for the 1930 *Encyclopedia of Social Sciences*, Lowie states, "adoption customs [in "traditional societies"] rest on a mental attitude difficult to conceive for those nurtured in Western traditions" (p. 460). This observation seems to be as valid today as it was 79 years ago, but it applies equally to adoption of the unrelated child in Western societies then and now. We can observe a continuing fascination with adoption in the media in Western Europe and North America, a fascination that is mirrored among the public more generally. To raise as one's own an unrelated and unknown child appears to most people in the Western world to be a daunting task. Many, including legislators, expect that the absence of shared blood must result in tension, in a troubled sense of identity, and even in second-best love and affection. Anthropological studies of adoption show that, by and large, this is not the case. The picture that is emerging from recent research shows complexity in attitudes, expectations, and experiences. As such, it is a valuable contribution to a more nuanced approach to the practice.

Although there are a number of anthropological studies on adoption practices from many parts of the world, there are not many that address the practice in a Euro-American setting. This is changing. Perhaps owing to the recent rise in transnational adoption by involuntarily childless people in Western Europe and North America, anthropological interest in the practice has been aroused. As I have shown, not only are studies of transnational adoption in receiving countries growing fast, but adoption practices in other parts of the world are also receiving renewed anthropological attention. Anthropologists are realizing the rich potential for social and cultural analysis that can be derived from the study of adoption—comparable to that already obtained from studies on the various forms of assisted conception. Continued study of transnational adoption in Western Europe and North America will undoubtedly reveal profound differences, as well as similarities, in ontology, morality, and ideology, even within the region that is commonly referred to as the West. One may safely conclude, then, that adoption is what adoption does.

DISCLOSURE STATEMENT

The author is not aware of any affiliations, memberships, funding, or financial holdings that might be perceived as affecting the objectivity of this review.

LITERATURE CITED

Alber E. 2003. Denying biological parenthood: fosterage in Northern Benin. *Ethnos* 68(4):487–506

Alber E. 2004. The real parents are the foster parents: social parenthood among the Baatombu in Northern Benin. See Bowie 2004, pp. 33–47

Anderson A. 2004. Adoption and belonging in Wogeo, Papua New Guinea. See Bowie 2004, pp. 111–26

Ardener S, ed. 1974. *Perceiving Women*. London: Dent

Barnard A. 2006. *Social Anthropology: Investigating Human Social Life*. Abergyle: Studymates

Barnes J. 1973. Genetrix: genitor: nature: culture? In *The Character of Kinship*, ed. JR Goody, pp. 61–73. Cambridge, UK: Cambridge Univ. Press

Bledsoe C, Isingo-Abanike U. 1989. Strategies in child-fosterage among Mende grannies in Sierra Leone. In *Reproduction and Social Organization in Sub-Sahara Africa*, ed. JL Lesthaeghe, pp. 442–74. Berkeley: Univ. Calif. Press

Bowie F, ed. 2004. *Cross Cultural Approaches to Adoption*. London: Routledge

Brady I, ed. 1976. *Transactions in Kinship: Adoption and Fosterage in Oceania*. Honolulu: Univ. Press Hawaii

Brooks CC. 1976. Adoption on Manihi Atoll, Tuamoto Archipelago. See Brady 1976, pp. 51–64

Brottveit Å. 1999. *Jeg Vil Ikke Skille Meg Ut*. Oslo: Diaforsk 4

Cadoret A. 2002. *Des Parents comme les Autres: Homosexualité et Parenté*. Paris: Ed. Odile Jacob

Carroll V, ed. 1970. *Adoption in Eastern Oceania*. Honolulu: Univ. Hawaii Press

Carsten J, ed. 2000. Knowing where you've come from: ruptures and continuities of time and kinship in narratives of adoption reunion. *J. R. Anthropol. Inst.* 6(4):687–904

Cartwright L. 2006. Images of waiting children: spectatorship and pity in the representation of global social orphans in the 1990s. See Volkman 2005a, pp. 185–212

Collard C. 1991. Les orphelins "propres" et les autres . . . carence parentale et circulation des orphelins au Québec (1900–1960). *Culture* XI(1–2):135–49

Collard C. 2002. La politique du fosterage et de l'adoption internationale en Haiti. In *De l'Adoption. Des Pratiques de Filiation Différentes*, ed. I Leblic, pp. 175–98. Clermont-Ferrand, France: Univ. Blaise Pascal

Collier JF, Yanagisako J, eds. 1987. *Gender and Kinship: Essays Towards a Unified Analysis*. Stanford, CA: Stanford Univ. Press

Demian M. 2004. Transactions in rights, transactions in children: a view of adoption from Papua New Guinea. See Bowie 2004, pp. 97–110

Dorow SK. 2006. *Transnational Adoption: A Cultural Economy of Race, Gender and Kinship*. New York: NY Univ. Press

Edwards J, Franklin S, Hirsch E, Pine F, Strathern M. 1999. *Technologies of Procreation: Kinship in an Age of Assisted Conception*. London: Routledge. 2nd ed.

Edwards J, Salazar C, eds. 2009. *Kinship Matters*. Oxford/New York: Berghahn Books

Ennew J. 2002. Outside childhood. In *The Handbook of Children's Rights*, ed. B Franklin, pp. 388–403. London: Routledge

Faubion JD, ed. 2001. *The Ethics of Kinship: Ethnographic Inquiries*. Lanham, MD: Rowman & Littlewood

Fines A, ed. 1998. *Adoptions: Ethnologie des Parentés Choisies*. Paris: Éd. Maison Sci. Homme

Fonseca C. 2003. Inequality near and far: adoption as seen from the Brazilian favelas. *Law Soc. Rev.* 36(2):397–431

Fonseca C. 2004. The circulation of children in a Brazilian working-class neighbourhood: a local practice in a globalized world. See Bowie 2004, pp. 165–80

Foucault M. 1991. Governmentality. In *The Foucault Effect: Studies in Governmentality*, ed. G Burchell, C Gordon, P. Miller, pp. 87–104. Chicago: Univ. Chicago Press

Fox R. 1967. *Kinship and Marriage*. Middlesex, UK: Penguin Books

Franklin S, McKinnon S, eds. 2001. *Relative Values: Reconfiguring Kinship Studies*. Durham/London: Duke Univ. Press

Franklin S, Ragoné H, eds. 1998. *Reproducing Reproduction: Kinship, Power, and Technology Innovation*. Philadelphia: Univ. Penn. Press

Gailey CW. 1999. Seeking baby rights: race, class, and gender in US international adoption. In *Mine—Yours—Theirs: Adoption, Changing Kinship and Family Patterns*, ed. A-L Rygvold, M Dalen, B Sætersdal, pp. 33–51. Oslo: Dep. Spec. Needs, Univ. Oslo

Gailey CW. 2000. Race, class and gender in intercountry adoption in the USA. In *Intercountry Adoption: Developments, Trends and Perspectives*, ed. P Selman, pp. 40–52. London: Br. Agencies Adopt. Foster.

Gillis J. 1996. *A World of Their Own Making: Myths, Ritual and the Quest for Family*. Cambridge, MA: Harvard Univ. Press

Goodenough WH. 1970. Epilogue: transactions in parenthood. See Carroll 1970, pp. 391–410

Goody E. 1982. *Parenthood and Social Reproduction: Fostering and Occupational Roles in West Africa*. Cambridge, UK: Univ. Cambridge Press

Goody J. 1969. Adoption in cross-cultural perspective. *Comp. Stud. Sociol. Hist.* 1(11):55–78

Halbmeyer E. 2004. The one who feeds has the rights: adoption and fostering of kin, affines and enemies among the Yukpa and other Carib-speaking Indians of Lowland South America. See Bowie 2004, pp. 145–64

Howell S. 2001. Self-conscious kinship: some contested values in Norwegian transnational adoption. See Franklin & McKinnon 2001, pp. 203–23

Howell S. 2002. Community beyond place: adoptive families in Norway. In *Realizing Community: Concepts, Social Relationships and Sentiments*, ed. V Amit, pp. 84–104. London: Routledge

Howell S. 2003a. Kinning: creating life-trajectories in adoptive families. *J. R. Anthropol. Inst.* 9(3):465–84

Howell S. 2003b. The diffusion of moral values in a global perspective. In *Globalization: Studies in Anthropology*, ed. TH Eriksen, pp. 198–216. London: Pluto

Howell S. 2006a. Changes in moral values about the family: adoption legislation in Norway and USA. *Soc. Anal.* 3:146–63

Howell S. 2006b. *The Kinning of Foreigners: Transnational Adoption in a Global Perspective*. Oxford/New York: Berghahn Books

Howell S. 2007a. Imagined kin, place and community: some paradoxes in the transnational movement of children in adoption. In *Holding Worlds Together: Ethnography of Truth and Belonging*, ed. M Lien, M Melhuus, pp. 17–36. Oxford/New York: Berghahn Books

Howell S. 2007b. Relations with the imagined child: the emotionality of becoming an adoptive parent. In *The Emotions: A Cultural Reader*, ed. H Wulff, pp. 179–96. Oxford, UK: Berg

Howell S, Marre D. 2006. To kin a foreign child in Norway and Spain: notions of resemblances and the achievement of belonging. *Ethnos* 4:293–316

Howell S, Melhuus M. 2007. Race, biology and culture in contemporary Norway: identity and belonging in adoption, donor gametes and immigration. See Wade 2007, pp. 53–72

Johnson K. 2005. Chaobao: the plight of Chinese adoptive parents in the era of the one-child policy. See Volkman 2005a, pp. 117–41

Keesing RM. 1975. *Kin Groups and Social Structure*. New York: Holt, Rinehart and Winston

Keesing RM. 1981. *Cultural Anthropology: A Contemporary Perspective*. New York: Holt Rinehart and Winston

Kennedy A. 2007. *Born of my heart: a study of the process of unrelated adoption in Delhi*. MPhil thesis, Univ. Oslo

Leifsen E. 2004. Person, relation and value: the economy of circulating Ecuadorian children in international adoption. See Bowie 2004, pp. 182–96

Leinwater JB. 2007. On moving children: the social implications of Andean child circulation. *Am. Ethnol.* 34:163–80

Leinwater JB. 2008. *The Circulation of Children: Kinship, Adoption and Morality in Andean Peru*. Durham, NC: Duke Univ. Press

Maine H. 1917 [1861]. *Ancient Law*. London: Dent

Marre D. 2007. I want her to learn her language and maintain her culture: transnational adoptive families' views of "cultural origin." See Wade 2007, pp. 73–94

Marre D, Briggs L, eds. 2009. *International Adoption: Global Inequalities and the Circulation of Children*. New York: NY Univ. Press

Marshall M. 1976. Solidarity or sterility? Adoption and fosterage on Namoluk Atoll. See Brady 1976, pp. 28–50

Marshall M. 1977. The nature of nurture. *Am. Ethnol.* 4(4):643–62

Meigs A. 1986. Blood, kin and food. In *Conformity and Conflict: Readings in Cultural Anthropology*, ed. JP Spradley, DW McCurdy, pp. 117–80. Boston: Little Brown Higher Educ.

Melosh B. 2002. *Strangers and Kin: The American Way of Adoption*. Cambridge, MA: Harvard Univ. Press

Modell JS. 1994. *Kinship with Strangers: Adoption and Interpretations of Kinship in American Culture*. Berkeley: Univ. Calif. Press

Modell JS. 1999. Freely given: open adoption and the rhetoric of the gift. In *Transformative Motherhood: On Giving and Getting in a Consumer Culture*, ed. LL Layne, pp. 29–64. New York: NY Univ. Press

Modell JS. 2002. *A Sealed and Secret Kinship: The Culture and Practices in American Adoption*. New York: Berghahn Books

Morgan LH. 1871. *Systems of Consanguinity and Affinity of the Human Family*. Washington, DC: Smithson. Inst.

Morton KL. 1976. Tongan adoption. See Brady 1976, pp. 64–80

Murdoch GP. 1949. *Social Structure*. New York: Macmillan

Needham R. 1971. Remarks on the analysis of kinship and marriage. In *Rethinking Kinship and Marriage*, ed. R Needham, pp. 1–34. London: Tavistock Press

O'Collins M. 1984. Influences of western adoption laws in the Third World. In *Adoption: Essays in Social Policy, Law, and Sociology*, ed. P Bean, pp. 288–305. London: Tavistock

Ortner SB, Whitehead H, eds. 1981. *Sexual Meanings: The Cultural Construction of Gender and Sexuality*. Cambridge, UK: Cambridge Univ. Press

Panter-Brick C. 2000. Nobody's children? A reconsideration of child abandonment. In *Abandoned Children*, ed. C Panter-Brick, MT Smith, pp. 1–26. Cambridge, UK: Cambridge Univ. Press

Quellette FR. 2003. *Plenary legal adoption and its implications for the adopted child*. Work. Pap. INRS-Urbanisation, Culture et Societé, Montreal: Univ. Québec

Rosaldo M, Lamphere L, eds. 1974. *Woman, Culture and Society*. Stanford, CA: Stanford Univ. Press

Rose N. 1999. *Governing the Soul: The Shaping of the Private Self*. London: Free Assoc. Books

Schachter J. 2007. *Law, custom, Hawaii, and international adoption*. Presented at Conf. Adopt. Culture, Oct., Univ. Pittsburgh

Scheper-Hughes N. 1998. Introduction. In *Small Wars: The Cultural Politics of Childhood*, ed. N Scheper-Hughes, C Sargent, pp. 1–34. Berkeley: Univ. Calif. Press

Schneider DM. 1968 [1980]. *American Kinship: A Cultural Account*. Chicago: Univ. Chicago Press

Schneider DM. 1972. What is kinship all about? In *Kinship Studies in the Morgan Centenial Year*, ed. P Reining, pp. 62–63. Washington, DC: Anthropol. Soc. Wash.

Schneider DM. 1984. *A Critique of the Study of Kinship*. Ann Arbor: Univ. Mich. Press

Selman P, ed. 2000. *Intercountry Adoption: Developments, Trends and Perspectives*. London: Br. Agencies Adopt. Foster.

Selman P. 2004. Adoption—a cure for (too) many ills? See Bowie 2004, pp. 256–73

Silverman MG. 1971. *Disconcerting Issues: Meaning and Struggle in a Resettled Pacific Community*. Chicago: Univ. Chicago Press

Stephens S. 1995. Introduction. In *Children and the Politics of Culture*, ed. S Stephens, pp. 3–48. Princeton, NJ: Princeton Univ. Press

Sterett SM. 2002. Introductory essay. Special Issue on Non-Biological Parenting. *Law Soc. Rev.* 36(2):209–26

Strathern M. 1992. *After Nature: English Kinship in the Late Twentieth Century*. Cambridge, UK: Cambridge Univ. Press

Telfer J. 1999. In-dividual but in-complete: adoption, identity and the quest for the wholeness. In *Mine— Yours—Theirs: Adoption, Changing Kinship and Family Patterns*, ed. AL Rygvold, M Dalen, B Sætersdal, pp. 247–65. Oslo: Dep. Spec. Needs, Univ. Oslo

Telfer J. 2004. Partial to completeness: gender, peril and agency in Australian adoption. See Bowie 2004, pp. 242–56

Tonkinson R. 1976. Adoption and sister exchange in a New Hebredean community. See Brady 1976, pp. 228–46

Volkman T, ed. 2005a. *Cultures of Transnational Adoption*. Durham, NC: Duke Univ. Press

Volkman T. 2005b. Embodying Chinese culture: transnational adoption in North America. See Volkman 2005a, pp. 81–116

Wade P, ed. 2007. *Race, Ethnicity and Nation: Perspectives From Kinship and Genetics*. Oxford/New York: Berghahn Books

Weismantel M. 1995. Making kin: kinship theory and Zumbagua adoptions. *Am. Ethnol.* 22(4):685–709

Weston K. 1991. *Families We Choose: Lesbians, Gays, Kinship*. New York: Columbia Univ. Press

Yanagisako SJ, Delaney C, eds. 1995. *Naturalizing Power: Essays in Feminist Cultural Analysis*. New York: Routledge

Yngvesson B. 2002. Placing the "gift child" in transnational adoption. *Law Soc. Rev.* 2(36):227–56

Yngvesson B. 2004. National bodies and the body of the child: "completing" families through international adoption. See Bowie 2004, pp. 211–26

Yngvesson B. 2005. Going "home": adoption, loss of bearings and the mythology of roots. See Volkman 2005a, pp. 25–48

Anthropology and Global Health

Craig R. Janes and Kitty K. Corbett

Simon Fraser University, Burnaby, British Columbia V5A 1S6, Canada;
email: cjanes@sfu.ca, kcorbett@sfu.ca

Annu. Rev. Anthropol. 2009. 38:167–83

First published online as a Review in Advance on
June 23, 2009

The *Annual Review of Anthropology* is online at
anthro.annualreviews.org

This article's doi:
10.1146/annurev-anthro-091908-164314

Copyright © 2009 by Annual Reviews.
All rights reserved

0084-6570/09/1021-0167$20.00

Key Words

political economy of health, critical medical anthropology,
globalization of bioscience, international health policy, civil society,
global health governance, population health

Abstract

This article addresses anthropology's engagement with the emerging
discipline of global health. We develop a definition for global health
and then present four principal contributions of anthropology to global
health: (*a*) ethnographic studies of health inequities in political and
economic contexts; (*b*) analysis of the impact on local worlds of the
assemblages of science and technology that circulate globally; (*c*) interrogation, analysis, and critique of international health programs and
policies; and (*d*) analysis of the health consequences of the reconfiguration of the social relations of international health development.

DEFINING GLOBAL HEALTH

Defining global health in relation to anthropological research and practice is a challenge. Although in common use in a variety of disciplines, the term defies simple delineation. It frequently serves as a gloss signaling complexities inherent in linking health and accelerating and intensifying global processes, although it sometimes simply refers to work that has an international (read: low-income country) dimension. In his recent book on the subject, Nichter (2008) suggests that anthropology intersects global health along a number of dimensions, ranging from the study of popular health culture and local perceptions as a way to both critique and improve international public health, to the study of ethics, governance, and emergent forms of biological citizenship. Cast in such a broad framework, though, these intersections could characterize much of the development of medical anthropology to the present, including, especially, much of the ethnographic applied research on local social and cultural factors linked to improving community health in developing countries (Foster 1976; Hahn & Inhorn 2009; Inhorn & Janes 2007; Nichter 1989, 1991; Paul 1955). To further complicate matters, until recently anthropologists have not typically invoked the term global health as a referent for a subdisciplinary domain of research or practice or in description of their own identity as scholars. Although a recent upsurge in publications and several recent editorials suggest that global health may at last be finding a home in anthropology, definitional clarity is needed (Adams et al. 2008, Erickson 2003, Inhorn 2007a, Nichter 2008, Pfeiffer & Nichter 2008, Whiteford & Manderson 2000b).[1]

As noted, global health is used to either supplant or mirror the longstanding conceptual domain of international health. This distinction is complicated by the fact that international health references a better-defined set of research and applied skills, many of which are derived from the disciplines that constitute public health and development studies (including anthropology; e.g., Nichter 2008). In contrast, global health remains a diffuse and highly diverse arena of scholarship and practice (Inst. Med. 2009, Macfarlane et al. 2008). The political scientist Kelley Lee, a prolific writer on global health, distinguishes the two by highlighting the construct of transnationalism. Lee argues that global health, as opposed to international health, should be a field of scholarship and practice that focuses on health issues that transcend the territorial boundaries of states (Lee 2003c). International health becomes global health when the causes or consequences of ill health "circumvent, undermine, or are oblivious to the territorial boundaries of states, and thus beyond the capacity of states to address effectively through state institutions alone" (Lee et al. 2002, p. 5).

Lee (2003a,c) argues for a model that specifically positions health as an outcome of processes that have intensified human interaction, given that previous boundaries separating individuals and population groups "have become increasingly eroded and redefined, resulting in new forms of social organization and interaction across them" (Lee 2003a, p. 21). She identifies three such boundaries or dimensions of globalization: the spatial, the temporal, and the cognitive. As she and others note, in this sense global health has come to occupy a new and different kind of political space that demands the study of population health in the context of power relations in a world system (Brown et al. 2006, Kickbush 2003, Lee 2003c).

Lee's model merges with writing in anthropology and sociology that looks at globalization from the perspective of local, though not necessarily spatially bound, social contexts. Appadurai (1991, 1996), for example, has invoked the idea of "scapes" that have come to

---

[1] A review of articles indexed in PubMed reflects both an increasing tendency to cast medical anthropological work as global health and an increasing diversity of subjects so classified. Using the search terms "anthropology" and "global health," PubMed returns (in January 2009) ~2000 citations from its complete database (dating to the mid-1960s). Of these, about half have been published since 2004. A review of titles indicates a dizzying array of subjects, ranging from the narrowly epidemiologic to the broadly programmatic.

stand in place of older place-based divisions. Burawoy (2000), who with his graduate students developed a theoretical and methodological program to "ground globalization," observes that the "mishmash of migrations, capital flows, hostilities, and opportunities jostling within the hot signifier of globalization" (p. ix) can be sorted along three axes. These axes are global forces, including global economic and political processes as mediated by agents, institutions, and ideas; global connections, referring to the underlying social grids, networks, flows, and new forms of sociality; and the global imagination, which addresses the adoption of values and images that circulate globally.

Burawoy takes these abstractions of globalization and applies them to understand something local. Yet what constitutes the "local" in the context of globalization is contested (Ferguson 2005, Janes 2004, Morgan 2001, Ong & Collier 2005a). Although the concept of locality is worthy of extended analysis, we take a pragmatic approach: As ethnographers we study people-in-places or people-in-contexts. We thus prefer the definition advanced by Ginsburg & Rapp (1995b): "[T]he local is not defined by geographical boundaries but is understood as any small-scale arena in which social meanings are informed and adjusted" (p. 8).

What does this mean for understanding health? Both theoretically and methodologically the task is to understand how various assemblages of global, national, and subnational factors converge on a health issue, problem, or outcome in a particular local context. Ong & Collier (2005a) refer to these processes collectively as the "actual global," and they prefer the more fluid, irreducible, and emergent concept of the "global assemblage" to "the global": An assemblage "does not always involve new forms, but forms that are shifting, in formation, or at stake" (p. 12). These heterogeneous global assemblages interact with local institutions, social worlds, and cultural identities through unpredictable and uncertain processes (Whiteford & Manderson 2000b). Consistent with Burawoy's (2000) approach to grounded globalization,

anthropological work in global health thus requires a focus on the instantiation of global assemblages in local social arenas, however defined. Methodologically, Burawoy (2000) argues for the grounding of globalization through what he identifies as the extended case method: "extending from observer to participant, extending observations over time and place, extending from process to external forces, and extending theory" (p. 28). In so doing, the ethnographer is positioned to "construct perspectives on globalization from below" (p. 341).

With this information as a brief background, and for purposes of this exercise, we offer the following definition of global health as it pertains to anthropology: Global health is an area of research and practice that endeavours to link health, broadly conceived as a dynamic state that is an essential resource for life and well-being, to assemblages of global processes, recognizing that these assemblages are complex, diverse, temporally unstable, contingent, and often contested or resisted at different social scales. This includes work that focuses on health inequities; the distribution of resources intended to produce health and well-being, including science and technology; social identities related to health and biology; the development and local consequences of global health policy; the organization of health services; and the relationship of anthropogenic transformations of the biosphere to health. The ultimate goal of anthropological work in and of global health is to reduce global health inequities and contribute to the development of sustainable and salutogenic sociocultural, political, and economic systems.

Although global health conceptually includes all peoples regardless of social, economic, and political contexts, its ethical and moral commitment is to the most vulnerable. However, and given the impending and hitherto unprecedented scale of global catastrophe that environmental destruction, mass species extinction, and anthropogenic climate change presage, global health might benefit from redefining the vulnerable to include all of us (McMichael & Beaglehole 2003).

So defined, the anthropological project in global health can be arranged along several axes. Here we review what we consider key arenas of research and practice: ethnographic studies of health inequities in political and economic contexts; analysis of the impact on local worlds of the assemblages of science and technology that circulate globally; interrogation, analysis, and critique of international health programs and policies; and analysis of the health consequences of the reconfiguration of the social relations of international health development.

EXPLAINING HEALTH INEQUITIES

The anthropological contribution to the study of health inequities has primarily been to ground globalization (as anticipated by Burowoy 2000 and Nichter 2008) through exposing processes by which people are constrained or victimized or resisting external forces in the context of local social worlds (Baer et al. 2003; Farmer 1997, 2003, 2004; Farmer et al. 1996; Kim et al. 2005; Maternowska 2006; Pfeiffer & Nichter 2008; Scheper-Hughes 1993). This research encompasses different registers, mainly in the depth of engagement with local materials, the care by which the local is nested within higher-level social structures, and the degree to which the analysis is used as a platform for public health advocacy. However, this work tends to share a common, critical theoretical perspective that focuses on explicating or grounding health inequities in reference to upstream constellations of international political economy, regional history, and development ideology. It is closely linked with critical medical anthropology, a research tradition that seeks to identify the social origins of distress and disease, recognizing that these origins are ultimately located within the processes and contradictions inherent in the capitalist world system (Baer et al. 2003, Singer & Baer 1995). Farmer (2004) has used the concept of "structural violence" to explain this impact of political-economic regimes of oppression on the health of the poor.

Such work has contributed to redefining the concept of risk in epidemiology by redirecting attention from risky behaviors to structural factors that constrain or determine behavior. For example, early reports on the epidemiology of HIV/AIDS tended to focus on individual behaviors rather than on the impact of poverty and marginality that differentially affected men and women within particular populations and communities (Farmer et al. 1996, 2001; Simmons et al. 1996). Pointing to the tendency of some public health researchers to conflate poverty and cultural difference, Farmer and colleagues argued against "immodest claims of causality" and for a focus on, and mitigation of, the structural violence that produces ill being on a massive scale among the poor (Farmer 2003, Farmer et al. 2001, Simmons et al. 1996, Singer 1997). In similar fashion, anthropological research on infectious diseases, particularly HIV/AIDS, TB, and cholera, has contributed significantly to moving global public health away from a narrow focus on risk groups (Baer et al. 2003, Trostle 2005).

The social origins of infection with HIV are often bound up with or linked to a number of other threats to health and well-being, and in turn, the coexistence of two or more diseases may synergistically interact to produce a higher degree of pathogenesis (an example would be HIV and TB coinfection). Termed syndemics, these synergistic processes suggest a biosocial model of disease (Nichter 2008, Singer 2009, Singer & Clair 2003) that conceives "of disease both in terms of its interrelationships with noxious social conditions and social relationships, and as one form of expression of social suffering... it would make us more alert, as well, to the likelihood of multiple, interacting deleterious conditions among populations produced by the structural violence of social inequality" (Singer & Clair 2003, p. 434).

Many researchers experience a tension between a close rendering of the local and effective engagement with the global. Analytically and methodologically, how does one extend ethnographic work to incorporate globalization while portraying faithfully the rich human stories that bring voice to the poor and suffering, without conceptually flattening, simplifying, or objectifying one or the other (Butt 2002)? Farmer and his colleagues often juxtapose stories of individual suffering with political-economic givens, offering sometimes thin analyses of intervening processes and structures. Some have observed that the concept of structural violence is a black box, rarely unpacked (Bourgois & Scheper-Hughes 2004, Wacquant 2004). Future work on global health inequities might thus profitably employ ecosocial epidemiology (Krieger 2001) by addressing, for instance, the interplay among exposure, susceptibility, and adaptation at meso- and macroscales across the life course (Nichter 2008). Application within global health contexts of the construct of "intersectionality" also provides a way to unpack the concept of structural violence. Derived primarily from feminist studies, this theoretical and methodological perspective emphasizes the importance of simultaneously considering how different aspects of social location (e.g., gender, ethnicity, class, age, geography, sexual identity) interlock and the impact of systems and processes of oppression and domination (Hankivsky & Cormier 2009, Hulko 2009).

Whether explicitly identified as critical medical anthropology or not, a substantial body of scholarly work in anthropology seeks to link wider social, economic, and political forces to local experiences of sickness and suffering. We believe that this work is an important adjunct to the emerging scholarship on the social determinants of health that tends to focus more on patterns evident at population levels (Comm. Soc. Determinants Health 2008). A few examples include studies of extreme hunger and scarcity in northeastern Brazil (Scheper-Hughes 1993); the global circulation of tobacco and its impacts (Nichter & Cartwright 1991, Stebbins 1991); parasitic and infectious diseases (Briggs & Mantini-Briggs 2003, Farmer 1999, Feldman 2008, Ferguson 2005, Inhorn & Brown 1997, Kendall 2005, Manderson & Huang 2005, Whiteford & Hill 2005); reproductive health, fertility, and infertility (Inhorn 2003, 2007b; Janes & Chuluundorj

2004; Maternowska 2006; Morsy 1995); mental ill health (Desjarlais et al. 1995, Kleinman 1988); alcohol and drug use (Singer 2008); and life style transitions and noncommunicable diseases (Dressler & Bindon 2000, Evans et al. 2001, McElroy 2005).

Although anthropologists have engaged with many of the core themes of health equity studies in global public health, they lag in taking up some emerging concerns. Gaps are apparent in the domain of environmental change affecting and affected by global processes. Examples range from climate change broadly (Baer & Singer 2009, Guest 2005, McMichael & Beaglehole 2003, Patz et al. 2005) to specific problems such as microbial resistance (Orzech & Nichter 2008). Many of the models of human impacts of climate change point to the need for more research to identify factors that affect the vulnerabilities of local populations in the context of political economy (Intergov. Panel Climate Change 2007). We anticipate that in the next decade medical anthropology will begin to investigate more systematically the relationship of global environmental transformations to health.

GLOBAL TECHNOSCAPES

Invoking the term technoscape, Appadurai (1996) refers to the "global configuration... of technology, and the fact that technology, both high and low, both mechanical and information, now moves at high speeds across various kinds of previously impervious boundaries" (p. 34). The global technoscape as it pertains to health is comprised of an inextricable mix of things (e.g., medicines, medical devices, machines), techniques (e.g., medical procedures), and bundles of shared understandings and epistemological practices that together constitute science in the global north. Far from being a homogenizing influence, the global circulation of science and technology engages various localities as one component of a global assemblage (Ong & Collier 2005a). This assemblage of things, ideologies, and representations interacts with communities in diverse ways, both shaping and being transformed by local beliefs and practices. Questions central to investigation of global science concern how paradigms, practices, and results are negotiated and unfold far from their places of origin (Adams et al. 2005). As many scholars have noted, the products and purported benefits of science and technology are unevenly distributed; some sites and groups have greater access than others do (Ginsburg and Rapp 1995b, Inhorn 2003).

Examples of key works in this area include the local impact of biomedical research practices, such as those involving translation of the ethical principles of scientific research, especially clinical trials, in specific cultural contexts (Adams et al. 2005, Petryna 2005); the circulation of medicalized objectifications of body and behavior, such as those having to do with sexuality in this era of HIV (Parker 2000, Pigg & Adams 2005); the transformations of local beliefs and understandings about the body, life, and death that are entailed by the globalization of human organ replacement therapies (Lock 2001, Marshall & Daar 2000); local acceptances of and resistance to contraceptive technologies (Maternowska 2006, Rak & Janes 2004); the complex local/global dynamics of organ transplantation and medical tourism (Cohen 2005; Scheper-Hughes 2000, 2005), including the definitional exercises needed to create harvestable tissues and organs (Lock 2001, Marshall & Daar 2000); and cases illustrating complexities of corporate practices, medicalization, and the politics of biomedical knowledge through the interwoven dynamics of drug production, marketing, and sales practices, the classification of disease, and patterns of clinical practice (Applbaum 2006, Hayden 2007, Singer & Baer 2008).

A particularly robust area of research has focused on the globalization of reproductive and prenatal diagnostic technologies (Browner & Sargent 2010; Erikson 2003; Ginsburg & Rapp 1995a; Inhorn 2003, 2005, 2007b; Ong & Collier 2005b). Writing of the globalization of treatments for infertility, Inhorn (2003) observes that "[l[ocal considerations, be they cultural, social, economic, or political,

shape and sometimes curtail the way in which these Western-generated technologies are both offered to and received by non-Western subjects" (p. 1844). Cultural or religious proscription of procedures such as donor insemination has led to increased global demand and rapid circulation of more expensive technologies such as in-vitro fertilization (Inhorn 2003). In Egypt, for example, men and women contending with infertility are confronted by constraints that are deeply embedded in local social and cultural contexts. These arenas of constraint include local understandings of reproductive biology, social and economic barriers to access, gender dynamics within marriage, and local understandings of Islam (Inhorn 2003, p. 1844; 2005; 2007b).

Globalization also sets into motion people, for example, the export of physicians and nurses (the "brain drain") from low-income countries to rich countries (Pfeiffer & Nichter 2008), and "medical tourists" and others who travel to places where desired technologies exist or are affordable (Kangas 2002). As noted above, it also enables the flow of organs, tissues, and genetic materials (Marshall & Daar 2000, Scheper-Hughes 2005). Described as an artifact of "second coming" capitalism, the worldwide spread of medical procedures and technologies has produced "strange markets and 'occult' economies" (Comaroff & Comaroff 2001, cited in Scheper-Hughes 2005, p. 149).

Bioscience is not the only set of ideas about bodies, physiology, and health that circulates globally. Countervailing creativities also exist, whereby what were formerly "local" and "non-western" engage both the imagination and the markets at the center of the world system. This is the case for Asian medicines, both brought by immigrants and practiced by immigrant communities, but also adopted by New Agers and others challenging the hegemony of conventional biomedicine. In their places of origin and their global circulation, the content and practice of these medical traditions are transformed (Alter 2005, Høg & Hsu 2002, Janes 2002). In many cases these processes of transformation involve at their core the commoditization of medicinal substances, which is in turn based on the reduction of complex systems of diagnosis, explanation, and healing to the exchange and consumption of medicinal substances (Janes 1999).

Medicines—*materia medica*—are at the heart of much of what we might define as "medical technologies." Although medicines, especially pharmaceuticals, were ignored as a focal topic more often than not by medical anthropologists in the first decades of the discipline, work by van der Geest and other anthropologists in the 1980s and 1990s initiated a florescence of research on their uses in the context of global influences and on factors affecting their production, distribution, demand, and consumption (Trostle 1996; van der Geest et al. 1988, 1996). This trend continues, spurred in part by the ethical and practical challenges represented by the need for people everywhere who live with HIV/AIDS to receive treatment (Farmer et al. 2001, Robins 2009, Whyte et al. 2006). Addressing access needs requires investigation into pharmaceutical governance, trade practices, patent protection, distribution channels, and alternative industries and markets, as well as local organizations and the cultural and ritual properties of medicines (Petryna et al. 2006). Approaches to understanding how medicines function in society increasingly include attention to the context of global assemblages, including greater attention to formal and institutional sectors (Hayden 2007, Kim 2009, Mather 2006, Oldani 2004). As anthropologists reflect on medication use, including not just underuse but also overuse, inappropriate use, and errors in delivering appropriate medications to patients, they increasingly situate these practices within global institutional and perceptual systems (Nichter 2008). Medicines, whether originating in local traditions or developed through the pharmaceutical pipeline, are global citizens.

One dimension of the global circulation of expert, biomedical knowledge on disease, therapeutic regimes, and prevention is the creation of novel social forms (Biehl 2007, Lee 2003a, Nguyen 2005, Rose & Novas 2005).

In the context of HIV, notes Nguyen (2005), these groups are "more than social movements articulated around objectives" and are a "complex biopolitical assemblage, cobbled together from global flows of organisms, drugs, discourses, and technologies of all kinds" (p. 125). Nguyen is interested particularly in how the constellations of technoscientific understandings of prevention and treatment that together constitute the global AIDS industry are translated locally by groups and organizations to mobilize a response to the epidemic. Similarly, Petryna (2002) shows how the Chernobyl disaster and its impacts on health provided an avenue for affected individuals, joined by a biologically mediated identity, to make claims on the state for resources. The development of therapeutic groups is increasingly entangled with the industry of health development (Nguyen 2005, p. 125). This form of citizenship represents evolving subjectivities, politics, and ethics that result from the globalization of biomedical developments and discoveries (Ecks 2005, Rose & Novas 2005).

INTERROGATING HEALTH POLICY

Analysis of the formation, dissemination, and local consequences of expert knowledge forms the core of the anthropological critique of global public health policy (Castro & Singer 2004, Whiteford & Manderson 2000b). This critique focuses on both the process and consequences of policymaking: ideological and political-economic relations that influence decision makers and the policymaking process and the impacts, intended or otherwise, of specific policies on the health and well-being of the intended beneficiaries. In regard to the latter, it is common for observers to report on the problems inherent in localizing global health policies (Whiteford & Manderson 2000b). Central to the interrogation of health policy, an area only a few anthropologists have explored in any depth (e.g., Justice 1986), are the processes by and through which the substances of international health policymaking—knowledge, ideology, politics of representation, competing vested interests, processes of persuasion and advocacy, etc.—come to constitute it. In a pure and perhaps idealized form, policy represents translating knowledge into action. What are these processes of translation? Is it possible, thinking here in ethnographic terms, to expose these processes through careful analysis of global policymaking communities? And how might anthropologists proactively affect these translational processes?

Nichter (2008) suggests that policymakers tend to simplify and frame problems in ways that limit the thinking about possible solutions; these "key social representations" dominate health and development discourse as "master narratives" (p. 2). Lee & Goodman (2002) argue that the networks of so-called experts in global health tend to be fairly small but are positioned strategically to create and successfully advocate for solutions to key international agencies. Such networks comprise what are in international relations and globalization literatures termed epistemic communities (Adler & Haas 1992), loose networks of actors that develop common frameworks of knowledge, values, and beliefs that underlie configurations of public health policy and action. Although presumably oriented to technical matters, these epistemic communities are powerful because they, as representatives at least implicitly of the global capitalist class (Singer & Castro 2004), can set agendas, frame issues, identify problems, and propose solutions. These networks extend into major universities, especially in the fields of economics and public health (Lee & Goodman 2002) and are now at the core of global health governance (Adams et al. 2008).

Van der Geest (2006), in commenting about pharmaceutical matters, critiques an overemphasis in global health on policies as a solution, commenting about the lip service and culture of policy makers whose mandate is to produce planning reports and documents (e.,g., about essential medicines, their distribution, etc.) but who are not invested in program implementation. Whyte & Birungi (2000) found that World Health Organization (WHO)-inspired model policies were ineffective in changing local-level and lay practices around inappropriate prescription and use of pharmaceutical medicines. Hardon (2005), also critical of policymakers, asserts that their work often entails a focus on "magic bullets." She notes that recent policy shifts reflect a growing acknowledgment in the policy sectors that people without economic resources or literacy can and do use HIV/AIDS treatments appropriately. Yet although many more people now have access to previously far too expensive treatments, the policies have had side effects. The prices of pharmaceuticals are still extremely high for people on the margins of the economy, and entire family networks may experience cash depletion and food insecurity as they shift the household economy to procure medicines for a family member who is ill (Whyte et al. 2006).

The global circulation of expert knowledge produces particular relations of power between policy makers and policy subjects. The collapse of the primary care initiatives fostered at Alma Ata in 1978, the resurgence of selective forms of primary care and vertical public health programs, and the ascendency of the World Bank as the principal health policymaking institution provide a glimpse of how these processes work themselves out (Janes 2004, 2009; Janes et al. 2005; Lee & Goodman 2002; Paluzzi 2004). Deploying a set of strategies to reframe health and health care in narrow technical terms (i.e., the development of the disability adjusted life year, or DALY) subject to the principles of classical economics, a relatively small group of individuals crafted an approach to health care that removed it from public governance and placed it largely in the hands of the market, complementing and bolstering processes of structural adjustment begun in the 1980s (Farmer 2003, Farmer & Castro 2004, Janes 2004, World Bank 1993). The result has been increasing inequities and contradictions at local levels, for example reforms that mandate selling medicines to poor people who cannot afford them (Keshavjee 2004). Although it is remarkable that the WHO is currently attempting to reclaim the discourse on health reform and reassert the principles of primary health care (World Health Organ. 2008), it remains to be seen whether rights-based approaches will be able to trump the neoliberal orthodoxy that dominates health sector policy.

Population and reproductive policy is a significant area in which deeply held beliefs about the causes and consequences of poverty, and the role of scientific development and expert knowledge of demographic processes in remediating poverty, have come to drive health and social policy (Escobar 1995, Maternowska 2006). For example, in a series of works focusing on population policy in China, Greenhalgh (2005) has shown how the development of coercive family planning practices linked a version of Western population science with socialist planning and party-led community mobilization in order to achieve demographic modernity. Although the International Conference on Population Development held in Cairo in 1994 urged countries to move away from a narrow focus on fertility targets and to respect and protect women's rights to make an informed choice about their reproduction, in many contexts oppressive and coercive regimes of family planning have continued, directed primarily at poor women (Castro 2004, Greenhalgh 2005, Maternowska 2006, Morsy 1995). Other important works also focus on the problematic disjuncture between global reproductive health policy and the lived experiences of local women and men (Berry 2009, Browner & Sargent 2010, Castro 2004, Ginsburg & Rapp 1995a, Rak & Janes 2004, Towghi 2004).

The anthropological literature documenting the problematic implementation of international health development policy is vast. Other examples include, in addition to the above, work on child immunization (Justice 2000, Nichter 1995); implementation of therapeutic regimes for tuberculosis (DOTS) and treatment of multiple-drug-resistant forms of the disease (Farmer 2003, Kim et al. 2005, Nichter 2008); disaster management and resettlement (Whiteford & Tobin 2004); the globalization of bioethics and ethical issues, including especially those arising in the context of organ transplantation and drug development (Marshall 2005, Marshall & Koenig 2004, Petryna 2005); the local impact of the global extension of regimes of monitoring and evaluation of public health programs, a variant of "audit cultures" (Nichter 2008, Strathern 2000); ideologies of community participation and political will in international health program planning (Janes 2004; Morgan 1989, 1997, 2001); and HIV/AIDS treatment and prevention policies (Bastos 1999, Biehl 2007, Desclaux 2004, Farmer 1999, Farmer et al. 2001).

AN UNRULY MÉLANGE

Neoliberal development strategies initiated in the health sector since the 1980s have systematically reduced the size, scope, and reach of public health services. As a result, a number of private organizations, grouped collectively under the general heading of civil society, have become a cornerstone to health development. These include everything from small, local private organizations, to faith-based charities, to local offices of large international philanthropies. Favored as implementing agents by bilateral and international donors, including the major foundations and development banks, these agents of civil society have in many locales effectively supplanted government in the provision of primary health care. Often uncoordinated, competing with one another for donor and ministerial attention, duplicating efforts, and distorting local economies through the demands for food, housing, transportation, and entertainment by their expatriate staffs, they comprise, as Buse & Walt (1997) note, an unruly mélange (Adams et al. 2008; Pfeiffer 2003, 2004).

Despite their prominence in health development, nongovernmental organizations (NGOs) have received relatively little attention as social and cultural phenomena in their own right (though see Abramson 1999; Markowitz 2001; Pfeiffer 2003, 2004; Redfield 2005). Pfeiffer (2003, 2004) has documented how in Mozambique the operation of NGOs, instead of strengthening health services, may have in fact had the opposite effect, undermining local control of health programs and contributing to the health human resource crisis by recruiting public-sector employees from public health service. Pfeiffer also gives us a glimpse of the social dynamics of NGOs, observing that in the interaction between the elite, educated technicians from the rich countries and community members living in extreme poverty, the exercise of power is laid bare: international NGOs intensify unequal social relations at the local level.

The expansion of NGOs is but one example of a growing number of transnational institutions that have become active in global health. Along with existing bilateral donors, intergovernmental institutions, and public private partnerships, these include economic interest groups, large philanthropic organizations, and multinational pharmaceutical companies. The effective practice of global health regardless of disciplinary background increasingly requires not just understanding of how to work effectively at a local level to improve health and well-being, but also skills to work across these many, and often competing, interest groups (Adams et al. 2008).

CONCLUSION: REFLECTIONS ON THE ECONOMY OF KNOWLEDGE IN GLOBAL HEALTH

A colleague of ours, reflecting on the virtual invasion of Africa by international scholars, suggested that the continent's new export was information for university-based researchers and pharmaceutical companies. In addition, academic programs in global health (like our own), located primarily in schools of public health in North America, send thousands of students abroad each year to complete global health practice placements. Presumably these students gain through these experiences the knowledge and skills they need to "do" global health. This experience raises the spectre of a new form of colonialism: extending uses of sites in the global south to study their disease burdens to satisfy the needs of science (particularly, these days,

the AIDS industry) to find new subjects and explore new problems. Citing his colleague, Jim Yong Kim, Farmer (1999, p. 35) has wryly observed that we are now in the midst of a global "Tuskegee experiment." We are mindful of the fact that global health, a field of exploding popularity largely in Europe and North America, is deeply involved in this manner of knowledge creation, exploitation, and exchange.

We argue that a central ethical problem for anthropologists, as for scholars of global health more generally, is consideration of the fairness of the terms of this exchange and whether their work contributes to social justice and the remediation of structural violence where it is the most severe. This problem provokes two questions: Are the products of anthropological scholarship in global health—conceptually, theoretically, methodologically, and pragmatically—relevant to those broadly interdisciplinary efforts to improve health and well-being? And, is anthropology, principally an academic discipline, prepared in the context of global health to engage in what we refer to here as principled engagement and intervention?

Partly in response to these questions, it is useful to reflect on anthropology's relevance to global health, which we have encapsulated into four main areas of research and practice. In the first of these, through ethnographic analysis of health inequities, anthropologists have added considerable depth to the project of identifying the social determinants of health (Comm. Soc. Determinants Health 2008). By specifying links among local life worlds and the global forces of neoliberal development, anthropologists have laid bare the lines of power, exploitation, and structural violence. Although more conceptual development is needed, this work has pointed to inherent flaws in health development programs that do not take poverty and environmental degradation, their root causes and consequences, as primary problems.

Second, and what now currently seems to be a popular avenue of research, is the study of global technoscience. Here anthropologists focus on the global circulation of technology and the bundles of meanings, representations, and understandings that together constitute biomedical science in the global north. The intent here is twofold: to unpack and explicate the cultural context of science and its products, and then to understand how science, as a social and cultural product, interacts with the local, where it is transformed and transforms, through being adopted, used, and resisted. Theoretically complex, this research area nevertheless has simple, direct, and profound implications for global health problems related to access to medicine and technology, the impact of western bioscience on conceptions of the body, ethical issues related to experimentation, the commoditization of body parts, identity and citizenship, and emerging processes of governance.

Third, an investigation of the globalization of western bioscience facilitates interrogation of entailed policies. How are policies made? Who makes these policies, and what ideologies, discourses, representations, and systems of knowledge do they draw on to craft decisions? How are policies made by global communities implemented, and to what effect, in highly variable local settings and contexts? Here, as with the study of the global technoscape, the focus is on examining the unintended consequences of policy for locals, reflecting on the fact that for the poor and vulnerable it is an unlevel playing field (Whiteford & Manderson 2000b).

Fourth, it is clear from the analysis of global health policymaking that the institutional landscape in health development has been transformed. The proliferation of nonstate actors and neoliberal development practices that both constitute and engage civil society has produced a complex mix of groups and organizations at state and community levels. Successful health development entails both coordinating across this unruly mélange and understanding the social and cultural effects of their various operations. Yet there is much we do not understand about how civil society operates in global health. The principal questions appear to be when and how private organizations operating in parallel to the state foster, or compromise, positive health outcomes, and whether they in fact contribute to reducing, or increasing, health inequities.

Although clearly relevant, we have to ask whether anthropology has contributed, or is capable of contributing, in substantive ways to the kinds of engagement and interventions that promise to reduce health inequities, foster social justice, and address the challenges to global health presaged by global climate change, habitat destruction, and mass species extinction, as well as the global economic crisis. Here we are less sanguine. We have promising examples, and the work that many researchers have done lends itself clearly to concrete, appropriate policies, programs, and interventions. Like many, we are buoyed by the work of Farmer and his colleagues at Partners in Health in a variety of country and community settings, from poverty-stricken neighbourhoods in the United States to postgenocide Rwanda. We are also mindful of the several generations of anthropologists who, largely external to the academy, through hard work at community to policy levels, through clear and principled commitment to socially and culturally relevant public health efforts, have made a difference. These efforts are, in many ways, both the foundation and the backbone of current medical anthropology and constitute in large measure the substance of promise and hope that we hold out to our students. Nevertheless, we also recognize that many anthropologists continue to be reluctant to do work identified as "applied" or "public health," or, perhaps perceived as worse, glossed as "development" (Escobar 1995, Ferguson 1997).

Although writing of current work in pharmaceutical anthropology, van der Geest (2006) offers an opinion that is a cautionary note to other anthropologists working in global health:

Overcoming the "temptation" of just writing about the intriguing [pharmaceutical] nexus should be a first concern of medical anthropologists. We owe it to our informants to contribute to the actual improvement of distribution and use of pharmaceuticals. Ironically, however, that imperative of turning our paper medicines into medicines that cure and protect people is not exactly what mainstream anthropology encourages us to do. Applied medical anthropology is somewhat slighted as diluted anthropology and as too subservient to policy and medical science. My view, however, is that uncommitted ethnographers lack reflexivity and fail to see themselves in the nexus of pharmaceuticals and of culture in general. Their methodological innocence gives way to epistemological naïveté. (pp. 313–14)

To this we add simply that the problems living beings face globally are too vast and the assaults on social justice and the environment too egregious for us to worry overly much about the sullying effects of doing applied work. Commitment and action are sometimes messy; the fine points of theory and abstract conceptualization may appear irrelevant in the worlds of suffering, injustice, and environmental degradation that we face, and being a principled "public intellectual" is sometimes not enough. What we should be worried about, as we consider our disciplinary position as producers and consumers of knowledge in the global political economy, is the pressing question of "so what?" We are called to apply our tools and knowledge, to seek interdisciplinary and intersectoral partnerships, and to both propose and engage directly in potential solutions.

DISCLOSURE STATEMENT

The authors are not aware of any affiliations, memberships, funding, or financial holdings that might be perceived as affecting the objectivity of this review.

LITERATURE CITED

Abramson D. 1999. A critical look at NGOs and civil society as a means to an end in Uzbekistan. *Hum. Organ.* 58:240–50

Adams V, Miller S, Craig S, Samen A, Nyima, et al. 2005. The challenge of cross-cultural clinical trials research: case report from the Tibetan Autonomous Region, People's Republic of China. *Med. Anthropol. Q.* 19:267–89

Adams V, Novotny TE, Leslie H. 2008. Global health diplomacy. *Med. Anthropol.* 27:315–23

Adler E, Haas PM. 1992. Epistemic communities, world order, and the creation of a reflective research program. *Int. Organ.* 46:367–90

Alter JS. 2005. *Asian Medicine and Globalization*. Philadelphia: Univ. Penn. Press

Appadurai A. 1991. Global: notes and queries for a transnational anthropology. In *Recapturaing Anthropology: Working in the Present*, ed. RG Fox, pp. 191–210. Santa Fe, NM: New Sch. Am. Res. Press

Appadurai A. 1996. *Modernity at Large: Cultural Dimensions of Globalization*. Minneapolis: Univ. Minn. Press

Applbaum K. 2006. Educating for global mental health: the adoption of SSRIs in Japan. See Petryna et al. 2006, pp. 85–110

Baer H, Singer M, Susser I, eds. 2003. *Medical Anthropology and the World System*. Westport, CT: Praeger

Baer H, Singer M. 2009. *Global Warming and the Political Ecology of Health: Emerging Crises and Systemic Solutions*. Walnut Creek, CA: Left Coast Press

Bastos C. 1999. *Global Responses to AIDS: Science in Emergency*. Bloomington: Indiana Univ. Press

Berry NS. 2009. Making pregnancy safer for women around the world: the example of safe motherhood and maternal death in Guatemala. See Hahn & Inhorn 2009, pp. 422–46

Biehl J. 2007. *Will to Live: AIDS Therapies and the Politics of Survival*. Princeton, NJ: Princeton Univ. Press

Bourgois P, Scheper-Hughes N. 2004. Comment on "An anthropology of structural violence," by Paul Farmer. *Curr. Anthropol.* 45:317–18

Briggs CL, Mantini-Briggs C. 2003. *Stories in a Time of Cholera: The Transnational Circulation of Bacteria and Racial Stigmata in a Venezuelan Epidemic*. Berkeley: Univ. Calif. Press

Brown TM, Cueto M, Fee E. 2006. The World Health Organization and the transition from "international" to "global" public health. *Am. J. Public Health* 96:62–72

Browner CH, Sargent CF. 2010. *Reproduction, Globalization, and the State*. Durham, NC: Duke Univ. Press. In press

Burawoy M. 2000. Conclusion: grounding globalization. In *Global Ethnography: Forces, Connections, and Imaginations in a Postmodern World*, ed. M Burawoy, JA Blum, S George, Z Gille, T Gowan, et al., pp. 337–50. Berkeley: Univ. Calif. Press

Buse K, Walt G. 1997. An unruly mélange? Coordinating external resources to the health sector: a review. *Soc. Sci. Med.* 45:449–63

Butt L. 2002. The suffering stranger: medical anthropology and international morality. *Med. Anthropol.* 21:1–24

Castro A. 2004. Contracepting and childbirth: the integration of reproductive health and population policies in Mexico. See Castro & Singer 2004, pp. 133–44

Castro A, Singer M, eds. 2004. *Unhealthy Health Policy: A Critical Anthropological Examination*. Walnut Creek, CA: AltaMira

Cohen L. 2005. Operability, bioavailability, and exception. See Ong & Collier 2005b, pp. 79–90

Comaroff J, Comaroff J, eds. 2001. *Millenial Capitalism and the Culture of Neoliberalism*. Durham, NC: Duke Univ. Press

Comm. Soc. Determinants Health. 2008. *Closing the Gap in a Generation: Health Equity Through Action on the Social Determinants of Health*. Geneva: World Health Organ.

Desclaux A. 2004. Equity in access to AIDS treament in Africa. See Castro & Singer 2004, pp. 115–32

Desjarlais R, Eisenberg L, Good B, Kleinman A. 1995. *World Mental Health: Problems and Priorities in Low-Income Countries*. Oxford: Oxford Univ. Press

Dressler WW, Bindon JR. 2000. The health consequences of cultural consonance: cultural dimensions of lifestyle. *Am. Anthropol.* 102:244–60

Ecks S. 2005. Pharmaceutical citizenship: antidepressant marketing and the promise of demarginalization in India. *Anthropol. Med.* 12:239–54

Erickson PI. 2003. Medical anthropology and global health. *Med. Anthropol. Q.* 17:3–4

Erikson SL. 2003. Post-diagnostic abortion in Germany: reproduction gone awry, again? *Soc. Sci. Med.* 56:1987–2001

Escobar A. 1995. *Encountering Development: The Making and Unmaking of the Third World*. Princeton, NJ: Princeton Univ. Press

Evans M, Sinclair RC, Fusimalohi C, Liava'a V. 2001. Globalization, diet, and health: an example from Tonga. *Bull. World Health Organ.* 79:856–62

Farmer P. 1997. On suffering and structural violence: the view from below. In *Social Suffering*, ed. A Kleinman, V Das, M Lock, pp. 261–84. Berkeley: Univ. Calif. Press

Farmer P. 1999. *Infections and Inequalities: The Modern Plagues*. Berkeley: Univ. Calif. Press

Farmer P. 2003. *Pathologies of Power: Health, Human Rights, and the New War on the Poor*. Berkeley: Univ. Calif. Press

Farmer P. 2004. An anthropology of structural violence. *Curr. Anthropol.* 45:305–17

Farmer P, Castro A. 2004. Pearls of the Antilles? Public health in Haiti and Cuba. See Castro & Singer 2004, pp. 3–28

Farmer P, Connors M, Simmons J, eds. 1996. *Women, Poverty, and AIDS: Sex, Drugs, and Structural Violence*. Monroe, ME: Common Courage

Farmer P, Léandre F, Mukherjee JS, Claude MS, Nevil P, et al. 2001. Community-based approaches to HIV treatment in resource-poor settings. *Lancet* 358:404–9

Feldman DA, ed. 2008. *AIDS, Culture and Africa*. Gainesville: Univ. Press Fla.

Ferguson A. 2005. Water reform, gender, and HIV/AIDS: perspectives from Malawi. See Whiteford & Whiteford 2005, pp. 45–66

Ferguson J. 1997. Anthropology and its evil twin: "development" in the constitution of a discipline. In *International Development and the Social Sciences: Essays on the History and Politics of Knowledge*, ed. F Cooper, R Packard, pp. 150–75. Berkeley: Univ. Calif. Press

Foster GM. 1976. Medical anthropology and international health planning. *Med. Anthropol. Newsl.* 7:12–18

Ginsburg F, Rapp R, eds. 1995a. *Conceiving the New World Order: The Global Politics of Reproduction.* Berkeley: Univ. Calif. Press

Ginsburg F, Rapp R. 1995b. Introduction. See Ginsburg & Rapp 1995a, pp. 1–18

Greenhalgh S. 2005. Globalization and population governance in China. See Ong & Collier 2005b, pp. 354–72

Guest G, ed. 2005. *Globalization, Health, and the Environment: An Integrated Perspective.* Lanham, MA: AltaMira

Hahn RA, Inhorn MC. 2009. *Anthropology and Public Health: Bridging Differences in Culture and Society.* New York: Oxford Univ. Press. 2nd ed.

Hankivsky O, Cormier R. 2009. *Intersectionality: Moving Women's Health Research and Policy Forward.* Vancouver, BC: Women's Health Res. Netw., Simon Fraser Univ. **http://www.whrn.ca**

Hardon A. 2005. Confronting the HIV/AIDS epidemic in sub-Saharan Africa: policy versus practice. *Int. Soc. Sci. J.* 57:601–8

Hayden C. 2007. A generic solution? Pharmaceuticals and the politics of the similar in Mexico. *Curr. Anthropol.* 4:475–95

Høg E, Hsu E. 2002. Introduction to special issue: countervailing creativity: patient agency in the globalisation of Asian medicines. *Anthropol. Med.* 9:205–21

Hulko W. 2009. The time- and context-contingent nature of intersectionality and interlocking oppressions. *Affilia* 24:44–55

Inhorn MC. 2003. Global infertility and the globalization of new reproductive technologies: illustrations from Egypt. *Soc. Sci. Med.* 56:1837–51

Inhorn MC. 2005. Gender, health, and globalization in the Middle East: male infertility, ICSI, and men's resistance. In *Globalization, Women, and Health in the Twenty-First Century*, ed. I Kickbush, KA Hartwig, JM List, pp. 113–25. New York: Palgrave Macmillan

Inhorn MC. 2007a. Medical anthropology at the intersections. *Med. Anthropol. Q.* 21:249–55

Inhorn MC, ed. 2007b. *Reproductive Disruptions: Gender, Technology, and Biopolitics in the New Millennium.* New York: Berghahn

Inhorn MC, Brown PJ, eds. 1997. *The Anthropology of Infectious Disease: International Health Perspectives.* Amsterdam, The Neth.: Gordon and Breach

Inhorn MC, Janes CR. 2007. The behavioral research agenda in global health: an advocate's legacy. *Global Public Health* 2:294–312

Inst. Med. 2009. *The U.S. Commitment to Global Health: Recommendations for the New Administration.* Washington, DC: Natl. Acad. Press

Intergov. Panel Climate Change. 2007. *Climate Change 2007—Impacts, Adaptation and Vulnerability.* Contribution of Working Group II to the Fourth Assessment Report of the IPCC. Cambridge, UK: Cambridge Univ. Press, **http://www.ipcc.ch/ipccreports/ar4-wg2.htm**

Janes CR. 1999. The health transition and the crisis of traditional medicine: the case of Tibet. *Soc. Sci. Med.* 48:1803–20

Janes CR. 2002. Buddhism, science, and market: the globalisation of Tibetan medicine. *Anthropol. Med.* 9:267–89

Janes CR. 2004. Going global in century XXI: medical anthropology and the new primary health care. *Hum. Organ. J. Soc. Appl. Anthropol.* 63:457–71

Janes CR. 2009. An ethnographic evaluation of post-Alma Ata health system reforms in Mongolia: lessons for addressing health inequities in poor communities. See Hahn & Inhorn 2009, pp. 652–80

Janes CR, Chuluundorj O. 2004. Free markets and dead mothers: the social ecology of maternal mortality in postsocialist Mongolia. *Med. Anthropol. Q.* 18:102–29

Janes CR, Chuluundorj O, Hilliard C, Rak K, Janchiv K. 2005. Poor medicine for poor people? Assessing the impact of neoliberal reform on health care equity in a postsocialist context. *Global Public Health* 1:5–30

Justice J. 1986. *Policies, Plans and People: Foreign Aid and Health Development.* Berkeley: Univ. Calif. Press.

Justice J. 2000. The politics of child survival. See Whiteford & Manderson 2000a, pp. 23–38

Kangas B. 2002. Therapeutic itineraries in a global world: Yemenis and their search for biomedical treatment abroad. *Med. Anthropol.* 21:35–78

Kendall C. 2005. Waste not, want not: grounded globalization and global lessons for water use from Lima, Peru. See Whiteford & Whiteford 2005, pp. 85–106

Keshavjee S. 2004. The contradictions of a revolving drug fund in post-Soviet Tajikistan: selling medicines to starving patients. See Castro & Singer 2004, pp. 97–114

Kickbush I. 2003. Global health governance; some theoretical considerations on the new political space. See Lee 2003b, pp. 192–203

Kim J. 2009. Transcultural medicine: a multi-sited ethnography on the scientific-industrial newtworking of Korean medicine. *Med. Anthropol.* 28:31–64

Kim JY, Shakow A, Mate K, Vanderwarker C, Gupta R, Farmer P. 2005. Limited good and limited vision: multidrug-resistant tuberculosis and global health policy. *Soc. Sci. Med.* 61:847–59

Kleinman A. 1988. *Social Origins of Distress and Disease: Depression, Neurasthenia, and Pain in Modern China.* New Haven, CT: Yale Univ. Press

Krieger N. 2001. Theories for social epidemiology in the 21st century: an ecosocial perspective. *Int. J. Epidemiol.* 30:668–77

Lee K. 2003a. *Globalization and Health: An Introduction.* New York: Palgrave Macmillan

Lee K, ed. 2003b. *Health Impacts of Globalization: Towards Global Governance.* New York: Palgrave MacMillan

Lee K. 2003c. Introduction. See Lee 2003b, pp. 1–12

Lee K, Fustukian S, Buse K. 2002. An introduction to global health policy. In *Health Policy in a Globalizing World*, ed. SH Lees, K Buse, S Fustukian, pp. 3–17. Cambridge, UK: Cambridge Univ. Press

Lee K, Goodman H. 2002. Global policy networks: the propagation of health care financing reform since the 1980s. In *Health Policy in a Globalising World*, ed. K Lee, K Buse, S Fustukian, pp. 97–119. Cambridge, UK: Cambridge Univ. Press

Lock M. 2001. *Twice Dead: Organ Transplants and the Reinvention of Death.* Berkeley: Univ. Calif. Press

Macfarlane SB, Jacobs M, Kaaya EE. 2008. In the name of global health: trends in academic institutions. *J. Public Health Policy* 29:383–401

Manderson L, Huang Y. 2005. Water, vectorborne disease, and gender: schistosomiasis in rural China. See Whiteford & Whiteford 2005, pp. 67–84

Markowitz L. 2001. Finding the field: notes on the ethnography of NGOs. *Hum. Organ.* 60:40–46

Marshall P, Koenig B. 2004. Accounting for culture in a globalized bioethics. *J. Law Med. Ethics* 32:252–66, 191

Marshall PA. 2005. Human rights, cultural pluralism, and international health research. *Theor. Med. Bioeth.* 26:529–57

Marshall PA, Daar A. 2000. Ethical issues in human organ replacement: a case study from India. See Whiteford & Manderson 2000a, pp. 205–30

Maternowska MC. 2006. *Reproducing Inequities: Poverty and the Politics of Population in Haiti.* New Brunswick, NJ: Rutgers Univ. Press

Mather C. 2006. Medical innovation, unmet medical need, and the drug pipeline. *Can. J. Clin. Pharmacol.* 13:e85–91

McElroy A. 2005. Health ecology in Nunavut: Inuit elders' concepts of nutrition, health, and political change. See Guest 2005, pp. 107–32

McMichael T, Beaglehole R. 2003. The global context for public health. In *Global Public Health: A New Era*, ed. R Beaglehole, pp. 1–23. New York: Oxford

Morgan LM. 1989. "Political will" and community participation in Costa Rican primary health care. *Med. Anthropol. Q.* 3:232–45

Morgan LM. 1997. *Community Participation in Health: The Politics of Primary Care in Costa Rica.* Cambridge, UK: Cambridge Univ. Press

Morgan LM. 2001. Community participation in health: perpetual allure, persistent challenge. *Health Policy Plann.* 16:221–30

Morsy SA. 1995. Deadly reproduction among Egyptian women: maternal mortality and the medicalization of population control. See Ginsburg & Rapp 1995a, pp. 162–76

Nguyen VK. 2005. Antiretroviral globalism, biopolitics, and therepeutic citizenship. See Ong & Collier 2005b, pp. 124–44

Nichter M. 1989. *Anthropology and International Health: South Asian Case Studies.* Dordrecht: Kluwer

Nichter M. 1991. Use of social science research to improve epidemiologic studies of and interventions for diarrhea and dysentery. *Rev. Infect. Dis.* 13(Suppl. 4):S265–71

Nichter M. 1995. Vaccinations in the Third World: a consideration of community demand. *Soc. Sci. Med.* 41:617–32

Nichter M. 2008. *Global Health: Why Cultural Perceptions, Social Representations, and Biopolitics Matter.* Tucson: Univ. Ariz. Press

Nichter M, Cartwright E. 1991. Saving the children for the tobacco industry. *Med. Anthropol. Q.* 5:236–56

Oldani MJ. 2004. Thick prescriptions: toward an interpretation of pharmaceutical sales practices. *Med. Anthropol. Q.* 18:325–56

Ong A, Collier SJ. 2005a. Global assemblages, anthropological problems. See Ong & Collier 2005b, pp. 3–21

Ong A, Collier SJ, eds. 2005b. *Global Assemblages: Technology, Politics, and Ethics as Anthropological Problems.* Malden, MA: Blackwell

Orzech KM, Nichter M. 2008. From resilience to resistance: political ecological lessons from antibiotic and pesticide resistance. *Annu. Rev. Anthropol.* 37:267–82

Paluzzi JE. 2004. Primary health care since Alma Ata: lost in the Bretton Woods? See Castro & Singer 2004, pp. 63–78

Parker R. 2000. Administering the epidemic: HIV/AIDS policy, models of development, and international health. See Whiteford & Manderson 2000a, pp. 39–56

Patz JA, Campbell-Lendrum D, Holloway T, Foley JA. 2005. Impact of regional climate change on human health. *Nature* 438:310–17

Paul B, ed. 1955. *Health, Culture and Community: Case Studies of Public Reactions to Health Programs.* New York: Sage

Petryna A. 2002. *Life Exposed: Biological Citizens After Chernobyl.* Princeton, NJ: Princeton Univ. Press

Petryna A. 2005. Ethical variability: drug development and globalizing clinical trials. *Am. Ethnol.* 32:183–97

Petryna A, Lakoff A, Kleinman A, eds. 2006. *Global Pharmaceuticals: Ethics, Markets, Practices.* Durham, NC: Duke Univ. Press

Pfeiffer J. 2003. International NGOs and primary health care in Mozambique: the need for a new model of collaboration. *Soc. Sci. Med.* 56:725–38

Pfeiffer J. 2004. International NGOs in the Mozambique health sector: the "velvet glove" of privatization. See Castro & Singer 2004, pp. 43–62

Pfeiffer J, Nichter M. 2008. What can critical medical anthropology contribute to global health? *Med. Anthropol. Q.* 22:410–15

Pigg SL, Adams V. 2005. Introduction: the moral object of sex. In *Sex in Development: Science, Sexuality, and Morality in Global Perspective*, ed. V Adams, SL Pigg, pp. 1–38. Durham, NC: Duke Univ. Press

Rak K, Janes CR. 2004. Reproductive health in post-transition Mongolia: global discourses and local realities. In *Globalization and Health*, ed. RL Harris, MJ Seid, pp. 171–96. Leiden, The Neth.: Brill

Redfield P. 2005. Doctors, borders, and life in crisis. *Cult. Anthropol.* 20:328–61

Robins S. 2009. Foot soldiers of global health: teaching and preaching AIDS science and modern medicine on the frontline. *Med. Anthropol.* 28:81–107

Rose N, Novas C. 2005. Biological citizenship. See Ong & Collier 2005b, pp. 439–63

Scheper-Hughes N. 1993. *Death Without Weeping: The Violence of Everyday Life in Brazil.* Berkeley: Univ. Calif. Press

Scheper-Hughes N. 2000. The global traffic in human organs. *Curr. Anthropol.* 41:191–224

Scheper-Hughes N. 2005. The last commodity: posthuman ethics and the global traffic in "fresh" organs. See Ong & Collier 2005b, pp. 145–68

Simmons J, Farmer P, Schoepf BG. 1996. A global perspective. See Farmer et al. 1996, pp. 39–90

Singer M. 1997. *The Political Economy of AIDS.* Amityville, NY: Baywood

Singer M. 2008. *Drugs and Development: Global Impact on Sustainable Growth and Human Rights.* Prospect Heights, IL: Waveland

Singer M. 2009. *Introduction to Syndemics: A Systems Approach to Public and Community Health.* San Francisco, CA: Jossey-Bass

Singer M, Baer H. 1995. *Critical Medical Anthropology.* Amityville, NY: Baywood

Singer M, Baer H. 2008. *Killer Commodities: Public Health and the Corporate Production of Harm.* Lanham, MD: AltaMira/Roman Littlefield

Singer M, Castro A. 2004. Introduction. Anthropology and health policy: a critical perspective. See Castro & Singer 2004, pp. xi–xx

Singer M, Clair S. 2003. Syndemics and public health: reconceptualizing disease in bio-social context. *Med. Anthropol. Q.* 17:423–41

Stebbins KR. 1991. Tobacco, politics and economics: implications for global health. *Soc. Sci. Med.* 33:1317–26

Strathern M. 2000. *Audit Cultures: Anthropological Studies in Accountability, Ethics and the Academy*. London: Routledge

Towghi F. 2004. Shifting policies toward traditional midwives: implications for reproductive health care in Pakistan. See Castro & Singer 2004, pp. 79–95

Trostle J. 1996. Inappropriate distribution of medicines by professionals in developing countries. *Soc. Sci. Med.* 42:1117–20

Trostle J. 2005. *Epidemiology and Culture*. New York: Cambridge Univ. Press

Van Der Geest S. 2006. Anthropology and the pharmaceutical nexus. *Anthropol. Q.* 79:303–214

Van Der Geest S, Hardon A, Whyte SR, eds. 1988. *The Context of Medicines in Developing Countries: Studies in Pharmaceutical Anthropology*. Dordrecht, The Neth.: Kluwer

Van Der Geest S, Whyte SR, Hardon A. 1996. The anthropology of pharmaceuticals: a biographical approach. *Annu. Rev. Anthropol.* 25:153–78

Wacquant L. 2004. Comment on: "An anthropology of structural violence," by Paul Farmer. *Curr. Anthropol.* 45:322

Whiteford LM, Hill B. 2005. The political ecology of dengue in Cuba and the Dominican Republic. See Guest 2005, pp. 219–38

Whiteford LM, Manderson L, eds. 2000a. *Global Health Policy, Local Realities: The Fallacy of the Level Playing Field*. Boulder, CO: Lynne Rienner

Whiteford LM, Manderson L. 2000b. Introduction. See Whiteford & Manderson 2000a, pp. 1–22

Whiteford LM, Tobin GA. 2004. Saving lives, destroying livelihoods: emergency evacuation and resettlement policies in Ecuador. See Castro & Singer 2004, pp. 189–202

Whiteford LM, Whiteford S, eds. 2005. *Globalization, Water, and Health: Resource Management in Times of Scarcity*. Santa Fe, NM: Sch. Am. Res. Press

Whyte SR, Birungi H. 2000. The business of medicines and the politics of knowledge. See Whiteford & Manderson 2000a, pp. 127–50

Whyte SR, Whyte MA, Meinert L, Kyaddondo B. 2006. Treating AIDS: dilemmas of unequal access in Uganda. See Petryna et al. 2006, pp. 240–62

World Bank. 1993. *Investing in Health: World Development Report 1993*. New York: Oxford Univ. Press for the World Bank

World Health Organ. 2008. *Primary Health Care: Now More than Ever*. Geneva: WHO

Transitions: Pastoralists Living with Change

Kathleen A. Galvin

Department of Anthropology and Natural Resource Ecology Laboratory, Colorado State University, Fort Collins, Colorado 80523; email: Kathleen.Galvin@colostate.edu

Annu. Rev. Anthropol. 2009. 38:185–98

First published online as a Review in Advance on July 16, 2009

The *Annual Review of Anthropology* is online at anthro.annualreviews.org

This article's doi:
10.1146/annurev-anthro-091908-164442

Key Words

fragmentation, climate, adaptation, resilience, pastoralism

Abstract

This review covers two major causes of change in pastoral systems. First is fragmentation, the dissection of a natural system into spatially isolated parts, which is caused by a number of socioeconomic factors such as changes in land tenure, agriculture, sedentarization, and institutions. Second is climate change and climate variability, which are expected to alter dry and semiarid grasslands now and into the future. Details of these changes are described using examples from Africa and Mongolia. An adaptation framework is used to place global change in context. Although pastoral systems are clearly under numerous constraints and risks have intensified, pastoralists are adapting and trying to remain flexible. It is too early to ask if the responses are enough, given the magnitude and number of changes faced by pastoralists today.

The land is too small and all your children now depend only on that piece of land. Before subdivision everybody could go everywhere. Then, if your sons wanted to go to somewhere else they could go. But now it is not possible, they have to stay just within the enclosure.

Rain has decreased, I don't know why. These issues are very far up there (looking up to the sky). Grass quantity has decreased. When it doesn't rain, like now, it seems like there has never been any grass. Grass quality has also really decreased. Some grass species are really missing because the rain has decreased. On the hills in the distance there used to be very good grass. So grasses that used to be very good for cows are disappearing.

Maasai elder quotes, from Roque de Pinho (2009)

INTRODUCTION

Much has been written about pastoral land use systems and how enduring they have been through time (e.g., Evans-Pritchard 1940, Gulliver 1955, Stenning 1959). However, recently many scholars have predicted their transition to other types of land use in the face of climate change, human population growth, and globalization (e.g., Homewood et al. 2001). Some of these factors are changing the grasslands, some are changing pastoral social systems, and some are affecting both. In this review I describe a few of these factors and show that, taken together, they are inhibiting pastoral land use, particularly movement, and in some cases making pastoral land use very difficult. My goal here is not to describe a new postpastoralism but rather to describe some of the changes and how they are affecting pastoral systems. I approach the issue of change by focusing on the local level.

I discuss two major causes of transformations in pastoralism. First is fragmentation of once contiguously intact grasslands. Fragmentation is the dissection of natural systems into spatially isolated parts and is caused primarily by socioeconomic changes. Land tenure changes from communal to private ownership often fragment grasslands. Other sources of fragmentation include land use changes, which disconnect formerly intact grasslands, thereby compartmentalizing important components of the environment. These include agriculture, which brings with it economic inputs such as fence and water-well construction (Western 2002, Boone et al. 2007, Hobbs et al. 2008). The result is a reduction of scale of the landscape over which human pastoral management takes place. Once the environment is fragmented, the only way for it to support pastoralists and their livestock is to increase economic and policy inputs (Galvin et al. 2008a, Hobbs et al. 2008).

The second source of change to grasslands is climate change. Climate change may be a cause of fragmentation, but here it is considered separately because of the potential magnitude of change, which may be unprecedented in scale and out of the range of experience (Adger et al. 2007, Galvin et al. 2008a). Semiarid and arid grasslands are areas of high climatic variability, but with increasing fragmentation, greater inputs are required to offset effects of climate perturbations. Individually each source of change can change the structure and function of the ecosystem and together they affect the livelihoods of the people who depend on the ecosystem (Holling & Gunderson 2002, Walker & Abel 2002). **Figure 1** (see color insert) depicts the change from an intact to a fragmented grassland. In a connected grassland, complex interactions of the environment do not require large inputs by humans because management is exercised largely in the form of movement across the landscape to access livestock forage and water. When the grassland is fragmented, the grassland's interdependent spatial units become disconnected thus compartmentalizing important parts of ecosystem function (Hobbs et al. 2008). The result is a reduction in scale over which human management takes place. Thus, economic, policy, and other inputs are needed to maintain pastoral viability. The two sources of transformation are discussed in some detail below.

This article is organized in the following manner. First, I present a conceptual framework

Figure 1

A schematic diagram of an interdependent spatial unit that is fragmented into separate entities. The result is a reduction in the scale over which complex interactions among landscapes and land management can occur. Figure made by R. Boone.

that provides an understanding of pastoral change. Second, I address changes occurring in the world's arid and semi arid grasslands and in pastoral societies. Finally, I speculate on the future of pastoralism. I start with Africa because that is the place I know best, but I include examples from Central Asia, specifically Mongolia, not to be inclusive, but to illustrate that some pastoral transitions are similar across the world.

CONCEPTUAL FRAMEWORK

Adaptation is a key concept in anthropology and one that dates back to, at least, the turn of the twentieth century but became prevalent in several subfields of anthropology in the 1940s and 1950s. It is again a unifying concept, especially in the arena of global change (e.g., White 1949, Steward 1955, Thomas 1998, Nelson et al. 2007). The concept of adaptation of human systems to global change is quite broad. Smit & Wandel (2006, p. 282) state, "Adaptation in the context of human dimensions of global change usually refers to a process, action or outcome in a system (household, community, group, sector, region, country) in order for the system to better cope with, manage or adjust to some changing condition, stress, hazard, risk or opportunity." People are constantly adapting, often incrementally but sometimes quickly, to new opportunities for and constraints on their livelihoods.

Adaptive capacity is the suite of mechanisms that a society possesses to cope with change. Pastoral management or governance over natural resource use encompasses the core of pastoral adaptive capacity, which includes formal and informal institutions. Adaptations can occur at multiple scales and, what may be adaptive today in response to a perceived change may not be tomorrow (Nelson et al. 2007). Thus, it is necessary to assume that the natural state of pastoral systems is one of change and that we can never really assess its state of adaptation. We can, at best, describe some of the processes of change and consider the adaptive state. Because change is often unpredictable, systems ought to be managed for flexibility rather than maintaining stability so that they can respond to changes in ways that keep the system functioning (Natl. Res. Counc. 2002, Nelson et al. 2007, Young et al. 2006).

The converse of adaptation is vulnerability, which can be defined as the degree to which a system or some part of a social system is likely to experience harm due to exposure to some perturbation (Turner et al. 2003). Both climate and the political economy can contribute to differential exposure (Biersack & Greenberg 2006). Pastoral management strategies, which may have worked under an intact grassland, may or may not be sufficient under fragmentation. Subsidizing local systems with inputs from the outside is well documented in archaeology, but Redman (1999) also shows that this practice can lead to increased vulnerability and ultimately to system collapse because the inputs leading to structural changes of the system move it into a new system.

Below I consider a number of changes to pastoral systems. Then I posit whether the responses are increasing the adaptive capacity of pastoral systems to change or, conversely, increasing vulnerability. I am fully aware that both the changes and their impacts can affect pastoralists differentially and that those best placed to take advantage of adaptation strategies either control those strategies or have close links to decision-making. An example may be rich pastoralists who benefit more from privatization of once communal grasslands, thus giving these individuals more options to weather an extreme climate event. However, this article does not explicitly address who wins and who loses.

CHANGES IN PASTORAL SOCIAL AND ENVIRONMENTAL SYSTEMS

Changes affecting grasslands and pastoral societies include land tenure, land use, intensification, sedentarization, institutional changes, and climate change. Others not explicitly discussed but embedded in the text include human population growth, wildlife conflicts, and conservation policies. Some of the above factors are the drivers of change, some are adaptive strategies to cope with change (e.g., changing herd size and structure, cultivating maize, wage income), and some are the results of change. However, the truth is that each of the factors can be drivers, adaptations, and responses depending on one's point of view and each contributes to the realization that pastoral systems are complex, dynamic, and ever changing.

Land Tenure Change

Most grasslands of the world have been communally governed, by *de jure* or *de facto* control (Sanford 1983, McCabe 1990, Behnke & Scoones 1993, Fratkin et al. 1994). Movement of livestock herds is a central component of land management. Pastoralists access forage and water across space and time through reciprocal rights to common pool resources sometimes belonging to other people. These rights to use another group's property is the basis for the nonexclusive tenure and land use systems common to pastoralism (Behnke 1995, Turner 1999). However, there has been a steady move toward privatization of grasslands (Little 1992, Peters 1994, Lesorogol 2003, Reid et al. 2008). This practice is occurring in part because of the notion that individuals invest and steward the land better than can a group of individuals; thus governments under the guise of economic development mandate it (Behnke & Scoones 1993, MEA 2005, Alimaev & Behnke 2008, Behnke 2008, Galvin et al. 2008a). Some land tenure changes are coming directly from the pastoralists themselves with the goal of gaining control over their lands to keep agriculturalists, conservation organizations, and other powerful groups from gaining title to their lands (e.g., BurnSilver et al. 2008, Galvin et al. 2008a). Pastoralists are also diversifying their own economic activities into agriculture, wage labor, and businesses (Barrett et al. 2001, Little et al. 2001a). The result is that pastoralists are losing access to high-value resources, often dry-season refuge areas (e.g., Fratkin 2001, 2004). Some examples follow.

Kajiado District, Kenya, is undergoing rapid changes in land tenure as communal land is converted into group ranches, some of which are now privatizing. Group ranches, established in the 1960s through the 1980s, were supported by Maasai pastoralists to secure the land against non-Maasai who were moving in and expropriating the better-watered land (Kimani & Pickard 1998). The group ranches are today subdividing into private parcels, causing sedentarization (Thornton et al. 2006). BurnSilver et al. (2008) found that subdivision and occupation of private parcels of land are the leading land tenure trends in most areas of the district. From the standpoint of the individual, the positive aspect of subdivision is security of land tenure. However, the loss of the ability to move livestock must be compensated by economic inputs such as intensification of livestock raising or diversification of livelihoods. The authors compared mobility of pastoralists in areas that were subdivided and areas that were not. They found that subdivided and sedentarized households are less mobile in normal years. Yet, in drought, both sedentarized and subdivided households were mobile. Thus, although land tenure may change, land use can help keep it connected.

Mwangi (2003) also found that access to Maasai territorial units or *olosho* may be negotiated, especially during times of environmental stress. She shows that "in times of environmental stress herds were moved freely from any region within the *olosho* with accessible pastures, if not across the *olosho* boundaries to explicit grazing elsewhere. Relations among members of the *olosho* were generated and sustained by ideological and social practices such as ritual and ceremony as well as by reciprocity" (Mwangi 2003, p. 37).

A similar situation is happening in Mongolia where the state has control and ownership of the grasslands. Pastoral production has always been the mainstay of the Mongolian economy (Mearns 2004). Pastures are set aside for the nongrowing seasons of winter and spring, and social pressure discourages trespassing by locals or outsiders except by invitation or request.

This policy was well enforced during Soviet times. The collectivization of all livestock operations started in the 1950s and lasted until the democratic transition in 1990. The state collectives allocated pastures, directed seasonal movements, and provided veterinary services, fodder provisions, and labor (Fernández-Giménez 2001). During socialist times herders became dependent on the central government to provide a regular salary and means of transport for livestock mobility. Since the transition from a socialist economy (and government) to a market economy in the 1990s, all state collective farms collapsed and livestock were privatized, but the attitude of dependency was hard to discard (Muller & Bold 1996).

With the dismantling of herding collectives in 1992, formal regulatory institutions for allocating pastures disappeared, and weakened customary institutions were not able to replace them fully (Fernández-Giménez & Bathuyan 2004). In 1994, the government passed the Land Law, and in 1998 privatization of pastoral resources such as homesteads and pastures began, with land registration and titling. However, with the move toward privatization of the pastures, the fuzzy and shifting boundaries, which have been so adaptive in the past, are increasing herder vulnerability to other changes such as climate change (Fernández-Giménez 2002). Furthermore, poorer herders have a harder time obtaining camp site leases, and herders and officials are observing increasing conflicts over pastures.

Most scholars of pastoralism suggest that exclusionary land title is counterproductive to sustainable land use in arid and semi-arid areas. Formal title to private land makes the system more rigid and constricts the normal "unboundedness, porosity, impermanence, and continual social/political renegotiation" that pastoralism embraces (Turner 1999, p. 122). There are trade-offs, however. Although the individual has secure land ownership, the system cannot function as it did. People compensate for the potential loss of movement by engaging in new land uses and other ways of earning a living.

Livelihood Changes

Numerous livelihood changes occur among pastoralists, but perhaps the most prevalent now are diversification into agriculture and intensification of livestock production (Homewood et al. 2001, Little et al. 2001a, BurnSilver et al. 2008).

Pastoralists are cultivating where rain-fed or irrigated agriculture is possible (e.g., BurnSilver 2007). In Africa, more technical and economic assistance has always been given to crop cultivation than to livestock production, and now pastoralists are beginning to take advantage of it (Babiker 2006). Rising human populations along with relatively constant livestock populations means that people have to diversify their income to make ends meet (Galvin et al. 2002). Coast (2002) found that 88% of Tanzanian Maasai households and 46% of Kenyan Maasai cultivate. However, in Tanzania, conservation land use policy has restricted growth in agriculture in the Ngorongoro Conservation Area (NCA), so Maasai are not allowed to cultivate more than 0.5 of an acre per household (McCabe 2002), though Coast (2002) suggests that in reality this number is larger, at 0.86 ha. Nevertheless, land can only be plowed by hand. Agriculture, however limited, has become vital to human well-being in the NCA, where the government allowed limited agriculture in response to food shortages (McCabe et al. 1997, Galvin et al. 2002, Fratkin & Mearns 2003, Galvin et al. 2008b). Land cultivated to the north of the NCA in the Loliondo Game Controlled Area, also home to Maasai, was estimated to be 2.92 ha where animal draft is common. Agriculture is likely a necessity today for most east African pastoralists.

Intensification of livestock production is also occurring. For the Maasai of Kajiado District, Kenya, this occurs mostly through cattle crossbreeding where bigger cattle have a greater market value. The cost is that these breeds are less able to handle drought (BurnSilver 2007). BurnSilver (2007) found that wealthy herders invested in new breeds of livestock, yet overall Maasai are much poorer in livestock now than in the past. In the 1980s, mean household biomass of livestock [tropical livestock units (TLU)] was 159 (Bekure et al. 1991), whereas BurnSilver (2007) reported 62 TLUs 20 years later. The fact remains that in Africa herd sizes are more regulated by mortality than by strategic marketing decisions (Smith 2005).

In many places, including in Kajiado District, sheep or goat numbers are increasing relative to cattle (Western 2002, Österle 2008). Among the Il Chamus of northern Kenya, small stock are relied on to rebuild the herd and to recover from drought (McPeak & Little 2005). Feed requirements for small stock are lower. Seo & Mendelsohn (2006) expect small stock numbers to increase under a warming African climate. Similarly, Mongolian livestock numbers have increased as a result of privatization, and livestock composition has switched to goats relative to other livestock such as horses, cattle, camels, and sheep. This trend was due to the increased demand for cashmere, primarily from the Chinese (Fratkin & Mearns 2003, Mearns 2004).

Sedentarization

Sedentarization among pastoralists is caused by many factors. Fratkin (2004) found that the Ariaal, Rendille, Borana, and Samburu of northern Kenya have increasingly settled in or near towns. Factors pushing herders out of the pastoral sector include population growth, loss of land, droughts, and livestock raiding. Services provided by towns, including schools, hospitals, famine relief, and economic opportunities such as petty wage jobs, pull people into towns. Sedentarization attracts both poor and wealthy herders. The wealthy settle family members opportunistically, whereas the poor usually do not have a choice. Poor herders move to towns owing to loss of livestock and a hope that work is available in towns (McPeak & Little 2005). For the better-off pastoralists, sedentarization does not necessarily reflect a full-time departure from pastoralism, nor does it always jeopardize pastoral production (McPeak & Little 2005). In northern Kenya,

settled families often still have access to livestock and some mobility; family members in town have wage employment, which supports other family members who still herd the family's livestock. However, McPeak & Little (2005) empirically show that vulnerability to livestock losses in a drought increases with sedentarization. Conversely, higher levels of mobility result in less drought-related livestock losses.

As human populations rise and land is cultivated, sedentarization also leads to increased human-wildlife conflicts owing to competition over increasingly scarce resources (Chatty & Colester 2002, Western 2002). Lamprey & Reid (2004) looked at settlement patterns, vegetation, and livestock and wildlife numbers over a 50-year period for the area around the Masai Mara National Reserve, Kenya. They assert that the pastoral/wildlife system will collapse unless land can be managed to maintain movement of livestock and wildlife. Okello (2005) suggests that Maasai will consider conserving wildlife only if they will gain direct economic benefits from them. Most Maasai do not see conservation's benefits or relevance to their livelihoods.

Niamir-Fuller (1998) also sees a trend in Sahelian Africa of increasing sedentarization and agro-pastoralism, yet even agropastoralists usually rely on some level of transhumance. Bassett & Turner (2007) describe a change in the migration pattern for FulBe herders due to increasing permanent settlement in the southern regions (Bassett & Turner 2007). FulBe herders traditionally followed north-south seasonal migrations based on vegetation growth and senescence. The migrations were negotiated through social alliances built up over time. Grazing in the south was hampered by lower forage quality, government restrictions, and livestock diseases. However, the increase in croplands in the south has lowered the threat of the tstsee fly. At the same time, new social alliances have been formed owing to expansion of interregional cattle raiding, recurring droughts, and FulBe-friendly state policies by Cameroon and Ivory Coast. These processes have resulted in increased pastoral sedentarization.

Herders are increasingly settling down in Mongolia with the shift to a free-market economy (Ojima & Chuluun 2008). During the Soviet era (1960–1990), long and less frequent migrations occurred as livestock were moved by truck. After 1990, the privatization of livestock and the loss of subsidies for long-distance travel caused people to stay close to settled areas. At this time there was an increase in urban-to-rural migration as the once-collective-controlled livestock had been reallocated to all Mongolians (Fernández-Giménez & Bathuyan 2004, Mearns 2004). The result was greater heterogeneity among herders within the same communities who were not all following similar rules of settlement and migration. In some places, traditional institutions have reemerged (Ojima & Chuluun 2008); in others they have not (Bruun 2006). This occurrence has led to sedentarization near riparian areas where resources are available year round. Since 2000, a new settlement pattern has been emerging. Now approximately half of Mongolia's population lives in the nation's capital, Ulaan Bator (Ojima & Chuluun 2008).

Social Capital/Institutions

Much scholarship has been written on pastoral governance and institutions for range management and the fact that they are so fluid. Rules are constantly being negotiated in response to social, political, economic, and ecological criteria (Berry 1989, Behnke 1995, Turner 1999, Dekker 2004). Horizontal linkages such as kin and close associates among local resource users allow them to interact and work cooperatively to achieve a common end (Bourdieu 1986, Galvin 2008). Fragmentation of grazing lands has put pressure on pastoral social networks and the use of reciprocal rights and obligations. It is still common among many African pastoralists, such as the Maasai, to distribute portions of their herds to friends and relatives who might have better access to good grazing or simply to assist poor friends or family (Potkanski 1999, Mwangi 2003, BurnSilver 2007). They are coping with subdivision and privatization of land by reaggregating their lands with friends and family. However, it is not a perfect arrangement because some relations in the region are becoming strained as some Maasai who live on individual parcels move their herds onto group ranch land during the wet season only to retreat to their fenced pastures during the dry season. At the same time, they deny group members access to their exclusive pastures during this time.

New wealth has undermined some social relationships. Socioeconomic stratification is increasing among pastoralists with negative implications for the poor (Thornton et al. 2007). Although wealth differentials are not new in pastoral societies, the widening gap between the rich and the poor is. Furthermore, not all wealth classes are homogeneous with variability based on distance from infrastructure and access to natural resources. Agriculture is only pursued, for instance, in areas of rainfall or where irrigation can support it. Knowledge seems often to serve the individual more than the community; haves and have-nots are increasing, and the haves increasingly control the resources (Spencer 2004).

BurnSilver's (2007) work shows that the distribution of households within wealth groups has shifted so that there are more poor people as measured by animal holdings than existed in the past. The fact that income stratification is increasing has been documented for other Maasai populations in both Kenya and Tanzania (Rutten 1992, Hodgson 2001, Thompson et al. 2002). As poverty has increased, it has become more difficult to help kin and friends following drought and other perturbations (Potkanski 1999). When TLU-based and diversification wealth methods were compared for Maasai pastoralists, the poor households stayed poor and rich households remained rich. Furthermore, some studies have suggested that livestock becomes less important as households diversify (Homewood et al. 2001), but BurnSilver (2007) found that the importance of livestock remains strong and that the wealthy are particularly prone to reinvesting in cattle as livestock are increasingly seen as a source of investment as well as a traditional store of wealth.

Owing to increasing globalization of the processes of fragmentation, such as the making of conservation areas with backing from international interests, local-level social capital is often insufficient for management and use of the grasslands (Adger et al. 2006). Pastoralists are increasingly linking to institutions and people at higher levels of society who can help them govern their lands; comanagement is the shared authority between local users and regional or national governments (Fernández-Giménez 2002). The paradox of pastoralism is that it needs security to protect its flexibility. Pastoralists need secure rights to resources on the one hand, but they also need flexible patterns of resource use and flexible social relations on the other hand to be able to withstand uncertainty (Fernández-Giménez 2002). Fernández-Giménez and others (e.g., Newman & Dale 2005) suggest that vertical links help increase a network's ability to access new power relationships. Because this type of capital can bring in new and potentially novel information, it can establish strong resource management institutions and thereby contribute to group resilience.

In Mongolia, the pastoral sector acted as a safety net through the period of economic transition, further increasing the number of herders and contributing to a rising inequality in asset holdings (Fratkin & Mearns 2003). Wealthier families split their households or maintained several camps in different locations. Poorer families, however, did not have this ability and attached themselves to the wealthy (Fernández-Giménez 2002). This is not to say that kin and friend support is gone but rather that it has changed into semicommercial forms, in part as a legacy of the socialist economy when everyone had jobs and income from the state. Thus poorer herders attached to wealthier households assist with herding in return for a share in animal products and for access to grazing for their own few animals. However, increasing economic stratification has resulted in weakened norms and customs regarding pasture use.

"In the face of growing uncertainty (e.g., economies, climate, political processes), the capacity of people both to innovate and to adapt technologies and practices to suit new conditions becomes vital. An important question is whether forms of social capital can be accumulated to enhance such innovation" (Pretty 2002, p. 74). Without the trust associated with social capital, herders tend to use individualistic strategies that help them in the short term to access resources but which may actually increase their vulnerability in the long term.

Climate

Agricultural production and food security, including access to food in many countries and regions, are likely to be severely compromised by climate change and climate variability (Jones & Thornton 2003, Thornton et al. 2006, Boko et al. 2007, Parry et al. 2007). In drylands, a changing climate is predicted to increase the variability and frequency of rainfall perturbations. Solomon et al. (2007) estimates that by the 2080s, the proportion of arid and semiarid lands in Africa is likely to increase by 5%–8%. The significance of climate change to human societies, besides the potential to change long-known climate patterns, is the speed with which it seems to be occurring. Climate is beginning to change within a time frame relevant to people and thus may provide opportunities to or constraints on human livelihoods. Thus, what was a slow-to-change phenomenon, climate, may be reducing its timescale to years and decades (Streets & Glantz 2000, Overpeck & Cole 2006).

Pastoralists live in uncertain climates and are experienced at coping with climatic variability and drought (Dietz 1987, Little et al. 2001b). However, the 2007 Intergovernmental Panel on Climate Change climate change projections suggest that rainfall in southern Africa is likely to decrease in much of the winter rainfall region. Yet there is likely to be an increase in annual mean rainfall in East Africa, which may be good for agriculture. West Africa shows conflicting and unclear patterns of future rainfall (Christensen et al. 2007). Held et al. (2005) project a drier future Sahel. Their model accurately simulated several aspects of the twentieth-century rainfall record in the Sahel and then used it to project future rainfall patterns under conditions of increased CO_2. Although there is no real agreement on what will happen under the different global climate change scenarios for the Sahel, we might expect to see large internal variability in rainfall and similar pastoral migration drifts and geographical population rearrangements (Bassett & Turner 2007).

Climatic variability is also changing in grasslands worldwide, which is making it more difficult for some pastoralists to cope (Ash & Stafford Smith 2003, Hunt 2003). Severe events are occurring with increased frequency and longer duration in the world's dry grasslands. El Niño events, which caused rain for 6–8 months in east Africa in 1997–1998, have been described as the strongest predictor of east African climate variability (Schreck & Semazii 2004). These rains caught pastoralists off guard, but especially affected those who could not move their livestock (Galvin et al. 2001, Little et al. 2001b, Luseno et al. 2003). As increasing climate variability brings floods and drought to the rangelands of east Africa, pastoralists will have fewer opportunities for relocation, especially under increasing fragmentation. In Mongolia, winter and spring storms and summer droughts are not uncommon (Ojima & Chuluun 2008). The Dzud, or snowstorm, of 2000–2001 in Mongolia resulted in as much as 90% herd loss. This event paradoxically forced herders to abandon dependency on the state and evolve their livelihoods into a more market-driven economy.

As pastoralists become sedentary, cultivate, and diversify their livelihoods, the move to increasing control over land becomes understandable. It is only when pastoralists are dependent solely on their livestock that there is little advantage to having control over a stretch of territory. However, the unstable environment due to climate variability does not change. Behnke (1995, p. 149) states, "In an unpredictable environment certain critical ambiguities as to who owns what and can go where

provide a degree of fluidity which suits everyone's requirements."

CONCLUSIONS

Pastoralists have adapted for centuries to climate, social, political, and ecological processes. They have adapted to political, societal, or environmental changes by migrating, cooperating with other ethnic groups, or taking up agriculture, among many other activities (Stenning 1960, Loiske 1990). They are still adapting. Disturbance or crises are not always bad for a social system (Berkes & Folke 1994, Berkes et al. 1998, Holling et al. 1998, Holling 2000, Walker & Abel 2002, Folke et al. 2005), but the capacity to adapt to the changes will determine whether the system can endure. "A social-ecological system with low levels of social memory and social capital is vulnerable to such changes...[floods, shifts in property rights, resource failures, new government legislations, etc.]...and may as a consequence deteriorate into undesired states" (Folke et al. 2005, p. 455).

Is pastoralism in decline, as some assert (e.g., Markakis 2004)? Are pastoralists more vulnerable to current change? Are pastoralists socially resilient? Some scholars assert that climatic, economic, social, and institutional factors together have diminished pastoral flexibility (e.g., Thébaud & Batterbury 2001). Flexibility is embedded in pastoral management strategies and institutionalized in social capital. Pastoral social capital has been modified and, in some instances, transformed under recent changes, but its primary goal remains: to gain access to water and forage resources for livestock. If social resilience is defined as the ability of groups to tolerate and respond to environmental and socioeconomic constraints through adaptive strategies (Bradley & Grainger 2004), then it looks like pastoralists certainly are responding to changes. Are the responses enough, however, given the magnitude and number of changes? It seems that livestock-rearing options have become narrowed and the risks intensified for most pastoralists.

Clearly, common property systems characteristic of pastoralism are breaking down as privatization of the commons occurs. Sedentarization is resulting in reduced seasonal movements. Agriculture is encroaching on grasslands. Climate is changing and variability increasing. These factors do not necessarily individually and in isolation affect pastoralism nor do the responses occur in isolation, but rather they are the result of multiple people acting in response to multiple stresses (Nelson et al. 2007). Furthermore, pastoral economies are embedded into nation-states that today are, at the same time, undergoing tremendous changes.

The changes discussed here are representative of the far-reaching and pervasive challenges facing most pastoral societies globally (see, e.g., Fratkin & Mearns 2003, Galvin et al. 2008a). The changes could be seen as a collective tipping point at which pastoralism as we have known it disappears. Or, the changes could be seen as adaptive. The changing modes of production and land tenure along extensive social networks may actually show pastoral resilience based on dynamic responses. Depending on one's time horizon, pastoralism as an economic activity may be seen to be dissolving in the short term, or it may be seen as undergoing just another adjustment to changing circumstances in the long term. If resilience is based on flexibility and adaptability, then pastoralism is showing some of both.

DISCLOSURE STATEMENT

The author is not aware of any affiliations, memberships, funding, or financial holdings that might be perceived as affecting the objectivity of this review.

ACKNOWLEDGMENTS

The writing of this review was supported, in part, by the National Science Foundation project, Decision-Making in Rangeland Systems: An Integrated Ecosystem-Agent-Based Modeling Approach to Resilience and Change (DREAMER), Grant No. SES-0527481. I also thank Linda Knapp, Joana Roque de Pinho, and Jill Lackett for their help with the literature review for the manuscript.

LITERATURE CITED

Adger WN, Agrawala S, Mirza MQ, Conde C, O'Brien, K, et al. 2007. Assessment of adaptation practices, options, constraints and capacity. See Parry et al. 2007, pp. 717–43

Adger WN, Brown K, Tompkins EL. 2006. The political economy of cross-scale networks in resource comanagement. *Ecol. Soc.* 10(2):9 **http://www.ecologyandsociety.org/vol10/iss2/art9/**

Alimaev II, Behnke RH. 2008. Ideology, land tenure and livestock mobility in Kazakhstan. See Galvin et al. 2008a, pp. 151–78

Ash A, Stafford Smith DM. 2003. Pastoralism in tropical rangelands: seizing the opportunity to change. *Rangeland J.* 25:113–27

Babiker M. 2006. African pastoralism through anthropological eyes: Whose crisis? In *African Anthropologies: History, Critique and Practice*, ed. M Ntarangwi, D Mills, M Babiker, pp. 170–87. Dakar: CODESRIA

Barrett CB, Reardon T, Webb P. 2001. Nonfarm income diversification and household livelihood strategies in rural Africa: concepts, dynamics and policy implications. *Food Policy* 26(4):315–31

Bassett TJ, Turner MD. 2007. Sudden shift or migratory drift? FulBe herd movement to the Sudano-Guinean region of West Africa. *Hum. Ecol.* 35:33–49

Behnke R. 1995. Natural resource management in pastoral Africa. In *Social Aspects of Sustainable Dryland Management*, ed. D Stiles, pp. 145–52. West Sussex, UK: Wiley

Behnke RH. 2008. The drivers of fragmentation in arid and semiarid landscapes. See Galvin et al. 2008a, pp. 305–40

Behnke RH, Scoones I. 1993. Rethinking range ecology: implications for rangeland management in Africa. In *Range Ecology at Disequilibrium: New Models of Natural Variability and Pastoral Adaptation in African Savannas*, ed. RH Behnke, I Scoones, C Kerven, pp. 153–72. London: Overseas Dev. Inst.

Bekure S, deLeeuw PN, Grandin BE, Neate PJH, eds. 1991. *Maasai Herding: An Analysis of the Livestock Production System of Maasai Pastoralists in Eastern Kajiado District, Kenya*. ILCA Systems Study 4. Addis Ababa, Ethiopia: ILCA (Int. Livestock Cent. Afr.). 172 pp.

Berkes F, Folke C. 1994. Investing in cultural capital for sustainable use of natural capital. In *Investing in Natural Capital: The Ecological Economics Approach to Sustainability*, ed. A Jansson, M Hammer, C Folke, R Costanza, pp. 128–49. Washington, DC: Island

Berkes F, Folke C, Colding C, Colding J, eds. 1998. *Linking Social and Ecological Systems*. Cambridge, UK: Cambridge Univ. Press

Berry S. 1989. Social institutions and access to resources: Africa. *J. Int. Afr. Inst.* 59(1):41–55

Biersack A, Greenberg JB, eds. 2006. *Reimagining Political Ecology*. Durham, NC: Duke Univ. Press

Boko M, Niang I, Nyong A, Vogel C, Githeko A, et al. 2007. Africa. See Parry et al. 2007, pp. 433–67

Boone RB, Lackett JM, Galvin KA, Ojima DS, Tucker CJ III. 2007. Links and broken chains: evidence of human-caused changes in land cover in remotely sensed images. *Environ. Sci. Policy* 10(2):135–49

Bourdieu P. 1986. The forms of capital. In *Handbook of Theory and Research for the Sociology of Education*, ed. JG Richardson, pp. 241–58. Westport, CT: Greenwood

Bradley D, Grainger A. 2004. Social resilience as a controlling influence on desertification in Senegal. *Land Degrad. Dev.* 15:451–70

Bruun O. 2006. *Precious Steppe: Mongolian Nomadic Pastoralists in Pursuit of the Market*. Lanham, MD: Lexington

BurnSilver SB. 2007. *Pathways of continuity and change: diversification, intensification and mobility in Maasai*. PhD diss. Grad. Degree Program Ecol., Colo. State Univ., Fort Collins, CO

BurnSilver SB, Worden J, Boone RB. 2008. Processes of fragmentation in the Amboseli ecosystem, southern Kajiado District, Kenya. See Galvin et al. 2008a, pp. 225–53

Chatty D, Colester M, eds. 2002. *Displacement, Forced Settlement and Conservation*. Oxford: Berghahn

Christensen JH, Hewitson B, Busuioc A, Chen A, Gao X, et al. 2007. Regional climate projections. See Solomon et al. 2007, pp. 848–940

Coast E. 2002. Maasai socioeconomic conditions: a cross-border comparison. *Hum. Ecol.* 30(1):79–105

Dekker M. 2004. Sustainability and resourcefulness: support networks during periods of stress. *World Dev.* 32:1735–51

Dietz T. 1987. *Pastoralists in Dire Straits: Survival Strategies and External Interventions in a Semiarid Region at the Kenya/Uganda Border: Western Pokot, 1900–1986*. Amsterdam: Univ. Amsterdam, Inst. Soc. Geogr.

Evans-Pritchard EE. 1940. *The Nuer: A Description of the Modes of Livelihood and Political Institutions of a Nilotic People*. Oxford: Oxford Univ. Press

Fernández-Giménez ME. 2001. The effects of livestock privatization on pastoral land use and land tenure in postsocialist Mongolia. *Nomadic People* 5(2):49–66

Fernández-Giménez ME. 2002. Spatial and social boundaries and the paradox of pastoral land tenure: a case study from post socialist Mongolia. *Hum. Ecol.* 30(1):49–78

Fernández-Giménez ME, Bathuyan B. 2004. Law and disorder: local implementation of Mongolia's land law. *Dev. Change* 35(1):141–65

Folke C, Hahn T, Olsson P, Norberg J. 2005. Adaptive governance of social-ecological systems. *Annu. Rev. Environ. Resour.* 30:441–73

Fratkin E. 2001. East African pastoralism in transition: Maasai, Boran and Rendille cases. *Afr. Stud. Rev.* 44(3):1–25

Fratkin EM. 2004. *Ariaal Pastoralists of Kenya: Studying Pastoralism, Drought, and Development in Africa's Arid Lands*. Boston: Pearson Educ.

Fratkin E, Galvin K, Roth E, eds. 1994. *African Pastoralist Systems: An Integrated Approach*. Boulder, CO: Lynne Rienner

Fratkin E, Mearns R. 2003. Sustainability and pastoral livelihoods: lessons from East African Maasai and Mongolia. *Hum. Organ.* 62:112–22

Galvin KA. 2008. Responses of pastoralists to land fragmentation: Social capital, connectivity, and resilience. See Galvin et al. 2008a, pp. 369–89

Galvin KA, Boone RB, Smith NM, Lynn SJ. 2001. Impacts of climate variability on East African pastoralists: linking social science and remote sensing. *Climate Res.* 19:161–72

Galvin KA, Ellis J, Boone RB, Magennis AL, Smith NM, et al. 2002. Compatibility of pastoralism and conservation? A test case using integrated assessment in the Ngorongoro Conservation Area, Tanzania. See Chatty & Colester 2002, pp. 36–60

Galvin KA, Reid RS, Behnke RH Jr, Hobbs NT, eds. 2008a. *Fragmentation of Semi-Arid and Arid Landscapes. Consequences for Human and Natural Systems.* Dordrecht, The Neth.: Springer

Galvin KA, Thornton PK, Boone RB, Knapp LM. 2008b. Ngorongoro Conservation Area, Tanzania: fragmentation of a Unique Region of the Greater Serengeti Ecosystem. See Galvin et al. 2008a, pp. 255–79

Gulliver PH. 1955. *The Family Herds.* London: Routledge

Held IM, Delworth TL, Lu J, Findell KL, Knutson TR. 2005. Simulation of Sahel drought in the twentieth and 21st centuries. *Proc. Natl. Acad. Sci. USA* 102(50):17891–96

Hobbs NT, Galvin KA, Stokes CJ, Lackett JM, Ash AJ, et al. 2008. Fragmentation of rangelands: implications for humans, animals and landscapes. *Glob. Environ. Change* 18:776–85

Hodgson DL. 2001. "Once intrepid warriors": Modernity and the production of Maasai masculinities. In *Gendered Modernities*, ed. DL Hodgson, pp. 105–148. New York: Macmillan

Holling CS. 2000. Theories for sustainable futures. *Conservation Ecol.* 4(2):1–5 **http://www.consecol. org/vol4/iss2/art7/**

Holling CS, Berkes F, Folke C. 1998. Science, sustainability and resource management. See Berkes et al. 1998, pp. 342–59

Holling CS, Gunderson LH. 2002. Resilience and adaptive cycles. In *Panarchy: Understanding Transformations in Human and Natural Systems*, ed. LH Gunderson, CS Holling, pp. 25–62. Washington, DC: Island

Homewood K, Lambin EF, Coast E, Kariuki A, Kikula I, et al. 2001. Long-term changes in Serengeti-Mara wildebeest and land cover: pastoralism, population, or policies? *Proc. Natl. Acad. Sci. USA* 98(22):12544–49

Hunt LP. 2003. Opportunities for the future in Australia's grazed rangelands. *Rangeland J.* 25:183–95

Jones PG, Thornton PK. 2003. The potential impacts of climate change on maize production in Africa and Latin America in 2055. *Glob. Environ. Change* 13:51–59

Kimani K, Pickard J. 1998. Recent trends and implications of group ranch subdivision and fragmentation in Kajiado District, Kenya. *Geogr. J.* 164:202–13

Lamprey R, Reid RS. 2004. Expansion of human settlement in Kenya's Maasai Mara: what future for pastoralism and wildlife? *J. Biogeogr.* 31:997–1032

Lesorogol CK. 2003. Transforming institutions among pastoralists: inequality and land privatization. *Am. Anthropol.* 105(3):531–42

Little P. 1992. *The Elusive Granary: Herder, Farmer and State in Northern Kenya.* Cambridge, UK: Cambridge Univ. Press

Little PD, Smith K, Cellarius BA, Coppock DL, Barrett C. 2001a. Avoiding disaster: diversification and risk management among East African herders. *Dev. Change* 32(3):401–33

Little PD, Mahmoud H, Coppock DL. 2001b. When deserts flood: risk management and climatic processes among east African pastoralists. *Climate Res.* 19:149–59

Loiske VM. 1990. Political adaptation: the case of the Wabarbaig in Hanang District, Tanzania. In *Adaptive Strategies in African Arid Lands*, ed. M Bovin, L Manger, pp. 77–90. Uppsala, Sweden: Scand. Inst. Afr. Stud.

Luseno WK, McPeak JG, Barrett CB, Little PD, Gebru G. 2003. Assessing the value of climate forecast information for pastoralists: evidence from Southern Ethiopia and Northern Kenya. *World Dev.* 31(9):1477–94

Markakis J. 2004. *Pastoralism on the Margin.* London: Minority Rights Group Int.

McCabe JT. 1990. Turkana pastoralism: a case against the tragedy of the commons. *Hum. Ecol.* 18(1):81–103

McCabe JT. 2002. Giving conservation a human face? See Chatty & Colester 2002, pp. 61–76

McCabe JT, Shofield EC, Nygaard Pedersen G. 1997. Food security and nutritional status. In *The Experience of the Ngorongoro Conservation Area, Tanzania Multiple Land-Use*, ed. DM Thompson, pp. 285–302. Gland, Switz.: Int. Union Conserv. Nat.

McPeak J, Little PD. 2005. Cursed if you do, cursed if you don't: the contradictory processes of pastoral sedentarization in northern Kenya. In *As Pastoralists Settle: Social Health and Economic Consequences of Pastoral Sedentarization in Marsabit District, Kenya*, ed. E Fratkin, EA Roth, pp. 87–104. New York: Kluwer Acad.

MEA (Millenn. Ecosyst. Assess.). 2005. *Ecosystems and Human Well-Being: Synthesis*. Washington, DC: Island

Mearns R. 2004. Sustaining livelihoods on Mongolia's pastoral commons: insights from a participatory poverty assessment. *Dev. Change* 35(1):107–39

Muller F, Bold B. 1996. On the necessities of the new regulations on pastoral land use in Mongolia. *Appl. Geogr. Dev.* 48:29–51

Mwangi E. 2003. *Institutional change and politics: the transformation of property rights in Kenya's Maasailand*. PhD diss., Indiana Univ., Bloomington, 328 pp.

Natl. Res. Counc. 2002. *The Drama of the Commons*, ed. E Ostrom, T Dietz, N Dolšak, PC Stern, S Stonich, EU Weber, Comm. Hum. Dimens. Glob. Change, Div. Behav. Soc. Sci. Educ. Washington, DC: Natl. Acad. Press

Nelson DR, Adger WN, Brown K. 2007. Adaptation to environmental change: contributions of a resilience framework. *Annu. Rev. Environ. Resour.* 32:395–419

Newman L, Dale A. 2005. Network structure, diversity, and proactive resilience building: a response to Tompkins and Adger. *Ecol. Soc.* 10(1):r2. **http://www.ecologyandsociety.org/vol10/iss1.resp2**

Niamir-Fuller M. 1998. The resilience of pastoral herding in Sahelian Africa. See Berkes et al. 1998, pp. 250–84

Ojima D, Chuluun T. 2008. Policy changes in Mongolia: implications for land use and landscapes. See Galvin et al. 2008a, pp. 179–94

Okello MM. 2005. An assessment of the large mammal component of the proposed wildlife sanctuary site in Maasai Kuku Group Ranch near Amboseli, Kenya. *South Afr. J. Wildl. Res.* 35:63–76

Österle M. 2008. From cattle to goats: the transformation of East Pokot pastoralism in Kenya. *Nomadic Peoples* 12(1):81–91

Overpeck JT, Cole JE. 2006. Abrupt change in Earth's climate system. *Annu. Rev. Environ. Resour.* 31:1–31

Parry ML, Canziani OF, Palutikof JP, Van Der Linden JP, Hanson CE, eds. 2007. *Climate Change 2007: Impact, Adaptation and Vulnerability. Contribution of Working Group II to the Fourth Assessment Report of the Intergovernmental Panel on Climate Change*. Cambridge, UK: Cambridge Univ. Press

Peters P. 1994. *Dividing the Commons: Politics, Policy and Culture in Botswana*. Charlottesville: Univ. Press Va.

Potkanski T. 1999. Mutual assistance among the Ngorongoro Maasai. In *The Poor Are Not Us: Poverty and Pastoralism in Eastern Africa*, ed. DM Anderson, V Broch-Due, pp. 199–217. Athens: Ohio Univ. Press

Pretty JN. 2002. People, livelihoods, and collective action in biodiversity management. In *Biodiversity, Sustainability and Human Communities: Protecting Beyond the Protected*, ed. T O'Riordan, S Stoll-Kleeman, pp. 61–86. Cambridge, UK: Cambridge Univ. Press

Redman CL. 1999. *Human Impact on Ancient Environments*. Tucson: Univ. Ariz. Press

Reid RS, Galvin KA, Kruska RS. 2008. Global significance of extensive grazing lands and pastoral societies: an introduction. See Galvin et al. 2008a, pp. 1–24

Roque de Pinho J. 2009. *Staying together: people-wildlife relationships in the Amboseli ecosystem, Southern Kenya*. PhD diss., Grad. Degree Program Ecol., Colo. State Univ., Fort Collins, CO

Rutten MMEM. 1992. *Selling Wealth to Buy Poverty*. Saarbrucken: Verland Breitenbach

Sanford S. 1983. *Management of Pastoral Development in the Third World*. New York: Wiley

Schreck CJ III, Semazii FHM. 2004. Variability of the recent climate of east Africa. *Int. J. Climatol.* 24:681–701

Seo SN, Mendelsohn R. 2006. *The impact of climate change on livestock management in Africa: a structural Ricardian analysis*. Cent. Environ. Econ. Policy in Africa (CEEPA) Discuss. Pap. No. 23, Univ. Pretoria, Pretoria, S. Afr.

Smit B, Wandel J. 2006. Adaptation, adaptive capacity and vulnerability. *Glob. Environ. Change* 16:282–92

Smith AB. 2005. *African Herders: Emergence of Pastoral Traditions*. Walnut Creek, CA: Altamira

Solomon S, Qin D, Manning M, Chen Z, Marquis M, et al. eds. 2007. *Climate Change 2007: The Physical Science Basis. Contribution of Working Group I to the Fourth Assessment Report of the Intergovernmental Panel on Climate Change*. Cambridge, UK: Cambridge Univ. Press

Spencer P. 2004. Keeping tradition in good repair: the evolution of indigenous knowledge and the dilemma of development among pastoralists. In *Development and Local Knowledge: New Approaches to Issues in Natural Resources Management*, ed. A Bicker, P Sillitoe, J Pottier, pp. 202–17. London: Routledge

Stenning DJ. 1959. *Savannah Nomads*. London: Oxford Univ. Press

Stenning DJ. 1960. Transhumance, migratory drift, migration: patterns of pastoral Fulani Nomadism. In *Cultures and Societies of Africa*, ed. S Ottenberg, P Ottenberg, pp. 139–62. New York: Random House

Steward JH. 1955. *Theory of Culture Change: The Methodology of Multilinear Evolution*. Chicago: Univ. Ill. Press

Streets DG, Glantz MH. 2000. Exploring the concept of climate surprise. *Glob. Environ. Change* 10:97–107

Thébaud B, Batterbury S. 2001. Sahel pastoralists: opportunism, struggle, conflict and negotiation. A case-study from Niger. *Glob. Environ. Change* 11:69–78

Thomas RB. 1998. The evolution of human adaptability paradigms: toward a biology of poverty. In *Building a New Biocultural Synthesis*, ed. AH Goodman, TL Leatherman, pp. 43–74. Ann Arbor: Univ. Mich. Press

Thompson DM, Serneels S, Lambin EF. 2002. Land use strategies in the Mara ecosystem: a spatial analysis linking socio-economic data with landscape variables. In *Linking People, Place and Policy: A GIScience Approach*, ed. SJ Walsh, KA Crews-Meyer, pp. 39–68. Dordrecht, The Neth.: Kluwer

Thornton PK, Boone RB, Galvin KA, Burnsilver SB, Waithaka MM, et al. 2007. Coping strategies in livestock-dependent households in east and southern Africa: a synthesis of four case studies. *Hum. Ecol.* 35(4):461–76

Thornton PK, Burnsilver SB, Boone RB, Galvin KA. 2006. Modelling the impacts of group ranch subdivision on agro-pastoral households in Kajiado, Kenya. *Agric. Syst.* 87:331–56

Turner BL II, Kasperson RE, Matson PA, McCarthy JL, Corell RW, et al. 2003. A framework for vulnerability analysis in sustainability science. *Proc. Natl. Acad. Sci. USA* 100(14):8074–79

Turner MD. 1999. The role of social networks, indefinite boundaries and political bargaining in maintaining the ecological and economic resilience of the transhumance systems of Sudan-Sahelian West Africa. In *Managing Mobility in African Rangelands*, ed. M Niamir-Fuller, pp. 97–123. London: Food Agric. Organ. United Nations, Beijer Int. Inst. Ecol. Econ.

Walker B, Abel N. 2002. Resilient rangelands-adaptation in complex systems. In *Panarchy: Understanding Transformations in Human and Natural Systems*, ed. LH Gunderson, CS Holling, pp. 293–313. Washington, DC: Island

Western D. 2002. *In the Dust of Kilimanjaro*. Washington, DC: Island

White L. 1949. *The Science of Culture: A Study of Man and Civilization*. New York: Grove

Young OR, Berkhout F, Gallopín GC, Janssen MA, Ostrom E, Van Der Leeuw S. 2006. The globalization of socio-ecological systems: an agenda for scientific research. *Glob. Environ. Change* 16:304–16

Medical Discourse

James M. Wilce

Department of Anthropology, Northern Arizona University, Flagstaff,
Arizona 86011-5200; email: jim.wilce@nau.edu

Annu. Rev. Anthropol. 2009. 38:199–215

First published online as a Review in Advance on
June 19, 2009

The *Annual Review of Anthropology* is online at
anthro.annualreviews.org

This article's doi:
10.1146/annurev-anthro-091908-164450

Key Words

authority, interaction, circulation, textuality, conversation analysis

Abstract

Discourse plays an important role in medicine, and medical discourse
in the broadest sense (discourse in and about healing, curing, or therapy; expressions of suffering; and relevant language ideologies) has profound anthropological significance. As modes of social action, writing
and speaking help constitute medical institutions, curative practices,
and relations of authority in and beyond particular healing encounters.
This review describes cultural variation in medical discourse and variation across genres and registers. It then surveys two approaches to
analyzing medical discourse: conversation analysis (CA) and discourse
studies echoing Foucault's work, attempting to spur dialogue between
them. Such dialogue could be fruitful because, despite hesitancy to invoke macrosocial variables, conversation analysts as well as Foucaultian
discourse analysts have reflected on medical authority. Finally, the article
reviews recent attempts to contextualize closely analyzed interactions—
written exchanges as well as face-to-face clinical encounters—vis-à-vis
the global circulation of linguistic forms and ideologies.

INTRODUCTION

This article explores the anthropological significance of medical discourse—a high-stakes topic with clear applied relevance (Cooper et al. 2003, Maynard & Heritage 2005, Roberts et al. 2005) that is also rich ground for developing anthropological theory. Studying discourse (language in its fullness) and medicine together brings us to encounter culture as discursively constituted. As historically situated practices, forms of medical discourse play a role in cultural production and reproduction. Effective intervention in those processes (Hodge et al. 1996) requires insightful assessment of communicative practices in sociocultural contexts (Browner et al. 2003, Kleinman & Benson 2006) (see sidebar, Gesture and Embodied Communicative Action in Medical Interaction). This article reviews such practices and contexts.

Medical discourse inspired two streams of work beginning in the 1960s—one U.S.-based and microanalytic (*The Natural History of an Interview* project; Condon & Ogston 1966, Scheflen 1973), the other macroanalytic (Foucault 1965[1961], 1990[1978]). [The ethnography of communication, emerging at the same time, described local ways of speaking in general, rather than focusing on curing (compare Sherzer 1983).] Face-to-face interaction of patients and physicians remains the focus of what emerged as conversation analysis (CA), mostly within sociology (Heritage & Maynard 2006a,b; Waitzkin 1991). The qualitative analytic approach of CA reflects Garfinkel's (1967) ethnomethodology, viewing social actors like doctors and patients as constituting shared worlds by means of particular actions, especially talk. Quantitatively and qualitatively oriented sociolinguists, whose sociology is more mainstream, have analyzed therapeutic discourse (Labov & Fanshel 1977); translation in multicultural encounters (Aranguri et al. 2006); and the relationship between particular medical concerns motivating the encounter between patient and practitioner and the achievement of attunement to each others' perspectives (Hamilton 2004). Below, I highlight problems in the literature on medical discourse. I then explain why medical discourse is an anthropological concern and survey its variability vis-à-vis culture, genre, and register. In the final, longest section of the article I review contributions to the field, starting with CA (rather than the broader field of sociolinguistics), to highlight debates over medical authority between conversation analysts and contributors to the macroanalytic stream. Finally, I describe recent attempts to link microinteraction to global circulation of texts that help constitute modern persons as well as medicine and its authority.

Insights from the analysis of medical discourse have been applied, for example, to training and certifying new doctors. Roberts & Sarangi (1999) worked collaboratively with the Royal College of General Practitioners to improve forms of doctor-doctor communication. Such collaboration can benefit patients and

---

Discourse: instances of language (written and spoken, face-to-face and mass-mediated) in actual use in particular social contexts

CA: conversation analysis

Text: a particular instance of discourse that is coherent, memorable, quotable and thus recontextualizable

---

GESTURE AND EMBODIED COMMUNICATIVE ACTION IN MEDICAL INTERACTION

Speech, gesture, posture, and other acts jointly produce meaning in medical interaction. Patients position themselves to make body parts visible to physicians (Heath 1986; 2002; 2006, p. 207), even while physicians gaze at computerized records (Ruusuvuori 2001). During the physical examination patients constitute themselves as clinical objects, gazing away with apparent disregard while making their subjectivity a clinical resource, e.g., demonstrating pain and its location (Heath 2006). Medical teamwork is coordinated by talk and gesture; one gesture may call for another, as when a junior member of an anesthesia team points to the knob that increases gas flow, eliciting a go-ahead nod from a senior member. Talk can elicit and coordinate physical activity, as when one member tells a patient he will now lay her down flat, prompting another to move to help lay her down (Hindmarsh & Pilnick 2002). Senior surgeons use gestural as well as spoken signs to teach medical school students about the currently problematic body part and guide the ongoing activity. This practice can involve such methods as doing a trace of the body area in the air, precisely located vis-à-vis patient, endoscopic video monitor, and students (Koschman et al. 2007).

doctors, immigrants and nonimmigrants. U.K. doctors whose linguistic experience is with fluent English speakers might expect patients to maintain a factual orientation. Immigrant patients, however, sometimes bring to clinical encounters a troubles-telling orientation (Jefferson & Lee 1992, Wilce 1998). Thus, in multicultural societies, doctors' "training for uncertainty" (Fox 1957) must now include training for managing "interactional uncertainty" (Roberts et al. 2004).

Unfortunately, much of the literature on medical discourse confines itself to practitioner-patient interaction in biomedical settings and tailors proposals for improving communication to biomedical models of the doctor-patient encounter, such as a "patient-centered" or "biopsychosocial" approach [see critiques by Kuipers (1989) and questions by Cooper et al. (2003)]. For Maynard & Heritage (2005), introducing CA in medical education "facilitates the biopsychosocial approach to the interview, as well as a more recent emphasis on relationship-centered care" (p. 434). Anthropologists resist the exclusive focus on biomedicine and practitioner-patient communication and are skeptical about the psychosocial approach as an oft-inappropriate cultural export—into postwar situations, for example—that "merely assign[s] people the role of...patient" rather than recognizing their narratives as potential legal testimony (Summerfield 1995, p. 356). Similarly, talk of "patient empowerment" can be "used...to constrain doctors' responsibility for patients' suffering" (Salmon & Hall 2003, p. 1969). These ideological representations of discourse (as empowering or culturally competent, for example)—or language ideologies—are as important to analyze as clinical interactions.

Communication among practitioners affects health seekers' experiences. This assertion is supported by analyses of many sorts of discursive events involving practitioners interacting with each other: medical school lectures (Linthorst et al. 2007, Martin 1992), grand rounds (Atkinson 1999, Martin 1992), clinical settings where an attending physician consults

specialists (Cicourel 1992) and notes are added to charts (Hobbs 2003), and team meetings of occupational therapists (Mattingly 1998b). To these we might add "development discourse" (Pigg 1996, p. 178) of the sort circulating in schools and public health campaigns in poor countries such as Nepal, in which assertions of biomedical authority are common. These assertions have profound cultural/medical effects that applied anthropologists might be interested in moderating. Programs that train mental health providers in cultural competence involve metadiscourse reflecting on practitioners' and institutions' communicative forms. Such programs aim to improve communication but are often undermined by essentializing premises about cultural citizenship (Giordano 2008), languages, and their speakers (Briggs 2005). One such program erases multilingual competencies of Latino psychiatric patients, representing Spanish (the mother tongue, a phrase reflecting the institutional gendering of the language) as Latinos' only medium for authentic emotional expression and thus for curing problems newly understood as psychological (Santiago-Irizarry 2001). Insightful critiques, such as those offered by Santiago-Irizarry, can potentiate better fixes.

MEDICAL DISCOURSE AS ANTHROPOLOGICAL CONCERN

In this section I present a model of language that best equips us to study medical discourse ethnographically. I situate medical discourse within that model and introduce the sorts of issues that make it a pressing anthropological concern.

Construing the relationship between medicine and discourse broadly in this review makes anthropological sense, although many facets of the relationship may only be mentioned, such as the intersection of music, discourse, and healing (Roseman 1991); disability discourse (Hadder 2007); "laughter as a patient's resource" (Haakana 2001); the iconicity between a sufferer's voice quality and denotative expressions of pain (Wilce 1998, p. 123); and the representation of talk itself as

Language ideologies: metadiscourses and ideas about language(s) and speakers, tied to structures of power, distorting yet influencing the language on which they reflect

a symptom (of mental illness; Ribeiro 1994; Desjarlais 1997; Wilce 2004a,b). Recognizing the vast potential scope of anthropological work on the role of communication in health, illness, and healing follows from understanding the difficulty of cordoning off a domain of medicine from the rest of life. For example, people visit diviners to seek both causes and remedies for various problems, such as a sick child (Nuckolls 1991). But lost cows are also diviner-eligible topics (Wilce 2001). An analytic distinction between medicine and, say, ritual, though analytically useful, should not be confused with reality. Forms of discourse do not mind the boundaries between the domains we conceive or conform completely to institutional norms. Medical discourse itself may have as its "effect...the creation and maintenance of the interests of certain hegemonic groups" (MacDonald 2002, p. 464), and ideologies of language per se that surface in discourse on health and illness also appear elsewhere.

Grasping the import of medical discourse in particular requires a general understanding of the functions of language, which in turn helps us avoid essentializing the medical. What any bit of language is apparently about is only the beginning of its signifying activity. Reference and predication—targeting something to which a linguistic expression corresponds (referring), and saying something (predicating) about it—are only the most salient of linguistic functions. Dominant "referentialist" ideologies (Hill 2008), representing language's prime function as clear, realistic, or sincere reference, rather than performing social acts, help undermine the sociopolitical agency of patients in therapeutic programs (Carr 2006, Desjarlais 1997). Note, however, that referring is social action, for example directing a doctor's attention toward, or mutually constructing, the object of a clinical encounter (Engeström 1995). Talking about sickness may point to apparently nonmedical topics such as speaker traits (other than illness), relationships, family resources, and the moral order. Stories told by Miskitu lobster divers about courage in the face

of dangers, including decompression sickness, may signal their deserving status to overhearers who control important resources such as boats. Moreover, some of the social and performative meaning of divers' stories of danger and sickness is carried in their choice of codes (Miskitu, Spanish, Creole, English, etc.; Humphrey 2005).

Attention to whole patterns of signs in discursive events also helps free us from the hold of referentialist language ideologies. Discourse regarded as healing may never refer to sickness or healing or to those present. Javanese wayang (shadow puppet plays), for example, refer to events in old royal courts. It is their circular text structure that works on wayang audiences, repelling "madness, demons, [and] disease" (Becker 1979, p. 233). Navajo stories used in Holyway rituals for eye problems describe Coyote removing his eyes and throwing them in the air or replacing them with balls of pitch (Toelken 1987). Curative efficacy here depends on the iconicity between two acts in Coyote's time and two steps—performance and healing—in ritual time. The same stories can be used to cause as well as cure sickness, just as in Bangladesh Qur'anic verses may be inserted into amulets to heal or, if written or read backward, to curse. Here again, sign patterning is crucial to event meaning.

Cultural Variation and Globalization

Both commonalities and variation in medical discourse interest anthropologists. Studies of symbolic healing have offered putative universals (Dow 1986) or have located shamanic chants somewhere between "our physical medicine and psychological therapies" (Lévi-Strauss 1963, p. 198). We ought, however, add a layer of reflexivity to such comparisons, asking why they appeal—to Navajos among others (Milne & Howard 2000). Thus our interest in the rich global diversity of discursive and interactional structures present in healing encounters, classifying discourses, reflections on healing signs, and illness talk invites analysis in and of itself, but the interest endures. Consider the rule among Aboriginal occupants of Darwin fringe camps banning talk about one's past serious illnesses (Sansom 1982). Such stories belong instead to those whose interventions saved one's life. Sansom learned this after asking a man about his racking cough and being told that someone coming soon could explain it; no one else could. If medical discourse is an arena in which selves are constituted as this sort or that, the transferred ownership of "tellability" (Ochs & Capps 2001) in the Darwin fringe camps constantly reinvents a social self, embedded in relations of reciprocity. In Finland and elsewhere, psychoanalysts engage in a temporary ownership transfer, laying claim to middle-class patients' truth (Vehviläinen 2008, p. 138), but with the aim of returning tellability to the analysand, whose healing entails producing a particular narrative of the suffering self (Lévi-Strauss 1963). Shamanic healing marshals multiple sign modalities and sensory experiences—touch, sparks in a rattle (Briggs 1996), and sound (the clanging of a bell meant to awaken a Yolmo body that has lost its soul; Desjarlais 1996). In any context, we should take medical discourse to include local reflections on signs and healing, as in the Yolmo attribution of healing to an aesthetic, rather than symbolic-persuasive, function. Effective healing may require of shamans a beautiful voice quality (Malaysia; Laderman 1987) or a poetics of "wild images" that invite the soul on an envigorating chase (Nepal; Desjarlais 1996). Although recovering lost souls of western analysands may also require a therapeutic aesthetic, and doctors' speech can be as esoteric as shamans', divergent meaning-producing contexts still demand attention.

The stakes of medical discourse go beyond meaning and the reproduction of cultural sensibilities and encompass social reproduction/transformation. Balancing verbal avoidance by some and production of proprietary sickness stories by others is a key form of reciprocity that sustains an Aboriginal community (Sansom 1982). Shamanic curing also reproduces a social order. The particular pattern of alternation between esoteric and everyday linguistic registers in Warao shamans' songs

underscores their authority (Briggs 1996). Still, although it is appropriate to be wary of the romance of resistance (Abu-Lughod 1990), straightforward reproduction of shamans' power is not all that happens in curing sessions. Patients' family members can (cautiously) resist shamanic authority (Brown 1988).

Genre and Register

Beyond cultural particularity, grasping the significance of medical discourse requires exploring particularities of genre, rejecting overgeneral reference to discourses and invocations of narrative that erase the specificity of local genres. Discourse comes already packaged in relation to genres—discourse types or rules that emerge in activity systems such as clinical encounters (Engeström 1995) and are structurally oriented to expectations—so that performances gain conventionalized reception (Bauman 1999).

Specialized discourse genres arose in modern Europe along with sciences such as medicine in histories for which we must account if we are to contextualize medical discourse (Berkenkotter 2008). The emergence of the scientific article (Atkinson 1992); clinical chart note (Berkenkotter 2008, Coker 2003, Luhrmann 2000, Mattingly 1998b); medical textbook (e.g., Kraepelin 1883, Pinel 1801) and atlas (Armstrong 1983); *historiettes* ("little histories") (Goldstein 1987); and case studies fusing fictional-narrative and scientific features (such as Freud's; Berkenkotter 2008) enabled medicine to constitute itself as a science and tool of power. But genres evolve. Expectations governing research articles in the *Edinburgh Medical Journal* changed markedly over three centuries. The individual case reports popular in the eighteenth century yielded, in the twentieth century, to "case-derived statistics . . . as the basis of medical persuasion" (Atkinson 1992, p. 363). An "informational" style, one of conceptual precision and explicit reference to the theory around which articles must now cohere, has displaced an "involved" rhetorical style [using affective language clearly oriented to

Registers: various local speech repertoires understood as indexing roles and statuses, often ranked as "high" and "low"

Genres: types of discourse linked to event types, patterned to fit recipients' expectations of both the discourse and the broader event interaction, with a letter-like narrative organization; Atkinson (1992, pp. 351–56)].

Nineteenth-century psychiatry sought legitimacy through linguistic reform, which involved coining new mental disease labels such as French *monomanie* ("obsession"), rapidly embraced by the bourgeoisie (Goldstein 1987, p. 153), but also genres as metatexts legitimating the labels. New nosologies structured the semantic field of psychiatric disease entities and restrospectively enabled a particular imagination of the clinical notes in which those entities [e.g., "maniacal-depressive insanity," coined by Kraepelin (1968)] ostensibly emerged as natural kinds. This is the story of Kraepelin's diagnostic *Zählkarten* (literally, "counting cards")—apparently completed post hoc, guided by an a priori vision of the epistemic field (Weber & Engstrom 1997), but still a key inspiration for the series of *Diagnostic and Statistical Manual*[s] *of Mental Disorders* (APA 2000) first appearing in mid-twentieth century.

Narrative genres are of special importance in many curative traditions, in the production of illness, and in certain approaches to medical anthropology (Garro 2000, Good 1994, Good et al. 1994, Kleinman 1988). Stories sufferers tell construct for them a theory of the world (Capps & Ochs 1995, pp. 21–22). For Good et al. (1994), it is the "subjunctivizing tactics" in sufferers' narratives that enable such stories to sustain the sick. For example, keeping multiple perspectives in play and introducing "encounters with the mysterious" are strategies that render stories open to various futures. To Radley et al. (2008, p. 1494), illness stories are "constructed retrospectively, looking back from their endings"—as though indeed the end were known and thus might be foreshadowed all along. In yet another twist on the function of narrative, Capps & Ochs (1995) argue that certain features of the stories panic disorder sufferers tell are key to mediating their repeated experiences of panic. Nonsufferers' narratives often situate events and related feelings within a moral order related to narrators' capacity to act. Narrating panic involves a more paradoxical form of agency, actively constructing a form of passivity by assigning to emotions the power to overwhelm the present. Capps & Ochs (1995) thus suggest that therapists explore how to intervene in the narrative construction of panic.

Connections between narrative and agency (including the agency of narrators and narrated figures) have usually been viewed more positively. Mattingly (1998a,b) contrasts narrative and "chart talk" as distinct forms of reasoning in meetings where occupational therapists discuss patients. Chart talk—authoritative, monological, and oriented toward biomedical rationality—elides agency. Therapists' personal stories allow patients to "emerge" as agents (1998b, p. 274). Patients' agency may indeed be discussed, albeit reduced to compliance [Kuipers (1989); compare Browner's (1998) critique of Mattingly's distinction as oversharp]. The celebration of agency, and of its reassertion in interactions natural to home or clinic as well as in theoretical discourse, may preclude its problematization. The outcomes and social significance of ascriptions of agency by practitioners deserve study in themselves. Recognizing institutional agency in occupational therapists' stories, as Mattingly does (1998b), is important. Still, we need a rich theory of talk, agency, and self at both super- and subindividual levels (Kockelman 2007). The multivocality of illness narratives (Kirmayer 2000) and the casting of constituent parts of self (viz., feelings) as troublesome agents in panic disorder narratives (Capps & Ochs 1995) imply that stories and tellers have no single, centered agency. The often joint production of illness narratives raises further questions about figuring narrative agency as ownership (Garro 2000, Ochs & Capps 2001, Sansom 1982). Looking beyond individual narrators, the social circulation of illness stories, e.g., AIDS stories, has had enormous consequences (Farmer 1994).

Narrative may be disappearing from clinics (Luhrmann 2000, Marinker 2000, Radley et al. 2008, Wilce 2005), persisting (perhaps) as but a minority interest among readers of the *American Journal of Psychiatry* (Berkenkotter 2008). In Bangladesh, eliciting stories from patients is integral to vernacular healing (Wilce 1998) but marginal to, or disruptive of, efficient psychiatric interviews. The long stories families recounted to an ethnographer with hours to listen disturbed scientific sensibilities: Stories of sorcery causing madness and of lawsuits against sorcerers (Wilce 2004a). When families take deviant members to psychiatrists, their stories stay home, although, in at least a few cases, families' stories can still come to reflect something of the psychiatrist's rationalized, disenchanted discourse.

Genres are distinct from discursive registers—repertoires of linguistic forms understood locally as different ways of saying the same thing. Registers index such things as speaker role or status (Agha 2007). A shamanic register (Briggs 1996) is not how shamans speak at all times but is instead a toolkit with which they do something, sometimes. We perform work-related social identities using one register and other identities with other registers elsewhere. Medical registers of German (Weber & Engstrom 1997), French (Goldstein 1987), English (Atkinson 1992, Berkenkotter 2008), or other languages (Lee 1999, Liebeskind 2002, Wilce 2008) may be performed in many genres—textbooks or chart notes, for example. Performing medical interviews (another genre) might mean alternating between an esoteric medical register and an everyday register in which patients are more comfortable, mirroring the alternation of registers in Warao shamanic discourse (Briggs 1996). The process by which registers emerge and become recognizable—"enregisterment" (Agha 2007)—attracts increasing attention, and we return to it below.

CONTRIBUTIONS TO THE STUDY OF MEDICAL DISCOURSE

The last section of this article surveys attempts to address issues such as medical authority (from a CA perspective) or power (particularly medicine's incitement to discourse) and the ways in which local medical interactions reflect the global circulation of discourse forms.

Authority in Conversation

CA has provided at least some of the inspiration for many close analyses of medical discourse (Mishler 1984). CA highlights emergent coconstruction of meaning, denying for instance that doctors unilaterally impose diagnoses or therapies (Engeström 1999, Maynard & Frankel 2003). Like all interlocutors, doctors and patients are accountable to each other, i.e., they have an "obligation to index the grounds on which their conclusions are formed" (Heritage 2005, p. 92). News deliveries follow the same rules in the clinic as in conversation (Gillotti et al. 2002, Peräkylä 1998, Wittenberg-Lyles et al. 2008), particularly a preference for foreshadowing revelations. Bluntness, however, is another strategy medical personnel may follow in certain circumstances, not to assert power but for immediate interactional reasons, e.g., to break through resistance (Maynard 2003).

A rare example of raw power may be the case of company doctors urging workers complaining of illness back to their jobs, downplaying the seriousness of complaints (Mishler 1984, Waitzkin 1991). More universal is the healer's power to "name the world" (Heritage 2005, p. 99). Yet clients also have some authority (regarding their own experience) and influence. Parents sometimes demand antibiotics for their children (Stivers 2002), leading doctors to push back—or negotiate (Stivers 2005). Physicians in other circumstances may secure patient agreement by offerings grounds, early on, for diagnoses announced later (Mangione-Smith et al. 2003). Eliciting patients' perspectives at an appropriate juncture (Gill & Maynard 2006) may not compromise health workers' authority, but rather prevent miscommunication that contributes, for example, to relatively high rates of amniocentesis refusal by Mexican-origin clients in genetic counseling (Browner et al. 2003; on discursive strategies for dealing with genetic risk, see Sarangi et al. 2003; on apparently positive instances of misunderstanding, see Sachs 1989). Such "tacit bargaining" (Heritage 2005, p. 99), in which exercises of authority are balanced by "social accountability"—i.e., providing grounds (Peräkylä 1998, 2002; Robinson 2003)—apparently indicates limits on practitioners' authority (on the similar dialogism that emerges in Bangladeshi divination encounters concerning children's health, despite the appearance of ex cathedra authority, see Wilce 2001). Still, if Gill & Maynard (2006) are correct, the "organization of the medical interview" (Cohen-Cole 1991) works—together with tacit agreement by patients and doctors that the information-gathering phase, when patients' perspectives would (ironically) be most relevant, should not be disrupted—to sustain doctors' (or biomedicine's) epistemic authority.

CA-inspired work in the 1980s and 1990s used frequency of interruptions or unilateral topic changes as a token of practitioners' power (Ainsworth-Vaughan 1998, Waitzkin 1991, Wilce 1998; on the difficulty of operationalizing interruptions, see Murray 1985). In one study of gender in clinical interactions, patients succeeded in initiating topic changes only if doctors went along. Doctors' topic changes apparently required no agreement. Male doctors made three times more unilateral topic changes than did female doctors (Ainsworth-Vaughan 1998; compare Todd 1993, Cordella 1999, Uskul & Ahmad 2003). Similarly, doctors may fail to attend to voiced-and-embodied demonstrations of patients' suffering, with consequences for patient health but apparently none for the clinical relationship, whereas patients who ignore doctors threaten that relationship (Heath 1986, p. 98). A more complete understanding of medical authority requires attending to discourse histories beyond a single clinical encounter—whole strings of discursive encounters (Atkinson 1999, Cicourel 1992, Erickson 1999), including discourse involving only care receivers, or familial talk (for a tracking of health complaints from home to practitioners of various kinds, and back again in rural Bangladesh, see Wilce 1998). The next subsection focuses on such histories.

Confessional Production of Modern Subjects

As one who illumined those discourse histories, Foucault (1990 [1978]) posited the productive-power role of medical or therapeutic encounters in constituting modern persons as "subjects in both senses of the word" (p. 60). Medicalization, affecting ever more domains of life, has increasingly commanded anthropologists' attention. The related process of psychologization (Rieff 1987[1966]), rendering ever broader swaths of life therapy-relevant, likewise involves power-laden ideologies of communication, as when using language to express feelings is represented as a value in and of itself. Foucault describes the Catholic mandate to confess sins spreading to medicine, "recodified as [a] therapeutic operation" (1990, p. 67), so that the modern subject "has become a confessing animal" (p. 59). Recent studies (Carr 2006, Smith 2005) have rigorously analyzed the discursive practices and ideologies constituting this Foucaultian regime. Practices that create a putatively therapeutic environment in a drug treatment program for women, for example, involve "incitement to discourse" (Foucault 1990, p. 56). Staff pushes participants toward the discursive style embodied in the motto "Honesty, Openness, and Willingness" (HOW). HOW is an instrument of power. Its insistence that language is a tool for at least potentially truthful reference to inner states (feelings) occludes institutional forces rewarding some discursive acts and punishing others. This referentialist ideology of language works "to minimize the potential of words to point, protest, or critique" (Carr 2006, p. 635).

The dominant ideology in the field of psychotherapy represents client-speakers as entities existing independently of discourse. But Foucault's point was that, by inciting to discourse, therapeutic encounters actively produce subjects oriented to such discourse. Carl Rogers' therapeutic practice, for example, projected an authentic self realizable in therapy (Smith 2005, p. 259). The confessional nature of Rogers' approach, encouraging clients to verbalize epistemic commitments to embodied experience—e.g., to feeling, but also saying, that her cheeks are hot—is a study in contradiction. Psychoanalysts often speak for analysands (Vehviläinen 2008), in putative contrast to Rogers' nondirective means of guiding clients to insight. In fact, however, Rogers actively modeled statements of insight, revoicing clients' utterances to make them refer to the embodied present. Rogerian discourse on authenticity may have had an "impact . . . on folk concepts of selfhood" (Smith 2005, p. 270) in post–World War II America. Even biomedical encounters now feature an "incitement to speak"—and speak emotionally—"increasingly construct[ing] the patient, through various discursive practices, as an experiencing, [feeling,] communicating subject" (Peräkylä 1995, pp. 339–40; compare Arney & Bergen 1984).

Local Interaction, Global Circulation

Because sociocultural processes increasingly unfold at intersections of locality and globality, i.e., because of their "glocality" (Brenner 1998), that is where we increasingly find urgently relevant examples of medical discourse. How the ideologies and discursive practices I have just described circulate globally concerns us in this final subsection. We must find ways to track such discourse forms and ideologies circulating in and through local face-to-face encounters. For example, the globally hegemonic ideology of "communicability" (Briggs 2005) reinforces inequalities through its peculiar imaginings of health and communication. Briggs & Mantini-Briggs (2003) provide a shocking account of this deadly ideology traveling to, within, and beyond Venezuela during a cholera epidemic. The ideology of communicability involves nation-states and experts representing some (racialized) groups as agents in medical knowledge production, others as "translators and disseminators, others . . . receivers, and some simply out of the game" (Briggs 2005, p. 274). Evidence of that grand-scale process

also emerges in a CA-driven study in Los Angeles County, where the race and education level of parents determine how directly some doctors interact with child-patients (Stivers & Majid 2007).

When Langford (2002) visits an Ayurvedic doctor in India to discuss her condition, the popular practitioner also reports having found the true essence of Ayurveda—in treating foreigners. South Asia is the site of newly imported genres of medical discourse, e.g., the psychiatric/psychological advice column (Halliburton 2005, Wilce 2008). Psychiatric discourse in magazines and newspapers has not displaced possession and exorcism in south India. Yet, whereas decades ago in Kerala troublesome spirits had distinct names and personalities, today they introduce themselves with generic names, much like the spirits exorcised by charismatic Catholics in the United States (Csordas 1997). Similarly, Cherokee medical texts underwent a transformation from the late-nineteenth to the mid-twentieth century, involving a loosening of the texts' indexicality, their contextual groundedness. Before the forced migration of the Cherokee people, medicinal texts evoked and activated the healing relevance of "the geocosmological surround" (Bender, n.d., p. 17)—crucially, the cardinal directions and the colors associated with them. Texts dating after the removal, by contrast, invoked signs such as colors and "spirits for their general symbolism rather than their attachments to place and indexical centering potential" (p. 36). Such combinations of continuity and change exemplify medical discourse's glocality.

Translation/interpretation. The exploding global circulation of people, goods, and ideas that defines late modernity necessitates armies of medical interpreters or translators. Too many in those armies are unpaid conscripts—patients' family members, including nonadult children (Cohen et al. 1999); hospital staff untrained as interpreters (Elderkin-Thompson et al. 2001); even strangers in waiting rooms

Indexical: a word, gesture, etc. having as its meaning the particular way that it invokes or creates contextual features (spatial, temporal, or social)

(Flores 2006). Interpreters do not convey everything patients say, resulting in distortion (Aranguri et al. 2006). Patients' children are especially likely to avoid sensitive issues (Flores 2006). The ad hoc approach to medical interpretation in the United States reflects the devaluation of subordinate languages and their speakers, i.e., racialized classes of people who become associated with "ignorance" (Briggs 2005)—a paradox, given the institutional reproduction of ignorance of linguistic diversity that renders medical communication difficult.

Interpreters and their particular communicative styles affect clinical outcomes (Preloran et al. 2005). But translation in and beyond the clinic involves more than clear transfer of information across difference; it involves power (Giordano 2008). A Xhosa translation of the Beck Depression Inventory (Beck 1976) was produced in South Africa during apartheid. Taking steps to ensure the translation's "accuracy," including back translation and having "bilinguals take the same test in two languages" (Drennan et al. 1991, p. 367), failed to address "the power differential" (p. 361). The translation team's own discourse reflected the kind of essentializing relativism that buttressed apartheid, including the "folk-Whorfian" (Silverstein 2000) notion that populations either have or lack "a word for [X, e.g., sadness]" and that absences reflect primitiveness. Such discourse structured the team's attempts to grapple with difference and sameness (Drennan et al. 1991, pp. 371–73) and its reproduction of social inequality (compare Yen & Wilbraham 2003).

Textuality. Translated or not, why do some forms of discourse circulate widely while others do not? Discourse is variably coherent, memorable, quotable, and thus "textual." From any instance of speech-in-interaction two kinds of "textuality," or structures of coherence, can emerge: interactional textuality, i.e., the social acts, statuses, and shifts performed in talk (including outcomes like being insulted); and

denotational textuality (Silverstein 2004), the quotable "said"-ness of discourse and forms of patterning involving denotative meanings. Elaborate denotational patternment typifies ritual communication (Silverstein 2004), but even a conversation about one topic hangs together denotatively. The entextualization (memorable patterning) of discourse enables its circulation.

The denotational textuality of the DSM, psychiatry's bible [the American Psychiatric Association's *Diagnostic and Statistical Manual* (APA 2000)], facilitates its global circulation as authoritative discourse. For Gaines (1992, p. 14) its way of dividing illnesses into a very few macrocategories reflects dualisms of mind and body, emotion and thought. This is the DSM's coherence. Psychiatric conferences reproduce DSM categories, as sessions on particular diagnoses legitimize illnesses and their textual matrices; the DSM typically defines what is arguable in such sessions. What happens when anthropologists' writings juxtaposing local versus DSM categories circulate globally? A version of Kleinman's (1986) ethnographic account of *shenjing shuairuo* (SJSR, "neurasthenia") as a diagnostic category in China has entered psychiatric discussions there, motivating the replacement of SJSR with *yiyu zheng* ("depression") (Lee 1999). Kleinman's descriptions of the complex functions of SJSR are rich and politically sensitive but, in their circulation in China, are stripped of ethnographic contextualization. Drug companies now push *yiyu zheng* to Chinese doctors as a more scientific construct than SJSR. Discursive forms—"hard-sell lectures" and presentational "razzmatazz"—have been central to the successful campaign (Lee 1999, pp. 362, 365).

"Psy disciplines" like psychiatry and psychology have "disseminated themselves rapidly" through genres such as the magazine advice column (Rose 1996, p. 34). A Bangladeshi advice column is contributing to the enregisterment of a psychiatric Bangla (the sedimenting of a psychiatric register). The psychiatrist-editors answering readers' letters introduce English DSM disease labels such as "social phobia." Recurrent discourse frames lend the new terms authority. These include an apparently meaningful echo of the English "you are suffering from…," recognizable as authoritative medicalese since the nineteenth century (Wilce 2008, p. 94). The elaborate entextualization that typifies ritual communication ironically appears in the column, as psychiatrists combating the use of charms and Islamic medicine embed DSM labels in a poetics of modernity. Such poetic structuring of at least some of their letter responses and face-to-face encounters with patients and their families—a layering of contrasts (modern/traditional, urban/rural, knowledge/ignorance, etc.)—may add rhetorical punch (Wilce 2008).

Interactional textuality and healing. In cultural context, forms of interactional textuality such as the achievement of coordination in turn taking, or alignment toward a shared sense of the activity at hand, can take on affective meanings such as intimacy. Senegalese patients ground the efficacy of encounters with *sériñ*s (vernacular healers, *marabout*s) in that intimacy, coupled with hierarchy. The *sériñ*s' reciting of Islamic texts in Arabic reproduces hierarchy, whereas initial greeting exchanges marked by intensive latching (turn exchanges with no perceptible intervening pause) create intimacy. "The relative lack of temporal separation between the turns comes to signify a relative lack of interpersonal separation between the speech participants" (Perrino 2002, p. 234). A Senegalese commentator compared the tight coordination of turns to musical harmony and braided hair (Perrino 2002, p. 239). Like denotational textuality, such patterning—albeit interactional and thus more grounded in nonrepeatable context—is memorable, characterizable, and thus repeatable, i.e., circulates across time and space. Its significance becomes clearer in the breach. We have long suspected that attempts by multinational agencies to encourage traditional medicine (TM) through partnerships with biomedicine end up transforming TM (Perrino 2007, p. 1). Perrino's comparative analysis of patients' experiences with *sériñ*s versus *tradipraticiens* at an NGO-funded TM hospital in Senegal shows through careful discourse analysis the loss of the unique traditional form of interactional textuality experienced by patients as healing in itself. No Arabic words are uttered, no Islamic texts are invoked, and a distancing bureaucratic register replaces the conversational performance of intimacy.

CONCLUSION

Studies of medical discourse have contributed to broader anthropological projects including the analysis of ideologies that empower some communicators and stigmatize others as premodern (Briggs 2005). Rooted in close analysis of dyadic clinical encounters and other forms of medical discourse, recent studies trace interactions between globally circulating discourse forms and local traditions that have constituted medical relationships, broadly construed. Textuality, be it denotational (like the DSM's) or interactional, enables discourse to circulate, but competing patterns meet on an unlevel playing field. Further studies focusing on encounters of different forms of textuality, as in Senegal, are called for, as are others investigating how generalizable is the paradoxical affinity of scientific and ritual discourse apparent in the elaborate entextualization of some Bangladeshi psychiatrists' discourse. Finally, given that some studies consistently uncover patient-practitioner collaboration and a degree of agency on the part of patients, whereas others find in somewhat similar settings a straightforward reproduction of power relations, both empirical and theoretical work to illuminate this contradiction are needed. Such studies stand to contribute to critical medical anthropology and to help those seeking not only to describe but to change medical worlds.

SUMMARY POINTS

1. The anthropological significance of medical discourse becomes clear through acquaintance with its scope of variation, its potential for generating particular kinds of subjects, the complexities involved in the reproduction of power and inequality at sites of such discourse, and the ways language and discourse work in general.

2. Medicine as practiced in some sites is becoming increasingly like psychotherapy in requiring patients to speak, and speak emotionally, whereas such speech genres as narrative may be disappearing from other areas of medicine.

3. Instances of medical discourse typically circulate to the extent that they are coherently structured, i.e., that their linguistic expressions and denotative meanings are memorably patterned.

4. The genres and registers typifying medical discourse have histories that we can, and should continue to, trace as they spread to new areas and become part of public culture.

5. The prerequisite for developing effective interventions aimed at improving communication in medical settings is an adequate understanding of site-particular communicative practices—including the linguistic genres and registers in use and ideologies of communication that shape these practices.

DISCLOSURE STATEMENT

The author is not aware of any affiliations, memberships, funding, or financial holdings that might be perceived as affecting the objectivity of this review.

ACKNOWLEDGMENTS

Joel Kuipers's work has inspired my thinking on these matters (Kuipers 1989) and influenced the structure of my review. For reading and commenting on whole or partial drafts, thanks go to Robert Desjarlais, Anssi Peräkylä, Carole Browner, Seamus Decker, Aaron Denham, Sabina Perrino, Arthur Kleinman, Sing Lee, and Elinor Ochs.

LITERATURE CITED

Abu-Lughod L. 1990. The romance of resistance: tracing transformations of power through Bedouin women. *Am. Ethnol.* 17:41–55

Agha A. 2007. *Language and Social Relations.* Cambridge, UK: Cambridge Univ. Press

Ainsworth-Vaughn N. 1998. *Claiming Power in Doctor-Patient Talk.* New York: Oxford Univ. Press

APA (Am. Psychiatr. Assoc.). 2000. *Diagnostic and Statistical Manual of Mental Disorders: DSM-IV-TR.* Washington, DC: Am. Psychiatr. Assoc.

Aranguri C, Davidson B, Ramirez R. 2006. Patterns of communication through interpreters: a detailed sociolinguistic analysis. *J. Gen. Intern. Med.* 21:623–29

Armstrong D. 1983. *Political Anatomy of the Body: Medical Knowledge in Britain in the Twentieth Century.* Cambridge, UK: Cambridge Univ. Press

Arney WR, Bergen BJ. 1984. *Medicine and the Management of Living: Taming the Last Great Beast.* Chicago: Univ. Chicago Press

Atkinson D. 1992. The evolution of medical research writing from 1735–1985. The case of the Edinburgh Medical Journal. *Appl. Linguist.* 13:337–74

Atkinson P. 1999. Medical discourse, evidentiality and the construction of professional responsibility. See Sarangi & Roberts 1999, pp. 75–107

Bauman R. 1999. Genre. *J. Linguist. Anthropol. (Special Issue: Language Matters in Anthropology: A Lexicon for the Millennium)* 9:84–87

Beck AT. 1976. *Cognitive Therapy and Emotional Disorders*. New York: Int. Univ. Press

Becker AL. 1979. Text-building, epistemology, and aesthetics in Javanese shadow theater. In *The Imagination of Reality*, ed. AL Becker, A Yengoyan, pp. 211–43. Norwood, NJ: ABLEX

Bender M. n.d. *Up to center: indexicality and voice in Cherokee medicinal texts*. Unpubl. manuscr. Contact benderm@wfu.edu

Berkenkotter C. 2008. *Patient Tales: Case Histories and the Uses of Narrative in Psychiatry*. Charleston: Univ. SC Press

Brenner N. 1998. Global cities, glocal states: global city formation and state territorial restructuring in contemporary Europe. *Rev. Int. Pol. Econ.* 5:1–37

Briggs CL. 1996. The meaning of nonsense, the poetics of embodiment, and the production of power in Warao healing. See Laderman & Roseman 1996, pp. 185–232

Briggs CL. 2005. Communicability, racial discourse, and disease. *Annu. Rev. Anthropol.* 34:269–91

Briggs CL, Mantini-Briggs C. 2003. *Stories in the Time of Cholera: Racial Profiling during a Medical Nightmare*. Berkeley: Univ. Calif. Press

Brown MF. 1988. Shamanism and its discontents. *Med. Anthropol. Q.* 2:102–20

Browner CH. 1998. Varieties of reasoning in medical anthropology. *Med. Anthropol. Q.* 12:356–58

Browner CH, Preloran HM, Casado MC, Bass HN, Walker AP. 2003. Genetic counseling gone awry: miscommunication between prenatal genetic service providers and Mexican-origin clients. *Soc. Sci. Med.* 56:1933–46

Capps L, Ochs E. 1995. *Constructing Panic: The Discourse of Agoraphobia*. Cambridge, MA: Harvard Univ. Press

Carr ES. 2006. "Secrets keep you sick": metalinguistic labor in a drug treatment program for homeless women. *Lang. Soc.* 35:631–53

Cicourel AV. 1992. The interpenetration of communicative contexts: examples from medical encounters. In *Rethinking Context: Language as an Interactive Phenomenon*, ed. A Duranti, C Goodwin, pp. 291–310. Cambridge, UK: Cambridge Univ. Press

Cohen S, Moran-Ellis J, Smaje C. 1999. Children as informal interpreters in GP consultations: pragmatics and ideology. *Soc. Health Illn.* 21:163–86

Cohen-Cole S. 1991. *The Medical Interview: The Three-Function Approach*. St. Louis: Mosby-Year Book

Coker EM. 2003. Narrative strategies in medical discourse: constructing the psychiatric "case" in a nonwestern setting. *Soc. Sci. Med.* 57:905–16

Condon WS, Ogston WD. 1966. Sound film analysis of normal and pathological behavior patterns. *J. Nerv. Mental Dis.* 143:338–47

Cooper LA, Roter DL, Johnson RL, Ford DE, Steinwachs DM, Powe NR. 2003. Patient-centered communication, ratings of care, and concordance of patient and physician race. *Ann. Intern. Med.* 139:907–15

Cordella M. 1999. Medical discourse in a Hispanic environment: power and *simpatía* under examination. *Aust. Rev. Appl. Linguist.* 22:35–50

Csordas TJ. 1997. *Language, Charisma, and Creativity: The Ritual Life of a Religious Movement*. Berkeley: Univ. Calif. Press

Desjarlais RR. 1996. Presence. See Laderman & Roseman 1996, pp. 143–64

Desjarlais RR. 1997. *Shelter Blues: Sanity and Selfhood Among the Homeless*. Philadelphia: Univ. Penn. Press

Dow J. 1986. Universal aspects of symbolic healing: a theoretical synthesis. *Am. Anthropol.* 88:56–69

Drennan G, Levett A, Swartz L. 1991. Hidden dimensions of power and resistance in the translation process: a South African study. *Cult. Med. Psychiatry* 15:361–81

Elderkin-Thompson V, Silver RC, Waitzkin H. 2001. When nurses double as interpreters: a study of Spanish-speaking patients in a US primary care setting. *Soc. Sci. Med.* 52:1343–58

Engeström R. 1995. Voice as communicative action. *Mind Cult. Act.* 2:192–215

Engeström R. 1999. Imagine the world you want to live in: a study on developmental change in doctor-patient interaction. *OUTLINES* 1:33–50

Erickson F. 1999. Appropriation of voice and presentation of self as a fellow physician: aspects of a discourse of apprenticeship in medicine. See Sarangi & Roberts 1999, pp. 109–44

Farmer P. 1994. AIDS-talk and the constitution of cultural models. *Soc. Sci. Med.* 38:801–9

Flores G. 2006. Language barriers to health care in the United States. *N. Engl. J. Med.* 355:229–31

Foucault M. 1965 [1961]. *The Birth of the Clinic: An Archaeology of Medical Perception*. New York: Vintage

Foucault M. 1990 [1978]. *The History of Sexuality: An Introduction*. New York: Vintage

Fox RC. 1957. Training for uncertainty. In *The Student-Physician*, ed. RK Merton, GG Reader, pp. 207–41. Cambridge, MA: Harvard Univ. Press

Gaines A. 1992. From DSM-I to DSM-IIIR: voices of self, mastery and the Other: a cultural constructivist reading of U.S. psychiatric classification. *Soc. Sci. Med.* 35:3–24

Garfinkel H. 1967. *Studies in Ethnomethodology*. Englewood Cliffs, NJ: Prentice-Hall

Garro LC. 2000. Cultural knowledge as resource in illness narratives: remembering through accounts of illness. See Mattingly & Garro 2000, pp. 70–87

Gill VT, Maynard DW. 2006. Explaining illness: patients' proposals and physicians' responses. See Heritage & Maynard 2006a, pp. 115–50

Gillotti C, Thompson T, McNeilis K. 2002. Communicative competence in the delivery of bad news. *Soc. Sci. Med.* 54:1011–23

Giordano C. 2008. Practices of translation and the making of migrant subjectivities in contemporary Italy. *Am. Ethnol.* 35(4):588–606

Goldstein J. 1987. *Console and Classify: The French Psychiatric Profession in the Nineteenth Century*. New York: Cambridge Univ. Press

Good BJ. 1994. *Medicine, Rationality, and Experience: An Anthropological Perspective*. Cambridge, UK: Cambridge Univ. Press

Good B, Good MJD, Togan I, Ilbars Z, Güvener A, Gelisen I. 1994. In the subjunctive mode: epilepsy narratives in Turkey. *Soc. Sci. Med.* 38:835–42

Good M-JD, Munakata T, Koybayashi Y, Mattingly C, Good BJ. 1994. Oncology and narrative time. *Soc. Sci. Med.* 38:855–62

Haakana M. 2001. Laughter as a patient's resource: dealing with delicate aspects of medical interaction. *Text* 21:187–219

Hadder N. 2007. *Apparitions of difference*. PhD thesis, Univ. Tex., Austin

Halliburton M. 2005. "Just some spirits": the erosion of spirit possession and the rise of "tension" in South India. *Med. Anthropol.* 24:111–44

Hamilton H. 2004. Symptoms and signs in particular: the influence of the medical concern on the shape of physician-patient talk. *Commun. Med.* 1:59–70

Heath C. 1986. *Body Movement and Speech in Medical Interaction*. Cambridge, UK: Cambridge Univ. Press

Heath C. 2002. Demonstrative suffering: the gestural (re)embodiment of symptoms. *J. Commun.* 52:597–617

Heath C. 2006. Body work: the collaborative production of the clinical object. See Heritage & Maynard 2006a, pp. 185–213

Heritage J. 2005. Revisiting authority in physician-patient interaction. In *Diagnosis as Cultural Practice*, ed. JF Duchan, D Kovarsky, pp. 83–102. New York: Mouton De Gruyter

Heritage J, Maynard DW, eds. 2006a. *Communication in Medical Care: Interaction Between Primary Care Physicians and Patients*. Cambridge, UK: Cambridge Univ. Press

Heritage J, Maynard DW. 2006b. Problems and prospects in the study of physician-patient interaction: 30 years of research. *Annu. Rev. Sociol.* 32:351–74

Hill J. 2008. *The Everyday Language of White Racism in the United States*. Malden, MA: Wiley-Blackwell

Hindmarsh J, Pilnick A. 2002. The tacit order of teamwork: collaboration and embodied conduct in anesthesia. *Sociol. Q.* 43:139–64

Hobbs P. 2003. The role of progress notes in the professional socialization of medical residents. *J. Pragmat.* 36:1579–607

Hodge FS, Fredericks L, Rodriguez BT. 1996. American Indian women's talking circle. A cervical cancer screening and prevention project. *Cancer* 78:1592–97

Humphrey C. 2005. *Narrative negotiations of decompression sickness and modernity among Miskitu Indian lobster divers of Corn Island, Nicaragua*. MA thesis, Dep. Anthropol., North. Ariz. Univ., Flagstaff, AZ

Jefferson G, Lee JRE. 1992. The rejection of advice: managing the problematic convergence of a "troubles-telling" and a "service encounter". In *Talk at Work: Interaction in Institutional Settings*, ed. P Drew, J Heritage, pp. 521–48. Cambridge, UK: Cambridge Univ. Press

Kirmayer LJ. 2000. Broken narratives: clinical encounters and the poetics of illness experience. See Mattingly & Garro 2000, pp. 153–80

Kleinman A. 1986. *The Social Origins of Distress and Disease*. New Haven/London: Yale Univ. Press

Kleinman A. 1988. *The Illness Narratives: Suffering, Healing, and the Human Condition*. New York: Basic Books

Kleinman A, Benson P. 2006. Anthropology in the clinic: the problem of cultural competency and how to fix it. *PLoS Med.* 3:1673–76

Kockelman P. 2007. Agency: the relation between meaning, power, and knowledge. *Curr. Anthropol.* 48:375–401

Koschmann T, LeBaron C, Goodwin C, Zemel A, Dunnington G. 2007. Formulating the triangle of doom. *Gesture* 7:97–118

Kraepelin E. 1883. *Compendium der Psychiatrie*. Leipzig: Ambrosius Abel

Kraepelin E. 1985. Depressed stages of maniacal-depressive insanity (circular stupor). In *Lectures on Clinical Psychiatry*, ed. E Kraepelin, T Johnstone, pp. 11–20. New York: Hafner

Kuipers JC. 1989. "Medical discourse" in anthropological context: views of language and power. *Med. Anthropol. Q.* 3:99–123

Labov W, Fanshel D. 1977. *Therapeutic Discourse: Psychotherapy as Conversation*. New York: Acad. Press

Laderman C. 1987. The ambiguity of symbols in the structure of healing. *Soc. Sci. Med.* 24:293–301

Laderman C, Roseman M, eds. *The Performance of Healing*. New York: Routledge

Langford JM. 2002. *Fluent Bodies: Ayurvedic Remedies for Postcolonial Imbalance*. Durham/London: Duke Univ. Press

Lee S. 1999. Diagnosis postponed: Shenjing shuairuo and the transformation of psychiatry in post-Mao China. *Cult. Med. Psychiatry* 23:349–80

Lévi-Strauss C. 1963. The effectiveness of symbols. In *Structural Anthropology*, pp. 186–205. New York: Basic Books

Liebeskind C. 2002. Arguing science: Unani *tibb*, hakims, and biomedicine in India, 1900–50. In *Plural Medicine, Tradition and Modernity, 1800–2000*, ed. W Ernst, pp. 58–75. London/New York: Routledge

Linthorst GE, Daniels JMA, van Westerloo DJ. 2007. The majority of bold statements expressed during grand rounds lack scientific merit. *Med. Educ.* 41:965–67

Luhrmann T. 2000. *Of Two Minds: An Anthropologist Looks at American Psychiatry*. New York: Vintage

MacDonald MN. 2002. Pedagogy, pathology and ideology: the production, transmission and reproduction of medical discourse. *Discourse Soc.* 13:447–67

Mangione-Smith R, Stivers T, Elliott M, McDonald L, Heritage J. 2003. Online commentary during the physical examination: a communication tool for avoiding inappropriate antibiotic prescribing? *Soc. Sci. Med.* 56:313–20

Marinker M. 2000. The medium and the message. *Patient Educ. Couns.* 41:117–25

Martin E. 1992. AES Distinguished Lecture: The end of the body? *Am. Ethnol.* 19:121–40

Mattingly C. 1998a. *Healing Dramas and Clinical Plots: The Narrative Structure of Experience*. Cambridge, UK: Cambridge Univ. Press

Mattingly C. 1998b. In search of the good: narrative reasoning in clinical practice. *Med. Anthropol. Q.* 12:273–97

Mattingly C, Garro LC, eds. 2000. *Narrative and the Cultural Construction of Illness and Healing*. Berkeley: Univ. Calif. Press

Maynard DW. 2003. *Bad News, Good News: Conversational Order in Everyday Talk and Clinical Settings*. Chicago: Univ. Chicago Press

Maynard DW, Frankel RM. 2003. Indeterminacy and uncertainty in the delivery of diagnostic news in internal medicine: a single case analysis. In *Studies in Language and Social Interaction: Essays in Honor of Robert Hopper*, ed. P Glenn, C LeBaron, pp. 383–410. Mahwah, NJ: Lawrence Erlbaum

Maynard DW, Heritage J. 2005. Conversation analysis, doctor-patient interaction and medical communication [Series/Article Genre: Making Sense of Qualitative Research]. *Med. Educ.* 39:428–35

Milne D, Howard W. 2000. Rethinking the role of diagnosis in Navajo religious healing. *Med. Anthropol. Q.* 14:543–70

Mishler EG. 1984. *The Discourse of Medicine: Dialectics of Medical Interviews*. Norwood, NJ: ABLEX

Murray SO. 1985. Toward a model of members' methods for recognizing interruptions. *Lang. Soc.* 14:31–40

Nuckolls C. 1991. Deciding how to decide: possession-mediumship in Jalari divination. *Med. Anthropol.* 13:57–82

Ochs E, Capps L. 2001. *Living Narrative: Creating Lives in Everyday Storytelling*. Cambridge, MA: Harvard Univ. Press

Peräkylä A. 1995. *AIDS Counseling*. Cambridge, UK: Cambridge Univ. Press

Peräkylä A. 1998. Authority and accountability: the delivery of diagnosis in primary health care. *Soc. Psychol. Q.* 61:301–20

Peräkylä A. 2002. Agency and authority: extended responses to diagnostic statements in primary care encounters. *Res. Lang. Soc. Interact.* 35:219–47

Perrino SM. 2002. Intimate hierarchies and Qur'anic saliva (tefli): textuality in a Senegalese ethnomedical encounter. *J. Linguist. Anthropol.* 12:225–59

Perrino SM. 2007. *Intimacy and global biomedicine in Senegalese ethnomedical encounters*. Presented at 106th Annu. Meet. Am. Anthropol. Assoc., Washington, DC

Pigg SL. 1996. The credible and the credulous: the question of 'villager's beliefs' in Nepal. *Cult. Anthropol.* 11:160–201

Pinel P. 1801. *Traité Médico-Philosophique sur L'aliénation Mentale, ou la Manie*. Paris: Richard, Caille et Ravier

Preloran HM, Browner CH, Lieber E. 2005. Impact of interpreters' approach on Latinas' use of amniocentesis. *Health Educ. Behav.* 32:599–612

Radley A, Mayberry J, Pearce M. 2008. Time, space and opportunity in the outpatient consultation: "the doctor's story". *Soc. Sci. Med.* 66:1484–96

Ribeiro BT. 1994. *Coherence in Psychotic Discourse*. New York: Oxford Univ. Press

Rieff P. 1987 [1966]. *The Triumph of the Therapeutic*. Chicago: Univ. Chicago

Roberts C, Sarangi S. 1999. Hybridity in gatekeeping discourse: issues of practical relevance for the researcher. See Sarangi & Roberts 1999, pp. 473–503

Roberts C, Sarangi S, Moss B. 2004. Presentation of self and symptoms in primary care consultations involving patients from non-English speaking backgrounds. *Commun. Med.* 1:159–69

Roberts C, Wass V, Jones R, Moss B, Sarangi S. 2005. Misunderstandings: a qualitative study of primary care consultations in multi-lingual settings, and educational implications. *Med. Educ.* 39:465–75

Robinson JD. 2003. An interactional structure of medical activities during acute visits and its implications for patients' participation. *Health Commun.* 15:27–59

Rose N. 1996. *Inventing Our Selves: Psychology*. Cambridge, UK: Cambridge Univ. Press

Roseman M. 1991. *Healing Sounds from the Malaysian Rainforest: Temiar Music and Medicine*. Berkeley: Univ. Calif. Press

Ruusuvuori J. 2001. Looking means listening: coordinating displays of engagement in doctor-patient interaction. *Soc. Sci. Med.* 52:1093–108

Sachs L. 1989. Misunderstanding as therapy: doctors, patients and medicines in a rural clinic in Sri Lanka. *Cult. Med. Psychiatry* 13:355–49

Salmon P, Hall GM. 2003. Patient empowerment and control: a psychological discourse in the service of medicine. *Soc. Sci. Med.* 57:1969–80

Sansom B. 1982. The sick who do not speak. In *Semantic Anthropology*, ed. DJ Parkin, pp. 183–96. London: Acad. Press

Santiago-Irizarry V. 2001. *Medicalizing Ethnicity: The Construction of Latino Identity in a Psychiatric Setting*. Ithaca, NY: Cornell Univ. Press

Sarangi S, Bennert K, Howell L, Clarke A. 2003. 'Relatively speaking': relativisation of genetic risk in counseling for predictive testing. *Health Risk Soc.* 5:155–70

Sarangi S, Roberts C, eds. 1999. *Talk, Work and Institutional Order: Discourse in Medical, Mediation and Management Settings*. Berlin: Mouton de Gruyter

Scheflen AE. 1973. *Communicational Structure: Analysis of a Psychotherapy Transaction*. Bloomington: Indiana Univ. Press

Sherzer J. 1983. *Kuna Ways of Speaking*. Austin: Univ. Tex. Press

Silverstein M. 2000. Whorfianism and the linguistic imagination of nationality. In *Regimes of Language: Ideologies, Polities, and Identities*, ed. P Kroskrity, pp. 85–138. Santa Fe: Sch. Am. Res.

Silverstein M. 2004. "Cultural" concepts and the language-culture nexus. *Curr. Anthropol.* 45:621–52

Smith B. 2005. Ideologies of the speaking subject in the psychotherapeutic theory and practice of Carl Rogers. *J. Linguist. Anthropol.* 15:258–72

Stivers T. 2002. Participating in decisions about treatment: overt parent pressure for antibiotic medication in pediatric encounters. *Soc. Sci. Med.* 54:1111–30

Stivers T. 2005. Parent resistance to physicians' treatment recommendations: one resource for initiating a negotiation of the treatment decision. *Health Commun.* 18:41–74

Stivers T, Majid A. 2007. Questioning children: interactional evidence of implicit bias in medical interviews. *Soc. Psychol. Q.* 70:424–41

Summerfield D. 1995. Assisting survivors of war and atrocity: short notes on "psychosocial" issues for NGO workers. *Dev. Pract.* 5:352–56

Todd AD. 1993. Exploring women's experiences: power and resistance in medical discourse. In *The Social Organization of Doctor-Patient Communication*, ed. AD Todd, S Fisher, pp. 267–85. Norwood, NJ: Ablex

Toelken B. 1987. Life and death in the Navajo coyote tales. In *Recovering the Word: Essays on Native American Literature*, ed. B Swann, A Krupat, pp. 388–401. Berkeley: Univ. Calif. Press

Uskul AK, Ahmad F. 2003. Physician–patient interaction: a gynecology clinic in Turkey. *Soc. Sci. Med.* 57:205–15

Vehviläinen S. 2008. Focus on the patient's action: identifying and managing resistance in psychoanalytic interaction. In *Conversation Analysis and Psychotherapy*, ed. A Peräkylä, C Antaki, S Vehviläinen, I Leudar, pp. 120–38. Cambridge, UK: Cambridge Univ. Press

Waitzkin H. 1991. *The Politics of Medical Encounters*. New Haven, CT: Yale Univ. Press

Weber MM, Engstrom EJ. 1997. Kraepelin's 'diagnostic cards': the confluence of clinical research and preconceived categories. *Hist. Psychiatry* 8:374–85

Wilce JM. 1998. *Eloquence in Trouble: The Poetics and Politics of Complaint in Rural Bangladesh*. New York: Oxford Univ. Press

Wilce JM. 2001. Divining TROUBLES or diVINing troubles? gender, conflict, and polysemy in Bangladeshi divination. *Anthropol. Q.* 74:190–99

Wilce JM. 2004a. Madness, fear, and control in Bangladesh: clashing bodies of power/knowledge. *Med. Anthropol. Q.* 18:357–75

Wilce JM. 2004b. To "speak beautifully" in Bangladesh: subjectivity as pāgālmī. In *Schizophrenia, Culture, and Subjectivity: The Edge of Experience*, ed. JH Jenkins, RJ Barrett, pp. 196–218. New York: Cambridge Univ. Press

Wilce JM. 2005. Narrative transformations: emotion, language, and globalization. In *Companion to Psychological Anthropology: Modernity and Psychocultural Change*, ed. C Casey, R Edgerton, pp. 123–39. Malden, MA: Blackwell

Wilce JM. 2008. Scientizing Bangladeshi psychiatry: parallelism, enregisterment, and the cure for a magic complex. *Lang. Soc.* 37:91–114

Wittenberg-Lyles EM, Goldsmith J, Sanchez-Reilly S, Ragan SL. 2008. Communicating a terminal prognosis in a palliative care setting: deficiencies in current communication training protocols. *Soc. Sci. Med.* 66:2356–65

Yen J, Wilbraham L. 2003. Discourses of culture and illness in South African mental health care and indigenous healing. Part I: Western psychiatric power. *Transcult. Psychiatry* 40:542–61

State Emergence
in Early China

Li Liu

Archaeology Program, School of Historical and European Studies, La Trobe University, Melbourne VIC 3086, Australia; email: l.liu@latrobe.edu.au

Annu. Rev. Anthropol. 2009. 38:217–32

First published online as a Review in Advance on June 19, 2009

The *Annual Review of Anthropology* is online at anthro.annualreviews.org

This article's doi:
10.1146/annurev-anthro-091908-164513

0084-6570/09/1021-0217$20.00

Key Words

Chinese civilization, Longshan culture, Xia dynasty, Erlitou

Abstract

Questions relating to state emergence in China are often intertwined with the origins of early dynasties. This subject involves many disciplines, including archaeology, history, and anthropology, and scholars from these fields often employ different definitions for states/civilization, use various approaches, and address diverse issues. This article intends to provide an overview of major archaeological findings, approaches, interpretations, and debates on certain issues. Controversial questions include whether some of late Neolithic polities can be considered early states, and whether ancient textual accounts can be used to guide archaeological interpretations. It may not be possible in the near future to alter the historiographically determined approach, which pervades Chinese archaeology, but social-archaeology methods for investigating the political-economic system on regional and interregional scales have proven productive.

INTRODUCTION

China is one of the oldest civilizations in the world and also has a long historical record, which provides rich information concerning China's cultural origins. Questions relating to state emergence are often intertwined with the development of early dynasties. This subject involves many disciplines, including archaeology, history, and anthropology, and scholars from these fields often employ different approaches and address different issues. This article provides an overview of major archaeological findings, different approaches, diverse interpretations, and debates on certain issues. Because this review is written for English readers, I use primarily English sources when available. The chronology and location of major archaeological cultures and sites relevant to this study are shown in **Table 1** and **Figure 1**.

BACKGROUND

Modern archaeology conducted by Chinese archaeologists began in the 1920s and was the result of interplay among the Chinese traditions of historiography, the introduction of Western scientific methodology, and rising nationalism. The primary objective was to reconstruct national history, particularly to reveal the origins of early dynasties: the Xia, Shang, and Zhou, which emerged in the Central Plains of the Middle Yellow River valley (Falkenhausen 1993, Liu & Chen 2001a). The

first site excavated by a Chinese-led archaeology team was Yinxu (the ruins of Yin/Shang) in Anyang, Henan, which has been confirmed as a capital of the late Shang dynasty (Li 1977). This project was the first time that archaeologists proved legends to be real history, i.e., verifiable by material evidence. The success of the Anyang excavations heightened archaeologists' confidence that more remains of early dynasties, especially the Xia and early Shang, could also be found.

Archaeological investigations of the prehistoric period have been significantly influenced by legendary accounts in ancient texts, an approach resulting from the strong historiographical tradition (Falkenhausen 1993) coupled with a research tendency toward the reconstruction of national history (Liu & Xu 2007). In addition, theoretical orientations employed in Chinese archaeology during the second half of the twentieth century were defined primarily by classical evolutionary models derived from Morgan (1963 [1877]), Engels (1972 [1884]), and Childe (1950), which regard social change as a unilineal process (Tong 1995). Such a complex of native and imported intellectual influences has helped to shape the research questions and interpretations relating to the trajectories of early states (Liu 2004, pp. 1–10).

Chinese archaeology has been a fast-developing field in recent decades owing to the rapid economic growth in the country. Several large urban sites, such as Erlitou, Yanshi,

Table 1 Chronology of archaeological cultures concerned

Time (B.C.)	Liao River	Middle Yellow River	Lower Yellow River	Middle Yangzi River	Lower Yangzi River
4000–3000	Hongshan	Yangshao	Dawenkou	Qujialing	Hemudu-Majiabang
3000–2600/2500	Xiaoheyan	Early Longshan			Liangzhu
2600/2500–2000/1900	?	Late Longshan	Longshan	Shijiahe	
1900/1800–1600/1500	Lower Xiajiadian	Erlitou	Yueshi	Lower Zaoshi	Maqiao
1600–1400	?	Erligang	Yueshi-Erligang	Panlongcheng-Baota	
1400–1300		Middle Shang	Yueshi-Shang		
1300–1026		Late Shang			Hushu

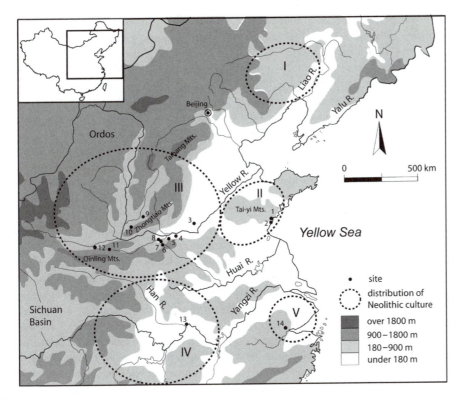

Figure 1

Distribution of cultures and sites mentioned in the text. Cultures: I, Hongshan; II, Dawenkou-Shandong Longshan; III, Yangshao-Longshan; IV, Qujialing; V, Liangzhu. Sites: 1, Liangchengzhen; 2, Yaowangcheng; 3, Anyang/Yinxuj; 4, Zhengzhou; 5, Wangchenggang; 6, Nanwa; 7, Huizui; 8, Erlitou, Yanshi; 9, Taosi; 10, Dongxiafeng; 11, Donglongshan; 12, Laoniupo; 13, Panlongcheng; 14, Mojiaoshan.

Zhengzhou, and Anyang, have been found in the Central Plains where the Xia and Shang dynasties are believed to have emerged. Excavations at these sites have indeed testified to the development of early states there. Many astonishing discoveries have also been made in regions outside the Central Plains, revealing some highly developed Neolithic and Bronze Age cultures with local characteristics. These new findings in the latter category have challenged the traditional view that the most advanced civilization centers first emerged in the Central Plains and then diffused to the surrounding regions. As a result, Chang (1986) and Su (Su & Yin 1981, Wang 1997) developed new interpretations, emphasizing the importance of regional interactions prior to the rise of early states/civilizations.

Su's *quxi leixing* (regional systems and local cultural series) model describes regional variations of archaeological culture and diverse trajectories toward civilization in different parts of China (Su 1999, Su & Yin 1981, Wang 1997). This model is then coupled with Su's three-part evolutionary hierarchy: *guguo—fangguo—diguo* (archaic state—regional state—empire), which outlines the sociopolitical transformation from the Neolithic to the dynastic periods (Su 1999, pp. 129–67). Despite some strong criticism on the vagueness of these generalizations (An 1993), Su's two models together have become an influential methodological framework in China, encouraging many archaeologists to pursue regional developmental trajectories and to classify their findings into seemingly appropriate evolutionary stages.

Since the 1990s, an increasing number of Sino-foreign collaborative projects have been carried out in China, many focusing on regional settlement patterns in relation to the process of social change and state formation. These projects have covered many regions, including southeast Shandong (Underhill et al. 1998, 2002, 2008), the Huan River valley in northern Henan (Sino-Am. Huan 1998), the Yiluo River in western Henan (Liu & Chen 2007, Liu et al. 2002–2004), and the Liao River in the Northeast (Linduff et al. 2002–2004, Chifeng 2003). These projects have employed more up-to-date methods and theory from Western anthropological archaeology traditions aiming to provide systematic data for the study of social evolution in China. Based on the data generated from these projects, fluctuations in three variables of settlement pattern—site number, size of the largest site, and settlement hierarchy—that are indicative of the degree of social complexity are present in all regions, but each appears to have its unique cycles of social development and decline. The most striking difference among these regions occurred during the first half of the second millennium B.C. when the Central Plains experienced political solidarity and integration, as indicated by the emergence of a large urbanized and state-level political center at Erlitou in the Yiluo basin. In contrast, all other regions witnessed either a perceivable reduction in population density with no observable settlement hierarchy (southeast Shandong and the Huan River region) or decentralized intergroup conflict (the Liao River valley) (Liu & Chen 2001c). These investigations have made significant contributions to our understanding of social change from a cross-regional comparative perspective.

RESEARCH PROBLEMS

There is a lack of consensus about where, when, and how the first state emerged in China. Two problems are primarily responsible for causing confusion. First, the term "state" has been used interchangeably with the word "civilization" in Chinese archaeology literature;

"civilization" occurs more frequently than "state." Because civilization is often used in a more general way than state, and different scholars usually employ different definitions for these two concepts, many interpretations are ambiguous. Nevertheless, two recent studies have attempted to clarify the relationship between these concepts. Allan (2007) argues that a common elite culture, which was associated with a particular set of religious practices, was first crystallized in the region centered at Erlitou. Erlitou thus represents the highest form of political organization (a state) at the early part of the second millennum B.C., whereas the common elite culture associated with Erlitou may be called a civilization. A similar treatment to the two concepts is also given by Yoffee & Li (2009), who suggest that early states as the governmental center of a society were created in cities, whereas a set of cultural values as a civilization was shared by several early microstates. Although the terminology remains a problem, in this review article I do not impose a rigid distinction between the two terms when they were used interchangeably in the original literature.

Second, diverse scholarly traditions exist regarding the relationships between archaeological site/culture and early dynasties mentioned in textual records. This situation also leads to disputes over the nature of early states.

Definitions and Approaches

Investigators use three general approaches to study state formation, which may be traced back to different preferences toward defining the state, as held by particular scholarly traditions.

Xia Nai's approach. The interchangeable usage of civilization/state was first explicitly employed by Xia Nai (1985, p. 81), who wrote that "civilization refers to a society in which the clan system has disintegrated and a state organization with class differentiation has formed." Influenced by Gordon Childe's concept of urban revolution, Xia identified four essential and archaeologically detectable criteria for defining civilization/state: (*a*) state-level political organization (characterized by class differentiation), (*b*) urban center of political, economic, and cultural/religious activity, (*c*) writing, and (*d*) metallurgy. He further suggested that civilization in China had emerged in the Erlitou culture (1900/1800–1500 B.C.) in Henan, at least in its late phase (Xia 1985, pp. 79–106).

Xia (1985, p. 96) regarded himself as a conservative archaeologist. When Xia published his article on the origins of Chinese civilization in the 1980s, Erlitou was the only site revealing archaeological evidence that met his criteria for a state. The current archaeological record shows that the level of social complexity observable at Erlitou has not been surpassed by any archaeological cultures prior to or contemporary with it (more discussion below). This approach, which emphasizes hard archaeological evidence with less concern for textual information, has not been very popular in China. Most publications relating to the Erlitou culture attempt to provide it with dynastic affiliations (see Du & Xu 2006, Inst. Archaeol. 2003). However, some new research has shown that Xia's principle needs to be reconsidered; archaeological information and historical records relating to prehistoric societies should be dealt with independently before they can be considered together (Liu 2004, pp. 9–10; Liu & Chen 2003; Liu & Xu 2007).

Su Bingqi's approach. Su Bingqi (1999) took a more radical approach than Xia Nai, using the term civilization loosely and without a clear definition. He traced the early development of some cultural traits to the Neolithic period more than 5000 years ago and described these traits as signifying the dawn of civilization, manifest in archaic states. These characteristics include walled settlements, jade objects with dragon designs, large public architecture, and burial differentiation. Because such traits could be found in many regions, Su (1999) described this situation as *mantian xingdou* ("the sky full of stars") at the dawn of civilization. He further suggested that there were many regional trajectories toward civilization and that such processes started more than 5000 years ago. He also proposed three pathways to early states in

different regions: fission, clash, and amalgamation (pp. 119–27). The examples he used highlight changes in artifactual styles and archaeological features found in different sites over several thousand years; therefore, Su's models seem to be related more to general cultural evolution than to the process of state formation.

Su's view has been shared by many archaeologists and historians in China, who believe that the origins of civilization/state should be traced back to Neolithic times (e.g., Li 1997, Yan 2000, Zhang 2000). Examples of these early civilizations include many archaeological cultures, such as Late Yangshao, Hongshan, Dawenkou, Qujialing, Liangzhu, and Longshan, dating to the fifth through third millennia B.C. (Zhang 2000). In these studies, the presence of hierarchical society and construction of public buildings and settlement fortifications are most frequently cited as marking the emergence of early states (e.g., Li 1997, pp. 7–10). Although opposing views have appeared (e.g., An 1993, Chen 1987), this approach seems to have gained more momentum in recent years, as new discoveries from several late Neolithic cultures have shown construction of large-scale public architecture, such as rammed-earth enclosure, and evolution of rather advanced social organization during the third millennium B.C. These discoveries of complex Neolithic societies are particularly exemplified by Taosi in southern Shanxi, Wangchenggang in central Henan, and the Liangzhu site cluster in Yuhang, Zhejiang. They all show large rammed-earth enclosures (more discussion below).

Social archaeological approach. Two Sino-foreign collaborative and interdisciplinary projects in southeast Shandong and the Yiluo basin (Henan) are also concerned with issues of state formation. These projects, involving full-coverage regional survey and excavation, employ the methodology of settlement archaeology to study social change from a regional perspective (e.g., Adams & Jones 1981, Feinman 1995, Fish & Kowalewski 1990, Kowalewski 1989, Wilson 1988, Wright 1984). For this approach, a state is defined as a society with a minimum of two social strata: a professional ruling class and a commoner class. The ruling class is characterized by a centralized decision-making process, which is both externally specialized, with regard to the local processes it regulates, and internally specialized in that the central process is divisible into separate activities, which can be performed in different places at different times (Marcus & Feinman 1998, p. 4; Wright 1977, p. 383). Furthermore, a state-level social organization often develops at minimum a four-tiered regional settlement hierarchy, equivalent to three or more levels of political hierarchy (Earle 1991, p. 3; Flannery 1998, pp. 16–21; Wright 1977, p. 389; Wright & Johnson 1975).

In southeastern Shandong, settlement patterns show a long period of population development and decline from the Neolithic to the Han dynasty (~3000 B.C.–A.D. 200). During the late Neolithic Longshan culture (2600–2000 B.C.) the research region (1120 km^2) witnessed the rise of two very large centers at Liangchengzhen (272.5 ha) and Yaowangcheng (367.5 ha), each dominating a settlement system with three tiers of political hierarchy (Underhill et al. 2008). Extensive excavations at Liangchengzhen show that this settlement was densely populated, was enclosed by ditches (Sino-Am. Collab. 2004), and functioned as a center of craft production for making stone tools (Bennett 2008, Cunnar 2007) and possibly jade objects (Liu 1988). All these findings seem to suggest a state-level social organization, although the project team hesitates to claim that these developments amount to state formation before investigators can carry out further excavations (Underhill et al. 2008).

In the Yiluo region, settlement patterns show a rapid process of population nucleation during the Erlitou period, when a large urban center developed at the Erlitou site (300 ha) and the settlement system in the survey region (860 km^2) shows three tiers of political hierarchy (Erlitou 2005, Liu et al. 2002–2004). On the basis of archaeological information from regional surveys and excavations performed at Erlitou and other sites within and beyond the Yiluo basin, there is little doubt that Erlitou developed into a state-level society (Lee 2004, Liu 2006, Liu et al. 2007, Liu & Chen 2003) (more discussion below).

Archaeology versus Textual Record

China's long historical record provides rich information concerning its cultural origins, which often refer to the Three Sovereigns, Five Emperors, and Three Dynasties (Xia, Shang and Zhou; ~2100–200 B.C.). In archaeology, although the discovery of Yinxu was an encouraging success, it has proven difficult and controversial to match archaeological sites with prehistoric cities or places mentioned in historical accounts, which may be treated as legends and oral history (Liu & Xu 2007). Nevertheless, many Chinese archaeologists are determined to search for the cultural remains of early dynasties, particularly the Xia, and the final goal is to reconstruct a dynastic history by integrating archaeological data with the received historical record, including legendary traditions (Inst. Archaeol. 2003, pp. 21–23). This approach has been heightened by several state-organized projects, namely the Xia-Shang-Zhou Chronology Project in the 1990s and the subsequently developed Searching for the Origins of Chinese Civilization Project. Both projects have employed interdisciplinary approaches. The former aimed to provide the traditional historiographic accounts a firmer chronological base (Lee 2002), whereas the latter attempts to determine dynastic origins and the earliest civilizations in the Neolithic times and early Bronze Age (Yuan & Campbell 2008).

During recent decades several ancient urban sites have been unearthed in the Central Plains, and some of them indeed roughly coincide in time and space with early dynastic capitals recorded in ancient texts. Much of the discussion has been focused on the site of Erlitou, but judgments about it are controversial. Many archaeologists have been concerned primarily with the correlation between this site and early dynasties, either Xia or Shang (see summary in Liu & Xu 2007), and the majority of them believe that Erlitou represents the material remains of a capital city of the late Xia dynasty (e.g., Chang 1999, Childs-Johnson 1995, Du 1991, Gao et al. 1998, Li 1997, Zou 1980). Furthermore, the efforts to identify the Xia dynasty have been extended to the Late Neolithic period in recent years, as some large Neolithic sites enclosed with walls or ditches have been found at Wangchenggang and Xinzhai, both in central Henan (Cent. Stud. Anc. Civiliz. 2004, Sch. Archaeol. Museol. Peking Univ. 2007).

However, not all researchers in China agree to connect archaeological sites with prehistoric polities mentioned in ancient textual accounts (e.g., Wang 2006), and some are reluctant to affirm a direct link between Erlitou and early dynasties, owing to insufficient evidence (Liu & Chen 2003, Liu & Xu 2007, Xia 1985). Many sinologists in the West are particularly skeptical about the reliability of textual information—and thus about the claimed historical connection between Erlitou and Xia (e.g., Allan 1991; Bagley 1999, pp. 130–31; Keightley 1983; Linduff 1998, p. 629; Thorp 1991, 2006). These debates are likely to continue for some time, but it should be noted that increasing numbers of sinologists have recently begun to accept that Erlitou shows a high degree of cultural-political sophistication, which can be seen as indicating a civilization or state-level society (e.g., Allan 2007).

Nature and Form of Early States

Another research topic concerning early states analyzes their general nature and form, viewed from a cross-cultural comparative perspective. Several models have been employed to describe early states in China. During the late twentieth century, discussions focused mainly on the late Shang dynasty, and the conclusions were controversial. The late Shang was described as city-states (Lin 1998, Yates 1997), segmentary states (Keightley 2000; Southall 1993, p. 33), territorial states (Trigger 1999), and village states (Maisels 1990, pp. 12–13, 254–61). These four models can be grouped into two types: city-states and segmentary state, on the one hand,

and territorial state and village-state, on the other. Major disputes between the two camps concern the political structure and the territorial size of early states (see summary in Liu & Chen 2003). However, because scholars usually have different understandings of political territory and use different criteria to measure it, their conclusions regarding the same political entity often vary considerably. In regards to the late Shang dynasty centered in Anyang, for example, some scholars argue for a very large territorial state (Trigger 1999), whereas others suggest a rather small city-state or segmentary state (Keightley 2000, Lin 1998, Yates 1997). Chinese archaeologists often determine the Shang political boundaries using the distribution of the ceramic and bronze styles and tend to claim a relatively large territory, including the entire middle and lower Yellow River and to the north of the Yangzi River (Song 1991, p. 201). In contrast, some sinologists regard only the Shang core area as its territory, covering a small region on the middle Yellow River (Wheatley 1971, p. 97). Crucial to the resolution of this dispute is some agreed understanding of the relationship between the distribution of a material culture and the administrative territory of a polity. Recent studies have suggested that regions characterized by Shang cultural remains were by no means all under direct political control of the Shang court (Liu 2009, Xu 1998), and the late Shang territory appears to have been considerably smaller than the early Shang (Tang 2001). Notably, Xu (1998) argues that there was a cultural sphere of bronze ritual objects in the Shang period, which was much greater in area than the Shang political boundry. This observation echoes Allan's (2007) and Yoffee & Li's (2009) concept of civilization as a set of common cultural values.

In the past decade, as more archaeological data became available, researchers shifted to the Erlitou and Erligang cultures for understanding the emergence of early states. As both the Erlitou and Erligang cultures show evidence of territorial expansion, and the relationship between core and periphery was characterized by control of vital resources, these two polities have been interpreted as territorial states (Liu & Chen 2003).

General cross-cultural comparative research is a useful approach for understanding both the level of social complexity and the nature of political organization involved in state formation. But we should not become too obsessed with classification of state types. Two recent studies by Campbell (2007) and Li (2008) attempted alternative approaches. They employed Baines & Yoffee's (1998) notion of civilization as a shared cultural order in which early states were embedded and further explored multifaceted interrelationships between the Shang and its neighboring polities. Campbell (2007) criticizes previous interpretations of early states in China as functionalist and typological and shows that the Late Shang political landscape is a picture of overlapping material, practical, and discursive networks forming concentric but distinctive spheres of authority. Likewise, Li (2008) investigates the interaction between humans and animals, using the faunal remains from a regional center, at Daxinzhuang in Shandong, which reflects the process of "becoming Shang." This process is conceptualized as reconciling ongoing tensions between the state's claim to supremacy and diverse local circumstances.

ARCHAEOLOGY OF STATE EMERGENCE IN CHINA

Although some archaeologists believe that early states emerged in many parts of China more than 5000 years ago, current archaeological data suggest that some late Neolithic cultures of the third millennium B.C. and the Erlitou culture are the best candidates for recognition as pristine states, with Erlitou showing the strongest evidence.

State Emergence in the Late Neolithic Cultures

Three Neolithic cultures/variants often assigned to the category of early states are Taosi, Wangchenggang, and Liangzhu.

Taosi (2600–2000 B.C.) was a regional center in the Linfen basin, southern Shanxi. No full-coverage regional survey has been conducted there, but nonsystematic surveys have identified some 50 late Longshan sites, forming a three-tiered site hierarchy in the basin (Liu 2004, pp. 170–76). During its heyday, Taosi was encircled by large rammed-earth walls (280 ha), its elite residences appear to have been separated from commoners by walled enclosures, and social hierarchy was clearly expressed in mortuary practice. The site was also a craft production center for stone artifacts and pottery vessels. A large, semicircular rammed-earth structure (1 ha) has been identified as an astronomical observatory (Liu 2004; Shanxi Team IACASS et al. 2003, pp. 109–13; 2005; 2007). Taosi apparently was a major political, economic, and ritual center in the region. As seasonal changes were crucial moments for Neolithic farming societies, by which to schedule their agricultural activities, the Taosi elite may have held great ritual power by possessing astronomical knowledge needed to determine the calendar. In addition, two glyphs painted in red pigment were found on a pottery vessel. They have been identified as characters for "wen yi," which are believed to have referred to a capital of the Xia dynasty (Feng 2008). This site has been interpreted not only as an early state, but also as a political center affiliated with either the Xia dynasty or predynastic kings, such as Yao and Shun; all were active in south Shanxi, according to ancient texts (Xie 2006). Nevertheless, owing to a lack of full-coverage regional survey, we are not clear about the Taosi polity's level of social complexity, considered from a regional perspective.

Wangchenggang in Dengfeng is located on a terraced area in the alluvial region of central Henan. During the late Longshan period, this region was characterized by a multicentered competitive settlement system, in which some centers were enclosed by rammed-earth fortifications (Liu 2004, pp. 182–85). Wangchenggang (~2200–1835 B.C.) was such an enclosed site and served as the settlement center for 22 unwalled sites distributed in the upper Ying River valley. At Wangchenggang, two connected small rammed-earth enclosures

(~1 ha each) were built around 2200 B.C., and a large enclosure (35 ha) was constructed by ~2100–2050 B.C. Many ash pits were unearthed at the site, some containing human sacrifices. This site was also a craft-production center, judging from stone drills and blanks, uncovered there, for making spades, axes, knives, and sickles (Henan Inst. Cult. Relics 1992, Sch. Archaeol. Museol. Peking Univ. 2007).

Wangchenggang's status as a state has to do with its location, which coincides with Yangcheng, the capital city said to have been established by Yu the Great, who founded the Xia dynasty according to textual accounts. Since the discovery, in 1977, of small internal enclosures, suggesting a segregated ruling elite, Wangchenggang has often been regarded as the ancestral place of the Xia dynasty (Henan 1992). The recent discovery of the large urban enclosure has promoted a new interpretation, that the small enclosures were built by Guan, the legendary father of Yu the Great, and the large town walls by Yu himself (Sch. Archaeol. Museol. Peking Univ. 2007). Nevertheless, such an attribution fails to explain a gap of some 100 years between the two constructions at Wangchenggang.

The Liangzhu site cluster in Yuhang.
The Liangzhu culture (3100–2200 B.C.) is distributed in the Lower Yangzi River region. The site density is particularly high in the Yuhang district, Zhejiang. A group of 135 sites/locales have been identified in an area of 33.8 km² there. The central place is located at Mojiaoshan, which is a man-made terrace, about 10 m high and 30 ha in area. Several rammed-earth architectural foundations, up to 3 ha in size, were situated on top of this large terrace. Mojiaoshan, together with several smaller sites, was surrounded by a large rammed-earth enclosure (290 ha), which was built during the late Liangzhu period. Liangzhu sites can be categorized into several functional types: the large ritual center at Mojiaoshan, sacrificial altars, burial sites, residential sites, and jade and pottery workshops. In addition, a rammed-earth wall, 5-km long and 20–50-m wide, was built parallel to the Tianmu mountain range in the north of the site cluster; it may have been constructed for flood control (Zhejiang 2005, 2008). The Liangzhu culture is well known for its large numbers of elaborate jade items unearthed from burial sites (Huang 1992, Mou & Yun 1992). Many jade forms appear to have embodied complex symbolic meanings (Chang 1989), and some bear pictographic symbols (Keightley 2006, Yang 2000). Some elite individuals may have been involved in manufacturing these prestige items, and Liangzhu jade, together with its symbolic meanings, had great influence on many Neolithic cultures in other regions (Liu 2003).

Different from its Central Plains' counterparts, the Liangzhu culture left no trace in ancient texts, so interpretations of its material remains rely completely on archaeology. Given that enormous amounts of construction and jade working were carried out by the Liangzhu people, and social hierarchy was clearly expressed in their mortuary practice, it is possible that a state-like social organization emerged there.

These Neolithic societies appear to have declined after their heydays. While the Liangzhu culture and Taosi site disappeared from the archaeological record, Wangchenggang became an ordinary village during the succeeding Erlitou period. The causes for such declines are still matters of ongoing investigations and are probably attributable to both environmental and social factors (Liu 2000, 2004; Stanley et al. 1999).

State Emergence in the Bronze Age

During the second millennium B.C., the Central Plains witnessed the rise of the Erlitou and then Erligang cultures, centered in the Yiluo basin and Zhengzhou area, respectively. They represent the earliest Bronze Age civilization/states in China.

The Erlitou state.
Settlement patterns in the Yiluo basin show a clear trend of increasing site hierarchy and nucleated population

through time. A mono-centered and highly integrated political entity emerged around 1900–1800 B.C., with Erlitou serving as the dominant central place and 190 smaller sites forming a four-tiered settlement hierarchy (Erlitou Work. Team IACASS 2005, Liu et al. 2002–2004, Qiao 2007).

The Erlitou urban center expanded rapidly from 100 ha to 300 ha within 100 years. The palatial complex, within a rammed-earth enclosure (12 ha), was located almost in the center of the site, forming a clear residential segregation between the high elite and the rest of the population. Enclosed bronze and turquoise workshops were situated immediately south of the palatial complex, suggesting a close control of the production of these prestige goods by the high elite, and the craftsmen may have been attached specialists. The bronze and turquoise artifacts have been found mainly in high elite burials, suggesting that these prestige items were distributed to form elite networks (Inst. Archaeol. CASS 1999, Liu 2006, Liu & Xu 2007). About a dozen types of pottery marks have been found, but they cannot be identified as a writing system (Qiu 1988).

Elite burials at Erlitou were normally associated with bronzes, jades, turquoise objects, and white pottery vessels. One of the high-ranking burials contained a dragon-shaped artifact, which was made of ~2000 pieces of turquoise and jade and placed on top of the skeleton (Liu & Xu 2007). Because the dragon has traditionally been regarded as a mythical animal with enormous supernatural powers, its association with a high-ranking burial seems to suggest that the Erlitou elite assumed great ritual power.

Some secondary centers in the Erlitou hinterland became specialized in manufacturing craft products. Huizui in Yanshi, for example, was a locale of stone tool production, particularly quarrying locally available dolomite for making spades (Ford 2007, Webb et al. 2007). Nanwa in Dengfeng may have been one of the sites that produced prestige white pottery with kaolinic clay (Li et al. 2008). These products appear to have been distributed to many sites in the Yiluo basin, including Erlitou. But there is no evidence that Erlitou controlled the circulation of these goods. These phenomena suggest multifaceted interactions between Erlitou and its hinterland. Whereas Erlitou elites may have assumed positions of highest political and religious authority in the region, minor elite individuals in local centers also constructed their own power networks by exchanging various utilitarian and ritual items. All these relationships formed a complex political-economic system in the core area of the state (Liu et al. 2007).

Erlitou also expanded its power to more distant areas, where important resources were found in abundance, such as salt, copper, and precious stones. Outposts may have been set up in these regions to procure and transport various local resources; such places include Dongxiafeng near the Zhongtiao Mountains, Donglongshan in the Qinling Mountains, and Panlongcheng in the middle Yangzi River (Liu & Chen 2001b, 2003). It is by no means to suggest that the Erlitou political territory is equivalent to the enormous region encircling these outposts, but Erlitou's regional expansion was unprecedented and is particularly attributable to the rulers' hunger for bronze alloys, which were used to cast weapons for warfare and ceremonial vessels for ancestor-worship ritual, both activities being intended to ensure the political legitimacy of the ruling class (Chang 1983).

It is particularly notable that the Erlitou state developed during a period of climatic deterioration. In the Yiluo basin, emerging dry and cold conditions led to severe stream incision, narrowed floodplains, and reduced wetland (Rosen 2007, 2008). In the meantime, however, population size exceeded the optimum carrying capacity (Qiao 2007), and a multicropping agricultural system was established, incorporating both local domesticates (millet, rice, and possibly soybean) and newly introduced ones (wheat and barley). Multicropping would help to increase annual yields and reduce risks of crop failure (Lee et al. 2007, Lee & Bestel 2007). In the face of these environmental challenges, the new subsistence strategies manifested human responses that may have contributed to creating and maintaining the Erlitou state.

Zhengzhou and the Erligang state. The pattern of core-periphery interaction established by the Erlitou polity appears to have continued in the succeeding polity centered in Zhengzhou, often referred to as the Erligang culture or Early Shang (~1600–1400 B.C.), although the relationship between these two polities is still a matter of debate. Zhengzhou was enclosed by two concentric rammed-earth walls, forming an inner city (300 ha) and an outer city (13 sq. km) (Yuan & Zeng 2004). The inner city contained royal palaces and temples, whereas the outer city defined the urban areas for craft production workshops, cemeteries, and residences. These workshops manufactured bronze, ceramic, and bone objects, used for both prestige and utilitarian purposes (Henan 2001). Pottery marks and some inscriptions on bones have been found, but their meanings are unclear (Inst. Archaeol. 2003, pp. 424–25). Like Erlitou, the Erligang state also established outposts in the periphery to procure important resources, including salt, copper, and proto-porcelain. The Erligang expansion reached even broader regions in all directions. These actions are likely to have been military in nature, as many of the outposts became fortified towns (Liu & Chen 2001b, 2003).

The interactions between the core and periphery during the Erlitou and Erligang periods appear to have involved interdependent relationships, although the outlying populations were much the weaker partners, politically and militarily. The regional centers in the periphery provided raw materials and exotic elite goods as tribute to the core area to support urban growth and craft production in the major center and to contribute to the formation of hierarchical sociopolitical structures. In return, the major center may have provided ritual services and redistributed prestige items as rewards to regional elites (Liu & Chen 2001c, 2003).

It is important to note that Erlitou and Zhengzhou are the only sites where evidence for casting ritual vessels has been found during each period. Several sites in the periphery have revealed remains of bronze casting, but only of tools and weapons (Liu & Chen 2001b, 2003). This observation suggests that the early states may have monopolized the production of bronze ritual vessels. This situation did not change until the Late Shang when the power structure was altered and some regional polities (such as Laoniupo near Xi'an) began to produce their own ritual vessels (Liu 2009). Although the proposition needs to be tested in the future, this scenario is consistent with the general circumstances that bronze vessels were sacred items used in ancestral worship ritual, which was one of the most important state affairs during the early Bronze Age (Chang 1983, 1991).

CONCLUSIONS

Study of state formation, and of the emergence of civilization, has come a long way since the beginning of modern archaeology in China, but many questions remain unsolved. One problem is whether some of the late Neolithic polities can be considered early states. If so, then early states in China would have appeared as peer-polities, as defined by Renfrew (1982, 1986). The argument for the formation of early states in the late Neolithic period has been gaining momentum recently in China, particularly owing to the new discovery of large public architectures at Taosi and Mojiaoshan. Yoffee & Li (2009) also express that some characteristics of early states have been noted in the Taosi walled site. At present, however, we do not have sufficient evidence to determine typologically the nature of these polities.

Less controversial is the definition of Erlitou and Erligang as states. Many similarities exist between the Neolithic polities and these two Bronze Age states, such as social stratification, construction of large public architecture, and production of prestige ritual objects and utilitarian items in regional centers. Signs and marks have been found in many late Neolithic sites, as well as in Erlitou and Erligang. However, it is difficult and controversial to assess their phonetic values, which by definition are required for writing (Boltz 1986, Keightley 2006, Li et al. 2003, Yang 2000). A major difference between these Neolithic and early Bronze Age polities is the scale of energy expenditure that the ruling elite was able to manipulate for creating and maintaining power. The production of prestige ritual items provides a tangible example of this contrast. On the one hand, Neolithic production of elite-goods, such as jade and fine pottery, normally involved local resources and manufacture, which would have required relatively low levels of managerial operation and energy expenditure. On the other hand, bronze production in the Erlitou and Erligang cultures, including mining, smelting, and casting, embraced much greater geographic catchments for transporting raw material and required more complex technology and management for production, as compared with Neolithic manufacturing (Franklin 1983, Liu 2003). Such extraordinary efforts invested in production of bronze weapons and ritual vessels testify to the importance of these products as sources and instruments of political legitimacy for the ruling elite. Adopting Baines & Yoffee's (1998) and Allan's (2007) concept of shared elite cultural value as civilization, it is also clear that Erlitou is markedly different from these late Neolithic cultures in terms of its much greater sphere of a common elite culture.

Based on current archaeological information, we are still unable to pinpoint the exact moment when the first state emerged. It is also less than productive to match archaeological remains with legendary places and individuals. Nevertheless, archaeological data can help us to understand general trajectories toward state formation. We need to study not only how these early states operated in urban centers, the rural hinterland, and periphery, but also how states and other polities interacted with each other. It may not be possible in the near future to alter the historiographically determined approach, which pervades Chinese archaeology, but we can develop new approaches for investigating the political-economic system on regional and interregional scales. An anthropological dimension in the study of state emergence in China certainly needs to be encouraged.

DISCLOSURE STATEMENT

The author is not aware of any affiliations, memberships, funding, or financial holdings that might be perceived as affecting the objectivity of this review.

ACKNOWLEDGMENTS

I am grateful to the constructive comments by Xingcan Chen and an anonymous reviewer. Yu Qiao helped with map drawing, and Thomas Bartlett edited the English.

LITERATURE CITED

Adams REW, Jones RC. 1981. Spatial patterns and regional growth among Classic Maya cities. *Am. Antiq.* 46:301–22

Allan S. 1991. *The Shape of the Turtle: Myth, Art and Cosmos in Early China*. Albany: State Univ. NY

Allan S. 2007. Erlitou and the formation of Chinese civilization: toward a new paradigm. *J. Asian Stud.* 66:461–96

An Z. 1993. Lun huan Bohai de shiqian wenhua—jianping "quxi" guandian. *Kaogu* 7:609–15

Bagley R. 1999. Shang archaeology. See Loewe & Shaughnessy 1999, pp. 124–231

Baines J, Yoffee N. 1998. Order, legitimacy, and wealth in Ancient Egypt and Mesopotamia. In *Archaic States*, ed. G Feinman, J Marcus, pp. 199–60. Santa Fe: Sch. Am. Res.

Bennett GP. 2008. Context and meaning in late Neolithic lithic production in China: the Longshan period in southeastern Shandong province. *Archeol. Pap. Am. Anthropol. Assoc.* 17:52–67

Boltz WG. 1986. Early Chinese writing. *World Archaeol.* 17:420–36

Campbell RB. 2007. *Blood, flesh and bones: kinship and violence in the social economy of the Late Shang.* PhD diss., Harvard Univ., Cambridge, Mass.

Cent. Stud. Anc. Civiliz., Zhengzhou Inst. Cult. Relics. 2004. Henansheng Xinmishi Xinzhai yizhi (The Xinzhai site in Xinmi city, Henan province). *Wenwu* 3:4–20

Chang K-C. 1983. *Art, Myth, and Ritual.* Cambridge, MA: Harvard Univ. Press

Chang K-C. 1986. *Archaeology of Ancient China.* New Haven, CT: Yale Univ. Press

Chang K-C. 1989. An essay on cong. *Orientations* 20:37–43

Chang K-C. 1991. Introduction: The importance of bronzes in ancient China. In *Ancient Chinese Bronze Art: Casting the Precious Sacral Vessel*, ed. WT Chase, pp. 15–18. New York: China House Gallery, China Inst. Am.

Chang K-C. 1999. China on the eve of the historical period. See Loewe & Shaughnessy 1999, pp. 37–73

Chen X. 1987. Wenming zhuyinsu de qiyuan yu wenming shidai (On the origins of the elements of civilization and the civilized era). *Kaogu* 5:437, 458–61

Chifeng Int. Collab. Archaeol. Res. Project. 2003. *Regional Archeology in Eastern Inner Mongolia: A Methodological Exploration.* Beijing: Kexue Press

Childe VG. 1950. The urban revolution. *Town Plann. Rev.* 21:3–17

Childs-Johnson E. 1995. Symbolic jades of the Erlitou period: a Xia royal tradition. *Arch. Asian Art* XLVIII:64–90

Cunnar G. 2007. *The production and use of stone tools at the Longshan Period site of Liangchengzhen, China.* PhD diss., Yale Univ., New Haven, Conn.

Du J, Xu H, eds. 2006. *Erlitou Yizhi yu Erlitou Wenhua Yanjiu (Research on the Erlitou Site and Erlitou Culture).* Beijing: Kexue Press

Du Z. 1991. Xiadai kaogu jiqi guojia fazhan de tansuo (Archaeology of the Xia dynasty and the development of state). *Kaogu* 1:43–56

Earle TK. 1991. The evolution of chiefdom. In *Chiefdoms: Power, Economy, and Ideology*, ed. T Earle, pp. 1–15. Cambridge, UK: Cambridge Univ. Press

Engels F. 1972 [1884]. *The Origin of the Family, Private Property and the State.* New York: Int. Publ.

Erlitou Work. Team IACASS. 2005. Henan Luoyang pendi 2001–2003 nian kaogu diaocha jianbao (Report of the 2001–2003 archaeological survey in the Luoyang basin, Henan). *Kaogu* 5:18–37

Falkenhausen Lv. 1993. On the historiographical orientation of Chinese archaeology. *Antiquity* 67:839–49

Feinman G. 1995. The emergence of inequality: a focus on strategies and processes. In *Foundations of Social Inequality*, ed. DPaG Feinman, pp. 225–79. New York: Plenum

Feinman GM, Marcus J, eds. 1998. *Archaic States.* Santa Fe: Sch. Am. Res. Press

Feng S. 2008. "Wen yi" kao (On "wen yi"). *Kaogu Xuebao* 3:273–90

Fish SK, Kowalewski SA, eds. 1990. *The Archaeology of Regions: A Case for Full-Coverage Survey.* Washington, DC: Smithson. Inst. Press

Flannery KV. 1998. The ground plans of archaic states. See Feinman & Marcus 1998, pp. 15–58

Ford A. 2007. *Stone tool production-distribution systems during the Early Bronze Age at Huizui, China.* MA thesis, La Trobe Univ., Melbourne

Franklin UM. 1983. The beginnings of metallurgy in China: a comparative approach. In *The Great Bronze Age of China*, ed. G Kuwayama, pp. 94–99. Los Angeles, CA: Los Angeles County Mus.

Gao W, Yang X, Wang W, Du J. 1998. Yanshi Shangcheng yu Xia Shang wenhua fenjie (The Yanshi Shang city and the demarcation between the Xia and Shang cultures). *Kaogu* 10:66–79

Henan Inst. Cult. Relics. 1992. *Dengfeng Wangchenggang yu Yangcheng.* Beijing: Wenwu Press

Henan Inst. Cult. Relics. 2001. *Zhengzhou Shangcheng.* Beijing: Wenwu Press

Huang T-M. 1992. Liangzhu—a late Neolithic jade-yielding culture in southeastern coastal China. *Antiquity* 66:75–83

Inst. Archaeol. CASS. 1999. *Yanshi Erlitou.* Beijing: Zhongguo Dabaikequanshu Press

Inst. Archaeol. CASS. 2003. *Zhongguo Kaoguxue: Xia Shang Juan (Chinese Archaeology: The Xia and Shang Volume).* Beijing: Zhongguo Shehui Kexue Press

Keightley DN. 1983. The late Shang state: when, where, and what? In *The Origins of Chinese Civilization*, ed. D Keightley, pp. 523–64. Berkeley: Univ. Calif. Press

Keightley DN. 2000. *The Ancestral Landscape: Time, Space, and Community in Late Shang China (ca. 1200–1045 B.C.)*. Berkeley: Inst. East Asian Stud.

Keightley DN. 2006. Marks and labels: early writing in Neolithic and Shang China. In *Archaeology of Asia*, ed. MT Stark, pp. 177–201. Malden, MA: Blackwell

Kowalewski SA. 1989. *Prehispanic Settlement Patterns in Tlacolula, Etla, and Ocotlan, the Valley of Oaxaca, Mexico*. Ann Arbor: Regents of the Univ. Mich., Mus. Anthropol.

Lee G-A, Bestel S. 2007. Contextual analysis of plant remains at the Erlitou-period Huizui site, Henan, China. *Bull. Indo-Pac. Prehist. Assoc.* 27:49–60

Lee G-A, Crawford GW, Liu L, Chen X. 2007. Plants and people from the early Neolithic to Shang periods in North China. *Proc. Natl. Acad. Sci. USA* 104:1087–92

Lee YK. 2002. Building the chronology of early Chinese history. *Asian Perspect.* 41:15–42

Lee YK. 2004. Control strategies and polity competition in the lower Yi-Luo valley, north China. *J. Anthropol. Archaeol.* 23:172–95

Li B, Liu L, Zhao J, Chen X, Feng Y, et al. 2008. Chemical fingerprinting of whitewares from Nanwa site of the Chinese Erlitou state: comparison with Gongxian and Ding kilns. *Nucl. Instrum. Methods Phys. Res. B* 266:2614–22

Li C. 1977. *Anyang*. Seattle: Univ. Wash. Press

Li M. 2008. *Conquest, concord, and consumption: becoming Shang in Eastern China*. PhD diss., Univ. Mich., Ann Arbor

Li X, ed. 1997. *Zhongguo Gudai Wenming yu Guojia Xingcheng Yanjiu (Research on Ancient Civilization and State Formation in China)*. Kunming: Yunnan Renmin Press

Li X, Harbottle G, Zhang J, Wang C. 2003. The earliest writing? Sign use in the seventh millennium BC at Jiahu, Henan Province, China. *Antiquity* 77:31–44

Lin Y. 1998. Jiaguwen zhong de Shangdai fangguo lianmeng (The confederation states of the Shang dynasty seen in oracle-bone inscriptions) (originally published in 1982 *Guwenzi yanjiu* 6). In *Lin Yun Xueshu Wenji (Collected Essays by Lin Yun)*, ed. Y Lin, pp. 69–84. Beijing: Zhongguo Dabaike Quanshu Press

Linduff K, Drennan R, Shelack G. 2002–2004. Early complex societies in NE China: the Chifeng international collaborative archaeological research project. *J. Field Archaeol.* 29:45–73

Linduff KM. 1998. The emergence and demise of bronze-producing cultures outside the Central Plain of China. In *The Bronze Age and Early Iron Age Peoples of Eastern Central Asia*, ed. VH Mair, pp. 619–46. Washington, DC: Inst. Study Man

Liu D. 1988. Youguan Rizhao Liangchengzhen yukeng yuqi de ziliao (Information on the jade objects from pits at Liangchengzhen in Rizhao). *Kaogu* 2:121–23

Liu L. 2000. The development and decline of social complexity in China: some environmental and social factors. *Indo-Pac. Prehist.: Melaka Pap. Bull. Indo-Pac. Prehist. Assoc.* 20:14–33

Liu L. 2003. "The products of minds as well as of hands": production of prestige goods in the Neolithic and early state periods of China. *Asian Perspect.* 42:1–40

Liu L. 2004. *The Chinese Neolithic: Trajectories to Early States*. Cambridge, UK: Cambridge Univ. Press

Liu L. 2006. Urbanization in China: Erlitou and its hinterland. In *Urbanism in the Preindustrial World: Cross-Cultural Approaches*, ed. G Storey, pp. 161–89. Tuscaloosa: Univ. Ala. Press

Liu L. 2009. China: state formation and urbanization. In *The Oxford Handbook of Archaeology*, ed. B Cunliffe, C Gosden, R Joyce, pp. 579–610. Oxford: Univ. Oxford Press

Liu L, Chen X. 2001a. China. In *Encyclopedia of Archaeology: History and Discoveries*, ed. T Murray, pp. 315–33. Santa Barbara: ABC-CLIO

Liu L, Chen X. 2001b. Cities and towns: the control of natural resources in early states, China. *Bull. Mus. Far East. Antiq.* 73:5–47

Liu L, Chen X. 2001c. Settlement archaeology and the study of social complexity in China. *Rev. Archaeol.* 22(2):4–21

Liu L, Chen X. 2003. *State Formation in Early China*. London: Duckworth

Liu L, Chen X. 2007. Multidisciplinary research in the Yiluo Project: after 10 years. *Bull. Indo-Pac. Prehist. Assoc.* 27:37–38

Liu L, Chen X, Lee YK, Wright H, Rosen A. 2002–2004. Settlement patterns and development of social complexity in the Yiluo region, north China. *J. Field Archaeol.* 29:75–100

Liu L, Chen X, Li B. 2007. Non-state crafts in the early Chinese state: an archaeological view from the Erlitou hinterland. *Bull. Indo-Pac. Prehist. Assoc.* 27:93–102

Liu L, Xu H. 2007. Rethinking Erlitou: legend, history and Chinese archaeology. *Antiquity* 81:886–901

Loewe M, Shaughnessy E, eds. 1999. *The Cambridge History of Ancient China: From the Origins of Civilization to 221 BC.* Cambridge, UK: Cambridge Univ. Press

Maisels C. 1990. *The Emergence of Civilization: From Hunting and Gathering to Agriculture, Cities, and the State in the Near East.* London: Routledge

Marcus J, Feinman G. 1998. Introduction. See Feinman & Marcus 1998, pp. 3–14

Morgan LH. 1963 [orig. 1877]. *Ancient Society.* New York: World Publ.

Mou Y, Yun X, eds. 1992. *Zhongguo Yuqi Quanji: Yuanshi Shehui (Selected Works on Chinese Jades: Primitive Society).* Shijiazhuang: Hebei Meishu Press

Qiao Y. 2007. Development of complex societies in the Yiluo region: a GIS based population and agricultural area analysis. *Indo-Pac. Prehist. Assoc. Bull.* 27:61–75

Qiu X. 1988. *Wenzixue Ganyao Essentials of Philology.* Beijing: Shangwu Press

Renfrew C. 1982. Polity and power: interaction, intensification and exploitation. In *An Island Polity: The Archaeology of Exploitation in Melos*, pp. 264–90. Cambridge, UK: Cambridge Univ. Press

Renfrew C. 1986. Introduction: peer polity interaction and socio-political change. In *Peer Polity Interaction and Socio-Political Change*, ed. C Renfrew, J Cherry, pp. 1–18. Cambridge, UK: Cambridge Univ. Press

Rosen AM. 2007. The role of environmental change in the development of complex societies in China: a study from the Huizui site. *Bull. Indo-Pac. Prehist. Assoc.* 27:39–48

Rosen AM. 2008. The impact of environmental change and human land use on alluvial valleys in the Loess Plateau of China during the Middle Holocene. *Geomorphology* 101:298–307

Sch. Archaeol. Museol. Peking Univ., Henan Inst. Cult. Relics Archaeol. 2007. *Dengfeng Wangchenggang Kaogu Faxian yu Yanjiu (2002–2005) (Archaeological Discovery and Research at the Wangchenggang Site in Dengfeng [2002–2005]).* Zhengzhou: Daxiang Press

Shanxi Team IACASS, Shanxi Inst. Archaeol., Linfen Bur. Cult. Relics. 2003. Taosi chengzhi faxian Taosi wenhua zhongqi muzang (Mid-Taosi phase burials at the Taosi walled site). *Kaogu* 9:3–6

Shanxi Team IACASS, Shanxi Inst. Archaeol., Linfen Bur. Cult. Relics. 2005. Shanxi Xiangfen Taosi chengzhi 2002 nian fajue baogao (Report of 2002 excavation at the walled site at Taosi in Xiangfen, Shanxi). *Kaogu Xuebao* 3:307–46

Shanxi Team IACASS, Shanxi Inst. Archaeol., Linfen City Cult. Bur. 2007. Shanxi Xiangfenxian Taosi zhongqi chengzhi daxing jianzhu IIFJT1 jizhi 2004–2005 nian fajue jianbao (Report of 2004–2005 excavations of the large edifice IIFJT1 in the walled enclosure during the middle phase at Taosi, Xiangfen, Shanxi). *Kaogu* 4:3–25

Sino-Am. Collab. Liangcheng Archaeol. Team. 2004. Shandong Rizhao Liangchengzhen yizhi 1998–2001 nian fajue jianbao (preliminary report of the 1998–2001 excavation seasons at the Liangchengzhen site in Rizhao, Shandong). *Kaogu* 9:7–18

Sino-Am. Huan River Valley Archaeol. Team. 1998. Huanhe liuyu kaogu yanjiu chubu baogao (Preliminary report of regional archaeological research in the Huan River valley). *Kaogu* 10:13–22

Song X. 1991. *Yin Shang Wenhua Quyu Yanjiu (On the Cultural Territories of the Late Shang).* Xi'an: Shaanxi Renmin Press

Southall A. 1993. Urban theory and the Chinese city. In *Urban Anthropology in China*, ed. GGaA Southall, pp. 19–40. Leiden: Brill

Stanley DJ, Chen Z, Song J. 1999. Inundation, sea-level rise and transition from Neolithic to Bronze Age cultures, Yangtze delta, China. *Geoarchaeology* 14:15–26

Su B. 1999. *Zhongguo Wenming Qiyuan Xintan (New Investigations on the Origins of Chinese Civilization).* Beijing: Sanlian Press

Su B, Yin W. 1981. Guanyu kaoguxue wenhua de quxi leixing wenti (On the issue of the distribution and development of regional cultures in Chinese archaeology). *Wenwu* 5:10–17

Tang J. 2001. The construction of an archaeological chronology for the history of the Shang dynasty of early Bronze Age China. *Rev. Archaeol.* 22:35–47

Thorp RL. 1991. Erlitou and the search for the Xia. *Early China* 16:1–38

Thorp RL. 2006. *China in the Early Bronze Age: Shang Civilization*. Philadelphia: Univ. Penn. Press

Tong E. 1995. Thirty years of Chinese archaeology (1949–1979). In *Nationalism, Politics, and the Practice of Archaeology*, ed. PL Kohl, C Fawcett, pp. 177–97. Cambridge, UK: Cambridge Univ. Press

Trigger BG. 1999. Shang political organization: a comparative approach. *J. East Asian Archaeol.* 1:43–62

Underhill AP, Feinman GM, Nicholas LM, Bennett G, Cai F, et al. 1998. Systematic, regional survey in SE Shandong province, China. *J. Field Archaeol.* 25:453–74

Underhill AP, Feinman GM, Nicholas LM, Bennett G, Fang H, et al. 2002. Regional survey and the development of complex societies in southeastern Shandong, China. *Antiquity* 76:745–55

Underhill AP, Feinman GM, Nicholas LM, Fang H, Luan F, et al. 2008. Changes in regional settlement patterns and the development of complex societies in southeastern Shandong, China. *J. Anthropol. Archaeol.* 27:1–29

Wang T. 1997. The Chinese archaeological school: Su Bingqi and contemporary Chinese archaeology. *Antiquity* 71:31–39

Wang W. 2006. Guenyu zai wenming tanyuan zhong kaogu yu lishi zhenghe de sikao (Some thoughts on the integration of archaeology and history in research of the origins of civilization). *Zhongguo Shehui Kexueyuan Gudai Wenming Yanjiu Zhongxin Tongxun* 11:7–10

Webb J, Ford A, Gorton J. 2007. Influences on selection of lithic raw material sources at Huizui, a Neolithic/Early Bronze Age site in northern China. *Bull. Indo-Pac. Prehist. Assoc.* 27:76–86

Wheatley P. 1971. *The Pivot of the Four Quarters: A Preliminary Enquiry into the Origins and Character of the Ancient Chinese city*. Chicago: Aldine

Wilson D. 1988. *Prehispanic Settlement Patterns in the Lower Santa Valley, Peru*. Washington, DC: Smithson. Inst. Press

Wright HT. 1977. Recent research on the origin of the state. *Annu. Rev. Anthropol.* 6:379–97

Wright HT. 1984. Prestate political formations. In *On the Evolution of Complex Societies: Essays in Honor of Harry Hoijer*, ed. T Earle, pp. 41–77. Malibu: Undena

Wright HT, Johnson G. 1975. Population, exchange, and early state formation in southwestern Iran. *Am. Anthropol.* 77:267–89

Xia N. 1985. *Zhongguo Wenming de Qiyuan (The Origins of Chinese Civilization)*. Beijing: Wenwu Press

Xie X, ed. 2006. *Xiangfen Taosi Yizhi Yanjiu (Research on the Taosi Site in Xiangfen)*. Beijing: Kexue Press

Xu L. 1998. Wenhua yinsu dingxing fenxi yu Shangdai "qingtong liqi wenhua quan" yanjiu (An analysis of cultural elements and "cultural sphere of bronze ritual vessels"). In *Zhongguo Shang Wenhua Guoji Xueshu Taolunhui Lunwenji (Collected Papers from the International Conference on the Shang culture, China)*, ed. IACASS, pp. 227–36. Beijing: Zhongguo Dabaike Quanshu Press

Yan W. 2000. The origins of rice agriculture, pottery and cities. In *Daozuo Taoqi he Dushi de Qiyuan (The Origins of Rice Agriculture, Pottery and Cities)*, ed. W Yan, Y Yasuda, pp. 3–15. Beijing: Wenwu Press

Yang X. 2000. *Reflections of Early China: Decor, Pictographs, and Pictorial Inscriptions*. Seattle/London: Nelson-Atkins Mus. Art

Yates R. 1997. The city-state in ancient China. In *The Archaeology of City-States: Cross-Cultural Approaches*, ed. D Nichols, T Charlton, pp. 71–90. Washington, DC: Smithson. Inst. Press

Yoffee N, Li M. 2009. Wangquan, chengshi yu guojia: bijiao kaoguxue shiye zhongde zhongguo zaoqi chengshi (Kingship, city and state: China's early cities from a perspective of comparative archaeology). In *Duowei Shiyu—Shang Wangchao yu Zhongguo Zaoqi Wenming Yanjiu (Multiple Perspectives—Study of the Shang Dynasty and Early Chinese Civilizations)*, ed. Z Jing, J Tang, K Takashima, pp. 276–90. Beijing: Kexue Press

Yuan G, Zeng X. 2004. Lun Zhengzhou Shangcheng neicheng he waicheng de guanxi (Relationship between the inner walls and outer walls at the Zhengzhou Shang city). *Kaogu* 3:59–67

Yuan J, Campbell R. 2008. Recent archaeometric research on "the origins of Chinese civilization." *Antiquity* 83:96–109

Zhang Z. 2000. Zhongguo gudai wenming xingcheng de kaoguxue yanjiu (Archaeological research on the origins of ancient Chinese civilization). *Gugong Bowuyuan Yuankan* 2:5–27

Zhejiang Inst. Archaeol. 2005. *Liangzhu Yizhiqun (The Liangzhu Site Cluster)*. Beijing: Wenwu Press

Zhejiang Inst. Archaeol. 2008. Hangzhoushi Yuhangqu Liangzhu gucheng yizhi 2006–2007 nian de fajue (The 2006–2007 excavation season at the Liangzhu walled site in Yuhang district, Hangzhou city). *Kaogu* 7:3–10

Zou H. 1980. *Xia Shang Zhou Kaogu Lunwenji (Essays on the Archaeology of the Xia, Shang and Zhou Dynasties)*. Beijing: Wenwu Press

Interdisciplinary Translational Research in Anthropology, Nutrition, and Public Health

Stephen T. McGarvey

International Health Institute, Brown University, Providence, Rhode Island 02912;
email: Stephen_McGarvey@brown.edu

Annu. Rev. Anthropol. 2009. 38:233–49

First published online as a Review in Advance on
June 19, 2009

The *Annual Review of Anthropology* is online at
anthro.annualreviews.org

This article's doi:
10.1146/annurev-anthro-091908-164327

Key Words

applied studies, translational research, community health worker,
schistosomiasis, obesity and diabetes

Abstract

This review focuses on several human population health research topics
that exemplify interdisciplinary concepts and approaches from anthropology, nutrition, and public health with an emphasis on applied or
translational global health implications. First, a recent study on neonatal survival in a resource-poor region emphasizes how health can be
markedly improved with detailed translation and implementation of
evidence from all three disciplines. Second, schistosomiasis, a parasitic
worm infection, is reviewed with an emphasis on developing a consensus of its nutritional health burdens and the next translational research
steps needed to improve control of both infection transmission and disease. Last, the author's long-term Samoan nutrition and health studies
are described with a focus on new translational research to improve
diabetes. This selective review attempts to provide a rationale for the
intersections of anthropology, nutrition, and public health to proceed
with fundamental biological, cultural, and behavioral research to reduce
health inequalities globally and domestically.

INTRODUCTION

Nutrition in its broadest sense as a human science concerns the relationships among diet, physical activity, human biology, and health (Pike & Brown 1967). Common usage within both the lay and the scientific communities often implies a focus on food and diet only. The general objective of most nutritional research is to provide evidence about the balance between the amount and types of energy and nutrients consumed in the diet and energy expended in spontaneous and purposeful physical activities, the biological mechanisms involved, and the associations of diet, physical activity, and energy balance to health and disease. There is also an explicit awareness in nutritional research and recommendations about what is normal or healthy growth and body size in relation to the maintenance and function of bodily tissues conditional on age, sex, developmental stage, reproductive status, and socioeconomic factors (Malina et al. 2004).

The anthropological perspective on nutrition emphasizes variations in diet, activity, physical growth and development patterns, adult body size, health and functioning in relation to our evolutionary history, biocultural adaptive processes, contemporary ecological settings, and socioeconomic forces and their interactions (Haas & Pelletier 1989, Ungar et al. 2006). Anthropology's concern with heterogeneity in both sociocultural and biological aspects of nutrition across and within human communities has never been more important because global sociopolitical and economic changes exert consequences on dietary and physical activity patterns and produce strong social gradients in nutritional health (McGarvey 2007, Reyes-Garcia et al. 2008).

The public health perspective on nutrition focuses on the relationships of health and disease with diet, physical activity, and overall nutritional status in populations to produce evidence that influences public health policy (Willett 1998). Using epidemiologic methods, researchers have striven to provide descriptive and inferential evidence from well-defined populations with careful concern for interpreting causal associations between nutritional factors and health outcomes. In addition, the increased scientific and policy attention within public health to domestic U.S. and global health inequalities is shown in nutritional research on both undernutrition and overnutrition (Popkin & Gordon-Larsen 2004, West et al. 2006).

This review is a selective presentation of several topics, including two in which the author has long-term involvement, with a focus on applied perspectives. The intent here is to answer this question: How do nutrition, anthropology, and public health intersect in ways that provide evidence to support implementation and translational research to improve population health? Intervention studies that are directly or indirectly relevant to this interdisciplinary domain are described in some detail as models for how to produce scholarly knowledge that can inform policy decisions. The subtext of the review includes concepts and evidence about global health (Merson et al. 2006, Jamison et al. 2006) and health inequalities and inequities (Ruger 2006, Wilkinson & Pickett 2006).

First, I briefly discuss perspectives about applied research. Second, I describe informative recent work on infant and neonatal survival that amplifies and reinforces the importance of community-based anthropological understanding and action to reduce health inequalities. I then review our work on schistosomiasis and nutrition to indicate future intellectual contributions by anthropology in basic and applied work. Last, I use our new translational research on diabetes and obesity in Samoans to highlight both the scientific advantages of an interdisciplinary nutrition, public health, and anthropology project for improving population health and the potential for an innovative set of future research questions to be explored.

APPLIED PERSPECTIVES

Translating basic knowledge of biological and behavioral processes from laboratories to clinical settings and free-living individuals and then implementing program delivery into communities with variation in sociocultural, economic, and historical influences remain challenges for the human sciences, especially health-related disciplines (Maddon et al. 2008). Instead of the invidious distinction between basic and applied scholarship that occasionally surfaces because of concerns about contributions to fundamental understanding and definitions of the core concerns within existing disciplines, implementation research offers the opportunity to produce generalizable knowledge about design and delivery of programs. Given the current level of global health inequalities and the epidemiological evidence about how risk-factor exposures lead to disease and ill health, an increased emphasis is being placed on how to translate and implement individual and community-level programs to avert these risks and provide preventive and curative services that are acceptable and sustainable (Jamison et al. 2006, Lopez et al. 2006a).

As anthropologists, we must critically think and teach our students and the public about certain hidden assumptions about poverty, health, and mortality without resorting to the easy refuge of imprecise evolutionary concepts about relative survival and mortality and a too-easy acceptance of inequalities. Our intellectual mission as anthropologists is to attempt to observe and measure human biocultural phenomena as they are in all their fundamental heterogeneities and employ complex webs of many causal factors operating at different levels in our interpretations. The view of life we derive may be bleak considering history, ecology, adaptations, politics, poverty, and seemingly ineradicable health inequalities. But if we adopt an explicit interdisciplinary mission with public health and other scholarly areas such as nutrition, which are dedicated to improving life and health and reducing differences, then we can contend with the challenge to derive anthropologically informed questions, concepts, and measures that work with these more applied fields (McGarvey 2007).

Community health workers (CHW), also called peer counselors, health advocates, lay health educators, community outreach workers, and *promotores de salud* in Spanish, are members of the communities they serve and sometimes are selected from among patients. They are uniquely qualified to participate in the design, development, and delivery of public health preventive and health care services because they understand community concerns and cultural practices, and they speak the local language (Witmer et al. 1995). They provide culturally appropriate education and social support and facilitate access to care, including for hard-to-reach or noncompliant individuals, while also providing information to health care providers (Satterfield et al. 2002). Several research studies reviewed below incorporated CHWs into group-based interventions, community-based programs, and one-on-one case-management interventions for all types of health and disease.

CHILD AND NEONATAL SURVIVAL

More than 10 million children annually die before their fifth birthday, with almost 4 million dying in the first 28 days of life (Black et al. 2003). Poor sanitation, limited access to safe water, and undernutrition are major risk factors for child mortality and morbidity. They are responsible for much of the global health inequalities and disability-adjusted life years (DALYS), a population health metric that includes quality of life and age of death due to specific conditions (Lopez et al. 2006b). Although pneumonia and diarrhea are two of the most important medical conditions responsible for child deaths, a large proportion of child deaths is attributable to interactions of specific infections with undernutrition and other conditions (Pelletier 1994, Black et al. 2003). Insufficient or no breastfeeding is very strongly related to infant, birth to one year of age, mortality, and especially in the first six months of life (WHO 2000, Black et al. 2003). As part of the same series of articles on child mortality in the *Lancet*, existing interventions were reviewed in terms of effectiveness at reducing childhood mortality and ranked according to the extent of evidence for

CHW: community health workers

effectiveness (Jones et al. 2003). Two-thirds of child deaths could be prevented by interventions that are available today and are feasible for implementation in resource-limited settings.

A remarkable research project to reduce neonatal mortality in Bangladesh is an excellent example of interdisciplinary nutritional, public health, and anthropological research (Baqui et al. 2008). Three clusters of 8 villages each were randomly assigned to one of three arms: home-care, community-care, or the comparison or control arm. All married women 15–49 years of age were eligible to participate. In all villages, baseline household surveys assessed health knowledge and practices related to the maternal and newborn dyad and retrospective reports in the past year of infant and neonatal mortality. During the intervention, in home-care villages female CHWs identified eligible women who were pregnant, visited each woman twice during her pregnancy, and after birth visited on the first, third, and seventh day of life. During the prenatal visits, the CHWs promoted preparation for the birth and caring for a newborn and provided maternal iron and folic acid supplements. Postnatally, the CHWs assessed newborns, reinforced newborn-care information, provided guidance about breast-feeding problems, treated ill newborns, and made referrals to clinics when necessary (Baqui et al. 2008, table 2). In the community-care arm, health information about and promotion of birth and newborn-care preparedness and obtaining health care from qualified providers, i.e., those trained in biomedicine, were available only in group sessions led by female and male community mobilizers. In the comparison or control arm, health care providers from the usual mix of government, nongovernment organizations, and private clinics were used. From an ethical perspective of improving local standards of care, it is important to note that in all three study arms refresher training about clinical management of maternal and newborn health complications was held for government health workers.

In both intervention arms, male and female community mobilizers held group meetings to disseminate information about birth and newborn-care preparedness. In the community-care villages, female community resource people, generally local traditional birth attendants, were trained to identify pregnant women, inform the women about and support their attendance at the community meetings on newborn health, and suggest care if mothers or newborns demonstrated signs of serious illness.

The investigators describe in detail the community preparations and development and reinforcement of community mobilization for identification of pregnant women and notification of births to schedule the first-day neonatal assessments and clinical assessments, treatments, and referrals by degrees of severity of neonatal illness (Baqui et al. 2008, figure 3). These detailed descriptions serve as an excellent general model of maternal and child public health and clinical service delivery. They can be elaborated and implemented in many different populations throughout the developing world and medically underserved communities in the developed world.

The results were very striking, showing decreased neonatal mortality in the home-care villages relative to the community-care villages, but only in the past year, and especially in the last 6 months of the 30-month intervention. In the last 6 months, neonatal mortality rates were reduced by 34% [adjusted relative risk 0.66; 95% confidence intervals (CI) 0.47–0.93] in the home-care villages with the actual rates being 29.2 per 1000, 45.2 per 1000, and 43.5 per 1000 in the home-care, community-care, and comparison arms, respectively. In the home-care villages, the CHWs made referrals for about one-third of the neonatal infections and treated more than one-third with injected antibiotics. Of note, there were improved care practices in the community-care villages, but these did not appear to produce lowered neonatal mortality (Baqui et al. 2008, table 4). The authors describe the ratio of CHWs to population as similar to the government primary health care system, ~1 per 4000 people, suggesting the CHW home-care work is sustainable throughout the entire health system. They conclude that in the context of an underdeveloped health system, low health-care use, and high neonatal mortality, a home-centered delivery of integrated and sustainable health care for pregnant women and neonates can reduce neonatal mortality (Baqui et al. 2008).

What are the lessons from this study for anthropology and its interdisciplinary overlaps with nutrition and public health? First, both fundamental and translational applied research include the necessary smaller individual investigator studies that contribute to larger interdisciplinary team research. Detailed community studies using anthropological methods that improve understanding at the village level about how health and medical knowledge and attitudes play out both in daily life and in family medical emergencies are a necessity before large intervention trials are designed. For example, understanding that within villages there are exchanges of information about services and even prenatal dietary supplements requires clinical trial researchers to avoid contamination effects by randomizing interventions at the village level. Before large scale-up programs of similar infant- and child-mortality interventions can be done, fundamental social science knowledge is required about community-wide diffusion of new information about pregnancy and child care, particularly if the new information derives from the cultural paradigm of evidence-based biomedical science. How do citizens in communities talk about such information? Who are the important family and community members who may be opinion leaders or charismatic individuals, may have higher social position or prestige, or may be part of the existing traditional health care system? New biomedical and health information from outside the usual local health system has it own patterns of salience, transmissibility, and social communication. How is social support mediated, and who provides it to new and experienced mothers and other infant care takers who want to change their preventive and curative behaviors in response to novel health information and education? In short, what

are the processes of change in health literacy? Without understanding such phenomena, scaling-up or actual implementation of nutritional and other public health evidence-based interventions should not be started in communities, regions, and nations. Medical and biocultural anthropology and anthropological linguistics clearly must be part of such research and should seek to collaborate with less anthropologically trained and experienced health communication or behavioral medicine experts.

Second, bioanthropologists with their biological evolutionary and genetic and physiologic diversity perspectives can also play a role because there may be important human biological differences within populations that have an influence on the efficacy and safety of nutritional supplements, feeding strategies, and other proposed interventions. Careful evaluations of the impact of Vitamin A, zinc, or iron supplementation programs on child health must account for variations in nutritional status, body composition, levels of the micronutrients in different body compartments, multiple infectious disease burden, and attention to both functional and biomedical health outcomes (Prentice 2008, Roth et al. 2008, Stoltzfus 2008).

SCHISTOSOMIASIS

Schistosomiasis is one of the most prevalent parasitic infections worldwide and has important negative impacts on nutritional health (McGarvey et al. 1998, McGarvey 2000). An estimated 779 million people are at risk for schistosomiasis, with 207 million infected in 76 countries and territories (Lammie et al. 2006, Steinmann et al. 2006). Approximately 120 million people are symptomatic, and 20 million have severe and debilitating disease (Engels et al. 2002). The infection, schistosomiasis, is caused by the three major species of the trematode *Schistosoma*, *S. mansoni*, *S. hematobium*, and *S. japonicum*. Schistosome egg deposition in gastrointestinal tissues and subsequent inflammatory immune responses results in extensive clinical manifestations, including hepatomegaly, splenomegaly, and liver fibrosis from chronic infection with *S. mansoni* and *S. japonicum* (Wiest et al. 1994, Olveda et al. 1996, King et al. 2005). In the urinary form, *S. hematobium*, egg deposition leads to structural urinary tract disease, including bladder cancer (Warren et al. 1979, Michaud 2007). Infection intensity is measured (with error, Carabin et al. 2005) by the number of eggs in stool or urine, which is a proxy for the number of adult worms harbored in the body.

In addition to the more specific organ morbidities, which are more prevalent in adults, infection produces nutritional and functional consequences especially among children, which scholars refer to as subtle morbidities such as anemia, diarrhea, growth retardation, and cognitive deficits (McGarvey et al. 1992, 1993, 1996; Nokes et al. 1999; Ezeamama et al. 2005a,b; Friedman et al. 2005a,b; King et al. 2005; Finkelstein et al. 2008). Because antischistosomal curative chemotherapy treatment with Praziquantel has become more available globally, the distribution of infection intensity has shifted largely to low-to-moderate levels of infection. Following the changes in distribution of intensity of infection, the burden of disability has and will continue to shift from schistosomiasis-specific diseases to more general morbidity measures, especially nutritional deficits (McGarvey 2000, King et al. 2005). On the basis of earlier estimates, schistosomiasis accounts for 1.7–4.5 million DALYs lost each year worldwide, among the highest of all neglected tropical diseases (Morel 2000, Utzinger et al. 2001, WHO 2002). Recent work increased substantially the estimated disability resulting from all forms of schistosomiasis (King et al. 2005) and specifically from *S. japonicum*, the Asian schistosome (Jia et al. 2007, Finkelstein et al. 2008).

Specific nutritional effects and interactions with immunity of schistosomiasis have been a major recent area of study in our Philippine *S. japonicum* research (McGarvey et al. 2004). Partially influenced by an increased interest about immunity in anthropology (McDade 2003, 2005), I review our key findings and discuss implications for the interdisciplinary overlap of nutrition, anthropology, and public health.

S. japonicum infection was significantly related to decreased nutritional status, and schistosomiasis treatment improved nutritional status. At baseline the intensity of infection was inversely related to height adjusted z-score (HAZ) among children 7–12 years old after adjusting for age, gender, other helminths, and socioeconomic factors (Friedman et al. 2005a). Adjustment for a possessions index as a proxy for socioeconomic status (SES) allowed a more accurate assessment of the relationship between *S. japonicum* and nutritional status than was possible from our previous studies. In longitudinal analyses over an 18-month observation period, treatment produced moderate improvements in HAZ and BMI z-score (Coutinho et al. 2006a). Those who were nutritionally wasted at baseline BMI increased by 0.41 z-score units, whereas those stunted at baseline improved 0.17 z-score units in HAZ. Individuals aged 7–20 years with high-intensity reinfection at 18 months grew 2.6 cm less and gained 1.5 kg less than individuals who did not become reinfected.

Schistosomiasis is causally related to low hemoglobin and prevalence of anemia, which is due to a combination of factors including blood loss–mediated iron deficiency, anemia of inflammation, splenomegaly leading to red blood cell sequestration, and autoimmune hemolysis (Friedman et al. 2005b, Kanzaria et al. 2005). Because anemia is a major source of disability in children and women, with specific deficits in cognition, we explored in some detail the complex context of associations between schistosomiasis and anemia. Anemia was defined using the WHO age- and sex-specific cutoffs, and iron deficiency was defined as serum ferritin <12 ng/ml for persons aged <15 years and women of all ages and serum ferritin <18 ng/ml for men aged ≥15 years. Iron-deficiency anemia was defined as anemia with concurrent iron deficiency (Leenstra et al. 2006a). *S. japonicum* infection was related to decreased hemoglobin in a dose-dependent fashion after adjusting for age, sex, occult blood status, and other geohelminths such as hookworm, Ascaris, and Trichuris. Those with a high-intensity infection had hemoglobin levels that were 1.0 gr/dl lower than uninfected individuals (Friedman et al. 2005a). Individuals with a high-intensity infection had 6.6-fold increased odds of iron-deficiency anemia compared with individuals with no, light, or moderate-intensity infection. There was no evidence of iron deficiency in lower-intensity infections. In contrast, individuals with any *S. japonicum* intensity had a 3.8-fold increased risk of anemia without iron deficiency, suggesting the influence of infection on the anemia of inflammation and functional consequences of this anemia (Leenstra et al. 2006a).

Eighteen months after Praziquantel treatment, reinfection with *S. japonicum* was associated with a 0.39 g/dl lower hemoglobin level and 1.70-fold higher odds of all-cause anemia compared with individuals who did not become reinfected (Leenstra et al. 2006b). Reinfection was also associated with iron-deficiency anemia but only among those with high reinfection intensities. Conversely, reinfection was associated with noniron-deficiency anemia for all infection intensities. Reinfection was associated with serum interleukin-6 (IL-6) responses, and these responses were associated with noniron-deficiency anemia but not with iron-deficiency anemia (Leenstra et al. 2006b). Anemia of inflammation appears at all intensities of infection, but iron deficiency is detectable only among high-intensity infections.

Individuals with high-intensity *S. japonicum* infection had 2.6 g/L decreased serum albumin levels, a 0.21 z-score unit decrease in HAZ, and a 0.31 decrease in BMI z-score compared with low or moderately infected individuals over the 18 months of observation (Coutinho et al. 2006b). Reinfection was associated with decreased albumin. *S. japonicum* infection and reinfection were positively associated with both serum C-reactive protein (CRP) and IL-6 production. CRP, in turn, was inversely associated with BMI z-score and albumin. The results indicate that inflammation in general, and proinflammatory cytokines in particular, mediate *S. japonicum*–associated undernutrition.

In related cross-sectional work in the Philippines (Ezeamama et al. 2005a), we further quantified the polyparasitic impact of *S. japonicum* and other helminth infections on cognitive impairment demonstrated in our earlier study in China (Nokes et al. 1999). After adjusting for age, sex, nutritional status, hemoglobin, and SES, *S. japonicum* infection was associated with a threefold decrease in performance on tests of learning among children aged 7–18 years in villages in Leyte, the Philippines. *A. lumbricoides*, roundworm, infection was associated with a more than twofold odds of poor performance on tests of memory, and *T. trichiura*, whipworm, infection was associated with poor performance on tests of verbal fluency, odds ratio (OR) = 4.5.

The search for pubertal influences on schistosomiasis is based on the ubiquitous finding of the highest age-specific prevalence of infection found in those 10–20 years of age and the interpretation that susceptibility to reinfection decreases with age and development (Butterworth et al. 1988). We explored the interrelationships among undernutrition, immunity, susceptibility to *S. japonicum* infection, and puberty. The impact of pubertal development was measured by dehydroepiandrosterone sulfate (DHEAS) levels (Campbell 2006). At baseline in both males and females, DHEAS was related to both mediators of inflammation, CRP and IL-6, and prevalence of anemia after adjusting for age, SES, intensity of helminth infections, and household clustering of participants (Coutinho et al. 2007). Males and females with DHEAS levels in the lower decile had twofold and fourfold, respectively, higher prevalence of noniron-deficiency anemia compared with individuals with DHEAS in the upper decile. The intensity of infection among individuals with high DHEAS levels was 43% lower (28 eggs per g, $n = 243$), compared with individuals with low DHEAS levels (50 eggs per g, $n = 242$), even after adjusting for age, sex, and village (Kurtis et al. 2006).

DHEAS: dehydroepiandrosterone sulfate

Notably, longitudinal data showed that post-treatment, increased baseline DHEAS levels were associated with resistance to reinfection (Kurtis et al. 2006). The intensity of reinfection among individuals with high DHEAS levels was 42% lower, compared with individuals with low DHEAS levels, after adjusting for age, baseline intensity of *S. japonicum* infection, village, sex, and water contact. Further longitudinal analyses showed that increased levels of DHEAS over the 18 months were associated with improved nutritional status in both males and females after adjusting for age, SES, and helminth infections (Coutinho et al. 2007). Males with DHEAS levels in the upper decile had 26% greater upper arm muscle area Z score and 63% greater sum of triceps and subscapular skin fold z score compared with individuals with DHEAS in the lower decile. Similarly, females with DHEAS levels in the upper decile had 37% greater sum of skinfolds. DHEAS showed dose-dependent inverse associations with CRP, IL-1, and the production of IL-6 (Coutinho et al. 2007). These inflammatory markers, in turn, were consistently associated with undernutrition and anemia. These results suggest that the puberty-associated rise in DHEAS down-modulates proinflammatory immune responses and thereby reduces undernutrition and anemia in a population experiencing a high burden of chronic helminth infections. This novel regulatory mechanism of inflammation-related nutritional morbidity emphasizes the importance of treating prepubescent children for helminth infections.

Last, we explored ways to describe and estimate the potential synergistic relationships on anemia among schistosomiasis and the three geohelminths, hookworm, *A. lumbricoides*, and *T. trichiura*. These worm infections, which require transmission in part by contamination of the environment by eggs in feces and human exposure to the eggs or larval forms, tend to be correlated in developing countries owing to the poverty and lack of sanitary infrastructure. Children with polyparasitic infections (three or four parasite species at moderate intensity or greater) had a 7.9-fold greater risk of anemia compared with children with no or one parasite infection at low intensity after adjusting for the effects of age, sex, pubertal development, SES, and nutritional status (Ezeamama et al. 2005b). In quantitative estimation of synergy we found that moderate or high-intensity coinfection of hookworm and *S. japonicum* (OR = 13.2), and of hookworm and *T. trichiura* (OR = 5.34), were associated with higher odds of anemia relative to children without those respective moderate to high coinfections (Ezeamama et al. 2008). For coinfections of hookworm and *S. japonicum* and of *T. trichiura* and hookworm, the estimated indices of synergy were 2.9 and 1.4, respectively. Coinfections of hookworm and either *S. japonicum* or *T. trichiura* were associated with higher levels of anemia than expected if the effects of these species had only independent effects on anemia. These data suggest that integrated antihelminthic treatment programs with simultaneous deworming for *S. japonicum* and some geohelminths could yield a greater-than-additive benefit for reducing anemia in helminth-endemic regions.

In the absence of an efficacious schistosomiasis vaccine and the economic development-related construction of sanitation systems in rural areas of the world, antischistosomal treatment with Praziquantel provides the bulwark of public health and clinical options to improve nutritional and general population health and reduce transmission (Lammie et al. 2006, Taylor 2008). Mass treatment of populations and targeted mass treatment of school-aged children remain favorite and effective strategies to improve disease control and reduce infection transmission (Fenwick & Webster 2006). There is some concern among schistosomiasis researchers and policy makers about sustainability of the mass treatment programs after the initial efforts because reductions in infection intensity and severe specific morbidities follow repeated mass treatment. Communities may believe schistosomiasis infection and disease control are less salient while transmission continues and may rise with changes in ecological and socioeconomic factors (Zhu et al. 2008). In addition, mass treatment for

S. japonicum is further complicated because it is a zoonotic infection, with several mammals likely contributing to transmission (McGarvey et al. 2006, Fernandez et al. 2007, Riley et al. 2008). Sustainable interruption of ecological processes to reduce transmission remains a concept in poor rural areas, although Wang et al. (2009) recently reported on a successful demonstration project among lake-side villages in China focused on animal and snail control, sanitation improvements, and farming mechanization. As part of our interdisciplinary schistosomiasis research in the Philippines, we undertook a mass treatment program in 50 villages with an eligible population of 30,187 residents in Western Samar, the Philippines (Tallo et al. 2008). Before the mass treatment, advocacy, information dissemination, and social mobilization activities were conducted with village political and health leaders primarily responsible for community mobilization. Community involvement was measured using a participation index. We found that only a village-level average of 53.1% of residents came to the treatment site, leading to a mass-treatment coverage with an average of 48.3%. At the individual level, participation proportions were higher among males, preschool and school-age children, individuals not participating in the transmission research, and those who provided a fecal sample. At the village level, better community involvement was associated with increased participation, but even in villages with high community involvement, the average participation was only 56%. Larger village population was associated with decreased participation.

There are several implications for anthropologists involved in schistosomiasis studies or more generally in interdisciplinary research on parasitic worms. First, from a biological and biocultural anthropology perspective, the changing distribution of the intensity of schistosomiasis infection to more low- and moderate-intensity infections will shift the disease burden to nutritional and functional morbidities, and specific organ pathology may decrease in relative importance. There will

be an increase in such morbidities as delayed growth and size for age in young children and adolescents and prevalence of anemia, both iron deficient and noniron deficient. Further work is needed to confirm and elaborate the biologically plausible associations among immune responses, susceptibility to infection, undernutrition, and pubertal development. Evolutionary and life-history perspectives on immunology, body size, pubertal development, and nutritional stressors may yield novel insights about the influence of changing patterns of parasitic infection intensity and severity on population biology and health (McDade 2003, 2005). The cognition studies indicate the obvious need for biocultural anthropologists to participate in development of measures of cognition and performance that are salient for daily-life and adult life-course development perspectives.

Second, the link between infection and nutritional health indicates the need to reduce disease and infection transmission through chemotherapy with Praziquantel. Thus there is a need for intensive study of sociocultural facets of mass antischistosomal (or other antiworm) drug administration campaigns. The scenario of low participation in mass treatment raises concern for the ongoing mass-treatment initiatives to reduce schistosomiasis now taking place in developing countries (Taylor 2008). Much more intensive and extensive community-based education, preparation, and perhaps incentives may be required to increase participation and coverage. These need to be formulated after detailed qualitative and quantitative interdisciplinary research in endemic villages about schistosomiasis knowledge and attitudes, perceptions of the burden of disease, and reasons for seeking or refusing treatment. Some insights for potential ethnographic and other qualitative research may be gained from behavioral economic research on mass deworming programs that suggest that level of community knowledge and social network attitudes about deworming have strong and paradoxical influences on acceptance of mass drug administration (Miguel & Kremer 2003). In summary, there appear to be many opportunities for anthropologists' involvement in interdisciplinary fundamental and translational research on schistosomiasis and other worm infections. Finally, it is difficult to resist the notion that trained and committed community-level health workers could play a significant role in the research and evidence-based clinical and public health activities to improve schistosomiasis control.

SAMOAN OBESITY AND TYPE 2 DIABETES

Anthropological and public health studies of the impact of modernization on the human biology and health of Samoans have occupied this author, my colleagues, our students, and our mentors for more than 30 years (Hanna & Baker 1979, McGarvey & Baker 1979, Bindon & Baker 1985, Baker et al. 1986). Samoans residing in California, Hawaii, American Samoa, and Samoa are characterized by high levels of overweight, obesity, and the associated chronic noncommunicable diseases including hypertension, type 2 diabetes, high-risk blood lipid profiles, and mortality from these and other conditions. These levels have increased over the past 30 years in adults and children (McGarvey 1991, 2001; Roberts et al. 2004; Keighley et al. 2006, 2007; DiBello et al. 2009).

In 2002–2003 ~90% of all men and women in American Samoa, and in Samoa 58% of men and 83% of women, had BMI ≥ 26 kg/m^2 (Keighley et al. 2006, 2007). The prevalence of type 2 diabetes among those aged 25–54 years from American Samoa increased from 12.9% in 1990 to 17.2% in 2002 in men, and in women doubled from 8.1% in 1990 to 16.7% in 2002 (Keighley et al. 2007). Over all adult ages, 18–74 years, seen in 2002 in American Samoa, type 2 diabetes prevalence was 19.6%. Diabetes prevalence in Samoa was far lower than in American Samoa, but between 1991 and 2003, there were striking increases in prevalence in all sex and age groups. For example, 2.4% of men aged 25–54 years had diabetes in 1991, but this number rose to 6.0% in 2003. In the same aged women, prevalence rose from 3.0% to 8.2%. In 2003, among all adults, type 2 diabetes preva-

lence in Samoa was 9.3% and 12.6% in men and women, respectively (Keighley et al. 2007).

Present Samoan groups have an exceedingly high population health risk from obesity-related diseases. Regardless of the exciting and necessary etiologic research in these modernizing Polynesians that has tried to unravel evolutionary, genetic, and physiological influences, the contemporary nutritional environment, and their interactions (Galanis et al. 1999; Ezeamama et al. 2006; Keighley et al. 2006, 2007; Dai et al. 2007, 2008; Åberg et al. 2008, 2009), it is crucial to use interdisciplinary approaches now to collaborate with Samoan organizations to reduce the present and future health burdens from overweight and related conditions.

Translating recent research advances into communities at risk is important to eliminate disease disparities but requires thoughtful adaptation to meet the needs of the community effectively with emphasis on social, economic, and cultural heterogeneities. Our translational research on diabetes emphasizes the cultural translation of chronic disease self-management in the Samoan context and the improvement of diabetes health care delivery at a primary health care center through education of care providers (Rosen et al. 2008). Although the need for a diabetes intervention among American Samoans was clear, to be effective, any intervention must be tailored to local needs. I describe four stages of the research: formative qualitative research; development of the behavioral intervention; implementation of the trial to test efficacy of a CHW intervention with diabetes patients; and qualitative data collection after the trial with all study participants, CHWs, and clinic staff about their experiences in the study in order to make interpretations about sustainability and scale-up.

The first research stage has been completed and involved learning about the current state of diabetes care and the experiences of living with diabetes. We allocated substantial resources to design and conduct formative qualitative research components including focus groups with people with diabetes and in-depth interviews with providers and with community diabetes stakeholders. The information we gathered and interpreted was used to take existing behavioral theory, measures, and intervention materials and adapt and implement them into the context of conducting a randomized controlled trial of CHW effectiveness in improving diabetes management. Several key results came from the patient focus groups, including confirmation that almost all patients accepted the biomedical model of diabetes with reference to overweight, diet, and exercise. This was necessary to establish before we attempted any type of behavioral intervention, although we note for future work among Samoans that acceptance of the biomedical disease model may not be universal among those who are not diabetes patients. Patients were ready for more personalized care and projected that they would accept a CHW-based behavioral intervention (Rosen et al. 2008). In addition, the role of stress stemming from familial obligations featured prominently in discussions about impediments to all aspects of self-management, from keeping clinic appointments to eating correctly and getting enough exercise (Elstad et al. 2008). Among providers, in-depth interviews and standard measures of diabetes care practices showed their support for a goal of working with patients to manage diabetes and their desire for more specialty training in diabetes care, but they also revealed room for improvement in patients' beliefs and practices about the importance of maintaining normal blood glucose levels (Bitton et al. 2006).

In the second stage, the CHW intervention was culturally translated and implemented into the Samoan context using already existing evidence-based algorithms and protocols. The main evidence base used to develop individual treatment action plans with the CHWs is the Precede-Proceed Model of behavioral change for those with chronic diseases (Green & Kreuter 1999). This model is built on more than 40 years of work and has been applied in numerous cultural contexts. The goals are to diagnose health-related behaviors and environments and evaluate interventions intended to influence these factors. Precede involves

five phases of diagnosis: (*a*) Social diagnosis identifies problems that impact quality of life, from the perspective of community members; (*b*) epidemiological diagnosis identifies health issues associated with poor quality of life; (*c*) behavioral and environmental diagnosis assesses health practices and nonbehavioral factors associated with health problems; (*d*) educational diagnosis prioritizes those factors, which if modified, are most likely to result in behavior change—these factors are categorized as predisposing factors that motivate behavior (e.g., knowledge, attitudes, beliefs), enabling factors that facilitate action (e.g., access, skills), reinforcing factors that serve to strengthen motivation for the behavior (e.g., family, peers, community); (*e*) administrative and policy diagnosis determines resources needed to implement the program and assesses policy compatibility within the organization and community. Then Proceed involves four additional phases: (*f*) implementation and evaluation, (*g*) process, (*h*) impact, and (*i*) outcome evaluation.

The diabetes problem is more complicated because it involves intervening on several behaviors, such as diet, physical activity, self-monitoring, use of medications, and health care seeking, each involving its own educational diagnosis and intervention plan. The methods of communication by Samoan CHWs, the information and educational materials, the salience of the most modifiable behaviors among patients and families, and clinical management of diabetes were all established and agreed on by the Samoan collaborators and team members during the second stage of the research in light of the need to translate the concepts and methods for initiating and supporting patient behavioral change.

The third stage of research, which began in February 2009, is the randomized trial to test the effectiveness of a CHW and primary-care coordinated intervention to provide outreach, education, and support to type 2 diabetes patients and their families. In one group of villages, the CHWs will educate participants and family members about diabetes and help them make and keep clinic appointments and learn how to eat more healthfully, to exercise safely, and to follow their doctors' recommendations to care for their diabetes. Those in the second group of villages, which is called the wait-list control group, will receive their usual care for diabetes at the primary health care center. At baseline and at a one-year follow-up, all participants will answer questions about their diabetes, diet and exercise behaviors, and adherence to diabetes care guidelines and be measured for glycosolated hemoglobin levels, blood pressure, BMI, and abdominal circumference. The last and fourth stage will be the execution of follow-up focus groups and data analysis at the end of the intervention delivery, which should provide key findings about the perceived efficacy, acceptability, and sustainability of CHW interventions.

We plan to continue both basic and applied translational research on behavioral and biological aspects of the nutrition transition among Samoans. The basic research will continue asking questions about genetic, physiological, and energetic factors as well as behavioral and socioeconomic factors at the individual and group level that ultimately structure the causes and consequences of adiposity and related conditions (Drewnowski & Spector 2004; Ezeamama et al. 2006; Wilkinson & Pickett 2006, 2008). In addition to more health psychology–based individual interventions, such as the diabetes study, we are planning to conduct applied intervention research on overweight-related behaviors at more structural levels using villages and religious and social organizations. The goal of these interventions will be to improve the ability of families and other groups to make changes to their consumer, occupational, recreational, and psychosocial environments to enable easier healthful choices by individuals about their energetic behaviors (Harris et al. 2008).

CONCLUSION

Anthropologists can draw several general conclusions from this idiosyncratic summary and review. Despite the relative success of child survival activities, there remains enormous variation and unacceptable health inequalities as the world's populations experience a range of health transitions (Jamison et al. 2006, Merson et al. 2006). These inequalities exist and are likely to persist across all ages and types of morbidity and mortality, including the topics covered here: infant and child mortality, worm infections of school-age children and adolescents, and noncommunicable diseases and their risk factors among adults and children. These inequalities in health are associated with both global and intrapopulation socioeconomic and political factors in complex ways that defy the easy translation of macrolevel generalizations to the design of efficacious and cost-effective community-level interventions. Anthropology's unique attention to community-level factors, shared social, behavioral, and ecological phenomena, and greater attention to heterogeneity within communities should be engaged as part of the efforts to help produce both fundamental and translational knowledge to reduce health inequities.

Before intervention trials can begin, there must be a solid and detailed understanding of the experiences of the community about all aspects of the health condition of interest and any putative interventions to reduce the disease burden. This formative work is the first stage of translational research and should include social scientists, especially anthropologists. Anthropological methods and concepts should be used to involve the community, including stakeholders, leaders, and the general populace, to establish informal and formal organizations, such as community-based associations, that will work actively with scholars and intervention scientists to conduct and disseminate both etiologic and translational research.

Finally, hallmarks of anthropological inquiry such as our holistic and value-free perspectives are needed to investigate local population responses to health and disease conditions before any interventions are designed. Patterned or shared behaviors, and individual actions, that appear to increase risk need to be understood within a cultural and historical context as logical or practical accommodations to the challenges to individual and community survival, well-being, and flourishing. We must as anthropologists try to understand why community members, parents, traditional and biomedical care providers, CHWs, local government officials, ministries of health officials, and central government officials act the way they do regarding morbidity and mortality risks. A combination of persistent, respectful studies using both qualitative and quantitative research methods may reveal processes, or stages, of behavioral decision-making that elevate risks to health at many different levels. Understanding how these stages unfold and relate to one another in an explicit ecological, historical, cultural, and political-economic context is our scholarly responsibility as anthropologists involved in population health studies.

DISCLOSURE STATEMENT

The authors are not aware of any affiliations, memberships, funding, or financial holdings that might be perceived as affecting the objectivity of this review.

LITERATURE CITED

Åberg K, Dai F, Keighley ED, Sun G, Indugula SR, et al. 2009. Susceptibility loci for adiposity-related phenotypes on 8p, 9p and 16q in a combined study sample from American Samoa and Samoa. *Obesity* 17(3):518–24

Åberg K, Dai F, Sun G, Keighley ED, Indugula SR, et al. 2008. A genome-wide linkage scan identifies multiple chromosomal regions influencing serum lipid levels in the population on the Samoan Islands. *J. Lipid Res.* 49:2169–78

Baker PT, Hanna JM, Baker TS, eds. 1986. *The Changing Samoans: Behavior and Health in Transition*. New York: Oxford Press

Baqui AH, El-Arifeen S, Darmstadt GL, Ahmed S, Williams EK, et al. for the Projahnmo Study Group. 2008. Effect of community-based newborn-care intervention package implemented through two service-delivery strategies in Sylhet district, Bangladesh: a cluster-randomised controlled trial. *Lancet* 371:1936–44

Bindon JR, Baker PT. 1985. Modernization, migration and obesity among Samoan adults. *Ann. Hum. Biol.* 12:67–76

Bitton A, DePue J, Tuitele J, McGarvey ST. 2006. Patient and provider attitudes toward type 2 diabetes care in American Samoa. *J. Gen. Intern. Med.* 21(S4):153–54 (Abstr.)

Black RE, Morris SS, Bryce J. 2003. Where and why are 10 million children dying every year? *Lancet* 361:2226–34

Butterworth AE, Fulford AJ, Dunne DW, Ouma JH, Sturrock RF. 1988. Longitudinal studies on human schistosomiasis. *Phil. Trans. R. Soc. London B Biol. Sci.* 321(1207):495–511

Campbell B. 2006. Adrenarche and the evolution of human life history. *Am. J. Hum. Biol.* 18(5):569–89

Carabin H, Marshall C, Joseph L, Riley S, Aligui GD, et al. 2005. Estimating and modelling the dynamics of the intensity of infection with *Schistosoma japonicum* in villagers of Leyte, Philippines. Part I: A Bayesian cumulative logit model. The Schistosomiasis Transmission and Ecology Project (STEP). *Am. J. Trop. Med. Hyg.* 72(6):745–53

Coutinho HM, Acosta LP, McGarvey ST, Jarilla B, Jiz M, et al. 2006a. Nutritional status improves after treatment of *Schistosoma japonicum*-infected children and adolescents. *J. Nutr.* 136:183–87

Coutinho HM, Leenstra T, Acosta LP, Olveda RM, McGarvey ST, et al. 2007. Higher serum concentrations of DHEAS predict improved nutritional status in Helminth-infected children, adolescents, and young adults in Leyte, the Philippines. *J. Nutr.* 137:433–37

Coutinho HM, Leenstra T, Acosta LP, Su L, Jarilla B, et al. 2006b. Pro-inflammatory cytokines and C-reactive protein are associated with undernutrition in the context of *Schistosoma japonicum* infection. *Am. J. Trop. Med. Hyg.* 75:720–26

Dai F, Keighley ED, Sun G, Indugula SR, Roberts ST, et al. 2007. Genome-wide scan for adiposity-related phenotypes in adults from American Samoa. *Int. J. Obes.* 31:1832–42

Dai F, Sun G, Åberg K, Keighley ED, Indugula SR, et al. 2008. A whole genome linkage scan identifies multiple chromosomal regions influencing adiposity-related traits among Samoans. *Ann. Hum. Genet.* 72(6):780–92

DiBello J, Baylin A, Viali S, Tuitele J, Bausserman L, McGarvey ST. 2009. Adiponectin and type 2 diabetes in Samoan adults. *Am. J. Hum. Biol.* 21:389–91

Drewnowski A, Spector SE. 2004. Poverty and obesity: the role of energy density and energy costs. *Am. J. Clin. Nutr.* 79(1):6–16

Elstad E, Tusiofo C, Rosen RK, McGarvey ST. 2008. Living with Ma'i Suka: individual, familial, cultural, and environmental stress among patients with type 2 diabetes mellitus and their caregivers in American Samoa. *Prev. Chronic Dis.* 5(3):e1–10

Engels D, Chitsulo L, Montresor A, Savioli L. 2002. The global epidemiological situation of schistosomiasis and new approaches to control and research. *Acta Trop.* 82:139–46

Ezeamama A, Viali S, Tuitele J, McGarvey ST. 2006. The influence of socioeconomic factors on cardiovascular disease risk factors in the context of economic development in the Samoan archipelago. *Soc. Sci. Med.* 63:2533–45

Ezeamama AE, Friedman JF, Acosta LP, Bellinger DC, Langdon GC, et al. 2005a. Helminth infection and cognitive impairment among Filipino children. *Am. J. Trop. Med. Hyg.* 72:540–47

Ezeamama AE, Friedman JF, Olveda RM, Acosta LP, Kurtis JD, et al. 2005b. Functional significance of low-intensity polyparasite helminth infections in anemia. *J. Infect Dis.* 192:2160–65

Ezeamama AE, McGarvey ST, Acosta LP, Zierler S, Manalo DL, et al. 2008. The synergistic effect of concomitant schistosomiasis, hookworm, and Trichuris Infections on children's anemia burden. *PLoS Negl. Trop. Dis.* 2(6):e245

Fenwick A, Webster JP. 2006. Schistosomiasis: challenges for control, treatment and drug resistance. *Curr. Opin. Infect Dis.* 19(6):577–82

Fernandez TJ Jr, Tarafder MR, Balolong E Jr, Joseph L, Willingham AL III, et al. 2007. Prevalence of *Schistosoma japonicum* infection among animals in 50 villages of Samar province, The Philippines. *Vector-Borne Zoonotic Dis.* 7:147–55

Finkelstein J, Schleinitz M, Carabin H, McGarvey ST. 2008. Decision-model estimation of the age-specific disability weight for *Schistosomiasis japonica*: a systematic review of the literature. *PLoS Negl. Trop. Dis.* 2(3):e158

Friedman JF, Kanzaria HK, Acosta LP, Langdon GC, Manalo DL, et al. 2005a. Relationship between *Schistosoma japonicum* and nutritional status among children and young adults in Leyte, the Philippines. *Am. J. Trop. Med. Hyg.* 72:527–33

Friedman JF, Kanzaria HK, McGarvey ST. 2005b. Human schistosomiasis and anemia: the relationship and potential mechanisms. *Trends Parasitol.* 21:386–92

Galanis DJ, McGarvey ST, Quested C, Sio B, Fa'amuli-Afele S. 1999. Dietary intake of modernizing Samoans: implications for risk of cardiovascular disease. *J. Am. Diet. Assoc.* 99(2):184–90

Green LW, Kreuter MW. 1999. *Health Promotion Planning: An Educational and Ecological Approach.* Mountain View, CA: Mayfield. 3rd ed.

Haas JD, Pelletier DE. 1989. Nutrition and human population biology. In *Human Population Biology: A Trans–disciplinary Science*, ed. MA Little, JD Haas, pp. 152–70. NY: Academic

Hanna JM, Baker PT. 1979. Biocultural correlates to the blood pressure of Samoan migrants in Hawaii. *Hum. Biol.* 51(4):481–97

Harris J, Pomeranz J, Lobstein T, Brownell KD. 2008. A crisis in the marketplace: how food marketing contributes to childhood obesity and what can be done. *Annu. Rev. Public Health* 30:211–25

Jamison DT, Breman JG, Measham AR, Alleyne G, Claeson M, et al, eds. 2006. *Disease Control Priorities in Developing Countries.* New York, NY: Oxford Univ. Press

Jia TW, Zhou XN, Wang XH, Utzinger J, Steinmann P, Wu XH. 2007. Assessment of the age-specific disability weight of chronic *Schistosomiasis japonica*. *Bull. World Health Organ.* 85:458–65

Jones G, Steketee RW, Black RE, Bhutta ZA, Morris SS, and the Bellagio Child Survival Study Group. 2003. How many child deaths can we prevent this year? *Lancet* 362:65–71

Kanzaria HK, Acosta LP, Langdon GC, Manalo DL, Olveda RM, et al. 2005. *Schistosoma japonicum* and occult blood loss in endemic villages in Leyte, the Philippines. *Am. J. Trop. Med. Hyg.* 72:115–20

Keighley ED, McGarvey ST, Quested C, McCuddin C, Viali S, Maga U. 2007. Nutrition and health in modernizing Samoans: temporal trends and adaptive perspectives. In *Health Change in the Asia-Pacific Region: Biocultural and Epidemiological Approaches*, ed. R Ohtsuka, SJ Ulijaszek, pp. 147–91. Cambridge, UK: Cambridge Univ. Press

Keighley ED, McGarvey ST, Turituri P, Viali S. 2006. Farming and adiposity in Samoan adults. *Am. J. Hum. Biol.* 18:112–21

King CH, Dickman K, Tisch DJ. 2005. Reassessment of the cost of chronic helmintic infection: a meta-analysis of disability-related outcomes in endemic schistosomiasis. *Lancet* 365:1561–69

Kurtis JD, Friedman JF, Leenstra T, Langdon GC, Wu HW, et al. 2006. Pubertal development predicts resistance to infection and reinfection with *Schistosoma japonicum. Clin. Infect Dis.* 42:1692–96

Lammie PJ, Fenwick A, Utzinger J. 2006. A blueprint for success: integration of neglected tropical disease control programmes. *Trends Parasitol.* 22:313–21

Leenstra T, Acosta LP, Langdon GC, Manalo DL, Su L, et al. 2006a. *Schistosomiasis japonica*, anemia, and iron status in children, adolescents, and young adults in Leyte, Philippines. *Am. J. Clin. Nutr.* 83:371–79

Leenstra T, Coutinho HM, Acosta LP, Langdon GC, Su L, et al. 2006b. *Schistosoma japonicum* reinfection after praziquantel treatment causes anemia associated with inflammation. *Infect. Immun.* 74:6398–407

Lopez AD, Mathers CD, Ezzati M, Jamison DT, Murray CJL. 2006a. *Global Burden of Disease and Risk Factors.* New York: Oxford Univ. Press

Lopez AD, Mathers CD, Ezzati M, Jamison DT, Murray CJL. 2006b. Global and regional burden of disease and risk factors, 2001: systematic analysis of population health data. *Lancet* 367:1747–57

Maddon T, Hofman KJ, Kupfer L, Glass RI. 2008. Implementation science. *Science* 318:1728–29

Malina RM, Bouchard C, Bar-Or O. 2004. *Growth, Maturation, and Physical Activity.* Champaign, IL: Hum. Kinet. 2nd ed.

McDade TW. 2003. Life history theory and the immune system: steps toward a human ecological immunology. *Yearb. Phys. Anthropol.* 46:100–25

McDade TW. 2005. The ecologies of human immune function. *Annu. Rev. Anthropol.* 34:495–521

McGarvey ST. 1991. Obesity in Samoans and a perspective on its etiology in Polynesians. *Am. J. Clin. Nutr.* 53(6):1586S–94

McGarvey ST. 1998. Intestinal parasitism. In *Cambridge Encyclopedia of Human Growth and Development*, ed. SJ Ulijaszek, FE Johnston, MA Preece, p. 337. London: Cambridge Univ. Press

McGarvey ST. 2000. Schistosomiasis: impact on childhood and adolescent growth, malnutrition, and morbidity. *Semin. Pediatr. Infect. Dis.* 11(4):269–74

McGarvey ST. 2001. Cardiovascular disease (CVD) risk factors in Samoa and American Samoa, 1990–95. *Pac. Health Dialog.* 8(1):157–62

McGarvey ST. 2007. Population health. *Ann. Hum. Biol.* 34(4):393–96

McGarvey ST, Aligui G, Daniel BL, Peters P, Olveda RM, Olds GR. 1992. Child growth and *Schistosomiasis japonica* in northeastern Leyte, the Philippines: cross-sectional results. *Am. J. Trop. Med. Hyg.* 46:571–81

McGarvey ST, Aligui G, Graham KK, Peters P, Olds GR, Olveda RM. 1996. *Schistosomiasis japonica* and childhood nutritional status in northeastern Leyte, the Philippines: a randomized trial of praziquantel versus placebo. *Am. J. Trop. Med. Hyg.* 54:498–502

McGarvey ST, Aligui G, Kurtis JD, Willingham AL, Carabin H, Olveda R. 2004. Multidisciplinary perspectives on *Schistosoma japonicum*. In *The Changing Face of Disease: Implications for Society*, ed. N Mascie-Taylor, J Peters, ST McGarvey, pp. 114–29. Boca Raton, FL: CRC Press

McGarvey ST, Baker PT. 1979. The effects of modernization and migration on Samoan blood pressure. *Hum. Biol.* 51:461–79

McGarvey ST, Bindon J, Crews D, Schendel D. 1989. Modernization and adiposity: causes and consequences. In *Human Population Biology: A Trans–Disciplinary Science*, ed. MA Little, JD Haas, pp. 263–79. New York: Academic

McGarvey ST, Carabin H, Balolong E Jr, Bélisle P, Fernandez T, et al. 2006. Cross-sectional associations between animal and human intensity of infection with *Schistosoma japonicum* in Samar Province, the Philippines. *Bull WHO* 84(6):446–52

McGarvey ST, Wu G, Zhang S, Wang Y, Peters P, et al. 1993. Child growth, nutritional status, and *Schistosomiasis japonica* in Jiangxi, People's Republic of China. *Am. J. Trop. Med. Hyg.* 48:547–53

Merson MH, Black RE, Mills A, eds. 2006. *International Public Health*. Boston: Jones & Bartlett. 2nd ed.

Michaud DS. 2007. Chronic inflammation and bladder cancer. *Urol. Oncol.* 25(3):260–68

Miguel E, Kremer M. 2003. *Networks, social learning and technology adoption: the case of deworming drugs in Kenya*. Unpubl. manuscr., Dept. Econ., Univ. Calif., Berkeley

Morel CM. 2000. Reaching maturity—25 years of the TDR. *Parasitol. Today* 16:522–28

Nokes C, McGarvey ST, Shiue L, Wu G, Wu H, et al. 1999. Evidence for an improvement in cognitive function following treatment of *Schistosoma japonicum* infection in Chinese primary schoolchildren. *Am. J. Trop. Med. Hyg.* 60(4):556–65

Olveda RM, Daniel BL, Ramirez BD, Aligui GD, Acosta LP, et al. 1996. *Schistosomiasis japonica* in the Philippines: the long-term impact of population based chemotherapy on infection, transmission, and morbidity. *J. Infect. Dis.* 174:163–72

Pike RL, Brown ML. 1967. *Nutrition: An Integrated Approach*. New York: Wiley

Pelletier DL. 1994. The potentiating effects of malnutrition on child mortality: epidemiologic evidence and policy implications. *Nutr. Rev.* 52:409–15

Popkin BM, Gordon-Larsen P. 2004. The nutrition transition: worldwide obesity dynamics and their determinants. *Int. J. Obes. Relat. Metab. Disord.* 28(Suppl. 3):S2–9

Prentice AM. 2008. Iron metabolism, malaria, and other infections: What is all the fuss about? *J. Nutr.* 138(12):2537–41

Reyes-García V, McDade TW, Molina JL, Leonard WR, Tanner SN, et al. 2008. Social rank and adult male nutritional status: evidence of the social gradient in health from a foraging-farming society. *Soc. Sci. Med.* 67(12):2107–15

Riley S, Carabin H, Bélisle P, Joseph L, Tallo V, et al. 2008. Multi-host transmission dynamics of *Schistosomiasis japonica* in Samar Province, the Philippines. *PLoS Med.* 5(1):e18

Roberts ST, McGarvey ST, Viali S, Quested C. 2004. Youth blood pressure levels in Samoa in 1979 and 1991–93. *Am. J. Hum. Biol.* 16(2):158–67

Rosen RK, DePue J, McGarvey ST. 2008. Overweight and diabetes in American Samoa: translating research into effective health care practice. *Med. Health RI.* 91(12):372–77

Roth DE, Caulfield LE, Ezzati M, Black RE. 2008. Acute lower respiratory infections in childhood: opportunities for reducing the global burden through nutritional interventions. *Bull. WHO* 86(5):356–64

Ruger JP. 2006. Ethics and governance of global health inequalities. *J. Epidemiol. Community Health* 60:998–1002

Satterfield D, Burd C, Valdez L, Hosey G, Eagle Shield J. 2002. The "in-between people": participation of community health representatives in diabetes prevention and care in American Indian and Alaska Native communities. *Health Promot. Pract.* 3:166–75

Steinmann P, Keiser J, Bos R, Tanner M, Utzinger J. 2006. Schistosomiasis and water resources development: systematic review, meta-analysis, and estimates of people at risk. *Lancet Infect. Dis.* 6:411–25

Stoltzfus RJ. 2008. Research needed to strengthen science and programs for the control of iron deficiency and its consequences in young children. *J. Nutr.* 138(12):2542–46

Tallo VL, Carabin H, Alday PP, Balolong E Jr, Olveda RM, McGarvey ST. 2008. Is mass treatment the appropriate schistosomiasis elimination strategy? *Bull. World Health Organ.* 86(10):765–71

Taylor M. 2008. Global trends in schistosomiasis control. *Bull. WHO* 86(10):738

Ungar PS, Grine FE, Teaford MF. 2006. Diet in early *Homo*: a review of the evidence and a new model of adaptive versatility. *Annu. Rev. Anthropol.* 35:209–28

Utzinger J, Xiao SH, N'Goran EK, Bergquist R, Tanner M. 2001. The potential of artemether for the control of schistosomiasis. *Int. J. Parasitol.* 31:1549–62

Wang LD, Chen HG, Guo JG, Zeng XJ, Hong XL, et al. 2009. A strategy to control transmission of *Schistosoma japonicum* in China. *N. Engl. J. Med.* 360(2):121–28

Warren KS, Mahmoud AA, Muruka JF, Whittaker LR, Ouma JH, Arap Siongok TK. 1979. *Schistosomiasis haematobia* in coast province Kenya: relationship between egg output and morbidity. *Am. J. Trop. Med. Hyg.* 28:864–70

West KP, Caballero B, Black RE. 2006. Nutrition. See Merson et al. 2006, pp. 187–272

WHO. 2002. Prevention and control of schistosomiasis and soil-transmitted helminthiasis: report of a WHO Expert Committee. *WHO Tech. Rep. Ser. 912*. World Health Organ., Geneva

WHO Collab. Study Team Role Breastfeed. Prev. Infant Mortal. 2000. Effect of breastfeeding on infant and child mortality due to infectious diseases in less developed countries: a pooled analysis. *Lancet* 355:451–55

Wiest PM, Wu G, Zhong S, McGarvey ST, Yuan J, et al. 1994. Impact of annual screening and chemotherapy with praziquantel on *Schistosomiasis japonica* on Jishan Island, People's Republic of China. *Am. J. Trop. Med. Hyg.* 51:162–69

Wilkinson RG, Pickett KE. 2006. Income inequality and population health: a review and explanation of the evidence. *Soc. Sci. Med.* 62(7):1768–84

Wilkinson RG, Pickett KE. 2008. Income inequality and socioeconomic gradients in mortality. *Am. J. Public Health* 98(4):699–704

Willett W. 1998. *Nutritional Epidemiology*. New York: Oxford Univ. Press. 2nd ed.

Witmer A, Seifer SD, Finocchio L, Leslie J, O'Neil EH. 1995. Community health workers: integral members of the health care work force. *Am. J. Public Health* 85:1055–58

Zhu HM, Xiang S, Yang K, Wu XH, Zhou XN. 2008. Three Gorges Dam and its impact on the potential transmission of schistosomiasis in regions along the Yangtze River. *Ecohealth* 5(2):137–48

Amazonian Archaeology

Michael Heckenberger[1] and Eduardo Góes Neves[2]

[1] Department of Anthropology, University of Florida, Gainesville, Florida 32605;
email: mheck@ufl.edu

[2] Museu de Arqueologia e Etnologia, Universidade de São Paulo, São Paulo,
Brazil 05508-900; email: edgneves@usp.br

Annu. Rev. Anthropol. 2009. 38:251–66

First published online as a Review in Advance on
June 23, 2009

The *Annual Review of Anthropology* is online at
anthro.annualreviews.org

This article's doi:
10.1146/annurev-anthro-091908-164310

Key Words

indigenous culture history, anthropogenic landscapes, premodern
complex societies, political ecology

Abstract

Amazonian archaeology has made major advances in recent decades,
particularly in understanding coupled human environmental systems.
Like other tropical forest regions, prehistoric social formations were
long portrayed as small-scale, dispersed communities that differed little in organization from recent indigenous societies and had negligible impacts on the essentially pristine forest. Archaeology documents
substantial variation that, while showing similarities to other world regions, presents novel pathways of early foraging and domestication,
semi-intensive resource management, and domesticated landscapes associated with diverse small- and medium-sized complex societies. Late
prehistoric regional polities were articulated in broad regional political economies, which collapsed in the aftermath of European contact. Field methods have also changed dramatically through in-depth
local and regional studies, interdisciplinary approaches, and multicultural collaborations, notably with indigenous peoples. Contemporary
research highlights questions of scale, perspective, and agency, including concerns for representation, public archaeology, indigenous cultural
heritage, and conservation of the region's remarkable cultural and ecological resources.

INTRODUCTION

Archaeology in the Amazon River basin has changed the way anthropologists and natural scientists view the world's largest tropical forest. Recent studies challenge scientific and popular stereotypes of ecological and cultural uniformity, notably of small, dispersed human settlements living in virgin tropical forest wilderness. These studies reveal dynamic change and variability, including complex social formations and large-scale transformations of the natural environment. The paradigm shift from ecological equilibrium and cultural stasis to diversity and change highlights social dynamics and the role of human agency in long-term change in coupled human natural systems.

Amazonian anthropology over the past several decades promotes synergy—if not synthesis—between studies focused on the past and perspectives on present social formations and environments (Carneiro da Cunha 1992, Descola & Taylor 1993, Roosevelt 1994, Sponsel 1995, Viveiros de Castro 1996). Building on the region's prodigious ethnographic tradition, notably North American cultural ecology and Franco-Brazilian structuralism, recent ethnography encourages approaches that address temporal and spatial scale and change, including indigenous histories and perspectives (Fausto & Heckenberger 2007, Whitehead 2003). In tropical forests it is difficult to ignore the natural environment, but contemporary ecological anthropology highlights symbolic, historical, and sociopolitical dimensions and diversity in human ecological systems (Balée & Erickson 2006, Biersack 1999). Today, regional specialists agree that humans and environments act recursively, rather than directionally (i.e., one simply causing change in the other), noting that pre-Columbian and historical societies made major impacts on plant and animal communities, hydrology, and soils. Likewise, human groups underwent dramatic transformations, including varied pre-Columbian trajectories of sociohistorical change and the political ecology of colonialism and modern globalization (Cleary 2001, Hecht 2009).

In-depth studies of the Amazonian past are beginning to strike a balance with the archaeology of the Andes, as reflected in the recent *Handbook of South American Archaeology* (Silverman & Isbell 2008). Interests have changed in stride with broader changes in archaeology, including shifts from description and culture history to explanation and culture process and, more recently, questions of perspective and voice, including the hybrid interests of Latin American archaeology (Barreto 1998, Funari 2001, Oyuela-Caycedo & Raymond 1998, Polítis & Alberti 1999) and collaboration with indigenous peoples (Colwell-Chanthaphonh & Ferguson 2007, Green et al. 2003, Heckenberger 2003). Archaeology suggests broad similarities with other world areas, particularly in the Americas and other tropical forest regions but also emphasizes the uniqueness of Amazonian societies and environments (Fausto 2000, McEwan et al. 2001, Neves 2006, Stahl 1995). This review focuses on recent field research, particularly along the Amazon and southern borderlands of the Brazilian Amazon, to highlight the deep history and temporality of the Amazon's indigenous people (see, e.g., Gassón 2003, Lathrap 1970, Myers 2004, Prous 1991, Rostain 2008b, for adjacent areas).

AMAZONIA: A BRIEF HISTORY

The Amazon River basin, covering nearly seven million square kilometers, is by far the largest on Earth, well over twice the size of the next largest basin, the Congo. Its monthly discharge far exceeds that of the Mississippi River (the third largest basin) in a year. Over this vast area there is tremendous variation in forest and river ecologies, but three forest regimes dominate throughout the Holocene (Colinvaux et al. 2000): closed broadleaf evergreen forests of the Amazon River and western tributaries [<150 meters above sea level (masl)]; more open broadleaf evergreen forests in adjacent uplands (150–250 masl); and complex contact zones in borderland areas, such as the Andes and the Guiana and Brazilian plateaus (>250 masl).

Rivers are likewise highly variable, but are commonly divided into white (Andean-derived), black (northwestern), and clear-water river systems (Meggers 1996, Moran 1993). Culture history includes varied early forager occupations, mid-Holocene settled foragers and horticulturalists, and the late Holocene emergence of settled, agricultural societies. In late pre-Columbian times, small- to medium-sized polities living in complex constructed landscapes occupied the Amazon River bottoms and several other areas (Denevan 2001).

Early Occupations

Early (~11,000 to 8500 B.P.) occupations included diverse tropical forest foraging societies. In the central and lower Amazon, bifacial (stemmed) projectile points have been identified (Costa 2009, Neves & Petersen 2006, Roosevelt et al. 1996), associated with developed rock art traditions in the lower Amazon (Pereira 2004). Other early occupations are described for several upland areas (Barse 1990, Magalhães 1994, Meggers & Miller 2003, Miller 1992, Mora 2003, Prous & Fogaça 1999). Mid-Holocene (~7500–3500 B.P.) shellfish foragers in the lower Amazon and along the Atlantic coast with early ceramics (6000 B.P. or before) have been described, with broad affinities with preagricultural shell mounds in eastern coastal South America (Bandeira 2008, Gaspar et al. 2008, Roosevelt et al. 1991, Rostain 2008b). Early evidence from coastal Peru, Northern Colombia, and Panama documents domesticated Amazonian species, including manioc, and mid-Holocene innovations, notably house gardens (Castillo & Aceituno 2006, Oliver 2008, Piperno et al. 2000, Piperno & Pearsall 1998, Raymond 2008). Mid-Holocene horticultural societies have been identified in the upper Madeira region (Miller 1999).

Late Holocene Domestication and Agriculture

In Amazonia, house garden horticulture underwent significant changes as some groups developed extensive slash-and-burn agriculture and semi-intensive strategies during the Late Holocene (Denevan 2001, Lathrap 1977, Oliver 2008). Of the wide inventory of domesticated and semidomesticated plants, root crops, particularly manioc, and arboriculture were critical elements of Amazonian agricultural systems, although some systems relied heavily on maize (Lathrap et al. 1985, Perry 2005, Roosevelt 1980). These findings generally support Sauer's (1952) prediction that domestication and agricultural development in tropical regions differ in important ways from classic Neolithic settings and cereal crop agriculture, including complex systems of wetland management and fish farming (Erickson 2000, Schaan 2004). Further complicating conventional models of food production, numerous non- or semidomesticated plants are actively managed or cultivated in Amazonia, notably palms (Goulding & Smith 2007, Morcote-Ríos & Bernal 2001, Smith 2007). Peach palm (*Bactris gasipaes*) is the only domesticated palm, but numerous species, such as buriti (*Mauritia flexuosa*), açaí (*Euterpe oleracea*), and others, were subject to intense management (Clement 2006). Diverse agricultural strategies were coupled with systems of faunal exploitation that included a variety of managed species, such as birds (Muscovy ducks, parrots and macaws, and others), fish, and other aquatic species, including the giant Amazon river turtle (up to 80 cm) and manatee, or sea cow. Many managed plants and animals are difficult to distinguish morphologically from wild varieties, but detailed archaeobotanical, zooarchaeological, and genetic studies are rare (Clement 1999, Mora 2003, Morcote-Ríos 2008, Perry 2005).

Change is commonly manifest in broad transformation of habitats, rather than focus on specific domesticated plants and animals. The "domestication of landscape" refers to the "conscious process by which human manipulation of the landscape results in changes in landscape ecology and the demographics of its plant and animal populations, resulting in a landscape more productive and congenial for humans" (Clement 1999, p. 190). Human impacts on the natural environment resulted from long-term occupations of select settings, in some cases initiated by semisedentary early to mid-Holocene societies. Agricultural intensification typically refers to large-scale technological advances, such as terracing and irrigation, but in the Amazon forest extractive strategies and semi-intensive agriculture and wetland management in broad domesticated landscapes were critical (Denevan 2001). Late Holocene landscaping involved raised mounds for crops in wet savanna areas of southwestern and northeastern Amazonia (Erickson 2008, Rostain 2008a), management of Amazonian dark earth or *terra preta* (Glaser & Woods 2004, Lehmann et al. 2003, Woods et al. 2009), and complex forest and wetland management strategies, which often leave obvious marks or "footprints" detectable (like crop-marks) in orbital imagery (Erickson 2000, Heckenberger et al. 2003).

Language, Agriculture, and Regional Development

In a worldwide review, Diamond & Bellwood (2003) suggest that dispersals of early agriculturalists "constitute collectively the most important process in Holocene human history" (p. 597). The farming/language dispersal hypothesis argues that early agriculturalists expanded rapidly owing to the adaptive advantage over existing foragers and horticulturalists (Bellwood 2004). Amazonia has played a small role in these discussions, but the widespread and fairly early (2500–2000 B.P.) dispersal of several language families, notably Arawak, Tupi-Guarani, and Carib, has long been recognized (Brochado 1984, Dixon & Aihkenvald 1999, Hill & Santos-Granero 2002, Lathrap 1970, Noelli 2008). Speakers of the three families dispersed widely across the tropical lowlands, including eastern coastal South America and the Caribbean.

Linguistic diversity is a notable feature of Amazonia, but no single language family dominates the region, as is true of Europe (Indo-European), sub-Saharan Africa (Niger-Congo), or the Pacific (Austronesian). Likewise, no single agricultural system, such as manioc cultivation, was accountable for the diversity of crop systems that prevailed in the area. Furthermore, no sociopolitical formation was strong enough to expand its political influence on a large scale, as was true of several episodes of Andean prehistory. Changes appear to be tied to early variability of resource management systems, including settled riverine (Arawak) and more mobile upland (Tupi-Guarani and Carib) strategies, as well as climate change and changes in agricultural lifestyles in the mid to late Holocene. Although still poorly understood, agricultural expansions were more complicated than posited by a wave of advance model, such as Lathrap's (1970) "cardiac model," or unified processes of site or trait diffusion, but instead involved complex and variable processes of change, broadly oriented to river and upland ecologies, and resulted in cultural pluralism (Carneiro 1995, Hornborg 2005, Zucchi 2002). Whether cause or consequence, changes in technoeconomics are correlated with important changes in sociopolitical organization, notably emerging social hierarchy and regional integration, as was true in the other major tropical linguistic diaspora. Carneiro's (1970) observation bears scrutiny in the general sense that in broad forested landscapes, societies tend to ramify, whereas tightly circumscribed areas, such as coastal Peruvian river valleys, seem to promote rapid and more rigid stratification.

By ~2500–1500 B.P., early expressions of sociopolitical complexity, in terms of local landscape domestication, monumentality, and integration in regional social systems, appeared in several parts of the Amazon, during a regional formative period (Arroyo-Kalin 2008, Neves 2006). These small-scale regional polities were roughly comparable with other formative cultures of the Americas, in terms of technological innovations, such as ceramics, agriculture, and settled villages or towns (Raymond 2008, Zeidler 2008). Multiethnic societies, regional sociopolitical systems, and interregional interaction underscore the diverse pathways of social complexity in the region. In this context, politically independent, permanent villages may have periodically joined into larger, regional confederations, for instance around singular leaders and warfare. In other cases, more centralized and hierarchical regional societies were integrated through ritual and elite exchange, although they maintained diverse strategies of political power, as known from several areas during the final millennium of prehistory.

LANDSCAPE AND POLITY, 500–1500 C.E.

By the 1970s, it was clear that Amazon River polities depended on fairly intensive exploitation of aquatic resources and diversified cultivation, based on early eyewitness accounts from the sixteenth and seventeenth centuries. Accounts report large, densely settled populations, which were decimated by the early violence of colonialism (Porro 1996; Whitehead 1994, 2003). Settled populations commonly concentrated along major rivers, as common in other world areas. Where propitious ecological conditions prevailed, notably in rich soils and aquatic resources, cultural groups developed into dense, regionally organized societies by late prehistoric times (Carneiro 2007, Denevan 1996, Lathrap et al. 1985, Myers 1992, Roosevelt 1980). However, the Amazon River bottoms are a small fraction (<5%) of the basin, which is criss-crossed by numerous large tributaries. Owing to their difficult access, many upland areas remain *terra incognita*, although this panorama is changing, particularly as "salvage archaeology" is developed in remote parts of the region (Miller 1992).

Amazon Floodplain Polities

Early archaeological surveys were conducted primarily along the Amazon and were later expanded to several major tributaries, aimed primarily to identify broad regional ceramic traditions and local phases (Evans & Meggers 1968, Hilbert 1955, Meggers & Evans 1957, Simões & Kalkman 1987, Simões & Lopes 1987). Research in the Upper Amazon initiated by

Lathrap (1970, Lathrap et al. 1985, Myers 2004, Oliver 1991) and Roosevelt (1980, 1991) in the Middle Orinoco and lower Amazon developed more in-depth studies of regional sequences and spatial distributions, which laid the foundation for detailed regional survey and studies of intrasite variability, including in upland areas (e.g., Balée & Erickson 2006, McEwan et al. 2001). Two broad ceramic traditions are widely recognized with substantial regional variation: the Amazonian Barrancoid or Incised-Rim Tradition, ~500 B.C.E. (2500 B.P.) to 900 C.E. and the Amazonian Polychrome Tradition, widespread by 1000–1250 C.E. (Lima 2008). Several subtraditions, such as the early Marajoara style, combine elements of modeled, incised-line, and bichrome decoration, typical of Amazonian Barrancoid, and the painted pottery of the southeast Amazon Tupiguarani tradition, suggesting cultural pluralism or "ethnogenesis" (Barreto 2009, Brochado 1989, Neves 2006).

Marajoara mound-building societies flourished from ~400 to 1300 C.E. in the wooded savannas and gallery forests of eastern Marajó, the large fluvial island in the Amazon estuary. Emerging from earlier ceramic groups, Marajoara is notable for numerous small- to medium-sized domestic mounds and major ceremonial and elite residential mounds (Meggers & Evans 1957; Roosevelt 1991; Schaan 2004; Simões 1969, 1981). In the Anajás River headwaters, Schaan (2004) describes a small polity, perhaps numbering in the thousands, which integrated dozens of domestic mounds organized around large ceremonial mounds. The large ceremonial Camutins and Belém mounds (up to 12 meters high and 2.5 ha) indicate large-scale construction, apparently early, ~400–600 C.E., and highlight the difference between small- to medium-sized domestic mounds and larger mounds, distinguished by major public ritual and elite urn-burials. Camutins/Belém mounds are centrally located between other mound groups, more or less equidistant (~8 km) to the southeast (Monte Carmelo), northwest (Pequaquara), and northeast (upper Camutins stream), which may have defined the territory of the regional polity, with smaller intervening domestic mounds along waterways. Shared styles of prestige goods, notably burial urns, suggest subregional identities across the island and clearly reflect important social distinctions, such as gender and social hierarchy, as true of other urn cemetery complexes in the region (Guapindaia 2008b, Schaan 2004). Marajó communities were supported by a diverse resource base and focus on managed river products, such as fish and palm farming (Meggers 2003, Roosevelt 1991, Schaan 2008). Mound construction apparently declined after ~1300 C.E., but Marajoara ceramic styles continue into the dynamic and plural social landscapes of the sixteenth and seventeenth centuries (Schaan 2004).

In-depth archaeological research at the confluence of the Solimões and Negro rivers (Manaus) has identified more than 100 archaeological sites, providing the clearest picture to date of late Holocene occupations along the Amazon (Arroyo-Kalin 2008, Lima 2008, Neves 2008, Neves & Petersen 2006). Major ceramic complexes include two early variants of the Incised-Rim Tradition, the Açutuba (300 B.C.E. to 400 C.E.) and Manacapuru phases (400 C.E. to 900 C.E.), a local Paredão phase (700 C.E. to 1200 C.E.), and a regional variant of the Amazonian Polychrome Tradition, called Guarita (900 C.E. to contact). The chronology shows overlapping and mixed occupations, which suggests extensive interaction and ethnic diversity (Lima 2008). Despite ceramic differences, sites share a circular or horseshoe layout. The period from 600 to 1200 C.E. appears to mark a peak in regional population, but Paredão ceramics disappear after ~1200 C.E., coincident with an apparent increase in conflict as reflected in defensive ditches constructed at Açutuba and Lago Grande at ~1100 C.E. (Moraes 2007, Neves 2008).

In late prehistory, fairly large regional populations lived in dispersed small settlements (<10 ha) and larger residential and ceremonial centers (>30 ha), such as the sites of Açutuba and Hatahara, and others located within the limits of the modern cities of Manacapuru and Manaus. Large centers were spaced roughly 30–50 km apart, which served as the sociopolitical and ritual centers of small regional polities, such as those described in the sixteenth and seventeenth centuries. Core residential areas overlooking the Negro and Solimões rivers were surrounded by peripheral areas of lighter traffic and nonresidential areas of anthropogenic dark earth for agricultural production (Petersen et al. 2001, Neves et al. 2003). In the centuries before 1492, major centers were structurally elaborated for ritual consumption, including prestige goods, such as elaborate elite-ware ceramics. At Açutuba, the central area is defined by a broad sunken amphitheater-like plaza (400–100 m), flanked by a series of habitation mounds with subfloor and adjacent burials, as well as ramps, ditches, and managed wetlands. Landscape transformations and available radiocarbon dates in major centers suggest long continuous occupation of these centers and stable, sedentary populations, perhaps numbering in the low thousands by ~1000 C.E. (Neves & Petersen 2006).

Early chronicles from the floodplains describe populous territorial polities with regional overlords, major settlements or towns with large-scale roads and productive technoeconomies, rich artistic and ritual traditions, and organized martial forces (Porro 1996). Among these, the polity that dominated the lower Tapajós River was perhaps the largest (Nimuendajú 1952). The Santarém or Tapajônica archaeological culture is renowned for its ornate ceramics associated with the "Incised Punctate" regional tradition (Gomes 2005, 2008). It shares affinities with the coeval Amazonian Polychrome Tradition and, particularly, the Arauquinoid ceramic complexes of the Orinoco and Guianas, which suggests that Carib-speaking peoples expanded into the middle-lower Amazon between 500 and 1000 C.E. (Lathrap 1970, Zucchi 1985). The large capital town at Santarém is composed of a core area with dense archaeological deposits (~100 ha) within a broader settled landscape up to 25 km, which rivals many major centers in the Americas (e.g., Cahokia, Chan Chan) (Gomes 2008, Roosevelt 1999). The polity was supported by intensive floodplain and upland agriculture, including both occupation site dark earth (*terra preta*) and nonoccupational agricultural soils (*terra mulata*) (Denevan 2001, Woods & McCann 1999). The study of Amazonian dark earths, the focus of significant recent research in a wide range of settings, has critical implications not only for cultural development, particularly related to the enrichment of infertile soils, but also for sustainable development strategies (Glaser & Woods 2004, Lehmann et al. 2003, Petersen et al. 2001, Woods et al. 2009).

Floodplain archaeology and ethnohistory suggest complementarity between densely and sparsely settled stretches of the main rivers, including buffer-zones, and with hinterland zones (DeBoer 1981, Denevan 1996, Porro 1996). In the Parauá area, 80 km upstream from the Santarém site, Gomes (2005) found little evidence of influence by the Santarém polity. Likewise, regional survey in the Trombetas River (Konduri ceramic tradition) indicates fairly small and shallow deposits (Guapindaia 2008a, Kern et al. 2003). Throughout the region, the largest centers were generally not that large (<50 ha), and cycling between periods of greater and lesser political centralization is apparent in the Central Amazon, with notable fluctuations in site locations and population densities. It remains unclear whether Santarém was a large, centralized polity or represents smaller integrated polities within a regional peer-polity, as seems to be the case in the estuary, central Amazon, and southern borderlands.

Southern Borderlands Polities

The broad transitional forests between the central Brazilian plateau (>300 masl) and the evergreen Amazon forests extend from the upper Tocantins (east) to the upper Madeira (west) rivers. A century ago, Max Schmidt (1917) noted that southern Arawak groups dominated forested headwater basins of the major southern tributaries, surrounded by more mobile groups in the rolling upland topography and open wooded savanna and gallery forest landscape of

central Brazil and eastern Bolivia. Cultural variation across the region highlights the interplay of phylogenetic and reticulate processes, as well as ecological diversity, as early Arawak-speaking settled agriculturalists developed into distinctive ethnically plural societies, as seen in other areas of the lowlands (Hill & Santos-Granero 2002, Hornborg 2005).

Archaeological complexes associated with these multiethnic groups, notably mounds, roads, and agricultural earthworks, are well known from the Llanos de Mojos. Erickson's (e.g., 2000, 2006, 2008) recent work has revealed the remarkable scale and integration of agricultural earthworks in broad domesticated landscapes, including causeways, fish weirs and ponds, forest islands (ancient settlements), raised fields, and diverse other archaeological landscape features. These complexes can be subdivided into an eastern group of ring-walled villages, major causeways, and wetland fish-farming complexes in forest and savanna landscapes (Baures) and a western group, including mounds and raised fields, in the central llanos, which provide detailed examples of urban-scale production landscapes (see also Denevan 2001, Walker 2004). Excavations of mounds in the Upper Mamoré area have revealed a complex sequence indicating that the area has been occupied by different groups in the past (Calandra & Salceda 2004, Erickson & Balée 2006, Prümers 2004, Walker 2008). The plural ethnic landscape of eastern Bolivia and adjacent areas strongly influenced the development of "mission" or other postcontact "mixed blood" peoples (Block 1992, Gow 1996).

Early accounts (1600–1750) from eastern Bolivia describe diverse large, densely settled populations, with complicated settlement and agricultural works, and regional sociopolitical organization (Denevan 1966, Metraux 1942). Along the eastern Bolivian-Brazil border (Guaporé), ethnohistory documents palisaded ring villages (Block 1992, Erickson 2000). Farther east in central Brazil, Campos (1862, pp. 443–44) describes a networked settlement pattern in the 1720s, which included densely settled plaza communities, well-maintained roads, and a plaza ritual complex ("temple-idol-priest complex") considered characteristic of the "theocratic chiefdoms" of the southern Amazon (Steward & Faron 1959). More autonomous ring village settlements are also widely known from central Brazil (Wüst & Barreto 1999).

In southwestern Amazonia, an area also dominated by Arawak-speaking people historically, major geoglyphs in the upper Purus River region of Brazil and adjacent portions of Peru and Bolivia reveal another complex of related monumental sites (Pärssinen & Korpisaari 2003, Schaan et al. 2007). The well-planned and laterally extensive earthworks, including massive circular and square ditches (up to 7 m deep) and long linear processionals (up to 50 m wide and nearly 1 km in length), suggest sociopolitical integration based on broadly shared ritual interaction among numerous sites (~150, which is estimated as 10%; Mann 2008). Linkages between sites is not yet described, but it is clear that basic orientations are similar and were conceived as related elements of a regional built environment and served as ceremonial central places within regional social systems.

In eastern portions of the southern borderlands region, the headwater basin of the Xingu River preserves a sequence of occupations from early agricultural groups (Arawak), who colonized the basin by 500–800 C.E. or earlier, to contemporary Xinguano peoples (Heckenberger 2005; Heckenberger et al. 2003, 2008). In one study area (~1200 km²), corresponding to the traditional lands of the Kuikuro (Xinguano) community, two dozen residential sites have been identified, most or all of which were occupied in late prehistoric to early protohistoric times, ~1250–1650 C.E. Late prehistoric settlements were integrated in two ranked clusters, which represent small, territorial polities. In clusters, large walled towns (25–50 ha), estimated to number more than 1000 in some cases, and smaller nonwalled villages were linked by an extensive road system. Road and settlement nodes, marked by large ceremonial plazas surrounded by residential areas, are archaeologically visible as linear earthworks at the margins of roads and plazas (curbs) and around major settlements (ditches). Settlement hierarchies were defined by an exemplary center and four major satellites and smaller peripheral plaza settlements and hamlets within territories of ~250 km² or more. The two clusters were part of a regional peer-polity—a confederation of culturally related territorial polities extending across an area ≥20,000 km² and likely numbering well into the tens of thousands. Across the region, land use was fairly intensive, with settlements and countryside features (fields, orchards, wetlands) rigidly planned and defined, including dark earth farming plots within the patchy agricultural landscape.

The domesticated landscapes of the Upper Xingu basin provide a particularly striking example of the self-organized built environments of the southern borderlands. Descendent Xinguano populations, well described since the 1880s, continue to practice basic cultural patterns documented from prehistoric times, notably in terms of technoeconomy, house and village spatial organization, and general settlement locations (Fausto et al. 2008, Heckenberger 2005). Agricultural landscapes, in the past and today, included broad areas under cultivation in primary staple crops of manioc (*Manihot esculenta* spp.) and pequi fruit (*Caryocar* sp.), large tracts of sapé grass (*Imperata* sp.) for thatch, diverse palms and other secondary crops, and managed secondary forest, as well as managed wetland areas (Carneiro 1983). Although isolated from early colonial activities, Xinguano peoples were not insulated from the catastrophic effects of early colonialism, notably disease that decimated populations across the Amazon. Xinguano settlement and land-use provides graphic testimony of the post-1492 population collapse, with regional populations reduced to nearly 500 by the 1950s, and documents the extensive landscape fallowing that occurred across the southern borderland regions.

CONCLUDING REMARKS

The archaeology of the Amazon, an area larger than Europe, is still poorly known—the least known region of the "least known continent" (Lyon 1974)—but recent advances in archaeology have dramatically changed the way scholars view the region. In world historical schemes, Amazonia was long appraised by what it lacked, notably the absence of harbingers of classic civilizations, such as stone architecture, writing, grain surplus, and domesticated ungulates. Archaeology reveals novel variation and dynamic indigenous histories, including alternative pathways to domestication, settled life, and social complexity. Recent studies into the deep history of the region, like other tropical forest regions worldwide, challenge stereotypes of small-scale, dispersed villages—primitive tribes—in a largely pristine forest. These studies raise the possibility that the average Amazonian person in 1492 did not live in an isolated, autonomous village, but instead was part of a regional polity or articulated with one in broad regional social networks that extended across the region.

These findings suggest remarkable sociocultural diversity, although it seems likely that no large bureaucratic state or integrated macroregional political entity or empire ever developed in the area. In the comparative context of other tropical forest regions or complex social formations in the Americas, Amazonian complex societies do not seem out of place (McIntosh 1999, Pauketat 2007). In general terms, the forest polities of the Amazon were more diffuse and less centralized in terms of technoeconomic, sociopolitical, and symbolic resources than areas with more circumscribed resources, such as the desert river valleys of the Peruvian coastal region (Carneiro 1970). As the medieval historian Jacques Le Goff (1964) once noted of Europe's forest civilizations, they are like the "photographic negative" of classic "oasis" civilizations. Nonetheless, the settled territorial polities that dominated various areas in late prehistoric times constructed elaborate domesticated landscapes, linking important centers in regional peer polities and perhaps more centralized tributary systems, as suggested along portions of the Amazon River (Roosevelt 1999).

As well documented among more recent social formations, the primary capital in Amazonian political economies was sociopolitical and symbolic, in the sense that surplus and wealth orbited around human bodies, constructed through ritual and social interaction, rather than the other way around. In diffuse and often multicentric regional systems small and large settlements were integrated through major public ritual, notably including elite mortuary rituals (Chaumeil 2007, Guapindaia 2008b). Ritual performance in highly structured public ceremonial spaces and material culture, notably prestige goods and bodily adornment, were primary mechanisms of social communication—a symbolic language—within multiethnic and, in some cases, multilingual regional sociopolitical systems (Barreto 2009, Lathrap 1985). The fine-ware ceramics of the Amazonian Polychrome Tradition are the most obvious expression of such broad prestige goods economies, spread throughout the Amazon floodplains, but these economies also included numerous other wealth items, such as shell, stone, and perishable wood, basketry, and feather valuables and other commodities (McEwan et al. 2001).

Communication and integration in regional systems of interaction did not create cultural homogeneity but produced remarkable diversity and pluralism. Against the backdrop of diversity, the distinction between river and upland regimes of dwelling was critical to local and broader regional patterns of social interaction, as witnessed in archaeological distributions and "sedimented" in the languages, bodies, and built environments—the cultural memory—of living descendent peoples. The sociocultural integrity of descendent peoples, following traditional lifestyles in generally nonindustrialized landscapes, provides rich opportunities for ethnoarchaeological research into indigenous history and archaeological formation processes (e.g., DeBoer et al. 1996, Polítis 2007, Roe 1982, Silva 2008). Research with descendent populations also highlights questions of multicultural collaboration and dialogue (Colwell-Chanthaphonh & Ferguson 2007, Green et al. 2003, Schmidt & Patterson 1996).

The recognition of sociohistorical variation has great relevance to contemporary debates on biodiversity, which reflects dramatic prehistoric influence and complex post-1492 histories across the region (Cleary 2001, Denevan 1992, Erickson 2008, Stahl 1996). Long-term and, in some cases, semi-intensive resource management strategies had widespread and dramatic impacts on the natural environment. The domestication of nature began early, and over time human groups became increasingly tethered to certain places, which by late prehistoric times included major centers and dense populations in a variety of areas. The focus shifts from human societies adapting to the natural environment to humans participating as active agents of change, both before and after European contact (Balée & Erickson 2006). The decimation of regional polities and native world systems in the early centuries of European colonialism resulted in the fallowing of the region's tropical forests, which were then affected by colonial extractive economies, such as the Rubber Boom, and twentieth-century development (Balée 2006, Hecht 2009).

Discovering that the region's forested landscapes are not pristine in no way diminishes their relevance in debates on conservation and sustainable development in the Amazon, the poster child of global environmentalism. However, it does complicate things and makes archaeology—the primary means to understand change in coupled natural human systems over long timescales—not only more interesting and contested but also more central in contemporary debates on the Amazon. The legacy of cultural landscapes, including contemporary practices, offers important clues to discussions of resource management in the future (Willis et al. 2007). This is true par-

ticularly in indigenous areas, which constitute more than 20% of the Brazilian Amazon and are a critical barrier to deforestation (Nepstad et al. 2005). In these areas, indigenous and folk knowledge systems, including diverse forms of cultural and ecological memory, draw attention to the need for memory conservation and cultural property rights alongside conservation of natural resources (Nazarea 2006, Posey 2002, Posey & Balée 1989).

Much has changed in recent decades regarding how scholars view the world's largest tropical forest, including the antiquity and diversity of human occupations and how they transformed the natural environment. Much has also changed in archaeological practice, notably increasingly interdisciplinary approaches, regional perspectives, fine-grained excavations, and the application of new technologies (e.g., remote-sensing applications and geo-archaeology). These changes occur within the context of broader changes in scientific research, notably the shift from science as detached, objective observation to multivocal and multiscalar contexts of research applications, including engagement with local communities and attention to regional and global concerns (Latour 2004). In this world of research, archaeology plays an important role, particularly in understanding centennial- and millennial-scale change in human-natural systems, which are vital to debates regarding conservation, sustainable development, and human rights in an era of unprecedented change across the region. For practitioners of archaeology this entails getting dirty, digging more deeply into the Amazonian past, and learning to read the varied traces of the deep past. One thing is certain: It is an exciting, challenging, and important time to be engaged with Amazonian archaeologies.

DISCLOSURE STATEMENT

The authors are not aware of any affiliations, memberships, funding, or financial holdings that might be perceived as affecting the objectivity of this review.

LITERATURE CITED

Arroyo-Kalin M. 2008. *Steps towards an ecology of landscape: a geoarchaeological approach to the study of anthropogenic dark earths in the Central Amazon region, Brazil*. PhD thesis, Cambridge Univ., 232 pp.

Balée W. 2006. The research program of historical ecology. *Annu. Rev. Anthropol.* 35:75–98

Balée W, Erickson CL, eds. 2006. *Time and Complexity in Historical Ecology: Studies from the Neotropical Lowlands*. New York: Columbia Univ. Press

Bandeira A. 2008. *Ocupações humanas pré-históricas no litoral maranhense: um estudo arqueológico sobre o sambaqui do Bacanga na ilha de São Luís—Maranhão*. Masters thesis, Mus. Arqueol. Etnolog., Univ. São Paulo, 316 pp.

Barreto C. 1998. Brazilian archaeology from a Brazilian perspective. *Antiquity* 72(277):573–81

Barreto C. 2009. *Meios místicos de reprodução social: arte e estilo na cerâmica funerária da Amazônia antiga*. PhD thesis, Mus. Arqueol. Etnolog., Univ. São Paulo, 332 pp.

Barse W. 1990. Preceramic occupations in the Orinoco River Valley. *Science* 250:1388–90

Bellwood P. 2004. *The First Farmers: The Origins of Agricultural Societies*. London: Wiley-Blackwell

Biersack A. 1999. The new ecological anthropologies. *Am. Anthropol.* 10:1–22

Block D. 1992. *Mission Culture on the Upper Amazon: Native Tradition, Jesuit Enterprise and Secular Authority in Moxos, 1660–1880*. Lincoln: Univ. Neb. Press

Brochado JP. 1989. A Expansão dos tupi e da cerâmica da Tradição Policrômica Amazônica. *Dédalo* 9(17/18):41–47

Brochado JP. 1984. *An ecological model of the spread of pottery and agriculture into Eastern South America*. PhD thesis, Univ. Ill., 507 pp.

Calandra H, Salceda SA. 2004. Bolivian Amazonia: archaeology of the llanos de Mojos. *Acta Amazonica* 34(2):155–63

Campos AP. 1862 (1720). Breve notícia que dá o Capitão Antônio Pires de Campos do gentio que há na derrota da viagem das minas de Cuyabá e seu recôncavo. *Rev. Trimestral Inst. Histórico, Geográfico, Etnográfico Brasileiro* 5:437–49

Carneiro RL. 1970. A theory of the origin of the state. *Science* 169:733–38

Carneiro RL. 1983. The cultivation of manioc among the Kuikuro Indians of the Upper Xingu. In *Adaptive Responses in Native Amazonians*, ed. RB Hames, WT Vickers, pp. 65–111. New York: Academic

Carneiro RL. 1995. The history of ecological interpretations in Amazonia: Does Roosevelt have it right? See Sponsel 1995, pp. 45–65

Carneiro RL. 2007. A base ecológica dos cacicados amazônicos. *Rev. Soc. Arqueol. Bras.* 20:117–54

Carneiro da Cunha M, ed. 1992. *História dos Índios no Brasil*. São Paulo: Companhia da Letras

Castillo N, Aceituno J. 2006. El bosque domesticado, el bosque cultivado: un proceso milenario en el valle medio del rio Porce en el noroccidente Colombiano. *Lat. Am. Antiquity* 17(4):561–79

Chaumeil JP. 2007. Bones, flutes, and the dead: memory and funerary treatments in Amazonia. See Fausto & Heckenberger 2007, pp. 243–83

Cleary D. 2001. Towards an environmental history of the Amazon: from prehistory to the nineteenth century. *Lat. Am. Res. Rev.* 36(2):65–96

Clement C. 1999. 1492 and the loss of crop genetic resources: I. Crop biogeography at contact. *Econ. Bot.* 53(2):203–16

Clement C. 2006. Fruit trees and the transition to food production in the Amazon. See Balée & Erickson 2006, pp. 165–85

Colinvaux P, Oliveira P, Bush M. 2000. Amazonian and neotropical plant communities on glacial time-scales: the failure of aridity and refuge hypotheses. *Quat. Sci. Rev.* 19:141–49

Colwell-Chanthaphonh C, Ferguson TJ. 2007. *Collaboration in Archaeological Practice: Engaging Descendant Communities*. Lanham, MD: Altamira

Costa F. 2009. *Arqueologia das campinaranas do baixo rio Negro: em busca dos pré-ceramistas nos areais da Amazônia central*. PhD thesis, Mus. Arqueol. Etnolog., Univ. São Paulo, 189 pp.

DeBoer W. 1981. Buffer zones in the cultural ecology of aboriginal Amazonia: an ethnohistorical approach. *Am. Antiquity* 46(2):364–77

DeBoer W, Kintigh K, Rostoker A. 1996. Ceramic seriation and settlement occupation in Amazonia. *Lat. Am. Antiquity* 7(3):263–78

Denevan W. 1966. *The Aboriginal Cultural Geography of the Llanos de Mojos of Bolivia*. Berkeley: Univ. Calif. Press

Denevan W. 1992. The pristine myth: the landscape of the Americas in 1492. *Ann. Assoc. Am. Geog.* 82(3):369–85

Denevan W. 1996. A bluff model of riverine settlement in Amazonia. *Ann. Assoc. Am. Geog.* 86(4):654–81

Denevan W. 2001. *Cultivated Landscapes of Native Amazonia and the Andes*. Oxford: Oxford Univ. Press

Descola P, Taylor AC, eds. 1993. *La Remonteé de l'Amazonie: Anthropologie et Histoire des Sociétés Amazoniennes*. Spec. Ed. *L'Homme*, Vols. 26/28

Diamond J, Bellwood P. 2003. Farmers and their languages: the first expansions. *Science* 300:597–603

Dixon R, Aihkenvald A. 1999. *The Amazonian Languages*. Cambridge, UK: Cambridge Univ. Press

Erickson CL. 2000. An artificial landscape-scale fishery in the Bolivian Amazon. *Nature* 408:190–93

Erickson CL. 2006. The domesticated landscapes of the Bolivian Amazon. See Balée & Erickson 2006, pp. 235–78

Erickson CL. 2008. Amazonia: the historical ecology of a domesticated landscape. See Silverman & Isbell 2008, pp. 157–83

Erickson CL, Balée W. 2006. The historical ecology of a complex landscape in Bolivia. See Balée & Erickson 2006, pp. 187–233

Evans CE, Meggers BJ. 1968. *Archaeological Investigations on the Rio Napo, Ecuador*. Washington, DC: Smithson. Inst. Press

Fausto C. 2000. *Os Índios antes do Brasil*. Rio de Janeiro: Jorge Zahar

Fausto C, Franchetto B, Heckenberger M. 2008. Ritual language and historical reconstruction: toward a linguistic, ethnographical, and archaeological account of Upper Xingu Society. In *Lessons from Documented Endangered Languages*, ed. KD Harrison, DS Rood, A Dwyer, pp. 129–57. Amsterdam: John Benjamins

Fausto C, Heckenberger M, eds. 2007. *Time and Memory in Indigenous Amazonia: Anthropological Perspectives*. Gainesville: Univ. Press Fla.

Funari P. 2001. Public archaeology from a Latin American perspective. *Public Archaeol.* 1:239–43

Gaspar MD, DeBlassis P, Fish SK, Fish PR. 2008. Sambaqui (shell mound) societies of coastal Brazil. See Silverman & Isbell 2008, pp. 319–35

Gásson R. 2003. Orinoquia: the archaeology of Orinoco River Basin. *J. World Prehist.* 16(3):237–311

Glaser B, Woods WI, eds. 2004. *Amazonian Dark Earths: Explorations in Space and Time*. New York: Springer

Gomes DC. 2005. *Análise dos padrões de organização comunitária no Baixo Tapajós: o desenvolvimento do Formativo na area de Santarém*. PhD thesis, Mus. Arqueol. Etnolog., Univ. São Paulo, 325 pp.

Gomes DC. 2008. The diversity of social formations in Pre-Colonial Amazonia. *Rev. Arqueol. Am.* 25:187–223

Goulding M, Smith N. 2007. *Palms: Sentinels of Amazonian Conservation*. St. Louis: Mo. Bot. Garden Press

Gow P. 1996. *Of Mixed Blood: Kinship and History in the Peruvian Amazon*. Oxford: Clarendon

Green LF, Green D, Neves EG. 2003. Indigenous knowledge and archaeological science. *J. Soc. Archaeol.* 3(3):366–98

Guapindaia V. 2008a. *Além da margem do rio—a ocupação Konduri e Pocó na região de Porto Trombetas, PA*. PhD thesis, Mus. Arqueol. Etnolog., Univ. São Paulo, 194 pp.

Guapindaia V. 2008b. Prehistoric funeral practices in the Brazilian Amazon: the Maracá urns. See Silverman & Isbell 2008, pp. 1005–26

Hecht S. 2009. *Amazon Odyssey: Euclides da Cunha and the Scramble for Amazonia*. Chicago: Univ. Chicago Press. In press

Heckenberger MJ. 2003. Archaeology as indigenous advocacy in Amazonia. *Pract. Anthropol.* 26(3):34–38

Heckenberger MJ. 2005. *The Ecology of Power: Culture, Place, and Personhood in the Southern Amazon, AD 1000–2000*. New York: Routledge

Heckenberger MJ, Kuikuro A, Kuikuro UT, Russell JC, Schmidt M, et al. 2003. Amazonia 1492: pristine forest or cultural parkland? *Science* 301:1710–14

Heckenberger MJ, Russell JC, Fausto C, Toney JR, Schmidt MJ, et al. 2008. Pre-Columbian urbanism, anthropogenic landscapes, and the future of the Amazon. *Science* 321:1214–17

Hilbert PP. 1955. *Archäologische Untersuchungen am Mittlern Amazonas*. Berlin: Dieter Reimer Verlag

Hill J, Santos-Granero F, eds. 2002. *Comparative Arawakan Histories: Rethinking Language Group and Culture Area in Amazonia*. St. Louis: Univ. Ill. Press

Hornborg A. 2005. Ethnogenesis, regional interaction, and ecology in prehistoric Amazonia: towards a systemic perspective. *Curr. Anthropol.* 46(4):589–620

Kern DC, D'Aquino G, Rodrigues TE, Frazdo FJL, Sombroek W, et al. 2003. Distribution of Amazonian Dark Earths in the Brazilian Amazon. See Lehmann et al. 2003, pp. 51–76

Lathrap DW. 1970. *The Upper Amazon*. London: Thames and Hudson

Lathrap DW. 1977. Our mother the cayman, our father the gourd: Spinden revisited or a unitary model for the emergence of agriculture in the New World. In *Origins of Agriculture*, ed. C Reed, pp. 713–51. The Hague: Mouton

Lathrap DW. 1985. Jaws: the control of power in the early Nuclear American ceremonial center. In *Early Ceremonial Architecture in the Andes*, ed. CB Donnan, pp. 241–67. Washington, DC: Dumbarton Oaks

Lathrap DW, Gebhart-Sayer A, Mester AM. 1985. The roots of the Shipibo art style: three waves at Imiríacocha, or there were "Incas" before the Incas. *J. Lat. Am. Lore* 11(1):31–119

Latour B. 2004. *The Politics of Nature: How to Bring the Sciences into Democracy*. Cambridge, MA: Harvard Univ. Press

Le Goff J. 1964. *Le Civilization de l'Occident Medieval*. Paris: B. Arthaud

Lehmann J, Kern DC, Glaser B, Woods WI. 2003. *Amazonian Dark Earths: Origins, Properties and Management*. Dordrecht: Kluwer

Lima HP. 2008. *História das caretas: a Tradição Borda Incisa na Amazôna Central*. PhD thesis, Mus. Arqueol. Etnolog., Univ. São Paulo, 538 pp.

Lyon P, ed. 1974. *Native South America: Ethnology of the Least Known Continent*. Boston: Little Brown

Magalhães M. 1994. *Arqueologia de Carajás: A Presença Pré-Histórica do Homen na Amazônia*. Rio de Janeiro: Companhia do Vale do Rio Doce

Mann C. 2008. Ancient earthmovers of the Amazon. *Science* 321:1148–51

McEwan C, Neves EG, Barreto C, eds. 2001. *The Unknown Amazon: Culture and Nature in Ancient Brazil*. London: Br. Mus. Press

McIntosh S, ed. 1999. *Beyond Chiefdoms: Pathways to Complexity*. Cambridge, UK: Cambridge Univ. Press

Meggers BJ. 1996. *Amazonia: Man and Culture in a Counterfeit Paradise*. Washington, DC: Smithson. Inst. Press

Meggers BJ. 2003. Natural versus anthropogenic sources of Amazonian biodiversity: the continuing quest for El Dorado. In *How Landscapes Change*, ed. GA Bradshaw, PA Marquet, pp. 89–107. Berlin: Springer

Meggers BJ, Evans CE. 1957. *Archaeological Investigations at the Mouth of the Amazon*. Washington, DC: Smithson. Inst. Press

Meggers BJ, Miller ET. 2003. Hunters-gatherers in Amazonia during the Pleistocene-Holocene transition. In *Under the Canopy: The Archaeology of Tropical Rain Forests*, ed. J Mercader, pp. 291–316. New Brunswick: Rutgers Univ. Press

Metraux A. 1942. *The Native Tribes of Eastern Bolivia and Western Matto Grosso*. Washington, DC: Smithson. Inst. BAE

Miller ET. 1992. *Arqueologia nos Empreendimentos Hidroelétricos da Eletronorte: Resultados Preliminares*. Brasília: Eletronorte

Miller ET. 1999. A Limitação ambiental como barreira à transposição do period formativo no Brasil. Tecnologia, produção de alimentos e formação de aldeias no sudoeste da Amazônia. In *Formativo Sudamericano: Homenaje a Albert Rex González y Betty J. Meggers*, ed. P Ledergerber-Crespo, pp. 331–39. Quito: Ed. ABYA-YALA

Mora S. 2003. *Early Inhabitants of the Amazonian Tropical Rain Forest: A Study of Human and Environmental Dynamics*. Pittsburgh: Lat. Am. Archaeol. Publ.

Moraes C. 2007. *Arqueologia na Amazônia Central vista de uma perspectiva da região do Lago do Limão*. Masters thesis, Mus. Arqueol. Etnolog., Univ. São Paulo, 196 pp.

Moran E. 1993. *Through Amazonian Eyes: The Human Ecology of Amazonian Populations*. Iowa City: Iowa Univ. Press

Morcote-Ríos G. 2008. *Antiguos Habitantes en Ríos de Aguas Negras: Ecosistemas y Cultivos en el Interfluvio Amazonas—Putumayo, Columbia—Brasil.* Bogotá: Univ. Nac. Colombia

Morcote-Ríos G, Bernal R. 2001. Remains of palms (Palmae) at archaeological sites in the New World: a review. *Bot. Rev.* 67(3):309–50

Myers T. 1992. Agricultural limitations of the Amazon in theory and practice. *World Archaeol.* 24(1):82–97

Myers T. 2004. Dark Earth in the Upper Amazon. See Glaser & Woods 2004, pp. 67–94

Nazarea V. 2006. Local knowledge and memory in biodiversity conservation. *Annu. Rev. Anthropol.* 35:317–35

Nepstad D, Swartzman S, et al. 2005. Inhibition of Amazon deforestation and fire by parks and indigenous lands. *Conserv. Biol.* 20(1):65–73

Neves EG. 2006. *A Arqueologia da Amazônia.* Rio de Janeiro: Jorge Zahar

Neves EG. 2008. Ecology, ceramic chronology and distributions, long-term history, and political change in the Amazonian floodplain. See Silverman & Isbell 2008, pp. 359–79

Neves EG, Petersen JB. 2006. Political economy and Pre-Columbian landscape transformations in Central Amazonia. See Balée & Erickson 2006, pp. 279–309

Neves EG, Petersen JB, Bartone RN, Silva CA. 2003. Historical and socio-cultural origins of Amazonian Dark Earths. See Lehmann et al. 2003, pp. 29–50

Nimuendaju C. 1952. Os Tapajó. *Bol. Mus. Para. Emílio Goeldi* 10:93–106

Noelli F. 2008. The Tupi expansion. See Silverman & Isbell 2008, pp. 659–70

Oliver J. 1991. Donald Lathrap: approaches and contributions to New World archaeology. *Antropológica* 75/76:5–60

Oliver J. 2008. The archaeology of agriculture in ancient Amazonia. See Silverman & Isbell 2008, pp. 185–216

Oyuela-Caycedo A, Raymond S, eds. 1998. *Recent Advances in the Archaeology of the North Andes.* Los Angeles: Inst. Archaeol., Univ. Calif.

Pärssinen M, Korpisaari A, eds. 2003. *Western Amazonia: Amazonia Ocidental: Multi-Disciplinary Studies on Ancient Expansionistic Movements, Fortifications, and Sedentary Life.* Publ. 14. Helsinki: Renvall Inst.

Pauketat T. 2007. *Chiefdoms and Other Archaeological Delusions.* Lanham, MD: Altamira

Pereira E. 2004. *Arte Rupestre na Amazonia: Pará.* São Paulo: UNESP

Perry L. 2005. Reassessing the traditional interpretation of "manioc" artifacts in the Orinoco Valley of Venezuela. *Latin Am. Antiquity* 16(4):409–26

Petersen JB, Neves EG, Heckenberger MJ. 2001. Gift from the past: terra preta and prehistoric Amerindian occupation in Amazonia. See McEwan et al. 2001, pp. 86–105

Piperno DR, Pearsall DM. 1998. *The Origins of Agriculture in the Lowland Neotropics.* San Diego: Academic

Piperno DR, Ranere AJ, Hansell P. 2000. Starch grains reveal early root crop horticulture in the Panamanian tropical forest. *Nature* 407:894–97

Polítis G. 2007. *Nukak: Ethnoarchaeology of an Amazonian People.* Walnut Creek, CA: Left Coast

Polítis G, Alberti B. 1999. *Archaeology in Latin America.* London: Routledge

Porro A. 1996. *Os Povos das Aguas.* Rio de Janeiro: Vozes

Posey DA. 2002. *Kayapó Ethnoecology and Conservation.* London: Routledge

Posey DA, Balée W. 1989. *Resource Management in Amazonia: Indigenous and Folk Strategies.* New York: Adv. Econ. Bot. 7

Prous A. 1991. *Arqueologia Brasileira.* Brasília: Univ. Bras.

Prous A, Fogaça E. 1999. Archaeology of Pleistocene-Holocene boundary in Brazil. *Quat. Int.* 53/54:21–41

Prümers H. 2004. Hügel umgeben von "schönen Monstern": ausgrabungen in der Loma Mendoza (Bolivien). In *Expeditionen in Vergessene Welten*, pp. 47–78. AVA-Forschungen Band 10. Bonn: KAVA

Raymond S. 2008. The process of sedentism in northwestern South America. See Silverman & Isbell 2008, pp. 79–90

Roe P. 1982. *The Cosmic Zygote: Cosmology in the Amazon Basin.* Rutgers, NJ: Rutgers Univ. Press

Roosevelt AC. 1980. *Parmana: Prehistoric Maize and Manioc Subsistence along the Amazon and Orinoco.* New York: Academic

Roosevelt AC. 1991. *Moundbuilders of the Amazon: Geophysical Archaeology in Marajó Island.* San Diego: Academic

Roosevelt AC. 1994. *Amazonian Indians from Prehistory to the Present: Anthropological Perspectives.* Tuscon: Univ. Ariz. Press

Roosevelt AC. 1999. The development of prehistoric complex societies: Amazonia, a tropical forest. In *Complex Polities of the Ancient Tropical World*, ed. EA Bacus, LJ Lucero, pp. 13–33. Washington, DC: Am. Anthropol. Assoc.

Roosevelt AC, Imazio M, Maranca S, Johnson R. 1991. Eighth millennium pottery from a shell mound in the Brazilian Amazon. *Science* 254:1621–24

Roosevelt AC, Lima da Costa M, Lopes Machado C, Michab M, Mercier N, et al. 1996. Paleoindian cave-dwellers in the Amazon: the peopling of the Americas. *Science* 272:373–84

Rostain S. 2008a. Agricultural earthworks on the French Guiana Coast. See Silverman & Isbell 2008, pp. 217–33

Rostain S. 2008b. The Archaeology of the Guianas: an overview. See Silverman & Isbell 2008, pp. 279–302

Sauer C. 1952. *Agricultural Origins and Dispersals*. New York: Am. Geog. Soc.

Schaan DP. 2004. *The Camutins chiefdom: rise and development of complex societies on Marajó Island, Brazilian Amazon*. PhD thesis, Univ. Pittsburgh, 338 pp.

Schaan DP. 2008. The non-agricultural chiefdoms of Marajó. See Silverman & Isbell 2008, pp. 339–57

Schaan DP, Ranzi A, Pärssinen M, eds. 2007. *Arqueologia da Amazônia Ocidental: Os Geoglifos do Acre*. Belém: Ed. Univ. Fed. Pará

Schmidt M. 1917. *Die Aruaken: Ein Beitrag zum Problem de Kulturverbrietung*. Leipzig: Veit

Schmidt P, Patterson T. 1996. *Making Alternative Histories: The Practice of Archaeology and History in Non-Western Settings*. Santa Fe: SAR Press

Silva FA. 2008. Ceramic technology of the Asurini do Xingu, Brazil: an ethnoarchaeological study of artifact variability. *J. Archaeol. Method Theory* 15:217–65

Silverman H, Isbell W. 2008. *Handbook of South American Archaeology*. New York: Springer

Simões M. 1969. The Castanheira site: new evidence for the antiquity and history of the Ananatuba phase. *Am. Antiquity* 34(4):402–10

Simões M. 1981. Coletores-pescadores ceramistas do litoral do Salgado (Pará). *Bol. Mus. Para. Emílio Goeldi* 78:1–31

Simões M, Kalkman A. 1987. Pesquisas arqueológicas no médio Rio Negro (Amazonas). *Rev. Arqueol.* 4(1):83–116

Simões M, Lopes D. 1987. Pesquisas arqueológicas no Baixo/Médio Rio Madeira (Amazonas). *Rev. Arqueol.* 4(1):117–34

Smith N. 2007. *Amazon River Fruits: Flavors for Conservation*. St. Louis: Mo. Bot. Garden Press

Sponsel L. 1995. *Indigenous People and the Future of the Amazon: An Ecological Anthropology of an Endangered World*. Tuscon: Univ. Ariz. Press

Stahl P. 1995. *Archaeology in the American Tropics: Current Analytical Methods and Applications*. Cambridge, UK: Univ. Cambridge Press

Stahl P. 1996. Holocene biodiversity: an archaeological perspective from the Americas. *Annu. Rev. Anthropol.* 25:105–26

Steward JH, Faron L. 1959. *Native Peoples of South America*. New York: McGraw-Hill

Versteeg A. 2008. Barrancoid and Arauquinoid mound builders in coastal Suriname. See Silverman & Isbell 2008, pp. 303–18

Viveiros de Castro EB. 1996. Images of nature and society in Amazonia. *Annu. Rev. Anthropol.* 25:179–200

Walker J. 2004. The llanos de Mojos. See Silverman & Isbell 2008, pp. 937–38

Walker J. 2008. *Agricultural Change in the Bolivian Amazon*. Pittsburgh: Latin Am. Archaeol. Publ.

Whitehead NL. 1994. The ancient Amerindian polities of the Amazon, Orinoco, and the Atlantic coast: a preliminary analysis of their passage from antiquity to extinction. See Roosevelt 1994, pp. 33–53

Whitehead NL, ed. 2003. *Histories and Historicities in Amazonia*. Lincoln: Univ. Neb. Press

Willis KJ, Gillson L, Knapp S, eds. 2007. Biodiversity hotspots through time: using the past to manage the future. *Philos. Trans. R. Soc. B* 362:167–333

Woods WI, McCann J. 1999. The anthropogenic origin and persistence of Amazonian Dark Earths. *Yearb. Conf. Lat. Am. Geog.* 25:7–14

Woods WI, Texeira WG, Lehman J, Steiner C, WinklerPrins A, Rebellato L, eds. 2009. *Amazonian Dark Earths: Wim Sombroek's Vision*. New York: Springer

Wüst I, Barreto C. 1999. The ring villages of central Brazil: a challenge for Amazonian archaeology. *Lat. Am. Antiquity* 10(1):1–23

Zeidler JA. 2008. The Ecuadorian formative. See Silverman & Isbell 2008, pp. 459–88

Zucchi A. 1985. Evidencias arqueológicas sobre grupos de posible lengua Carib. *Antropológica* 63/64:23–44

Zucchi A. 2002. A new model for northern Arawakan expansion. See Hill & Santos-Granero 2002, pp. 199–222

Symptom: Subjectivities, Social Ills, Technologies

João Biehl and Amy Moran-Thomas

Department of Anthropology, Princeton University, Princeton, New Jersey 08544;
email: jbiehl@princeton.edu, amoran@princeton.edu

Annu. Rev. Anthropol. 2009. 38:267–88

First published online as a Review in Advance on
June 23, 2009

The *Annual Review of Anthropology* is online at
anthro.annualreviews.org

This article's doi:
10.1146/annurev-anthro-091908-164420

Key Words

medical science and capitalism, lived experience, ethnographic theory

Abstract

In the domain of health, not only are the raw effects of economic, social,
and medical inequalities continually devastating, but novel processes of
reconfiguring illness experience, subjectivity, and control are also underway. Human relationships to medical technology are increasingly
constituted outside the clinical encounter. In this article we explore
how the domestic encroachment of medical commodities affects social bonds in both affluent and resource-poor contexts, as well as how
these commodities become interwoven in the very fabric of symptoms
and identities. Symptoms are more than contingent matters; they are, at
times, a necessary condition for the afflicted to articulate a new relationship to the world and to others. In exploring how people conceptualize
technological self-care, we are specifically concerned with disciplinary
modes of evidence-making and ask the following: what are the possibilities and limitations of theoretical frameworks (such as structural
violence, biopower, social suffering, and psychoanalysis) through which
these conceptions are being analyzed in contemporary anthropological scholarship? What can the unique capacities of ethnography add to
the task of capturing the active embroilment of reason, life, and ethics
as human conditions are shaped and lost? The intellectual survival of
anthropological theory, we argue, might well be connected to people's
own resilience and bodily struggles for realities to come.

CONTEMPORARY SYMPTOMS

Symptom: A (bodily or mental) phenomenon, circumstance, or change of condition arising from and accompanying a disease or affection, and constituting an indication or evidence of it; a characteristic sign of some particular disease. Especially, in modern use, a subjective indication, perceptible to the patient, as opposed to an objective one or sign.

-Oxford English Dictionary

"I am not the daughter of Adam and Eve. I am the Little Doctor. CATKINE. I need to change my blood with a tonic. Medication from the pharmacy costs money. To live is expensive." Without a known origin and increasingly paralyzed, a young woman named Catarina[1] spent her days in Vita, an asylum in southern Brazil (Biehl 2005), assembling words in what she called "my dictionary." As Catarina wrote, "The characters in this notebook turn and unturn. This is my world after all."

Conveying minimal literacy, the dictionary was a sea of words with puzzling references to all kinds of illnesses, places, roles that Catarina no longer inhabited and people she once lived for. "Rheumatism, complication of labor, evil eye, spasm, nerves.... Documents, reality, truth, voracious, consumer, saving, economics, Catarina, pills, marriage, cancer, Catholic church, separation of bodies, division of the estate, the couple's children."

Caregivers at this grassroots institution of last resort referred to Catarina as "mad" and haphazardly treated her—and the more than 100 people who were also waiting with death in Vita—with all kinds of psychiatric drugs (donations that were by and large expired). "Maybe my family still remembers me, but they don't miss me." Catarina knew what had made her an abject figure in family life, in medicine, in Brazil—"I know because I passed through it"—and she organized this knowledge for herself and the anthropologist, thus bringing

the public into Vita: "I learned the truth and I try to divulge what reality is." "Mine is an illness of time." "My ex-husband sent me to the psychiatric hospital." "The doctors said that they wanted to heal me, but how could they if they did not know the illness?" "My brothers brought me here. And all of us in Vita, we form a society, a society of bodies."

Catarina's life tells a larger story about the encroachment of new medical technologies in urban poor settings and the fate of social bonds in today's dominant mode of subjectification at the service of medical science and capitalism. "To want my body as a medication, my body." In her thinking and writing, global pharmaceuticals are not simply taken as new material for old patterns of self-fashioning: "The dance of science, pain broadcasts sick science, the sick study, brain, illness, Buscopan, Haldol, Neozine, invoked spirit." There is a science to Catarina's symptoms, a science that is itself sick, a money-making science. The goods of psychiatry, such as "Haldol" and "Neozine," are now as ordinary as "Buscopan" (an over-the-counter antispasmodic medication) and have become part of familial practices. Ritual-like, they work on her brain and her illness. "What I was in the past does not matter."

In his lecture "The Sense of Symptoms," Freud (1957) hinted at the existence of a kind of symptom that could not be traced to an individual's idiosyncratic history and that the science and skills of psychoanalysis failed to explain satisfactorily (p. 271). He spoke of "typical symptoms of an illness" that are more or less the same in all cases: "Individual distinctions disappear in them or at least shrink up to such an extent that it is difficult to bring them into connection with the patient's individual experience and to relate them to particular situations they have experienced" (p. 270). Freud had in mind, for example, the repetition and doubt that would be common to all obsessional neurotics. Instead of linking these typical symptoms to biology, Freud saw them as another level of experience, reflecting, perhaps, a kind of universal culture: "If the individual symptoms are so unmistakenly dependent on the patient's experience, it

---

[1] Biehl conducted research with Catarina from 1997 to 2003. Quotes from Catarina are from Biehl's own ethnographic materials.

remains possible that the typical symptoms may go back to an experience which is itself typical—common to all human beings" (p. 271).

Freud (1957) admits that the symptom that makes people similar actually enables the work of medical science: "And we must not forget that it is these typical symptoms, indeed, which give us our bearings when we make our diagnosis" (p. 271). But rather than elaborating further on how the expert uses the symptom to produce science, Freud shifts attention back to the individual's tinkering with it. Insightfully, he notes that the typical symptom activates a subjective plasticity: "On this similar background, however, different patients nevertheless display their individual requirements—whims, one is inclined to say—which in some cases contradict one another directly" (p. 270). Through typical symptoms patients actively project—manufacture, one could say—their own individual conditions and moods. But then, instead of exploring the materiality and historicity of this prosthetic agency, Freud refers to it as a kind of nucleus around which the patient refashions his or her given neurosis.

In the end, not surprisingly, Freud universalizes (1957). He suggests that these affects actually make the individual symptom and typical symptom one and the same: "I will try to console you, therefore, with the reflection that any fundamental distinction between the one kind of symptom and the other is scarcely assumed" (p. 271). Thus, the repetition and doubt that are common to obsessional neurotics can be read as "general reactions which are imposed on the patients by the nature of their pathological change" (p. 271). The problem with this interpretation in modern times is that the subject is not simply the reflection of unconscious processes but is literally composed of both life-enhancing and morbid scientific/market/political changes.

Abandoned in Vita to die, Catarina has ties to *pharmakons*. These universally disseminated goods are entangled in and act as vectors for new mechanisms of sociomedical and subjective control that, in her case, have a deadly force. In this sense, it is not the symptom per se that is ahistorical but an understanding of how these scientific identifications became so widely available, as well as the concrete ways in which they replace social ties, voiding certain forms of human life in the family and medicine. Catarina writes that her desire is now a pharmaceutical thing with no human exchange value: "Catarina cries and wants to leave, desire, watered, prayed, wept, tearful feeling, fearful, diabolic, betrayed, my desire is of no value, desire is pharmaceutical. It is not good for the circus." The symptoms she experiences are the outcome of events and practices that altered the person she had learned to become. Words such as "Haldol" and "Neozine" is now literally her. The drug Akineton used to control the side effects of antipsychotics is actually embedded in the new name Catarina gave herself in the dictionary: CATKINE. While integrating drug experience into a new self-perception and literary work, she kept seeking camaraderie and demanded another chance at life. "The abandoned are part of life."

THE ANTHROPOLOGY OF TECHNOLOGICAL LIVES

In the domain of health, not only are the raw effects of economic, social, and medical inequalities continuously devastating, but novel processes of reconfiguring illness experience, subjectivity, and control are also underway (Biehl et al. 2007, Das 2006, DelVecchio et al. 2008, Jenkins & Barrett 2004, Kleinman 2006, Lakoff 2006, Petryna 2009, Scheper-Hughes 2003). The currents of medical isolation and technological self-care that shape Catarina's existence represent actual global trends (Ecks 2005, Fischer 2009, Luhrman 2000, Martin 2007, Petryna et al. 2006).

New information and life technologies enable new types of exchanges and allow people to imagine and articulate different desires and possibilities for themselves and others (Appadurai 1996, Dumit 2004, Fischer 2003, Inhorn 2003, Rajan 2006, Rapp 1999, Whitmarsh 2008). Embattled geopolitics as well as economic, technoscientific, and legal developments shape life chances and the strategic value of agency claims into the twenty-first century. Although the current understanding of subjectivity as a synonym for inner life processes and affective states is of relatively recent origin, subjectivities have quickly become "raucous *terrae incognitae*" for anthropological inquiry, writes Fischer (2007): "landscapes of explosions, noise, alienating silences, disconnects and dissociations, fears, terror machineries, pleasure principles, illusions, fantasies, displacements, and secondary revisions, mixed with reason, rationalizations, and paralogics—all of which have powerful sociopolitical dimensions and effects" (p. 442).

As Catarina conveys, subjectivity does not merely speak as resistance, nor is it simply spoken (or silenced) by power. It continually forms and returns in the complex play of bodily, linguistic, political, and psychological dimensions of human experience, within and against new infrastructures and the afflictions and injustices of the present (Abu-Lughod 2002, Biao 2006, Dunn 2004, Edmonds 2007, Han 2004, Petryna 2002, Pinto 2008, Rofel 2007, Rouse 2004, Schull 2006). To grasp the wider impact of how medical technologies are becoming interwoven in the very fabric of symptoms and notions of well-being, we must account comparatively for the ways such life forms are fundamentally altering interpersonal relations, domestic economies, and identity-making processes in both affluent and resource-poor contexts (Fassin & Rechtman 2009, Reynolds Whyte 2009). The study of individual subjectivity as both a strategy of existence and a material and means of sociality and governance helps to recast totalizing assumptions of the workings of collectivities and institutions. It also holds the potential to disturb and enlarge presumed understandings of what is socially possible and desirable.

In suburban America, Lynette,[2] a mother of four, is one of thousands of people who report feeling an array of worms and parasitic fibers inhabiting her organs, biting her skin and even turning her flesh into plastic. She believes these pathogens cannot be detected by biomedical diagnostics because technology itself is a component of the parasites that she feels transforming her body in the most intricate and terrifying ways, making her flesh electro-sensitive and even responsive to devices such as computers and televisions. Lynette often seeks virtual help for her symptoms, finding it hard and even impossible to talk to her children and husband. "I feel like I'm in this world, but not of it anymore," she said offhandedly one night while eating a Styrofoam bowlful of pills for dinner.

In her bowl, the mixed antidepressants and prescription antibiotics are easy to recognize because they are printed with cryptic letters and numbers; but their tiny shapes often slip underneath the natural remedies, which are larger pills and far outnumber the prescriptions—yellowish and dully speckled, or sapphire blue and translucent. She eats them with a plastic spoon, as if the bowl contained a colorful cereal missing only its milk. Yet such attempts at self-treatment do not represent an escape to a new technological world, but rather signify her last tenuous link to and effort to remake the former self she feels receding. As an Internet magazine recently reported on her emergent condition, it "is in the process of reconstructing people into an entirely different life form; a cyborg-like creature, both biological and machine." Or as Lynette reports more simply, holding up a strip of her peeled skin close to a light so she can check it for infectious nanomachines: "Sometimes I can't tell which parts are me anymore."

The many infectious disease experts and parasitologists Lynette has seen remain incredulous that these parasites are real, some calling her crazy and most telling her they have no way to help her. Yet Lynette's symptoms do not dissipate when pushed out of the clinic—to the contrary, her subjective and interpretive struggle is only intensified as she drinks liquid silver, rinses her skin with bleach solutions, devises pharmaceutical regimens from an array of prescribed antibiotics, and ultimately is left alone with such

---

[2] Moran-Thomas is currently conducting research with Lynette. Quotes from Lynette are from Moran-Thomas' own ethnographic materials.

technologies of self-care. "Some days I am so symptomatic," she sighed. "No one knows what I should do to heal, to get my life back. But trying gives me ways to face the unknown."

One can see some hauntingly evocative parallels discernable within these two women's drastically divergent circumstances. Although their stories span the devastating conditions of an asylum in southern Brazil and a lonely bathroom in middle-class America, Catarina and Lynette both grapple with the destructive and healing potentials of technology at the level of their very self-conception, painfully wrestling with their illnesses in ways that reshape understandings of kinship and redefine patterns of consumption within their own sick roles to open possibilities for an alternate future.

THE DISCOURSE OF CAPITALISM AND SUBJECTIVE PLASTICITY

In a 1972 lecture (unpublished translation), psychoanalyst Jacques Lacan said that capitalism was now the new discourse of the master and as such it overdetermined social bonds. Lacan spoke of the effects of an absolutization of the market: Subjects do not necessarily address each other to be recognized but experience themselves in the market's truths and commodities (increasingly a bioscientific market—Petryna 2009, Rajan 2006). Although people might have access to the products of science, those countless objects are made to never completely satiate their desires or the desires of those who mediate the access to technologies (Biehl et al. 2001, Zizek 2006). A few years earlier, Lacan stated, "The consumer society has meaning when the 'element' that we qualify as human is given the homogenous equivalent of any other surplus enjoyment that is a product of our industry, a fake surplus enjoyment" (1991, p. 92). Or, as Catarina suggests, these days one can conveniently become a medico-scientific thing and ex-human for others. In the contemporary version of the astute capitalistic discourse we seem to be all proletariat patient-consumers, hyperindividualized psycho-biologies doomed to consume diagnostics and treatments (for

ourselves and surrounding others) and to experience fast success or self-consumption and lack of empathy.

Can we fall for science and technology in different and more lively and caring ways? In Lynette's case, interpreting her symptoms and the technology she uses to treat them become for her both a process that alienates her from the loved ones in her life and her last chance to make possible a continuing connection to that world. In this sense, symptoms and technology are fundamental to the lives of both these women because of the subjective work they occasion (Corin 1994, Turkle 2008b, Young 1995). For whatever their painful constraints, symptoms can also serve as a vital prosthesis—a means of searching for a name, in a singular quest for recognition and care where the search itself becomes more important than the final name at which the search might arrive. Symptoms are born and die with time. They can be significant articulations of one's relationship to the present world. In fact, the word "semiotic" itself was originally defined as "relating to symptoms" (Oxford English Dictionary), underscoring this potential for symbolic work.

The possibilities opened by such processes begin to suggest the profound malleability of the subject, which relates to one set of ideas that we foreground here: the power of plasticity inherent to human interiority. "I mean," writes Friedrich Nietzsche (1955) in *The Use and Abuse of History*, "the power of specifically growing out of one's self, of making the past and the strange one body with the near and the present, . . . of healing wounds, replacing what is lost, repairing broken molds" (pp. 10, 12). Rather than speaking of an essential individuality or of an all-knowing subject of consciousness, Nietzsche calls our attention to modifications in subjective form and sense vis-à-vis historical processes and the possibilities of establishing new symbolic relations to the past and to a changing world.

Such plasticity—whether we think of it as the capacity for being molded or the adaptability of an organism to changes in its environment—is a theme moving through readings of anthropology, psychoanalysis, psychiatry, and cultural history. It appears in the "allo-plastic" capacity of Freud's neurotic patients to alter reality through fantasy (1959, p. 279); in Malinowski's argument about the "plasticity of instincts" under culture (as an alternative to the notion of a mass psyche) (2001, p. 216); in Mauss's ensemble of the social, the psychological, and the biologically, "indissolubly mixed together," in "body techniques" (1979, p. 102); in Kleinman's reading of patterns of social and moral upheaval in individuals' symptoms of distress (1981, Kleinman & Kleinman 1985); in Scheper-Hughes's account of medicalization of the bodily common sense of "nervoso" alongside hunger (1992); in the body of the old person becoming an uncanny double in the liminal space between households and the science of old age, as evidenced by Cohen (1998, p. 269); and in the self-empowerment afforded to the subjected by ambiguity, as Butler (1997) argues in *The Psychic Life of Power*. The notion of the self as malleable runs through these otherwise divergent arguments—malleability is central to our understanding of how sociocultural networks form and how they are mediated by bodily affect and inner worlds.

By way of speech, the unconscious, and the many knowledges and powers whose histories they embody, one can see a subjective plasticity at the heart of Catarina's and Lynette's existences. Facing changing social and medical realities, they deal with a multiplicity of bodily symptoms and desperately try to articulate a symbolic function that has been lost, searching for words and identifications that might make life newly possible. We are not here suggesting that symptoms are basically a matter of social construction or that pharmaceutical treatments do not carry potential benefits for the afflicted. Our point is simply that disorders such as the ones experienced by Catarina and Lynette take form at the most personal juncture between the subject, her biology, and the interpersonal and technical recoding of "normal" ways of being in local worlds. Hence they do implicate those people, institutions, and things standing for common sense and reason, and it is our

responsibility to account for their embroilment in the unfolding of such disorders. Ethnography, we believe, can help us to resituate and rethink pathology within these various circuits and concrete struggles over belonging, voice, and care.

In this article, we explore how people conceptualize illness experiences today and also probe the anthropological frames through which these conceptions are being analyzed. We understand human interiority as fundamentally ethnological—as the whole of an individual's behavior in relation to his or her environment and to the measures that define reality—be they legal, scientific, relational, or affective. It is in family complexes and in convoluted medical, technical, economic, and political domains, as they determine life possibilities and the conditions of representation, that human interiority and its paradoxes belong to a certain order of being in the world.

"EVERYDAY REFLEXIVITY (REGARDLESS OF CULTURE)"

Ethnographically examining symptoms—the entangled realities of affects, subjectivities, social ills, and technologies—requires rethinking older formulations and problematics associated with human nature, social control, identity, and culture. In uniting psychological with cultural themes, Geertz (1973, 1983) famously articulated a cultural approach to subjectivity and a subjectivity-oriented theory (Ortner 2006, Shweder & Good 2004). Geertz commented on the distinction between symptoms and symbolic acts in his discussion of the relationship between depth psychology and anthropology: "In the study of culture the signifiers are not symptoms or clusters of symptoms, but symbolic acts or clusters of symbolic acts, and the aim is not therapy but the analysis of social discourse. But the way in which theory is used—to ferret out the unapparent import of things—is the same" (1973, p. 26).

Geertz insightfully highlights the importance of using theoretical tools to extrapolate from the nuances of lived experience, but his "disciplinary" distinction between symptoms and symbolic actions also raises new questions for the anthropology of subjectivity. Are there realities below the level of action—things envisioned or unspoken—that still matter in shaping the trajectory of a human life? Is the conception of anthropology's purpose as a close analysis of social discourse still enough, or are certain aspects of therapeutic approaches—such as the primacy of affects and role of sublimation—helpful in staking out a new space between these modes of analysis? By more centrally exploring the affective tissue that makes a symbolic action possible or impossible, anthropological accounts can return to life the uncertainty and angst it holds when it is actually lived rather than merely studied and theorized. In this sense, symptoms are more than contingent matters; they are, at times, a necessary condition for us to articulate a relationship to the world and to others.

In addressing psychosis, Lacan (1977), for example, urged psychiatrists and psychoanalysts to question their own trust in the order of reality, to halt diagnosis, and to let patients define their own terms. "I have a great deal of difficulty in logifying," said a patient in a conversation with Lacan. "I don't know if that is a French word, it is a word I invented" (1980, p. 27). We are here faced with the patient's making of meaning in a clinical world that would rather assign such meaning. We are also faced with Lacan's important insight (drawn not only from intellectualization but also from his therapeutic practice) that the unconscious is grounded in rationality and in the interpersonal dimension of speech "born at the level of the lowest encounters and of all the talking crowd that precedes us" (1978, p. 47). For Lacan (1992), subjectivity is that failed and renewable and all-too-human attempt to articulate the truth of oneself.

In a "world in pieces" (Geertz 2000), older notions of the subject who is cultural "all the way down" seem inadequate. Moreover, the body has re-emerged in anthropological analysis in very much the way Mauss (1979) and, later, Foucault (1973, 1980) and Bourdieu (1972) conceived of it (in their distinct theoretical frames) as a privileged heuristic to historical and social processes, thus extending cultural phenomenology to political subjectivity. The presumed subject of humanist theorizing has been deconstructed by poststructuralist, postcolonial, and feminist writers and shown to be a product of Enlightenment, colonial, racialized, and gendered discourses rather than a foundational reality for investigation (Bhabha 1994, Fanon 1963, Haraway 1991, Mbembe 2001, Said 1979, Scott 1999, Spivak 1990). Anthropological studies have, using varying methodologies, shown how medico-scientific formations, political economy, and social networks are mediated by the body and the sense of psychological interiority (Bourgois 1995; Comaroff 1985; Comaroff & Comaroff 1992; Csordas 1994; Das 1996; Lock 1994; Lovell 2006; Martin 1987, 1994; Scheper-Hughes 1979, 1992; Taussig 1986). These studies go beyond mentalist reductionism and convey a key understanding of the self as corporeal, with the body as part and parcel of technical, political, and social processes. The "mindful body" (Hahn & Kleinman 1983, Scheper-Hughes & Lock 1987) has become an important part of our understanding of what the person is in diverse, but always specific, times and places.

By drawing attention to the importance of somatic processes for ordinary life, anthropological studies of the body have cast light on some of the blind spots of a strictly symbolic approach. They have helped to reveal human and institutional interconnectedness and to generalize ethnographic findings. Yet by treating the body as a privileged heuristic of reality, such studies have, at times, also produced a one-dimensional picture of individuals: socially entrained physiologies determined, all the way down, by forms of exploitation and discipline. Not surprisingly, debates on subjectivity that begin with this assumption often center on questions of domination, resistance, and social identity.

Since the 1980s, medical anthropology began moving from studies of ethnomedicine and cultural syndromes to examine also western medicine as itself a cultural system, paying special attention to patient-doctor relations, the medicalization of illness, and the bureaucratization of care (DelVecchio Good 1998; Desjarlais 1997; Kleinman 1981, 1989; Mattingly & Garro 2000; Scheper-Hughes 1992). Whereas these important studies focused on topics such as embodiment and illness narratives within the clinic, emerging realities today also demand new analytics through which these new global phenomena might be better understood (Nichter & Lock 2002, van der Geest et al. 1996). A "descent into the ordinary" (Das 2006) of violently fractured places has made necessary a rethinking of the terms of anthropological inquiry (see also Greenhouse et al. 2002 and Scheper-Hughes & Bourgois 2004). As part of his effort to move away from biologically deterministic and philosophically atomistic conceptions of the self, Kleinman (1999, 2006) uses the term human conditions rather than human nature to describe the inherent malleability of lived experience as it both shapes and is shaped by more macrolevel social, political, and economic processes.

Das has also built on the anthropology of the body literature and probed the extent to which market logics, institutional norms, and rational-technical interventions define the relationship between body and subjectivity. For Das, inner and outer states are inescapably sutured together. And an ethnography of subjectivity illuminates the materials of this suturing and the language by which it is experienced: "[L]anguage is not just a medium of communication or misunderstanding, but an experience which allows not only a message but also the subject to be projected outwards" (Das & Kleinman 2001, p. 22). In this way, people come close to Boon's (1999) "everyday reflexivity (regardless of culture)," disrupting the "comfortably consolidated transdisciplinary theme ('You-Name-It-Of-The-Body')" (pp. 263–65).

As institutional care becomes increasingly outsourced to entrepreneurs and local communities, and as powerful medications circulate without even a doctor visit, human relation-ships to medical technology are increasingly constituted outside the clinical encounter. New populations and forms of intimacy are now emerging around technology at community and domestic levels, as in the case of large-scale AIDS treatment and the massive and often unregulated dissemination of psychiatric drugs worldwide (see, for example, Applbaum 2006, Biehl 2005, Ecks 2005, Farmer 2008, Fassin 2007, Lakoff 2006, Le Marcis 2004, Martin 2007, Reynolds Whyte et al. 2006). Amid the "pharmaceuticalization of public health" (Biehl 2007) and in the daily rituals of medication and adherence, alternative conceptions of political belonging and ideas of what life is for begin to take shape. As interrelations such as kinship become mediated by technology in new ways, we need to account for novel social realities as pharmaceuticals and other health technologies open up and relimit family complexes and human values—as well as for the agency that solitary and chemically submerged subjects such as Catarina/CATKINE express and live by. How are these new technologies of the human now taken up by ethnographers, and with which conceptual apparatuses?

Likewise, with narrative projects initially at the core of an effort to rehumanize medical subjects (Good 1994, Kleinman 1989, Mattingly & Garro 2000), it is crucial to examine also the ways this original endeavor has been variously reoriented, transformed, and even instrumentalized. Moreover, we have to scrutinize how theoretical frameworks used by anthropologists might flatten realities at hand (Borneman & Hammoudi 2009) thus—paradoxically—dehumanizing the people whose lives are recounted as evidence for a preceding explanatory rubric. The intellectual survival of theory might well be connected to people's own resilience and struggles for realities to come (Biehl & Locke 2010). Beginning with these two women who feel technology transforming and even becoming literal components of their identities, this article asks how such complex human stories may speak to (or diverge from) major critical trends in sociocultural studies of health—in particular, influential analytics that explain the subject as fundamentally determined by structural violence, history, biopolitics, and/or the unconscious. What can the unique capacities of ethnography add to the task of capturing the active embroilment of reason, life, and ethics as human lives are reshaped and lost?

STRUCTURAL VIOLENCE AND HUMAN AGENCY

Anthropologists have used the term structural violence to express the ways in which a society's organization and institutions systematically deprive some of its citizens of basic resources and rights—and to critique, in Farmer's (2003) words, the "flabby moral relativism of our times." Depicting people as subjects of structural violence has become a central way of articulating the devastation caused by absent and failed health care systems and of framing this absence/failure as a critical end point of diffuse forms of political and economic violence. Although many anthropologists have employed the analytic of structural violence in significant ways, we consider the work of Farmer, Scheper-Hughes, and Bourgois as particularly influential and emblematic of three distinct formulations of subjectivity within this shared rubric. As they study multiple pathologies—from TB and AIDS to malnutrition and child death to organ trade and transplantation and devastating homelessness and drug addiction—each of these authors argues that structural violence and human rights violations fundamentally cause the symptoms of the conditions they chronicle. They share a commitment to a public anthropology as well as to producing knowledge that leads to life-saving action and to maximizing social and economic rights. Farmer and his colleagues at Partners In Health have effectively critiqued entrenched orthodoxies and established alternative forms of evidence and treatment.

Despite their shared notion of human lives defined by oppressive political economies, the subjectivities recorded by each of these authors in their ethnographic works notably diverge. In fact, quite radical differences exist among the subjectivities suggested by Farmer's renderings of the victimized and often heroic surviving poor (1992, 1999, 2003), Scheper-Hughes's haunting portrayals of damaged mother-child relations under "false consciousness" in conditions of extreme poverty in Brazil (1992), and Bourgois's carefully balanced depictions of crack dealers and users (1995), who he renders by foregrounding their individual relatability and humanity ultimately to explore addiction as a lived ramification of oppression and symbolic violence (see also Bourgois & Schonberg 2009).

In trying to understand why these depictions of subjectivity vary so surprisingly among authors who share a conception of how the subject is conceived, we must also bring into view the subjectivity, arts, and politics of both the writer and the reader. Yet this issue runs deeper than the frame of intended audience so frequently discussed in the context of editorial constraints and authorial choices, and instead, pushes us to account for the subjectivity of the reader as a formative experience—that is, the formative power of a text to create a public that had not previously existed. To some extent, the three authors discussed here deliberately put the subjectivity of the reader as witness before the subjectivity of the people their ethnographies describe.

Farmer, for example, in *Pathologies of Power* (2003) is deeply committed to the project of securing treatment and sustained support for the global poor, so much so that a flattened depiction of their stories often becomes more rhetorically useful than a nuanced exploration of their complex lives. People seem to live and die in an exemplary way to the point of fitting into preconceived molds. It is not a matter of applauding or critiquing Farmer here, but of calling attention to the ways that an anthropology informed by the structural violence analytic goes about shaping evidence from human lives. What is the slippery trade-off of the representational strategy of idealizing lives and aggregating cases, and how do the sentiments that this strategy is designed to evoke fit into a larger idea of politics?

Farmer (2005) addresses the "politics of pity" critique directly and ultimately tries to find ways to make it useful: "We are not opposed to pity, but we're anxious to press for policies that would protect vulnerable populations from structural violence" (p. 152). He also acknowledges the criticism that, in using the category of structural violence, he conflates domination with disparity and collapses forms of violence that need to be differentiated. Farmer counters the "rhetorical tool critique" by asking, "But aren't rhetorical tools necessary if we seek to lessen violence in all its forms? Isn't that what photographs as personal narratives often are, rhetorical tools?" (p. 186). His explicit evocation of personal narratives is part of a critical activist toolkit—all of which has powerful implications for public mobilization, but also limitations in terms of addressing singularity, and at times, obscuring the nuanced and volatile texture of interlocutors' own subjectivities.

Although striving to evoke a sense of shared humanity rather than pity, Bourgois (2002) likewise discusses his ethnographic strategy quite reflectively when looking back on his ethnography *In Search of Respect*: "I frequently selected and edited personal narrative so as to evoke sympathy from readers, so that they would recognize emotionally as well as intellectually their common humanity with the crack dealers" (p. 227). Thus, although Bourgois remains painstakingly attentive to the subjective states he observes in his interlocutors, in the end he carefully filtered which of their behaviors and affective depictions will evoke a targeted emotional response in the reader. Yet the collaborative photo-ethnography of his most recent book, *Righteous Dopefiend* (Bourgois & Schonberg 2009) further complicates this theoretical outlook with its stunning photographic moments and accompanying narratives, the force of which comes precisely from their raw portrayals of life with addiction and the unknown variable this adds to possible readings of casuality and intervention.

Each of these depictions of human subjectivity implies a distinct consciousness and awareness, which become even more pronounced in Scheper-Hughes's (1992) readings of false consciousness in contexts of scarcity and inequality. Yet her work becomes difficult to interpret solely through the limits of the theoretical lens she claims for herself because she often writes beyond it, with the force of her writing itself infused with the transformative power of art. Perhaps the piece that escapes Scheper-Hughes's (2008) theoretical framework is precisely the moment when her characters come alive in their own right.

Such moments when care and art seem to merge point toward explorations that can offer ways outside the structure/agency impasse that still often limits structural violence as a theoretically generative analytic. Approaching such problems through the framework of interlocutors' subjectivities could allow us to find new ways around the dichotomization of structure and human agency, by understanding these tensions as affectively interconnected, rather than diametrically opposed. Ethnographic experiments that illuminate these intertwined capillaries can help us to repopulate the political stage with always-ambiguous actors (Rancière 2004), using artistic visual materials and the literary immanence of our writing itself to turn their complex and even contradictory actions into a critical dimension of our analytics.

SUBJECTS OF HISTORY

Anthropologists have turned to history as a way to add sequential complexity to the human stories they observe unfolding in the present (Boon 1977, Briggs & Mantini-Briggs 2003, Dirks 1992, Feldman 2008, Lomnitz 2008, Povinelli 2002, Stoler 1995, Taussig 1986, Trouillot 1997). It is important to consider the implications that this historical turn may hold for understandings of subjectivity, particularly in the face of illness, because tracing such trajectories holds special significance for identifying causalities of manifested symptoms as well as resources for alternate futures.

The Comaroffs have made critical disciplinary strides in linking historical flows of capitalism and colonialism with the shaping of contemporary consciousness. They have shown how the social and even religious meanings of medical contagion were manipulated to establish or reinforce power disparities (Comaroff & Comaroff 1997) and that hierarchies in the biomedical sciences and discourses of imperial control mutually reinforced each other in the colonial reaches of nineteenth-century Africa (Comaroff 1997). Using an eclectic methodology, their work often implicitly interprets symptoms, at once physical and social, as directly springing from new political economies and the uneven terms of European encroachment and neoliberal trade (Comaroff & Comaroff 2006). Yet this critical work leaves a vital question open: How can an individual's inner world, as well as the way it manifests itself through particular symptoms, remain distinct from the forces of collective history within which it is embedded?

An interesting example of the Comaroffs' take on the individual subject comes from a recent text (2003), which begins by evoking one of the figures from an earlier article, "The Migrant and the Madman" (1987), while also adding a new figure—the zombie—to their cast of characters. Both figures are defined largely by their refusal to speak, and the Comaroffs interpret this muteness as a symptom of their depersonalization in the face of new forms of labor. In the end, the madman and the zombie do not become fully fleshed characters with their own names, contradictions, or nonrepresentative symptoms. The Comaroffs' analytic frame valuably highlights how political economies historically come to exist and shape ways of being, but its applicability for exploring how individuals might understand themselves beyond their membership in an exploited population is open to further investigation.

In *When Bodies Remember: Experiences and Politics of AIDS in South Africa*, Fassin (2007) defines history as "what is inscribed within our bodies and makes us think and act as we do" (p. xix). Violent legacies of colonialism and racism are part and parcel of lethal symptoms. Past forms of structural violence become a habitus so deeply embodied that the human

lives Fassin depicts are inescapably cast as subjects of memory. For him, the contours of subjectivity are shaped—even delimited by or equated with—experiences of history. In a recent article, for example, Fassin and colleagues (2008) ask a young AIDS patient and activist named Magda to record her biography. Yet, surprisingly, the major political events and the racial discrimination that have shaped the nation's economy and Magda's life chances "never explicitly appear in the narrative" (p. 227). For the authors, this "invisible context" (p. 227) is itself a symptom of power arrangements and of the violence of history. They take it as their task to make this lacuna intelligible and to make Magda's story and history "part of each other" (p. 226).

Yet one wonders, why is "excavating the past" the necessary condition of making "the present understandable" (p. 225)? Could we not interpret Magda's refusal to do so as a simple and profound statement of being-for-the-future as opposed to her muteness being a symptom of the past? From this perspective, Magda would thus seem less a subject of power and memory and more a subject of desire. She herself speaks of a primacy of desire over power when faced with the death of her HIV-positive first child and her own medical demise: "We die, we can die . . . . And I used to say 'hey, they have the babies and me, I don't have the baby, I want the baby'" (p. 232). She was able to take advantage of the highly politicized AIDS treatment available and gave birth to a second child who was not HIV infected. A microanalysis of such engagements can help us to understand the present and people not so much as claimed by history but as makers of new systems of perception and action that come with specific sets of possibilities and limits. How can we integrate into social science and policy the insights, ambiguities, and desires (alternative human capacities) that millions like Magda now embody?

Stoler's (2009) recent examination of administrative archives from the Dutch East Indies takes such convoluted margins of history precisely as its object of inquiry. Rather than focusing on the broad currents of colonial power in hegemony and resistance, Stoler looks for places in which this analytic falters. She uses "minor histories"—moments of failure and seemingly tangential intimacies—to find variegated shades within hegemonic discourses and their attempted applications. The objective is "to identify a symptomatic space in the craft of governance," foregrounding "structures of feeling and force that in a 'major' history might otherwise be displaced" (p. 7). These explorations help us to understand more subtly the subjectivities of colonial administrators, insights that resonate for the holders of power in today's economy as well. Stoler replaces the language of hegemony and cruelty with the observation that "ethics are not absent" in colonial history. Rather, "imperial dispositions are marked by a negative space: that from which those with privilege and standing could excuse themselves" (p. 256). Stoler pays meticulous attention to the role that documents played in creating "conditions of disregard," circumscribing what she terms the "limits of care" (p. 256).

We highlight the trope of uncertainty that appears throughout this text and its significance for understanding the structures of time that underlie affective responses. From the first page, Stoler (2009) describes one dimension of her project as "about colonial archives as sites of the expectant and conjured—about dreams of comforting futures and foreboding of future failures" (p. 1). In allowing readers to glimpse a moment in which past futures were unknown, Stoler also raises a critical question for nonarchival ethnography. How do lapses and indeterminacy, waiting and wondering over time and living "in the subjunctive," help us to understand more fully subjectivity in relation to the trajectories of affect and control (Deleuze 1995, Stewart 2007)?

In keeping such a sense of open-endedness, Good's (2007) study of epidemic-like experiences of psychoses in contemporary Indonesia helps to illuminate how the present may be haunted by history without being thoroughly determined by it. While directing attention to how the experiences of acute brief psychoses

are entangled with the country's current political and economic turmoil, its postcolonial history, and an expanding global psychiatry, Good and colleagues emphasize the ambiguities, dissonances, and limitations that accompany all attempts to represent subjectivity in mental illness. In unremittingly resisting closure in their analysis, they challenge us to bring into view movement and unfinishedness. Such unfinishedness is integral to becoming. Returning to the opening story, Catarina was constantly recalling the events that led to her being abandoned as "mad" and with no social ties. And yet, she was not simply trying to make sense of these ruptures and to find a place for herself in history. Her subjectivity was actually constructed in relation to this tinkering. By going through all the components and singularities of the events that led to her abandonment, she was resuming her place in them "as in a becoming," in the words of Deleuze (1995): "[H]istory amounts only to the set of preconditions, however recent, that one leaves behind in order to 'become,' that is, to create something new" (p. 170).

THROUGH AND BEYOND BIOPOLITICS

According to Hannah Arendt (1958), political action has increasingly focused on the control of natural life and on the fabrication of automatons. The *Homo faber* gave way to the *Homo laborans*—that is, people became ever more involved in mass production and concerned with physiological existence. Scientific practices have been central to this transformation. Arendt argues that the experimental process that came to define the natural sciences— "the attempt to imitate under artificial conditions the process of 'making' by which a natural thing came into existence"—has acquired such a significance that it now serves "as well or even better as the principle for doing in the realm of human affairs" (p. 299).

Foucault pursued the historical complexities that emerged as science became a central component of the ways in which modern institutions and self-governance function. In his work on psychiatric power (1997), for example, he exposed the role of expertise in the constitution of mental illness, in its spatialization and embodied forms. Or, as Hacking (2002) puts it, "Instead of knowledge being that which is true, the objects of knowledge become ourselves" (p. 4). Lacan (1989) would agree that we moderns are not without a relationship to changing forms of truth (p. 13). Truth has become our labor. "The loss of human experience involved in this development is extraordinarily striking," writes Arendt (1958, p. 321). In the decades since Foucault's (1980, 2007) formulation of biopower—how natural life has been taken as an object of modern politics—numerous anthropologists have used this theoretical construct to assess the emergent intertwining or assemblages of medicine, technology, and governance (Dumit 2004; Ong & Collier 2005; Fassin 2001; Franklin 1997; Lakoff 2006; Nguyen 2005; Rabinow 1996, 1999; Rajan 2006). Yet this influential biopolitical analytic deserves deeper ethnographic probing, as it might assume transcendent forms of power and overly normalized people. What is outside biopower?

Anthropologist Allan Young (1995) has drawn from Foucault (1980) and Hacking (1986, 2002) to explore the ways that post-traumatic stress disorder (PTSD) classifications themselves distinctly "make people up" and shape war trauma experience. Through archival research on World War II veterans alongside ethnographic work at the Veterans Administration Hospital, Young suggests that certain aspects of PTSD, such as experiences of time, are not "natural" biological facts but rather "an achievement, a product of psychiatric culture and technology" (p. 116). More recently, Kaufman (2005) has profiled the ends of life in U.S. hospitals, revealing the dominant clinical strategies aimed toward coaxing families to make the "right decision" regarding the discontinuation of life support—which, as she points out, is not a matter of saying yes or no to the single device many people imagine but rather deliberating among an overwhelming array of ambiguous machines, tubes, and technological

support systems (2005). Young and Kaufman incorporate dozens of brief case studies into their analyses; in fact, they both record most of the clinical exchanges they witness in the form of extended interview-style dialogs, as do many anthropologists who have done important work in domains of technological expertise (Fortun 2008, Rabinow & Dan-Cohen 2005, Reardon 2004). This kind of evidence making importantly highlights clinical/laboratory narratives and the way expert knowledge is constituted and negotiated, yet at times, it may also have the unintended side effect of implying that there is a theory of subjectivity inherent to the forms of science and medicine themselves.

Lock (2002) undertakes a related project in *Twice Dead*, yet the comparative nature of her study—which bridges Japan and North America—adds a different dimension to her depictions of subjectivity. In examining the relationship between definitions of brain death and organ donation, the tension between the two sites allows her to carefully separate the biological conditions she observes from corresponding medical discourses to understand better what is locally specific within a given culture of medicine. For example, she suggests that qualities of Shinto animism often extend to inanimate objects and cast even medical technology in a more positive light in much of Japan, noting Mathews Hamabata's observation that "workers often understand the machinery they work with as a spiritual extension of themselves" (Lock 2002, p. 370)—in stark contrast with the humiliating connotations that life support often holds in American hospitals. Such divergences help Lock to move away from a top-down understanding of power/knowledge, as the comparative depth of her project brings her to consider not only the way various people react differently to analogous life technologies, but further how such differences impact assumed power structures themselves.

By exploring connections that make legal and medical forms newly personal, Adriana Petryna's (2002) concept of biological citizenship helps to elucidate the political nature of science as well as shifting state-market structures and the modes of survival they make available. Petryna describes people's common struggle in Ukraine to provide evidence that their illnesses are linked to the Chernobyl nuclear disaster and thereby make them eligible for welfare and care in an entirely new democratic state form. It is the deep engagement with vulnerable human lives and detailed accounts of their layered experiences with science, medicine, and politics that lends force to Petryna's biological citizenship. Meanwhile, the sociological uptake of Petryna's original concept (Rose & Novas 2005) can sometimes be "programmatic and decontextualized"; by foregrounding media and scientific discourses rather than the everyday human lives they travel through, in this latter framework "politics concerns an all-pervasive power that shapes perceptions and subjectivity" (Reynolds Whyte 2009, p. 11). Exploring the situated interrelations of subjective and economic experiences of illness and medico-legal criteria, Petryna empirically traces the interface of these registers—often painfully incommensurable—to illuminate novel ideas of care, ethics, and political belonging.

Although plasticity may be intrinsic to human subjectivity, technology makes such malleability literal in new ways. In examining such realities, we should reconsider, as Turkle (2008b) writes, "how technology touches on the ethical compacts we make with each other" (p. 29). The memoirs in her edited volume examine how our ways of being human are increasingly dependent on technological devices—from prosthetic eyes and virtual avatars to dialysis apparatuses and gambling machines (see Boellstorf 2008). But if mechanical intimacy shapes new meaning for digital lives and cyborg existences, perhaps chemical transformation allows for a different kind of subjective transformation. Martin (2007) grapples insightfully with this issue in a chapter on "Pharmaceutical Personalities," evoking her own struggles to medicate the symptoms of her bipolar disorder alongside interviews with pharmaceutical representatives and the

stories of many other diagnosed patients' medication histories—or as one woman put it, her "chemical résumé" (p. 166). As another of her interlocutors says, "If I take a new drug, even a new brand name of the same drug...I have to reshape my entire identity, like I am now not that person who took Depakote. If I have to go and take lithium, then I have to come up with an identity that takes lithium" (p. 162). In this description, naming and language become as important as the chemical composition of a new drug in rearticulating an identity.

For Martin and Turkle, technology does not determine or even necessarily constrain human lives; in fact, it often liberates them. They can explore these topics so intimately in part because of their fundamental premise that science and medicine are more than tools of control or even personified inanimate objects, but rather represent one actor in a process that always involves at least two sides acting on each other. The malleability and identity work that such objects can make possible in human lives are the affective end point of a process "about science, technology, and love" (Turkle 2008a, p. 3). In this process, technology itself becomes a complex intersubjective actor, with transformative potential that must be negotiated with and even cared for to actualize its fragile chance for a new beginning. As medical technology becomes a potential way to explore the new people we might be or the relationships we might imagine, Turkle (2008b) notes, "Inner history shows technology to be as much an architect of our intimacies as our solitudes" (p. 29).

Philosopher Giorgio Agamben (1998) has significantly informed contemporary biopolitical debates with his evocation of the *Homo sacer* and the assertion that "life exposed to death" is the original element of western democracies (p. 4). This "bare life" appears in Agamben as a kind of historical-ontological destiny—"something presupposed as nonrelational" and "desubjectified" (1999). A number of anthropologists have critiqued Agamben's apocalyptic take on the contemporary human condition and the dehumanization that accompanies such melancholic, if poignant, ways of thinking (Das & Poole 2004, Rabinow & Rose 2006).

Whether in social abandonment, addiction, or homelessness, life that no longer has any value for society is hardly synonymous with a life that no longer has any value for the person living it (Biehl 2005, Bourgois & Schonberg 2009, Garcia 2008). Language and desire meaningfully continue even in circumstances of profound abjection. Such difficult and multifaceted realities and the fundamentally ambiguous nature of people living them give anthropologists the opportunity to develop a human, not abstractly philosophical, critique of the nonexceptional machines of social death and (self) consumption in which people are caught. Against all odds, people keep searching for contact and for ways to endure, at times reworking and sublimating symptoms in their search for social ties.

Acknowledging the insights and alternative human capacities that grow out of abjection also forces us to inquire into how they can be part and parcel of the much needed efforts to redirect care. The need for subjective texture thus also raises broader anthropological questions about ethnography's unique potential to bring the private life of the mind into conversations about public health and politics. Rather than ethnographically illustrating the silhouettes of biopolitical theory, new ways of thinking about political belonging and subjectivity force us instead to reconsider this theoretical framework's very terms.

CODA: LITERATURE AND HEALTH

The function and formation of "Le Sinthome" (an ancient way of writing what would later be called symptom) was one of Lacan's final theoretical investigations (2005). In his 1975–1976 seminar he elaborated on the concept of the sinthome as the enigmatic fourth element that tied the imaginary, the symbolic, and the real together (p. 21). With a nature of their own, symptoms convey the inextricably knotted processes of identity. They are the support of subjects trying to organize the complex relationship between body and language; in Lacan's words, "We recognize ourselves only in what we have. We never recognize ourselves in what we are" (p. 120).

In classic psychoanalysis, symptoms are addressed to the analyst and might be dissolved through interpretation and analytic work—but the sinthome, Lacan argues, testifies to the persistence of the traumatic Real. Trauma is an event that remains without the possibility of symbolization. Or as Zizek (1989) puts it, the sinthome is "an inert stain resisting communication and interpretation, a stain which cannot be included in the circuit of discourse, of social bond network, but is at the same time a positive condition of it" (p. 75). Lacan (2005) said he learned from Joyce ("he was the sinthome") that it is only through art and "these little pieces of writing" that we can "historically enter the Real" (p. 68), undo supposed truths, and reinvent and give substance to the sinthome. As Lacan states, "it is the knot that gives writing its autonomy" (p. 140).

We find Deleuze's insights on "Literature and Life" especially helpful for this inquiry into the relationship between symptoms and creative art. For Deleuze (1997), writing is "a question of becoming, always incomplete, always in the midst of being formed, and goes beyond the matter of any livable or lived experience. It is a process, that is, a passage of Life that traverses both the livable and the lived" (p. 1). He thinks of language as a system that can be disturbed, attacked, and reconstructed—the very gate through which limits of all kinds are transcended and the energy of the "delirium" unleashed (Didion 2006, Kristeva 1982). The delirium suggests alternative visions of existence, the possibility of being singularized out of a population and open to a future that clinical definitions would tend to foreclose.

This vision for literature can also inspire anthropologists (Biehl 2005, Desjarlais 2003, Jackson 2009, Pandolfo 1998, Taussig 2006): Listening as readers and writers, rather than clinicians or theoreticians, our own sensibility and openness become instrumental in spurring social recognition of the ways ordinary people think through their conditions. Ethnographic details reveal nuanced fabrics of singularities and the worldliness, rather than exceptionality, of people's afflictions and struggles; they make explicit the concreteness of processes and buried anticipations. In Catarina's words, real and imaginary voyages compose a set of intertwined routes. "I am a free woman, to fly, bionic woman, separated." These trajectories are inseparable from her efforts of becoming. "The ultimate aim of literature," Deleuze (1997) argues, "is to set free, in the delirium, this creation of a health or this invention of a people, that is, a possibility of life." Or as Catarina wrote: "Die death, medication is no more." "I will leave the door of the cage open. You can fly wherever you want to."

Anthropologists can render publicly intelligible the value of what people, amid new rational-technical and politico-economic machineries, are left to resolve alone (Biehl & Locke 2010). Catarina's writings, and Lynette's efforts to heal herself enough to be human again, all evince pain and an ordinary life force seeking to break through forms and foreclosures and define a kind of subjectivity that is as much about swerves and escapes as about determinations. People's practices of survival and inquiry, their search for symbolic authority, challenge the analytic forms we bring to the field, forcing us to articulate more experience-near and immediately relevant conceptual work. Theory is thus embattled and unfinished on both sides of the conversation. Yet this open-ended tentativeness, this untimeliness (Rabinow 2008), is not always easily borne: With an eye to the possibilities and noninevitability of people's lives, we must recognize the thresholds at which liberating flights and creative actions can become deadly rather than vital forms of experimentation, opening up not to new webs of care and empathy but to systematic disconnection.

As evident in Catarina's writing and in Lynnete's thinking, the openings that such moments of imagination, creation, and sublimation can offer are undeniably fleeting. Yet the fact that such efforts often falter or even fail

to change material constraints does not negate the intrinsic force of this struggle to connect, the human resilience it reveals, or the ways these stories can complicate theories of how social structures shape people's own understandings of their possible futures. In accounting for symptoms, the profound plasticity inherent to human interiority surfaces as part of the struggle for answers and survival, reworked in the most visceral ways. Such efforts to understand and heal can make symptoms more than the incidental markers of disease, but rather a fundamental part of people's being and means of articulating a relationship to the world—at times an effort to reestablish a social tie that has been lost, perhaps less a matter of finding a voice than establishing oneself as part of a matrix in which there is someone else to hear it.

This is a rich human opening, in which anthropology has a unique disciplinary potential to contribute to commentaries on the power of narrative art that have largely emerged from reflections on literary giants. For while Lacan builds on Joyce and Deleuze draws from Kafka, we as anthropologists have a distinct task: Our curiosity can meet what remains to be known as we bring back the everyday stories and writings of characters that might otherwise remain forgotten, with attention to the ways their own struggles and visions of themselves create holes in dominant theories and policies. Perhaps the creativity of ethnography arises from this effort to give form to people's own painstaking arts of living and the unexpected potentials they create, and from the descriptive work of giving these observed tensions an equally powerful force in our own accounting.

Continually adjusting itself to the reality of contemporary lives and worlds, the anthropological venture has the potential of art: to invoke neglected human possibilities and to expand the limits of understanding and imagination. Compellingly attending to tiny gestures, islands of care, and moments of isolation or waiting in which hope and life somehow continue are not just footnotes in the ethnographic record, but rather the very place where our new ethics and politics might come into being.

DISCLOSURE STATEMENT

The authors are not aware of any affiliations, memberships, funding, or financial holdings that might be perceived as affecting the objectivity of this review.

ACKNOWLEDGMENTS

We are thankful to Peter Locke, Robson de Freitas Pereira, Luis Guilherme Streb, and Franco Rossi for their help. The comments and suggestions of the anonymous reviewer were very helpful. We acknowledge the support of the Center for Theological Inquiry and of Princeton University's Program in Latin American Studies and of Grand Challenges Initiative in Global Health and Infectious Disease.

LITERATURE CITED

Abu-Lughod L. 2002. Egyptian melodrama—technology of the modern subject? In *Media Worlds: Anthropology on New Terrain*, ed. FD Ginsburg, L Abu-Lughod, B Larkin, pp. 115–33. Berkeley: Univ. Calif. Press

Agamben G. 1998. *Homo Sacer: Sovereign Power and Bare Life*. Stanford, CA: Stanford Univ. Press

Agamben G. 1999. *Remnants of Auschwitz: The Witness and the Archive*. New York: Zone Books

Appadurai A. 1996. *Modernity at Large: Cultural Dimensions of Globalization*, Vol. 1. Minneapolis: Univ. Minn. Press

Applbaum K. 2006. American pharmaceutical companies and the adoption of SSRI's in Japan. In *Global Pharmaceuticals: Markets, Practices, Ethics*, ed. A Petryna, A Lakoff, A Kleinman, pp. 85–110. Durham, NC: Duke Univ. Press

Arendt H. 1958. *The Human Condition*. Chicago: Univ. Chicago Press

Bhabha HK. 1994. *The Location of Culture*. New York: Routledge

Biao X. 2006. *Global Body Shopping: An Indian Labor System in the Information Technology Industry*. Princeton, NJ: Princeton Univ. Press

Biehl J. 2005. *Vita: Life in a Zone of Social Abandonment*. Berkeley: Univ. Calif. Press

Biehl J. 2007. *Will to Live: AIDS Therapies and the Politics of Survival*. Princeton, NJ: Princeton Univ. Press

Biehl J, Coutinho D, Outeiro AL. 2001. Technology and affect: HIV/AIDS testing in Brazil. *Cult. Med. Psychiatry* 25(1):87–129

Biehl J, Good B, Kleinman A. 2007. *Subjectivity: Ethnographic Investigations*. Berkeley: Univ. Calif. Press

Biehl J, Locke P. 2010. Deleuze and the anthropology of becoming. *Curr. Anthropol.* In press

Boellstorf T. 2008. *Coming of Age in Second Life: An Anthropologist Explores the Virtually Human*. Princeton, NJ: Princeton Univ. Press

Borneman J, Hammoudi A, eds. 2009. *Being There: The Fieldwork Encounter and the Making of Truth*. Berkeley: Univ. Calif. Press

Boon J. 1977. *Anthropological Romance of Bali 1597–1972: Dynamic Perspectives in Marriage and Cast, Politics and Religion*. Cambridge, UK: Cambridge Univ. Press

Boon J. 1999. *Verging on Extra-Vagence: Anthropology, History, Religion, Literature, Arts . . . Showbiz*. Princeton, NJ: Princeton Univ. Press

Bourdieu P. 1972. *Outline of the Theory of Practice*, ed. E Leach, M Fortes. Cambridge, UK: Cambridge Univ. Press

Bourgois P. 1995. *In Search of Respect: Selling Crack in El Barrio*. Cambridge, UK: Cambridge Univ. Press

Bourgois P. 2002. The violence of moral binaries. *Ethnography* 3(2):221–31

Bourgois P, Schonberg J. 2009. *Righteous Dopefiend*. Berkeley: Univ. Calif. Press

Briggs CL, Martini-Briggs C. 2003. *Stories in the Time of Cholera*. Berkeley: Univ. Calif. Press

Butler J. 1997. *The Psychic Life of Power: Theories of Subjection*. Stanford, CA: Stanford Univ. Press

Cohen L. 1998. *No Aging in India: Alzheimer's, the Bad Family, and Other Modern Things*. Berkeley: Univ. Calif. Press

Comaroff J. 1985. *Body of Power, Spirit of Resistance: The Culture and History of a South African People*. Chicago: Univ. Chicago Press

Comaroff J. 1997. The diseased heart of Africa: medicine, colonialism, and the black body. In *Knowledge, Power, and Practice*, ed. S Lindenbaum, M Lock, pp. 305–29. Berkeley: Univ. Calif. Press

Comaroff JL, Comaroff J. 1987. The migrant and the madman: work and labor in the historical consciousness of a South African people. *Am. Ethnol.* 14(2):191–209

Comaroff JL, Comaroff J. 1992. *Ethnography and the Historical Imagination*. Boulder, CO: Westview

Comaroff JL, Comaroff J. 1997. The medicine of God's word. In *Of Revelation and Revolution: Volume II*, pp. 323–64. Chicago: Univ. Chicago Press

Comaroff JL, Comaroff J. 2003. Ethnography on an awkward scale: postcolonial anthropology and the violence of abstraction. *Ethnography* 4(2):147–79

Comaroff JL, Comaroff J. 2006. *Law and Disorder in the Postcolony*. Chicago: Univ. Chicago Press

Corin E. 1994. From symptom to phenomena: the articulation of experience in schizophrenia. *J. Phenomenol. Psychol.* 25:3–50

Csordas TJ. 1994. *Embodiment and Experience: The Existential Ground of Culture and Self*, Vol. 2. Cambridge, UK: Cambridge Univ. Press

Das V. 1996. *Critical Events: An Anthropological Perspective on Contemporary India*. New York: Oxford Univ. Press

Das V. 2006. *Life and Words: Violence and the Descent into the Ordinary*. Berkeley: Univ. Calif. Press

Das V, Kleinman A. 2001. Introduction. In *Remaking a World: Violence, Social Suffering, and Recovery*, ed. V Das, A Kleinman, M Lock, M Ramphele, P Reynolds, pp. 1–30. Berkeley: Univ. Calif. Press

Das V, Poole D. 2004. State and its margins: comparative ethnographies. In *Anthropology in the Margins of the State*, ed. V Das, D Poole, pp. 3–34. Santa Fe, NM: Sch. Am. Res. Press

Deleuze G. 1995. *Negotiations, 1972–1990*. New York: Columbia Univ. Press

Deleuze G. 1997. *Essays: Critical and Clinical*. Minneapolis: Univ. Minn. Press

DelVecchio Good MJ. 1998. *American Medicine: The Quest for Competence*. Berkeley: Univ. Calif. Press

DelVecchio Good MJ, Hyde ST, Pinto S, Good B, eds. 2008. *Postcolonial Disorders: Ethnographic Studies in Subjectivity*. Berkeley: Univ. Calif. Press

Desjarlais R. 1997. *Shelter Blues: Sanity and Selfhood Among the Homeless*. Philadelphia: Univ. Penn. Press

Desjarlais R. 2003. *Sensory Biographies: Lives and Deaths among Nepal's Yolmo Buddhists*. Berkeley: Univ. Calif. Press

Didion J. 2006. *The Year of Magical Thinking*. New York: Knopf

Dirks N. 1992. *Colonialism and Culture*. Ann Arbor: Univ. Mich. Press

Dumit J. 2004. *Picturing Personhood: Brain Scans and Biomedical Identity*. Princeton, NJ: Princeton Univ. Press

Dunn E. 2004. *Privatizing Poland: Baby Food, Big Business, and the Remaking of Labor*. Ithaca, NY: Cornell Univ. Press

Ecks S. 2005. Pharmaceutical citizenship: antidepressant marketing and the promise of demarginalization in India. *Anthropol. Med.* 12(3):239–54

Edmonds A. 2007. The poor have the right to be beautiful: cosmetic surgery in neoliberal Brazil. *J. R. Anthropol. Inst.* 13(2):363–81

Fanon F. 1963. *The Wretched of the Earth*. New York: Grove

Farmer P. 1992. *AIDS and Accusation: Haiti and the Geography of Blame*. Berkeley: Univ. Calif. Press

Farmer P. 1999. *Infections and Inequalities: The Modern Plagues*. Berkeley: Univ. Calif. Press

Farmer P. 2003. *Pathologies of Power: Health, Human Rights, and the New War on the Poor*. Berkeley: Univ. Calif. Press

Farmer P. 2005. Never again? Reflections on human values and human rights. *Tanner Lecture Series*. Salt Lake City: Univ. Utah Press

Farmer P. 2008. Challenging orthodoxies: the road ahead for health and human rights. *Health Hum. Rights* 10(1):5–19

Fassin D. 2001. The biopolitics of otherness: undocumented foreigners and racial discrimination in French public debate. *Anthropol. Today* 17(1):3–7

Fassin D. 2007. *When Bodies Remember: Experiences and Politics of AIDS in South Africa*. Berkeley: Univ. Calif. Press

Fassin D, Le Marcis F, Lethata T. 2008. The life and times of Magda A: telling a story of violence in South Africa. *Curr. Anthropol.* 49(2):225–46

Fassin D, Rechtman R. 2009. *The Empire of Trauma: An Inquiry into the Condition of Victimhood*. Princeton, NJ: Princeton Univ. Press

Feldman I. 2008. *Governing Gaza: Bureaucracy, Authority, and the Work of Rule, 1917–1967*. Durham, NC: Duke Univ. Press

Fischer M. 2003. *Emergent Forms of Life and the Anthropological Voice*. Durham, NC: Duke Univ. Press

Fischer M. 2007. To live with what would otherwise be unendurable: return(s) to subjectivities. See Biehl et al. 2007, pp. 423–46

Fischer M. 2009. *Anthropological Futures*. Durham, NC: Duke Univ. Press

Fortun M. 2008. *Promising Genomics: Iceland and deCODE Genetics in a World of Speculation*. Berkeley: Univ. Calif. Press

Foucault M. 1973. *The Birth of the Clinic: An Archeology of Medical Perception*. New York: Pantheon

Foucault M. 1997. *Ethics: Subjectivity and Truth*, ed. P Rabinow. New York: NY Press

Foucault M. 1980. *The History of Sexuality*. New York: Vintage

Foucault M. 2007. *Security, Territory, Population (Michel Foucault: Lectures at the College De France)*. New York: Palgrave Macmillan

Franklin S. 1997. *Embodied Progress: A Cultural Account of Assisted Conception*. New York: Routledge

Freud S. 1957. The sense of symptoms. In *The Standard Edition of the Completed Psychological Works of Sigmund Freud*, Vol. 16, *1916–1917*, ed. J Strachey, pp. 257–72. London: Hogarth

Freud S. 1959. The loss of reality in neurosis and psychosis. In *Collected Papers*, ed. E Jones, pp. 277–82. New York: Basic Books

Garcia A. 2008. The elegiac addict: history, chronicity and the melancholic subject. *Cult. Anthopol.* 23(4):718–46

Geertz C. 1973. *The Interpretation of Cultures*. New York: Basic Books

Geertz C. 1983. *Local Knowledge: Further Essays in Interpretive Anthropology*. New York: Basic Books

Geertz C. 2000. *Available Light: Anthropological Reflections on Philosophical Topics*. Princeton, NJ: Princeton Univ. Press

Good B. 1994. *Medicine, Rationality, and Experience*. Cambridge, UK: Cambridge Univ. Press

Good B, Good MJ, Subandi. 2007. The subject of mental illness: psychosis, mad violence and subjectivity in Indonesia. See Biehl et al. 2007, pp. 62–108

Greenhouse C, Mertz E, Warren K. 2002. *Ethnography in Unstable Places: Everyday Lives in Contexts of Dramatic Political Change*. Durham, NC: Duke Univ. Press

Hacking I. 1986. Making up people. In *Reconstructing Individualism: Autonomy, Individuality, and the Self in Western Thought*, ed. T Heller, M Sosna, D Wellberg, pp. 222–36. Stanford, CA: Stanford Univ. Press

Hacking I. 2002. *Historical Ontology*. Cambridge: Harvard Univ. Press

Hahn R, Kleinman A. 1983. Belief as pathogen, belief as medicine. *Med. Anthropol. Q.* 14(4):16–19

Han C. 2004. The work of indebtedness: the traumatic present of late capitalist Chile. *Cult. Med. Psychiatry* 28(2):169–87

Haraway D. 1991. *Simians, Cyborgs, and Women: The Reinvention of Nature*. New York: Routledge

Inhorn MC. 2003. *Local Babies, Global Science: Gender, Religion, and In Vitro Fertilization in Egypt*. New York: Routledge

Jackson M. 2009. *The Palm at the End of the Mind: Relatedness, Religiosity, and the Real*. Durham, NC: Duke Univ. Press

Jenkins JD, Barrett RJ. 2004. *Schizophrenia, Culture, and Subjectivity: The Edge of Experience*. New York: Cambridge Univ. Press

Kaufman S. 2005. *And a Time to Die: How American Hospitals Shape the End of Life*. New York: Scribner

Kleinman A. 1981. *Patients and Healers in the Context of Culture: An Exploration of the Borderland between Anthropology, Medicine, and Psychiatry*. Berkeley: Univ. Calif. Press

Kleinman A. 1989. *Illness Narratives: Suffering, Healing, and the Human Condition*. New York: Basic Books

Kleinman A. 1999. Experience and its moral modes: culture, human conditions, and disorder. *Tanner Lect. Hum. Values* 20:355–420

Kleinman A. 2006. *What Really Matters: Living a Moral Life Amid Uncertainty and Danger*. New York: Oxford Univ. Press

Kleinman A, Kleinman J. 1985. Somatization: the interconnections in Chinese society among culture, depressive experiences, and the meanings of pain. In *Culture and Depression*, ed. A Kleinman B Good, pp. 429–90. Berkeley: Univ. Calif. Press

Kristeva J. 1982. *The Powers of Horror: An Essay on Abjection*. New York: Columbia Univ. Press

Lacan J. 1977. *Écrits: A Selection*. New York: Norton

Lacan J. 1978. *The Four Fundamental Concepts of Psychoanalysis*. New York: Norton

Lacan J. 1980. A Lacanian psychosis: interview by Jacques Lacan. In *Returning to Freud: Critical Psychoanalysis in the School of Lacan*, ed. S Schneiderman, pp. 19–41. New Haven, CT: Yale Univ. Press

Lacan J. 1989. Science and truth. *Newsl. Freudian Field* 3:4–29

Lacan J. 1991. *Le Seminarie Livre XVII: L'Envers de la Psychanalyse*. Paris: Seuil

Lacan J. 1992. *The Seminar of Jacques Lacan, Book VII: The Ethics of Psychoanalysis, 1959–1960*. New York: Norton

Lacan J. 2005. *O Seminário, Livro 23: O Sinthoma, 1975–1976*. Rio de Janeiro: Jorge Zahar Editor

Lakoff A. 2006. *Pharmaceutical Reason: Knowledge and Value in Global Psychiatry*. Cambridge, UK: Cambridge Univ. Press

Le Marcis F. 2004. The suffering body of the city. *Public Cult.* 16(3):453–77

Lock M. 1994. *Encounters with Aging: Mythologies of Menopause in Japan and North America*. Berkeley: Univ. Calif. Press

Lock M. 2002. *Twice Dead: Organ Transplants and the Reinvention of Death*. Berkeley: Univ. Calif. Press

Lomnitz C. 2008. *Death and the Idea of Mexico*. New York: Zone Books

Lovell AM. 2006. Addiction markets: the case of high-dose Buprenorphine in France. In *Global Pharmaceuticals: Practices, Markets, Ethics*, ed. A Petryna, A Lakoff, A Kleinman, pp. 136–70. Durham, NC: Duke Univ. Press

Luhrman T. 2000. *Of Two Minds: The Growing Disorder in American Psychiatry*. New York: Knopf

Malinowski B. 2001. *Sex and Repression in Savage Society*. New York: Routledge

Martin E. 1987. *The Woman in the Body: A Cultural Analysis of Reproduction*. Boston: Beacon

Martin E. 1994. *Flexible Bodies: Tracking Immunity in American Culture from the Days of Polio to the Age of AIDS*. Boston: Beacon

Martin E. 2007. *Biopolar Expeditions: Mania and Depression in American Culture*. Princeton, NJ: Princeton Univ. Press

Mattingly C, Garro L. 2000. *Narrative and Cultural Contributions of Illness and Healing*. Berkeley: Univ. Calif. Press

Mauss M. 1979. The notion of body techniques. In *Sociology and Psychology: Essays*, pp. 95–119. London: Routledge and Keegan Paul

Mbembe A. 2001. *On the Postcolony*. Berkeley: Univ. Calif. Press

Nguyen V. 2005. Antiretroviral globalism, biopolitics, and therapeutic citizenship. In *Global Assemblages: Technology, Politics and Ethics as Anthropological Problems*, ed. SJ Collier, A Ong, pp. 124–44. Boston: Wiley-Blackwell

Nietzsche F. 1955. *The Use and Abuse of History*. New York: Macmillan

Nichter M, Lock M. 2002. *New Horizons in Medical Anthropology*. New York: Routledge

Ong A, Collier SJ. 2005. *Global Assemblages: Technology, Politics and Ethics as Anthropological Problems*. Boston: Wiley-Blackwell

Ortner S. 2006. *Anthropology and Social Theory: Culture, Power, and the Acting Subject*. Durham, NC: Duke Univ. Press

Pandolfo S. 1998. *Impasse of the Angels: Scenes from a Moroccan Space of Memory*. Berkeley: Univ. Calif. Press

Petryna A. 2002. *Life Exposed: Biological Citizens After Chernobyl*. Princeton, NJ: Princeton Univ. Press

Petryna A. 2009. *When Experiments Travel: Clinical Trials and the Global Search for Human Subjects*. Princeton, NJ: Princeton Univ. Press

Petryna A, Lakoff A, Kleinman A. 2006. *Global Pharmaceuticals: Ethics, Markets, Practices*. Durham, NC: Duke Univ. Press

Pinto S. 2008. *Where There is No Midwife: Birth and Loss in Rural India*. Oxford/New York: Berghahn

Povinelli E. 2002. *The Cunning of Recognition: Indigenous Alterities and the Making of Australian Multiculturalism*. Durham, NC: Duke Univ. Press

Rabinow P. 1996. *Making PCR: A Story of Biotechnology*. Chicago: Univ. Chicago Press

Rabinow P. 1999. Artificiality and englightenment: from sociobiology to biosociality. In *Health Studies: A Critical and Cross-Cultural Reader*, ed C Samson, pp. 50–60. Oxford, UK: Blackwell

Rabinow P. 2008. *Marking Time: On the Anthropology of the Contemporary*. Princeton, NJ: Princeton Univ. Press

Rabinow P, Dan-Cohen T. 2005. *A Machine to Make a Future: Biotech Chronicles*. Princeton, NJ: Princeton Univ. Press

Rabinow P, Rose N. 2006. Biopower today. *Biosocieties* 1(2):195–217

Rajan KS. 2006. *Biocapital: The Constitution of Postgenomic Life*. Durham, NC: Duke Univ. Press

Rancière J. 2004. Who Is the Subject of the Rights of Man? *South Atl. Q.* 102(2/3):297–310

Rapp R. 1999. *Testing Women, Testing the Fetus: The Social Impact of Amniocentesis in America*. New York: Routledge

Reardon J. 2004. Decoding race and human difference in a genomic age. *Differences* 15:38–65

Reynolds Whyte S. 2009. Health identities and subjectivities: the ethnographic challenge. *Med. Anthropol. Q.* 23(1):6–15

Reynolds Whyte S, White M, Meinert L, Kyaddondo B. 2006. Treating AIDS: dilemmas of unequal access in Uganda. See Petryna et al. 2006, pp. 240–87

Rofel L. 2007. *Desiring China: Experiments in Neoliberalism, Sexuality, and Public Culture*. Durham, NC: Duke Univ. Press

Rose N, Novas C. 2005. Biological citizenship. See Ong & Collier 2005, pp. 439–63

Rouse C. 2004. If she's a vegetable, we'll be her garden: embodiment, transcendence, and citations of competing cultural metaphors in the case of a dying child. *Am. Ethnol.* 31(4):514–29

Said E. 1979. *Orientalism*. New York: Vintage

Scheper-Hughes N. 1979. *Saints, Scholars, and Schizophrenics: Mental Illness in Rural Ireland*. Berkeley: Univ. Calif. Press

Scheper-Hughes N. 1992. *Death Without Weeping: The Violence of Everyday Life in Brazil*. Berkeley: Univ. Calif. Press

Scheper-Hughes N. 2003. Rotten trade: millennium capitalism, human values and global injustice in organ trafficking. *J. Hum. Rights* 2(2):197–226

Scheper-Hughes N. 2008. A talent for life: reflections on human vulnerability and resistance. *Ethnos* 73(1):25–56

Scheper-Hughes N, Bourgois P, eds. 2004. *Violence in War and Peace: An Anthology*. Oxford, UK: Blackwell

Scheper-Hughes N, Lock M. 1987. The mindful body: a prolegomenon to future work in medical anthropology. *Med. Anthropol. Q.* 1(1):6–41

Schull N. 2006. Machines, medication, modulation: circuits of dependency and self care in Las Vegas. *Cult. Med. Psychiatry* 30(2):223–47

Scott JW. 1999. *Gender and the Politics of History*. New York: Columbia Univ. Press

Shweder RA, Good B. 2004. *Clifford Geertz by His Colleagues*. Chicago: Univ. Chicago Press

Spivak GC. 1990. *The Postcolonial Critic: Interviews, Strategies, Dialogues*. New York: Routledge

Stewart K. 2007. *Ordinary Affects*. Durham, NC: Duke Univ. Press

Stoler AL. 1995. *Race and the Education of Desire: Foucault's History of Sexuality and the Colonial Order of Things*. Durham, NC: Duke Univ. Press

Stoler AL. 2009. *Along the Archival Grain: Epistemic Anxieties and Colonial Common Sense*. Princeton, NJ: Princeton Univ. Press

Taussig MT. 1986. *Shamanism, Colonialism, and the Wild Man: A Study in Terror and Healing*. Chicago: Univ. Chicago Press

Taussig MT. 2006. *Walter Benjamin's Grave*. Chicago: Univ. Chicago Press

Trouillot MR. 1997. *Silencing the Past*. Boston: Beacon

Turkle S, ed. 2008a. *Falling for Science: Objects in Mind*. Cambridge, MA: MIT Press

Turkle S, ed. 2008b. *The Inner History of Devices*. Cambridge, MA: MIT Press

Van Der Geest S, Reynolds Whyte S, Hardon A. 1996. The anthropology of pharmaceuticals: a biographic approach. *Annu. Rev. Anthropol.* 25:153–78

Whitmarsh I. 2008. *Biomedical Ambiguity: Race, Asthma, and the Contested Meaning of Genetic Research in the Caribbean*. Ithaca, NY: Cornell Univ. Press

Young A. 1995. *The Harmony of Illusions: Inventing Post-Traumatic Stress Disorder*. Princeton, NJ: Princeton Univ. Press

Zizek S. 1989. *The Sublime Object of Ideology*. New York: Verso

Zizek S. 2006. *Jacques Lacan's four discourses*. **http://www.lacan.com/zizfour.htm**

The Oldowan: The Tool Making of Early Hominins and Chimpanzees Compared

Nicholas Toth and Kathy Schick

Department of Anthropology, Indiana University, Bloomington, and Stone Age Institute, Gosport, Indiana 47433; email: toth@indiana.edu, kaschick@indiana.edu

Annu. Rev. Anthropol. 2009. 38:289–305

First published online as a Review in Advance on June 23, 2009

The *Annual Review of Anthropology* is online at anthro.annualreviews.org

This article's doi: 10.1146/annurev-anthro-091908-164521

Key Words

bonobo, hominid, human evolution, stone technology, Palaeolithic

Abstract

The Oldowan was the term first coined by Louis Leakey to describe the world's earliest stone industries, named after the famous site of Olduvai (formerly Oldoway) Gorge in Tanzania. The Oldowan Industrial Complex documents the first definitive evidence of early hominin culture as well as the earliest known archaeological record. This review examines our state of knowledge about the Oldowan and the hominin tool makers who produced this archaeological record and compares and contrasts these patterns with the technological and cultural patterns of modern apes, especially chimpanzees and bonobos. Of special interest are methodological approaches that can attempt to make direct comparisons between the early archaeological record and modern ape material culture, including a long-term collaborative experimental program in teaching modern apes to make and use stone tools.

INTRODUCTION

The Oldowan Industrial Complex is the first definitive evidence for early hominin tool making and culture (**Figure 1**, see color insert) and marks the beginning of the archaeological record. Palaeolithic research into aspects of early stone tools has now been carried out for well over 150 years (research into the Oldowan for more than 50 years), including excavation and documentation of early sites and stone artifact assemblages in Africa, Europe, and Asia, as well as a variety of laboratory and experimental studies exploring their significance. Awareness of chimpanzee tool use in the wild began to emerge approximately 50 years ago, after Goodall's (1964) initial documentation of such behaviors, and field and laboratory studies of chimpanzee tool-making and tool-using abilities have grown dramatically over the past few decades. After such concerted research and the development of a fairly extensive literature in each of these areas, it would seem an appropriate time and stage in the discipline to undertake a comparison of tool-related behaviors evident among early hominin tool makers and that now documented among our closest living relatives, the chimpanzees and bonobos.

Why Compare Oldowan and Chimpanzee Tool Makers?

The makers and users of Oldowan tools are now extinct, with no modern representatives of their mental and physical abilities and behaviors. The very earliest Oldowan sites emerge, in fact, prior to definitive evidence of any significant increase in brain size in early hominins and are contemporary with a small-brained, bipedal hominin form, *Australopithecus garhi* (Asfaw et al. 1999), whose cranial capacity (~450 cc) is within the range of modern apes.

Thus, we are devoid of modern representatives of the ancient species of tool makers, but we do have relatives, other living ape species, that show considerable tool-making and tool-using abilities, namely members of the genus *Pan* (the chimpanzees and the bonobos). It can be safely argued that chimpanzees exhibit the most elaborate set of tool-related behaviors of any existing nonhuman species. Because the chimpanzee's cranial capacity is roughly equivalent to that of a potential candidate for the earliest tool maker, and in consideration of the chimpanzee's documented propensity to make and use tools, it can be extremely useful to examine the similarities and differences between chimpanzee and early hominin tool-related behaviors.

Such comparisons can help inform the fields of paleoanthropology and primatology as well as anthropology as a whole. These may help provide models for other possible tool behaviors of early hominins, which may be archaeologically invisible in the material record; they may highlight behavioral adaptations among early hominins that go beyond behavior patterns observed among other apes and which may have had significance in our species' evolutionary success; they can likewise highlight aspects of modern primate behavior that show parallels with the behavioral transformations in the evolutionary lineage that led to *Homo sapiens*, or conversely, provide insight into important differences in the evolutionary trajectory of apes; and overall they may help provide a more refined view of how well, and in what ways, modern apes might serve as models for early hominin tool makers.

THE OLDOWAN: AN OVERVIEW

The earliest known assemblages of definite stone tools, consisting of stone artifacts that have been deliberately flaked through percussive blows, appear in the archaeological record at 2.6 Mya at Oldowan localities at Gona in Ethiopia (**Figure 1**) (Semaw 2006), and numerous sites bearing such tools have been found over the ensuing 1.5 My, first in Africa, then also in Europe and Asia. For other discussions of the Oldowan, see Isaac (1981, 1982, 1984, 1989), Harris (1983), Toth (1985), Toth & Schick (1986, 2005, 2006), Schick (1986, 1987), Potts (1991), Harris & Capaldo (1993), Schick & Toth (1993, 1994, 2001, 2006, 2009), Klein (1999), Martinez et al. (2003), de Beaune

Oldowan Industrial Complex: the earliest stage of human technology, consisting of simple percussors, cores, retouched pieces, flakes, and fragments (~2.6–1 Mya).

Hominin: member of the tribe Hominini, including the bipedal genera *Australopithecus* and *Homo*. Chimpanzees and bonobos are members of the tribe Panini

Tool: an object, modified or unmodified, that is used by an animal for a purpose or objective

Culture: in an ethological sense, refers to learned behavior that is shared by and transmitted among members of a community

Artifact: an object that is recognizably modified, intentionally or unintentionally, through manufacture or use

Chimpanzee: *Pan troglodytes*, found in West, Central, and East Africa. Closely related to bonobos, probably sharing a common ancestor ~2.5 Mya

Bonobo: *Pan paniscus*, sometimes called the pygmy chimpanzee, restricted to a core area of the Congo Basin

(2004), Lewin & Foley (2004), Plummer (2004), Roche (2005), Pickering et al. (2007), Barsky (2009), Braun & Hovers (2009), Carbonell et al. (2009), de la Torre & Mora (2009), and Hovers & Braun (2009). Here we outline the hominin candidates for early tool makers, summarize the nature of Oldowan sites and their stone tool industries, and discuss possible behavioral and cognitive implications of these industries.

Who Were the Tool Makers? The Fossil Hominins

From the current evidence, the earliest stone tool-making hominins of the Oldowan were likely australopithecine-grade with smallish brains and large dentition. The discovery of *A. garhi* at approximately the same time as the Gona sites in Ethiopia and only 60 km to the south would suggest this species as a candidate for the maker of the very early tool industries at 2.6 Mya. This taxon is also roughly contemporaneous with *A. aethiopicus* in East Africa and *A. africanus* in South Africa.

Starting ~2.3 Mya, hominin remains have been assigned to the genus *Homo*, although good evidence for the beginning of the cranial expansion generally associated with this genus has not been documented until ~2 Mya. During the time span from 2.0 Mya to 1.0 Mya, the hominin taxa that have been identified that co-existed with stone tool assemblages include the robust australopithecines *A. boisei* in East Africa and *A. robustus* in South Africa and early members of the genus *Homo*: *H. rudolfensis*, *H. habilis*, and *H. erectus*.

It cannot be ruled out that more than one of these hominin forms could have had some involvement in stone tool manufacture and use, but it is apparent that members of the genus *Homo* (*a*) demonstrate a significant brain expansion during this period, between 2.0 and 1.0 Mya, likely correlated with a tool-making emphasis in their evolution; (*b*) also apparently carry this tool-making tradition out of Africa into Eurasia (Bar-Yosef & Goren-Inbar 1993, de Lumley et al. 2005, Diez-Martín 2006); and (*c*) continue this tradition beyond the time of

the extinction of the robust australopithecines by 1 Mya. Thus, the *Homo* lineage would represent the major progenitors of Oldowan tools and, subsequently, the Acheulean tools (hand axes, cleavers, picks) that also appear on the paleolandscape starting ~1.6–1.7 Mya (about the time of the emergence of *H. erectus*) and is contemporaneous with these simpler industries.

The Nature of Oldowan Sites and Stone Industries

Stone artifacts constitute nearly the entirety of the record of early hominin tool making and tool using because these are nearly impervious to the many destructive forces at work since these sites were occupied. If early hominins also had a tool repertoire involving organic materials such as wood, hide, or other materials, direct evidence of these is, for the most part, invisible in the archaeological record. A small number of polished and striated bones that may have served as digging tools have been reported, however, and may give valuable hints about some of the missing elements of the Oldowan hominins' tool kits (Brain 1981, 2007; d'Errico et al. 2001; d'Errico & Backwell 2003).

Fundamentally, early Oldowan stone artifacts are primarily products of hand-held percussive flaking, i.e., holding a stone hammer in one hand and hitting another stone cobble or chunk held in the other hand with a strong percussive blow to detach flakes (a procedure called knapping). Another technique seen in the Oldowan is bipolar technique, in which a core is placed on an anvil and struck from the top with a hammer. Although this is ostensibly a relatively simple activity, experiments have shown this is not such an easy task to master, particularly with regard to the placement, angle, and power of the percussive blow (discussed further below).

Early Oldowan archaeological sites consist, at a minimum, of quantities of stone artifacts and often also contain fossil animal bones, mostly from medium-to-large-size animals. A number of these bones bear evidence of cut marks made with stone tools as well as evidence

Acheulean (Industrial Complex): the next stage of human technology, characterized by hand axes, cleavers, and picks, as well as Oldowan-like forms (~1.7–0.25 Mya)

Plio-Pleistocene:
time period straddling
the late Pliocene
(~3.0–1.8 Mya) and
Early Pleistocene
(~1.8–0.8 Mya)

of deliberate percussive pitting and fracture (e.g., Blumenschine & Peters 1998, Bunn 1983, Pickering & Domínguez-Rodrigo 2006), presumably to access marrow. A lively debate has centered on whether such butchery traces represent earlier, more primary access to animal remains through hunting and/or confrontational scavenging (Bunn 1983, Bunn & Kroll 1986, Domínguez-Rodrigo 2009, Domínguez-Rodrigo et al. 2007, Pickering et al. 2007, Pickering & Domínguez-Rodrigo 2006) or whether hominins had later, secondary access to carcasses by scavenging the remains of carnivore kills (e.g., Blumenschine 1986, 1989).

Concentrations of hundreds or sometimes thousands of stone artifacts are typically found at many Oldowan sites, and sometimes these sites are clustered in major basins occupied by hominins and that were accumulating layers of sediment during the Plio-Pleistocene. Many of these sites are located in the Rift Valley of Eastern Africa, in karstic caves in South Africa, and in sedimentary basins in North Africa. Major localities include Gona (Semaw 2000, 2006; Semaw et al. 1997, 2003), Hadar (Kimbel et al. 1996), Middle Awash (de Heinzelin et al. 1999), Melka-Kunture (Chavaillon et al. 1979), Konso Gardula (Asfaw et al. 1992), Omo (Howell et al. 1987), and Fejej (Asfaw et al. 1991, de Lumley & Beyene 2004) in Ethiopia; East Turkana (Isaac & Isaac 1997), West Turkana (Delagnes & Roche 2005, Roche 2005, Roche et al. 1999), and Kanjera (Plummer et al. 2009) in Kenya; Olduvai Gorge in Tanzania (Blumenschine & Peters 1998; Leakey 1971, 1994; Peters & Blumenschine 1995, 1996; Potts 1988); Nyambusosi in Uganda (Texier 1995); Sterkfontein and Swartkrans in South Africa (Field 1999; Kuman 1998, 2005); Ain Hanech and El Kherba in Algeria in North Africa (Sahnouni 1998, 2006; Sahnouni et al. 1997, 2002); and Dmanisi in the Republic of Georgia (de Lumley et al. 2005).

A typical Oldowan stone tool assemblage generally includes percussors (hammerstones, spheroids), simple core forms (choppers, discoids, polyhedrons, heavy-duty scrapers), retouched elements (scrapers, awls), and debitage (flakes and fragments). After ~2 My, some sites exhibited higher proportions of artifact classes such as retouched forms and battered spheroids, which Mary Leakey called "Developed Oldowan" (Leakey 1971, pp. 1–8).

Oldowan artifacts, particularly the larger pieces or cores (so-called core tools), have often been categorized by various researchers according to their shapes and placed into inferred functional groupings such as choppers or scrapers. Experimental studies, however, have called into question whether such categories represent intentional end-products on the part of the hominin tool makers and also question the functional inferences often implied (Toth 1982, 1985). These experiments in manufacturing Oldowan artifact forms have demonstrated that the full range of typical core forms found at early sites can result as by-products of percussive flaking to produce a set of sharp flakes, although sharp-edged core forms could also be used for a range of chopping and scraping activities.

Raw materials used for stone artifacts tended to be found in the form of rounded cobbles from river gravels or angular chunks from primary rock outcrops. Depending on a given region, typical rock types included volcanic lavas (basalts, trachytes, rhyolites, phonolite, occasionally obsidians, etc.), ignimbrites ("welded tuffs"), quartzes, quartzites, limestones, and cherts.

A recurrent pattern at many Oldowan sites is evidence for transport of stone resources, including quantities of flaked materials, from place to place on the paleolandscape, as well as selectivity in choices of rock types and quality for tools (see Blumenschine et al. 2008; Braun et al. 2008, 2009a,b; Goldman-Neuman & Hovers 2009; Harmand 2009; Hay 1976; Negash et al. 2006; Piperno et al. 2009; Schick 1987; Stout et al. 2005; Toth 1982). At some sites, these transport distances were more than ten kilometers. At Olduvai Gorge, Tanzania, for instance, raw materials are quite often found several kilometers and sometimes 8–20 km from their sources, and at Kanjera, Kenya transport distances were up to 13 km.

Longer distance transport does not, of course, necessarily imply that hominins accomplished this in one event because raw materials may well have been moved on separate occasions from one site to another, and such movement of stone was likely embedded in their foraging patterns rather than special long-distance trips just for stone. From analysis of reconstructed cores and from technological analysis of the artifact assemblages, it is evident that hominins were often flaking cores prior to transporting them to a particular site, conducting further flaking at the site, and then subsequently transporting some of the artifacts away from the site. This indicates a level of behavioral complexity that has only recently begun to be appreciated.

One of the long-standing challenges of Palaeolithic archaeology is the determination of artifact function. For the Oldowan, most of the evidence is indirect—based on ethnographic analogy, experimental feasibility studies, and archaeological context (e.g., the association of stone artifacts with animal bones). We know that battered hammers and spheroids served as percussors for flaking stone, and roughly pitted stone hammers and anvils testify to their use in bipolar flaking. And, as previously mentioned, the processing of animal carcasses can leave diagnostic cut-mark traces from the stone knives used to skin, deflesh, and dismember, as well as produce diagnostic fracture patterns from breaking bones for marrow and brains. This evidence is particularly clear at the FLK Zinj site in Bed I at Olduvai (the "Woodstock" of Oldowan studies), but it should be noted that a number of Oldowan sites with associated stone artifacts and animal bones bear little or no evidence of hominin modification (e.g., Domínguez-Rodrigo 2009) and leave the probable function of these artifacts an open question.

Experiments in the use of a range of Oldowan artifact forms for a variety of possible tasks substantiate the effectiveness of simple flake edges in cutting tasks, particularly in animal butchery (Jones 1994; Toth 1982, 1985). Microscopic usewear analysis on a sample of Oldowan artifacts from East Turkana has indicated use of a number of flakes for cutting meat as well as use of some others for cutting soft plants (perhaps grasses for bedding) and for scraping wood (Keeley & Toth 1981). This latter evidence may suggest the use of stone tools to produce tools in other materials, e.g., perhaps the shaping of wood into spears or digging sticks, but such direct evidence is so far absent in the Oldowan.

The Oldowan documents one of the major phases of hominin brain evolution, with cranial capacities increasing from ~450 cc in *A. garhi* to up to 900 cc in early *Homo erectus.* Holloway et al. (2004) suggests that this period of brain evolution is correlated with increased language abilities, social complexity, tool standardization, hunting, and the development of home bases. Recently, brain-imaging studies (Stout et al. 2009) have shown that brain activity during the manufacture of Oldowan (and Acheulean) tools partially overlaps with areas associated with language, suggesting a possible coevolution of these two systems. For overviews and further discussions of the possible cognitive implications of early stone tools, see Parker & Gibson (1979), Isaac (1986), Wynn (1989, 2002), Gibson (1986), Dunbar (1993), Gibson & Ingold (1993), Toth & Schick (1993), Aiello & Wheeler (1995), Gowlett (1996), Joulian (1996), Mellars & Gibson (1996), Mithen (1996), Noble & Davidson (1996), Deacon (1997), Parker & McKinney (1999), Ambrose (2001), de la Torre et al. (2003), Holloway et al. (2004), de la Torre & Mora (2005), Pelegrin (2005), Roux & Bril (2005), Stout (2006), Stout & Semaw (2006), Stout et al. (2006, 2009), and Renfrew et al. (2009).

Summary: Implications of Oldowan Sites

Some important inferences that bear on possible cognitive abilities of the early hominin tool makers can be drawn from the Oldowan patterns:

1. Stone tool manufacturing skill: Even very early stone artifacts at the earliest sites at Gona demonstrate remarkable skill and control in flaking stone;

Material culture:
learned behavior that
is manifested in
objects, notably tools

2. Forethought and transport: Hominin tool makers showed considerable forethought in multiple aspects of their tool manufacture and use, including transport of raw materials and tools to and from different site locales;

3. Selectivity in use of raw materials: Hominin tool makers were aware of and responsive to signs of raw material quality that would affect ease and control of fracture as well as tool effectiveness;

4. Concentrating artifacts: Hominin behaviors tended to concentrate substantial amounts of tool materials at certain locations, possibly indicating repeated use or large social group use of these locales;

5. Acquisition of animal resources: Evidence indicates that hominins were often engaged in accessing meat resources from fairly sizeable animals using stone tools to deflesh carcasses and to fracture bones to access marrow. They may also have been actively involved in transporting these animal parts and concentrating them at some site locations, presumably for amenities such as shade, shelter, or protection or water. Consistent acquisition of such food sources would have placed them in more direct competition with active predators and scavengers and likely increased their risk factors from predation as well.

CHIMPANZEE TOOLS AND TECHNOLOGY

Studies of Wild Chimpanzee Tools

The range and instances of documented wild chimpanzee technology have increased dramatically during the past few decades of research. This increase likely is largely the result of the growing number of habituated chimpanzee populations combined with the number of long-term, committed projects investigating chimpanzee populations in different parts of Africa. The number of articles and chapters discussing chimpanzee technology and cultural traits far exceeds the citation limit of this review, so here we focus on the references that attempt a synthesis of our state of knowledge. A number of researchers from different backgrounds and perspectives have addressed the relevance of chimpanzee technology to human evolutionary studies, including Beck (1980) (animal tools), Bonner (1980) (animal culture), Goodall (1986) (general), Foley (1987) (tool phylogeny), Wynn & McGrew (1989) (primate and hominin tool use), Sept (1992, 1998) (nesting patterns), McGrew (1992, 1993, 2004) (general), Berthelet & Chavaillon (1993) (primate and hominin tool use), Wrangham (1996) (general), Whiten et al. (1999, 2009) (chimpanzee cultural traits), Stanford (2001) (general), Panger et al. (2002) (evolutionary history of technology), Matsuzawa (2002) (general), van Schaik et al. (2003) (ape cultural traits), Hunt (2006) (sex differences in tool use), Lycett et al. (2007) (cladistics of chimpanzee cultural traits), and Carvalho et al. (2008) (chaînes opératoires).

Studies of chimpanzee tool use afford us much more fully textured insight into the range of material culture employed by these populations than is possible for Oldowan tools (e.g., Goodall 1986; McGrew 1992, 1993). McGrew (1993) has argued effectively for an intelligent, flexible, problem-solving use of tools among chimpanzees and, moreover, that tool use is the norm among wild chimpanzee populations. The range of tools used may differ among populations, but tool use is observed daily in any well-habituated population. Chimpanzee tool use involves a variety of organic materials that do not tend to be preserved in the archaeological record, and furthermore, it is possible to observe directly a wealth of detail regarding many aspects of tool use.

The variety of details that can be obtained from studies of chimpanzee tool use among wild populations can include preparation or processing of the tool, specifics regarding how it was used and on what sort of material(s), potential reuse of a tool, the use of tool sets combining a sequence of tools for a specific purpose, the frequency of observed uses of a tool, possible age or sex differences in tool use, the process of learning tool use, fine-grained information regarding transport of tools and other materials, seasonal or ecological factors affecting tool use, contemporary regional or population similarities and differences, possible details regarding the locale of tool use (shade or protection, food or other resources, etc.), and potentially other activities also conducted at the site. These data can provide a wealth of information not directly available to the Palaeolithic archaeologist.

McGrew (1992, 2004) has provided broad overviews of material culture as well as culture writ large among chimpanzee populations, particularly among wild chimpanzees. As he has noted, most observations of habitual chimpanzee tool use are oriented toward subsistence activities, obtaining or processing materials for consumption, especially social insects such as termites or ants and nuts. Typical tool use for subsistence would include fishing for termites with twigs or grasses, using leaf sponges to scoop brains from a cranium or fruit from a husk, or using stone or wood hammers and anvils to crack open hard-shelled nuts. One report (Mercader et al. 2007) has suggested that a locality in the rainforest of Côte d'Ivoire dated to 4300 years ago may be a chimpanzee nut-cracking site, which would indicate some longevity for this practice if chimpanzees were responsible for the apparent activities here. In addition, in Senegal, chimpanzees appear to have used stone anvils to smash open baobab fruits (Marchant & McGrew 2005).

Another category of tools consists of materials used as weapons, such as sticks and stones thrown at other chimpanzees or at baboons competing for the same food, behaviors that are well known but not systematically studied. Although chimpanzee males are known to prey on smaller animals such as monkeys and small antelope, they generally have been observed to carry out the hunt and the consumption of the animal without the use of tools. An exception to this pattern with regard to hunting has recently been documented in Senegal by Pruetz & Bertolani (2007), who observed a number of chimpanzees, particularly females and including immature individuals, on several occasions shape wooden branches into pointed tools to try to jab and extract prosimians from tree cavities; they observed one successful kill in 22 bouts of observations.

Besides such use of stone hammers and anvils, another chimpanzee activity that could have archaeological visibility is their consumption of prey animals, which can leave toothmarks on bones, including tooth scoring, canine punctures, and damage to bone ends. This practice has been observed in the wild (Plummer & Stanford 2000) as well as in an experimental setting (Pickering & Wallis 1997). [Toothmarks on bones from Oldowan sites are often assumed to be produced by carnivores, although there is a growing appreciation that Oldowan hominins could also be responsible for some of these (White & Toth 2007)].

Some sex differences have been noted among chimpanzees in terms of tool-related behaviors. Notably, fishing for termites and dipping for ants are important subsistence activities conducted with tools that are preferentially associated with females, who have been observed to pursue these activities much more often than do males. McGrew (1992) has observed that these activities require prolonged and systematic persistence using a tool to extract predictable resources and that they are, in a sense, akin to gathering. Hunt (2006) has observed that not only do female chimpanzees use tools more frequently than do males, but they do so especially for lower-return food items requiring significant processing. Hunt further notes that females also use tools during arboreal feeding, whereas males use technology to harvest terrestrial resources. Among the nut-cracking chimpanzee populations in West Africa, investigators have observed that females are more apt and efficient than are males in opening the harder-shelled varieties. As mentioned above, hunting of smaller mammals is a predominantly male activity, albeit without the use of tools.

A number of researchers have compiled evidence and analyses from a number of chimpanzee study areas and discerned that chimpanzee material culture and nonmaterial culture show some regional patterning, indicating the potential role of cultural transmission in spreading and maintaining regional patterns of behavior (Whiten et al. 1999, 2001). Such a pattern might be expected because many shared behaviors among chimpanzees appear to be learned, often transmitted through observation and a trial-and-error learning curve. Much of this transmission seems to be from mother to offspring, sometimes with a prolonged period of apprenticeship (Boesch & Boesch-Achermann 2000, Goodall 1986, McGrew 2004).

To investigate large-scale chimpanzee cultural patterning, Toth & Schick (2007) examined the relationships between geographical proximity of different chimpanzee populations in West and East Africa and the number of shared cultural traits reported in the Whiten et al. (1999) study. At the species level, there was no significant pattern, but at the subspecies level (comparing West African groups to other West African groups of *Pan troglodytes verus* and comparing East African groups to other East African groups of *Pan troglodytes schweinfurthii*), a highly significant pattern appeared to emerge (**Figure 2**). The number of shared cultural traits between groups dropped by more than half (from eight shared traits to fewer than four) at a distance of ~700 km (about 450 miles).

At the species level, with West African and East African populations separated by more than 4000 kilometers (more than 2700 miles), and perhaps two million years of time based on some genetic estimates, the results would appear to indicate some degree of convergence (independent invention) of cultural traits among disparate populations, without any clear evolutionary history. At the subspecies level, with a much more recent evolutionary history, there appeared to be some geographic patterning to the number of shared cultural traits by proximity to other chimpanzee groups. The drop-off of more than half the number of cultural traits in ~700 kilometers was used as a model for early hominin groups on the basis of known Oldowan archaeological sites (Toth & Schick 2007, Whiten et al. 2009). Such a subspecies patterning has also been independently suggested by Lycett et al. (2007) on the basis of a cladistic/phylogenetic analysis of chimpanzee cultural traits.

Thus, there is no universal chimpanzee culture in terms of tools but rather different clusters of tool-use behaviors in differing populations. One major difference noted between East African and West African populations is the prevalent (though not universal) use of hammers and anvils of stone or wood to crack open hard-shelled nuts in West African chimpanzee populations, a behavior that has not yet been documented among East African populations. Whiten et al. (2001) found that 39 behavior patterns, many of which involved tool use, variably observed among a group of 9 long-term chimpanzee study sites across Africa, showed patterning consistent with social transmission.

As might be expected, as quadrupedal, knuckle-walking animals, chimpanzees are not proficient at transporting materials. They do transport tools to tool-use sites, though generally over fairly short distances. Interesting patterns are observed in the tool transport behaviors for nutting activities in West Africa (Boesch & Boesch 1983, 1984, 1990; Boesch & Boesch-Achermann 2000; Boesch-Achermann & Boesch 1994). For the softer-shelled *Coula* nuts, wooden hammers are sometimes chosen

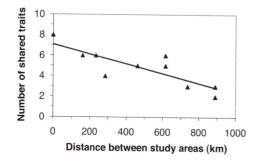

Figure 2

The relation between the number of shared chimpanzee cultural traits (habitual or customary, from the Whiten et al. 1999 paper) and distances between pairs of chimpanzee groups of the same subspecies. Note that groups in closer proximity tend to share more traits and that the number of shared traits drops by more than half (to fewer than four) at a distance of ~700 km. A Pearson r^2 value of 0.702 was derived for the 11 pairs of 7 groups; among the East African chimpanzee groups (10 pairs), Pearson r = −0.829, r^2 = 0.687, p = 0.003; Mantel test p = 0.014.

and taken up into a *Coula* tree to crack open nuts on a tree branch. For the harder, *Panda* nuts, however, stone hammers are sometimes carried short distances to the base of the *Panda* tree. The distance a stone or wooden hammer is transported may be relatively low in a single instance, but cumulative trips could accomplish greater distances.

Boesch & Boesch (1984) documented transport of wooden or stone hammers primarily over distances of less than 20 meters but with many transports evident over a distance of up to 500 m and, in very rare instances, more than 500 m. Their study indicated the chimpanzees could develop mental maps of resource locations and follow a least-distance rule in choosing stones to transport to nut tree locations, likely in response to the difficulty chimpanzees face in transporting heavier materials over longer distances. Chimpanzees also generally do not transport vegetable foods or invertebrates any great distance away from the food source. After a hunt, males may transport the kill (e.g., in the mouth or around the neck) to a safe or comfortable place for consumption, but with some difficulty in any case. Under such constraints, it is not surprising that, as McGrew has observed (1992), containers are not part of the tool equipment employed by chimpanzees.

Chimpanzees in the wild have not been observed to flake stone deliberately and thus do not produce materials that may be directly compared with Oldowan technology. Although Mercader et al. (2002) suggested that a West African nut-cracking locality presumably used by chimpanzees contained materials comparable to artifacts at early Oldowan sites, this material does not appear to represent the products of deliberate percussive flaking (unlike most Oldowan artifacts) but instead is only the by-product of nut-cracking (Schick & Toth 2006, pp. 24–26). Interestingly, no food-getting or other activity conducted by modern chimpanzees appears to require a reliance on cutting activities, and this may be the primary reason that a culture of flaked stone technology has apparently not developed among chimpanzees.

To explore the ability of this closely related ape to manufacture Oldowan-type artifacts, then by knapping, we conducted an experimental study.

An Experimental Study of Bonobo Stone Tool Manufacture

One major obstacle in attempts to compare and contrast Oldowan technology with the material culture of chimpanzees is that modern apes in the wild are not known to flake stones intentionally in the wild. Beginning in 1990, we embarked on a long-term experimental project to teach bonobos (*Pan paniscus*) to make and use flaked stone tools (**Figure 3**, see color insert). In collaboration with cognitive psychologists Sue Savage-Rumbaugh and Duane Rumbaugh and their colleagues at the Language Research Laboratory of Atlanta and then the Great Ape Trust of Iowa, we began to investigate the tool-making and tool-using capabilities of bonobos in an experimental setting.

Pioneering work by Wright (1972) with a young orangutan demonstrated that a great ape could be taught to make and use a stone tool. Although this experiment used a flint core strapped to a stable board and did not continue beyond the first flake produced and used, it was nonetheless one of the inspirations behind this project. We produced a more naturalistic environment for the bonobos, where freehand, hard-hammer percussion was used to flake cobbles of quartzite, lava, and chert, and the sharp flakes produced were then used to cut a cord to open a box (or cut through the membrane of a drum) and retrieve a food reward. Our first bonobo subject, Kanzi, learned both the flaking and the cutting tasks through observing a human tool maker, began using flakes the first day of the experiment, and made his first tool within a month of the onset of the experiment. He has now been flaking stone for 18 years, and his sister Panbanisha is now also a practiced stone tool maker (Savage-Rumbaugh & Fields 2006; Schick et al. 1999; Toth & Schick 1993, 2006).

Recently we undertook a three-way comparison of stone tools manufactured (*a*) by very early tool makers at Gona, Ethiopia (possibly *A. garhi*); (*b*) by bonobo (*Pan paniscus*) tool makers with several years experience in stone tool making; and (*c*) by modern *H. sapiens* very experienced in Oldowan tool manufacture (Toth et al. 2006), all using the same raw materials. These three populations of stone artifacts were then analyzed in detail and compared in terms of dozens of assemblage characteristics, particularly those that would indicate a level of tool-making skill.

For most of the traits attributed to skill, the bonobos tended to be the outgroup, with characteristics of the Gona artifacts either clustering with the modern human sample or intermediate between the bonobo and human samples. The bonobo cores tended to be heavier (the bonobos tended to select larger cobbles, probably because their hands were larger), less heavily reduced, and with fewer scars and a great deal of hammerstone battering on core edges from unsuccessful blows. The morphology of the bonobo cores and flakes appears to have been a function of less impact velocity (a probable biomechanical constraint) as well as less control as to where exactly to detach flakes from a cobble core (a possible cognitive constraint).

The Gona artifacts, however, show much better skill in cobble reduction than the bonobo artifacts do. Cores are more heavily reduced, with almost twice the number of flake scars, and exhibit significantly less battering from misplaced hammerstone blows. Biomechanical studies (Dapena et al. 2006, Harlacker 2009) of the arm swing during Oldowan flaking indicate that manufacture by modern humans produces a very rapid speed of the hammerstone, reaching a final velocity of up to 20 mph. The bonobo arm swing during tool making is considerably less, which may help account for the lower skill evident in their flaking and the considerable battering on the bonobo cores relative to the Gona artifacts and those produced by modern humans.

This study has demonstrated that our closest living relatives among the apes are definitely capable of stone tool manufacture. The apes in this study, however, are not as proficient in stone tool making, even after many years of experience, as were the early hominin tool makers. As noted above, this difference in skill may be attributed both to cognitive processing and to the biomechanical constraints of the ape.

DISCUSSION AND CONCLUSIONS

In view of the significant technological repertoire of chimpanzees, there are valid arguments for using their behaviors as models for aspects of early hominin activities that are elusive or largely invisible to us. There are, however, also significant differences in chimpanzee biology, behavior patterns, and ecology that should temper us from basing our models of hominid behavior on modern chimpanzees too strictly or uniformly.

This overview has highlighted a number of elements of chimpanzee technology and behavior that appear to have, or may be likely to have, some counterpart in early hominin behavior and technology. These would include the concentrating of tools at sites of use, consumption of meat involving hunting activities and even group cooperation, carrying and transport of tools including stone, battering and bashing activities with stone, their use of probing sticks (which may have some counterpart in early bone tools), and even their tendency to gather together in groups on a daily basis (in nesting trees at night).

We could also infer that the cultural transmission of tool use within a group and between groups would have parallels between the chimpanzee mode (especially from mother to offspring) and early Oldowan hominins. We do not know if the sexual differences observed in chimpanzee tool use and behaviors had counterparts in early hominins, but the ape model does raise this question. Hunt (2006) suggests, based on chimpanzee analogies, that female Oldowan hominins were more frequent tool users than males. The use by chimpanzees of a great variety of tools in perishable, organic materials highlights the probability that early

Figure 1

The dawn of human technology. Stone artifacts made on lava river cobbles from Gona, Ethiopia, ~2.6 Mya (cm scale). (*Top row*) Three Oldowan cores. (*Bottom row*) Three flakes. Such artifacts represent the earliest known stage of hominin technology and herald the beginning of the archaeological record. Photo copyright © S. Semaw.

Figure 3

Kanzi, a bonobo or pygmy chimpanzee (*Pan paniscus*), knaps an Oldowan-like cobble-core by freehand, hard-hammer percussion in an experimental setting. Kanzi can produce percussors, cores and flakes that, in a prehistoric context, would easily be recognized as artifactual by archaeologists. Kanzi has now been flaking stone for almost two decades, and other bonobos at the Great Ape Trust of Iowa are now knapping as well. Photograph courtesy of the Great Ape Trust of Iowa.

hominins likewise had a much richer, more diverse, and varied tool kit than is visible in the archaeological record. Bipedal hominins would have had a considerable advantage in terms of transporting tools and foodstuffs around the landscape, and this practice could have been greatly enhanced with the use of containers.

The emergence of the Oldowan around 2.6 Mya, at our present state of knowledge, appears to occur during an evolutionary stage involving relatively small-brained, bipedal australopithecines. The following one million years documents a period of dramatic encephalization with the rise and evolution of the genus *Homo*, a reduction in the size of hominin jaws and teeth, the first spread of hominins out of Africa and into Eurasia, and the earliest appearance of Acheulean industries.

Wild chimpanzees and Oldowan hominins, considering their material culture, would appear to share the following characteristics. First, stone is transported to and used at activity areas, making spatial concentrations of material culture. Second, stone tools become modified (battered and pitted) from their use as hammers and anvils.

As previously mentioned, it is likely that Oldowan hominins had a rich suite of cultural traits that leave little prehistoric visibility. Similarly, the majority of chimpanzee cultural traits and tool-related behaviors would leave little long-term archaeological record. Although their tool use is intelligent and flexible, chimpanzees tend to modify their tools with their bodies, e.g., stripping branches or pulling off bark with their hands or feet or even sharpening tips of branches with their teeth. Early hominins may well have accomplished some tasks in a similar fashion, but the human paleontological evidence suggests that a decrease in size of jaws and teeth over time may be correlated with the rise in extrasomatic tool use, with technology creating "synthetic organs" and gradually allowing hominins to move into niches traditionally occupied by other animals, such as the carnivore guild. We have called this phenomenon "techno-organic" evolution (Schick & Toth 1993).

Major differences in material culture between wild chimpanzees and Oldowan hominins would include the following traits observed in the Oldowan:

1. Skilled, forceful stone knapping by direct percussion with stone hammers, or bipolar flaking with stone hammers and anvils to create sharp edges that could be used for cutting, chopping, and scraping.

2. More selectivity and long-distance transport of lithic raw materials from their geological sources to activity areas ("sites"); concentrations of flaked and battered stone artifacts can number into the hundreds or thousands at a given locality, and transport distances can range from tens of meters to more than 10 kilometers.

3. The acquisition, processing, and consumption of large mammal carcasses (or parts of carcasses), assisted with technology (stone knives and percussors) to exploit meat, marrow, and organ foods, leaving recognizable traces on the bones in the form of stone tool cut marks and hammerstone-induced fracture.

4. Longer-term curational behavior of material culture over longer distances and probably longer time periods, suggesting a higher level of planning and anticipatory behavior.

It is likely, but less demonstrable, that during this period hominid populations developed more human-like characteristics, including the emergence of containers and carrying devices (e.g., of skin, shell, or bark); digging tools such as sharpened digging sticks to process underground plant resources; simple spears, throwing sticks or stone missiles, and clubs for predation; larger average group sizes and home ranges; food-sharing behavior; more sexual division of labor; more emphasis on central foraging places (home bases); more complex communicative skills; and the beginnings of symbolic behavior.

Future research into Oldowan archaeology will almost certainly continue to stress the role of technology in its ecological context and explore new ways to study and test the significance and patterning of this technology during the course of human evolution. As new sites are discovered, our sample sizes of well-excavated stone artifact assemblages, associated animal bones and other materials, and associated hominin tool makers will allow more rigorous methodologies and more robust scientific results. Studies of our ape relatives in the wild will become increasingly crucial and urgent as their habitats dwindle and their populations become endangered, and our disciplines will also gain a great deal of understanding from well-constructed studies of captive apes, who may become the surviving guardians of their genetic and behavioral legacy. Chimpanzees and bonobos are our closest living relatives. Each of our lineages has managed to survive for millions of years since we separated from a last common ancestor; we still have much to learn about them, and they still have much to teach us about ourselves.

DISCLOSURE STATEMENT

The authors are not aware of any affiliations, memberships, funding, or financial holdings that might be perceived as affecting the objectivity of this review.

LITERATURE CITED

Aiello L, Wheeler P. 1995. The expensive tissue hypothesis. *Curr. Anthropol.* 36(2):199–221

Ambrose S. 2001. Palaeolithic technology and human evolution. *Science* 291:1748–53

Asfaw B, Beyene Y, Semaw S, Suwa G, White T, WoldeGabriel G. 1991. Fejej: a new palaeontological research area in Ethiopia. *J. Hum. Evol.* 21:137–43

Asfaw B, Beyene Y, Suwa G, Walter RC, White TD, et al. 1992. The earliest Acheulean from Konso-Gardula. *Nature* 360:732–35

Asfaw B, White T, Lovejoy O, Latimer B, Simpson S. 1999. *Australopithecus garhi*: a new species of early hominid from Ethiopia. *Science* 284(5414):629–34

Barsky D. 2009. An overview of some African and Eurasian Oldowan sites: evaluation of hominin cognition levels, technological advancement and adaptive skills. See Hovers & Braun 2009, pp. 39–47

Bar-Yosef O, Goren-Inbar N. 1993. The lithic assemblages of 'Ubeidiya: a Lower Palaeolithic site in the Jordan Valley. *Oedem* 45:1–266

Beck BB. 1980. *Animal Tool Behavior.* New York: Garland

Berthelet A, Chavaillon J, eds. 1993. *The Use of Tools by Human and Non-Human Primates.* Oxford: Oxford Univ. Press

Blumenschine RJ. 1986. *Early Hominid Scavenging Opportunities: Implications of Carcass Availability in the Serengeti and Ngorongoro Ecosystems.* Oxford: Br. Archaeol. Rep.

Blumenschine RJ. 1989. A landscape taphonomic model of the scale of prehistoric scavenging opportunities. *J. Hum. Evol.* 18:345–71

Blumenschine RJ, Masao FT, Tactikos JC, Ebert J. 2008. Effects of distance from stone source on landscape-scale variation in Oldowan artifact assemblages in the Paleo-Olduvai Basin, Tanzania. *J. Archaeol. Sci.* 35:76–86

Blumenschine RJ, Peters CR. 1998. Archaeological predictions for hominid land use in the paleo-Olduvai basin, Tanzania. *J. Hum. Evol.* 34:565–607

Boesch C, Boesch H. 1983. Optimization of nut-cracking with natural hammers by wild chimpanzees. *Behavior* 83:265–86

Boesch C, Boesch H. 1984. Mental maps in wild chimpanzees: an analysis of hammer transports for nut cracking. *Primates* 25(2):160–70

Boesch C, Boesch H. 1990. Tool use and tool making in wild chimpanzees. *Folia Primatol.* 54:86–99

Boesch C, Boesch-Achermann H. 2000. *The Chimpanzees of the Tai Forest: Behavioral Ecology and Evolution.* Oxford: Oxford Univ. Press

Boesch-Achermann H, Boesch C. 1994. Hominization in the rainforest: the chimpanzee's piece of the puzzle. *Evol. Anthropol.* 3:9–16

Bonner JT. 1980. *The Evolution of Culture in Animals.* Princeton, NJ: Princeton Univ. Press

Brain CK. 1981. *The Hunters or the Hunted? An Introduction to African Cave Taphonomy.* Chicago: Univ. Chicago Press

Brain CK. 2007. Fifty years of fun with fossils: some cave taphonomy-related ideas and concepts that emerged between 1953 and 2003. See Pickering et al. 2007, pp. 1–24

Braun DR, Harris JWK, Mania DN. 2009. Oldowan raw material procurement and use: evidence from the Koobi Fora Formation. *Archaeometry* 51:26–42

Braun DR, Hovers E. 2009. Current issues in Oldowan research. See Hovers & Braun 2009, pp. 1–14

Braun DR, Plummer T, Ditchfield P, Ferraro JV, Mania D, et al. 2008. Oldowan behavior and raw material transport: perspectives on the Kanjera Formation. *J. Archaeol. Sci.* 35:2329–45

Braun DR, Plummer TW, Ditchfield PW, Bishop LC, Ferraro JV. 2009. Oldowan technology and raw material variability at Kanjera South. See Hovers & Braun 2009, pp. 99–110

Bunn H. 1983. Evidence of the diet and subsistence patterns of Plio-Pleistocene hominids at Koobi Fora, Kenya, and Olduvai Gorge, Tanzania. In *Animals and Archaeology*, Vol. 1: *Hunters and Their Prey*, ed. J Clutton-Brock, C Grigson, pp. 21–30. Oxford: Br. Archaeol. Rep.

Bunn H, Kroll E. 1986. Systematic butchery by Plio-Pleistocene hominids at Olduvai Gorge, Tanzania. *Curr. Anthropol.* 27(5):431–52

Carbonell E, Sala R, Barsky D, Celiberti V. 2009. From homogeneity to multiplicity: a new approach to the study of archaic stone tools. See Hovers & Braun 2009, pp. 25–37

Carvalho S, Cunha E, Sousa C, Matsuzawa T. 2008. Chaînes opératoires and resource-exploitation strategies in chimpanzee (*Pan troglodytes*) nut cracking. *J. Hum. Evol.* 55:148–63

Chavaillon J, Chavaillon N, Hours F, Piperno M. 1979. From the Oldowan to the Middle Stone Age at Melka-Kunturé (Ethiopia): understanding cultural change. *Quaternaria* 21:87–114

Dapena J, Anderst W, Toth N. 2006. The biomechanics of the arm swing in Oldowan stone flaking. See Toth & Schick 2006, pp. 333–38

Deacon T. 1997. *The Symbolic Species: The Co-Evolution of Language and the Brain.* New York: Norton

de Beaune SA. 2004. The invention of technology: prehistory and cognition. *Curr. Anthropol.* 45:139–62

de Heinzelin J, Clark JD, White TD, Hart WK, Renne PR, et al. 1999. Environment and behavior of 2.5-million-year-old Bouri hominids. *Science* 284:625–29

Delagnes A, Roche H. 2005. Late Pliocene hominid knapping skills: the case of Lokalalei 2C, West Turkana, Kenya. *J. Hum. Evol.* 48:435–72

de la Torre I, Mora R. 2005. *Technological Strategies in the Lower Pleistocene at Olduvai Beds I & II.* Liege: ERAUL

de la Torre I, Mora R. 2009. Remarks on the current theoretical and methodological approaches to the study of early technological strategies in East Africa. See Hovers & Braun 2009, pp. 15–24

de la Torre I, Mora R, Domínguez-Rodrigo M, Luque L, Alcala L. 2003. The Oldowan industry of Peninj and its bearing on the reconstruction of the technological skills of Lower Pleistocene hominids. *J. Hum. Evol.* 44:203–24

de Lumley H, Beyene J, eds. 2004. *Les Sites Préhistoriques de la Région de Fejej, Sud-Omo, Éthiopie, dans Leurs Contexte Stratigraphique et Paléontologique.* Paris: Éd. Rech. Civiliz.

de Lumley H, Nioradze M, Barsky D, Cauche D, Celiberti V, et al. 2005. Les industries lithiques préoldowayennes du début du Pléistocène inférieur du site de Dmanissi en Géorgie. *Anthropologie* 109:1–182

d'Errico F, Backwell LR. 2003. Possible evidence of bone tool shaping by Swartkrans early hominids. *J. Archaeol. Sci.* 30:1559–76

d'Errico F, Backwell LR, Berger LR. 2001. Bone tool use in termite foraging by early hominids and its impact on our understanding of early hominid behaviour. *S. Afr. J. Sci.* 97:71–75

Diez-Martín F. 2006. After the African Oldowan: the earliest technologies of Europe. See Toth & Schick 2006, pp. 129–51

Domínguez-Rodrigo M. 2009. Are all Oldowan sites palimpsests? If so, what can they tell us about hominid carnivory? See Hovers & Braun 2009, pp. 129–47

Domínguez-Rodrigo M, Egeland CP, Barba R. 2007. *Deconstructing Olduvai*. New York: Springer

Dunbar RI. 1993. Coevolution of neocortical size, group size and language in humans. *Behav. Brain Sci.* 16:681–735

Field AS. 1999. *An analytical and comparative study of the earlier Stone Age archaeology of the Sterkfontein Valley*. MSc thesis, Univ. Witwatersrand

Foley R. 1987. Hominid species and stone tool assemblages: How are they related? *Antiquity* 61:380–92

Gibson KR. 1986. Cognition, brain size and the extraction of embedded food resources. In *Primate Ontogeny, Cognition and Social Behavior*, ed. JG Else, PC Lee, pp. 93–103. Cambridge, UK: Cambridge Univ. Press

Gibson KR, Ingold T, eds. 1993. *Tools, Language and Cognition in Human Evolution*. Cambridge, UK: Cambridge Univ. Press

Goldman-Neuman T, Hovers E. 2009. Methodological considerations in the study of Oldowan raw material selectivity: insights from A. L. 894 (Hadar, Ethiopia). See Hovers & Braun 2009, pp. 71–84

Goodall J. 1964. Tool-using and aimed throwing in a community of free-living chimpanzees. *Nature* 201:1264–66

Goodall J. 1986. *The Chimpanzees of Gombe*. Cambridge, MA: Harvard Univ. Press

Gowlett JAJ. 1996. Mental abilities of early *Homo*: elements of constraint and choice in rule systems. See Mellars & Gibson 1996, pp. 191–215

Harlacker L. 2009. *The biomechanics of stone tool-making: kinematic and kinetic perspectives on Oldowan Lithic technology*. PhD thesis, Anthropol. Dept., Indiana Univ., Bloomington

Harmand S. 2009. Variability in raw material selectivity at the late Pliocene sites of Lokalalei, West Turkana, Kenya. See Hovers & Braun 2009, pp. 85–97

Harris JWK. 1983. Cultural beginnings: Plio-Pleistocene archaeological occurrences from the Afar, Ethiopia. *Afr. Archaeol. Rev.* 1:1–31

Harris JWK, Capaldo SD. 1993. The earliest stone tools. In *The Use of Tools by Human and Non-Human Primates*, ed. A Berthelet, J. Chavaillon, pp. 196–220. Oxford: Clarendon

Hay RL. 1976. *Geology of the Olduvai Gorge*. Berkeley: Univ. Calif. Press

Holloway RH, Broadfield DC, Yuan MS. 2004. *The Human Fossil Record*, Vol. 3: *Brain Endocasts, The Paleoneurological Evidence*. Hoboken: Wiley

Hovers E, Braun DR, eds. 2009. *Interdisciplinary Approaches to the Oldowan*. Dordrecht: Springer

Howell FC, Haesaerts P, de Heinzelin J. 1987. Depositional environments, archaeological occurrences and hominids from Members E and F of the Shungura Formation (Omo basin, Ethiopia). *J. Hum. Evol.* 16:665–700

Hunt K. 2006. Sex differences in chimpanzee foraging behavior and tool use: implications for the Oldowan. See Toth & Schick 2006, pp. 243–66

Isaac G. 1981. Stone age visiting cards: approaches to the study of early land-use patterns. In *Patterns of the Past*, ed. I Hodder, G Isaac, N Hammond, pp. 131–55. Cambridge, UK: Cambridge Univ. Press

Isaac G. 1982. The earliest archaeological traces. In *Cambridge History of Africa*, Vol. 1: *From the Earliest Times to c. 500 BC*. Cambridge, UK: Cambridge Univ. Press

Isaac G. 1984. The archaeology of human origins: studies of the Lower Pleistocene in East Africa. In *Advances in World Archaeology*, ed. F Wendorf, A Close, pp. 1–87. New York: Acad. Press

Isaac G. 1986. Foundation stones: early artifacts as indicators of activities and abilities. In *Stone Age Prehistory*, ed. GN Bailey, P Callow, pp. 221–41. Cambridge, UK: Cambridge Univ. Press

Isaac G. 1989. *The Archaeology of Human Origins: Papers by Glynn Isaac*. Cambridge, UK: Cambridge Univ. Press

Isaac G, Isaac B, eds. 1997. *Koobi Fora Research Project*, Vol. 5: *Plio-Pleistocene Archaeology*. Oxford: Clarendon

Jones PR. 1994. Results of experimental work in relation to the stone industries of Olduvai Gorge. See Leakey 1994, pp. 254–98

Joulian F. 1996. Comparing chimpanzee and early hominid techniques: some contributions to cultural and cognitive questions. See Mellars & Gibson 1996, pp. 173–89

Keeley L, Toth N. 1981. Microwear polishes on early stone tools from Koobi Fora, Kenya. *Nature* 293:464–66

Kimbel WH, Walter RC, Johanson DC, Reed KE, Aronson JL, et al. 1996. Late Pliocene *Homo* and Oldowan tools from the Hadar Formation (Kada Hadar Member), Ethiopia. *J. Hum. Evol.* 31:549–61

Klein RG. 1999. *The Human Career: Human Biological and Cultural Origins*. Chicago: Univ. Chicago Press

Kuman K. 1998. The earliest South African industries. In *Early Hominid Behavior In Global Context: The Rise and Diversity of the Lower Palaeolithic Record*, ed. MD Petraglia, R Korisettar, pp. 151–86. London: Routledge

Kuman K. 2005. La préhistoire ancienne de l'Afrique méridionale: contribution des sites à hominids d' Afrique du Sud. In *Le Paléolithique en Afrique: L'Histoire la Plus Longue*, ed. M Sahnouni, pp. 53–82. Paris: Éd. Artcom'

Leakey MD. 1971. *Olduvai Gorge*, Vol. 3: *Excavations in Beds I and II, 1960–1963*. Cambridge, UK: Cambridge Univ. Press

Leakey MD, with D Roe. 1994. *Olduvai Gorge*, Vol. 5: *Excavation in Beds III, IV, and the Masek Beds, 1968–1971*. Cambridge, UK: Cambridge Univ. Press

Lewin R, Foley RA. 2004. *Principles of Human Evolution*. Oxford: Blackwell

Lycett SJ, Collard M, McGrew WC. 2007. Phylogenetic analyses of behavior support existence of culture among wild chimpanzees. *Proc. Natl. Acad. Sci. USA* 104:17588–93

Marchant LF, McGrew WC. 2005. Percussive technology: chimpanzee baobab smashing and the evolutionary modeling of hominin knapping. See Roux & Bril 2005, pp. 341–50

Martinez J, Mora R, de la Torre I, eds. 2003. *Oldowan: Rather More Than Smashing Stones*. Bellaterra: Univ. Autonom. Barc.

Matsuzawa T, ed. 2002. *Primate Origins of Human Cognition and Behavior*. Tokyo: Springer

McGrew WC. 1992. *Chimpanzee Material Culture*. Cambridge, UK: Cambridge Univ. Press

McGrew WC. 1993. The intelligent use of tools: twenty propositions. See Gibson & Ingold 1993, pp. 151–70

McGrew WC. 2004. *The Cultured Chimpanzee: Reflections on Cultural Primatology*. Cambridge, UK: Cambridge Univ. Press

Mellars P, Gibson K, eds. 1996. *Modelling the Early Human Mind*. Cambridge, UK: McDonald Inst.

Mercader J, Barton H, Gillespie J, Harris J, Kuhn S, et al. 2007. 4,300-year-old chimpanzee sites and the origins of percussive stone technology. *Proc. Natl. Acad. Sci. USA* 104:3043–48

Mercader J, Panger M, Boesch C. 2002. Excavation of a chimpanzee stone tool site in the African rainforest. *Science* 296:1452–55

Mithen S. 1996. *The Prehistory of the Mind*. London: Thames and Hudson

Negash A, Shackley MS, Alene M. 2006. Source provenance of obsidian artifacts from the Early Stone Age (ESA) site of Melka Konturé, Ethiopia. *J. Archaeol. Sci.* 33:1647–50

Noble W, Davidson I. 1996. *Human Evolution, Language and Mind: A Psychological and Archaeological Inquiry*. Cambridge, UK: Cambridge Univ. Press

Panger MA, Brooks AS, Richmond BG, Wood B. 2002. Older than the Oldowan? Rethinking the emergence of hominin tool use. *Evol. Anthropol.* 11:235–45

Parker ST, Gibson KR. 1979. A developmental model for the evolution of language and intelligence in early hominids. *Behav. Brain Sci.* 2:367–408

Parker ST, McKinney ML. 1999. *Origins of Intelligence: The Evolution of Cognitive Development in Monkeys, Apes, and Humans*. Baltimore: Johns Hopkins Univ. Press

Pelegrin J. 2005. Remarks about archaeological techniques and methods of knapping: elements of a cognitive approach to stone knapping. See Roux & Bril 2005, pp. 23–33

Peters CR, Blumenschine RJ. 1995. Landscape perspectives on possible land use patterns for Early Pleistocene hominids in the Olduvai Basin, Tanzania. *J. Hum. Evol.* 29:321–62

Peters CR, Blumenschine RJ. 1996. Landscape perspectives on possible land use patterns for Early Pleistocene hominids in the Olduvai Basin, Tanzania: Part II, expanding the landscape model. *Kapuia* 6:175–221

Pickering TR, Domínguez-Rodrigo M. 2006. The acquisition and use of large mammal carcasses by Oldowan hominins in eastern and southern Africa: a selected review and assessment. See Toth & Schick 2006, pp. 113–28

Pickering TR, Domínguez-Rodrigo M, Egeland C, Brain CK. 2007. Carcass foraging by early hominids at Swartkrans Cave (South Africa): a new investigation of the zooarchaeology and taphonomy of Member 3. See Pickering et al. 2007, pp. 233–53

Pickering TR, Schick K, Toth N, eds. 2007. *Breathing Life into Fossils: Taphonomic Studies in Honor of C.K. (Bob) Brain*. Gosport, IN: Stone Age Inst. Press

Pickering TR, Wallis J. 1997. Bone modification resulting from captive chimpanzee mastication: implications for the interpretation of Pliocene archaeological faunas. *J. Archaeol. Sci.* 24:1115–27

Piperno M, Collina C, Gallotti R, Raynal J, Kieffer G, et al. 2009. Obsidian exploitation and utilization during the Oldowan at Melka Kunturé (Ethiopia). See Hovers & Braun 2009, pp. 111–28

Plummer T. 2004. Flaked stones and old bones: biological and cultural evolution at the dawn of technology. *Yearb. Phys. Anthropol.* 47:118–64

Plummer TW, Bishop LC, Ditchfield PW, Ferraro JV, Kingston JD, et al. 2009. The environmental context of Oldowan hominin activities at Kanjera South, Kenya. See Hovers & Braun, pp. 149–60

Plummer TW, Stanford CB. 2000. Analysis of a bone assemblage made by chimpanzees at Gombe National Park, Tanzania. *J. Hum. Evol.* 39:345–65

Potts R. 1988. *Early Hominid Activities at Olduvai.* New York: Aldine

Potts R. 1991. Why the Oldowan? Plio-Pleistocene toolmaking and transport of resources. *J. Anthropol. Res.* 47:153–76

Pruetz JD, Bertolani P. 2007. Savanna chimpanzees, *Pan troglodytes verus*, hunt with tools. *Curr. Biol.* 17:1–6

Renfrew C, Frith C, Malafouris L, eds. 2009. *The Sapient Mind: Archaeology Meets Neuroscience.* Oxford: Oxford Univ. Press

Roche H. 2005. From simple flaking to shaping: stone knapping evolution among early hominins. See Roux & Bril 2005, pp. 35–48

Roche H, Delagnes A, Brugal J, Feibel C, Kibunjia M, et al. 1999. Early hominid stone tool production and technical skill 2.34 Myr ago in West Turkana, Kenya. *Nature* 399:57–60

Roux V, Bril B, ed. 2005. *Stone Knapping: The Necessary Conditions for a Uniquely Hominin Behaviour.* Cambridge, UK: McDonald Inst.

Sahnouni M. 1998. *The Lower Palaeolithic of the Magreb: Excavations and Analyses at Ain Hanech, Algeria.* Oxford: Br. Archaeol. Rep.

Sahnouni M. 2006. The North African Early Stone Age and the sites at Ain Hanech, Algeria. See Toth & Schick 2006, pp. 77–111

Sahnouni M, Hadjouis D, Van Der Made J, Derradji A, Canals A, et al. 2002. Further research at the Oldowan site of Ain Hanech, North-east Algeria. *J. Hum. Evol.* 43:925–37

Sahnouni M, Schick K, Toth N. 1997. An experimental investigation into the nature of faceted limestone "spheroids" in the Early Paleolithic. *J. Archaeol. Sci.* 24:701–13

Savage-Rumbaugh S, Fields WM. 2006. Rules and tools: beyond anthropomorphism. See Toth & Schick 2006, pp. 223–41

Schick K. 1986. *Stone Age Sites in the Making: Experiments in the Formation and Transformation of Archaeological Occurrences.* Oxford: Br. Archaeol. Rep.

Schick K. 1987. Modelling the formation of Early Stone Age artifact concentrations. *J. Hum. Evol.* 16:789–807

Schick K, Toth N. 1993. *Making Silent Stones Speak: Human Evolution and the Dawn of Technology.* New York: Simon and Schuster

Schick K, Toth N. 1994. Early Stone Age Technology in Africa: a review and case study into the nature and function of spheroids and subspheroids. In *Integrative Paths to the Past: Palaeoanthropological Advances in Honor of F. Clark Howell*, ed. R Coruccini, R Ciochon, pp. 429–49. Englewood Cliffs: Prentice-Hall

Schick K, Toth N. 2001. Palaeoanthropology at the millennium. In *Archaeology at the Millenium: A Sourcebook*, ed. D Feinman, G Price, pp. 30–108. New York: Kluwer

Schick K, Toth N. 2006. An overview of the Oldowan Industrial Complex: the sites and the nature of their evidence. See Toth & Schick 2006, pp. 3–42

Schick K, Toth N, eds. 2009. *The Cutting Edge: New Approaches to the Archaeology of Human Origins.* Gosport, IN: Stone Age Inst. Press

Schick K, Toth N, Garufi GS, Savage-Rumbaugh ES, Rumbaugh D, Sevcik R. 1999. Continuing investigations into the stone tool-making and tool-using capabilities of a bonobo (*Pan paniscus*). *J. Archaeol. Sci.* 26:821–32

Semaw S. 2000. The world's oldest stone artifacts from Gona, Ethiopia; their implications for understanding stone technology and patterns of human evolution between 2.6–1.5 million years ago. *J. Archaeol. Sci.* 27:1197–214

Semaw S. 2006. The oldest stone artifacts from Gona (2.6–2.5 Ma), Afar, Ethiopia: implications for understanding the earliest stages of stone knapping. See Toth & Schick 2006, pp. 43–75

Semaw S, Renne P, Harris JWK, Feibel CS, Bernor RL, et al. 1997. 2.5-million-year-old stone tools from Gona, Ethiopia. *Nature* 385:333–36

Semaw S, Rogers MJ, Quade J, Renne PR, Butler RF, et al. 2003. 2.6-million-year-old stone tools and associated bones from OGS-6 and OGS-7, Gona, Ethiopia. *J. Hum. Evol.* 45:169–77

Sept JM. 1992. Was there no place like home? A new perspective on early hominid archaeological sites from mapping of chimpanzee nests. *Curr. Anthropol.* 33(2):187–207

Sept JM. 1998. Shadows on a changing landscape: comparing nesting habits of hominids and chimpanzees since their last common ancestor. *Am. J. Prim.* 46:85–101

Stanford C. 2001. *Significant Others: The Ape-Human Continuum and the Quest for Human Nature*. New York: Basic Books

Stout D. 2006. Oldowan toolmaking and hominin brain evolution: theory and research using positron emission tomography (PET). See Toth & Schick 2006, pp. 267–305

Stout D, Quade J, Semaw S, Rogers MJ, Levin NE. 2005. Raw material selectivity of the earliest stone toolmakers at Gona, Afar, Ethiopia. *J. Hum. Evol.* 48:365–80

Stout D, Semaw S. 2006. Knapping skill of the earliest stone toolmakers: insights from the study of modern human novices. See Toth & Schick 2006, pp. 307–20

Stout D, Toth N, Schick K. 2006. Comparing the neural foundations of Oldowan and Acheulean toolmaking: a pilot study using positron emission tomography. See Toth & Schick 2006, pp. 321–31

Stout D, Toth N, Schick K, Chaminade T. 2009. Neural correlates of Early Stone Age toolmaking: technology, language, and cognition in human evolution. See Renfrew et al. 2009, pp. 1–19

Texier PJ. 1995. The Oldowan assemblage from NY 18 site at Nyabusosi (Toro-Uganda). *Comptes Rendus Acad. Sci., Paris* 320:647–53

Toth N. 1982. *The stone technologies of early hominids at Koobi Fora, Kenya: an experimental approach*. PhD thesis, Univ. Calif., Berkeley

Toth N. 1985. The Oldowan reassessed: a close look at early stone artifacts. *J. Archaeol. Sci.* 12:101–20

Toth N, Schick KD. 1986. The first million years: the archaeology of protohuman culture. *Adv. Archaeol. Methods Theory* 9:1–96

Toth N, Schick KD. 1993. Early stone industries and inferences regarding language and cognition. See Gibson & Ingold, pp. 346–62

Toth N, Schick K. 2005. African origins. In *The Human Past: World Prehistory and the Development of Human Societies*, ed. C Scarre, pp. 46–83. London: Thames and Hudson

Toth N, Schick K, eds. 2006. *The Oldowan: Case Studies into the Earliest Stone Age*. Gosport, IN: Stone Age Inst. Press

Toth N, Schick K. 2007. *An archaeological view of chimpanzee cultural traits*. Presented at the "Palaeoanthropology meets Primatology" conference, March, Leverhume Center, Cambridge Univ.

Toth N, Schick K, Semaw S. 2006. A comparative study of the stone tool-making skills of *Pan, Australopithecus*, and *Homo sapiens*. See Toth & Schick 2006, pp. 155–222

van Schaik CP, Ancrenaz M, Borgen G, Galdikas BF, Knott CD, et al. 2003. Orangutan cultures and the evolution of material culture. *Science* 299:102–5

White TD, Toth N. 2007. Carnivora and carnivory: assessing hominid toothmarks in zooarchaeology. See Pickering et al. 2007, pp. 281–96

Whiten A, Goodall J, McGrew WC, Nishida T, Reynolds V, et al. 1999. Cultures in chimpanzees. *Nature* 399:682–85

Whiten A, Goodall J, McGrew WC, Nishida T, Reynolds V, et al. 2001. Charting cultural variation in chimpanzees. *Behaviour* 138:1481–516

Whiten A, Schick K, Toth N. 2009. The evolution and cultural transmission of percussive technology: integrating evidence from palaeoanthropology and primatology. *J. Hum. Evol.* In press

Wrangham R. 1996. *Demonic Males: Apes and the Origins of Human Violence*. Boston: Houghton Mifflin

Wright RV. 1972. Imitative learning of a flaked tool technology—the case of an orangutan. *Mankind* 8:296–306

Wynn T. 1989. *The Evolution of Spatial Competence*. Champaign-Urbana: Univ. Ill. Press

Wynn T. 2002. Archaeology and cognitive evolution. *Behav. Brain Sci.* 25:389–438

Wynn T, McGrew WC. 1989. An ape's view of the Oldowan. *Man* 24:383–98

Cumulative Indexes

Contributing Authors, Volumes 29–38

Foley WA, 29:357–404
Fortier J, 38:99–114

G

Galvin KA, 38:185–98
Gangestad SW, 34:523–48
Garrett PB, 31:339–61
Geertz C, 31:1–19
Geller PL, 38:65–81
Geschiere P, 34:385–407
Godoy R, 34:121–38
Good I, 30:209–26
Goodenough WH, 32:1–12
Gravlee CC, 34:231–52
Gremillion H, 34:13–32
Grine FE, 35:209–28
Gldemann T, 37:93–109
Gupta D, 34:409–27
Gusterson H, 36:155–75
Guyer JI, 33:499–523

H

Haeri N, 29:61–87
Hames R, 36:177–90
Hammer MF, 31:303–21
Hancock AM, 37:197–217
Hanks WF, 34:67–83
Hann C, 37:145–58
Hansen KT, 33:369–92
Hansen TB, 35:295–315
Harrell S, 30:139–61
Hay J, 36:89–103
Hayashida FM, 34:43–65
Hayes MG, 29:217–42
Heckenberger M, 38:251–66
Hill K, 34:639–65
Himmelmann NP, 37:337–50
Hodder I, 36:105–20
Hogle LF, 34:695–716
Holloway RL, 37:1–19
Holtzman JD, 35:361–78
Houston SD, 33:223–50
Howell S, 38:149–66
Hurtado AM, 34:639–65
Hutchinson JF, 30:85–108

I

Igoe J, 35:251–77
Inhorn MC, 37:177–96

J

Jablonski NG, 33:585–623
Jackson JE, 34:549–73
James P, 34:639–65
Janes CR, 38:167–83
Johnson-Hanks J, 37:301–15
Johnstone B, 29:405–24
Joyce RA, 34:139–58

K

Kane S, 30:457–79
Kaufman SR, 34:317–41
Keyes CF, 31:233–55
King SR, 30:505–26
Koo KS, 33:297–317
Korbin JE, 32:431–46
Kulick D, 29:243–85
Kuzawa CW, 38:131–47
Kyratzis A, 33:625–49

L

Lamb Z, 34:619–38
Lambourne CA, 34:639–65
Lansing JS, 32:183–204
LaRoche CJ, 34:575–98
Lemon A, 31:497–524
Leonard WR, 34:121–38; 451–71
Leone MP, 34:575–98
Levine NE, 37:375–89
Lindenbaum S, 30:363–85;
    33:475–98
Liu L, 38:217–32
Lofink H, 35:337–60
Lomnitz C, 34:105–20
Lovejoy CO, 32:85–109

M

Maffi L, 34:599–617
Mahon M, 29:467–92
Makihara M, 38:17–31
Marcus J, 37:251–66
Maskovsky J, 32:315–38
Mason T, 30:457–79
Mathur S, 29:89–106
Maurer B, 35:15–36
Mazzarella W, 33:345–67
McCollum MA, 32:85–109
McDade TW, 34:495–521

McGarvey ST, 38:233–49
McHenry HM, 29:125–46
McIntyre MH, 38:83–97
Mencher JP, 29:107–24
Mendoza SP, 38:115–30
Merlan F, 34:473–94
Merry SE, 35:99–116
Mertz E, 36:337–53
Meskell L, 31:279–301
Meyer B, 33:447–74
Michael L, 31:121–45
Mills MB, 32:41–62
Mintz SW, 31:99–119
Monaghan L, 31:69–97
Montgomery H, 36:391–405
Moore SF, 34:1–11
Moran K, 30:505–26
Moran-Thomas A, 38:267–88
Moreland J, 35:135–51
Morgan LM, 34:317–41
Morgen S, 32:315–38
Morris RC, 36:355–89
Mufwene SS, 33:201–22
Mühlhäusler P, 35:457–79
Mullings L, 34:667–93

N

Nazarea VD, 35:317–35
Nelson DL, 36:191–209
Neves EG, 38:251–66
Nguyen V-K, 32:447–74
Nichter M, 37:267–82

O

Okongwu AF, 29:107–24
O'Rourke DH, 29:217–42
Ortiz S, 31:395–417
Orzech KM, 37:267–82
Oths KS, 34:231–52

P

Paley J, 31:469–96
Palmié S, 35:433–56
Panter-Brick C, 31:147–71
Parker R, 30:163–79
Peace A, 35:457–79
Peregrine PN, 30:1–18

Perry SE, 35:171–90
Peschard K, 32:447–74
Peterson LC, 31:449–67
Phillips L, 35:37–57
Poe MR, 36:301–36
Pollard AM, 36:245–59
Poole D, 34:159–79
Povinelli EA, 30:319–34

Q

Quinn EA, 38:131–47

R

Redmond EM, 33:173–99
Reischer E, 33:297–317
Renfrew C, 34:343–61
Reno PL, 32:85–109
Reyes-García V, 34:121–38
Rhodes LA, 30:65–83
Richards M, 32:135–62
Robbins J, 33:117–43
Rogers SC, 30:481–504
Rosenman BA, 32:85–109
Ross CF, 29:147–94
Rubertone PE, 29:425–46
Ruff C, 31:211–32

S

Safari L, 36:391–405
Sapolsky RM, 33:393–418
Scheinsohn V, 32:339–61
Schell LM, 32:111–34
Scheyd GJ, 34:523–48
Schick K, 38:289–305
Schildkrout E, 33:319–44
Schneider J, 37:351–73
Schneider P, 37:351–73
Schoenemann PT, 35:379–406
Schoepf BG, 30:335–61
Schurr TG, 33:551–83
Senghas RJ, 31:69–97
Sharp LA, 29:287–328

Shepherd N, 31:189–209
Shennan S, 37:75–91
Sheridan TE, 36:121–38
Sherzer J, 31:121–45
Shukla S, 30:551–72
Sidnell J, 36:229–44
Siikala J, 35:153–70
Silk JB, 31:21–44
Silverman EK, 33:419–45
Silverstein M, 35:481–96
Silverstein PA, 34:363–84
Slice DE, 36:261–81
Smart A, 32:263–85
Smart J, 32:263–85
Smedley A, 30:xvii–xxxii
Smith EA, 29:493–524
Smith ME, 33:73–102
Snodgrass JJ, 34:451–71
Sorensen MV, 34:451–71
Spencer CS, 33:173–99
Spencer J, 29:1–24
Spindler GD, 29:xv–xxxviii
Stahl AB, 33:145–72
Stanish C, 30:41–64
Stark MT, 35:407–32
Steppuat F, 35:295–315
Stocks A, 34:85–104
Stokes M, 33:47–72
Stoneking M, 37:93–109
Strathern M, 33:1–19
Strier KB, 37:21–36
Strong PT, 34:253–68
Stronza A, 30:261–83
Swisher CC, 33:271–96

T

Tainter JA, 35:59–74
Taylor JS, 34:741–56
Teaford MF, 35:209–28
Threlkeld B, 34:619–38
Tomlinson M, 38:17–31
Toth N, 38:289–305
Trevathan WR, 36:139–54
Trinkaus E, 34:207–30

U

Ulijaszek SJ, 35:337–60
Ungar PS, 35:209–28

V

Vadez V, 34:121–38
Vail G, 35:497–519
Valeggia CR, 38:115–30
van der Veer P, 31:173–87
Van Esterik P, 31:257–78
Van Wolputte S, 33:251–69
Varki A, 36:191–209
Vigil JD, 32:225–42
Vitzthum VJ, 37:53–73
Voss BL, 37:317–36

W

Walker PL, 30:573–96
Walsh M, 34:293–315
Warren KB, 34:549–73
Watkins J, 34:429–49
Watson P, 38:1–15
Wells JCK, 31:323–38
West P, 35:251–77
Wichmann S, 35:279–94
Wilce J, 38:199–215
Wilson ML, 32:363–92
Wilson SM, 31:449–67
Wishnie M, 29:493–524
Wolfe TC, 29:195–216
Wortham S, 37:37–51
Wrangham RW, 32:363–92

Y

Yelvington KA, 30:227–60
Yon DA, 32:411–29

Z

Zegura SL, 31:303–21
Ziegler TE, 31:45–67

Chapter Titles, Volumes 29–38

Biological Anthropology

Linguistics and Communicative Practices

ANNUAL REVIEWS
A Nonprofit Scientific Publisher

Annual Reviews – Your Starting Point for Research Online
http://arjournals.annualreviews.org

- Over 1280 Annual Reviews volumes—more than 28,800 critical, authoritative review articles in 37 disciplines spanning the Biomedical, Life, Physical, and Social sciences—available online, including all Annual Reviews back volumes, dating to 1932

- Personal subscriptions include permanent online data rights to the volume regardless of future subscription status. Online data rights include access to full-text articles, PDFs, Reviews in Advance (as much as 6 months ahead of print publication), bibliographies, and other supplementary material

- All articles are fully supplemented, searchable, and downloadable—see http://anthro.annualreviews.org

- Access links to the reviewed references (when available online)

- Site features include customized alerting services, citation tracking, and saved searches

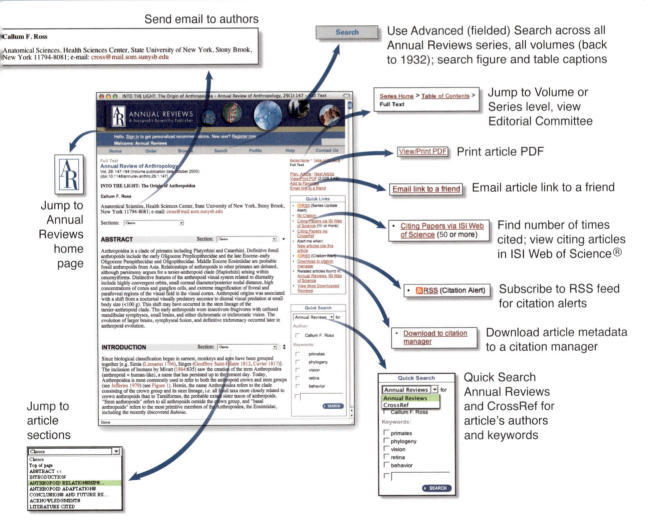

Send email to authors

Search — Use Advanced (fielded) Search across all Annual Reviews series, all volumes (back to 1932); search figure and table captions

Series Home > Table of Contents > Full Text — Jump to Volume or Series level, view Editorial Committee

View/Print PDF — Print article PDF

Email link to a friend — Email article link to a friend

Jump to Annual Reviews home page

Citing Papers via ISI Web of Science (50 or more) — Find number of times cited; view citing articles in ISI Web of Science®

RSS (Citation Alert) — Subscribe to RSS feed for citation alerts

Download to citation manager — Download article metadata to a citation manager

Quick Search Annual Reviews and CrossRef for article's authors and keywords

Jump to article sections